Money Adviser
1995

Junius Ellis
and the
Editors of MONEY

MONEY BOOKS
Time Inc. Home Entertainment
1271 Avenue of the Americas
New York, NY 10020

Other MONEY BOOKS by Junius Ellis

Making Money With Mutual Funds
Making the Most of Your Money Now
Your Best Money Moves Now
Guide to a Secure Retirement
Winning With Mutual Funds

MONEY STAFF
managing editor Frank Lalli

executive editors Caroline Donnelly, Tyler Mathisen;
assistant managing editors Lynn Crimando, Richard Eisenberg, Frank Merrick, Eric Schurenberg;
senior editors Joseph Coyle, Eric Gelman, Roy Johnson (special projects), Joanna Krotz, Kevin McKean, Nancy Perry;
wall street editor Michael Sivy; **associate editors** Denise Topolnicki, Walter Updegrave;
Washington, D.C. bureau chief Teresa Tritch; **senior writers** Jerry Edgerton, Elizabeth Fenner, Ruth Simon, Penelope Wang;
staff writers Lesley Alderman, Gary Belsky, Shelly Branch, Carla Fried, Peter Keating, Beth Kobliner, Lani Luciano, John Manners,
Vanessa O'Connell, Marguerite Smith, Ellen Stark; **art director** Rudy Hoglund; **deputy art director** Traci Churchill;
associate art directors Scott Davis, Helene Elek; **designers** Nadia Maryniak, Mimi Maxwell; **picture editor** Deborah Pierce;
deputy picture editor Miriam Hsia; **assistant picture editor** Leslie Yoo; **picture researcher** Samantha Welsh;
chief of reporters Katharine Drake; **senior staff** Sian Ballen (chief of correspondents), Mark Bautz, Jillian Kasky,
Holly Wheelwright Ketron, Roberta Kirwan, Prashanta Misra, Amanda Walmac; **staff** Susan Berger, Judy Feldman, Karen Hube,
Jeanhee Kim, Leslie Marable, Sheryl Nance-Nash, Elif Sinanoglu, Kelly Smith, Daphne Mosher (mail);
manufacturing director Kathy O'Shaughnessy; **editorial director** Mark Giles; **production manager** Susan Eason;
editorial operations director David White; **copy chief** Patricia Feimster; **senior systems engineer** Al Criscuolo;
editorial systems engineer Mark Hernandez; **senior coordinators** Bill O'Connor, Sukey Rosenbaum; **staff** Kathleen Beakley,
Sally Boggan, Eric Hutton, Robin Johnson, Nigel Killikelly, Judith Ryan, Eve Sennett, Geraldine Vopelak;
editorial finances director Michael Terry; **staff** Bernard Palmer; **assistant to managing editor** Arlene Lemanski;
staff Genevieve Fernandez, Marianne Nardone, Darlen Obertance, Yvonne Varriale

Manufactured in the United States of America
First Printing 1995

To order MONEY Magazine, call Customer Service at 800-633-9970
or write to MONEY, P.O. Box 60001, Tampa, Florida 33660-0001.

Money Adviser 1995

Editor: Junius Ellis
Designers: Laura Ierardi, LCI Design; Monica Kowarick
Cover: Photo by Ken Fisher/Tony Stone

Time Inc. New Business Development

Director: David Gitow
Assistant Director: Stuart Hotchkiss
Fulfillment Director: Mary McGrade
Production Director: John Calvano
Operations Director: David Rivchin
Development Manager: John Sandklev
Associate Manager: Gretchen Sanders

Contents

1 Where to Put Your Money Now

2 Your New Agenda for Axing Taxes

3 Flex and Protect Your Earning Power

4 How to Retire Sooner With More

5 Investing in Your Family's Future

6 How to Be a Smarter Fund Investor

Where to Put Your Money Now

Following sharp increases last year, interest rates will level off by mid-1995 and set the stage for surprisingly strong corporate earnings and an advancing stock market. In short, MONEY sees 1995 stacking up as a pretty good year for investors. Why should you put stock in what we think? For starters, our market forecast in last year's book was remarkably accurate. We argued that in 1994 a speedup in the economy and investors' fears of higher inflation would force the Federal Reserve to boost interest rates. And that, in turn, would cause stocks to drop as much as 10% before rebounding to post a small profit by year-end. We also thought that rising rates would reduce bond prices by 5% or more.

We were on the money. We predicted that blue chip stocks would provide a total return of about 4% including dividends. The actual return for the Dow Jones industrial average for the year was a bit better at 5.9%. Moreover, stocks suffered an 8% decline between February and April '94, a shade under our forecast 10% drop in the first half of that year. We weren't too far off on bonds either. The fears about inflation that we discussed, however, mounted faster than we expected. As a result, prices of long-term bonds (maturing in a decade or more) fell almost 10%. While many bondholders were subjected to bigger paper losses than we anticipated, anyone who followed our advice at least got protection. We warned: "Cut back your holdings of long-term bonds to a minimum."

Among our other predictions, we said that foreign stocks would outperform the U.S. market, and they did excel with a 6% rise overall. As for specific picks, the 30 stock recommendations of our All Star brokers provided a fat 16% average profit not counting dividends, vs. 1% for Standard & Poor's 500-stock index (the All Stars' 1995 picks and pans begin on page 11). Of course, we had our share of misses. For example, we thought small-company shares would outpace big stocks. Instead, small caps stumbled hard and ended the year down 3%. We also forecast that electric utility stocks and tax-exempt municipal bonds would weather interest-rate rises better than long-term taxable bonds. In fact, utilities and munis fared as badly for reasons we discuss in greater detail below.

MONEY'S Financial Forecast for 1995

There's no doubt as to who's the real power in the nation's capital these days, at least as far as the economy is concerned. He's Alan Greenspan, the Federal Reserve chairman who last November jacked up short-term interest rates three-quarters of a percentage point to 5.5% in one bold move. It was the Fed's sixth hike since February '94 and the biggest rate increase since 1981. Why is Greenspan so anxious to douse last year's seemingly tepid 3% inflation? One reason is that he's apparently convinced an inflation surge is lurking just over the horizon. The warning signs are rising prices for commodities, unemployment below 6% and an economy that's running above 83% of capacity.

Some economists don't share Greenspan's inflation outlook and think he's going overboard with the price-buster stuff. A few even sketch out a disaster scenario unfolding over the next couple of years during which an overzealous Fed pushes up rates another full point or more, shoving the country into recession. In a recession, interest rates would fall and prices of long bonds would soar 10% or more. But stocks could lose as much as 20% of their market value.

MONEY doesn't think that scenario will unfold. Thus we're a lot more optimistic about the prospects for the stock market. In our estimation, the Republican landslide on November 8 gave Greenspan the leeway to raise rates all at once as much as he thought necessary. Don't overlook the fact that the Republican victory removed the Fed-bashing Henry Gonzales from the chairmanship of the House Banking Committee. As a result, we think that Greenspan has completed most of his monetary tightening, with only another half point at most to come, perhaps in early 1995. And once the rate increases are behind us, we expect many happy returns for investors. This upbeat outlook rests on our expectation that Greenspan will succeed in slowing the economy slightly without tipping the country into recession. The brand-new Republican Congress is likely to help with some small tax cuts that could possibly juice up the economy a bit. The Republicans' more relaxed approach to regulation will aid industries such as drugs, insurance, tobacco and cable television.

Successful fine-tuning by Greenspan would reduce inflation pressures and allow corporate profit growth to keep rolling along at a double-digit annual rate. "We're not going to see the kind of interest rates that would bring Western civilization to its knees," says Wall Street economist Edward Yardeni at C.J. Lawrence/Deutsche Bank Securities. "Corporate profits will increase 10% to 15% in '95, and that's clearly very bullish for the stock market." Add the better-than-even prospect of a capital-gains tax cut

this year, which could cause growth stocks to take off. Here's a rundown of our '95 forecast:

◆ **Economic growth,** in terms of real (inflation-adjusted) gross domestic product, will slow to 2.8% for '95, vs. 3.8% last year.

◆ **Inflation** for consumer prices will rise moderately to 3.5%, up from a recent 3%.

◆ **Short-term interest rates** can be expected to hit 6% by summer, up from 5.5% lately, but then level off for the rest of '95.

◆ **Long-term interest rates,** recently 8%, can rise to 8.5% by summer. Then rates will drift down a tad in the second half of the year.

◆ **U.S. blue chips** can return at least 10% including dividends. Later in this chapter we rate the prospects for each of the stocks in Standard & Poor's 500-stock index, the broadest gauge of big-name companies.

◆ **Small-company stocks,** especially shares of fast-growing companies in technology, health care and retailing, will probably outpace blue chips and move up 12%.

◆ **Stock funds** whose objective is strong earnings growth could gain 12% or more.

◆ **Foreign stocks** and funds that primarily invest in them figure to appreciate 14%.

◆ **Top-quality bonds** are unlikely to return much more than 5% because the rising interest rates we envision would depress their prices.

Why stocks are headed higher. Share prices fundamentally reflect two factors—the profits corporations stand to earn over the coming year and the value investors set on each dollar of projected profits. This valuation is measured by a stock's PE (price-earnings) ratio. Investors lately were willing to pay about $15 for each $1 of projected profits, a PE of 15. After the 1990-91 recession, corporate profits rebounded strongly. Last year, profits for the stocks in the S&P 500 jumped an estimated 30%. That growth rate is certain to slow in '95 as the economy throttles back. By most economists' forecasts, however, corporate profits will still manage to increase this year at a double-digit rate. We think the S&P 500 could see 12% to 14% earnings growth this year, and smaller stocks could have increases of 17%.

By contrast, PE ratios have dropped since the start of 1992, when the earnings multiple for the S&P 500 peaked at nearly 19. The impetus? Once the bull market was two years old, investors began wondering how much longer the good times could last. We think the PE decline will stop this year when long-term interest rates level off. With the PE of the S&P 500 settling at about 14 (roughly the historic norm), stock prices will likely advance in line with companies' double-digit earnings growth. "I'm upbeat about '95 because the valuation level of the market is much more reasonable than it was two years ago," says Bradlee Perry of Babson Research, an investment firm based in Boston.

What investors should do now. Last year we correctly forecast that stocks would be poor performers. If you followed our advice and trimmed your holdings of blue chips to 30% or less of your portfolio, you probably don't have as much in stocks as you normally would. Thus for '95 you should consider raising your investment in stocks to 50% or more and shift at least half of your income investments into long-term bonds maturing in 20 to 30 years. There's no need to rush to make these adjustments, however. "As long as interest rates are rising and earnings are growing,

there will be a frustrating period in which stock prices move up and down, just as they did last year," says James Solloway, director of research at the investment firm Argus Research in New York City. And figure on a volatile bond market in the first half of '95, when we expect the Fed to make its last rate hikes. Add to your stockholdings gradually during this period and start buying long-term bonds only after rates appear to have peaked, probably after Memorial Day. Meanwhile, you probably should keep your income bets in low-risk bank CDs (certificates of deposit), money-market funds and short-term bonds maturing in five years or fewer.

In selecting mutual funds, favor those that buy stocks with above-average earnings growth. Beginning on page 20, we profile nine dynamic U.S. stock funds, many of which have large holdings of technology issues such as Microsoft and Motorola. In choosing individual stocks, emphasize companies that seem likely to churn out profit gains of 15% or more in '95. You'll find many in our rating of the entire S&P 500 later in this chapter. Besides big U.S. stocks, we think you should selectively buy shares of both small and foreign companies. Small stocks seem undervalued by historic standards and thus have ample room to grow. Based on projected earnings, these stocks as a group can command a PE that's up to 19% above the S&P 500's multiple, compared with small caps' recent 7% premium to the market. The outlook is even better for foreign stock markets (see page 20), which could have earnings gains of 20% or more.

Although we expect '95 to be a vintage year for investors, we don't think it will be a no-brainer. Stocks and bonds could suffer some temporary reversals in the first six months. By the second half of the year, however, we think you'll be enjoying the kind of double-digit returns that we envision.

Bet on the Dollar's Rebound Abroad

Why has Wall Street been so spooked by the dollar's decline in value overseas? "It's a symbolic vote of no confidence in Washington's leadership of the world economy," says economist Erich Heinemann at brokerage house Ladenburg Thalmann in New York City. More important, says Solloway at Argus Research, is the Clinton Administration's ability to manage the U.S. economy. "The dollar tends to fall when investors think U.S. inflation will exceed inflation in other industrial countries," Solloway explains. And since a falling dollar encourages U.S. inflation by boosting the cost of imports, such a decline can become a vicious cycle.

MONEY thinks the dollar's swoon has been overdone, however. Inflation may be a problem a decade from now. But we don't think it will rise beyond the 4% to 5% range in the next three years or so. Despite rapid growth in the money supply and the strength of the U.S. economy, unit labor costs, the prime determinant of long-term inflation, are rising less than 1% a year, the lowest rate since 1984. As a result, we expect to see the dollar bounce back. Our rationale: higher U.S. interest rates will attract foreign capital at a time when rates are falling overseas. Steady economic growth will make U.S. stocks look appealing to foreign investors. What's more,

economic recoveries in Europe and Japan will sharpen those countries' appetite for U.S. exports, improving our trade balance.

With the flow of world money into U.S. markets speeding up, the dollar's recovery will become self-reinforcing—a virtuous cycle, you might say—as foreign investors seek currency profits on U.S. stocks and bonds. When the foreigners eventually sell their dollar-denominated securities, they will get more francs, marks or yen if the greenback's value has increased over the time they owned the securities.

This accelerating foreign demand will help support the stock market. U.S. bonds are also likely to fare better than they have over the past year. American investors, however, may find foreign shares less appealing in part because their prices will translate into fewer dollars. (Note that a stronger dollar deflates returns earned abroad, but a weaker dollar inflates those returns.) While a recovery in the dollar can't power a bull market by itself, it sure adds zest to an ongoing stock rally, as history confirms. The value of the dollar fell to low points in 1988 following the October '87 stock crash, in the 1990-91 recession and in 1992. In all three cases, the Dow shot up 15% to 20% over the next couple of years as the dollar strengthened again.

Your Stake in Orange County's Squeeze

When a municipality mismanages its money, taxpayers and municipal bond investors can get crushed. In the case of Orange County,

Calif., the pain is intensified by the fact that nobody really knows how bad it is going to get. The county filed for bankruptcy last

December after its highly leveraged $8 billion investment fund, which was well stocked with the risky securities known as derivatives, plunged $1.5 billion in value. Total losses will exceed $2 billion. The scary headlines sent municipal bond prices tumbling and raised troubling questions about how taxpayer money gets managed in municipalities across the country. For Orange County and the other local governments that also had money in the fund, the debacle could mean a loss of more than 26% of their investment. The most seriously hurt will face a shortage of cash to pay teachers, collect garbage, fund capital projects and service debt. Here's what the crunch means to you.

◆ **If you invest in municipal bonds,** now may be a good time to scoop up some bargains created by panic selling. Muni prices were already reeling from many interest-rate hikes in the past year, and the selling only intensified in the wake of Orange County's troubles. Still, the fiasco is a reminder that munis do carry some risk for which investors should be compensated. Before you buy individual bonds or bond funds, compare the after-tax returns of munis and taxable government issues. You want to get at least 0.2 to 0.5 percentage points more with munis than you can get by owning higher-quality Treasury bonds. Also keep in mind that a high credit rating on muni bonds does not necessarily mean low risk—witness the fact that Orange County issues were once highly rated. You can protect against default by sticking to insured bonds, which typically pay 0.5 to 0.75 percentage points less. But insurance doesn't shield you against losses attributable to rising interest rates or the kind of panic selling that has hit California bonds.

◆ **If you own California muni bonds,** try to remain calm. Almost half of the long-term

bonds affected by Orange County's troubles carried insurance or some other guarantee that interest and principal will be paid even if the issuer goes bankrupt. So you may be suffering from a short-term price drop. But you should get paid in full at maturity. Several single-state California muni funds, including TransAmerica California Tax-Free Income and Oppenheimer California Tax-Exempt, had at least 5% of their entire portfolio in Orange County-related bonds that don't carry these protections. Not all of these bonds appear equally vulnerable, however. For example, the Irvine Unified School District and the Orange County Flood Control District kept only their spare cash in the pool. Even if your bonds are in trouble, resist the temptation to sell. Orange County, which ranks as one of the nation's wealthiest, appears to have the financial wherewithal to make good on its debts in the long run.

◆ **If you're a California taxpayer,** brace yourself for fewer government services or maybe more taxes as Orange County and its fellow municipal investors scramble to get by without funds from the investment pool. Could something this rotten happen where you live? You bet. Municipal investments aren't closely regulated by the SEC, and state laws vary greatly. "Hundreds, maybe even thousands, of municipalities could suffer substantial losses from derivatives," says Robert Lamb, professor of finance and management at New York University, "though not on the order of Orange County's." If you suspect local elected officials in your town are playing with matches near your tax dollars, call your local treasurer or city council member. Ask whether your government's fund uses derivatives, invests short-term money in long-term securities or uses leverage. If you don't like the answers, tell the mayor and threaten to vote your convictions.

10

Our All Star Brokers' 30 Top Picks

Whether your market stance is bullish, bearish or sheepish, pause for a moment to tot up your portfolio's ball-park return since MONEY published its roster of 10 All Star brokers and their top stocks a year ago. Here's a crib sheet—and a crying towel. Investors in U.S. stock funds have lost roughly 2% as a group. Holders of seemingly stodgy government bond funds actually lost money as yields on 30-year Treasuries, mirroring Federal Reserve rate hikes, spiked two percentage points to around 8%. And our All Stars? Their 30 picks and pans gained an awesome 16%, on average, against a corresponding 1% rise in the S&P 500 index.

If that 16% profit puts yours to shame, you have an added incentive to check out the advice of our '95 All Stars. Our new team of accomplished brokers sports one new member plus nine repeaters from '94 (their reward for outperforming the S&P 500). Pacing our nine market beaters was Paine Webber's Stanley Trilling, a 25-year veteran based in Los Angeles. Trilling scored not only a 43% average profit but last year's biggest gain as well—a 111% rise for Special Devices, a $58 million (annual sales) maker of gizmos in auto air bags. Other highlights of the '94 season:

Best in the West. Our top three stock pickers all reside in western states. This talent pool doesn't surprise Trilling, however. "We've all been burned by Wall Street hypesters," he explains. "So out West, we tend to develop our own sources as well as a healthy skepticism of hot stocks."

Spence's winning streak. The gifted stock picking of Steven Spence, a 23-year veteran of Paine Webber in Portland, Ore., has earned him a slot on each of the five All Star squads that we've fielded since 1988. How did his three recommendations do in '94? He placed second, with an impressive 33% average profit. Since '88, Spence's annual gains averaged 23%, vs. the market's 14%.

Don't count your chickens. Peter Slocum of A.G. Edwards in Carefree, Ariz., No. 3 with a 25% profit, named as his top '94 pick WLR Foods, an obscure $617 million poultry producer selling for $20 a share. By March the stock was up 60% to $32 following a $330 million buy-out bid by $4.7 billion chicken czar Tyson Foods. Alas, WLR's board thwarted Tyson's offer, plunging the stock back to $21, a mere 7% gain. Moral: take the money once a corporate bid is on the table.

In selecting the All Stars, we sought referrals from money managers and brokerage executives, who were asked to nominate exemplars at firms other than their own. Candidates had to take new accounts of $150,000 or less and to have a squeaky clean record of professional conduct according to the files of the National Association of Securities Dealers, the best source of disciplinary actions against brokers. We then focused on the important attributes of accountability and independent thinking that set All Stars apart from journeymen. Our 10 typically:

◆ Base their recommendations on their own research as well as that of stock analysts.

◆ Make a practice of owning the stocks on their recommended lists—a show of confidence increasingly rare among brokers.

◆ Avoid selling most brokerage products, including mutual funds, whose fat sales and management fees can weigh down returns.

◆ Give their regular customers brokerage commission discounts that average roughly 20% to 25% in many cases.

The following All Star bios appear in order of the broker's average gain over last year's season. They feature his or her '95 market outlook; three are bullish (down from six in '94), six are anxious (vs. three) and one bearish (Steve Spence both years). Each offers three recommendations capable of beating the S&P 500 in '95. Their picks also figure to deliver earnings growth—the best proxy of a stock's potential appreciation—averaging a heady 38% next year. That's nearly triple the earnings rise forecast for the companies in the S&P 500. Yet the All Stars' picks as a group are priced 20% below the market's earnings multiple, recently 15 based on most analysts' projections for '95.

Stanley Trilling	Up 43%

FIRM: Paine Webber, Los Angeles, 800-344-3786. AGE: 55. ROOKIE YEAR: 1969. CLIENTS: 250. MINIMUM ACCOUNT: None. AVERAGE: $1 million. OUTLOOK: Anxious.

RÉSUMÉ: Native of Los Angeles; graduate of the University of California at Berkeley; formerly a marketer at Switzerland-based drugmaker Hoffmann La Roche

CLIENT PROFILE: Entrepreneurs and money managers who demand fresh ideas from his four-broker Trilling Partners boutique with a branch in New York City

COMMENT: "Emerging growth stocks, our specialty, figure to excel in a market environment that's laboring under higher interest rates," says Trilling. Last year the Los Angeles broker recommended two such up-and-com-

ers, top performer Special Devices (up 111%) and $38 million Veterinary Centers of America (up 19%), plus a short sale of $3 billion media giant Times Mirror (no change).

PICKS: Buy **Williams Controls** (traded over the counter, lately $3). Trilling expects rapid 25% annual earnings growth through '97 from this $42 million firm with a dominant 60% share of the emergent $40 million market for efficient electronic throttles used to bring big diesel trucks into compliance with federal clean-air laws. And buy $475 million recorded music wholesaler **Alliance Entertainment** (New York Stock Exchange, $5). Its projected 30% annual profit growth over the next three years, says Trilling, derives largely from economies of scale that are realized by snapping up the mom-and-pop operations that characterize Alliance's highly fragmented $1.5 billion field.

PAN: Sell short the $28 million **Positive Response Television** (OTC, $17), creator of infomercials for $40 Super Slicers and other impulse purchases hawked on air by chairman Mike Levey. In 1993 the Federal Trade Commission forced Levey to pay $275,000 to consumers who claimed they were misled by his pitches at Twin Star Productions, a now bankrupt firm that Trilling says may provide a sneak preview of Positive Response's prospects.

Steven Spence	Up 33%

FIRM: Paine Webber, Portland, Ore., 800-245-0900. AGE: 47. ROOKIE YEAR: 1971. CLIENTS: 550. MINIMUM: None. AVERAGE: $250,000. OUTLOOK: Bearish.

RÉSUMÉ: Native of Pasadena; graduate of San Diego State; career broker who heads a three-adviser team

CLIENT PROFILE: Executives who typically own stakes in the companies that they manage

COMMENT: "I'm an old-fashioned value investor," says Spence, who looks for prosperous but low-profile companies with stocks that sell at bargain prices relative to such fundamentals as cash flow and book value. Last year's three picks certainly proved to be cheapos: $169 million Key Tronic (up 37%), a maker of computer keyboards; $106 million In Focus Systems (up 36%), an innovator in color LCD (liquid crystal display) screens designed for portable PCs; and $5 billion papermaker James River (up 25%). Such values are so scarce these days, however, that he's urging clients to stash as much as 50% of their funds in low-risk Treasury bills in anticipation of long-term interest rates, which lately have been around 8%, spurting to 8.75% in the first half of '95. Still, Spence is decidedly upbeat on three companies—two of them small West Coast firms that are currently on the rebound under new, highly motivated managements.

PICKS: Buy $80 million **Vans Inc**. (OTC, $6). The retro canvas sneakers made by this California firm are suddenly so hip among teenagers and women, says Spence, that '95 earnings will hop 185%. Buy $61 million **Data I/O** (OTC, $4), where he sees an 80% profit gain this year. This Redmond, Wash. company's software allows computer designers to program chips and thus create prototypes much faster than is possible by using standardized components. And buy $4 billion **Bindley Western** (OTC, $13), the lowest-cost producer in the fast-consolidating $50 billion field of wholesale drug distribution. "Bindley seems destined to be swallowed by a bigger rival," predicts Spence, with a takeover bid that's probably north of $27, a possible double.

Peter Slocum   Up 25%

FIRM: A.G. Edwards, Carefree, Ariz., 800-688-3123. AGE: 54. ROOKIE YEAR: 1966. CLIENTS: 250. MINIMUM: None. AVERAGE: $500,000. OUTLOOK: Bullish.

RÉSUMÉ: Native of Boston; graduate of Columbia University (A.B. and M.A.); began brokerage career at Merrill Lynch in London; worked abroad for 15 years before settling down in Carefree (population 1,900), where he's partnered with son Josh, 33

CLIENT PROFILE: Corporate executives and money managers in the U.S. and overseas

COMMENT: "My clients expect me to bring them ideas that aren't shopworn on Wall Street," says Slocum. The three he offered last year netted a bittersweet 7% profit on WLR Foods (see "Don't count your chickens" on page 11), a fat 68% gain on $210 million furnituremaker Bush Industries, and no change on $27 million medical supplier Orthomet (news of its acquisition at $11 a share, a 38% rise, came after our contest's cutoff).

PICKS: Buy $140 million **Rawlings Sporting Goods** (OTC, $14), the famed name on baseballs, footballs and basketballs (and related gear) that went public last year at $12. "The stupid baseball strike tainted the stock's debut but not the company," says Slocum. He expects earnings to pop 56% in '95, lifting the shares about 43% to $20. Buy $62 million **Insignia Financial** (OTC, $21), the rapidly expanding manager of 205,000 apartment units in 44 states. Slocum figures Insignia's profits can rise 40% this year, boosting the stock 33%. And buy $118 million **Rural/Metro** (OTC, $21), originally a private fire department in Arizona that's now buying up complementary ambulance services in eight states. Slocum's '95 target for the stock is $27, a 38% advance.

Malcolm Lowenthal   Up 23%

FIRM: Wertheim Schroder, New York City, 800-992-9876. AGE: 59. ROOKIE YEAR: 1962. CLIENTS: 200. MINIMUM: None. AVERAGE: $250,000. OUTLOOK: Anxious.

RÉSUMÉ: Native of Waterbury, Conn.; graduate of Cornell University; career broker

CLIENT PROFILE: Seasoned investors who routinely buy stocks that appear cheap and also sell short the shares of companies that seem unduly dear in price

COMMENT: "There are two sides to a stock story," says Lowenthal. "I talk to the bulls and bears, try to separate fact from fiction and invest accordingly." Last year's winning advice: Sell short $54 million hearing-aid maker ReSound (a 51% profit); buy Cardiovascular Imaging, a $14 million medical-technology concern (up 14%); and buy $3 billion media power McGraw-Hill (up 4%).

PICKS: Buy $219 million **Recognition International** (NYSE, $7). This once ailing manufacturer of high-volume document scanning and retrieval equipment, Lowenthal says, is headed in '95 for a sharp earnings turnaround and a possible buy-out at $14 to $18 a share, a 100% to 157% jump.

PANS: Sell short $360 million **Cordis** (OTC, $59). He thinks the stock of this cardiovascular instrument maker has been unduly inflated by investors' ardor for last year's takeover bid for $266 million rival, SciMed Life Systems, by Boston Scientific. "Cordis' $60 stock is headed to a more realistic $45, or 24% less, this year," he adds. And sell short **Vivus Inc.** (OTC, $13), a medical start-up with a rich total market value of $160 million. The rub? "Vivus' sole product, a therapy for impotency now in clinical trials, isn't really an improvement on existing treatments that are available from big drugmakers like Upjohn," he warns.

Monk White   Up 14%

FIRM: Smith Barney, Dallas, 800-527-5814. AGE: 53. ROOKIE YEAR: 1966. CLIENTS: 100. MINIMUM: $150,000. AVERAGE: $500,000. OUTLOOK: Anxious.

RÉSUMÉ: Native of Fort Worth; graduate of the University of Texas and Penn's Wharton School (M.B.A.); career broker

CLIENT PROFILE: Wealthy Dallas/Fort Worth families and dealmakers including Richard Rainwater, who made his first $100 million managing the Bass brothers' billions

COMMENT: It's no coincidence that Smith Barney often serves as an investment banker to deals struck by Rainwater, whose friendship with White dates back to their days at the University of Texas. "We both look for stocks with a competitive edge that's not recognized by most investors," says White. His '94 picks: $3.6 billion HMO operator United Healthcare (up 43%), $63 billion General Electric (up 4%) and $4 billion YPF, Argentina's top oil company (down 5%). For '95, White likes three multinationals well positioned to weather rising U.S. interest rates while riding the strengthening economic upturn he envisions overseas.

PICKS: Buy $675 million slot-machine king **International Game Technology** (NYSE, $19), which White thinks can rise 58% to $30 in '95, given his forecast of 26% growth in earnings. Bet on a 35% gain to $27 for **PartnerRe** (OTC, $20) in anticipation of a 50% surge in '95 profits at this $1 billion (in assets) reinsurer of property and casualty companies. And look for embattled $63 billion tobacco behemoth **Philip Morris** (NYSE, $62) to advance 21% to $75 in step with its expanding share, lately around 46%, of the $48 billion U.S. cigarette market.

Joan Getsinger   Up 9%

FIRM: Donaldson Lufkin & Jenrette in San Francisco, 800-227-4492. AGE: 50. ROOKIE YEAR: 1980. CLIENTS: 500. MINIMUM: $100,000. AVERAGE: $250,000. OUTLOOK: Bullish.

RÉSUMÉ: Native of Bloomfield Hills, Mich.; graduate of the University of Michigan; began career in 1972 as a secretary; rose to junior partner of a prominent broker; went solo as a stock picker in 1983

CLIENT PROFILE: Conservative investors, many of whom were referrals from two brokers who retired in the mid-1980s

COMMENT: "My clients hire me to create portfolios whose main objective is a balance of both growth and income," says Getsinger, "yet still manage to outperform the market over the long term." In pursuit of that goal, she recommended three blue chips in '94: BankAmerica (up 16%), the nation's No. 2 bank after Citicorp with $214 billion in assets; $3.6 billion AMP Inc. (up 14%), the world leader in electronic connectors; and $7.7 billion Deere, tops worldwide in farm equipment (down 2%). Now Getsinger says she's finding uncommon bargains in three sectors—auto, financial and technology stocks—that she follows closely.

PICKS: Again buy **BankAmerica** (NYSE, $42) for a projected 31% rise to $55 this year. "Even Wall Streeters will eventually recognize that the California economy, BA's traditional stronghold, is gaining steam again," says Getsinger. Buy beleaguered $150 billion **General Motors** (NYSE, $39), which she believes can vroom 54% to $60 on a forecast 45% rebound in '95 earnings. And buy her pet small-stock sleeper, $105 million **Cerplex Group** (OTC, $13). She thinks this low-profile leader in the $3 billion field of independent computer/electronics repair centers can probably double its earnings in '95, boosting the stock roughly 46% to $19.

George Stark — Up 9%

FIRM: Burnham Securities, Houston, 713-622-1594. AGE: 50. ROOKIE YEAR: 1967. CLIENTS: 38 families. MINIMUM: $150,000. AVERAGE: $1.8 million. OUTLOOK: Bullish.

RÉSUMÉ: Born in pre-Castro Havana; raised in Paris; graduate of Cornell and France's Insead (M.B.A.); career broker who teamed up with the Burnham family (who

once ran Drexel Burnham) to launch their five-year-old firm based in New York City

CLIENT PROFILE: Monied clans in Texas, the Southwest, Latin America and Europe who value his fluency in five languages

COMMENT: "My preference for fairly conservative big-caps mirrors that of our $105 million Burnham Fund, on whose investment committee I sit," notes Stark. Last year he recommended two such stocks, $1.4 billion Hilton Hotels (up 37%) and $70 billion AT&T (down 3%), plus $425 million software house ASK Group (down 8%). Now he's banking on three new entries whose booming profits figure to be fatter in '95 than most analysts forecast.

PICKS: Buy $50 billion **Chrysler** (NYSE, $46) before billionaire Kirk Kerkorian follows through on his bluff to buy more than 9% of the stock. Stark sees 23% earnings growth this year fueled by pedal-to-the-metal demand for its innovative minivans, surefooted Jeeps and stylish Dodge Ram pickups. Buy $253 billion (in assets) **Citicorp** (NYSE, $45). Stark is confident that the bank's thriving business overseas, particularly in today's fast-emerging Asian and Latin American markets, ensures big profit gains averaging 20% annually through '97. And buy $125 million **Aerovox** (OTC, $8), an unheralded leader in low-tech electric capacitors (used in many household appliances) that he predicts will boost earnings 35% in '95.

Sherri Carfi — Up 5%

FIRM: Chicago Corp., Chicago, 800-621-0686. AGE: 45. ROOKIE YEAR: 1971. CLIENTS: 175. MINIMUM: $100,000. AVERAGE: $1 million. OUTLOOK: Anxious

RÉSUMÉ: Native of Chicago; career broker who, like Getsinger, rapidly worked her way up from secretary to broker

CLIENT PROFILE: Owners of successful companies and professional money managers, who account for more than 80% of her business

Our All Stars' Picks and Pans for '95

Here are 27 buys whose earnings growth—the best proxy of a stock's potential appreciation—figures to average 38% this year (plus three short sales as hedges against a toppy market). That's nearly triple the 12% to 14% profit rise forecast for the S&P 500.

Broker Company Phone	Stock	Buy/ sell short	Recent price	Earnings per share	EPS change	PE	Price
					Projected 1995		
Stanley Trilling	Williams Controls	BUY	$3.00	$0.33	43%	9	$4[1]
Paine Webber	Alliance Entertainment	BUY	5.00	0.55	38	10	8[1]
800-344-3786	Positive Response TV	SELL SHORT	17.00	N.A.	N.A.	N.A.	5
Steven Spence	Vans Inc.	BUY	6.00	0.40	185	15	17[1]
Paine Webber	Data I/O	BUY	4.00	0.45	80	9	7[1]
800-245-0900	Bindley Western	BUY	13.00	1.35	13	10	27
Peter Slocum	Rawlings	BUY	14.00	1.40	56	10	20
A.G. Edwards	Insignia Financial	BUY	21.00	1.40	40	15	28
800-688-3123	Rural/Metro	BUY	21.00	0.90	27	23	27
Malcolm Lowenthal	Recognition Intl.	BUY	7.00	0.50	N.A.	14	14
Wertheim Schroder	Cordis	SELL SHORT	59.00	3.00	24	20	45
800-992-9876	Vivus Inc.	SELL SHORT	13.00	N.A.	N.A.	N.A.	5
Monk White	Intl. Game Technology	BUY	19.00	1.26	26	15	30
Smith Barney	PartnerRe	BUY	20.00	4.50	50	4	27
800-527-5814	Philip Morris	BUY	62.00	6.20	14	10	75
Joan Getsinger	BankAmerica	BUY	42.00	6.20	14	7	55
Donaldson Lufkin	General Motors	BUY	39.00	8.00	45	5	60
800-227-4492	Cerplex Group	BUY	13.00	1.05	102	12	19
George Stark	Chrysler	BUY	46.00	10.75	23	4	57[1]
Burnham Securities	Citicorp	BUY	45.00	6.10	14	7	51[1]
713-622-1594	Aerovox	BUY	8.00	1.25	35	6	11[1]
Sherri Carfi	First Alert	BUY	17.00	1.00	25	17	21[1]
Chicago Corp.	Three-Five Systems	BUY	33.00	1.83	20	18	40[1]
800-621-0686	American Electronic	BUY	10.00	0.76	21	13	12[1]
Robert Anning	StarBanc	BUY	38.00	4.25	10	9	49
Merrill Lynch	Cincinnati Financial	BUY	50.00	4.25	16	12	60
800-234-2099	MBNA	BUY	25.00	2.35	32	11	35
Isadore Friedman	Intel	BUY	61.00	6.70	13	9	73
Paine Webber	Microsoft	BUY	62.00	2.67	25	23	75
800-937-7071	Amgen	BUY	58.00	3.70	21	16	74
S&P 500 index			462.00	31.00	12	15	—

[1]Money's target prices based on broker's earnings projections

COMMENT: "I focus on smaller stocks whose earnings can accelerate faster than most analysts expect," says Carfi. But she buys only companies growing at least 20% annually and whose managers candidly field her questions or those of her 75 institutional clients. Her '94 picks: Integrated Health, a $433 million chain of post-op clinics (up 21%); $64 million direct marketer DiMark Inc. (down 1%); and $260 million data processor SEI Corp. (down 5%).

PICKS: Buy $233 million **First Alert**

(OTC, $17). Carfi sees profits at this pioneer of home smoke alarms surging 25% this year in response to growing consumer acceptance of its $45 home carbon monoxide detectors (with 70% of the $60 million U.S. market). Also buy $74 million **Three-Five Systems** (American Stock Exchange, $33), maker of LCD screens in many Motorola cell phones. She expects Three-Five's earnings to compound about 20% annually to '98. And bet on brisk 22% annual growth from $35 million **American Electronic Components** (OTC, $10), a big innovator in custom sensors that automakers increasingly use to improve engine performance and anti-lock brakes.

Robert Anning	Up 3%

FIRM: Merrill Lynch, Cincinnati, 800-234-2099. AGE: 54. ROOKIE YEAR: 1967. CLIENTS: 300. MINIMUM ACCOUNT: $150,000. AVERAGE: $1.2 million. OUTLOOK: Anxious.

RÉSUMÉ: Native of Cincinnati; graduate of Trinity College; former Navy intelligence officer who was assigned to Adm. Thomas Moorer's staff

CLIENT PROFILE: Wealthy Midwest families

COMMENT: "Traders rarely retire rich," says Anning, who credits skills honed in the Navy with helping him discern when Wall Street scuttlebutt is credible. "I strive to own stocks whose reliable growth reduces the risk of losing money over time." Still, he was nearly torpedoed by one '94 pick—$2.6 billion carpet king Shaw Industries, which sank 34% on fears that rising interest rates would undermine housing stocks. The loss, however, was amply offset by profits on $1.5 billion bottler Coca-Cola Amatil (up 25%) and $1.2 billion appliance maker Sunbeam-Oster (up 17%). Now Anning finds outstanding values in financial stocks, another group beaten down by soaring interest rates.

PICKS: Buy two prosperous but glamour-less franchises based in Cincinnati: $9.2 billion (in assets) **Star Banc** (NYSE, $38) and $4.8 billion insurer **Cincinnati Financial** (OTC, $50). Anning sees well-run Star as a merger waiting to happen. Even if he's wrong, earnings figure to push the stock to a '95 target price of $49, a 29% profit. Bank on a 20% gain to $60 for Cincinnati Financial, a property and casualty shop, powered by a 16% rise in '95 earnings. And buy $9.8 billion **MBNA** (NYSE, $25), the No. 2 issuer of bank credit cards (after Citicorp) for a 40% ride to $35. The impetus, he predicts, will be the huge 50% increases in total receivables both in '94 and '95 from MBNA's specialty—so-called affinity cards marketed to 3,600 groups.

Isadore Friedman

FIRM: Paine Webber, Boca Raton, 800-937-7071. AGE: 51. ROOKIE YEAR: 1969. CLIENTS: 100. MINIMUM: None. AVERAGE: $2 million. OUTLOOK: Anxious.

RÉSUMÉ: Native of Newburgh, N.Y.; graduate of the University of Pennsylvania and Georgetown Law School; career broker

CLIENT PROFILE: Conservative investors, mostly professionals, who have managed to accumulate sizable personal and company pension funds under his control

COMMENT: A borderline bear, Friedman is urging clients to stash half their money in cash and intermediate-term bonds, mainly tax-exempt munis. The rest rides on the big-name growth stocks he's long followed. "These days I have to see at least a 20% annual return from a stock to compensate clients for the risk that the market's overvalued and topping out," he says. The few he's confident can attain his 20% bogey share two comforting traits. First, the companies traditionally generate a lot of business overseas as well as Stateside. And they promise to deliver better-than-expected earnings growth in '95.

PICKS: Buy $11 billion chipmaker **Intel** (OTC, $61) to get in the fast lane of the information highway that communications firms are building. Despite embarrassing but minor bugs in the firm's advanced Pentium chips, Friedman says Intel's technological lead figures to lift earnings at least 20% this year and the stock 20% to $73. Expect 25% profit growth and 21% stock appreciation this year from $4.9 bil-lion software powerhouse **Microsoft** (OTC, $62), another information juggernaut scheduled to unveil its much-anticipated Windows '95 operating system later this year. And capitalize on the biotech stock bust by buying into the sector's star, $1.6 billion **Amgen** (OTC, $58), before a major drug company does. Friedman sees Amgen's profits rising 21% and elevating the stock 28% to $74 over the course of '95.

How to Profit from GATT's Go-Ahead

The ease with which the world trade agreement known as GATT (General Agreement on Tariffs and Trade) sailed through Congress last December came as no surprise to Corporate America, which can't wait to cash in on the pact's reduced tariffs, enhanced copyright protections and generally freer trade. What's good for business is also great for investors in selected companies. Among GATT's immediate beneficiaries will be drug manufacturers, computer software companies and chipmakers. Going forward, the list of potential winners could include nearly every large U.S. company with sizable exports or global operations. "GATT takes the shackles off the most efficient U.S. companies and allows them to go after billions of consumers around the world," crows strategist Hugh Johnson at brokerage First Albany in Albany, N.Y. And portfolio manager Edward Bousa of Putnam Investments in Boston goes one step further. "The winners from the passage of GATT will include almost any cost-efficient company that has access to global markets," he explains. Our research points to seven specific stocks listed below.

◆ **Merck** (NYSE, $37). The phasing out of international tariffs on pharmaceuticals and stronger patent protection for prescription drugs stands to enrich Merck, the premier U.S. drug company with estimated 1995 revenues of $17 billion. In response, strategist James Solloway at Argus Research in New York City sees the stock gaining 36% to $50 over the next 18 months.

◆ **J.P. Morgan** (NYSE, $58). Thanks to a PE ratio below nine and a juicy yield, this leading global bank ($138 billion in assets) allows even conservative investors to play the free-trade trend. "J.P. Morgan will be the preeminent player in North America, Europe and Asia in investment banking and financing trade," says Putnam's Bousa. He thinks the shares could climb as much as 36% to the high $70s over 18 months.

◆ **General Electric** (NYSE, $46). "Top free-trade beneficiaries will include companies that build global infrastructure such as transportation systems and power plants," says Smith Barney's portfolio strategist Marshall Acuff. For that reason, he recommends $63 billion GE, which is the leading supplier of a variety of industrial technologies worldwide. A key business line is building power plants,

Ben Graham's Classic Rules of Investing

As we explain at length in this chapter, 1995 could be a surprisingly good year for investors. Yet we remind ourselves that no matter how accurate—or inaccurate—our market forecasts may be, the real key to maximizing profits is choosing the right individual investments. With that truth in mind, we contacted Janet Lowe, author of *Benjamin Graham on Value Investing*, a book that takes a fresh look at the investing principles espoused by the late inventor of securities analysis. Here, as distilled by Lowe, are Graham's essential rules for success by patient shareholders.

◆ **Don't pay much attention to the market**. It's easier to find good buys when share prices are cheap overall. But you can still spot a few bargains even when the market is out of sight relative to its fundamentals.

◆ **Buy stocks as if you're buying the company.** Don't try to make a quick buck on a crummy company. Look for firms whose underlying products or services are so good you would be willing to own their shares forever.

◆ **Look for specific signs of value**. The most attractive stocks have below-average PE ratios, above-average dividend yields and earnings that have doubled since 1985 with no more than two annual declines of more than 5%.

◆ **Focus on quality and consistency**. Especially if you're a beginner, you should buy only blue-chip stocks with long records of steadily rising earnings.

◆ **Diversify with both stocks and bonds**. You should keep at least 25% of your money in bonds and cash reserves. And plan on holding at least eight stocks. If you can't afford that many, invest via stock funds.

◆ **Think for yourself and be patient**. The biggest rewards come from hanging on to underappreciated growth stocks for five years or more. Consider Graham's most famous student, Omaha billionaire Warren Buffett, who buys and sells stocks so rarely that Buffett describes his investing style as lethargy bordering on sloth. Some sloth! His patient approach to managing his portfolio has earned him a fortune.

often in today's rapidly industrializing markets, including China. Acuff figures the stock could gain 30% to $60 over 18 months.

◆ **Intel** (OTC, $61). The widely publicized calculation flaw in its Pentium chips has embarrassed the $11 billion chipmaker, says Solloway. But that computation problem, which affects a relatively small number of heavy-duty computer users, will fade away before long. And Intel will re-emerge with greater copyright protection of its chip designs. Thus Solloway thinks the stock could rise about 30% to $80 within 18 months.

◆ **Caterpillar** (NYSE, $52). The world's largest producer of earthmoving equipment gets 49% of its $14 billion sales overseas. That's the top share among major U.S. capital goods companies, says analyst Steven Colbert of Prudential Securities in New York

City. He thinks Caterpillar's stock can move up more than 24% to $64 in 18 months.

◆ **United Technologies** (NYSE, $59). Who will profit as skyscrapers proliferate around the world? United Technologies, says Bousa. The $22 billion company is a leading maker of elevators (under the Otis brand name) and air conditioners (Carrier). Bousa sees the stock rising 22% to $72 within 18 months.

◆ **Boeing** (NYSE, $47). As the leading maker of commercial jet aircraft, $21 billion Boeing is a huge exporter. Moreover, says Merrill Lynch analyst Byron Callan: "We're at a point in the cycle where airlines will be buying planes to replace old ones and handle increasing traffic." Over the next 18 months, he thinks the stock could rise 17% to at least $55 propelled in part by all the business execs flying around to push global trade.

Twelve Sturdy Stock Funds to Weigh

The winning prescription for mutual fund investors this year is fairly straightforward. With the U.S. economy slowing, you should fill up on domestic funds favoring growth stocks with the potential to appreciate 12% or more. And to benefit from a rising economic tide overseas, invest some of the money you have earmarked for stocks in funds that buy foreign shares. Here's our rationale, starting with the case for growth funds, backed by data in the table on page 23.

In general, two broad categories of stocks, growth and value, take turns topping the market. Growth stocks are shares in companies that historically have been able to boost earnings by 15% a year or more. Value stocks are those selling below the per-share worth of their assets or future earnings. For the past two years, value was in vogue as the recovery that began in the spring of 1991 boosted the earnings of economically sensitive corporations. Accordingly, the value-stock index kept by Prudential Securities has outperformed its growth counterpart 29% to 15% since the beginning of '92.

Remember what happened to the Democrats on Election Day? Well, look for a similar shift in national leadership to occur in the stock market this year. With economic growth expected to slow half a percentage point or so to about 2.8% in '95, MONEY believes the market is poised to favor growth shares. In a downshifting economy, high-torque cyclical outfits that roar during the early stages of an expansion typically cede market leadership to sportier growth stocks that can more dependably churn out double-digit earnings gains. Moreover, growth stocks have been selling at attractive prices lately. At last count the average PE of growth stocks

was just 1.8 times that of the typical value stock based on research by the Leuthold Group in Minneapolis. The last time that ratio was below 2 was in mid-1988. Over the next 2.5 years, growth stocks gained a total of 81%, while value stocks advanced 49%.

To help you profit from this likely change in relative performance, we identified nine superior funds that specialize in U.S. growth stocks. All have outperformed stock funds as a group over a recent five-year period and are well positioned to thrive in '95. In the profiles below, you'll notice that most have substantial holdings in technology and health care, two sectors that many analysts believe possess the best growth opportunities for the decade. "The producers of today's capital goods—computer hardware and software and telecommunications equipment—will be the premier growth stocks," says Wall Street economist Edward Yardeni. And with Republicans in control of Congress, there's much less of a threat of health care legislation crimping drug and hospital company profits.

Our nine U.S. selections are divided into three groups according to the median market capitalization (total value of outstanding shares) of the companies they hold. By and large, small-cap funds invest in companies with market values of $1 billion or less. Mid-caps mainly own those pegged between $1 billion and $5 billion. And large-caps focus on firms worth more than $5 billion. If growth is king this year as we expect, our nine growth funds have the potential to return 12% on average, compared with 10% or so for the S&P 500.

Here's the argument for owning foreign stock funds, which disappointed investors in '94. Economic growth in many nations around the world will outpace that of the U.S., and foreign stock markets will show bigger advances as well. Double-digit gains could emerge in Asia and Europe as economic recoveries gain strength. Reflecting the variety of conditions abroad, the three foreign funds we've chosen follow differing investment styles. But all have been outstanding performers that figure to return 15% or more in '95. Below are descriptions of our choices (all are no-loads except where noted).

Stars among small-cap specialists.
Fund manager Richard Aster gobbles up growth with his **Meridian Fund**—but only if the price is right. "I have heard growth fund managers say that they really like a stock so much they do not care what the valuation is," says Aster. "We do care." He seeks companies that are generating earnings spurts of 15% or more a year, and he prefers to buy them when their PEs are lower than their growth rates. As a result, the fast-growing stocks in Meridian recently had a reasonable average PE of 18 times estimated '95 earnings, not far above the 15 multiple for the big-cap S&P 500. That has proved to be a formula for success over the past five years, when Meridian returned 17% annually. Aster's price discipline applies to selling too. When he believes a stock is overvalued, he will ditch it even if he still likes the business. The stocks he owns have positioned him well in market sectors likely to excel in '95. For example, 14% of his portfolio recently was stashed in cellular telephone stocks like AirTouch and Cellular Communications. He had an additional 8% in technology issues and 12% in health care shares like Surgical Care Affiliates, which builds and staffs outpatient surgical centers.

PBHG Growth appeals to investors who want to go all out for appreciation. But fasten your seat belt. While the fund raced to outsize gains of 52% in '91 and 49% in '93, it skidded badly during the first half of last year, dropping 16%. Now manager Gary Pilgrim and his staff of 12 analysts appear to be back on track. They scrutinize a database of 400 companies with projected annual earnings growth rates of 20% or more. To find the stocks most likely to succeed in that group of growth getters, Pilgrim & Co. assess the quality of each company's earnings via such indicators as whether profits consistently come in above analysts' estimates. The portfolio recently included companies whose five-year earnings growth averaged 30% annually, vs. 18% for its group. Technology stocks such as Zebra Technologies, a maker of bar code printers, lately were 30% of assets. Another 22% was in consumer companies like Cobra Golf, an innovator of oversized irons and woods. And 21% was invested in health issues such as Health Management Associates, an operator of rural hospitals.

T. Rowe Price New Horizons' John Laporte, a veteran of small-caps, is fond of stocks with flashy track records. Laporte's selections recently sported an average five-year growth rate of 27% annually, which should help the fund catch the growth-stock tail wind in '95. With big stakes in technology (20%) and health care (16%), the portfolio resembles many of its growth-seeking peers. Laporte is firmly convinced that mounting pressure to reduce medical costs (with or without sweeping reform legislation) will benefit prized health care holdings such as HMO operator United Healthcare.

Mid-caps poised to beat the market.
Lead fund manager Alexander Macmillan of **Columbia Growth** seems to have mastered the tricky game of moving in and out of market segments to catch big upswings. He recently had 16% of the fund's assets in technology issues such as Hewlett-Packard; 9% in health care stocks such as Columbia/HCA

Healthcare; and 7% in energy companies such as Anadarko Petroleum, a natural gas producer. That puts Macmillan right in sync with MONEY's 1995 forecast, which calls for strong performance by energy stocks.

Safeco Equity's Doug Johnson has made large bets in stocks large and small throughout his 10-year tenure at the helm of the fund. More often than not, those wagers have paid off over the past five years, when the fund returned 13% annually. And Safeco Equity thrived last year, returning 10%. The fund's holdings range from small-company zoomers like Callaway Golf to such big-company boomers as media giant Knight-Ridder. The mix of large and small gives the portfolio a median size that puts it squarely in mid-cap territory. Johnson recently had 14% of fund assets in technology stocks and 10% in utilities. He particularly likes the high dividends of telephone utilities such as GTE, which lately yielded 6% against 2.7% for the S&P 500.

Vanguard/Primecap's lead manager Howard Schow fills his portfolio with high-growth companies that are temporarily (he hopes) out of favor with investors. Enough of Schow's fallen angels have regained their wings to help the fund return 13% annually over the past five years. And Primecap ran ahead of the pack in '94 as well, with an 11% gain. Schow's prospects for '95 hinge on the budding rebound in technology stocks, which recently accounted for 33% of the portfolio. Two of his favorites are European: Vodafone of Great Britain, a cellular-phone firm, and Ericsson Telephone of Sweden, an equipment maker. He also had an 8% position in the troubled airline and transportation sectors, where he believes cost cutting will produce higher profits.

Large-caps with vroom to grow.
Spiros Segalas, lead manager of **Harbor Capital Appreciation**, is looking overseas for profits

in '95. Segalas recently had 17% of the portfolio in foreign stocks. He also had major holdings in U.S. companies with sizable stakes overseas. The latter group included Coca-Cola, which gets 64% of its earnings from abroad; McDonald's, with more than 40% foreign profits; and technology leaders Microsoft and Motorola. Segalas believes his stocks will notch earnings gains of 26% on average this year, far better than the projected 12% profit growth for companies in the S&P 500. Harbor's sector holdings fit the familiar growth pattern for '95. Technology stocks, including the two noted above, accounted for 40% of the fund. Another 13% of the portfolio was in health care stocks, including drugmakers Pfizer and Astra, a Swedish firm. Segalas limits his holdings to 60 stocks, selling an issue whenever he wants to buy a new one. "Often that forces me to sell a stock that I might have held too long," he says.

IDS New Dimensions' Gordon Fines notes that he recently had 77% of his 5% load fund in stocks that are part of the S&P 500. Yet the portfolio's five-year return of 13% annually has smartly outperformed that big-cap index. Fines has increased his technology stake to 29% (from 18% in early '94), adding such major players as Xerox and Compaq Computer. He also had 6% of the portfolio in energy stocks, including petrogiants Royal Dutch Petroleum and Amoco.

Janus Fund's James Craig seems destined to return to his winning form this year if we're right about growth stocks regaining their lead over economically sensitive cyclicals. What's more, Craig has relinquished responsibility for sister fund Janus Venture to focus his attention on the flagship. And he's added four analysts (for a total of 18) to help him ride herd on Janus' 110-stock portfolio. Like Segalas of Harbor Capital, Craig expects a boost from foreign stocks. A hefty 21% of the fund's assets lately were touring in overseas shares,

Stock Funds That Shoot for Double-Digit Gains

These exemplary funds are poised to produce gains of 12% to 15% this year. All have solid holdings in the domestic sectors or foreign markets that MONEY figures will shine in '95. IDS New Dimensions imposes a 5% load; the others are no-load portfolios.

Fund	% annual gain (or loss)			Largest sector holding (%)	Annual expense ratio	Minimum initial investment	Telephone (800)
	1994	Three years	Five years				
Meridian	0.6	9.5	16.6	Cellular comm. (30)	1.3%	$1,000	446-6662
PBHG Growth	4.8	25.4	22.0	Technology (30)	1.3	1,000	809-8008
T. Rowe Price New Horizons	0.3	10.6	13.3	Technology (20)	0.9	2,500	638-5660
Columbia Growth	(0.6)	7.9	10.3	Technology (16)	0.8	1,000	547-1707
Safeco Equity	9.9	16.3	13.0	Technology (14)	0.9	1,000	426-6730
Vanguard/Primecap	11.4	12.8	13.2	Technology (33)	0.7	3,000	662-7447
Harbor Capital Appreciation	3.4	8.4	14.1	Technology (40)	0.9	2,000	422-1050
IDS New Dimensions	(3.0)	5.2	13.1	Technology (29)	0.9	2,000	328-8300
Janus	(1.1)	5.4	10.7	Health care (11)	0.9	1,000	525-8983
Tweedy Browne Global Value	4.4	—	—	Europe (63)	1.8	2,500	432-4789
USAA Investment International	2.7	12.8	8.1	Europe (37)	1.3	1,000	382-8722
Warburg Pincus Intl. Investment	0.1	13.1	10.8	Japan (27)	1.3	2,500	257-5614
U.S. stock funds	(2.0)	6.5	9.0				
Overseas stock funds	(3.7)	8.5	5.0				

Sources: Morningstar Inc. and the funds

including Philips Electronics and Wolters Kluwer, a Netherlands-based publisher.

Shopping for bargains overseas. With

economic recovery just taking hold in most of the countries of continental Europe, **Tweedy Browne Global Value** seems especially well set with 63% of its assets in Euro-stocks. That allocation is not based on an economic forecast but rather on a love of underpriced stocks. Says John Spears, one of the fund's four managers: "Europe is where we find the best values." Indeed, this young fund with a small-company bias is run on strict value principles. Spears explains that prospective pur-

chases must fall into one of two categories. In the first are stocks with low PEs; in the second are companies that look cheap in relation to their assets or book value. These tend to be slumbering cyclicals that should rebound with the revived economy. And you needn't be overly worried that a rebound in the dollar from its recent historic lows will wipe out the fund's overseas gains this year. (Note that a stronger dollar deflates returns earned abroad, but a weaker dollar inflates those returns.) Reason: Spears uses currency futures to protect the fund against such swings.

USAA International's David Peebles has proved adept at spotting the companies and industries that are ready to outperform the rest of the world. In the past five years, his fund has returned 8% annually, well ahead of overseas funds as a group. Peebles, who has run the fund since 1984, recently held a mixture of value and growth stocks. His favorites included Autoliv, a Swedish firm that makes air bags for auto manufacturers. Autoliv's earnings are expected to jump 20% to 25% a year over the next five years in part because its biggest customer, Volvo, plans to equip its cars with side air bags in addition to frontal ones. Peebles' biggest concentrations are in Europe (37% of assets) and Japan (25%). He also had 19% in Asian markets outside Japan and 9% in Latin America. "We have always leaned toward the so-called emerging mar-

kets," says Peebles. "And we think these holdings will do well for us this year."

Warburg Pincus International's knack for being in the right market at the right time has helped manager Richard King post a superior five-year return of 11% annually. More recently, King has received a boost from his 27% stake in Japan and a 6% position in the strong Korean market. He also had 26% in Europe, mainly in cyclicals. The fund should get additional sizzle this year from emerging markets. King had 30% of fund assets in Pacific Rim countries outside Japan and another 9% in Latin America. As always, his portfolio is in the mid-cap range. "We typically look at smaller companies because that's where we are likeliest to find strong growth," he explains.

Low-Risk Ways to Aim for 8% Income

The smartest move for an income-oriented investor this year is also the safest. Put your money in short-term U.S. Government securities maturing in one to five years and in federally insured bank CDs (certificates of deposit). Such investments normally pay paltry returns, but not these days. Yields on one-year Treasury bills have doubled in the past 12 months to around 7% lately. One-year CDs were paying as much as 6.6%. To boost your overall return to a comfortable 8%, you may have to add slightly riskier bets such as shares of utility companies. But watch for signs of an end to the steady climb of interest rates that has slashed the price of long-term bonds. MONEY thinks rates on long-term Treasuries will rise from around 8% recently to 8.5% by mid-year and then level off. At that point, consider buying bonds with long

maturities. Reason: you will get the benefit of higher bond yields and, if the Republican-controlled Congress manages to hold the line on inflation, you may even earn capital gains when long rates eventually decline.

Why '94 was the bane of bondholders.

Thanks mainly to the Federal Reserve's six straight hikes in short-term interest rates last year, bonds lost roughly 6%, one of their worst setbacks ever. Seemingly secure short-term government bond funds that tried to boost yields by investing in risky derivatives fared nearly as badly, losing as much as 29%. One money-market fund even went under, handing shareholders a 6% loss, the industry's first. And the damage is not over. The Fed may boost short-term rates again before mid-year. That's why, at least for now, the experts say it pays to stay short and safe. Fortunately, the pay has become respectable in recent months. You lately could earn 7.5% on two-year Treasury notes, which may be today's best deal among income investments.

If you want to aim for a higher return, put 60% of your income portfolio in a combination of Treasuries and CDs with maturities of one to five years. Park another 20% in money funds, six-month T-bills and ultra-short-term bond funds. Then divide the remaining 20% equally between beaten-down utility stocks and REITs (real estate investment trusts), which offer yield plus the potential for appreciation and could help push your overall return above 8%. Your best choices are summarized below in descending order of safety. And investors can be assured that the money and bond funds we recommend don't dabble in risky derivative securities.

U.S. Government securities.
Your Uncle Sam is paying more for the use of your money than at any time since 1991. And since Treasury interest is exempt from state and local taxes, your tax-equivalent yield could be an additional half a percentage point higher in tax-heavy states such as California, Massachusetts or New York. You can invest in Treasuries through bond funds, of course. But with $10,000 or more to invest, you would be better off buying individual bonds. That's because bond funds charge annual fees averaging 0.92% of total assets, and the value of their portfolios fluctuates with interest rates. If long-term rates climb by the predicted half-percentage point or so, a fund with an average maturity of 7.5 years would fall about 2.5%. Individual bonds can be held to maturity, however, thus sidestepping any principal loss. And by spreading your stake among issues with maturities ranging from three months to five years, a strategy called laddering, you ensure that you will

always have at least some of your money coming back to you to reinvest if yields rise.

Certificates of deposit.
CDs are also paying their highest rates in three years. But you probably can't get the best deals unless you shop nationally for CDs. Virtually all banks carry federal insurance on deposits of up to $100,000. Thus your money will be as safe across the country as across town. Here are two other shopping tips. Compare CDs based on their yields (the actual percentage increase in your money over a year) rather than their interest rates, which can be misleading. And steer clear of gimmicky products such as those that promise to step up your yield if interest rates rise. Rarely do they offer the best payout.

Money-market funds.
Recently offering rates as high as 5.8% and likely to top 6.5% by mid-year, these funds are attractive places to park cash while you wait for better investment opportunities. Most top performers have temporarily waived management fees to boost yields by half a point or so. But that may change. Last year over 30 funds reinstated such fees. If your fund does so, move your money elsewhere. And don't confuse true money funds with so-called money-market accounts at banks. The latter are federally insured (funds are not) but yield roughly two percentage points less.

Ultra-short-term bond funds.
For a slightly better yield with little added risk, check out funds like Strong Advantage and Pacifica Asset Preservation that invest in high-quality corporate and government bonds with maturities of three to 12 months (vs. money funds' average of 42 days). Ultras' share value changes with interest rates, making them more volatile than money funds, where the share price is fixed at $1. But ultras

were recently paying about one percentage point more than the best money funds. And ultras can weather rising rates because they stick with very short-term issues.

Utility stocks and funds.

The shares of electric power companies suffered a double jolt in '94. Income-seeking investors deserted them for higher rates elsewhere. And individual companies got hammered by investors who feared the firms would be hurt by new federal rules that end the virtual monopoly they once enjoyed over customers. As a result, the Dow Jones utility average fell a staggering 25% over a recent 12-month period (its worst loss since 1974). Many analysts argue that this sell-off has created some terrific bargains. But stick to stocks that meet these criteria: a conservative dividend yield of 6% to 8% (higher yields often indicate higher risk); dividends that are growing 3% a year (vs. the industry average of 1%); and a payout ratio (the percentage of earnings needed to meet dividends) at or below the industry average of 80%. Two utilities that measure up are New England Electric Systems (NYSE, $30; 7.5% yield) and Southern Co. (NYSE, $19; 6.1% yield). With expected price gains of 16% to 18%, both stocks could produce exceptional total returns of 20% or better over the next 12 months. If you prefer to let an expert pick your stocks, you probably should consider a top-rated utility or income fund like Stratton Monthly Dividend Shares or Fidelity Utilities.

Real estate investment trusts.

REITs, which often hold pools of commercial buildings, were a dicey investment during the late '80s and early '90s when real estate prices slumped. But now that real estate is reviving, REITs are coming back too with yields averaging nearly 8% and the potential for double-digit returns. Be aware, however, that some newer issues are of dubious quality. So be sure to stick to those that have proven management teams that own at least 10% of the company; total debt equivalent to 40% or less of their market capitalization (the number of shares times the share price); and conservative 6% to 8% yields. Or invest in seasoned funds like Cohen & Steers Realty Shares or Fidelity Real Estate Investment.

Watch for a likely peak in rates.

If long-term rates reach the predicted 8.5%, they will be five points above the expected 3.5% rate of inflation. That's a much wider gap than the nearly four-point spread on average for the past 17 years. So if rates seem to stabilize there, then move the cash you've stashed in money funds into bonds or bond funds with maturities of 15 years or longer. That way, you'll earn a higher return and be in a position to profit if long rates come back down again.

Cash in Now on Rental Real Estate

The residential real estate market, which was left for dead after the housing recession of the late 1980s, is finally coming back to life. If you have $10,000 or more to invest, the current revival offers some of the best tax write-offs around. There also are opportunities to earn 10% or more annually in combined income and capital gains. And unlike stocks and bonds, whose returns are out of your control, you can actually boost a rental property's market value through shrewd management and imaginative remodeling.

Today's tight rental market is a major plus. "Demand for rentals is rising steadily, but there's been very little new construction since the 1986 Tax Act curtailed builders' and investors' ability to take some tax write-offs," says Michael Sampson, professor of taxation at American University and author of *Tax Guide for Residential Real Estate*. The residential vacancy rate, a vital indicator of the health of the local rental market, has slimmed down to a lean 3% or less in far-flung cities including Austin, Denver, Nashville, Raleigh and Salt Lake City. Nationwide, the vacancy rate has dropped from a 20-year high of 8% in 1987 to 7.3% last year.

In many areas of the country, the lack of rental units is propelling rents higher. As a result, your chances of buying a building with a positive cash flow (where rental income exceeds expenses) are better than at any time since the late '80s. You don't have endless time to catch the action, however. Property prices, mortgage rates and rents have been edging higher over the past year. Further, builders are literally hammering away to meet the demand. Multifamily property developers accelerated their building pace during '94. As new units come to market, they will tend to increase competition for desirable tenants and hamper landlords' ability to raise rents. So get to know real estate brokers who have worked in your neighborhood for a long time, ask them what they see ahead for your area, and then start shopping for properties.

Before embracing a rental investment, make sure that you or your partner have a landlord's temperament. "My wife doesn't mind calls about broken pipes. But I'm less than thrilled," concedes Kenneth Edwards of Corvallis, Ore. Edwards, the author of *Homebuyer's Survival Guide*, checks out the finances on potential properties while leaving the plumbing patrol to his wife Judith. Also follow these guidelines to help improve your chances of scoring in rental real estate.

Tot up potential tax advantages.

No matter where you live, the tax benefits for rental real estate are still enticing. Middle-income investors have a terrific edge over property plutocrats. If your adjusted gross income (AGI) is less than $100,000, you can write off against earned income as much as $25,000 a year from rental losses as long as you actively manage your property. That means, for example, setting rents and choosing your tenants. (This tax break phases out until your AGI hits $150,000, at which point it disappears.) Rental real estate also offers the nifty deduction of depreciation. "It's an investor's boon because depreciation generates a tax write-off without a corresponding cash outlay," explains Sampson. For example, if you own a rental building that is worth $190,000, you can claim depreciation of about $6,900 a year for 27.5 years—the standard period for writing off residential property.

Look homeward investor.

Investigate neighborhoods that are within a convenient 30-minute drive of your home. You'll be more familiar with the market and more apt to keep a hawk eye on your investment. Go where people are building or fixing up their houses—both signs that the neighborhood is improving. Then look at the middle to low end of the price range where there's more room for appreciation. In addition, ask local real estate agents for a list of communities that have the shortest resale time for residential properties. That signals a seller's market, which will push property values higher. Such increases, in turn, build your equity while giving you better borrowing power if you choose to hold the unit long term. Today, single-family rental houses take approximate-

Check Out the Rental's Numbers Before You Buy

If you've zeroed in on a one-family house, a duplex or other prospective rental property investment, fill out this worksheet to determine whether to make a bid or walk on by. Two figures pretty much tell all. On line 11, you'll get the annual return you can expect on the cash you invest, once the property is in rentable condition. You want to see at least double the prevailing interest rate on one-year CDs, or roughly 10% or better. On line 14, you'll get the overall projected return on your investment. If that figure works out to be 10% or more, you probably should consider taking the plunge.

1 a) Annual rents $_____
   b) Allowance for vacancies and uncollected rents (typically 5%) $_____

2 Net rents (line 1a minus line 1b) $_____

3 Annual deductible operating expenses, excluding mortgage payments,
   such as repairs and maintenance (typically 10% of net rents), property taxes,
   insurance, management fees of 7% to 10% $_____

4 Net operating income before mortgage expense (line 2 minus line 3) $_____

5 Annual mortgage interest payment $_____

6 Annual pretax cash flow (line 4 minus line 5) $_____

7 Annual property depreciation
   (cost of the building but not the land, divided by 27.5 years) $_____

8 Tax loss or gain (line 6 minus line 7) $_____

9 Annual tax loss or tax due
   (line 8 multiplied by your combined federal, state and city tax rates) $_____

10 After-tax cash flow (line 6 plus or minus line 9) $_____

11 Cash-on-cash return (line 10 divided by cash invested) _____ %

12 Projected one-year gain in price
   (purchase price multiplied by the estimated 12-month percentage increase in value) $_____

13 Projected total return for year (line 10 plus line 12) $_____

14 Return on investment (line 13 divided by cash invested) _____ %

Source: Michael Sampson

ly three months to sell. Also get your area's local vacancy rate from a knowledgeable real estate agent. If it's hovering around 5%, you can probably rent your property with ease. At 7% to 10%, you may have trouble. Above 10%, drive on by unless the price is right and you expect the neighborhood to turn around.

Think small starting out. "A multifamily house of, say, two or three units is good for beginning investors," suggests Carolyn Janik, author of *Money-Making Real Estate*. "You learn to interview tenants, set rents, answer complaints and see whether you really want to be a landlord." At the same time, with several units, your rental income won't drop to zero if one tenant decamps unexpectedly. Be wary of most condominiums, however. Michael Sampson warns that condo associations can be notoriously unpredictable for investors.

For instance, one Florida group, dominated by retirees, voted to close its swimming pool as an economy measure. "This wrecked the value of the property for the owners who rented their units to vacationing families," he points out. Though condo prices have long been flat owing to widespread overbuilding, they've begun inching higher as sales have picked up. The median price lately was $110,300, supported by strong demand from retirees and first-time buyers.

Aim for positive cash flow.

When you find a property you like, bargain hard and try to pay no more than 80% of market value. You can determine a property's value by checking recent sales prices of comparable dwellings with an appraiser or real estate agent. Your goal is to own a building that provides a positive cash flow, preferably on a pretax basis. Its income ought to pay the bills from the day the place is in rentable condition. To help determine whether a rental property is worth buying, follow the example of American University's Sampson. He asks the current owner for three years' worth of Schedule E tax forms, used to report supplemental income from rental real estate to the IRS. "The landlord will minimize profits and maximize expenses on the Schedule E to reduce taxable profits, so I'm seeing the worst-case scenario," Sampson explains. Also hire a building inspector (cost: $250 to $500) to provide a written report on the property. Then estimate the cost of any needed repairs as part of your preliminary financial analysis. Favor situations in which your calculations show the improvements will pay for themselves in three years or less, advise experts in the field.

To unearth a real bargain, you may have to find a foreclosure, an auction or a seller in distress. Take the case of Brenda Bradsher, who in 1982 bought a three-bedroom house in Houston's Heights section for $20,000 in cash when the owners couldn't come up with $3,000 in back taxes and foreclosure was threatened. "A nearby vacant lot had recently sold for $45,000, so I knew I couldn't lose," says Bradsher, who runs an industrial hardware supply brokerage. She got a $60,000 home improvement loan to restore the house. After the facelift, it qualified for an $82,000 mortgage, which Bradsher used to repay the first loan—and herself. She now has only $10,000 of her own money invested in the property. In 1993, that $10,000 earned a stunning 159% return because Bradsher has so little cash tied up and houses in the Heights appreciated about 9%. Still, she keeps a sharp eye on the expenses of the three rental properties she owns. "After a house is in rentable condition, I want a minimum $200-a-month positive cash flow," Bradsher says. "That's enough to rest easy in the event a tenant inflicts some unexpected damage."

Crunch these numbers hard.

While the worksheet at left will guide you through the necessary financial analysis, you'll still need to estimate some variable costs, such as repairs and maintenance. With the worksheet complete, carefully mull two numbers. On line 11, the *cash-on-cash return* measures the gain on your cash investment. The pros say the return should be at least double the prevailing interest rate on one-year CDs, or around 10%. And on line 14, the *return on investment* should be at least 10%. To be sure you know what you're getting into, work up a final percentage called the *capitalization rate* (it's not in the worksheet). This figure measures the property's ability to generate a return on your investment. Calculate it by dividing the property's net operating income (line 4 on the worksheet) by its purchase price. The higher the cap rate, the sounder the deal. If the cap rate is less than 8%, you're looking at a relatively risky proposition. That's one cap you don't want to wear.

How Each S&P 500 Stock Stacks Up

Blue-chip growth stocks are the nimble giants of the market, typically pinnacle players in their industry. They provide liquidity, stability and often the kind of appreciation potential that only the hottest small companies can beat. And no index captures a more representative collection of these attractive blue chips than Standard & Poor's 500. That's the reason we have rated all 500 stocks in the index by their potential for strong performance this year. MONEY's forecast calls for the index to gain 10% in '95 on the strength of modest inflation, steady corporate profit gains and, with last November's Republican sweep on Capitol Hill, a possible capital-gains tax cut to boot.

The starting point for our ratings of all S&P 500 stocks is the Value Line Timeliness Rank, which is reported weekly in the *Value Line Investment Survey* available in most libraries. The Value Line system analyzes more than 1,700 stocks, favoring those with a history of long-term earnings growth, recent strong price gains and earnings that exceed Wall Street's expectations. Since 1980, stocks rated 1 for timeliness by the *Value Line Investment*

Survey have returned 18% annually, tops for that period among the 19 stock-picking publications followed by *Hulbert Financial Digest.* While the timeliness ranking doesn't work every year, it has proved especially reliable when market performance was dominated by growth stocks, as we expect in '95. In the tables that follow, you'll find the 500 listed by rank from most timely (a score of 1) to least (a score of 4 or 5). While some of the stocks overlap with the 30 picks and pans of our All Star Brokers (beginning on page 11), their prices and PEs may vary a bit because of slightly different starting points.

Standard & Poor's also measures Wall Street's opinion about each of the 500 stocks in the index, which we include in the tables under the heading "analysts' opinion rating." S&P's system digests the opinion of every major brokerage firm analyst toward a particular stock and translates the consensus into a score. A rating of 1.00 or more means that Wall Street overall likes the company and believes the stock is a buy. A lower opinion rating suggests the stock is a hold or possible sell.

S&P's Top 10 Using Three Yardsticks

THE BIGGEST BLUE CHIPS		THE FASTEST GROWERS		THE HIGHEST YIELDS	
Value Line ranking (1=best, 5=worst)		*Forecast five-year annual earnings gains*		*Recent dividend yield*	
General Electric	3	Raychem	43%	Texas Utilities	9.4%
AT&T	3	AirTouch Communications	35	Houston Industries	8.6
Exxon	5	Promus	35	Pacific Gas & Electric	8.6
Coca-Cola	1	Cisco Systems	31	Public Service Enterprise	8.2
Royal Dutch Petroleum	4	Lowe's Cos.	30	Niagara Mohawk Power	8.1
Wal-Mart Stores	2	Home Depot	29	Consolidated Edison	8.0
Philip Morris	2	Oracle Systems	29	Detroit Edison	7.8
Merck	3	Micron Technology	28	Entergy Corp	7.7
Procter & Gamble	3	United Healthcare	28	Ohio Edison	7.7
IBM	2	Skyline Corp	26	SCE Corp	7.7

MONEY Ranks the S&P 500

	Number of entries	Analysts' opinion rating	PE ratio	Projected annual earnings growth	Return on equity	Current yield	Value of $10,000 invested 12/31/89	Starts on
Value Line Timeliness Rank: 1	30	1.16	17.8	16.5%	28.6%	1.4%	$38,043	Page 31
Value Line Timeliness Rank: 2	92	0.97	13.6	12.5	22.0	2.2	20,382	Page 32
Value Line Timeliness Rank: 3	254	0.85	14.6	11.5	20.4	2.8	15,662	Page 34
Value Line Timeliness Rank: 4 and 5	95	0.64	13.3	9.6	15.8	4.1	12,816	Page 39
Unranked	29	0.92	15.0	12.0	N.M.	2.5	14,331	Page 42

Company (ticker symbol)	Industry	Analysts' opinion rating	Revenues (millions)	Recent price	PE ratio	Projected annual earnings growth	Return on equity	Current yield	Value of $10,000 invested 12/31/89
Value Line Timeliness Rank: 1									
Amgen (AMGN)[1]	Drugs	1.33	$1,571	$55.75	15.4	16%	31.4%	N.A.	$68,321
Andrew (ANDW)[1]	Telecommunications	1.25	519	51.75	28.1	20	16.4	N.A.	63,419
Black & Decker (BDK)	Household appliances/tools	1.11	5,066	25.00	15.6	17	N.M.	1.5%	14,564
Capital Cities/ABC (CCB)	Broadcasting/publishing	1.02	6,160	83.00	18.3	13	37.8	0.2	14,778
Clark Equipment (CKL)	Machinery	0.90	917	70.00	9.6	12	N.M.	N.A.	19,148
Coca-Cola (KO)	Beverages	1.07	15,528	50.25	21.6	17	53.1	1.5	28,053
Compaq Computer (CPQ)	Computer systems	1.27	9,817	40.00	10.7	16	21.0	N.A.	30,279
Computer Associates Intl. (CA)	Computer software/services	1.11	2,308	49.75	13.9	17	35.2	0.4	40,870
Computer Sciences (CSC)	Information services	1.33	2,879	46.50	18.9	15	23.2	N.A.	24,156
Gillette (G)	Personal-care products	0.88	1,503	74.25	20.4	15	N.M.	1.3	32,337
Goodrich, B.F. (GR)	Chemicals/aerospace	1.10	2,093	44.75	17.4	8	N.M.	4.9	13,732
Home Depot (HD)	Home improvement stores	1.35	10,764	45.50	26.6	29	25.1	0.3	56,604
Johnson & Johnson (JNJ)	Health-care products	1.08	15,175	54.50	16.0	11	36.9	2.1	20,170
Kroger (KR)	Grocery stores	1.30	22,776	26.00	10.8	17	N.M.	N.A.	17,708
Lowe's (LOW)	Home improvement stores	1.07	5,348	39.75	23.7	23	12.9	0.4	57,150
Mattel (MAT)	Toys/games	1.36	2,929	29.25	15.0	15	38.1	0.8	35,762
Medtronic (MDT)	Medical equipment	1.09	1,391	52.25	21.6	16	31.7	0.7	32,953
Micron Technology (MU)	Computer parts	1.22	1,629	40.00	7.7	28	19.0	0.5	103,384
Microsoft (MSFT)[1]	Computer software/services	1.17	4,649	63.00	27.3	22	42.7	N.A.	65,217
Nordstrom (NOBE)[1]	Retail stores	1.10	3,718	49.25	17.8	14	15.4	0.8	13,847
Oracle Systems (ORCL)[1]	Computer software/services	1.51	2,001	46.00	33.1	29	N.M.	N.A.	39,384
Pep Boys (PBY)	Auto-parts stores/service	1.42	1,321	36.00	22.6	19	12.7	0.4	31,389
Praxair (PX)	Chemicals	1.18	2,602	23.00	15.2	14	N.M.	1.2	N.A.
Schering-Plough (SGP)	Drugs/toiletries	0.91	4,544	71.25	13.3	11	51.2	2.8	18,766
Sun Microsystems (SUNW)[1]	Data processing	0.92	4,690	32.75	13.4	13	14.0	N.A.	18,986
Tandem Computers (TDM)	Computer systems/supplies	1.15	2,108	17.75	12.2	10	N.M.	N.A.	7,717
Tektronix (TEK)	Specialty instruments	1.00	1,318	38.00	16.7	11	N.M.	1.5	24,268
Union Carbide (UK)	Chemicals	0.92	4,628	33.00	14.5	13	N.M.	2.2	17,585
United Healthcare (UNH)	Health maintenance programs	1.34	2,973	52.75	23.1	22	44.1	N.A.	174,602
Williams (WMB)	Gas utility	1.30	2,287	29.00	13.0	11	10.9	2.8	18,100

Notes: [1]Trades over the counter [2]Trades on the American Stock Exchange; all others trade on the New York Stock Exchange **Value Line Timeliness Rank:** 1=highest expected performance in the next 12 months; 5=lowest expected performance **Analysts' opinion rating:** 1.00 or greater=buy; 0.99 to 0.01=hold, 0.00 or less=sell. **PE ratios** are based on 1995 earnings estimates. **Earnings growth projections** are for the next five years. **Return on equity** is popular among stock analysts as a basic yardstick of a company's profitability and ability to self-finance future growth. The figure we cite is the average for the past five years. N.M.—Not meaningful N.A.—Not applicable **Sources:** Standard & Poor's, Value Line

MONEY Ranks the S&P 500

Company (ticker symbol)	Industry	Analysts' opinion rating	Revenues (millions)	Recent price	PE ratio	Projected annual earnings growth	Return on equity	Current yield	Value of $10,000 invested 12/31/89
Value Line Timeliness Rank: 2									
Abbott Laboratories (ABT)	Drugs/health-care products	1.08	$8,902	$31.00	14.8	11%	39.5%	2.4%	$20,073
Advanced Micro Devices (AMD)	Electronics	0.82	2,003	26.25	7.3	15	N.M.	N.A.	33,507
Alberto-Culver Class B (ACV)	Beauty/hair-care products	0.40	1,216	25.25	14.4	10	18.5	1.1	11,898
Albertson's (ABS)	Grocery stores	0.95	11,693	30.00	16.7	14	25.2	1.4	23,089
Alcan Aluminum (AL)	Aluminum	0.82	7,933	27.00	15.9	7	N.M.	1.1	13,757
Amdahl (AMH)[2]	Computer systems	0.42	1,583	10.00	18.5	6	N.M.	N.A.	7,296
American International Group (AIG)	Insurance	1.48	20,307	93.50	12.4	13	15.4	0.4	17,366
American Stores (ASC)	Grocery/drugstores	1.27	18,679	27.00	12.2	12	N.M.	1.7	21,000
AMR (AMR)	Air transport	1.00	15,733	55.00	9.3	9	N.M.	N.A.	9,503
Apple Computer (AAPL)[1]	Computer systems	0.46	9,189	43.25	14.5	9	20.1	1.1	12,897
Archer-Daniels-Midland (ADM)	Agricultural/food processing	1.31	11,374	28.50	16.1	12	12.8	0.5	16,107
Asarco (AR)	Mining/metals	0.92	1,879	31.25	14.1	6	N.M.	1.2	12,767
Automatic Data Processing (AUD)	Computer software/services	1.26	2,469	58.25	21.4	13	32.4	1.0	24,963
Avery Dennison (AVY)	Office equipment/supplies	0.80	2,762	33.50	15.2	12	10.5	3.2	12,021
Bank of Boston (BKB)	Banking	0.86	6,341	28.75	7.6	8	N.M.	3.7	18,857
Bard, C.R. (BCR)	Medical supplies	1.00	1,003	24.50	11.8	13	23.9	2.4	12,227
Baxter International (BAX)	Medical supplies	0.78	9,219	26.00	11.3	8	N.M.	4.0	11,988
Bemis (BMS)	Containers/packaging	1.00	1,325	24.75	16.4	12	18.2	2.1	16,001
Beneficial (BNL)	Financial services	1.05	1,706	39.00	8.6	10	15.8	4.3	19,464
Beverly Enterprises (BEV)	Health-care facilities	0.77	2,939	15.00	15.3	16	7.0	N.A.	25,200
Biomet (BMET)[1]	Medical supplies	0.63	373	11.50	17.2	17	31.5	N.A.	16,739
Browning-Ferris Industries (BFI)	Pollution/waste management	1.04	4,315	31.75	18.1	14	N.M.	2.1	9,351
Campbell Soup (CPB)	Packaged foods	0.78	6,690	41.25	14.9	11	28.2	2.7	15,531
Caterpillar (CAT)	Building machinery	1.22	13,568	59.75	11.9	11	N.M.	1.0	45,765
Chase Manhattan (CMB)	Banking/financial services	1.00	11,601	36.00	6.1	10	N.M.	4.4	15,000
Cincinnati Milacron (CMZ)	Machinery	1.33	1,088	27.25	15.6	10	N.M.	1.3	18,414
Circuit City Stores (CC)	Electronic stores	0.87	4,692	25.50	14.3	16	20.9	0.3	23,944
Citicorp (CCI)	Banking/financial services	1.05	32,457	47.75	7.9	10	N.M.	1.2	20,371
Colgate-Palmolive (CL)	Household/health products	0.82	7,432	60.75	14.1	13	N.M.	2.6	21,390
ConAgra (CAG)	Food/agricultural processing	0.87	23,512	31.00	15.2	11	N.M.	2.6	18,007
Consolidated Freightways (CNF)	Trucking/air freight	1.10	4,511	22.25	11.1	9	N.M.	N.A.	8,822
Cooper Tire & Rubber (CTB)	Rubber/auto parts	1.07	1,337	24.50	14.7	13	22.1	0.9	31,583
DSC Communications (DIGI)[1]	Telecommunications	1.14	909	30.75	19.2	21	N.M.	N.A.	42,414
Enron (ENE)	Gas utility	1.11	8,622	32.25	15.9	14	14.6	2.4	26,256
Federal Home Loan (FRE)	Financial services	1.32	4,020	54.50	9.3	15	24.2	1.9	26,764
Federal National Mortgage (FNM)	Financial services	1.45	16,053	76.00	8.5	15	31.0	3.1	24,976
First Fidelity Bancorp (FFB)	Banking/financial services	0.89	2,462	45.00	7.9	9	N.M.	4.4	24,124
First Interstate Bancorp (I)	Banking/financial services	1.08	3,971	80.00	7.4	13	N.M.	3.7	24,835
First Mississippi (FRM)	Chemicals	0.80	508	21.00	14.6	20	N.M.	1.4	14,981
First Union (FTU)	Banking	1.01	5,755	45.00	7.9	9	18.3	4.0	26,835
Fleetwood Enterprises (FLE)	Manufactured housing	1.35	2,369	23.00	11.9	16	11.1	2.4	21,653
Fluor (FLR)	Engineering/construction	1.20	8,293	49.50	18.7	15	16.7	1.0	14,097
Foster Wheeler (FWC)	Engineering/construction equipment	1.16	2,334	36.00	17.4	15	11.5	2.0	19,178
Halliburton (HAL)	Oil/gas	0.75	5,860	37.00	27.8	13	N.M.	2.7	9,969
Hewlett-Packard (HWP)	Specialty instruments	0.95	23,676	97.75	14.6	13	13.9	1.2	21,869

Company (ticker symbol)	Industry	Analysts' opinion rating	Revenues (millions)	Recent price	PE ratio	Projected annual earnings growth	Return on equity	Current yield	Value of $10,000 invested 12/31/89
Household International (HI)	Banking/financial services	1.08	$4,498	$35.00	8.4	13%	19.7%	3.5%	$16,756
Inland Steel Industries (IAD)	Steel	0.97	4,320	35.75	8.2	6	N.M.	N.A.	11,269
Intel (INTC)[1]	Electronics	1.30	10,682	62.00	8.9	16	28.2	0.3	36,300
Intl. Business Machines (IBM)	Computer systems/software	0.87	63,551	74.50	13.7	10	N.M.	1.3	9,938
Intl. Flavors & Fragrance (IFF)	Cosmetics/personal products	0.77	1,270	43.75	19.9	12	20.6	2.4	22,055
Interpublic Group (IPG)	Advertising	1.12	1,868	33.00	15.6	13	N.M.	1.6	21,908
Jefferson-Pilot (JP)	Insurance	0.68	1,247	54.25	12.2	10	12.7	3.1	22,224
Loral (LOR)	Defense electronics	1.10	5,013	39.50	10.7	10	N.M.	1.5	29,662
Manor Care (MNR)	Health-care facilities	1.00	1,163	27.50	18.5	15	24.0	0.3	25,202
MBNA (KRB)	Financial services	1.30	1,558	26.75	12.2	16	N.M.	2.6	N.A.
Meredith (MDP)	Publishing/broadcasting	0.66	800	49.00	23.4	20	N.M.	1.4	15,535
Moore (MCL)	Office equipment	0.20	2,354	18.00	13.2	12	N.M.	5.1	7,940
Motorola (MOT)	Electronics	1.17	20,785	58.75	20.3	17	15.2	0.4	42,101
NationsBank (NB)	Banking/financial services	1.17	11,076	49.50	7.2	11	15.2	4.0	13,010
Newell (NWL)	Industrial products	1.06	1,972	21.00	14.8	14	33.0	1.9	20,534
Norwest (NOB)	Banking/financial services	1.29	5,580	24.50	8.7	11	20.6	3.4	25,221
Nucor (NUE)	Steel/related products	0.76	2,788	61.75	18.7	19	14.2	0.2	41,936
Outboard Marine (OM)	Boats/boat engines	0.63	1,059	20.50	10.5	15	N.M.	1.9	9,035
Panhandle Eastern (PEL)	Gas utility	1.13	2,048	23.50	12.6	8	N.M.	3.5	10,325
Pfizer (PFE)	Drugs	1.09	7,969	74.00	15.7	13	21.9	2.5	23,910
Philip Morris (MO)	Tobacco/consumer products	1.22	60,940	61.25	9.9	13	N.M.	5.3	17,442
Premark International (PMI)	Containers/cooking equipment	1.33	3,340	44.75	12.4	14	18.1	1.7	32,772
Reebok International (RBK)	Athletic footwear	1.33	3,174	39.75	11.7	13	30.1	0.7	22,304
Rite Aid (RAD)	Drugstores	0.85	4,172	24.00	13.3	10	13.6	2.5	16,457
Scientific-Atlanta (SFA)	Specialty instruments	1.00	812	21.50	24.7	18	8.3	0.2	28,234
Scott Paper (SPP)	Paper/related products	0.90	4,654	66.00	15.0	13	N.M.	1.2	15,140
Shawmut National (SNC)	Banking	0.45	1,922	20.50	6.7	12	N.M.	3.8	13,168
Sherwin-Williams (SHW)	Paint	1.26	3,064	32.50	13.8	11	19.8	1.7	20,587
Sonat (SNT)	Gas utility	1.06	1,870	32.50	14.4	11	14.0	3.3	16,443
Springs Industries A (SMI)	Textiles/home furnishings	0.94	2,058	40.25	11.4	9	N.M.	2.9	12,665
Sprint (FON)	Telecommunications	0.85	12,399	32.75	11.8	13	17.1	3.0	10,358
SPX (SPW)	Auto parts	0.85	989	17.25	10.4	15	N.M.	2.3	7,267
SunTrust Banks (STI)	Banking	0.59	N.A.	50.50	10.8	10	17.6	2.5	25,154
Sysco (SYY)	Food/related products	1.09	10,943	24.75	17.8	16	28.7	1.4	16,440
Tenneco (TGT)	Conglomerate	1.10	13,463	44.25	10.5	12	N.M.	3.6	9,157
Texas Instruments (TXN)	Electronics	1.13	9,907	74.75	8.9	15	N.M.	1.3	22,610
Timken (TKR)	Steel/bearings	0.08	1,866	34.75	13.2	7	N.M.	2.8	14,957
U.S. HealthCare (USHC)[1]	Health maintenance programs	1.11	2,878	47.25	17.1	18	56.0	1.7	120,892
USF&G (FG)	Insurance	0.58	3,167	13.50	9.7	14	N.M.	1.4	7,175
UST (UST)	Tobacco	0.91	1,188	26.50	12.5	15	63.4	4.2	20,105
USX-U.S. Steel Group (X)	Steel	1.27	5,895	37.50	7.9	7	N.M.	2.6	N.A.
Walgreen (WAG)	Drugstores	0.72	9,235	41.25	16.4	13	20.4	1.8	19,037
Wal-Mart Stores (WMT)	Retail stores	1.21	74,816	23.50	16.3	18	28.8	0.7	21,428

Notes: [1]Trades over the counter [2]Trades on the American Stock Exchange; all others trade on the New York Stock Exchange **Value Line Timeliness Rank:** 1=highest expected performance in the next 12 months; 5=lowest expected performance **Analysts' opinion rating:** 1.00 or greater=buy; 0.99 to 0.01=hold; 0.00 or less=sell. **PE ratios** are based on 1995 earnings estimates. **Earnings growth projections** are for the next five years. **Return on equity** is popular among stock analysts as a basic yardstick of a company's profitability and ability to self-finance future growth. The figure we cite is the average for the past five years. N.M.—Not meaningful N.A.—Not applicable **Sources:** Standard & Poor's, Value Line

MONEY Ranks the S&P 500

Company (ticker symbol)	Industry	Analysts' opinion rating	Revenues (millions)	Recent price	PE ratio	Projected annual earnings growth	Return on equity	Current yield	Value of $10,000 invested 12/31/89
Warner-Lambert (WLA)	Drugs/health-care products	0.79	$6,230	$76.25	13.6	9%	41.8%	3.2%	$15,165
Whitman (WH)	Bottling plants	0.80	2,631	16.50	12.7	13	N.M.	2.0	6,713
Worthington Industries (WTHG)[1]	Steel	1.16	1,285	22.25	19.3	15	16.4	1.7	24,005
Zenith Electronics (ZE)	Electrical equipment	0.50	1,377	14.00	22.2	5	N.M.	N.A.	10,980

Value Line Timeliness Rank: 3

Company (ticker symbol)	Industry	Analysts' opinion rating	Revenues (millions)	Recent price	PE ratio	Projected annual earnings growth	Return on equity	Current yield	Value of $10,000 invested 12/31/89
Ahmanson, H.F. (AHM)	Banking	1.10	3,176	19.00	7.6	11	N.M.	4.6	12,872
Air Products & Chemical (APD)	Chemicals/industrial gases	0.85	3,485	47.75	15.6	12	13.7	2.0	22,035
Alco Standard (ASN)	Paper/office products	1.35	7,996	57.00	16.4	17	N.M.	1.7	18,385
Alexander & Alexander Services (AAL)	Insurance	0.50	1,327	20.25	19.1	16	N.M.	0.4	8,011
Allergan (AGN)	Medical equipment	0.80	908	26.25	14.2	11	N.M.	1.6	16,398
Allied-Signal (ALD)	Auto/aerospace materials	1.09	12,342	34.50	11.3	11	N.M.	1.9	23,090
Aluminum Co. of America (AA)	Aluminum products	0.68	9,581	85.25	19.1	17	2.5	1.8	13,106
Alza (AZA)	Medical supplies	1.06	253	17.75	15.7	19	N.M.	N.A.	8,094
Amerada Hess (AHC)	Oil/gas	0.94	6,536	49.75	30.9	17	N.M.	1.2	10,875
American Barrick Resources (ABX)	Gold	1.13	743	23.75	25.5	14	17.4	0.4	30,830
American Brands (AMB)	Tobacco	0.96	13,998	34.75	10.3	8	N.M.	5.7	12,259
American Electric Power (AEP)	Electric utility	0.26	5,553	32.00	11.3	2	11.2	7.5	13,828
American General (AGC)	Insurance/financial services	1.11	6,583	27.50	8.5	10	13.6	4.2	22,513
American Greetings Class A (AGREA)[1]	Greeting cards/gifts	1.26	1,816	27.25	12.1	12	13.5	2.0	16,946
American Home Products (AHP)	Drugs/food products	0.63	8,497	63.50	12.3	6	56.7	4.7	14,356
Ameritech (AIT)	Telecommunications	0.76	12,275	40.75	12.9	6	18.1	4.7	15,229
Amoco (AN)	Oil/gas	0.75	26,513	63.25	15.2	9	9.1	3.4	14,186
AMP (AMP)	Electrical connection devices	1.07	3,803	75.75	19.0	11	16.1	2.2	19,375
Anheuser-Busch (BUD)	Alcoholic beverages	0.73	11,949	50.75	11.8	10	25.9	3.1	14,801
Armco (AS)	Steel products/services	0.60	1,466	7.00	17.5	4	N.M.	N.A.	7,142
Armstrong World Industries (ACK)	Home furnishings	0.90	2,672	41.50	8.5	11	N.M.	3.0	13,251
Ashland Oil (ASH)	Oil/gas	1.06	9,968	38.75	11.6	14	N.M.	2.5	11,338
AT&T (T)	Telecommunications	1.32	71,397	55.00	15.3	10	20.6	2.4	14,033
Autodesk (ACAD)[1]	Computer software/services	1.10	417	34.50	19.9	19	24.4	0.6	18,570
Avon Products (AVP)	Beauty products	1.00	4,190	63.25	14.8	12	N.M.	3.1	21,118
Baker Hughes (BHI)	Oil/gas	0.89	2,520	20.50	27.3	13	N.M.	2.2	8,970
Ball (BLL)	Containers/packaging	0.80	2,539	28.25	13.4	10	N.M.	2.1	9,932
Bally Entertainment (BLY)	Health clubs/casinos	0.50	1,292	7.00	12.1	10	N.M.	N.A.	5,121
Baltimore Gas & Electric (BGE)	Diversified utility	0.61	2,779	23.25	11.3	3	9.4	6.5	13,773
Banc One (ONE)	Banking	1.13	7,965	28.75	8.0	11	18.7	4.2	16,863
BankAmerica (BAC)	Banking/financial services	1.25	15,720	43.50	7.2	10	19.2	3.6	18,978
Barnett Banks (BBI)	Banking/financial services	0.82	3,037	41.75	8.1	9	12.6	3.9	14,162
Becton Dickinson (BDX)	Medical supplies	0.67	2,509	47.25	14.3	9	17.8	1.5	16,552
BellSouth (BLS)	Telecommunications	0.75	16,575	53.25	11.9	8	13.3	5.1	11,792
Bethlehem Steel (BS)	Steel/raw materials	1.00	4,725	19.00	5.5	6	N.M.	N.A.	10,919
Block, H&R (HRB)	Financial services	0.85	1,239	44.25	21.2	14	34.8	2.8	27,938
Boatmen's Bancshares (BOAT)[1]	Banking	0.90	2,178	29.50	8.1	8	15.4	4.5	23,239
Boise Cascade (BCC)	Paper/related products	0.72	4,176	26.50	38.4	6	N.M.	2.2	7,284
Briggs & Stratton (BGG)	Auto parts/machinery	1.18	1,286	69.50	9.7	8	19.2	2.8	31,135

Company (ticker symbol)	Industry	Analysts' opinion rating	Revenues (millions)	Recent price	PE ratio	Projected annual earnings growth	Return on equity	Current yield	Value of $10,000 invested 12/31/89
Bristol-Myers Squibb (BMY)	Drugs/medical supplies	0.66	$11,729	$58.25	12.2	7%	37.8%	5.0%	$12,669
Brown-Forman Class B (BF.B)	Beverages/luggage/china	0.28	1,401	30.75	14.2	11	33.7	3.0	12,104
Brown Group (BG)	Footwear	1.08	1,659	33.75	11.2	19	N.M.	4.7	16,482
Bruno's (BRNO)[1]	Grocery stores	0.44	2,835	9.50	16.1	10	17.2	2.7	7,020
Brunswick (BC)	Leisure	0.76	2,581	20.50	12.4	19	N.M.	2.1	16,886
CBS (CBS)	Broadcasting	0.65	3,899	59.75	13.9	15	N.M.	0.6	16,713
Champion International (CHA)	Paper	0.58	5,153	37.00	23.7	5	N.M.	0.5	12,525
Chemical Banking (CHL)	Banking/financial services	1.13	12,293	38.00	6.4	9	10.3	4.6	18,501
Chrysler (C)	Autos/trucks	1.35	49,916	48.50	4.8	8	N.M.	2.0	31,281
Chubb (CB)	Commercial insurance	1.31	5,789	69.75	9.9	13	15.3	2.6	16,320
CIGNA (CI)	Insurance/financial services	0.43	18,534	65.75	9.4	13	8.3	4.6	14,398
Cisco Systems (CSCO)[1]	Computer network products	1.25	1,243	30.00	18.5	31	51.4	N.A.	N.A.
Clorox (CLX)	Household products	0.58	1,837	54.00	14.4	11	33.9	3.5	15,277
Coastal (CGP)	Gas utility	1.00	10,412	28.50	11.9	14	N.M.	1.4	9,268
Conrail (CRR)	Railroads	1.12	3,657	54.50	11.8	13	N.M.	2.7	25,519
Corning (GLW)	Glass/housewares products	0.95	4,596	34.00	15.2	13	N.M.	2.0	17,424
CPC International (CPC)	Food processing	0.90	7,155	53.50	15.1	10	61.0	2.5	16,368
Crane (CR)	Diversified manufacturing	0.57	1,534	27.00	12.3	11	21.7	2.7	13,640
Crown Cork & Seal (CCK)	Containers/packaging	1.08	4,296	38.75	14.0	15	N.M.	N.A.	21,960
CSX (CSX)	Railroads	1.29	9,383	72.50	10.4	12	N.M.	2.4	23,076
Cummins Engine (CUM)	Truck parts	0.73	4,577	42.50	7.5	13	N.M.	2.3	18,350
Dana (DCN)	Auto parts	1.00	6,368	25.50	9.9	14	13.9	3.2	18,078
Data General (DGN)	Computer systems	0.29	1,121	9.75	30.5	8	N.M.	N.A.	7,800
Dayton Hudson (DH)	Retail stores	0.88	20,173	77.50	11.7	11	16.1	2.1	13,610
Deere (DE)	Construction/farm machinery	1.20	8,689	71.50	9.2	12	N.M.	3.0	13,973
Delta Air Lines (DAL)	Air transport	1.00	12,359	52.00	18.4	8	N.M.	0.3	8,172
Digital Equipment (DEC)	Computer systems/service	0.38	13,451	30.50	N.M.	8	N.M.	N.A.	3,734
Disney, Walt (DIS)	Leisure/entertainment	1.08	9,531	39.50	16.7	17	20.0	0.7	14,519
Donnelley, R.R. & Sons (DNY)	Printing	0.91	4,741	31.25	15.2	12	17.8	2.0	13,418
Dover (DOV)	Elevators/electronic equipment	0.70	2,927	55.50	14.4	12	36.6	1.8	16,777
Dow Chemical (DOW)	Chemicals	1.20	19,026	73.50	16.5	14	21.2	3.5	12,891
Dow Jones (DJ)	Publishing/info services	0.59	2,037	29.75	14.7	13	N.M.	2.8	10,310
Dresser Industries (DI)	Oil/gas	0.94	4,893	21.25	16.6	12	20.7	3.2	10,915
Dun & Bradstreet (DNB)	Information services	0.71	4,807	58.50	14.3	10	N.M.	4.4	15,632
duPont de Nemours, E.I. (DD)	Chemicals	1.06	39,114	59.50	13.3	11	12.0	3.1	17,421
Eastern Enterprises (EFU)	Gas utility	0.71	1,147	26.00	12.1	5	N.M.	5.3	9,617
Eaton (ETN)	Electronic systems	1.19	5,562	52.25	11.0	12	23.1	2.2	21,309
Echlin (ECH)	Auto parts	1.53	2,229	30.75	13.3	14	10.7	2.4	23,621
Echo Bay Mines (ECO)[2]	Mining	0.09	388	12.25	40.8	5	N.M.	0.6	6,955
Ecolab (ECL)	Institutional cleaning supplies	1.18	1,113	21.25	13.9	13	N.M.	2.0	16,646
Emerson Electric (EMR)	Electronics	1.00	8,411	60.75	15.6	10	30.8	2.5	17,659
Engelhard (EC)	Chemicals/precious metals	1.00	2,309	23.50	15.0	16	12.5	2.0	30,550
Enserch (ENS)	Gas utility	0.64	1,984	14.25	17.4	12	N.M.	1.4	6,390

Notes: [1]Trades over the counter [2]Trades on the American Stock Exchange; all others trade on the New York Stock Exchange **Value Line Timeliness Rank:** 1=highest expected performance in the next 12 months; 5=lowest expected performance **Analysts' opinion rating:** 1.00 or greater=buy; 0.99 to 0.01=hold, 0.00 or less=sell. **PE ratios** are based on 1995 earnings estimates. **Earnings growth projections** are for the next five years. **Return on equity** is popular among stock analysts as a basic yardstick of a company's profitability and ability to self-finance future growth. The figure we cite is the average for the past five years. N.M.—Not meaningful N.A.—Not applicable **Sources:** Standard & Poor's, Value Line

MONEY Ranks the S&P 500

Company (ticker symbol)	Industry	Analysts' opinion rating	Revenues (millions)	Recent price	PE ratio	Projected annual earnings growth	Return on equity	Current yield	Value of $10,000 invested 12/31/89
Federal Express (FDX)	Package delivery	0.85	$8,479	$60.75	12.5	15%	N.M.	N.A.	$13,279
Federal Paper Board (FBO)	Paper/related products	0.62	1,454	30.00	12.9	18	9.7%	3.3%	14,317
Fleet Financial Group (FLT)	Banking/financial services	1.03	4,500	34.25	7.1	11	N.M.	4.6	16,685
FMC (FMC)	Chemicals/machinery	1.11	3,953	61.00	11.4	8	N.M.	N.A.	17,305
Ford Motor (F)	Autos/trucks	1.32	122,677	29.50	5.8	7	N.M.	3.5	17,637
FPL Group (FPL)	Electric utility	1.03	5,366	33.00	11.0	3	N.M.	5.0	12,409
Gannett (GCI)	Publishing/broadcasting	1.09	3,759	48.00	13.6	11	N.M.	2.8	12,611
Gap (GPS)	Clothing stores	1.19	3,484	33.75	13.0	17	36.8	1.4	27,710
General Electric (GE)	Conglomerate	1.22	64,618	48.75	12.8	11	37.2	2.9	17,382
General Mills (GIS)	Packaged foods	0.58	8,517	56.00	14.9	10	49.5	3.3	17,655
General Motors (GM)	Autos/trucks	1.12	149,666	39.50	4.5	5	N.M.	2.0	11,530
General Signal (GSX)	Specialty instruments	1.00	1,645	36.00	13.8	11	N.M.	2.5	17,506
Genuine Parts (GPC)	Auto parts	0.85	4,746	36.00	14.1	9	20.0	3.1	14,993
Georgia-Pacific (GP)	Paper/building products	0.92	12,639	73.75	13.6	9	N.M.	2.1	17,541
Goodyear Tire & Rubber (GT)	Rubber/tires	1.11	11,978	35.00	8.5	12	N.M.	2.2	18,474
Grace, W.R. (GRA)	Chemicals/health-care supplies	1.00	4,813	39.50	11.5	10	N.M.	3.5	14,697
Grainger, W.W. (GWW)	Electrical equipment	1.06	2,917	55.00	14.4	12	16.6	1.4	18,202
Great Atlantic & Pacific Tea (GAP)	Grocery stores	0.22	10,322	26.00	18.4	14	N.M.	3.0	5,088
Great Lakes Chemical (GLK)	Chemicals	0.96	1,979	58.75	13.0	13	32.7	0.6	25,547
Great Western Financial (GWF)	Banking/financial services	0.85	2,831	17.75	7.9	11	8.8	5.1	13,225
Harland, John H. (JH)	Banking paper products	0.68	517	21.25	11.2	9	24.7	4.5	11,762
Harris (HRS)	Electronic equipment	1.00	3,336	42.75	11.6	9	10.2	2.8	15,208
Hartmarx (HMX)	Clothing stores	0.61	722	5.75	12.5	10	N.M.	N.A.	3,452
Heinz, H.J. (HNZ)	Packaged foods	0.62	7,047	37.00	15.9	8	46.6	3.8	12,211
Helmerich & Payne (HP)	Oil/gas	0.54	324	31.25	29.8	13	5.4	1.6	9,966
Hercules (HPC)	Chemicals	0.80	2,782	116.75	17.7	14	9.6	1.9	35,719
Hershey Foods (HSY)	Confectionary/food products	0.66	3,563	47.25	14.0	10	27.7	2.7	14,720
Hilton Hotels (HLT)	Hotels	0.68	1,471	60.50	18.8	12	10.8	1.9	8,349
Homestake Mining (HM)	Mining	0.72	726	18.75	24.4	6	N.M.	1.0	10,357
Honeywell (HON)	Electrical equipment	0.45	5,939	32.25	12.7	9	27.9	2.9	16,901
Illinois Tool Works (ITW)	Tools/fasteners	0.78	3,324	45.00	17.1	12	26.7	1.3	21,392
Inco (N)	Mining	0.39	2,241	30.00	22.1	8	N.M.	1.3	12,845
Ingersoll-Rand (IR)	Machinery	0.78	4,357	35.50	14.5	11	12.0	2.0	15,884
Intergraph (INGR)[1]	Computer graphic systems	0.56	1,013	8.50	53.1	14	N.M.	N.A.	4,997
International Paper (IP)	Paper/industrial services	0.85	14,259	74.50	13.6	16	7.1	2.2	14,875
ITT (ITT)	Conglomerate	1.40	23,555	88.25	10.3	13	N.M.	2.2	17,076
James River (JR)	Paper/related products	0.73	4,903	22.75	26.1	9	N.M.	2.6	9,324
Johnson Controls (JCI)	Automated building controls	0.61	6,871	49.75	12.2	13	17.9	2.8	18,038
Jostens (JOS)	Jewelry/memorabilia	0.45	827	17.25	19.2	9	N.M.	5.1	7,337
Kellogg (K)	Packaged foods	0.51	6,540	58.75	17.1	10	35.4	2.4	19,196
Kerr-McGee (KMG)	Oil/gas	0.85	3,357	49.00	18.4	11	N.M.	3.0	11,411
Key (KEY)	Banking/financial services	1.22	5,263	28.50	7.1	10	15.5	4.4	20,279
Kimberly-Clark (KMB)	Paper/personal products	0.70	7,207	51.50	12.9	10	20.7	3.4	16,327
King World Productions (KWP)	Filmed entertainment	0.96	546	35.50	12.4	10	N.M.	N.A.	13,971
Knight-Ridder (KRI)	Publishing	1.07	2,588	51.50	14.1	11	53.4	2.8	10,040
Lilly, Eli (LLY)	Drugs/medical supplies	0.78	6,934	62.00	13.9	6	26.4	4.0	10,631

Company (ticker symbol)	Industry	Analysts' opinion rating	Revenues (millions)	Recent price	PE ratio	Projected annual earnings growth	Return on equity	Current yield	Value of $10,000 invested 12/31/89
Liz Claiborne (LIZ)	Clothing/textiles	0.52	$2,192	$23.00	13.1	10%	23.0%	1.9%	$10,263
Longs Drug Stores (LDG)	Drugstores	N.A.	2,530	34.75	12.3	7	13.2	3.2	9,036
Louisiana Pacific (LPX)	Paper/forest products	0.97	2,927	30.50	8.4	11	13.6	1.6	23,493
Luby's Cafeterias (LUB)	Cafeterias	0.63	391	23.00	14.5	10	17.3	2.8	14,692
M/A-Com (MAI)	Commercial/defense electronics	0.16	337	7.00	25.0	15	N.M.	N.A.	14,737
Mallinckrodt Group (MKG)	Health-care products/chemicals	1.00	1,940	30.25	12.4	14	N.M.	1.8	18,633
Marsh & McLennan (MMC)	Insurance	0.75	3,357	75.00	12.8	12	56.2	3.8	11,301
Masco (MAS)	Building products	0.84	4,162	23.75	11.0	14	13.6	3.0	11,004
Maxus Energy (MXS)	Oil/gas	0.41	722	4.75	N.M.	8	N.M.	N.A.	4,318
May Dept. Stores (MA)	Retail stores	1.14	11,763	37.75	11.0	12	26.7	2.7	18,037
Maytag (MYG)	Household appliances	0.82	3,257	15.75	10.6	8	N.M.	3.1	9,955
McDermott International (MDR)	Oil/gas	1.18	3,063	25.50	18.3	11	N.M.	3.9	13,729
McDonald's (MCD)	Fast-food restaurants	1.17	7,983	28.75	15.4	13	22.7	0.8	17,458
McDonnell Douglas (MD)	Aerospace/defense	1.14	13,296	141.00	9.5	7	14.3	1.7	26,618
McGraw-Hill (MHP)	Publishing	0.66	2,747	74.75	16.5	9	N.M.	3.1	15,729
MCI Communications (MCIC)[1]	Telecommunications	1.18	13,065	23.00	14.3	14	28.7	0.2	10,599
Mead (MEA)	Paper/packaging	0.97	4,811	49.50	12.9	12	6.5	2.0	15,427
Mellon Bank (MEL)	Banking	1.09	3,622	55.50	8.3	9	20.2	4.8	23,558
Mercantile Stores (MST)	Retail stores	0.50	2,754	45.50	14.7	9	8.5	2.2	13,312
Merck & Co (MRK)	Drugs	0.88	14,099	35.50	13.3	11	59.8	3.3	15,499
Merrill Lynch (MER)	Financial services	0.72	18,275	39.25	7.1	10	21.2	2.3	33,898
Millipore (MIL)	Diversified manufacturing	0.83	481	51.25	16.2	15	11.0	1.1	20,544
3M (MMM)	Adhesive papers/coated abrasives	1.00	14,706	55.25	15.3	9	20.6	3.1	16,170
Monsanto (MTC)	Chemicals	1.17	8,064	76.00	12.8	11	23.1	3.3	15,622
Morton International (MII)	Chemicals/safety products	1.50	2,878	28.50	15.7	15	20.0	1.5	80,018
Nacco Industries Class A (NC)	Machinery/household appliances	1.00	1,746	59.00	10.8	26	N.M.	1.1	11,353
National City (NCC)	Banking	0.82	2,763	27.00	9.1	9	14.9	4.4	17,447
National Education (NEC)	Technical training	0.66	319	4.75	12.5	N.M.	N.M.	N.A.	7,089
National Medical Enterprises (NME)	Health-care facilities	0.65	2,967	14.50	11.4	10	N.M.	N.A.	8,339
National Semiconductor (NSM)	Electronics	1.14	2,295	17.50	8.8	13	N.M.	N.A.	24,303
National Service Industries (NSI)	Diversified manufacturing	0.50	1,882	26.75	14.5	7	12.4	4.0	11,644
Navistar International (NAV)	Trucks	0.34	4,987	13.00	8.7	10	N.M.	N.A.	3,386
NBD Bancorp (NBD)	Banking/financial services	0.73	2,957	30.75	8.6	9	15.0	3.9	17,162
New York Times Class A (NYT.A)[2]	Publishing/broadcasting	0.76	2,388	22.50	17.4	15	N.M.	2.4	9,579
Nike Class B (NKE)	Athletic footwear	0.97	3,790	60.75	13.4	12	35.0	1.3	24,159
Noram Energy (NAE)	Gas utility	0.22	2,953	6.00	11.8	13	N.M.	4.6	2,855
Norfolk Southern (NSC)	Railroads	0.94	4,495	63.00	11.7	9	12.8	3.0	18,026
Northern States Power (NSP)	Diversified utility	0.36	2,494	44.25	13.2	3	11.7	5.9	14,894
Northern Telecom (NT)	Telecommunications	0.52	8,583	36.00	18.8	9	N.M.	0.9	16,335
Northrop Grumman (NOC)	Aerospace/defense	0.91	6,087	43.75	8.8	9	15.3	3.6	31,081
Novell (NOVL)[1]	Computer software/services	0.73	1,516	18.50	15.9	20	N.M.	N.A.	47,804
Nynex (NYN)	Telecommunications	0.50	13,309	39.25	12.2	4	N.M.	6.0	11,430
Occidental Petroleum (OXY)	Oil/gas	0.90	8,692	21.75	25.0	9	N.M.	4.5	10,591

Notes: [1]Trades over the counter [2]Trades on the American Stock Exchange; all others trade on the New York Stock Exchange **Value Line Timeliness Rank:** 1=highest expected performance in the next 12 months; 5=lowest expected performance **Analysts' opinion rating:** 1.00 or greater=buy; 0.99 to 0.01=hold, 0.00 or less=sell. **PE ratios** are based on 1995 earnings estimates. **Earnings growth projections** are for the next five years. **Return on equity** is popular among stock analysts as a basic yardstick of a company's profitability and ability to self-finance future growth. The figure we cite is the average for the past five years. N.M.—Not meaningful N.A.—Not applicable **Sources:** Standard & Poor's, Value Line

MONEY Ranks the S&P 500

Company (ticker symbol)	Industry	Analysts' opinion rating	Revenues (millions)	Recent price	PE ratio	Projected annual earnings growth	Return on equity	Current yield	Value of $10,000 invested 12/31/89
Ogden (OG)	Environmental service management	1.00	$1,878	$21.25	11.9	12%	14.7%	5.8%	$8,971
Ohio Edison (OEC)	Electric utility	0.08	2,390	19.25	9.8	3	8.9	7.7	11,506
Oneok (OKE)	Gas utility	0.50	792	17.50	12.8	6	10.1	6.3	14,477
Oshkosh B'Gosh Class A (GOSH.A)[1]	Clothing/textiles	−0.33	352	15.00	24.2	11	11.2	2.7	4,053
Owens-Corning (OCF)	Glass/building materials	0.90	3,219	32.50	8.1	12	N.M.	N.A.	12,938
Paccar (PCAR)[1]	Trucks	0.95	4,068	44.75	8.4	13	9.4	4.4	14,126
PacifiCorp (PPW)	Electric utility	0.78	3,496	17.50	11.7	3	N.M.	6.1	10,524
Pall Corp (PLL)	Filters/machinery	0.61	701	18.00	18.8	13	18.1	2.0	17,159
Parker-Hannifin (PH)	Fluid power systems	0.95	2,576	46.75	16.8	12	8.5	2.1	21,410
Penney, J.C. (JCP)	Retail stores	1.03	19,987	50.75	11.0	10	16.4	3.3	16,977
Pennzoil (PZL)	Oil/gas	0.57	2,696	51.50	24.3	14	6.9	5.8	7,477
PepsiCo (PEP)	Beverages/snack foods	0.96	27,072	35.00	14.6	14	N.M.	2.0	17,638
Perkin-Elmer (PKN)	Specialty instruments	0.91	1,024	29.50	14.8	17	N.M.	2.3	14,607
Phelps Dodge (PD)	Mining	0.86	2,941	61.25	11.4	14	19.8	2.6	24,889
Phillips Petroleum (P)	Oil/gas	0.74	11,933	36.75	18.3	18	12.2	3.0	17,759
Pioneer High-Bred Intl. (PHYB)[1]	Hybrid seed corn	1.00	1,479	33.50	14.4	12	19.2	2.0	24,679
Pitney Bowes (PBI)	Office equipment	0.86	3,612	33.75	11.6	11	20.5	3.0	15,939
Placer Dome (PDG)	Mining	1.27	919	21.50	38.4	15	N.M.	1.3	12,954
PNC Bank (PNC)	Banking	0.94	4,578	23.50	6.7	9	14.0	5.9	14,774
Polaroid (PRD)	Photography	0.70	2,299	33.50	10.8	12	N.M.	1.7	8,139
PPG Industries (PPG)	Glass/building materials	1.18	6,050	40.75	13.4	13	14.6	2.8	23,830
Price/Costco (PCCW)[1]	Cash and carry retailer	0.89	16,481	15.75	13.8	14	N.M.	N.A.	3,405
Procter & Gamble (PG)	Household products	1.04	30,296	62.75	17.2	13	N.M.	2.2	19,847
Promus (PRI)	Casino gambling	1.39	1,500	29.50	15.5	35	N.M.	N.A.	N.A.
Raytheon (RTN)	Aerospace/defense electronics	1.02	9,801	63.75	10.0	8	20.6	2.3	20,891
Reynolds Metals (RLM)	Aluminum/related products	0.81	5,591	55.25	22.1	9	N.M.	1.8	11,833
Rockwell International (ROK)	Electronics/aerospace technology	1.14	11,079	34.75	11.1	8	23.3	3.0	16,884
Rohm & Haas (ROH)	Plastics/chemicals	1.08	3,434	60.25	14.0	10	14.9	2.4	19,830
Rollins Environmental Services (REN)	Pollution/waste management	N.A.	181	5.75	41.1	8	N.M.	N.A.	4,359
Rowan (RDC)	Oil/gas	0.78	426	7.50	46.9	13	N.M.	N.A.	6,773
Rubbermaid (RBD)	Plastics/rubber	0.86	2,076	27.50	16.8	14	21.1	1.8	15,898
Russell (RML)	Clothing/textiles	0.66	1,043	30.00	13.1	13	13.9	1.6	12,212
Ryan's Family Steak House (RYAN)[1]	Restaurants	0.78	435	6.25	9.5	13	15.2	N.A.	8,202
Safety-Kleen (SK)	Pollution control/recycling	0.67	785	13.75	13.9	12	N.M.	2.5	7,375
St. Jude Medical (STJM)[1]	Medical equipment	1.02	255	37.25	14.4	11	29.5	1.0	15,916
St. Paul (SPC)	Insurance	0.74	4,700	43.50	9.0	9	N.M.	3.4	17,477
Santa Fe Energy Resources (SFR)	Oil/gas	0.80	396	9.00	45.0	19	N.M.	N.A.	N.A.
Sara Lee (SLE)	Food/consumer products	0.78	15,536	24.50	15.3	11	N.M.	2.7%	$16,429
Seagram (VO)	Alcoholic beverages	0.91	6,061	30.75	11.8	11	16.3%	1.9	14,836
Service International (SRV)	Funeral services	1.29	800	26.50	15.6	14	25.4	1.5	28,171
Shared Medical Systems (SMED)[1]	Information services	0.87	578	29.50	17.6	12	15.5	2.8	27,764
Skyline (SKY)	Mobile homes	0.75	580	19.75	13.2	26	5.9	2.4	15,272
Snap-On (SNA)	Tools	0.94	1,193	31.75	11.5	12	13.6	3.4	11,484
Southwest Airlines (LUV)	Airline services	1.10	2,574	23.50	13.2	19	12.4	0.1	44,875
Stanley Works (SWK)	Consumer/industrial tools	0.57	2,425	39.75	13.1	10	18.8	3.5	11,978
Stone Container (STO)	Paper/packaging	0.85	5,370	16.75	20.2	6	N.M.	N.A.	7,983

Company (ticker symbol)	Industry	Analysts' opinion rating	Revenues (millions)	Recent price	PE ratio	Projected annual earnings growth	Return on equity	Current yield	Value of $10,000 invested 12/31/89
Sun (SUN)	Oil/gas	0.90	$8,942	$32.00	15.2	14%	N.M.	5.6%	$10,569
Tandy (TAN)	Computer stores	0.69	4,575	44.25	13.2	12	11.0%	1.3	12,332
Teledyne (TDY)	Conglomerate	0.75	2,380	17.00	9.9	10	N.M.	N.A.	2,931
Temple-Inland (TIN)	Paper/packaging	0.96	2,719	47.25	12.0	14	9.8	2.1	14,963
Textron (TXT)	Aerospace/financial services	0.95	9,733	51.00	9.6	10	24.1	2.7	23,648
Thomas & Betts (TNB)	Electrical components	0.56	1,136	71.25	17.8	11	24.0	3.1	17,140
Times Mirror (TMC)	Publishing/cable television	0.53	3,542	32.50	21.5	15	24.2	3.3	10,839
Time Warner (TWX)	Publishing/entertainment	0.90	7,069	35.50	N.M.	11	N.M.	1.0	12,339
Torchmark (TMK)	Insurance/financial services	0.83	2,003	36.75	8.1	10	28.7	3.0	11,254
Toys R Us (TOY)	Toy stores	1.15	8,257	38.50	16.8	17	17.3	N.A.	16,152
Transamerica (TA)	Insurance/financial services	0.71	4,804	49.00	8.5	10	11.5	4.0	13,847
Transco Energy (E)	Gas utility	0.63	2,922	14.25	11.7	11	N.M.	4.1	3,740
Travelers (TRV)	Insurance/financial services	1.10	16,279	34.75	7.8	15	31.2	1.7	26,175
Tribune Co. (TRB)	Publishing/broadcasting	1.18	2,084	52.50	14.8	13	N.M.	1.9	12,341
Trinova (TNV)	Aerospace/defense	0.97	1,740	35.00	12.8	10	N.M.	1.9	16,473
TRW (TRW)	Aerospace/electronics	0.73	8,645	71.25	13.4	9	N.M.	2.8	17,135
Tyco International (TYC)	Fire protection services	1.16	3,263	48.25	15.1	13	N.M.	0.8	9,995
U.S. Surgical (USS)	Medical equipment	0.20	936	22.50	30.8	17	N.M.	0.3	16,898
Unilever N.V. (UN)	Household products	0.88	39,865	118.75	12.9	9	N.M.	2.2	15,522
Unisys (UIS)	Computer systems	0.62	7,377	10.50	9.0	9	N.M.	N.A.	9,360
United Technologies (UTX)	Aerospace/high-tech services	1.02	21,099	63.00	12.4	11	N.M.	3.1	13,613
Unum (UNM)	Employee benefits/pensions	0.77	3,525	45.75	9.9	12	15.6	2.0	20,591
Upjohn (UPJ)	Drugs	0.29	3,577	33.00	13.0	3	28.5	4.4	10,374
USX-Marathon Group (MRO)	Oil/gas	0.83	11,815	18.75	19.9	19	N.M.	3.6	6,271
Varity (VAT)	Farm/industrial machinery	1.14	2,443	38.25	12.1	22	N.M.	N.A.	15,300
V.F. (VFC)	Clothing/textiles	1.22	4,780	50.50	11.1	13	33.8	2.6	18,463
Wachovia (WB)	Banking/financial services	0.86	2,789	33.50	9.8	9	15.8	3.9	19,380
Wells Fargo (WFC)	Banking	0.82	4,840	148.50	9.0	11	19.9	2.6	24,489
Wendy's International (WEN)	Fast-food restaurants	1.18	1,352	14.75	13.8	18	13.3	1.6	35,511
Westinghouse Electric (WX)	Conglomerate	0.37	8,721	14.00	17.5	8	N.M.	1.4	4,735
Weyerhaeuser (WY)	Paper	1.13	10,256	39.25	9.8	11	N.M.	3.0	17,146
Whirlpool (WHR)	Electrical equipment	1.02	7,872	52.00	10.6	11	23.9	2.3	18,106
Winn-Dixie Stores (WIN)	Grocery stores	0.50	11,082	52.75	16.3	10	22.7	2.9	18,529
WMX Technologies (WMX)	Pollution/waste management	1.07	9,826	29.25	15.8	13	N.M.	2.0	9,020
Wrigley, Wm. Jr (WWY)	Chewing gum	0.50	1,575	45.00	23.2	14	33.7	1.2	28,020
Xerox (XRX)	Office equipment	0.90	14,668	102.50	13.0	16	N.M.	2.9	22,377
Yellow (YELL)[1]	Trucking	0.57	2,869	19.50	11.5	9	N.M.	4.8	8,755

Value Line Timeliness Rank: 4 and 5									
Aetna Life & Casualty (AET)	Insurance/financial services	0.39	17,298	46.00	7.6	10	N.M.	5.9	10,906
Atlantic Richfield (ARC)	Oil/gas	0.48	17,189	108.25	16.8	12	14.0	5.0	12,335
Bankers Trust N.Y. (BT)	Banking	0.52	7,562	66.75	6.5	8	25.3	5.3	20,159

Notes: [1]Trades over the counter [2]Trades on the American Stock Exchange; all others trade on the New York Stock Exchange **Value Line Timeliness Rank:** 1=highest expected performance in the next 12 months; 5=lowest expected performance **Analysts' opinion rating:** 1.00 or greater=buy; 0.99 to 0.01=hold, 0.00 or less=sell. **PE ratios** are based on 1995 earnings estimates. **Earnings growth projections** are for the next five years. **Return on equity** is popular among stock analysts as a basic yardstick of a company's profitability and ability to self-finance future growth. The figure we cite is the average for the past five years. N.M.—Not meaningful N.A.—Not applicable **Sources:** Standard & Poor's, Value Line

Money Ranks the S&P 500

Company (ticker symbol)	Industry	Analysts' opinion rating	Revenues (millions)	Recent price	PE ratio	Projected annual earnings growth	Return on equity	Current yield	Value of $10,000 invested 12/31/89
Bassett Furniture (BSET)[1]	Home furnishings	0.50	$515	$27.25	13.6	10%	7.8%	2.9%	$15,987
Bausch & Lomb (BOL)	Eye-care products	0.38	1,858	32.50	10.1	12	25.2	3.0	10,931
Bell Atlantic (BEL)	Telecommunications	0.93	13,500	52.25	13.7	6	17.1	5.2	11,928
Boeing (BA)	Aerospace/defense	0.87	22,460	43.75	20.3	10	17.7	2.2	12,391
Burlington Resources (BR)	Oil/gas	0.71	1,246	42.25	26.1	14	7.9	1.2	9,459
Carolina Power & Light (CPL)	Electric utility	0.56	2,896	26.25	11.1	3	14.5	6.4	15,147
Centex (CTX)	Home building	0.80	3,391	22.25	8.4	12	9.9	0.8	15,040
Central & SouthWest (CSR)	Electric utility	0.54	3,741	22.50	10.8	3	13.3	7.5	15,065
Charming Shoppes (CHRS)[1]	Clothing stores	0.75	1,291	7.25	8.7	15	16.8	1.2	14,211
Chevron (CHV)	Oil/gas	0.65	30,760	45.00	14.0	9	12.2	4.1	16,422
Comcast Class A (CMCSK)[1]	Broadcasting	0.66	1,342	16.25	N.M.	20	N.M.	0.5	15,648
Community Psychiatric Centers (CMY)	Health-care facilities	0.58	394	9.75	13.0	15	N.M.	N.A.	3,615
Consolidated Edison (ED)	Diversified utility	0.24	6,395	24.75	9.2	2	12.6	8.0	11,877
Consolidated Natural Gas (CNG)	Gas utility	0.54	3,299	36.25	15.0	8	9.4	5.3	8,939
Continental (CIC)	Property/casualty insurance	-0.02	5,229	15.00	11.5	9	N.M.	N.A.	6,800
Cooper Industries (CBE)	Electrical machinery	0.85	5,526	37.25	14.4	9	N.M.	3.5	10,654
CoreStates Financial (CFL)	Banking	0.90	2,188	25.75	7.7	9	15.0	4.6	15,019
Cray Research (CYR)	Computer systems	0.70	987	19.00	7.8	9	N.M.	N.A.	4,903
Deluxe (DLX)	Banking paper products	0.50	1,710	28.25	13.3	9	32.7	5.2	9,702
Detroit Edison (DTE)	Electric utility	0.50	3,586	26.25	9.8	1	17.9	7.8	14,190
Dillard Department Stores A (DDS)	Retail stores	0.72	5,331	26.50	10.2	13	14.3	0.4	11,325
Dominion Resources (D)	Electric utility	0.72	4,522	37.00	11.4	2	12.2	6.9	15,934
Duke Power (DUK)	Electric utility	0.83	4,300	39.50	13.0	3	13.7	4.9	17,864
E-Systems (ESY)	Defense electronics	0.61	1,999	41.50	10.5	8	17.3	2.8	15,072
EG&G (EGG)	Specialty instruments	0.07	2,300	16.00	12.3	8	27.4	3.4	10,774
Entergy (ETR)	Electric utility	0.70	5,876	23.25	8.9	3	10.9	7.7	12,896
Exxon (XON)	Oil/gas	0.76	97,241	62.75	15.4	7	15.1	4.7	15,744
First Chicago (FNB)	Banking	1.13	4,892	49.00	7.3	9	N.M.	4.0	17,653
Fleming (FLM)	Wholesale food distribution	0.25	14,204	24.00	10.8	6	20.7	5.0	9,683
General Re (GRN)	Reinsurance	1.08	3,711	112.00	12.8	13	16.8	1.7	13,901
Giant Food Class A (GFS.A)[2]	Grocery stores	0.40	3,614	23.00	13.5	10	16.0	3.1	9,221
Giddings & Lewis (GIDL)[1]	Machinery	0.97	553	15.50	11.9	13	17.2	0.7	19,238
Golden West Financial (GDW)	Banking	1.07	1,893	39.00	8.7	10	20.9	0.7	14,941
GTE (GTE)	Telecommunications	0.89	19,759	31.00	12.3	9	18.9	6.0	11,417
Handleman (HDL)	Book/record distribution	0.37	1,067	11.25	10.6	10	15.0	3.9	6,250
Harcourt General (H)	Conglomerate	1.25	3,520	37.00	17.7	16	N.M.	1.7	15,795
Harnischfeger Industries (HPH)	Machinery	1.13	1,138	25.00	19.2	10	N.M.	1.6	13,050
Hasbro (HAS)[2]	Toys/games	0.90	2,662	33.00	13.2	12	32.6	0.8	27,423
Houston Industries (HOU)	Electric utility	−0.10	4,139	34.75	10.6	2	17.2	8.6	14,121
K Mart (KM)	Retail stores	0.64	36,673	16.50	9.9	9	N.M.	5.8	11,872
Kaufman & Broad Home (KBH)	Home building	0.65	1,305	13.00	8.3	15	11.9	2.3	10,511
Limited (LTD)	Clothing stores	0.69	7,105	18.50	12.6	15	23.4	1.9	11,369
Lincoln National (LNC)	Insurance/financial services	0.65	7,234	36.25	8.4	10	11.9	4.5	14,911
Lotus Development (LOTS)[1]	Computer software/services	0.79	986	38.25	17.2	16	14.7	N.A.	12,339
Louisiana Land/Exploration (LLX)	Oil/gas	0.80	836	45.25	43.9	26	N.M.	2.2	11,612
Melville (MES)	Retail stores	0.60	11,134	33.25	9.0	10	22.0	4.5	8,899

Company (ticker symbol)	Industry	Analysts' opinion rating	Revenues (millions)	Recent price	PE ratio	Projected annual earnings growth	Return on equity	Current yield	Value of $10,000 invested 12/31/89
Mobil (MOB)	Oil/gas	1.02	$64,555	$86.00	14.5	8%	11.1%	3.9%	$16,985
Morgan, J.P. (JPM)	Financial services	0.73	8,969	62.00	8.2	8	19.7	4.3	16,840
Morrison Knudsen (MRN)	Engineering/construction	0.27	2,641	15.50	15.2	13	7.9	5.1	8,025
Nalco Chemical (NLC)	Chemicals	0.71	1,381	32.25	15.4	10	31.5	2.9	14,725
Newmont Mining (NEM)	Mining	1.21	607	41.25	37.8	10	N.M.	1.1	11,578
Niagara Mohawk Power (NMK)	Diversified utility	0.24	4,122	13.75	8.1	3	9.5	8.1	11,443
Nicor (GAS)	Gas utility	0.56	1,752	24.25	11.1	5	16.2	5.1	13,362
Oryx Energy (ORX)	Oil/gas	0.75	1,015	14.50	N.M.	7	N.M.	N.A.	3,764
Pacific Enterprises (PET)	Gas utility	0.82	2,835	21.50	11.4	4	N.M.	5.9	5,669
Pacific Gas & Electric (PCG)	Diversified utility	0.25	10,516	22.50	7.8	2	13.2	8.6	13,752
Peco Energy (PE)	Diversified utility	0.98	4,063	25.50	9.7	3	10.2	6.3	14,568
Peoples Energy (PGL)	Gas utility	0.66	1,279	28.00	13.1	3	12.2	6.4	14,805
Pet (PT)	Specialty/packaged foods	0.79	1,582	17.50	14.3	9	N.M.	1.8	N.A.
Potlatch (PCH)	Paper	0.46	1,426	38.25	13.0	14	7.2	4.1	12,440
Providian (PVN)	Insurance	0.84	2,878	31.75	7.8	10	17.6	2.5	13,526
Public Service Enterprise (PEG)	Diversified utility	0.63	5,910	26.25	9.3	2	12.3	8.2	12,597
Pulte (PHM)	Home building	0.90	1,702	20.50	8.1	11	12.1	1.1	19,357
Quaker Oats (OAT)	Food/beverages	0.23	5,955	75.00	16.0	9	N.M.	3.0	14,800
Raychem (RYC)	Electronics/insulation	0.78	1,462	37.00	21.5	43	N.M.	0.8	12,231
Roadway Services (ROAD)[1]	Trucking	0.71	4,422	57.25	16.0	11	14.9	2.4	15,145
Royal Dutch Petrol (RD)	Oil/gas	0.90	57,104	116.50	15.8	9	N.M.	3.5	18,500
Safeco (SAFC)[1]	Insurance	0.95	3,656	50.00	8.5	11	14.1	3.9	15,251
Salomon (SB)	Financial services	-0.06	7,514	39.25	10.0	9	13.0	1.6	18,428
SCEcorp (SCE)	Electric utility	0.38	8,110	13.75	8.8	1	13.3	7.2	9,850
Schlumberger (SLB)	Oil/gas	1.01	6,662	58.75	21.1	14	20.6	2.0	13,253
Shoney's (SHN)	Restaurants	0.71	1,184	15.00	8.8	15	N.M.	N.A.	12,637
Sigma-Aldrich (SIAL)[1]	Chemicals	0.40	823	34.75	14.3	14	21.3	0.9	12,423
Southern (SO)	Electric utility	0.83	8,326	19.75	11.9	3	12.8	5.9	18,386
Stride Rite (SRR)	Footwear	0.08	550	13.75	13.8	11	25.5	2.7	10,458
Supervalu (SVU)	Food wholesaler	0.33	16,122	24.25	8.9	10	20.6	3.8	9,566
Tele-Communications A (TCOMA)[1]	Broadcasting	1.26	4,234	22.50	N.M.	16	N.M.	N.A.	12,658
Texaco (TX)	Oil/gas	0.61	31,690	65.25	15.4	9	12.1	4.8	14,234
Texas Utilities (TXU)	Electric utility	0.46	5,683	32.50	11.3	2	N.M.	9.4	13,505
TJX (TJX)	Clothing stores	0.55	3,718	15.75	8.7	14	39.5	3.5	11,722
U S West (USW)	Telecommunications	0.98	10,780	37.50	12.3	6	12.0	5.6	12,140
U.S. Bancorp (USBC)[1]	Banking/financial services	0.76	1,947	24.75	8.3	10	14.8	4.0	16,890
Unicom (UCM)	Electric utility	0.52	5,303	21.50	8.7	5	3.3	7.3	8,488
Union Camp (UCC)	Paper/packaging	0.50	3,267	47.50	15.2	16	6.0	3.2	15,284
Union Electric (UEP)	Electric utility	0.60	2,061	35.75	12.3	3	14.3	6.8	16,990
Unocal (UCL)	Oil/gas	1.05	7,889	29.25	18.8	14	9.9	2.7	11,259
USAir Group (U)	Air transport	0.50	7,117	4.25	N.M.	6	N.M.	N.A.	1,317
USLife (USH)	Insurance	0.40	1,646	32.75	7.1	8	8.7	4.0	13,124
Viacom Class B (VIA.B)[2]	Entertainment/communications	0.66	3,645	39.25	64.3	15	N.M.	N.A.	N.A.

Notes: [1]Trades over the counter [2]Trades on the American Stock Exchange; all others trade on the New York Stock Exchange **Value Line Timeliness Rank:** 1=highest expected performance in the next 12 months; 5=lowest expected performance **Analysts' opinion rating:** 1.00 or greater=buy; 0.99 to 0.01=hold, 0.00 or less=sell. **PE ratios** are based on 1995 earnings estimates. **Earnings growth projections** are for the next five years. **Return on equity** is popular among stock analysts as a basic yardstick of a company's profitability and ability to self-finance future growth. The figure we cite is the average for the past five years. N.M.—Not meaningful N.A.—Not applicable **Sources:** Standard & Poor's, Value Line

MONEY Ranks the S&P 500

Company (ticker symbol)	Industry	Analysts' opinion rating	Revenues (millions)	Recent price	PE ratio	Projected annual earnings growth	Return on equity	Current yield	Value of $10,000 invested 12/31/89
Westvaco (W)	Paper/industrial products	0.53	$2,463	$35.00	15.2	16%	7.4%	3.1%	$13,532
Woolworth (Z)	Retail stores	0.33	8,839	15.50	10.5	9	N.M.	3.8	5,969
Zurn Industries (ZRN)	Energy/water-control systems	0.25	508	18.25	12.5	2	N.M.	4.8	5,234

Unranked									
AirTouch Communications (ATI)	Telecommunications	1.40	988	29.75	76.3	35	N.M.	N.A.	N.A.
American Express (AXP)	Financial services	0.93	14,194	30.75	10.1	11	11.9	2.9	10,706
Borden (BN)	Food/industrial products	-0.34	5,552	13.50	13.9	8	N.M.	N.A.	4,690
Burlington Northern (BNI)	Railroads	1.09	4,897	49.75	9.5	12	N.M.	2.4	18,240
Ceridian (CEN)	Computers/information services	1.20	909	26.00	16.0	18	N.M.	N.A.	14,349
Cinergy (CIN)	Gas and electric utility	0.45	1,845	23.00	10.4	2	N.M.	7.4	15,150
Columbia Gas System (CG)	Gas utility	0.20	3,254	27.75	7.7	4	N.M.	N.A.	5,989
Columbia/HCA Healthcare (COL)	Health-care facilities/services	1.27	10,529	41.50	14.5	17	N.M.	0.2	N.A.
Coors, Adolph Class B (ACCOB)[1]	Beverages	0.18	1,644	17.25	13.1	10	N.M.	2.8	9,940
Cyprus Amax Minerals (CYM)	Mining	1.00	2,598	26.50	9.8	15	N.M.	3.0	11,828
Dean Witter Discover (DWD)	Brokerage/credit services	1.54	5,300	38.50	8.0	14	N.M.	1.2	N.A.
Dial (DL)	Personal/household products	1.23	3,447	20.50	11.1	9	N.M.	2.9	$15,242
Eastman Chemical (EMN)	Chemicals	1.14	4,140	54.00	13.9	13	N.M.	2.9	N.A.
Eastman Kodak (EK)	Photography	0.92	15,026	48.00	14.3	12	N.M.	3.3	14,371
First Data (FDC)	Credit-card processing services	1.37	1,601	50.00	22.6	18	N.M.	0.2	N.A.
General Dynamics (GD)	Aerospace/defense	0.82	3,113	42.25	11.7	7	N.M.	3.3	32,686
Lockheed (LK)	Aerospace/defense	0.73	13,025	72.00	9.9	6	N.M.	3.1	22,372
Marriott International (MAR)	Hotels	1.12	8,288	29.25	17.2	14	N.M.	0.9	N.A.
Martin Marietta (ML)	Aerospace/information technology	0.75	10,275	45.75	9.9	8	N.M.	2.0	23,271
Pacific Telesis Group (PAC)	Telecommunications	0.59	9,176	31.50	11.4	3	12.7	6.8	8,004
Pittston Services Group (PZS)	Airfreight/security services	0.71	1,777	27.50	12.3	12	N.M.	0.7	13,602
Ralston-Purina Group (RAL)	Packaged foods	0.47	7,383	42.50	15.0	7	N.M.	2.8	11,463
Ryder System (R)	Truck rental	1.13	4,537	23.50	10.5	11	N.M.	2.5	13,238
Santa Fe Pacific (SFX)	Railroads	1.05	2,793	15.50	13.2	13	N.M.	0.6	8,741
Santa Fe Pacific Gold (GLD)	Precious minerals	1.42	316	14.25	25.4	16	N.M.	0.3	N.A.
Sears Roebuck (S)	Retail stores	1.00	53,144	49.50	9.2	12	N.M.	3.2	16,406
Southwestern Bell (SBC)	Telecommunications	0.97	11,309	41.75	14.0	8	18.5	3.7	16,027
Union Pacific (UNP)	Railroads	1.04	7,937	48.75	10.4	10	19.9	3.5	14,627
Western Atlas (WAI)	Oilfield services	1.17	2,212	46.00	23.8	15	N.M.	0.0	N.A.

Notes: [1]Trades over the counter [2]Trades on the American Stock Exchange; all others trade on the New York Stock Exchange **Value Line Timeliness Rank:** 1=highest expected performance in the next 12 months; 5=lowest expected performance **Analysts' opinion rating:** 1.00 or greater=buy; 0.99 to 0.01=hold, 0.00 or less=sell. **PE ratios** are based on 1995 earnings estimates. **Earnings growth projections** are for the next five years. **Return on equity** is popular among stock analysts as a basic yardstick of a company's profitability and ability to self-finance future growth. The figure we cite is the average for the past five years. N.M.—Not meaningful N.A.—Not applicable **Sources:** Standard & Poor's, Value Line

2

Your New Agenda for Axing Taxes

The fury voters unleashed last election day seems destined to assure that Americans will see their federal tax load lighten this year. The new Republican leadership in the House of Representatives promises to bring 17 tax cut proposals from its famed *Contract with America* to a vote soon. All of those tax breaks won't pass, of course. If they did, the $203 billion federal budget deficit could balloon by an estimated $150 billion by the year 2000. Our forecast? MONEY sees passage of a tax credit of $300 or so for families with incomes up to $50,000, more generous IRAs and a capital-gains tax cut. The message finally appears to be getting through to Washington: Our Taxes Are Too High. Do Something!

The evidence that tax levels are excessive appears in a report from the Tax Foundation, a nonpartisan research group in Washington, D.C. According to the study, the median household is defined as a working couple with two kids and a gross income of $53,354. The couple now pays about 40% of its income in federal, state and local taxes. What's more, households in the top 39.6% federal bracket are handing over as much as 50% of their take to the tax men. That means, at these rates, a couple would have to pay as much as $4.2 million in taxes during their productive years. Can the Republicans (and their Democratic allies) roll back taxes enough to please the voters? "For now, you have to give the Republicans the benefit of the doubt that they'll fight tooth and nail for the tax cuts," says Stan Collender, a Washington, D.C. federal budget expert at the accounting firm Price Waterhouse. The challenge will be in financing the largesse. So look for genuine belt tightening pain to emerge in lockstep with any tax cut gain.

Stop Paying up to 50% in Taxes Now

There's no reason to wait for the politicians to get their tax act together, however. In this chapter, we offer proven ideas for cutting your federal income and Social Security taxes this year and beyond plus guidance on likely changes in the law. We also show you how to trim the state and local levies that really hit close to home and keep taxes on your investments to a minimum. As the tax landscape shifts this year, sound planning will become even more important. "Your best defense against the constantly changing tax code is to adopt a long-term strategy and update it as needed," says Kaycee Krysty of accountant Moss Adams in Seattle. Begin with the tips below that apply directly to you in the section covering your federal tax bracket.

15% Federal Bracket
Taxable '95 income up to $23,350 (singles) or $39,000 (couples)

Open an old-fashioned IRA. Individual Retirement Accounts offer tremendous advantages to people in their twenties. You get to deduct a full $2,000 contribution to an IRA as long as your adjusted gross income is $25,000 or less if you're single, $40,000 or less if you are married and file jointly. (AGI is your total income minus a few tax-favored items, such as alimony you pay. Taxable income, the amount on which your tax rate is based, is your AGI minus your deductions and exemptions.) If your spouse works, you can each contribute $2,000 to your respective IRAs, for an annual tax savings of $600. To make saving easier, you can arrange with the mutual fund, broker or bank where you have your IRA to deduct the contribution from your checking or savings account each month. By the way, you have until April 17 this year to open and write off a '94 IRA. That's because April 15, the normal deadline, falls on a Saturday, thus delaying the day of tax reckoning.

Odds are strong that Congress will pass a "back-end" IRA this year. This would permit nondeductible annual contributions of up to $4,000 per couple ($2,000 for singles). Like a traditional IRA, the earnings would grow tax deferred. Then after five years you could make withdrawals tax-free if you used the money for retirement, a first-home purchase, college or large medical expenses. The Republican proposal would even let you convert all or part of your current IRA to a back-end account, not including rollovers from employer-sponsored plans. To do so, you would have to pay income tax on the previously untaxed portion of the IRA, although you could spread the tax over four years. For now, however, you're better off with a deductible IRA. Later you can convert to a back-end account if you need the money.

Duck the nasty little kiddie tax. If you
have children, transfer cash or any income-producing assets to a no-fee custodial account in your child's name at a bank, brokerage or mutual fund. These earnings generally will be taxed at your child's lower tax rate, typically 15%. But if he or she is under 14, your child must pay taxes at your top tax rate on investment income above $1,200 in 1994 and $1,300 in 1995. That would be the amount accumulated on about $16,250 earning 8% this year. To avoid this fate, look for investments that pay out little or no income until after the child turns 14. Worthy choices include Series EE U.S. savings bonds (recent-

ly yielding around 6%) and zero-coupon Treasury bonds (yielding 7.6% to 8.1%).

Start your children on an IRA. Since
even minors may contribute up to $2,000 of their wages from, say, a summer job to an IRA, this move can be a clever way to keep your child's earnings from being taxed while getting him or her a super-early start on retirement savings. Should the back-end IRA become law, it could become a favored vehicle for funding a child's college education because you could make tax-free withdrawals for college after five years. For now, however, have your child use a deductible IRA. If the back-end version passes on Capitol Hill, you will probably be allowed to convert to one.

28% Federal Bracket
Taxable '95 income of $23,351 to $56,550 (singles) or $39,001 to $94,250 (couples)

Realize capital gains without worry.
Because you're in the 28% bracket, you can feel free to take your profits on winning stocks or funds whenever the time seems right. In contrast, folks in the 31%, 36% and 39.6% brackets risk a price decline by holding on to such investments for more than one year in an effort to qualify for long-term capital gains, which are taxable at a top rate of 28%. If this capital-gains rate is cut to half your top income tax rate, as new House Ways and Means Chairman Bill Archer (R-Texas) proposes, the advice above becomes inoperable. Here's why. If you sold a profitable stock or stock fund that you've owned for a year or less, you would owe taxes at your 28% income tax rate instead of the proposed 14% capital-gains rate. Still, if you own a stock or fund you think has peaked, go ahead and sell it this year. That's because the way the proposed law is currently written,

the new lower capital-gains rates would be available for any capital asset that was held for more than a year and sold in '95, regardless of when the law is passed.

File down oft-overlooked FICA tax. If you contribute to a flexible spending account at work, you may be able to cut your income tax and Social Security (FICA) levy. An FSA lets you set aside up to $5,000 in pretax salary to pay for dependent care expenses plus another amount determined by your employer (generally $2,000 to $4,000) to pay for unreimbursed medical expenses. Assume you're in the 28% bracket and make less than $61,200, the highest income subject to the 7.65% FICA tax in '95. If you contribute $4,000 to your FSA at the office, you'll shave $1,120 off your federal income tax and $306 off your FICA.

Shield your Social Security check. Any retirees in the 28% bracket are in the Social Security danger zone. As soon as your provisional income (AGI plus your tax-exempt income plus half of your Social Security benefit) inches past $32,000 on a joint return ($25,000 for a single), half of your benefits is subject to federal tax. As your provisional income tops $44,000 on a joint return ($34,000 for a single), up to 85% of your benefits are taxed. Gradual relief may be on the way, however. Republicans propose phasing out the 85% upper limit so that no more than 50% of your benefit would be taxable by the year 2000. They'd also raise the amount people ages 65 to 69 can earn without losing benefits from $11,280 in 1995 to $30,000 by 2000 or so. Meanwhile, you can trim your provisional income by favoring such investments as EE savings bonds (you don't have to declare the annual interest until you redeem the bonds); rental real estate (its losses reduce your AGI) and growth stocks (dividends are minimal and any capital gains are tax-deferred until you sell).

31% and 36% Federal Bracket
Taxable '95 income of $56,551 to $256,500 (singles) or $94,251 to $256,500 (couples)

Buy municipal bonds and muni funds.
Yes, we know that last year was a nightmare for many muni investors who saw their bonds and funds lose as much as 11% of their value. But this year looks better. And, yes, MONEY believes long-term interest rates will rise by as much as half a percentage point by mid-year. But we also think rates will level off after that. Even today, on an after-tax basis, the 6% to 6.5% tax-free yields of intermediate-term munis exceed those of taxable bonds for investors in the 31% bracket and up. If you don't have the $25,000 to $50,000 to assemble a top-quality portfolio of individual munis, invest through such diversified national muni funds as USAA Tax-Exempt Intermediate Term and Vanguard Muni Intermediate.

Check out rental real estate. Landlords
who actively manage their properties may deduct up to $25,000 a year in net rental losses against ordinary income such as wages, interest and dividends. You're considered active if you own at least 10% of a property and make management decisions like approving new tenants or authorizing repairs. The $25,000 maximum allowable write-off starts to phase out when your AGI tops $100,000 and disappears entirely at $150,000.

Consider taking on more shelter. Since
first and second homes still provide some of the best tax shelters around, you might ponder buying a vacation home. As long as you borrow only up to $1 million, you can fully deduct the interest on debt incurred to buy, build or improve a first and second home combined. And there's no limit on property tax write-offs. Points paid on a mortgage used to buy a second home are not deductible in

the year the house is bought. Deductions have to be spread over the life of the loan.

39.6% Federal Bracket

Taxable '95 income above $256,500
(both singles and couples)

Go for a defined-benefit Keogh. If you're 45 or older and generate income from self-employment, investigate this potential monster of a shelter. Like other defined-benefit pensions, this special type of Keogh is based on your life expectancy plus the amount you want to draw down as an annuity when you retire. The maximum benefit you can receive is your average income over your three top earning years or $120,000, whichever is less. Hiring an actuary to administer such a plan isn't cheap (up to $3,000 to set one up plus around $1,250 a year). You have until year-end to open a '95 Keogh, though you can fund the plan through April 15, 1996.

Seek out a rabbi to defer compensation. Many companies now offer their highly paid executives so-called rabbi trusts (because the method was first used by a congregation for its rabbi). Your employer sets up an irrevocable trust, stashes money in it every year for you and pays the income tax on the fund. You then have retirement dollars building up to be spent when you are presumably in a lower tax bracket. One drawback is that you have no control over your trust, which can even be seized by creditors to pay your employer's debts. So be confident about your company's long-term health before asking for the rabbi's blessing.

Your Tax Planning Calendar for '95

◆ **April 17:** Deadline for filing returns. (April 15, the normal day of tax reckoning, falls on a Saturday.) Last day to establish and contribute to a 1994 IRA or request a four-month filing extension. Your payment of the first installment of '95 estimated tax is also due.

◆ **Early May:** Meet with your tax preparation pro to start planning to reduce your taxes this year.

◆ **June 15:** Your payment of the second installment of '95 estimated tax is due.

◆ **August 15:** This is the last day to file a '94 income tax return if you received an automatic extension.

◆ **Early September:** Project your annual income and deductible expenses. Also adjust your W-4 withholding allowances or estimated tax payments to cover the projected tax due and avoid an underpayment penalty.

◆ **September 15:** Your payment of the third installment of '95 estimated tax is due.

◆ **November:** Discuss year-end moves with your tax adviser, especially if you are thinking of selling investments.

◆ **December 26:** Don't wait past today to sell stock or mutual fund shares for a '95 gain because the entire transaction will likely take three days. Starting this June, the SEC requires that all trades of securities be settled within three business days, vs. five in the past.

◆ **December 29:** This is the last day to set up a '95 Keogh plan to shelter self-employment income.

◆ **Early 1996:** Organize your tax records by deduction category. If you made a single donation of $250 or more, ask your charity for a receipt. If you're expecting a refund, make your appointment with your tax pro now so you get your cash soon.

◆ **January 15:** Your payment of the final installment of any '95 estimated tax is due.

◆ **February 1:** Now is a good time to check to make sure you have received all your W-2 and 1099 forms for '95. Don't hesitate to track down missing ones from your employer, bank, broker or mutual funds.

◆ **Mid-March:** This may be your last chance to make a date with your preparer before he or she gets booked.

Cut Your State and Local Levies Too

This year taxpayers stand to get more relief from state taxes than at any time in at least a decade. According to MONEY's annual 50-state tax survey (see page 50), only Illinois and the District of Columbia seem highly likely to hike taxes. In contrast, more than half the states seem to be seriously considering some form of major tax cut. For example, newly elected or sitting governors strongly favor phasing out state income taxes altogether in Arizona and Connecticut; slashing state income tax rates by as much as 25% in Iowa, New York and Virginia; and shifting two-thirds of local education costs in Wisconsin from property taxes to the state.

Such tantalizing tax treats are the payoff from the November elections, in which the Republicans who were committed to trimming taxes won big across the country. The G.O.P. seized 11 governorships, putting the party in control of 30 statehouses, including those in eight of the nine most populous states. And Republicans also gained a net of 481 state legislative seats, giving the G.O.P. a total of 3,508 out of 7,424. The backlash at the ballot box was fueled in part by more than a decade of steadily rising state and local taxes. Today's median two-income couple pay 12.4% of their income to state and local governments, up from 11.2% in 1980, according to the Tax Foundation in Washington, D.C.

While foreseeing better times for taxpayers in '95, tax experts say the years that follow may be far less buoyant. One reason is the economy. Over the past year, the states collected nearly 1% more in sales, income and corporate tax revenues than they had anticipated thanks to strong growth driven in part by abnormally high consumer spending. That boost enabled 21 states to trim taxes some $2.7 billion, says Steven Gold of the Center for the Study of the States in Albany, N.Y. But most experts expect consumer spending to slow down in the face of stagnant inflation-adjusted personal income, a five-year low of 4% for the savings rate and an all-time high for consumer debt at 80% of disposable income. Says Hal Hovey of *State Budget & Tax News*: "The excellent revenue performance of 1994 was stimulated by unusually high purchases of sales-taxed goods like cars, furniture and electronics. That will be extremely difficult to sustain past 1995."

Another danger is that voters, no matter how much they want lower taxes, will insist that their public services not be reduced. In fact, the typical state has already approved plans to spend 7.5% more for prisons and 7.2% more for Medicaid in 1995 than last year, according to the National Conference of State Legislators. Since red-ink budgets are prohibited in all states but Vermont, higher spending could cause some major headaches. Warns Andrew Klutkowski at Research Institute of America, a tax analysis firm in New York City: "If states reduce taxes and hand the responsibility for services to local governments, cities and towns will have to respond by increasing property taxes."

Consider New Jersey, where Republican Gov. Christine Todd Whitman won office in 1993 largely because she promised to slash state income tax rates by 30% in three years. She has already reduced them by 15%, but her administration balanced its 1994 budget partly by freezing state aid to schools and municipalities. As a consequence, property tax levies across New Jersey reportedly rose 5% last year. That's a full percentage point more than in any year since 1990.

Don't let this cautionary outlook obscure the upbeat fact that taxes are going down for now. Part of the Republican message is that all taxes are on the table. So be on the look-out for any new breaks that might come your way in 1995, courtesy of your new tax-conscious state and local legislators. Below are specific tips on how to keep your taxes low and your spirits high in '95 and beyond.

Get to know your state's tax code. The IRS estimates that nearly 8 million Americans overpaid their state and local tax bills in '94 because they didn't realize they were eligible for special breaks. To learn about such goodies, curl up with the instruction booklet for your state tax return. You'll be the richer for spending time with it. For example, if you're retired and collecting Social Security benefits, they won't be taxed in Alabama, Arizona, Arkansas, California, Delaware, Georgia, Hawaii, Idaho, Illinois, Indiana, Kentucky, Louisiana, Maine, Maryland, Massachusetts, Michigan, Mississippi, New Jersey, New York, North Carolina, Ohio, Oklahoma, Oregon, Pennsylvania, South Carolina, Virginia and the District of Columbia. And at least part of a retiree's pension is exempt from taxes in Alabama, Arkansas, Colorado, Delaware, Georgia, Hawaii, Illinois, Louisiana, Maryland, Michigan, Mississippi, Montana, New Jersey, New Mexico, New York, North Carolina, Oregon, Pennsylvania, South Carolina and Utah.

Couples can soften the marriage penalty by filing separate state tax returns (even if they file jointly at the federal level) in Alabama, Arizona, Arkansas, Delaware, Hawaii, Iowa, Kentucky, Mississippi, Montana, Pennsylvania, Tennessee, Virginia, West Virginia and the District of Columbia. In addition, if your children earn money, you might save by filing separately for them too. The federal government will tax investment income above $1,200 earned by any child under 14 at his or her parents' rate. But all states with income taxes, except California and Hawaii, tax kids at their own rate (no matter how much they earn) provided that separate federal and state returns are filed for them.

Defend your lower-tax residence. Watch out if you own dwellings in two states and work part of the time in the state with the higher taxes. In recent years, California, New York and other high-tax states have begun taxing the entire income of such residents including interest, dividends and capital gains earned in other states. What to do? First, find out what constitutes taxable residency in each state where you work or own property. Most states won't consider you a resident unless you spend more than half the year at a home within their borders. But New York and other voracious states may try to tax your entire income if you spend as little as one month within their borders. How can you document that your home in the low-tax state is your main residence? Start by keeping records that show where you spend most of your time, such as phone and electricity bills. Also keep documents that show where you go to church, send your kids to school, register your car and vote.

Shop around for sales tax breaks. Local surtaxes can cause sales taxes to vary widely from one community to another in some states. Californians, for example, pay 8.5% in sales taxes on purchases in San Francisco but only 7.25% in nearby San Rafael. Also take advantage of sales tax reductions that your state may enact to promote business in depressed areas. For example, New Jersey slashes its 6% sales tax in half for shoppers in Newark. Car dealers in all of the states but California, Maryland and Michigan can subtract the value of your trade-in before calculating the sales tax on your new vehicle.

From Alaska's $2,291 to New York's $10,529

	State	Total annual tax on typical household	Grade for risk of future tax hikes
1	Alaska	$2,291	A
2	Wyoming	3,104	A
3	Nevada	4,238	A
4	Florida	4,686	B
5	Tennessee	5,073	B
6	South Dakota	5,151	B
7	Texas	5,290	B
8	Washington	5,463	B
9	New Hampshire	5,506	B
10	Alabama[1]	6,157	C
11	North Dakota	6,552	A
12	Louisiana	6,625	B
13	Missouri[1]	6,698	B
14	Mississippi	6,759	A
15	Delaware[1]	6,781	B
16	Kansas	7,159	A
17	Virginia	7,303	B
18	Indiana	7,416	A
19	Colorado	7,503	A
20	Oklahoma	7,622	B
21	Kentucky	7,632	B
22	South Carolina	7,678	B
23	Iowa[1]	7,723	A
24	Illinois	7,755	D
25	Arkansas	7,761	B
26	Pennsylvania	7,781	B
27	Arizona	7,788	A
28	Vermont	7,788	B
29	New Mexico	7,809	A
30	West Virginia	7,809	B
31	Utah	8,172	A
32	North Carolina	8,308	A
33	Georgia	8,378	A
34	Idaho	8,448	A
35	Hawaii	8,471	C
36	California	8,496	B
37	Montana	8,541	A
38	Nebraska	8,613	B
39	Oregon	8,787	C
40	Michigan	8,793	A
41	Minnesota	8,822	B
42	New Jersey	8,832	C
43	Ohio	9,088	B
44	Massachusetts	9,513	A
45	District of Columbia	9,632	D
46	Wisconsin	9,976	B
47	Connecticut	9,996	A
48	Maine	10,132	B
49	Rhode Island	10,294	B
50	Maryland[2]	10,471	A
51	New York[1]	10,529	B

There are now three certainties in this world—death, taxes and the location of taxpayer heaven. That's Alaska, which tops our ranking as the place with the lowest state and local tax burden in the U.S. Our analysis shows that a typical affluent two-income family that subscribes to MONEY pays $2,291 in state and local taxes in Alaska. That's less than a quarter of the $10,529 a similar family pays in New York, which wound up dead last on our list.

The table gives the annual tax load for a family of four that earned $79,029 in 1994 plus $3,026 in interest, $513 in dividends and $1,590 in capital gains. They spent $38,179 on food, clothing, prescription drugs, household goods, a new car and other items. We ranked the states and the District of Columbia by the total amount the family would pay in state and local income, sales, property and gasoline taxes. The table's third column grades each state's likelihood of imposing tax increases in 1995 or 1996, according to tax experts: A, no major tax hikes expected (20 states); B, moderate chance (25); C, strong possibility (four) and D, almost certain (only the District of Columbia and Illinois).

Sources: State income tax estimates provided by Ernst & Young. Other sources: Vertex Inc.; CCH Inc.; *Lundberg Letter*, *Tax Rates and Tax Burdens in the District of Columbia: A Nationwide Comparison* (1994) by the Washington, D.C. Department of Finance and Revenue; *Significant Features of Fiscal Federalism* (1994) by the Advisory Commission on Intergovernmental Relations.

Notes: [1]Additional local income tax may also be assessed. [2]Local income tax is calculated on state return. [3]Tax rates are for couples filing jointly in 1994.

Tax on earned income				Sales tax			
For singles earning $35,000	For two-income married earning $50,000	For two-income married earning $75,000	For two-income married earning $100,000	Statewide rate	Highest combined state and local	Property tax	Comments[3]
$0	$0	$0	$0	0.000%	7.000%	$2,132	Most tax revenue from the oil and gas industry
0	0	0	0	4.000	6.000	1,129	Most tax revenue from oil, gas and coal companies and sales taxes
0	0	0	0	6.500	7.000	1,686	Most tax revenue from sales, gambling and gas taxes
0	0	0	0	6.000	7.000	2,475	Most tax revenue from sales and use taxes
0	0	0	0	7.000	8.750	1,844	Certain interest and dividend income taxed at 6%
0	0	0	0	4.000	6.000	3,269	Primary sources of revenue: sales and gas taxes and state lottery
0	0	0	0	6.250	8.250	2,730	Most tax revenue from sales and gas taxes
0	0	0	0	7.000	8.200	2,537	Most tax revenue from sales, property and business operation taxes
0	0	0	0	0.000	0.000	5,091	Dividends and interest over $2,400 taxed at 5%
1,280	1,366	2,395	3,342	4.000	12.000	836	Top rate: 5% on taxable income over $6,000; federal tax deductible
734	610	1,466	2,485	5.000	6.000	2,694	Top rate: 12% on taxable income over $50,000; federal tax deductible
905	995	1,785	2,515	4.000	10.750	1,659	Top rate: 6% on income over $100,000; federal tax deductible
1,275	1,193	2,248	3,717	4.225	7.725	1,478	Top rate: 6% above $9,000; $10,000 of federal tax deductible
1,185	995	2,271	3,545	7.000	7.000	1,801	Top rate: 5% on taxable income over $10,000
1,814	1,886	3,821	5,804	0.000	0.000	1,408	Top rate: 7.7% on taxable income above $40,000
1,632	1,077	2,668	4,305	4.900	7.400	1,509	Top rate: 6.45% on taxable income over $60,000
1,594	1,767	3,233	4,699	4.500	4.500	1,882	Top rate: 5.75% on taxable income above $17,000
1,511	2,139	3,302	4,464	5.000	5.000	1,699	Rate: a flat 3.4% of modified adjusted gross income
1,448	1,448	2,725	4,000	3.000	9.000	1,736	Rate: a flat 5% of modified federal taxable income
1,885	1,693	3,478	5,263	4.500	10.500	1,171	Top rate: 7% on income over $21,000; federal tax may be deductible
1,841	1,765	3,265	4,765	6.000	6.000	1,676	Top rate: 6% on taxable income above $8,000
1,699	1,966	3,708	5,449	5.000	6.000	2,032	Top rate: 7% over $10,850; 44% of capital gains excluded in '95
1,685	1,712	3,300	4,960	5.000	6.000	1,986	Top rate: 9.98% on income above $47,700; federal tax deductible
1,020	1,285	2,035	2,785	6.250	9.000	2,669	Rate: a flat 3% of all taxable income
1,694	1,509	3,144	4,862	4.500	7.500	1,656	Top rate: 7% on income over $25,000; 6% on capital gains
1,330	1,900	2,850	3,800	6.000	7.000	2,480	Rate: a flat 2.8% on a broad base of taxable income
1,271	1,112	2,317	3,686	5.000	8.500	2,423	Top rate: 6.9% on income over $300,000; down from 7% in '93
1,274	1,073	2,552	4,337	5.000	5.000	2,802	Rate: 25% of federal income tax liability; down from 34% in '93
1,319	1,178	2,917	5,008	5.125	6.876	2,165	Top rate: 8.5% on income over $64,000
1,260	1,695	3,230	4,855	6.000	6.000	1,477	Top rate: 6.5% on taxable income above $60,000
1,826	1,872	3,495	5,074	5.875	7.125	1,563	Top rate: 7.2% on income over $7,500; federal tax 50% deductible
1,972	1,915	3,700	5,485	6.000	6.000	1,729	Top rate: 7.75% on taxable income over $100,000
1,682	1,624	3,154	4,684	5.000	6.000	2,215	Top rate: 6% on taxable income over $10,000
2,108	1,859	3,902	5,993	5.000	7.000	1,666	Top rate: 8.2% on taxable income above $40,000
2,616	1,978	4,257	6,575	4.000	4.000	1,469	Top rate: 10% on income over $41,000; 7.25% on capital gains
1,446	722	2,534	4,905	6.500	8.750	2,302	Top rate: 11% on taxable income over $424,760
2,002	2,166	4,695	7,472	0.000	0.000	2,134	Top rate: 11% on income over $61,000; federal tax deductible
1,356	1,233	2,869	4,692	5.000	6.500	2,706	Top rate: 6.99% on income over $46,750
2,461	2,446	4,739	7,034	0.000	0.000	2,728	Top rate: 9% over $10,000; $3,000 of federal tax deductible
1,448	1,989	3,089	4,189	6.000	6.000	3,183	Rate: a flat 4.4%, down from 4.6% in '93; sales tax up from 4% to 6%
2,021	1,892	3,932	5,968	6.500	7.500	1,921	Top rate: 8.5% on taxable income above $88,460
713	912	1,688	3,060	6.000	6.000	4,710	Top rate: 6.65% on income over $150,000; cut to 6.58% in '95
1,766	2,396	4,149	6,153	5.000	7.000	2,033	Top rate: 7.5% on taxable income over $200,000
1,584	2,420	3,878	5,339	5.000	5.000	3,049	Flat rate on taxable earned income, 5.95%; unearned, 12%
2,600	2,628	5,050	7,473	5.750	5.750	1,473	Top rate: 9.5% on income over $20,000; sales tax cut from 7% to 5.75%
1,932	2,103	3,836	5,593	5.000	5.500	3,339	Top rate: 6.93% on taxable income over $20,000
1,377	1,071	3,037	4,410	6.000	6.000	4,317	Rate: a flat 4.5% of taxable income
878	1,541	3,770	6,108	6.000	6.000	3,504	Top rate: 8.5% on taxable income over $33,000
818	1,185	2,895	4,919	7.000	7.000	4,319	Rate: a flat 27.5% of modified federal tax liability
2,544	2,688	4,728	6,739	5.000	5.000	3,035	Top rate, with local surtax: 9% over $150,000; 7.5% in '95
1,925	2,343	4,242	6,140	4.000	8.500	2,610	Top rate: 7.875% on taxable income over $26,000; 7.59% in '95

Money Helps

Q. I am about to lose my job and dental benefits at a time when my 11-year-old son needs braces costing $3,000 to $4,000. My wife works, but her salary just covers our basic living expenses. Since this dental work is for my son's benefit, am I permitted to dip into the $25,000 I've invested for him in two mutual funds under the Uniform Gifts to Minors Act (UGMA) to pay his bills?

JAMES BROCK, OMAHA

A. While this is a gray area, it looks like someone in your financial straits should be free to use the cash for dental work. State law governs how money can be spent in UGMA accounts (now called Uniform Transfers to Minors in 44 states). States generally say that: 1) the money must be used for the child's benefit and 2) Mom and Dad have an obligation to support their offspring. That's to discourage parents from dipping into the accounts to pay for their kids' food, clothing, shelter or basic health care.

Wallace Becker, a lawyer with Kinsey Ridenour Becker & Kistler in Lincoln, Neb., points out that the law doesn't specifically mention braces. But he argues that while basic dental care is part of your support obligation, elective orthodontia may not be, particularly if you have no extra income to pay for it. As long as it's clear that you're not raiding your son's assets to avoid your parental duty, it's almost surely okay to take the money from the account. As a practical matter, your only risk is that years later your straight-toothed son could drag you into court for supposedly squandering his cash.

Cut consumption of unhealthy items.

Over the years, states have regularly ratcheted up excise taxes on products regarded as unhealthy. Last year eight states raised cigarette taxes as much as 50¢ a pack, while six states hiked taxes on alcohol. Since these excise taxes (a.k.a. "sin taxes") are likely to go up again in 1995, conserving your use of such products can lead to substantial savings. Last year a pack-a-day smoker in Michigan, home to the nation's highest cigarette tax (75¢ a pack), could have saved $274 in taxes alone by kicking the habit.

Invest in tax-exempt securities.

All states but Alaska, Florida, Nevada, South Dakota, Texas, Washington and Wyoming tax unearned income from investments. But interest on Treasuries and other securities issued by federal agencies is exempt from state and local taxes. Good candidates are short-term Treasury notes, available through a broker or directly from the Treasury (call your local Federal Reserve bank or branch for an application). You might also consider municipal bonds, which pay interest that is generally exempt from federal taxes.

Look for breaks on property taxes.

If you own your home, all of the states except Connecticut, Indiana, Massachusetts, New Jersey, Pennsylvania and West Virginia will give you either a tax credit or a deduction on your state taxes for some or all of your property taxes. And you can exempt a portion of the value of your house from taxation in Alabama, California, Florida, Georgia, Hawaii, Idaho, Illinois, Indiana, Louisiana, Massachusetts, New Mexico, Oklahoma, Texas and the District of Columbia. A growing number of municipalities cut the property taxes of people age 65 and over, veterans, persons with physical disabilities and heads of low-income households.

Fight excessive property assessments.

Take a careful look at your local assessor's appraisal of your house. For example, did he erroneously count your attic storage area as a bedroom? Then compare his estimate with recent sales prices of nearby homes that are similar to yours. You can usually obtain the information from real estate agents or the assessor's office. If you decide your property was overvalued, ask your local appeals board to correct the assessment. According to David Keating of the National Taxpayers Union in Washington, D.C., only one in 150 homeowners appeal their assessments. But half of those win reductions. If you decide you need professional help, you can hire a consultant who typically will charge half of your first year's tax savings.

Trim Taxes on All Your Investments

The best news for many taxpayers is the high probability of a sizable tax cut on capital gains. That's the profit you clear when you sell an investment that has risen in value as opposed to the dividends or interest you collect along the way. Better yet, the favorable tax treatment accorded such gains, which heretofore has solely benefited people with high incomes, may soon be available to all taxpayers, regardless of income.

Under federal tax law, you pay no more than 28% on gains from investments held for at least a year. That's a good deal less than the tax on your income if you are in the 31%, 36% or 39.6% federal brackets. (If you're in the 15% or 28% bracket, your gains tax is the same as your regular marginal tax rate.) But the Republican leaders who have taken over Congress want to cut the tax on long-term capital gains to half of an investor's top income tax rate. That means people in the 39.6% bracket (taxable earnings above $256,500 this year) would cede only 19.8% of their gains to Uncle Sam. Those in the lowest 15% bracket, including many teenagers and retirees, would pay a super-low rate of 7.5%.

Here are the tax basics of various types of investments. In each case, we point to the most tax-efficient choices and show the steps you can take now to lighten the tax burden on your profits. The advice is important because taxes take a bigger toll on investments than most people realize. Taxation at today's rates would have zapped from 7% to 37% of the total return of assorted stock, bond and real estate holdings over the past 10 years. "Income taxes are at their highest since 1982," observes John Bogle, chairman of the Vanguard family of mutual funds. "So the risks investors face are the same as ever, but their potential returns are lower."

The tax code fortunately is filled with quirks that let you defer, reduce or even avoid taxes. To postpone the tax bite, for example, you can concentrate on growth investments, where the profit comes mostly from price appreciation (taxable when you sell) rather than current income (taxed in the year you collect it). You can further reduce taxes by timing your sales, especially of losers. And you can avoid taxes altogether by choosing the right kinds of bonds or, if you own real estate, by swapping your old property for new property to duck the tax that would ordinarily be due.

The message here is to be smart about taxes, not fanatical. "I've seen plenty of otherwise intelligent people load up on tax-free bonds simply to avoid taxes," says Martin Shenkman, a C.P.A. in Teaneck, N.J. "Then when interest rates rose in 1994, they took a big hit because their portfolios weren't properly diversified." While it is important to reduce your investment taxes, that should not be your only goal. Go for the most promising investment. Use what you learn here to make sure that it will still be the most rewarding after you pay the taxes.

Sure ways to shield your stocks.

It's not what you earn as an investor that counts; it's what you keep after the taxman takes his cut. Growth stocks, which deliver most of their return through price gains, enjoy a major tax advantage over income stocks, which pay high dividends. Not only are price gains subject to a maximum levy of 28%, vs. 39.6% for dividends, but the tax isn't due until you cash out, leaving more of your money invested. Here are MONEY's tax-savvy tips for investing in stock. The first three apply only to people in at least the 31% bracket (which starts at $56,551 for singles and $94,251 for couples), though they may work for everyone if Congress cuts the tax on long-term capital gains sufficiently. The remaining points generally apply to all investors.

◆ **Go for growth in taxable portfolios.** Keeping a growth stock in a tax-deferred IRA or Keogh is like buying a Ferrari to drive to your commuter bus stop. You don't really need the account's tax protection because growth stocks derive 90% or so of their return from price increase, which isn't taxed until you sell. You also forgo the right to use any losses you incur to offset gains or ordinary income. And when you finally do withdraw your earnings from the account, you'll pay tax at the rates for ordinary income (which run as high as 39.6%) rather than at the maximum 28% capital-gains rate.

◆ **Seek income in tax-deferred accounts.** IRAs, Keoghs and other such accounts provide a very comfy home for high-dividend stocks whose payouts would otherwise be taxed each year. Good candidates include utility stocks (they generally pay 6% to 7% a year in dividends), financial services firms (2% to 4%) and many blue chips.

◆ **Shoot for long-term price gains.** The favorable tax treatment of capital gains applies only to assets held at least a year. If you cash out sooner, you'll pay your marginal income tax rate. So unless you've got hold of a real rocket—say, a stock that doubled in eight months but now seems headed for a fall—stay invested for at least 12 months before ejecting.

◆ **Sell your priciest shares first.** Suppose you have bought a company's shares at various prices over the years and now want to unload some. Since the tax code lets you designate which shares you sell, dump the ones that cost you the most in order to hold down your capital gains. Sure, you'll pay tax on those gains someday. In general, however, it's better to pay tax in the future rather than today.

◆ **Donate stocks to good causes.** The next time you want to be generous to a tax-exempt group, give away highly appreciated stock instead of cash. Why? Imagine that you bought a stock for $5,000 a decade ago and that it's now worth $15,000. If you cash out, you'll owe tax of up to 28% (or $2,800) on that $10,000 gain. But if you give the stock to charity, the organization pockets the full $15,000 value because tax-exempt charities do not have to pay the capital-gains tax. And you get to take the same $15,000 tax deduction that you would have taken if you'd donated cash instead of stock even though your shares are worth only $12,200 to you after taxes.

◆ **Time losses to claim a tax prize.** Every investor winds up holding losing cards once in a while. But at least you can deduct the damage you sustain outside of a tax-sheltered account. You are allowed to write off capital losses against the full amount of any gains you may reap during the year, and then against as much as $3,000 more of ordinary income. And don't worry if you can't write off the entire loss in one year. You can carry leftover losses forward to future years until they are all used up.

◆ **Avoid these tax tangles.** Watch out for the wash sale rule that prohibits you from deducting a loss on the sale of a stock if you buy any shares of the same company within 30 days either before or after that sale. Take into account the commission you paid when you bought a stock, as well as that imposed when you sold it, when figuring your gain or loss. And be sure to claim a U.S. tax credit if foreign tax was withheld from dividends paid to you by an international stock.

How to Figure All Your Capital Gains

To compute a gain or loss when you sell, take the proceeds of the sale and subtract your basis—or cost of acquiring the shares. Sounds simple. But the tax code can make it tricky depending on how you obtained the stock. Follow these general rules.

IF YOU GOT STOCK BY...	...YOUR BASIS IS
Buying it directly	The price you paid for the shares plus any fees or commissions you paid to buy them. Fees or commissions on the sale do not add to your basis but can be subtracted from the proceeds, thus also reducing your gain.
A dividend reinvestment plan (DRIP)	The full market value of the stock on the date the dividend was paid plus any fees or commissions even if, as is often the case, the DRIP lets you buy shares at a discount.
Receiving it as a gift	The donor's original basis plus any gift tax the donor has to pay. Exception: if you later sell the stock for a loss, your basis is the lesser of the donor's basis or the stock's fair market value on the date the gift was given.
Inheriting it	The market value of the shares on the date you inherited them. This often is the same as the donor's date of death. But in some cases the executor may choose an "alternate valuation date." To check, ask the executor or review the estate tax return. Note that even if you sell the stock within a year, any profit is considered a long-term rather than a short-term capital gain because the stock was inherited.
Receiving it after a stock split	The same, for your total stake, as it was before the split. To find out your new per-share basis, take the original basis of your holding and divide it by the number of shares you own after the split became effective.
Obtaining it as a stock dividend	Whatever the company tells you it is. How's that? Sometimes a company issues a dividend in the form of stock or spins off part of its business and gives shareholders stock in the new firm. You usually won't owe any tax on this so-called stock distribution even if it came as a dividend. But the per-share basis of your holding will be reduced by a percentage that the company will calculate and report to you.
Exercising a stock option	The price you paid for the shares (plus fees or commissions) even though it is lower than the market value at the time of purchase. You must retain the shares for at least a year after buying them, and for two years after receiving the option, or else any profit from their sale will be taxed as ordinary income rather than capital gains.

Deciding Whether Tax-Free Munis Still Work for You

The trick to buying a tax-free municipal bond is to find one paying more than a taxable investment does after taxes. Suppose you are in the 31% federal tax bracket and pay 5% in state income tax and 3% in local tax. For you, a municipal bond with a nominal yield of just 6% that is free of state and local taxes pays as much as a taxable investment earning 6.6%. If the bond is exempt from federal tax, its payout is equivalent to a taxable 8.7%. And if it is free of federal, state and local levies, then it matches a taxable 9.5%.

Type of bond (minimum face value)	Recent yield (maturity)	Interest exempt from what taxes	Tax advice
TREASURY BILLS ($10,000)			
Issued for terms of three, six or 12 months, these are bought at a discount to face value. Your interest is the difference between what you pay and the face value at maturity.	7% (one year)	State and local	Because bills return all their interest when they mature, you can use them to defer taxes by investing in ones that do not pay off until the next tax year.
TREASURY NOTES ($1,000 TO $5,000)			
These come in maturities of two, three, four, five, seven or 10 years. They pay interest twice annually and return your principal when they mature.	7.7% (five years)	State and local	You'll pay federal tax on the interest you receive each year. Try to hold any Treasury note until it matures. That way, you need not worry about price fluctuations. And you will never face a capital loss or capital-gains tax.
TREASURY BONDS ($1,000)			
These are just like T-notes (described above) but carry maturities of 10 to 30 years.	7.8% (30 years)	State and local	The longer a bond's term, the more its price varies with interest rates, so be prepared for capital losses or gains.
ZERO-COUPON GOVERNMENTS ($1,000)			
These are essentially Treasuries stripped of their interest payments. They are bought at a discount and return their full face value at maturity.	7.8% (10 years)	State and local	Although you do not collect any money until maturity, you still must pay taxes each year on the "phantom income" accrued as the bond climbs toward face value.
SERIES EE SAVINGS BONDS ($50)			
These are bought for one-half their face value and pay a variable rate of interest pegged at 85% of the payout on five-year Treasuries provided you hold them anywhere from five to 30 years.	5.9% (five to 30 years)	State and local	You pay no tax until you cash in your bond, so Series EEs are a convenient way to defer taxes to a time when your income and tax bracket figure to be lower. Also, interest on bonds bought since 1990 may be wholly or partly tax-exempt if you use them to pay college tuition.
MUNICIPAL BONDS (TYPICALLY $5,000 TO $10,000)			
These securities are issued by state and local governments to finance public projects such as bridges, airports and hospitals. They typically pay interest twice a year and come in a wide range of maturities up to 30 years.	5.9% to 6.75% (10 years)	Federal, state and local (if in-state); otherwise federal only	At today's rates, muni bonds yield more after taxes than taxable bonds of comparable maturity mainly for investors in the 36% tax bracket and up.
CORPORATES (TYPICALLY $1,000)			
These IOUs issued by corporations have fixed interest rates and usually carry maturities of from five to 30 years, though a few optimistic firms have issued 100-year bonds.	8.1% to 8.7% (five years)	None	Since these bonds are subject to all taxes, hold them in tax-deferred accounts or in the name of a child who pays lower taxes than you do.

How to tame hidden fund taxes.

Many mutual fund investors were jolted in January when they opened the 1099 forms that their funds sent them. They found they owed tax on a fund that lost money last year. Sound impossible? Not at all. It happens because a fund must distribute to shareholders nearly all the yearly income it earned from dividends and interest, plus any net gains it realized from selling securities, even if it had a losing year. Don't get irate, get informed employing the following mutual fund tax tips for '95.

◆ **Favor low turnover and tax savvy.**
Funds that follow a buy-and-hold strategy tend to realize fewer capital gains than those that trade actively. So if you are choosing between two funds with otherwise similar performance, go for the one with the lower turnover ratio (the proportion of its assets that have been bought or sold within the past year). You can find the ratio by calling a fund or by looking in its semiannual report. Low turnover is not the only positive indicator. A tax-savvy manager can be an active trader and still hold the tax bite down by timing any losses to offset the fund's gains. When considering a red-hot fund that has a high turnover ratio, check out its tax-efficiency ratio. That's the percentage of its total return that is left after taxes. As you can see from the table "Totting Up the After-Tax Fund Champs" on the next page, the winners have tax-efficiency ratios of around 80% or better.

◆ **Go for funds that protect profits.**
Several fund companies have launched carefully managed index funds that aim to deliver maximum tax efficiency by timing their losses to offset most of their gains. (Index funds are those that try to match or beat the performance of market benchmarks like the S&P 500 stock index.) Discount broker Charles Schwab has three such funds: International Index, Schwab 1000 and Small-Cap Index. And the Vanguard fund family has launched three entries as well. They are the Capital Appreciation Portfolio, Growth & Income Portfolio and Balanced Portfolio.

◆ **Invest overseas in taxable accounts.**
Under tax treaties between the U.S. and foreign countries, funds that are more than half invested outside the U.S. typically have to pay 5% to 10% of whatever they earn on those holdings to the foreign governments (just as you would if you owned a foreign stock). In return, you are eligible for as much as a dollar-for-dollar reduction of your U.S. tax provided you hold the funds in a taxable account. If you park your overseas funds in a tax-deferred retirement account, then you can kiss that credit adios.

Enjoying real estate's cozy shelter.

In comparison to other investments, property enjoys some truly remarkable tax perks. To begin with, you can deduct the interest you pay on mortgages totaling as much as $1 million on your first and second homes even if you rent out that second home part of the year. If you buy real estate strictly as an investment, you can depreciate (write off) the full price over the next 27.5 or 39 years. And if you help manage the property by, say, interviewing prospective tenants and setting rents, you can deduct any operating losses against as much as $25,000 of non-investment income. With stocks and bonds, by comparison, this kind of deduction is limited to $3,000 a year. Even real estate investment trusts (REITs), which own interests in property or mortgages and trade like stocks, have certain tax advantages. If your REIT profits from the sale of a property, you pay tax on your share at the maximum long-term gains rate of 28%, not at the generally higher rate for short-term gains. That's true even if the REIT owned the asset for less than a year.

Totting up the After-Tax Fund Champs

Judging a mutual fund solely on pretax performance can be misleading, as the table shows. For each category, we list the five funds with the best three-year total returns after taxes for taxpayers in the 31% bracket. We also list their pretax payouts and ranks, which are often quite different. Quest for Value Opportunity A, for example, placed seventh in its category before taxes. But the fund zoomed to No. 2 in our ranking because a tidy 93% of its return remained after taxes as indicated by its tax-efficiency ratio. Other numbers to watch are the turnover ratio, or percentage of assets that were bought or sold in the past year, and unrealized capital gains, the proportion of assets that would be taxed as gains if they sold today.

Fund name	Three-year average annual gain[1]		Tax-efficiency ratio	Turnover ratio	% unrealized capital gains	Maximum sales charge	800 number
	After tax	Before tax (Rank)					
AGGRESSIVE GROWTH							
PBHG Growth	27.3%	29.7% (1)	92%	94.3%	59.0%	None	433-0051
AIM Aggressive Growth	24.6	27.0 (3)	91	61.0	15.0	5.50%	347-1919
Twentieth Century Giftrust Investors	24.5	27.3 (2)	90	101.0	30.2	None	345-2021
PIMCo Advisors Opportunity C	22.1	24.1 (4)	92	105.4	N.A.	1.00[3]	426-0107
John Hancock Special Equities A	20.5	21.3 (7)	96	33.0	15.0	5.00	225-5291
CAPITAL GROWTH							
Oakmark	28.3	29.0 (1)	98	18.0	17.5	None	625-6275
Putnam New Opportunities A	23.5	24.2 (4)	97	52.8	16.0	5.75	225-1581
Parnassus	22.4	24.8 (3)	91	21.0	18.4	3.50	999-3505
Crabbe Huson Special	21.7	26.2 (2)	83	73.3	7.4	None	541-9732
Pioneer Capital Growth A	19.8	21.9 (5)	91	47.0	14.4	5.75	225-6292
GROWTH AND INCOME							
Oppenheimer Main St. Income & Growth A	19.5	23.8 (1)	82	283.0	1.1	5.75	525-7048
Safeco Equity	18.0	20.2 (3)	89	50.5	12.7	None	426-6730
Warburg Pincus Growth & Income	17.2	20.4 (2)	84	150.0	3.9	None	257-5614
Mutual Beacon	16.5	18.3 (4)	90	52.9	13.5	None	553-3014
Mutual Qualified	15.7	17.9 (5)	88	56.2	23.6	None	553-3014
EQUITY TOTAL RETURN							
Fidelity Equity-Income II	13.9	15.5 (1)	90	81.0	8.4	None	544-8888
Quest for Value Opportunity A	12.6	13.6 (7)	93	24.0	9.9	5.50	232-3863
Fidelity Equity Income	12.6	14.1 (4)	89	48.0	15.3	2.00	544-8888
Evergreen Foundation	12.2	14.9 (2)	82	60.0	-0.5[2]	None	235-0064
SoGen International	12.0	13.7 (6)	87	24.0	14.6	3.75	334-2143
INCOME TOTAL RETURN							
Bond Fund for Growth	16.7	18.9 (1)	88	68.4	0.8	3.25	None[4]
MainStay Convertible	12.6	15.9 (2)	79	269.0	0.5	5.00[3]	522-4202
Pacific Horizon Capital Income	12.4	14.7 (3)	84	103.0	-1.0[2]	4.50	332-3863
Fidelity Convertible Securities	11.9	14.6 (4)	81	401.0	0.4	None	544-8888
Franklin Convertible Securities	11.3	13.3 (6)	85	60.0	6.6	4.50	342-5236

Source: Morningstar **Notes:** [1]To Dec. 1, 1994 [2]Negative number indicates unrealized capital losses. [3]Deferred sales charge [4]Toll telephone number is 716-383-1300.

◆ **Profit without paying taxes.** If you want to unload a highly appreciated piece of property but stay invested in real estate, you can duck capital-gains tax with a nifty maneuver that's called a "like kind exchange." Here's how one works. You, as exchanger, transfer the deed to your property to a buyer. The buyer gives his payment to an intermediary, often an attorney. You then have 45 days to identify property you want to buy and 180 days to close on it. At the closing on the second property, the intermediary pays the seller (you chip in too if the new property is worth more than the old) and the seller gives you his deed. You now own the property you want—and owe no tax on the real estate you traded away.

Today's Best Software for Your 1040

With so many programs to choose among, picking the right tax software may seem about as simple as filling out IRS Form 4562 (that's the one used for Depreciation and Amortization Including Information on Listed Property, in case you forgot). Fortunately, after years of struggling to make the tax code understandable to ordinary mortals, software publishers are getting somewhere. This year any of the four major programs listed in the table on the next page will do a creditable job of coaching you through your federal tax return. That means they can handle anything from the simplest short form to such puzzles as Form 8615 (Tax for Children Under Age 14 Who Have Investment Income of More Than $1,200). All programs are $40 or less at discounters and offer a service that can file your taxes electronically (so you get your refund in two to three weeks instead of the four to six weeks it takes by mail). And all can help you finish your taxes in about half the time it takes to do them by hand.

Not every program will work equally well for you, however. For openers, you obviously want one that suits your type of computer, which may be either an IBM PC or compatible or an Apple Macintosh. If yours is a PC, you'll need one that runs on your operating system, either DOS or the newer Windows.

(Note that Windows users can run DOS programs, but not vice versa.) Beyond that, the programs have subtle but important differences. What follows is our advice tailored for typical types of consumers.

You have an older Windows machine. If yours is an early Windows-compatible PC, then you may want to avoid the Windows versions of *TurboTax* and *TaxCut*. Reason: while these programs nominally run on such equipment, their jazzy graphics may make the performance sluggish. Stick with the DOS version of these or other products.

You have a phobia of tax forms. Since most people hate filling out schedules and worksheets, each of the programs allows you to enter data by answering questions the computer asks. But some do it better than others. With *TaxCut*, for example, you can finish your entire return without ever seeing IRS forms until they roll out of your printer. With the others, however, you may hit form city. If you need to report profit or loss from an investment, for example, *CA-Simply Tax* will dump you straight into Schedule D.

You like a lot of hand-holding. Since all of these programs are proficient at crunching

Today's Best Software for Your 1040

Program Price/telephone	What it runs on	Forms and worksheets	Electronic filing fee	Cost of state program	Number of states covered
Kiplinger TaxCut $39.95/800-235-4060	DOS, Windows, Mac	97	$14.95	$24.95	23 (DOS, Windows) 2 (Mac)
Andrew Tobias' TaxCut $35 to $40/800-820-7461	DOS, Windows, Mac	97	$14.95	$29.95	23 (DOS, Windows) 2 (Mac)
TurboTax $35 to $40/800-964-1040	DOS, Windows	103 (DOS) 133 (Windows)	$19.95	$19.95	45 (DOS) 20 (Windows)
MacInTax $35 to $40/800-964-1040	Mac	133	$19.95	$15.00	20
Personal Tax Edge $19/800-223-6925	DOS, Windows	78	$15.00	$19.00	42 DOS 42 Windows
CA-Simply Tax $9.95/800-737-3382	DOS, Windows	90	$14.95	$19.95	30 DOS

numbers, some try to distinguish themselves with superior on-screen help. The leader here is probably the Kiplinger's version of *TaxCut*. It costs a little more than the Andrew Tobias version of the same program. But the Kiplinger's advice seems somewhat more comprehensive. Another good choice is *CA-Simply Tax*, with crisp commentary by Gary Klott, who writes a syndicated newspaper column on taxes.

You want to do your state taxes too. You can polish off your state returns in a few strokes with the state module. Trouble is, only *TurboTax* and *Personal Tax Edge* cover all states that impose an income tax along with the District of Columbia. Unless you live in New York or California, two states that every program handles, call the publisher to see whether your particular state is included.

Tax Trivia That Trips Up Many Pros

To gauge tax preparers' preparedness, MONEY drew up a list of 10 questions about the latest legislation and called 50 tax pros we plucked at random from the Yellow Pages of Atlanta, Minneapolis, Philadelphia, San Diego and Seattle. Our brave contestants, who were all promised anonymity, included 19 certified public accountants, 12 enrolled agents (who have either worked as IRS agents or passed a tough IRS test), 10 other independent preparers and nine representatives of storefront tax chains.

The results weren't encouraging. None of the 50 preparers aced all 10 questions, and only 34 got at least half right. One reason they performed so poorly was that ours was a true pop quiz. As we explained to them in advance, we wanted to see what they knew off the top of their heads, not how much they could tell us using reference books and tax software. Indeed, many of the stumped preparers said they rely on such aids to keep track of details. Others promised they would be up to speed by filing season. But those excuses didn't wash with Robert Coplan, the tax partner at accountant Ernst & Young in Washington, D.C. who checked our survey's accuracy. "If a professional pays close attention, changes in the tax law become second nature, " he explains. "A depth of knowledge reflects a level of commitment to the profession." Here's how the pros scored.

Deductions. A full 48 of the 50 preparers recalled that you can deduct only 50% of the cost of business meals and entertainment in 1994, down from 80% a year earlier. But only 38 of them knew that beginning last year, the deductible expenses of a work-related move no longer include such wallet-busters as pre-move house hunting trips or the costs of selling your old home and buying a new one. The deduction is now limited to the expense of moving yourself, your family and your possessions. Unlike in the past, however, you can write off a job-related move even if you don't itemize deductions—a change that only 37 of the pros correctly cited.

Investments. A single question, admittedly a toughie, stumped all but one contestant. Under what circumstances does the law now require that the gain on a tax-exempt bond be taxed as ordinary income rather than at the capital-gains rate, which tops out at 28%? The answer: some or all of the gain will be so taxed if you bought the bond on the secondary market after April 30, 1993 at a price that was below its face value. So, for example, if you purchased a $10,000 bond for $9,000 and sell it for $9,500, your $500 gain will be treated as ordinary income.

Social Security. All but four of the preparers knew that starting in 1994, as much as 85% of a Social Security recipient's benefit could be subject to tax, up from a maximum of 50% previously. But only 18 could accurately define provisional income—the figure used to compute how much of your Social Security is taxable. In general, provisional income is your adjusted gross income plus one-half of your benefit plus any tax-exempt income. As your provisional income exceeds $34,000 ($44,000 if you're married filing jointly), you become subject to tax on as much as 85% of your Social Security checks.

Estimated taxes. Only nine participants knew the new rules for avoiding an IRS tax penalty if you are among the 14 million Americans who make quarterly estimated-tax payments. As in the past, you can escape a penalty if your estimated payments and any withholdings equal at least 90% of your eventual tax bill. But Congress changed the provisions that let some people pay less than 90% without getting penalized. Now if your AGI is $150,000 or less, you must pay at least as much in withholding and estimated taxes this year as your '94 tax liability. If you made more than $150,000, you must pay in 110% of last year's total tax. That devilish detail tripped up about half of the preparers.

The alternative minimum tax. Just six preparers knew the precise changes that have been made to the AMT, a complex levy imposed on filers whose tax breaks reduce their bill below an amount considered by Congress to be their fair share. Many of the survey participants said they didn't pay much attention to the AMT because few clients are wealthy enough to be affected by it. They may be mistaken. An Ernst & Young analysis shows that the changes in the tricky rules will make it easier for less affluent taxpayers (those making between $150,000 and $200,000) to get nipped by the AMT.

Trusts. We were disappointed that only 19 quiz takers (38% of our sample) could say why the law now takes away many advantages of using a trust as a tax-saving device. The simple explanation is that trust earnings are subject to the 36% and 39.6% rates (just as individual earnings are) but at lower levels of income. A trust starts owing the top 39.6% rate when its earnings pass $7,500. That's far below the $250,000 threshold for individuals.

How the IRS Targets Taxpayers

John Drobish and Kim Vielma are about as different as two taxpayers can be. Drobish is a horse breeder from Lake Forest, Calif. Vielma is a Las Vegas travel agent. Yet they have three things in common. Both were audited by the IRS. Both easily settled their cases with one IRS district office. And both were subsequently assailed over the original audit issues by a different IRS office. Why? Both had moved. Drobish and Vielma are now well schooled in a fundamental fact of life about the IRS that's worth considering before roughly 1 million audit notices for the 1994 tax year start showing up in mailboxes in September. Your zip code partly determines not only your chance of being audited but how you would be treated after the audit.

To learn how the IRS deals with similar taxpayers differently, MONEY analyzed IRS documents covering audits and related activities. The result is our ratings of all 63 IRS district offices according to how tough they are on taxpayers (see "MONEY Ranks Your Local IRS Office" on the page opposite). Among our findings is that the Las Vegas district, which covers Nevada, audits taxpayers more than any other district. In contrast, the Milwaukee office, serving Wisconsin, shows the most gentleness. Other highlights:

◆ People living in the 10 toughest target districts, on average, face double the risk of being audited as taxpayers in the other 53 districts. They are also 14% more likely to see the IRS reject their offers to settle for less than the full tax and are 21% more likely to have the IRS seize their property. Westerners are targeted the most, with eight of the 10 strictest offices west of the Mississippi.

◆ The toughest district of all, Las Vegas, audited 1.8% of its taxpayers—2.5 times the national average of 0.7%. The easiest, Milwaukee, zapped only 0.2%. Note that MONEY uses the 0.7% national rate sanctioned by the General Accounting Office, not the IRS' 0.9% figure, which is inflated with such extraneous items as returns for nonfilers.

◆ Audited taxpayers in the top 10 target districts are, on average, 13% more likely to be victims of pointless IRS interrogations that end up concluding the taxpayers weren't really on the hook for extra taxes after all.

◆ Over the past two years, the relatively relaxed IRS office in Helena, Mont. accepted 78% of taxpayer offers to settle their bills for less than the full amount. By contrast, the Boston office okayed only 27%. The national average is 50%. Furthermore, the IRS office in Hartford collected an average of $35 per $100 owed. But the San Francisco office settled for a big-hearted $9 per $100. The national average is $22 by comparison.

Such disparate treatment of taxpayers conflicts with the IRS' pledge to inspire "the

Money Ranks Your Local IRS Office

The most feared agency of the federal government is in reality a rather independent collection of 63 district offices that treat taxpayers quite differently. The orneriest office is in Las Vegas; the most sweet-tempered is in Milwaukee. That's what MONEY discovered after ranking all 63 on how harshly they treat taxpayers.

To calculate the ranking, we culled 3,000 pages of IRS data and enlisted IRS expert and Washington tax attorney George Guttman to help analyze the numbers. We then chose the five most important quantifiable measures of how the IRS targets taxpayers and assigned a point system to each. For instance, a district's average audit rate (the percentage of taxpayers audited) earned the highest weighting because audits are so harrowing.

How you're treated depends on where you live. For example, the IRS offices in Hartford and Wilmington, Del. demand on average $35 for every $100 you owe when they accept settlements. The Salt Lake City office, however, is satisfied with just $5. So if you don't like how the IRS is treating you, one thing you might consider is moving to a nicer IRS district.

Rank	IRS district	Average of returns audited annually	Delinquents who had property seized	Chance of the IRS accepting your offer	What the IRS settled for per each $100 owed	Audited returns that didn't owe extra taxes
1	Las Vegas	1.8%	47%	41%	$16	32%
2	San Francisco	1.7	50	49	9	21
3	Cheyenne	1.2	62	29	23	13
4	Los Angeles	1.2	47	33	27	11
5	Anchorage	1.2	96	55	15	11
6	Providence	1.0	72	59	28	19
7	Laguna Niguel, Calif.	1.2	58	33	16	16
8	Boise, Idaho	1.2	45	71	24	18
9	Denver	1.0	59	43	17	15
10	Wilmington, Del.	0.8	42	43	35	12
11	Manhattan	0.9	48	30	18	15
12	Phoenix	0.9	61	29	15	16
13	Brooklyn	0.7	46	31	30	7
14	Houston	0.8	37	30	28	12
15	Jacksonville	0.7	45	29	28	15
16	Hartford	0.6	45	36	35	11
17	Aberdeen, S.D.	0.8	55	55	33	18
18	Fort Lauderdale	0.7	42	45	28	12
19	New Orleans	0.9	43	47	16	15
20	Portsmouth, N.H.	0.6	56	54	29	16
21	Oklahoma City	0.9	46	48	18	9
22	Boston	0.3	55	27	33	12
23	Birmingham	0.7	49	40	19	19
24	Sacramento	0.8	46	48	18	17
25	Jackson, Miss.	0.9	36	63	24	25
26	Dallas	0.7	43	40	24	9
27	San Jose	0.9	58	43	17	11
28	Burlington, Vt.	0.9	34	64	18	11
29	Helena, Mont.	1.0	52	78	19	16
30	Buffalo	0.5	38	48	34	22
31	Augusta, Maine	0.6	55	64	24	15
32	Albuquerque	0.6	46	56	29	12
33	Austin	0.6	45	32	19	9
34	Detroit	0.5	51	35	26	15
35	Seattle	0.8	45	58	15	16
36	Indianapolis	0.5	55	43	20	26
37	Pittsburgh	0.4	53	31	23	20
38	St. Paul	0.6	47	63	27	17
39	Newark	0.4	42	42	24	17
40	Cincinnati	0.5	60	66	30	19
41	Fargo, N.D.	0.8	58	77	19	8
42	Omaha	0.6	68	60	28	18
43	Little Rock	0.7	55	50	12	14
44	Cleveland	0.4	64	63	30	14
45	Richmond	0.4	51	38	25	8
46	St. Louis	0.7	43	74	21	16
47	Parkersburg, W.Va.	0.6	64	62	16	17
48	Des Moines	0.5	42	68	33	10
49	Louisville	0.6	59	70	24	22
50	Atlanta	0.6	23	57	24	6
51	Chicago	0.3	38	39	24	13
52	Wichita	0.5	41	57	21	14
53	Springfield, Ill.	0.4	48	54	26	19
54	Salt Lake City	0.7	63	63	5	13
55	Columbia, S.C.	0.5	23	50	24	14
56	Greensboro, N.C.	0.4	52	52	22	15
57	Philadelphia	0.3	49	50	27	17
58	Portland, Ore.	0.6	50	68	17	15
59	Albany, N.Y.	0.5	39	68	24	15
60	Nashville	0.5	52	56	12	18
61	Baltimore and D.C.	0.3	45	55	21	17
62	Honolulu	0.5	45	51	13	17
63	Milwaukee	0.2	42	65	17	16
	National average	**0.7**	**49**	**50**	**22**	**15**

Source: Internal Revenue Service

highest degree of public confidence in our integrity, efficiency and fairness," to quote the agency's mission statement. Yet dissimilar treatment has prevailed at the agency for more than 30 years. Says Don Alexander, IRS commissioner under Presidents Nixon, Ford and Carter and now a tax partner with the Washington, D.C. law firm Akin Gump Strauss Hauer & Feld: "Disparate treatment by the IRS, especially with audits, surely was and still is a serious problem. It's chronic." Adds Thomas Ochsenschlager, a tax partner at the accounting firm of Grant Thornton in Washington, D.C.: "Some IRS offices come on like sheriffs with both guns blazing, while other offices act like kindly crossing guards shepherding taxpayers through the system." (See "A Survival Guide for Tax Audits" on page 68 for advice on how to fight back.)

Why are some taxpayers targeted? First, the IRS is so decentralized that local bosses can decide whether to go easy on residents or use a sledgehammer. An internal report criticized the IRS' highly decentralized administration as "insufficient to assure the uniform, fair and equitable treatment of taxpayers across the country." IRS watchers continue to echo that charge today. "There is a little king mentality at these IRS offices," says Alexander. "Suppose a taxpayer has a tax obligation that he is unable to pay. Do you seize his property, or do you give the taxpayer a great, big break and let him work out a payment plan or compromise? It depends on the local office."

In addition, IRS offices often blindly follow local traditions. For instance, Las Vegas' cash economy and history of criminal activities have influenced the local office to adopt a hard-nosed compliance policy that often results in rough treatment of ordinary taxpayers. "We're tough here in Las Vegas," admits Richard Flakus, who has been the Las Vegas chief of collections since 1987. "We'd like our

audit rate to be four times the national average." In Milwaukee, by contrast, Midwesterners' traditional sense of probity has inspired the office to present a friendlier face to taxpayers. But that gentleness, in turn, may allow area cheats to fly freely under the IRS' radar. "We can't unequivocally prove that taxpayers here are more compliant than those elsewhere," says Robert McDonnell, Milwaukee's IRS chief of examinations.

What's more, the most aggressive IRS offices are rewarded with fatter budgets and bigger staffs. Therefore, the tougher they are, the more likely they are to get the resources to push even harder. By contrast, merciful IRS offices tend to end up without the staff that's needed to handle their population. Since the top 10 target districts, on average, audited 1.2% of the taxpayers in their purview and assessed $852 million in additional taxes and penalties, they were rewarded with an aggregate budget of $419 million. But the bottom 10 districts, which audited only 0.4% and brought in $493 million, got just $351 million to spend. Also, despite their lower budgets, those bottom 10 offices serve about 5 million more taxpayers than the top 10 target offices do (19 million, vs. 14 million).

The price of such massive imbalance is high. By sponsoring a system that enables some districts to be far more zealous than others, the agency denies evenhanded tax justice to many. Moreover, by following a flawed audit selection process, the IRS continuously audits tens of thousands of innocent citizens needlessly while letting the real tax cheats slip by. Here are more of the details:

Your odds of being audited. In 1989, Kim Vielma thought she had left her IRS troubles behind her when she moved from Bellevue, Wash. to be with her new husband in Las Vegas. In Washington State, the IRS had audited her in 1985 and disallowed a $2,000 tax shelter write-off that she had taken on her '84 return for a $6,000 investment in a partnership that distributed cassette tapes. After Vielma underwent a double mastectomy and a hysterectomy in 1987, the IRS' Seattle office, which ranks a relatively benign No. 35 out of 63 in our table, classified her as a hardship case. In 1988, while she was recovering, it approved an open-ended installment plan allowing her to pay down her resulting $6,000 bill. Once she got to Las Vegas, however, the tough local office yanked the agreement and billed her $21,300 for taxes, interest and penalties. It then seized two $300 paychecks and a $300 bank account, refused her $2,000 offer to settle, and after two years finally drove her into bankruptcy. The officer "said he came after me partly because I moved," recalls Vielma. "The whole experience was very upsetting." She has since settled her case with the IRS.

Californian John Drobish entered a similar IRS twilight zone in 1992 when he moved from Homeland, which is in Southern California's Riverside County, to Roseville, near Sacramento. Before he moved, the IRS office in Laguna Niguel notified him that it planned to audit his 1989 and 1990 returns because of what it called questionable business deductions for his horse-breeding operation in Oregon. He tried to convince the IRS to let its Sacramento office audit both his 1989 and 1990 returns but was granted only half his request. The Sacramento office audited his 1989 return, found nothing wrong with his $24,000 in write-offs and let him go. But the Laguna Niguel office disallowed $18,300 of the same type of deductions on his '90 return and handed him a $6,973 bill for back taxes, interest and penalties. After a two-year fight, the IRS in Laguna Niguel finally concluded last year that Drobish's '90 deductions were okay after all. Says Drobish: "I still don't understand why Laguna Niguel tried so hard to disallow my business write-offs."

As Drobish and Vielma can attest, some IRS districts are much tougher than others about auditing people, even those who earn identical incomes. IRS assistant commissioner of examinations John Monaco says flatly: "We audit taxpayers who make the same amount of money at the same rate no matter where they live." But his claim just doesn't wash. San Francisco is the toughest office for incomes of $50,000 to $99,000 (audit rate: 2.1%), compared with the gentlest, Philadelphia (0.4%). Yet John Scholz, a political science professor and IRS expert at the State University of New York at Stony Brook, calls the $50,000 to $99,000 income class a "fairly homogeneous group no matter where they reside." The IRS' Manhattan office sank its audit hooks into 11 of every 1,000 local tax-

Top Targets Ranked by Income

Contrast the rates below against these national averages: 0.5% for $25,000 to $49,999; 1.0% for $50,000 to $99,999; and 3.7% over $100,000.

IRS district	Audit rate for $25,000 to $49,999	IRS district	Audit rate for $50,000 to $99,999	IRS district	Audit rate for over $100,000
Anchorage	1.9%	San Francisco	2.1%	Helena, Mont.	12.7%
Las Vegas	1.2	Helena, Mont.	2.0	Fargo, N.D.	8.0
Fargo, N.D.	1.2	Los Angeles	1.9	New Orleans	7.1
Los Angeles	1.1	Anchorage	1.9	Oklahoma City	6.6
Boise, Idaho	1.0	Las Vegas	1.8	Cheyenne	6.5

Money Helps

Q. My employer has shut down the office where I worked and offered me a job at another facility about 75 miles away. Rather than face a three-hour daily commute, I decided to rent a room in a hotel near the new location on weekdays and drive home on weekends. Am I permitted to claim hotel expenses, meals, mileage and tolls as a business-related miscellaneous deduction on my federal income tax return?

DAN HILL, ORLANDO

A. The IRS would let you write off as miscellaneous business expenses (those exceeding 2% of your adjusted gross income) all your lodging and travel and 50% of your meals and entertainment if your employer made you stay in, say, Toledo for up to a year and did not reimburse your expenses. But your new job is your regular assignment and not a temporary one. Thus the IRS presumes that you can choose to live near your employer and that any commuting or other reimbursed expenses for meals and hotels are not deductible. If you decide to find a permanent home closer to your employer, you can write off the actual cost of the move plus up to $3,000 in miscellaneous expenses such as the cost of a house hunting trip (provided you've worked at least 39 weeks at your new location).

payers in that income group, while just a subway ride away, only seven of 1,000 Brooklynites with the same earnings were hit by the IRS office. Is there any evidence Manhattan's middle-class taxpayers cheat more than Brooklyn's? "In general, no," says Scholz.

Flakus of the Las Vegas IRS office concedes that "all districts should be auditing the same percentage of returns. But they're not." The problem begins when IRS computers evaluate your return. Using a top-secret set of formulas, the computers measure the probability that you may owe more tax, based on reported income and deductions, and give you what's known as a DIF (discriminant function) score. If it's high, an IRS auditor assesses whether your return is in fact audit bait. If so, you're mailed an audit notice.

Each IRS office does not audit the same percentage of high-scoring DIF returns, however. There are two reasons. First, to keep the audit stick in full public view, each office has wide discretion in deciding how many taxpayers to audit in each income class. Second, as mentioned earlier, the local IRS chieftains whose audits bring in the most are rewarded with even bigger budgets and staff. As a result, the top 10 target districts in our ranking had 519 auditors, nearly double the 279 working in the bottom 10 offices. Lowest-ranked Milwaukee has seen its audit troops dwindle from 77 to 24 over the past 20 years as its audit rate has sunk from 5.2% to a puny 0.2%, roughly a third of the U.S. average. "If we had more auditors we would do more audits. That's just a given," says Milwaukee IRS audit chief Robert McDonnell.

Your odds of an unneccessary audit.

Classical composer Sorrel Hays of Manhattan couldn't have been more annoyed. After enduring two years of abusive phone calls from an agent and $700 in audit expenses, she was informed by the IRS that her audited 1990 tax return was just fine in the first place. Says Hays: "My IRS agent was unnecessarily tough on me." In Hays' Manhattan district, 15% of the people who get audited end up owing no extra taxes. That's the national average. But 32% of those audited in the Las

Vegas district, 26% in Indianapolis and 25% in Jackson, Miss. end up not owing any money. That's not just unfair. It's also expensive for taxpayers. The American Institute of Certified Public Accountants figures that if all 550,000 of the taxpayers audited needlessly since 1988 (roughly 15% of the 4 million who were audited) had wisely hired a tax professional to represent them at a typical fee of $1,000 per audit, they would have spent more than $500 million to do so.

Why are there so many unnecessary IRS audits? An IRS report blames "job fatigue" as one key reason. Since decisions on whether to audit are left up to the 180 service center auditors who must each screen roughly 120 returns every day, judging a return must be accomplished in an average of four minutes. Another reason is low morale. "Picking returns for audit is a dreary, tedious job," says Ed Campbell, a Cambridge, Mass. computer contractor working with the IRS to fix this problem. For its part, the IRS insists that a new computer system, which will be completed in 1996, will take over the task and greatly reduce the agency's misfire rate.

Your odds of settling with the IRS. Back in 1984, Robert McWaters was in a bind. His check-guarantee business in Meridian, Idaho, which covered bounced checks for local retailers, had just gone bankrupt, and he had injured himself seriously in an auto collision. For the next eight years, he failed to file his tax returns. "Back then, I was running from my problems," he says. When McWaters finally filed his 1991 return, the IRS nailed him with a $30,000 tax bill, which he then reduced to $16,222 by paying his back taxes. But with his $9,000 annual household income—almost 50% below the poverty line—he could barely take care of his wife and three young boys, much less handle a huge tax bill.

So his C.P.A., Cheryl Curtis, asked the

Boise IRS office to let her client pay off less than the amount owed. She presented two so-called offers in compromise that totaled $1,000 (one for his personal returns, one for his business returns). Since 1992, the IRS has made it much easier to get such deals, and McWaters lucked out. The IRS accepted his offer of 6¢ on the dollar. He says: "I really feel the IRS was fair with me."

Meanwhile, in Wyoming, the IRS office was dragging James Simmons and his wife Darline through tax hell over similar problems. When the oil industry dried up in 1984, so did the Simmonses' $63,000 annual income from their oil-well servicing company. By 1987, James and Darline owed the IRS $38,000. The couple say they couldn't afford to pay their '84 to '86 income taxes, in part owing to high medical bills for their infant daughter Carmeleda. After James filed for bankruptcy in 1987, the couple tried unsuccessfully to whittle down the $38,000 in taxes, interest and penalties with a $50-a-month installment plan. The IRS tab had ballooned to an untenable $80,000 by 1993, when the Simmonses decided to offer the agency $6,000 (or 8¢ on the dollar) plus half of any income they earned annually over $50,000 from 1993 to 1997. Two C.P.A.s, who both called the Cheyenne office "extremely tough," warned them to expect a rejection. Sure enough, their Cheyenne revenue officer "took about five seconds to stamp our offer reject," says Darline.

As the Simmons and McWaters cases indicate, approval rates for settlements vary sharply. Our table shows how it's no surprise that the Simmonses are having trouble in Cheyenne. It's No. 3 of 63 in our overall IRS target ranking partly because it accepts a mere 29% of the offers it gets. Boise, the McWaterses' district, grants 71%. Why the different treatment of deals? IRS spokesman Henry Holmes offers one reason. "In areas where there is a low acceptance rate, we found taxpayers could afford to pay more." Yet one GAO study cites the telltale twins of decentralization and local culture. It fingers

"differences in district managers' attitudes," with some district directors viewing the offer in compromise as "a giveaway."

A Survival Guide for Tax Audits

If you're among the unlucky one million souls whose tax returns are selected for audit, don't let the IRS roll over you even if you live in one of its target towns (refer back to our table on page 63). Instead, follow this advice:

Hire a pro if the tax issues are complex.
Say you're being questioned on a tax shelter investment and a home office deduction. Even though professional help would likely cost you $1,000 or more, you would otherwise be at such a disadvantage going up against an IRS auditor that you could wind up owing even more than the original amount in question. Your best bet is an enrolled agent, who is apt to be a former IRS auditor and thus defter at dealing with the agency.

Postpone the audit if you're not ready.
Your audit notice will include an audit date that's 30 days away. But that may not give you enough time to find a suitable tax pro or to do homework if you are representing yourself. The IRS allows as many as two 30-day postponements. Use the time to read *Stand Up to the IRS* by San Francisco tax attorney Frederick Daily. When your audit date arrives, be sure you or your pro shows up. "Otherwise the IRS will disallow everything in question, and you'll have just 90 days to prove that it's wrong," says New York City enrolled agent Shelly Jacobson.

Appeal if the auditor's case seems weak.
If you lose your IRS audit, ask for the docu-

ments supporting the ruling, such as IRS regulations or case law. After reviewing them, if you still believe you're in the right, you have 30 days from the date on your audit report to appeal. And you should. Audit bills, on average, drop roughly 40% on appeal.

If you don't have the cash, pay slowly.
If your audit bill is $10,000 or less, you qualify for a three-year installment schedule. You'll owe annual interest and penalties at 14%, however. Just hand your auditor a completed Form 9465 for an installment plan.

If you'll never raise the cash, settle up.
Fill out Form 656, Offer in Compromise, and next to "Grounds for acceptance of this offer," type: "Doubt as to collectibility of the full amount of tax, penalty and interest." Make an offer of at least 10% of your bill. On average, the IRS accepts 15%. Be patient. "The IRS usually takes six months to a year to decide on taxpayer offers," says New York City accountant Nancy Gallagher.

When all else fails, consult a PRO.
You qualify for special help from an IRS problem resolution officer, or PRO, if you face financial hardship because of the agency's seizure of wages or bank accounts or if you've made at least two unsuccessful attempts to resolve your problem through regular IRS channels. File a taxpayer assistance order, Form 911, with your district office's PRO, who will try to fix your problem within two weeks.

3

Flex and Protect Your Earning Power

Savvy Ways to Get More Pay in '95

Turn That Pink Slip Into a Paycheck

Rating the Best Jobs in America

Twenty Hothouses for Small Business

Maximize Your Shrinking Benefits Now

Take the Pulse of Your Health Plan

You probably don't think of it as an asset. Yet your ability to earn a living and support your family over an average working life of roughly 40 years may be the single most valuable resource you possess. Indeed, one's earning potential is often overlooked because the trend in recent years has not been one's friend. Wages overall are only keeping up with the relatively slow pace of inflation. Salaries for some professions are actually declining. And personal income taxes were rising until voters finally rebelled en masse last election day. True, the nation's strengthening economy has pushed the unemployment rate down to a rock-bottom 5.4% recently (vs. a 6.5% rate a year ago). But much of this job growth was in the categories of part-time and temporary positions.

This chapter will help you buck these forces to keep your career moving forward and your income protected against adversity. For example, should your earning power be interrupted for any reason, you or your survivors could be left with mounting medical bills and other expenses. Thus your first line of defense is a long-term disability policy that replaces your salary in the event that an accident or illness prevents you from working. If you work for a large corporation, chances are it offers a group disability plan that covers 60% of your pay, a level that's adequate. But about 70% of companies offer no disability coverage. If you work for one, are self-employed or if your employer's benefits fall below that 60% threshold, you need to shop for a sound individual policy (discussed later in this chapter).

To prevent huge medical bills from creating debts that will soak up your income and deplete your savings, check out your medical insurance policy. You probably get this coverage through your employer. But if you are one of the nearly 19 million workers whose employers don't provide this benefit, you will have to seek out a private policy. Your biggest concern should be ensuring that a plan will handle large claims that could wipe out your resources. So look for policies with a lifetime benefit ceiling of at least $500,000 or, preferably, $1 million. If your household requires frequent medical care, consider becoming a member of a managed care plan such as an HMO (health maintenance organization), also discussed later in this chapter. The tab can be stiff, with the annual premium averaging about $400 a month for a typical family of four. But only modest out-of-pocket costs are required beyond the premium.

Savvy Ways to Get More Pay in '95

Companies across the country are buying into the latest corporate compensation trend—scrapping annual raises and offering instead bonuses based on performance and company profits. Consider that annual raises this year are expected to average a measly 4%, the lowest in two decades. Yet cash merit awards are being dangled well down the corporate ladder. According to benefits consulting firm Towers Perrin, bonuses will be awarded at 30% of companies surveyed, up from 25% in 1994. And according to a survey of 2,253 firms by the Wyatt Co. consultants, some 42% plan to install performance-based reward programs within the next two years.

The upside of bonuses, which can range from 2% to 30% of annual pay, is that you earn more when you prove your worth. The downside, of course, is that your base pay, on which benefits like profit-sharing and life insurance are calculated, stays the same. And even when your boss likes you, you must re-earn your bonus year after year. To prosper in this new pay environment, you'll need to learn the fine points of your firm's compensation policies and boost your visibility and skills. Today, you must continually demonstrate that you're highly motivated, tuned in and tangibly contributing. Here are the best strategies to get more pay.

Figure your comparative worth. Always be aware of how your salary ranks within your division, company and industry. In other words, what are you worth? To learn the pay standard for your position, read the want ads in the local newspaper or in established trade journals. Regional bureaus of the U.S. Labor Department will have listings on average pay for most professions in your area. Then talk to the company's compensation manager in the human resources department. Ask about the pay philosophy. Some companies make it a practice to pay market rate, while others pay a percentage below and then make up the difference with bonuses or other perks.

Think like a chief executive. If your company is getting clobbered by market forces, this may not be the time to request a sizable increase. On the other hand, with profits soaring, your compensation might spike as well. Stay abreast of company initiatives and launches so you'll know what areas are prospering. For instance, you might request a transfer into a new division or volunteer for a short-term project that showcases your particular talents. If you discover that cost-cutting is the name of this year's game, suggest procedures that will make your department more efficient. And yes, if you hear the company president is giving a speech, you should

try to get hold of a copy and read it. You'll be able to glean some writing on the company's upcoming walls. The employee newsletter and annual reports also offer potentially good leads you can act on.

Go ahead and suck up to the boss. The juggernaut of layoffs has just about buried the notion of job security. Indeed, an alarming one-third of Americans in a recent MONEY poll said they were afraid to ask for more pay because of the "current job climate." But staying mum won't keep you safe. Rather, make an appointment to talk to your boss about your capabilities and goals. Explains a New York City investment banker at Smith Barney whose total annual increase comes from her bonus: "It's not enough just to get a deal done here. You have to make sure everyone knows you've got the deal done." At the end of every year, a month before the bonus pie is carved up, she sends a one-page memo to her boss listing each transaction she negotiated during the year, including how profitably it turned out. Then she maneuvers at least one informal conversation, typically on a business trip or over lunch, with a member of the bonus committee. "This sounds conniving," she concedes. "But that's what it takes. Bonuses are performance plus politicking."

Ask for more in several ways. "Only a decade ago, it was seen as bad taste to talk about money with your boss," says Cathe Johnson, a director of organizational development and training at Motorola. "Today, it's okay to say, 'What do I need to do to get paid more?'" Here's how to pop the question, depending on your situation. If you're underpaid and can demonstrate your value to the company, ask straight out for the increase that brings your base pay up to a level that's at least standard for your firm. Managers at large companies usually have less latitude

about compensation than those at small firms. In either case, make a direct request. Don't give up if you're told that raises are capped or averaged this year. You can appeal to the big boss. But Joseph Kilmartin, a senior compensation consultant at the Wyatt Co., warns: "Go over your boss' head only if you've got a job lined up."

A better alternative may be trying to tap into the bonus pool. Ask your supervisor about how your bonus is calculated and what it would take to earn a higher one. You may prefer to set specific goals with your boss that you periodically update. If your company lacks a bonus plan or you've never been considered eligible for one, start acting as if you deserve one. After all, the more you do, the better your boss looks. Just remember to get your supervisor's approval before you revamp the database or put in an extra five hours every night. "Some employees make the mistake of embarking on a project they think will earn them more without first consulting their supervisor," cautions Johnson. "If they don't get the reward they expected, they end up discouraged." Most bosses want to keep valuable employees satisfied. "It's expen-

sive to replace good workers," says Kilmartin. "Consider the downtime and the cost to advertise or hire a headhunter. The loss of a key employee can hurt morale."

Leverage your skills. So you have garnered a fat raise and feel like resting on laurels for a couple of fiscals. Don't. Take advantage of every training opportunity that attracts you. Is there an extracurricular class on cruising the Internet? Sit in. A special task force on quality? Volunteer. Look beyond the firm for training as well. Approximately 72% of full-time employees are eligible for job-related tuition assistance. Yet only 7% sign up for that valuable perk. For example, many companies are now poised to enter the global marketplace. You should be thinking about foreign language courses. Have a tough time getting your ideas across? Try a business writing class at the local community college. Feel stuck in a current slot? Consider a move to the side. More and more companies now encourage lateral moves as a way to increase your skill base. You may not immediately see bigger numbers on your pay stub. But you will gain experience that can lead to a well-deserved promotion and pay raise.

Turn That Pink Slip Into a Paycheck

"Job security is a thing of the past. People are just going to have to get used to the idea of involuntary separations—sometimes four, five or six times during a career." Those unsettling words didn't come from a cost-cutting CEO like General Electric's Jack "the Knife" Welch. They came from Labor Secretary Robert Reich, once renowned as a bleeding heart. And the message isn't encouraging in the face of more and more reports of mass firings, early retirement offers and "voluntary sever-

ance" deals. Among the big companies that are adding to the legions of laid-off workers are telecommunications giant GTE (which aims to shed 17,000 jobs), phone company Nynex (16,800) and insurer Aetna (4,000).

Don't despair. If you are unemployed or fear that you soon will be, your career is not over unless you want it to be. Finding a new job may take some time. As a rule, expect to spend about one month job hunting for every $10,000 that you earned. The search can be

How to Find Work When You're Over 50

Obstacles abound for job hunters who are over 50. There's resistance to paying higher salaries and costly benefits and, of course, baseless biases that older workers are inflexible and less creative than younger ones. It can be particularly tough for fired executives to find comparable work. "There's a growing problem for middle-level managers and upper-middle-level managers who find themselves the victims of corporate downsizing," says Labor Secretary Robert Reich. "A small percentage are able to go on to other companies in industries that utilize the skill and experience they already have. But that's the exception rather than the rule." With a little luck and a lot of savvy, however, you can improve your chances of finding a job you're happy with. Here are suggestions tailored to those 50 and older.

◆ **Seek help from groups like Forty Plus**, a non-profit outplacement organization for professionals age 40 or older with chapters in 13 states. While services and costs vary by chapter, each offers use of computers, phones and fax machines. (Call 202-387-1582 for the one nearest you.) You can also turn to the American Association of Retired Persons (202-434-2100), which conducts a $20 job-hunting program called AARP Works.

◆ **Be prepared to upgrade your skills**. For example, if you're stuck in the era of typewriters and dictaphones, consider taking a computer course at night, perhaps at a local community college. To present yourself in the best possible light, revamp your résumé to emphasize recent experience. You may want to omit your earliest jobs to avoid the impression you've been around forever.

◆ **Focus on elder-friendly companies**. Days Inn of America, McDonald's and Staples like to hire older workers because the firms find them to be more dependable than younger ones. These companies, along with local merchants, hold job fairs each year in 100 cities (call the Days Inn nearest you for information). Most of the jobs they offer are in customer service and sales. Also look for positions in smaller companies, where employers tend to value older people's experience. Some employers shun older workers on the assumption that they will demand high salaries. You can sidestep that problem by targeting commission-based jobs such as travel agent or salesperson. And because some employers also worry that older workers will run up health insurance costs, you might volunteer to forgo benefits if you already have coverage through your spouse or as part of an early retirement package.

◆ **Don't reveal your age in interviews**. Yes, it's illegal for a potential employer to ask. But that may not stop some from trying. If the issue does come up somehow, present your age as a strength. Be ready to cite ways in which your extensive experience can help the company solve problems. And remind the interviewer that a barrage of studies, including a 1993 report by the nonprofit Commonwealth Fund, show workers over 55 to be reliable and less prone to absences than younger workers.

◆ **Show you're comfortable with change**. To dispel another misconception about older workers, be sure to keep up to date with developments in your field. Don't fail to mention ground-breaking projects you've worked on. And project a vibrant, energetic appearance. That doesn't mean running out for a facelift or a hair transplant. It does mean wearing stylish clothes, shaking hands firmly and making small talk, say, about your thrice-weekly tennis game. "It's essential to appear healthy and vital," says John Challenger of outplacement firm Challenger Gray & Christmas. "No one wants a tired employee."

especially tough if you are over age 50 (see above for strategies designed for those job seekers). But odds are that you can find a comparable new position. According to the Congressional Budget Office, nearly two-thirds of college graduates who lost jobs during the 1980s found new positions that paid at least 95% of their old ones. Here's another encouraging fact. Many Fortune 500 companies offering topnotch pay and benefits are still hiring even as they carry out downsizings. Indeed, the head count at the nation's 50 largest employers has increased by nearly 460,000 over the past six years. One reason: companies that push employees out the front door in a restructuring are hiring people with different skills through the back door.

Julio Davila, 40, illustrates this paradoxical trend. Davila volunteered to quit his $53,000-a-year job as a copy editor at the *San*

Money Helps

Q. I pay my six-year-old son $20 each week to help me sell sculptures at flea markets on weekends. He's accumulated about $375 that's kept in a checking account. He has a $44,000 legacy from his mom, who died in 1993, and the income from that is more than the $1,200 he can earn without his money being taxed at my rate. I want to set up an IRA for his flea market earnings so the money can grow without incurring taxes. But I can't find a company to open an IRA for anybody under age 14.

TOM HAUBNER, MOBILE

A. Discount broker Charles Schwab (800-435-4000) and the brokerage arm of the Vanguard mutual fund group (800-851-4999) both offer custodial IRA accounts, which allow you to make investment decisions while your son is still a minor. Your son can put as much as $2,000 into the IRA each year and deduct his contribution from his taxable income. Once deposited inside the IRA, his money would compound free of taxes until he pulls it out, preferably after age 59.5 to avoid a 10% early withdrawal penalty.

That's the catch. Are you sure that you want to lock up all the kid's money? The $44,000 legacy notwithstanding, you still may need money to get your kid through college. And when your boy is 17 and wants to buy a car, just try telling him he has to save for retirement. One way to introduce your child to the world of investing without tying up the money in an IRA is through the SteinRoe Young Investor Fund. Some 60% of its holdings are companies that children are familiar with, such as Coca-Cola and McDonald's.

Francisco Chronicle when the paper offered generous severance packages of six weeks' pay for each year of service, with a maximum of two years' pay. As a 20-year veteran, he pocketed $106,000. And he was confident he would find a new job. He had solid references, knew how to use the latest computer technology and was of Mexican descent. He felt the latter characteristic might aid his job search because many big-city newspapers are trying to hire more minority workers. He was right. Davila promptly found a $49,000 copy editing position at the *Seattle Times*, which had recently offered early retirement packages to its staff, after he placed an ad in the trade magazine *Editor & Publisher.* The paper needed another copy editor, particularly one like Davila who understood new layout technologies, to cover for vacationing employees.

While you may not recover as quickly as Davila did, you can help your cause by approaching the job search as if it were a full-time job. Start by skipping the outplacement counseling your former employer may provide. Such counselors can help you write your résumé. But they can't find you a job. Instead, spin your Rolodex for names of anyone who might give you a lead. Career counselors estimate that 70% of job seekers find work through contacts. Even if your associates don't know of any openings, you should at least ask them for two or three names to add to your phone list. Also answer want ads even though fewer than one in 10 job seekers finds work this way. You can increase your odds of success by checking trade publications, as Davila did, in addition to general-circulation newspapers. And ask people in your network whether they know anyone who works for a company that's hiring. If they do, call the employee to learn about the organization, its corporate culture and its business plans. You may be able to use the information you gain to craft a cover letter and résumé that make a special impression on the person who's doing the hiring.

If you've looked unsuccessfully for a full-time job for at least two months, try to find a part-time job for two or three days a week, preferably at a professional level in your old field. Part-time consulting assignments will provide additional income and give you access to completely new contact networks. For a directory of 120 search firms that place executives temporarily, call *Executive Recruiter News* (800-531-0007).

A mass résumé mailing is another option for executives who have exhausted the traditional job-search strategies. You can manageably send résumés to a few hundred employers on your own. But if that doesn't work, senior-level managers should consider hiring a firm that specializes in mailing job seekers' résumés and cover letters to the chief executives of thousands of corporations. A service such as this can cost $2 to $4 a letter. So you should consider one only if you have savings to spare and are searching for a job that pays $100,000 or more. Before you hire a mass

mailer, check references and ask how the company handles letters that are returned as undeliverable. A reputable firm will call the corporations in question, correct any errors in their addresses and resend the letters.

Harvard M.B.A. John Buckingham, who lost his job as president of a Kansas City manufacturer of fuel truck tanks, searched for a new position for four months before hiring WSA Corp., a Shawnee, Kans. firm, to do a mass mailing for him. For a typical client, WSA mails 4,000 to 6,000 résumés, charging $2 each, plus postage. But after hearing Buckingham's requirements, WSA advised him to mail 12,000 résumés. Buckingham did and received 17 responses. He decided to interview at four companies and ended up weighing three job offers. Seven months after he lost his job, he started work as president of Intoximeters, a St. Louis manufacturer of devices used by police and employers to measure alcohol levels in drivers. Buckingham says the result justified the cost: "I got back more than $24,000 in compensation during the first month I was re-employed."

Rating the Best Jobs in America

There are no more dreaded words in corporate America than "the system is down." Your boss is screaming; your clients are whining. What can you do? Call a computer systems analyst, that's what. Systems analysts are the indispensable people who install, customize and supervise computer operations at offices and factories across the nation. And now, with their services increasingly in demand, it's no surprise that they have the best job in America, according to MONEY's latest ranking of the 100 jobs chosen to represent a wide spectrum of pursuits. The Bureau of Labor

Statistics (BLS) believes there will be 501,000 systems analyst jobs created between now and the year 2005, a gain of 110% from today's 455,000. And that forecast represents a 37% upward revision from just two years ago. That explosive anticipated growth helped propel systems analyst to the top of our chart from No. 31 in our previous jobs ranking, published in 1992. (Our complete listing of 100 jobs appears on the next page.)

Among other notable findings, doctors scored well despite all the talk of drastic health care reforms. Their high prestige and

Today's Most Promising Career Choices

Computer systems analyst tops our ranking of 100 widely held jobs that MONEY researchers have evaluated on such factors as salary, prestige and security. This table shows the data we used to rank each job. In addition, the last column suggests where you might have the most luck finding a particular job by naming several of the metropolitan areas with the highest concentration of people in each field.

Rank	1992 rank	Occupation	Median annual earnings[1]	11-year job growth	Short-term outlook	Job security rating	Prestige rating	Stress and strain rating[12]	Where the jobs are
1	31	Computer systems analyst	$42,700	110%	Excellent	Excellent	Good	Low	Silicon Valley, Washington, Boston
2	3	Physician	148,000	35	Average	Good	Excellent	High	New York, San Francisco, Philadelphia
3	50	Physical therapist	37,200	88	Excellent	Excellent	Good	Average	Denver, Boston, Seattle
4	13	Electrical engineer	59,100[2]	24	Good	Excellent	Good	Average	Silicon Valley, Dallas, Boston
5	9	Civil engineer	55,800[2]	24	Good	Excellent	Good	Average	Houston, San Francisco, Denver
6	7	Pharmacist	47,500	29	Good	Good	Good	Low	Columbus, Pittsburgh, Kansas City
7	29	Psychologist	53,000	48	Average	Average	Good	Average	Boston, San Francisco, New York
8	2	Geologist	50,800	22	Good	Excellent	Good	Average	Houston, Denver, New Orleans
9	15	High school teacher	32,500	37	Good	Excellent	Good	Average	Dallas, Houston, Atlanta
10	5	School principal	57,300[3]	23	Average	Good	Good	Average	Dallas, Houston, Atlanta
11	38	Paralegal	27,900	86	Average	Average	Average	Low	Washington, New York, Chicago
12	—	Hospital administrator	36,000[4]	36[8]	Fair	Average	Good	Low	Boston, Indianapolis, Philadelphia
13	—	Computer programmer	38,800	30	Good	Good	Good	Low	Washington, Silicon Valley, Dallas
14	12	Chemist	43,500[5]	21	Average	Average	Excellent	Low	Wilmington, Northern N.J., Raleigh/Durham
15	18	Dentist	93,000	5	Average	Good	Excellent	Average	New York, San Francisco, Seattle
16	1	Biologist	46,000	25	Fair	Fair	Excellent	Low	Raleigh/Durham, Washington, Boston
17	49	Management consultant	61,900	43[8]	Good	Good	Good	Average[8]	Washington, Chicago, Minneapolis
18	46	Technical writer	37,400	23	Excellent	Excellent	Average	Low	Silicon Valley, Boston, Washington
19	19	Grade school teacher	31,000	21	Good	Excellent	Good	Average	Dallas, Houston, Atlanta
20	66	Construction superintendent	44,900	47	Good	Good	Good	High[8]	Atlanta, Houston, Baltimore
21	11	Aeronautical engineer	56,700[2]	14	Poor	Poor	Excellent	Low	Los Angeles, Seattle, Dallas
22	14	Bank officer	43,000	40[8]	Average	Average	Good	Low	New York, Los Angeles, Washington
23	56	Accountant	31,800	32	Good	Good	Good	Low	Washington, Dallas, New York
24	6	Sociologist	46,600	20[8]	Fair	Fair	Good	Low	Washington; Raleigh/Durham; Rochester, N.Y.
25	36	Economist	41,200	25	Fair	Fair	Good	Low	Washington, New York, Chicago
26	34	Clergy member	26,000	30	Average	Average	Good	Average	Greenville, S.C.; Birmingham; Charlotte, N.C.
27	4	Mathematician	42,700	8	Fair	Fair	Good	Low	Baltimore, Silicon Valley, Boston
28	52	Registered nurse	35,700	42	Good	Good	Good	High	Boston, Pittsburgh, Philadelphia
29	8	Urban planner	42,800	23	Fair	Fair	Average	Average	San Francisco, Minneapolis, Seattle
30	75	Lobbyist	91,300[6]	25[8]	Excellent	Good	Average	High[8]	Washington, Sacramento, Albany
31	32	Dental hygienist	28,600	43	Good	Good	Average	Average	Minneapolis, Seattle, Detroit
32	—	Nutritionist	25,700	26	Excellent	Excellent	Average	Low	Boston, St. Louis, Philadelphia
33	37	Preschool teacher	18,400	54	Good	Average	Average	Average[8]	Dallas, Houston, Atlanta
34	42	Medical lab technician	27,700	26	Average	Average	Good	Low	Philadelphia, Baltimore, Memphis
35	10	Veterinarian	46,900	33	Average	Good	Good	Average	Sacramento, Columbus, Kansas City
36	59	Forest ranger	29,400[7]	12	Average	Good	Average	Average	Portland, Ore.; Seattle; Sacramento
37	25	Purchasing manager	40,200	14	Average	Good	Good	Low	Washington, Seattle, Denver
38	64	Social worker	26,600	40	Fair	Fair	Average	Average	New York, Boston, Philadelphia
39	69	Computer repairer	30,500	45	Good	Good	Average	Average[8]	Atlanta, Silicon Valley, Dallas
40	72	Hotel manager	54,000	40[8]	Average	Average	Average[8]	Average	Las Vegas, Orlando, Honolulu
41	39	Financial planner	55,100[8]	30[8]	Good	Good [8]	Average	Average[8]	New York, San Francisco, Chicago
42	22	Airline pilot	56,500[9]	35[9]	Good	Good	Excellent	High	Dallas, Atlanta, Denver
43	16	Lawyer	60,500	31	Fair	Fair	Excellent	High	Washington, New York, Chicago
44	58	Licensed practical nurse	22,600	40	Good	Good	Good	High	Cleveland, Tampa, San Antonio
45	84	Paramedic	28,100[10]	36	Good	Good	Good	Very high	Detroit, Los Angeles, Chicago
46	20	Architect	36,100	20	Average	Average	Excellent	High	Boston, Washington, Atlanta
47	67	Photographer	23,400	25	Average	Average	Average	Average	Los Angeles, New York, San Francisco
48	71	Flight attendant	26,300[11]	51	Good	Good	Average	Average	Dallas, Denver, Atlanta
49	45	Personnel manager	31,100	25	Average	Average	Average	Average[8]	New York, Washington, Denver
50	35	Graphic artist	25,800	23	Average	Average	Average	Average	Los Angeles, New York, San Francisco
51	24	Librarian	29,500	12	Fair	Average	Average	Low	Washington, Boston, Raleigh/Durham
52	33	Fashion designer	29,600[14]	21[14]	Good	Average	Average	High	New York, Los Angeles
53	48	Bookkeeper	19,500	3	Average	Average	Average	Low	Denver; Minneapolis; Portland, Ore.

Rank	1992 rank	Occupation	Median annual earnings[1]	11-year job growth	Short-term outlook	Job security rating	Prestige rating	Stress and strain rating[12]	Where the jobs are
54	44	Advertising executive	$44,300	36%	Fair	Fair	Good	High	New York, Chicago, Atlanta
55	47	Travel agent	23,800	66	Average	Average	Average	Average	New York, Los Angeles, Chicago
56	27	Funeral director	36,500	18	Average	Excellent	Average	High	Scranton, Milwaukee, Pittsburgh
57	87	Stockbroker	40,700	33	Average	Average	Average	High	New York, Chicago, San Francisco
58	95	Fast-food manager	21,100	44	Average	Average	Average	High	Orlando, Los Angeles, Atlanta
59	—	Receptionist	16,400	34	Average	Average	Fair	Low	San Francisco, Minneapolis, Seattle
60	30	Air traffic controller	43,300	10	Fair	Average	Good	Very high	Long Island, Jacksonville, Memphis
61	51	Homemaker	0	5[8]	Fair	Good	Average[20]	Average[8]	Just about anywhere
62	83	Journalist	29,900[15]	26	Average	Average	Good	High[8]	Washington, New York, Boston
63	60	Property manager	26,600	35	Average	Average	Fair	Average	San Diego, Denver, Dallas
64	23	Musician	28,900	25	Fair[19]	Fair	Average	High[8]	New York, Los Angeles, Nashville
65	28	Police officer	32,900	13	Good	Good	Good	Very high	New York, Washington, Chicago
66	76	Machinist	26,600	-1	Average	Average	Average	Average	Milwaukee, Cleveland, Houston
67	81	Hairstylist	14,200	35	Average	Average	Fair	Average[8]	Miami, Las Vegas, Phoenix
68	65	Actor	31,300[16]	54	Poor	Poor	Good	High	Los Angeles, New York, San Francisco
69	78	Carpenter	22,800	20	Average	Average	Average	High	Seattle, Miami, Baltimore
70	57	TV news reporter	21,400	25[8]	Poor	Poor	Good	Average[8]	Los Angeles, New York, Washington
71	68	Plumber	27,000	8	Average	Average	Average	Average	Philadelphia, Houston, Baltimore
72	86	Restaurant cook	13,100	46	Fair	Fair	Fair	Average	Las Vegas, Honolulu, Orlando
73	17	Army officer	43,800[17]	-20	Poor	Fair	Good [21]	Average[8]	Washington; Fayetteville, N.C.; Austin
74	61	Heavy equipment operator	22,000	11	Average	Average	Average	High	Charlotte, N.C.; Birmingham; Atlanta
75	91	Cashier	11,700	24	Average	Average	Fair[8]	Average	Las Vegas, Orlando, New Orleans
76	77	Auto mechanic	21,900	23	Good	Good	Fair	High	Detroit, Houston, Los Angeles
77	43	Secretary	20,100	4	Fair	Fair	Average	Average	Washington, New York, Philadelphia
78	73	Public relations person	31,900	26	Fair	Fair	Average	High	Washington, Boston, New York
79	82	Welder	23,600	15	Average	Average	Average	High	Houston, Detroit, Birmingham
80	—	Appliance salesperson	23,300	21	Average	Average	Fair	Average	Dallas, Los Angeles, Atlanta
81	93	Surveyor	28,700	13	Fair	Average	Average	High	Seattle; Portland, Ore.; Houston
82	53	Tailor	16,600	-4	Poor	Poor	Average	Average[8]	New York, Los Angeles, Philadelphia
83	94	Waiter/waitress	12,000	36	Fair	Fair	Poor	Average	Las Vegas, Orlando, Detroit
84	41	Retail buyer	25,700	13	Fair	Fair	Average	High	Minneapolis, Atlanta, Chicago
85	70	Truck driver	23,100	27	Average	Average	Fair	High	Los Angeles, Houston, Atlanta
86	63	Insurance agent	29,400	15	Poor	Poor	Average	High	Chicago, Dallas, Hartford
87	79	Real estate agent	31,700	11	Average	Average	Average	Very high	Miami, Orlando, Seattle
88	55	Bank teller	15,200	-4	Fair	Fair	Average	Average	Chicago, New Orleans, Northern N.J.
89	62	Fire fighter	32,200	17	Fair	Average	Average	Very high	Boston, Providence, Oklahoma City
90	92	Apparel salesperson	13,600	21	Fair	Poor	Fair[8]	Average	New York, Chicago, Los Angeles
91	99	Auto salesperson	25,800	21	Average	Average	Poor[22]	High	Oklahoma City, Dallas, Nashville
92	74	Farmer	20,600[18]	-21	Poor	Average	Average	Very high	Job is rarely in cities.
93	96	Construction worker	19,700	17	Average	Average	Fair	Very high	Houston, Miami, Baltimore
94	90	Advertising salesperson	30,700	14[8]	Fair	Fair	Fair	High	New York, Chicago, Atlanta
95	89	Mail carrier	32,900	1	Fair	Average	Average	Very high	New York, Washington, St. Louis
96	85	Telephone operator	20,100	-28	Poor	Poor	Fair	Average	Dallas, Phoenix, St. Louis
97	—	Dancer	14,800	25	Poor	Poor	Average[23]	Very high	Las Vegas, New York, Los Angeles
98	97	Butcher[13]	18,400	-14	Average	Average	Fair	High	Chicago, Omaha, San Antonio
99	100	Taxi driver	16,200	18	Average	Average	Poor	Very high	New York, Washington, Las Vegas
100	98	Garbage collector	18,800	11	Average	Average	Poor	Very high	New York, Miami, Philadelphia

Notes: [1]Unless otherwise stated, income is median 1992 earnings. [2]Data include consulting income. [3]For middle-school principals [4]Data include other health-care managers. [5]For chemists with bachelor's degrees [6]For corporate lobbyists [7]Includes conservation scientists [8]MONEY estimate [9]Includes navigators [10]Average income [11]1991 data [12]Includes ratings of workplace environment, mental and physical stress [13]Includes meatcutters [14]Includes set and product designers [15]Includes editors [16]Includes directors [17]Figure is captain's salary and living allowance. [18]For farm managers [19]For orchestral musician [20]For housewives; househusbands were rated "fair" [21]For colonel [22]Rating for used-car salespeople [23]For ballet dancers **Sources:** Bureau of Labor Statistics, Census Bureau, National Opinion Research Center, *Jobs Rated Almanac*, American Medical Association, National Society of Professional Engineers, Educational Research Service, American Chemical Society, Commission on Professionals in Science, Association of Management Consulting Firms, Bank Administration Institute, American Mathematical Society, Foundation for Public Affairs, Roth Young Personnel Service, College for Financial Planning, *Journal of Emergency Medical Services*, Vernon Stone, U.S. Army Public Affairs, Claritas salaries (median: $148,000) lifted them to No. 2 on our list, up a notch from No. 3 in 1992. Two other health care professions, however, rose sharply in the rankings thanks to the growing tendency to shift medical services away from high-priced M.D.s. They are physical therapist (No. 3, up from No. 50) and registered nurse (No. 28, up from No. 52). Budget cutting at colleges took a toll on some of the scientific careers that dominated our list two years ago, including biologist (No. 16 this year, down from No. 1), geologist (No. 8, down from No. 2) and mathematician (No. 27, down from No. 4). It's worth noting that electrical and civil engineers, who are not dependent on universities for employment, more than held their own, moving up to the No. 4 and No. 5 spots from No. 13 and No. 9, respectively.

Even homemakers are not immune to economic trends. The Census Bureau reports recent declines in the percentage of couples who have children under 18 and those with only one wage earning spouse. Those shifts led us to downgrade our estimate of the future demand for homemakers. Therefore, they fell to No. 61 from No. 51. Being a homemaker, however, still outranks several positions that involve some of the work that homemakers do for free, including cook (No. 72), waitress (No. 83) and telephone operator (No. 96). Management consultants, on the other hand, jumped to No. 17 from No. 49 as job-cutting corporations increasingly turn to outsourcing (hiring outside specialists to do work once performed by permanent staff). And for all the talk of the Clinton Administration reining in lobbyists, their high salaries (median: $91,300 annually) and persistent influence vaulted them to No. 30 from No. 75.

Twenty Hothouses for Small Business

You probably know Boise as the American potato capital. Now a MONEY study shows that the Idaho city is also the best place in the country for starting or running a small business. Over a recent five-year stretch, the Boise area registered overall employment growth of 27%, three times the national rate. And small-company profits climbed even faster during that period. In Boise and its suburbs, the average annual income of proprietorships, a bellwether for small-business fortunes in general, shot up 65%, to nearly $20,000. That's more than twice the national growth rate of 31% and well above the national average of $15,212.

Boise's ascendance in our ranking isn't surprising when you consider that western cities in general fared extremely well. Overall, 11 of our top 20 places for entrepreneurs lie west of the Continental Divide (see the table on page 80). So do four of the top five, including No. 2, Bellingham, Wash., No. 4, Las Vegas, and No. 5, Reno. And we're not counting No. 3, Honolulu, which lies too far west to qualify as part of the American West. When taken together, these results are a virtual road map to higher profits for men and women seeking to start, relocate or expand a business. But even for entrepreneurs who aren't ready to move west, our findings serve an important purpose. They help identify the broad characteristics that make an area anywhere in the country desirable for small companies. After all, the fortunes of your location have a lot to do with your success. Says Nancy Pechloff, managing director of Arthur Andersen's Enterprise Group consulting service: "Small businesses, even more than large businesses, ride the local economic tide."

Why did the West do so well? Western cities led in nearly all of the more than a dozen factors we studied, ranging from employment growth to gains in the number of small businesses to the education level of the local work force. "The economic center of gravity of the U.S. has been moving west since the mid-1980s," says Philip Burgess of the Center for the New West, a Denver public policy think tank.

Boise, a picturesque, outdoorsy community of 365,300 (including residents of Ada and five adjacent counties), won because it was a consistently high performer in most categories. But that's not news to the business-people who live there. "Boise's been kind of like a Garden of Eden for us," says Jim Thompson, chief executive officer of Ecco, one of many local success stories. Ecco, established in 1972, makes those alarms that beep loudly when trucks and other heavy machinery back up. And thanks to deft marketing and innovative products—such as an alarm that automatically gets louder when the decibel level of any background noise goes up—Ecco has captured some 40% of this classic niche market worldwide. (Another Boise firm, Preco, holds 50%.) "With the Boise airport just three minutes away, we can ship relatively inexpensively to customers in six foreign countries," says Thompson. "And we manage to attract a lot of smart employees because Boise is a great place to live."

To identify Boise and the 19 other premier entrepreneurial hotbeds, we sought help from the Corporation for Enterprise Development (CFED), a nonprofit economic research and public policy firm in Washington, D.C. The CFED started by dividing the nation into 779

commuting zones based on the actual routes people most commonly travel between home and work. "We chose commuting zones because they give a more accurate picture of regional economic activity than political boundaries, such as city, county or even state lines," says Daphne Clones, a senior policy analyst who supervised the research project. In fact, many commuting zones cover parts of several states. Charlotte, N.C. (No. 14), for instance, includes areas of North and South Carolina; the Spokane region (No. 19) covers counties in both Washington and Idaho. Clones and her staff then ranked the places using more than a dozen different kinds of data, including job earnings, employment growth, the availability of capital and the presence of an educated work force. The results, and some of the data that went into them, are shown in our table.

To help you understand the trends behind the raw numbers, we asked small-business experts to discuss the economic, political and social characteristics that make places like these great. With their aid, we came up with the following factors that are common to many of our winning cities and that contribute substantially to an area's vitality.

A vigorous, diverse local economy. The success of a single local enterprise can sometimes boost an entire area's economy. In our ranking, Las Vegas (No. 4) and Reno (No. 5) benefited from their casinos' profits, up 41% since 1988. An influx of money like that trickles down to the local economy through wages to casino employees and through payments to firms that serve the gambling palaces and their customers. The result? Las Vegas has enjoyed an entrepreneurial boom, with the number of proprietorships growing nearly 50% since 1988. That is the largest increase among any of our winning cities. Proprietorship earnings have climbed too, by

almost 70% to $22,436, or some 47% above the national average. Talk about small business owners who are being dealt a winning hand.

In the long run, however, the most stable economies are those built upon a number of different industries so that a downturn in one is offset by gains in another. In Houston, for example, entrepreneurship was once synonymous with hard-charging oil and gas wildcatters. Since that industry collapsed in the mid-

How These 20 Entrepreneurial Edens Compare

Rank/Region	Number of companies included	Population	Overall job growth[1]	Per capita income	Growth in average earnings[1]	Growth in number of proprietors[1]	Proprietors' average earnings	Growth in proprietors' earnings[1]
1 Boise, Idaho	6	365,300	26.6%	$18,562	29.7%	27.8%	$19,711	65.4%
2 Bellingham, Wash.	1	137,900	32.2	18,186	20.6	31.8	17,215	56.1
3 Honolulu	1	863,100	12.6	23,864	33.1	32.0	23,731	48.4
4 Las Vegas	5	976,100	35.7	20,006	26.3	47.2	22,436	67.6
5 Reno	5	354,900	12.7	24,258	28.3	21.0	25,247	52.9
6 Houston/Galveston	10	3,823,000	16.5	21,482	30.6	18.0	25,887	63.1
7 Seattle/Tacoma	9	3,321,900	19.4	23,148	30.3	24.0	20,824	43.9
8 Fort Myers/Naples, Fla.	2	516,800	23.5	22,517	21.5	44.6	15,430	42.8
9 Redding, Calif.	2	209,500	19.9	16,425	19.6	34.8	18,726	48.3
10 Charleston, S.C.	4	564,200	8.2	16,039	31.2	13.9	20,338	109.9
11 Scranton/Wilkes-Barre	7	817,900	6.8	18,065	24.9	21.0	20,975	31.8
12 Sonoma Valley, Calif.	3	536,500	19.3	21,432	21.6	39.7	17,300	44.9
13 Medford/Grants Pass, Ore.	2	219,500	13.8	16,585	20.5	22.9	19,502	41.5
14 Charlotte, N.C.	9	1,145,600	9.3	19,769	28.7	24.5	18,619	47.5
15 Knoxville	8	657,300	12.6	17,875	25.5	18.1	19,825	39.5
16 Sacramento/Lake Tahoe	10	2,250,100	16.4	19,468	23.3	39.0	18,320	40.6
17 Portland, Ore./Vancouver, Wash.	6	1,544,400	17.3	20,839	27.9	15.6	18,116	35.9
18 Laredo, Texas	3	163,400	35.2	10,383	33.6	33.5	19,873	101.9
19 Spokane	7	528,000	17.6	17,620	24.5	18.8	15,300	38.9
20 Harrisburg, Pa.	7	984,300	9.4	20,024	23.9	27.7	17,445	29.9
U.S. average			**8.7**	**16,673**	**24.1**	**13.0**	**15,212**	**31.2**

Note: [1]Over a recent five-year period

1980s, many other types of businesses have sprung up. Among them are more than 60 biotech firms, many loosely associated with giant Texas Medical Center, which spends some $350 million a year on medical research. So

even though the oil and gas business has stabilized, the biotech firms and other new industries contributed to Houston/Galveston's placing sixth on our list of business greenhouses.

Major corporations can also help to bolster local economies. The Boise area boasts a number of such firms, including a branch of computer maker Hewlett-Packard (annual revenues of $23 billion) and the headquarters of Micron Technology, a $1.4 billion manufacturer of semiconductors. Among the many small firms that profit from supplying those behemoths is Richard Cortez's Metalcraft Inc. Says Cortez, a former H-P manager who retired at age 51 in 1986 to found Metalcraft: "When I started out, I looked at the larger businesses in town and thought, 'I should be able to make a go of it here.'" And indeed, after surviving a rocky first year, the company has grown to employ 38 people on revenues of $2 million a year. Nearly 60% of Metalcraft's business derives from sales of carts, cabinets and metal goods to H-P, Micron and two other local corporations.

An educated work force.

Another essential ingredient of entrepreneurial success is access to smart, educated workers. It's no coincidence that software giant Microsoft grew up in Redmond, Wash., within an hour's drive of 34 local colleges and universities, including the 25,000-student University of Washington located in Seattle. In fact, the Seattle/Tacoma area had the best-educated work force of any place we surveyed, a factor that helped earn it the No. 7 spot in our ranking. Some 65% of area residents have finished at least one year of college, compared with a national average of only 45%. In addition to turning out educated workers, colleges can help spawn new companies. "Universities are incubators for the kind of creative thinkers who found new businesses," says Arthur Andersen's Pechloff. Take the

Work force with some college	Bank deposits per capita	Comments
60.0%	$9,133	The area accounts for 40% of Idaho's entire manufacturing employment.
59.2	12,644	Some 110 Canadian-owned firms and branches have expanded here since '89.
58.3	22,207	After a decline during the recession, tourism is now growing at 3% a year.
53.3	10,542	Gambling, hotels and recreation provide 58% of the area's new jobs.
60.5	9,460	Nevada has no corporate income tax, franchise tax or inventory tax.
59.0	12,172	The top U.S. port for foreign trade, with $26 billion in goods shipped yearly
65.6	11,971	Cuts at defense firms like Boeing are offset by growth at consumer firms.
52.8	16,872	Its fastest-growing population group is 24- to 44-year-olds, not retirees.
55.7	9,234	Despite its small size, the region is home to 160 manufacturers.
53.4	7,364	Even with planned cutbacks, military bases benefit the area.
38.5	14,428	Five interstate highways pass through here, ensuring good transportation.
63.8	13,805	Only 90 miles from San Francisco, this is a haven for relocating professionals.
53.8	8,617	Since Oregon has no sales tax, bulk retailers such as Costco like it here.
54.7	15,407	This distribution center lies within a two-hour flight of 60% of U.S. residents.
47.3	10,652	There's no international airport, yet 500 local firms engage in foreign trade.
62.2	11,928	The presence of the state government helps keep its economy strong.
64.7	11,219	The area is home to 800 high-tech firms and major health-care providers.
36.2	17,057	Fully 95% of residents are Hispanic, facilitating trade with Mexico.
60.6	9,165	Commercial lease rates run 20% to 55% below those of San Francisco.
39.8	14,856	Since 1981, its public buildings have received a $1.2 billion facelift.
44.6	**11,843**	

case of Eric Heilborn. He was still a small-business student at Western Washington University in Bellingham when he was first bitten by the entrepreneurial bug six years ago. Heilborn and various partners spent two years and $80,000 trying—unsuccessfully, as it turned out—to make products such as the perfect ergonomic office chair and the ideal line of sports clothing. Not until 1990 did he hit on the idea that clicked—sturdy, attractive dog beds. Today his company, Apogee Industries, employs 20 people and earns gross revenues of $640,000 a year.

Lots of cash and construction.

Since access to financing is crucial to a business' success, entrepreneurial hot spots usually also have lots of venture-capital firms, special government loan programs and banks eager to lend. There is no way to measure the volume of such loans directly. They come from too many sources, and the loan amounts, especially with private capital, are often confidential. So we measured the growth of per capita local bank deposits, an excellent proxy for loan activity, since it indicates how much cash is available for lending. Honolulu, for example, has benefited from an influx of Asian capital in recent years—in part from wealthy Hong Kong residents nervous about the Chinese Communists' takeover of the colony in 1997. As a result, per capita bank deposits in Honolulu have risen to $22,207, almost double the U.S. average and tops among our 20 cities.

The result has been a boom in construction that provides local jobs, wages and tax revenues and also ensures a ready supply of affordable commercial real estate. Since 1988, developers have plowed $3 billion into non-residential construction in Honolulu, including warehouses, factories, and office space. That's an astounding 2,196 times the $138,000 average increase for the areas in our study.

A great transportation network.

Just as a ready supply of cash can help a small company grow, easy access to transportation can help make a small city seem big. Few people outside the state of Washington have heard of tiny Bellingham, for instance. The city and surrounding county are home to 137,900 people. Yet thanks to its location along busy Interstate 5, Bellingham is within a day's drive of 9 million U.S. consumers and another 1 million in Canada (the border is just 30 minutes away). That has helped Geographics, a $7 million office-supplies manufacturer, quadruple its profits since 1981. From its headquarters in nearby Blaine, Wash., a border town with one stoplight and a stunning view of Mount Baker, Geographics ships designer paper products to customers worldwide, mostly by truck but occasionally by air through nearby Bellingham International Airport to overseas buyers. "We may be located in a small town," says chairman Ronald Deans. "But that doesn't mean we can't be a global competitor."

Small size may be more an advantage than a handicap for cities like Bellingham. Such towns generally pose fewer bureaucratic obstacles for business owners who are seeking building permits, zoning variances and the like. And city leaders are often much more accessible. As Boise mayor Brent Coles explains: "Every time I stop at Nick's Shoe Store to get a shine, businesspeople wander over and give me an earful of ideas."

A good quality of life.

What would you do if, by moving your company to another community, you could improve your neighborhood, your kids' schools and your profits? You'd move, of course. That's the type of no-brainer that is increasingly spurring businesspeople to set up shop in countrified places where life is cleaner, saner and less congested than in big cities. And entrepreneurs who make the move often find that their business benefits as much as their lifestyle. Pleasant surroundings tend to attract a better-educated work force. Employees are more productive if their lives are less hectic. Less congestion often means lower costs for rent, utilities and other operating expenses. And business owners sometimes find it easier to be creative in a friendly, low-pressure environment. Those facts may help explain why an estimated 98% of the businesses in a city like Spokane have 100 or fewer employees.

Such locales also attract affluent professionals—lawyers, consultants, architects and the like—who could work almost anywhere but prefer a place where the living is good. Burgess of the Center for the New West calls them lone eagles. "A lone eagle can set up shop in a small town and bring in $150,000 a

year on average," he says. "You get 10 of these folks in a small area and they give a healthy boost to the local economy."

Of equal importance is the fact that good natural environment opens abundant opportunities for firms that cater to vacationers or those seeking recreation on weekends. That's how Intermountain Outdoor Sports, the largest retailer of its kind in the Boise area, has prospered. Annual revenues have tripled in five years to more than $5 million. "We've grown up here," says Gerry Sweet, general manager at the store that was founded by his parents and is now run by Sweet and his two brothers. "And I wouldn't want to live anywhere else, for lifestyle or for business." Boise would also be a great place to vacation, Sweet notes, if he could ever take some time off.

Maximize Your Shrinking Benefits Now

The leaner look continues to be the rage in company benefits. Only 6% of companies pay the full cost of family health coverage, down from 12% three years ago. Even stalwart IBM, which made our list of 10 major corporations with the best benefits on page 86, has dropped free health care for its 124,000 employees and their families after 38 years and begun charging premiums of $23 to $50 a month. Fully 60% of U.S. workers are enrolled in managed care plans like HMOs, which tend to be less costly than traditional indemnity, or fee-for-service, plans that don't restrict your choice of doctors. That's up from 51% in 1992. Employers also are replacing their conventional (and costly) pensions with 401(k) savings plans that invariably require employees to contribute to their own welfare. Some 4% of companies surveyed by accountant KPMG Peat Marwick eliminated their pension plans

over the past five years. American Express, for instance, will substitute a plan that no longer guarantees set amounts upon retirement. And many other firms have simply closed their pension plans to new workers.

What's a smart employee to make of this climate of austerity? Below are the best benefits moves you can make now or later in the year during companies' so-called open enrollment period, usually from November through year's end. We've canvassed experts for advice on how to capitalize on your core benefits and maximize the more marginal ones. Here's what top consultants say you need to know.

Focus on your health care needs. If you can choose between managed care and an indemnity plan, you'll find it usually makes financial sense to opt for managed care even though monthly premiums may be $6 to $20 higher. That's because such plans generally charge only $5 to $15 co-payments for doctor office visits and throw in freebies like annual mammograms, physical exams or eyeglasses. Most employers now offer a choice of an HMO (health maintenance organization) or the newer PPOs (preferred provider organizations). The latter, unlike HMOs, allow you to see physicians who are not on the approved list (usually at a reimbursement of only 30%). HMOs are a smart choice if your medical needs are fairly basic or if you have young children who need regular checkups. Join a

PPO for more freedom to choose among doctors and higher out-of-pocket costs. If your employer offers only an indemnity plan but still lets you choose how much coverage you receive, consider the plan's deductible as well as its out-of-pocket maximum. Assuming you're young and healthy, choose the least expensive plan. Just make sure you can afford the plan's out-of-pocket maximum should a serious illness or accident occur.

Check out your spouse's plan. When both spouses work, take time to scrutinize

Buy a Disability Policy That's Sound

Have you thought how your life would be upset if you were crippled in an accident? You should even though relatively few white-collar professionals ever become disabled. If you work, you shouldn't risk going without long-term disability insurance to replace lost income. Viewed as a surrogate paycheck, the policy's benefits should pay out an amount equal to 60% to 80% of your wages.

Alas, disability insurance is expensive. A no-frills policy covering 50% of the $75,000 income of a 40-year-old man might start at about $1,000 a year. The price could easily be twice that for a comprehensive plan that, among other things, replaces a higher percentage of income. Until recently, insurers charged men and women the same premiums for disability coverage. But in the past year, leading providers such as Northwestern Mutual, Paul Revere and Provident Life & Accident have begun charging women 5% to 45% more than men because women file more claims.

Before shopping for a policy, check to see what coverage you have through your employer. If you are one of the 43 million employees whose firms offer a long-term disability policy, grab it. Employer-sponsored coverage is usually 20% to 35% cheaper than comparable plans bought on your own. If you need to shop for a disability policy, start by calling life insurance agents for prices and coverage from three companies. Be certain that the insurers are financially strong (rated B or better from Weiss Research or triple A from Standard & Poor's and Moody's). To keep your premium affordable and assure adequate coverage, you want a policy with these features.

◆ **A long waiting period**. Most policies don't start

paying benefits until at least 30 days from the date the insurer says you became unable to work. But by buying a policy with a 90-day waiting period, you can save as much as 20% in premiums. If you go out as long as a one-year waiting period, you could save another 11%.

◆ **Benefits paid to age 65**. It's not worth paying 25% more (if you're age 40, for example) to get full lifetime benefits. Pay only for coverage until your retirement age, when Social Security and other savings can be your chief income sources. You also want a policy that can't be canceled and is protected against rate hikes. This is the only way you can be certain that the insurer won't drop your policy or make it unaffordable to you.

◆ **A cost-of-living rider**. A rider raising your benefits with inflation will jack up your premiums by 20% to 25%. But you don't want inflation gutting your income when you're out of work. A 40-year-old would pay 14% more in premiums to get an automatic 4% annual increase.

◆ **A residual benefit rider**. This essential add-on lets you work part-time or in a lower-paying job. You then collect the income shortfall, which can total as much as the policy's maximum, from your insurer.

◆ **Own-occupation coverage**. You could save about 10% with an "any occupation" policy, which pays out only if the insurer determines you're unable to work anywhere. Instead, you should buy "own occupation" coverage so you'll get benefits if you can't do your own job anymore.

your health options to find the most appropriate coverage for the least money. As a guideline, premiums for HMOs and PPOs are about $144 a month for family benefits. If both spouses work for companies that offer indemnity plans, don't sign up for more than one. Virtually all insurers now will reimburse you only up to the limit of the more generous plan. So paying extra premiums for a spouse's plan is rarely worth it. Sometimes it's smart to split the coverage. For example, if your plan offers free individual coverage but family premiums are high (say, $200 to $250 a month) insure yourself but put the rest of the family on your spouse's plan.

Stay alert to small changes.

"Employers tinker with health care coverage from year to year in an effort to keep down costs," says Michael Snyder, the director of benefits at Eastman Savings & Loan Association based in Rochester, N.Y. For instance, employers might hire new providers to get better priced coverage. But inevitably, the care isn't identical. Kodak, for instance, recently switched from an HMO that charged $50 a month to one that charged $25. A boon to employees, right? Not if you're a big consumer of prescription drugs. The new HMO had a drug deductible of $500, compared with only $100 under the old one. Once a year check the benefits booklets to make sure features haven't changed. A few moments of investigation could save you money.

Get a tax break on medical costs.

If you expect out-of-pocket medical expenses to total more than a few hundred dollars in 1995, sign up for a flexible spending account (FSA), now offered by 43% of large companies. That's because the money for an FSA account is deducted from your paycheck before Uncle Sam gets his due. Say you're married, earning $50,000 a year and expect to spend about $1,000 on health care this year. You'll save about $354 in taxes by opening an FSA, according to calculations by George Faulkner at consultant Foster Higgins. You can use your FSA to pay for such expenses as medical exams, cab rides to your doctor, orthodontics and contact lenses up to a maximum set by your company, typically $3,000. And you may spend all the money allocated to your FSA before you have actually made the payroll contributions. For example, if you have elective surgery in January and submit a bill to the FSA for $2,000, even though you have contributed only $250, the FSA reimburses you the full amount. Should you leave your job before year's end and have spent more from your FSA than you have contributed, your company must pick up the bill, according to rules set by the IRS.

Here are two cautionary notes. You may revise your allocation only when you experience a "life change," such as marriage or a death in the immediate family. In addition, you must come up with expenses equal to the total amount you've contributed by year's end or forfeit the remaining cash. But don't let that worry you too much. Only 4% of the total FSA accounts at large companies were left unused, reports Foster Higgins.

Utilize medical fringe offerings.

Vision care and prescription-drug programs are increasingly common in health plans. About 20% of companies now offer options where you pay only $5 for every prescription. If you take daily medication, such as Mevacor for lowering cholesterol, you may be able to order a three-month supply by mail for only $10, compared with the $381 tariff at the local drugstore. Four out of five companies now feature wellness programs, which let you take advantage of free cholesterol screenings, blood pressure tests and smoking cessation courses. Some, like Chrysler, provide on-site

Ten Big Employers with Unbeatable Benefits

Although Procter & Gamble (P&G) lacks a traditional pension plan, the company edged out IBM for the top spot in MONEY's ranking of the major corporations that provide America's most generous employee benefits. P&G makes up for that absent pension plan by rewarding employees with rich profit sharing. The company's annual contribution to employees' accounts amounts to 5% of pay and, after 20 years, reaches 25%—a gold mine for long-term workers. P&G also offers inexpensive and outstanding medical coverage, including three managed-care options and a menu of insurance and other programs.

P&G's first-place finish was helped by IBM's new cost cutting. Reversing its 38-year-history, the computer giant began charging employees $23 to $50 monthly for health insurance. Even so, IBM managed to add some valuable miniperks: flexible spending accounts for health and dependent care as well as annual reimbursement up to $250 for an approved exercise program or other extras.

Despite the leaner climate, all of our top 10 offer enviable medical, pension or profit-sharing plans plus vacation and other leave. Third-ranked Chrysler provides free medical insurance and permits employees up to 16 holidays a year, including the week between Christmas and New Year's. John Hancock, ranked fifth, offers pension, 401(k) and profit-sharing plans. And new parents at AT&T have the luxury of taking a full year of family leave with all of their benefits intact.

Rank/company (Number of U.S. employees)	INSURANCE		
	Medical	Dental	Life and disability
1. **Procter & Gamble** Cincinnati (39,000)	Cost: $19 a month. Deductible:none in network; 20% out of network. Reimbursement: 100% after $12 co-payment. No out-of-pocket max.	Cost: none. Deductible: preventive care and diagnostic, none; other, $75. Reimbursement: 50%. Max. annual: $1,600 a person.	Life: one year's pay. Short-term disability: 67% of pay for 52 weeks. Long-term disability: 50%.
2. **IBM** Armonk, N.Y. (124,000)	Cost: $50 a month. Deductible: 0.3% of pay with $250 minimum; average hospital deductible: $300. Reimbursement: major medical, 80%; surgical and hospital, 100%. No out-of-pocket max.	Cost: $15 a month. Deductible: $40 per person. Reimbursement: set amount for each procedure, based on prevailing local charges. Lifetime max.: $8,500 a person.	Life: up to $50,000, based on length of service. Short-term disability: 52 weeks at full pay. Long-term disability: 67%.
3. **Chrysler** Highland Park, Mich. (90,000)	No cost. Deductible: $250. Reimbursement: 80%. Out-of-pocket max.: $500.	Cost: none. Deductible: $150. Reimbursement: preventive, 90%; basic, 80%; major, 50%. Max. annual: $1,200 a person.	Life: two times annual pay. Accrued pensions payable to survivors of employees who die before age 65. Short-term disability: nine months at full pay and then three months at 70%. Long-term disability: 55%.
4. **Citicorp** New York City (38,500)	Cost: $962 a year. Deductible: none in network, 2% of pay out of network. Reimbursement: 100% after $10 co-payment; 80% out of network. Out-of-pocket max.: 5% of pay, out of network.	Cost: $107 a year per family. Deductible: $150. Reimbursement: preventive, 100%; basic and major, 50%. Max. annual: $2,500.	Life: one year's pay. Short-term disability: 67% for six months. Long-term disability: 50% of salary.
5. **John Hancock** Boston (13,500)	Cost: $98 a month. Deductible: none in network; $350 out of network. Reimbursement: 90% after $10 co-payment; 70% out of network. Max. out of pocket: $3,000 in network; $10,500 out of network.	Cost: $11 a month. Deductible: preventive, none; $50, basic and major, per person. Reimbursement: preventive, 100%; basic, 80%; major, 50%. Max. annual: $1,500 a person.	Life: choice of one or two years' pay with $50,000 minimum. Short-term disability: 60% to 100% of pay for 26 weeks, depending on length of service. Long-term disability: 60%.
6. **Quaker Oats** Chicago (11,000)	Cost: $69 a month. Deductible: $625. Reimbursement: 85%. Out-of-pocket max.: $3,150.	Cost: $9 a month. Deductible: none in network; none for preventive out of network, $100 for all other. Reimbursement: preventive, 100%, basic, 90%, major, 60%. Max. annual: $1,375.	Life: one year's pay. Short-term disability: up to 50 weeks at full pay, depending on service. Long-term disability: 50%.
7. **MCI** Washington, D.C. (42,500)	Cost: average 9% of pay. Deductible: none in network; $750 out of network. Reimbursement: 85% in network; 70% out of network. Out-of-pocket max.: $3,600 in network; $4,800 out of network.	Cost: included in medical. Deductible: $150. Reimbursement: preventive, 100%; basic, 80%; major, 50%. Max. annual: $1,500.	Life: two times annual pay. Short-term disability: 26 weeks at 67% of pay. Long-term disability: 67%.
8. **AT&T** New York City (226,800)	Cost: $70 monthly. Deductible: $450. Reimbursement: 80%; surgical and hospital, 95% to 100%. Out-of-pocket max.: $1,000 a person.	Cost: none. No deductible. Reimbursement: 100% preventive. Max. annual: $1,500 a person.	Life: one year's pay. Short-term disability: one year at full pay after 25 years of service. Long-term disability: 50%.
9. **Merck** Whitehouse Station, N.J. (20,000)	Cost: $40 a month. Deductible: to 0.5% of pay with $300 minimum. Reimbursement: 90% after 10% co-payment. Out-of-pocket max.: 2.5% of annual pay with $1,500 minimum.	Cost: none. Deductible: none for preventive, $25 a person for major. Reimbursement: 100%; major, 50%. Max. annual: $1,500, with $15,000 lifetime.	Life: choice from six months' to six years' full pay. Short-term disability: 26 weeks at full pay, based on length of service. Long-term disability: 50% to 70%.
10. **Bell Atlantic** Philadelphia (23,000)	Cost: $620 a year. Deductible: $625. Reimbursement: 80%. Out-of-pocket max.: $2,500 a family.	Cost: $38 a month. Deductible: $25 a person. Reimbursement: 100% preventive, scheduled fee otherwise. Max. annual: $1,000.	Life: choice of six months' or one year's pay or $50,000. Short-term disability: up to 52 weeks at full pay, based on length of service. Long-term disability: 40% to 70%.

In 1991, when we launched this ranking, only four of our top 10 companies provided flexible benefits. This year, all 10 do. In response to this trend toward benefits menus, we retooled our evaluation criteria to award more points to plans with the greatest range of desirable choices. As a result, Chrysler, John Hancock, MCI and Bell Atlantic emerged among our top 10 for the first time. Our methodology? We solicited 47 nominations of companies with superior plans from leading benefits experts nationwide. We then winnowed those to the 25 firms that had 7,000 or more employees covered by the nominated plans. Last, senior consultants and partners from Coopers & Lybrand Human Resource Advisory Group, a consulting division of the big accounting firm, scored the remaining firms. To ensure objectivity, companies were identified to judges only by code numbers, and various benefits were assigned different weights in scoring.

For the top 10 that are presented below, we describe the single most popular or representative medical, dental, and life and disability insurance options in the companies' flexible benefits plans. Keep in mind that all premiums, deductibles and maximum out-of-pocket costs are for family insurance coverage, unless noted otherwise. Vacation time is the maximum available; all 10 companies offer at least two weeks a year to new employees. Pension benefits are based on a final five-year average salary of roughly $50,000 a year.

RETIREMENT PLAN			
Time off	Pensions	Savings and stock purchase	Extras
Vacation: six weeks after 25 years; 12 holidays; parental leave: up to one year with benefits for three months	No pension plan; extremely generous profit sharing instead. Retiree pays $12.60 a month per person for health insurance.	No savings plan. Cash profit sharing; fixed percentage that gradually increases from 5% to 25% of pay after 20 years.	Flexible benefits that may be used for legal services, additional vacation or purchase of fitness equipment. Also, 2-for-1 higher education matching grants.
Vacation: five weeks after 20 years; 12 holidays; parental and personal leave: one year with benefits, renewable for up to three years	$20,250 at age 65 after 30 years; $16,875 at 60 after 25 years; $12,150 at 55 after 20 years. Free lifetime health insurance for retiree (and spouse) with 15 years of service.	Savings plan: company match of 30% on up to 5% of pay. Max. pretax contribution: 9%. Stock-purchase plan: 15% discount on share price, up to 10% of salary. Company contributes 2% of salary to personal retirement account.	Annual reimbursement up to $250 for health and fitness programs or personal financial planning fees.
Vacation: five weeks after 20 years; 14 to 16 holidays; parental leave: 12 weeks with benefits	$23,854 at age 65 after 30 years. $20,155 at 60 after 25 years. Not eligible before 60. Company pays portion of health insurance for retiree and family.	Savings plan: company match of 60% on up to 8% of pay. Max. pretax contribution: 15%. Cash profit sharing based on company's performance (about 10% of pay in '93).	Annual education scholarships for employee's children up to $4,000; discounts on new and used Chrysler cars.
Vacation: five weeks after 25 years, plus a week for every five years thereafter; 10 holidays; parental leave: 12 weeks with benefits; personal leave: two years without	$23,150 at age 65 after 30 years. $21,260 at 60 after 25 years. $17,730 at 55. Company pays a portion of retiree health insurance, depending on length of service.	Savings plan: no company match. Max. pretax contribution: 18%. Bonuses of 3% of pay may go into a tax-deferred account, where company matches 100%.	Fitness centers in 10 locations; discounts on bank products like credit cards and mortgages, plus free checking.
Vacation: five weeks after 20 or 25 years, depending on position; 10 to 11 holidays; parental leave: one year with benefits	$22,800 at age 65 after 30 years. $17,904 at 60 after 25 years. $10,104 at 55 after 20 years. Retiree pays $10 a month for health insurance and $15 a month for spouse.	Savings plan: company match of 100% up to 2% of pay. Max. pretax contribution: 15% of pay. Cash profit sharing: based upon company performance (4.88% of pay in 1993)	On-site child day care, dining and medical facilities; company store at Boston headquarters for up to 40% discounts on clothes and gifts.
Vacation: five weeks after 25 years; 12 holidays; parental leave: six months with benefits	$21,800 at age 65 after 30 years. $17,090 at 60 after 25 years. $11,015 at 55 after 20 years. Retiree contributes $2.30 a month for health insurance and $4.60 a month for each additional family member.	Savings plan: no company match. Max. pretax contribution: 7%. Stock-ownership plan: annual award of about 10% of pay.	Health exams; fitness centers at 12 locations. Company pays broker fees for purchase of Quaker Oats stock.
Vacation: five weeks after 20 years; 12 holidays; parental leave: 12 weeks with benefits; personal leave: one year without benefits	$18,300 at age 65 after 30 years. $12,266 at 60 after 25 years. $7,419 at 55 after 20 years. No health insurance.	Savings plan: company match of 67% on up to 6% of pay. Max. pretax contribution, 15% of pay. Stock-purchase plan: 15% discount on share price, up to 15% of pay.	Programs for high-risk pregnancy; child- and elder-care referral services; $25 monthly discounts on long-distance phone service.
Vacation: five weeks after 25 years; 10 holidays; parental leave: one year with benefits; personal leave: two years with benefits	$21,100 at age 65 after 30 years. $17,650 at 60 after 25 years. $14,190 at 55 after 20 years. Free health insurance for retiree and spouse.	Savings plan: company match of 67% on up to 6% of pay. Max. pretax contribution: 16%.	Education assistance service, including school selection and counseling; adoption referral and counseling services; company-paid legal insurance.
Vacation: six weeks after 27 years; 12 holidays; parental leave: 18 months with benefits; personal leave: one month with benefits	$24,000 at age 65 after 30 years. $20,000 at 60 after 25 years. $12,000 at 55 after 20 years. Free health insurance for retiree and family.	Savings plan: company match of 50% on up to 5% of pay. Max. pretax contribution: 5%	Job sharing; fitness center; extra flex credits are given to employees who undergo thorough health exams.
Vacation: five weeks after 25 years; 10 holidays; parental leave: up to one year with benefits for six months; personal leave: up to two years without benefits	$20,674 at age 65 after 30 years. $17,316 at 60 after 25 years. $13,120 at 55 after 20 years. Company pays portion of health insurance for retiree and spouse.	Savings plan: company match of 83.3% in stock up to 6% of pay. Max. pretax contribution: 16% of pay.	Health club discounts; job sharing; health programs including stop-smoking seminars, nutrition and stress management.

Weight Watchers meetings as well as fitness classes offered to workers at 60% discounts.

Beware of salary caps on pensions.

If you have an annual salary of $150,000 or more, your pension may just have become smaller than you were expecting. That's because a law that went into effect last year lowers the cap on which your pension can be calculated from $235,840 to $150,000. Any amount you earn over the new limit will not be factored into your final pension. An estimated 37% of companies have a bridge plan to make up the difference; 12% of firms plan to add one. If your salary tops $150,000 and your employer doesn't offer a supplemental plan, you should lobby the company to start

one. Also find out whether competitors have such a plan and then cite their offerings.

Go for the max in your 401(k).

Most companies will match your 401(k) contributions somewhat, typically 50¢ for every $1 you kick in, up to 6% of your annual salary. Some companies even let you invest up to 15% of your pretax income provided you do not exceed the limit set by law (about $9,500 this year). You now have more investment choices for your 401(k) contributions than ever thanks in part to U.S. Department of Labor regulations that went into effect in 1992 and encourage employers to offer three or more alternatives. If your company is still behind the curve, make sure to request more diverse choices.

Take the Pulse of Your Health Plan

If you think your doctor knows best and only the foolish or obnoxious bother to research their health problems, think again. If Mary Lee Horton had not questioned the treatment her children were getting for a rare blood disease, daughter Kate, 4, might not be alive today. As it was, Mom's intervention came too late to save Kate's twin sister Sydney, who died three years ago (see "One Family's Life-and-Death Struggle" on the right).

Such situations are rare, of course. But you and your family will benefit if you can aggressively act to solve more mundane medical problems, such as squeezing special treatment out of a tightfisted HMO or disputing an insurer's ruling that shortchanges you. Fact is, you no longer have a choice. Market forces are pushing free-spending American patients toward greater price consciousness. Insurers that don't scrutinize medical treatment by reviewing doctors' services are prac-

tically extinct. They account for just 5% of the market, down from 35% in 1988.

No matter how competent your family physician is, he or she is probably increasingly pinched by insurers and too swamped by paperwork to act as an informed advocate for every patient. So to get the care you desire and deserve, you have to look out for yourself. Armed with the right information and some gumption, you can become well qualified to take a major role in managing your care. Furthermore, it's getting easier to educate yourself, as we explain below. Our advice is organized according to the types of health care skirmishes you and your family are likely to encounter. In the accompanying boxes, you'll find stories of families who waged just such battles—and won.

Ensuring you get the best quality care.

The pressured atmosphere in many hospitals,

labs and doctors' offices these days often makes you feel as though everyone must act immediately. In fact, very few medical treatments or tests are so time-sensitive that you must make an on-the-spot decision. So examine your options. For instance, if your doctor presents only one possible treatment, push him or her to tell you whether there are others and how they differ. Alternative therapies don't necessarily mean embarking on New Age regimens. You may favor a more conservative approach than your doctor does. For example, three years ago, Group Health Cooperative of Puget Sound, a Seattle-based HMO, stopped its routine testing of male patients over 65 for prostate cancer. Instead, it asked each man whether he wanted to be tested. Because this type of cancer is generally very slow growing in symptomless cases, treatment hasn't been shown to lengthen life and carries significant risks of its own, including the death of one or two of each 100 patients as a result of surgery. After learning about the hazards of treatment, nearly 50% of the HMO's patients passed up the test.

The key to making wise medical decisions is getting clear, up-to-date information. One appealing new way to gain knowledge is through so-called interactive videos that run on computers with video disks. A patient views others discussing the merits and drawbacks of various treatments they chose for the same ailment, then uses a touchscreen to describe his own circumstances. Moments later, the computer prints out a customized profile of his risk factors.

Using medical data from the Foundation for Informed Medical Decision-Making, a Hanover, N.H. research and educational center, Sony is marketing programs on benign prostate disease, breast cancer, lower back pain and mild hypertension. In the works are videos on other topics, such as hormone-replacement therapy and stable angina. Sony

One Family's Life-and-Death Struggle

The nightmare began in 1990 soon after Mary Lee Horton, now 34, of Wilmington, N.C. gave birth to identical twin girls, Sydney and Kate. Syd came down with a 103 degree fever. A blood test revealed she had extraordinarily low counts of red blood cells and platelets. Biopsies at the University of North Carolina Medical Center in Chapel Hill confirmed the worst. Syd was suffering from FEL (familial erythrophagocytic lymphohistiocytosis), a rare and fatal genetic blood disease. Two weeks later, Kate had similar symptoms. The Chapel Hill doctors advised Mary Lee and her husband Howard Mitchell, 39, that no child with FEL had survived past its fourth birthday. They also said the best possible treatment for the girls was chemotherapy and steroids.

Mary Lee immediately decided to research the disease on her own. Aided by a national network of parents coping with FEL, she wrote to a doctor in France who had successfully treated the disease with bone marrow transplants. He told her that Sloan-Kettering Memorial in New York City was experimenting with his technique. Mary Lee mailed samples of Syd's and Kate's blood to Sloan-Kettering so the type could be matched with donors. Mary Lee says that hospital errors caused the hunt for donors to take more than a year, but the hospital denies responsibility for the delay. For Syd, sadly, the wait for a donor match proved fatal. She died of pneumonia in October 1991.

Three months later, however, Kate received the new bone marrow she needed. Though she must visit Duke University for a blood test and an immune booster shot three to four times a year, Kate today lives a normal life, taking ballet and gymnastics lessons. Looking back now, Mary Lee says her biggest regret is that she did not press her doctors hard enough, and early enough, for alternatives. "Friends also say we should have sued Sloan-Kettering," says Mary Lee. "But we didn't want money. All we wanted was Syd back."

She Reduced Her Premiums Over 50%

Insurance broker Madeleine Huff, 62, faced long odds in 1993, when she began trying to lower the cost of medical coverage for herself and her retired husband Ike, 64. Since 1977, the Auburn, Calif. couple had seen their combined health insurance premiums soar from $380 a month to $991 as their insurance company reacted to the couple's mounting medical bills. Foremost among them were Ike's as a result of his successful bout with colon cancer. And overweight Madeleine developed high blood pressure.

The Huffs tried to shop for cheaper coverage, but eight insurers flatly rejected the couple as bad risks. They then discovered that Blue Cross/Blue Shield had just launched a special policy for high-risk consumers. Although their move to Blue Cross/Blue Shield helped to cut their premiums in half, Madeleine wasn't satisfied. Dieting under her doctor's supervision, she lost nearly 60 pounds and was able to discard her blood pressure medicines.

Buoyed by her success, Madeleine asked Blue Cross to reclassify her in a cheaper, lower-risk insurance category. When the company declined, she refused to let the matter drop. "The rejection letter said to call if you disagreed with the refusal, so I did," she says. She explained to the medical examiner that after losing the weight and lowering her blood pressure, her feet were no longer swollen. To buttress her case, she also asked her internist and podiatrist to back up her claims by sending the results of her latest tests to Blue Cross.

Many consumers in Madeleine's situation would eventually have given up—or threatened to hire a lawyer to seek redress in the courts. But her persistence finally paid off. Last year Madeleine received word that she had been approved for Level 1 coverage, which cut her premiums 52%, from $269 a month to $128, and made her eligible for better coverage with a lower deductible. Exults Madeleine: "If I'd won the $7 million lottery, I couldn't be happier."

promises all will be updated each year with the latest medical data. The programs are currently available at more than 100 hospitals and HMOs around the country. But you need a doctor's prescription to see one.

Much of the data in Sony's videos was generated by a relatively new field called outcomes research, which tries to quantify how surgery, drugs and other treatments pay off in medical, social and emotional terms. This approach to treatment can be controversial because research often disagrees. Yet it has already contributed to some generally accepted "clinical guidelines" to help doctors decide when to use, and when to forgo, various treatments. These guidelines are often available in consumer-friendly pamphlets from self-help groups, medical specialty boards and government offices.

For serious medical matters, you may need to consult other sources and specialists. This process can get tricky because second opinions conflict with first ones about 15% of the time, on average. To minimize the crossfire from dueling medical opinions, you can arrange for all the doctors working on your case to sit down with you at one time, if only in a phone conference. Four years ago, Dorothy Rodman of New York City learned that she had breast cancer. Rodman, who had long suffered from emphysema, was concerned that the standard radiation treatment accompanying removal of a tumor might destroy precious lung cells. To decide what treatment to pursue after surgery, she met simultaneously with her internist and cancer surgeon. The three of them decided against radiation. Instead, the specialist suggested tamoxifen, a potent anticancer drug, plus semiannual mammograms. "It's not a perfect solution, but it's the one that works best for me," says Dorothy.

You may also be able to call in a health care adviser. A small but growing number of insurers and employers provide telephone consultation services that offer referrals, recommendations and even medical data to help you sort through options. More than a million Blue Cross customers in California, Kentucky, Oregon and Pennsylvania can call Personal Health Advisor, a free 24-hour hotline, to talk to registered nurses on topics ranging from whether to see a doctor about a rash to how to find a top specialist. You also can get specialized information from a research service, such as Planetree (415-923-3680), a medical library that's affiliated with California Pacific Medical Center in San Francisco. For the price of a phone call, they'll refer you to support groups, such as the one that put Mary Lee Horton on the trail of a cure for her twins' blood disease. They'll also give you the names of doctors who have written studies on treatments for your condition. For a $20 to $100 fee, Planetree's researchers will even compile medical literature on your problem.

Keeping your costs under control.

Becoming a confident health consumer can automatically reduce your medical bills by encouraging you to rely on your own judgment rather than rushing off to see your M.D. According to studies by the actuarial consulting firm Milliman & Robertson, at least 10% of doctor visits are unnecessary. To help you distinguish between situations that merit professional care and those you can handle, get a self-care manual such as the two-volume *Healthwise Handbook and Healthwise for Life* ($18 per volume; Healthwise, 1602 W. Franklin St., Boise, Idaho 83701).

Learning to question your doctor's fees can save you a bundle if you are among the 58% of the U.S. population whose insurance coverage requires you to pay a deductible (typically $250 to $1,000 annually) plus 20% or more of costs, or the 15% that lack any health insurance. Studies show that charges

They Prodded an HMO For a Specialist

To a casual observer, Geneva Finn, 15, looks like any number of young women her age. But for two years, this Minneapolis teen has been afflicted by a bizarre medical condition that could have appeared in one of her beloved science fiction novels: Small lesions that turn to scars have been mysteriously appearing on her body. So far, none of the doctors who has examined her has been able to diagnose her ailment, let alone treat it.

As if that frustration wasn't bad enough, the Finns' MedCenters HMO at first refused to refer Geneva to a topnotch specialist. The HMO, which costs the Finns $6,000 a year in premiums and out-of-pocket expenditures, initially referred her to five MedCenter dermatologists. None could offer a certain diagnosis. But all expressed concern that the baffling lesions might be symptomatic of subtle degeneration in Geneva's muscle tissue and joints, a problem that could eventually threaten her life.

The HMO initially turned down the Finns' request to consult Peter Lynch, a respected dermatologist at the University of Minnesota's hospital. MedCenters approved two visits to Lynch only after the Finns hired a lawyer. Geneva's father Charles, 43, a fellow at the Humphrey Institute of Public Affairs, was furious. "We followed the rules, and they denied Geneva the care to which she was entitled," he says. "How could anyone make a 15-year-old girl endure such stress?"

The HMO then approved four more sessions with Lynch. Says Pam Lux, a spokesperson for HealthPartners, the company that owns MedCenters: "The process of referring Geneva to a specialist should have gone a lot faster. We'll do whatever it takes to help the family get her diagnosed." Meanwhile, Geneva's condition is worsening. She now has more than 70 lesions on her body. Still, the Finns are hopeful. Says Charles: "I'm convinced that now MedCenters will act with Geneva's best interest in mind."

for the same service can vary by as much as 733% from one physician to the next. In St. Louis, for example, a patient can pay from $15 to nearly $110 for a routine office visit, says Medirisk, a medical pricing firm based in Atlanta. Ask your doctor for a schedule of charges before you undergo any procedures. Then call at least two other area physicians to compare prices. If your doctor insists on a fee schedule that seems out of line, you should consider changing doctors.

It's getting easier to compare prices because some local consumer or business groups now compile price guides. In Atlanta, Boston, Pittsburgh and St. Louis, a $4 news-stand magazine called *Health Pages* lists fees for hundreds of local doctors, hospitals and insurance plans. There's also a quick way Medicare beneficiaries can spot excessive doctors' fees. Federal rules limit the amount doctors can charge Medicare patients. If your share of the bill comes to more than 31% of the total fee, you can conclude that you're being overbilled and tell your doctor that he is required to give you a refund.

Make sure you're collecting all the insurance payments you've filed to receive. If you have many medical bills and find it easier to keep records on your home computer instead of in folders, try claims tracking software such as ClaimPlus ($75; 603-726-4700). If you're unable to do this complex job yourself, and you're willing to pay a fee equal to 10% to 15% of your reimbursements, you could hire a claims filing service such as Medical Insurance Claims (800-355-2662).

You can also control costs through your choice of coverage, particularly if you pay your own premiums. If you use a lot of medical services, look into an HMO where comprehensive care is covered at a flat rate. A family of four might have to pay about $400 a month for an HMO but would face few out-of-pocket costs. If you don't need much

medical care, consider a traditional policy but sign up for the highest deductible you can afford. A major-medical policy might cost a family of four $371 a month with a $500 deductible but only $190 a month with a $2,500 deductible. The $181 monthly savings ($2,172 a year) can be set aside to help cover any bills you do incur. And you may be able to trim premiums by as much as 50% by cutting out smoking, losing weight or reducing blood pressure or cholesterol levels. Agents and insurers usually won't volunteer such cost-saving strategies, so make a point of asking what you can do to trim premiums.

Getting the coverage that you need.
The simplest way to deal with claim denials by health insurers is to resubmit your claim, adding a bit more information. According to the Medicare Beneficiaries Defense Fund, a consumer group, 78% of Medicare claims that are denied at first get paid fully or partly on the second try and 67% make it on the third. If you are clearly entitled to a denied benefit, all you probably need is persistence. Your insurance company may even be willing to pay benefits not included in your policy if the insurer believes it will avoid more expensive treatment down the road. Examples are outpatient psychotherapy and rehabilitative services, both of which could forestall a big-ticket hospital stay some day in the future.

If you believe that you can make such an argument, don't hesitate to talk to a supervisor and try negotiation. Managed care can become a battleground when patients are unsatisfied with the plan's doctors and want their insurer to pay for care available outside of the network. If you may need a high-risk, high-cost treatment, you can appeal to the Medical Care Ombudsman Program (call 301-657-0404). The organization enlists independent doctors to review patients' cases and intervene on their behalf when appropriate, often for free.

4

How to Retire Sooner With More

Estimating How Much You'll Need

Weighing an Early Retirement Offer

Shield Your Stash From the Taxman

Making Your Money Last a Lifetime

America's Top-Rated Spots for Retirees

Gains and Pains of Retiring Abroad

Many people imagine their retirement years in terms of a spacious condo, perhaps adjacent to a manicured fairway, leisurely afternoons driving balls on the back nine, and fat monthly dividend checks. Dream on. Unless you begin saving and investing now, chances are you will be forced to reduce your standard of living in retirement or to work far longer than you'd like. According to one MONEY poll conducted jointly with Oppenheimer Management, a New York City investment firm, few working Americans are taking the steps they should to turn their retirement aspirations into reality. For example, our poll found that 73% of adults between the ages of 21 and 64 expect to retire comfortably and 74% plan to do so before age 65. Yet less than half of those questioned are investing in assets that are likely to provide the money they will need. To cite one disturbing fact, nearly as many have purchased lottery tickets for retirement (39%) as have invested in stocks (43%).

So just how much money will it take to ease you on down the road? Take, for example, a 35-year-old man earning $50,000 who lacks a company pension or savings plan. He will need to amass the equivalent of $1 million over the next 30 years to retire comfortably at age 65 and support his lifestyle to age 90. Yet 73% of respondents estimated their investment needs to be far lower (usually 33% to 50% lower). Moreover, three out of five believe they will be able to live on less than 70% of their pre-retirement income— the minimum required, according to many experts in the field. Warns Oppenheimer chairman Jon Fossel: "The average American may end up with less than half the money he or she will need in retirement."

This chapter aims to help you bridge that yawning money gap. You will learn, for example, to determine how much your retirement lifestyle will cost and when you should consider leaving work. We will show you the merits of various types of retirement plans and how to assess a corporate severance or early retirement package. We also provide concise answers to the complicated questions that haunt many retirees. Top of the list is how to make one's savings last a lifetime.

Get real about retirement planning.

The nation's largest single age cohort—77 million baby boomers born between 1946 and 1964—will not glide gently into their so-called golden years unless they step up their savings pace. For one thing, they probably will receive a less generous stipend from Social Security than their parents' generation. By 2030, when most baby boomers will have retired, there will be only two workers paying into Social Security for every retiree, vs. a ratio of 3.2 to 1 today. Unless Washington beefs up Social Security financing or reduces its benefits, the system will start running in the red by the year 2019. Indeed, the cutbacks have already started. The portion of Social Security payments subject to federal income tax has risen from 50% to 85% for married couples filing jointly whose total income exceeds $44,000 ($34,000 for singles), a level that is not indexed to inflation. Thus by 2010, assuming 4% inflation, that levy will apply to any married couple making more than the equivalent of $24,000 today.

Dwindling Social Security payments are not the only financial hurdle confronting baby boomers. Rising taxes are likely if the government does not cut spending, notes economist Laurence Kotlikoff at Boston University. Says he: "If Congress does not take action to cut the deficit and slow health care spending, the baby-boom generation could face tax hikes of as much as 40% in retirement." Increasing health care costs also seem certain for baby-boomer retirees because, sooner or later, Congress must hack away at the ballooning

Medicare/Medicaid budget, lately $252 billion. Reduced corporate retirement benefits are likely too as businesses continue to slash costs to remain competitive.

Affording a gracious retirement will be even more difficult for women because they tend to live longer than do men. Today's 40-year-old female is likely to live to the age of 80, compared with only 74 for a 40-year-old male. As a result, a woman needs a larger nest egg than a man to maintain the same level of investment income through retirement. At the same time, she may have a harder time accumulating what she needs. Women earn 30% less than men, on average, and they are also less likely to hold jobs that offer a company retirement plan. Single and divorced women are most at risk because they are less likely to share a spouse's benefits and full Social Security income. An Oppenheimer study found that the typical single woman in her thirties who lacks a pension will retire with only 20% of the income she needs.

Don't reach for the Prozac yet.
Consider this heartening example from a computer model designed by consulting firms WEFA Group and Arthur D. Little for Oppenheimer. Assume that a successful married couple in their early thirties earn $65,000, have a company pension and savings plan and get steady wage hikes of 1.5% above inflation each year. If inflation averages 3% for the next 30 years, they would be earning the equivalent of $155,000 in today's dollars when they reach retirement at 67. Since their total outlays, including taxes, should be 20% to 30% lower in retirement, they could probably maintain their pre-retirement standard of living on an annual income equal to roughly $109,000 today. But look what happens if they save and invest like most Americans in their income bracket, putting away only 5% of their pretax salary each year. They shouldn't

Money Helps

Q. My wife is thinking of leaving her company after 10 years. She wants to take care of our two young daughters, ages three and six months, and return to work later. She has a vested pension, but her benefits guide states that she is ineligible for retirement benefits if she leaves the company before she reaches the age of 55. Didn't Congress pass a law that allows an employee to leave with pension benefits after a certain period of employment?

KEHN BACON, HOUSTON

A. The Tax Reform Act of '86 generally gives workers full credit for pension benefits that they've accumulated after five years on the job or partial credit for benefits earned after three years. But an employer doesn't have to pay the pension until you reach customary retirement age, usually 65 (at your wife's company, 55). She may have one shot at getting her money early. If the plan permits, and if your wife's benefit totals less than $3,500, her employer may choose to cash her out, just to avoid future bookkeeping hassles.

figure on generating more than $62,000 a year in income, including pension and Social Security. That would leave them roughly $47,000 a year shy of what they need.

What would it take to prevent such a shortfall? According to WEFA and Arthur D. Little, if the couple promptly reapportion their investment mix so that 84% of their assets is in stocks and triple their savings to a conscientious 15% of income, their annual retirement income would nearly double to

$120,000. And by stashing more of their savings in tax-deferred accounts, such as 401(k)s and IRAs, the couple could get a full 100% increase in retirement income. The easiest way for most investors to try to accumulate such retirement riches is through mutual funds, which conveniently allow you to put away regular amounts of money. Before you call for prospectuses, consider the following retirement fundamentals.

It's never too soon to start saving.
While you probably have some kind of savings plan in place already, there's a good chance it's not enough. Today the national savings rate stands at a mere 4%, which is only half that of 20 years ago. Says Stanford University economics professor Douglas Bernheim: "To avoid a steep decline in living standards when they retire, baby boomers must triple the amount they are saving today."

Of course, the exact amount that you decide to sock away depends on several factors, including your age, the generosity (or stinginess) of your company's retirement benefits, the amount you have already saved and your income goals. For a rough idea of your savings target, you should take time to complete the worksheet "The Tab for Retiring in Style" later in this chapter. On average, a man in his thirties should be setting aside a little over 10% of his salary. One who waits until his forties ought to aim for 15% or more. And women, with their longer life expectancies, may need to be even thriftier.

You can probably put away a lot more than you think. Start by scrutinizing your budget. Do you really need to eat out three nights a week? Or even twice? Can you forgo that luxury coupe for the less costly sedan? And what about basic, money-saving moves such as shopping at warehouse clubs or improving your home's energy efficiency? Many families can save 10% or more just by cutting back on unnecessary expenditures. Before you start locking away that newfound money, however, make certain that you have built up an emergency cash reserve equivalent to three to six months' worth of expenses. You should keep that money in a safe account (such as a short-term CD or money-market fund) where you can get your hands on it quickly and without penalty. Once you get your savings plan under way, keep it in the groove by signing up for an automatic investing plan, authorizing your fund company to transfer a fixed amount every month from your bank account to funds of your choice. Most fund groups offer such automatic investing programs. And many will waive or reduce their investment minimum if you agree to make automatic monthly contributions of as little as $50 a month.

Shelter your savings from Uncle Sam.
A tax-deferred savings plan, such as a 401(k) or an IRA, can speed you along the road to retirement wealth. Not only can you get an immediate tax deduction for your contribution, but over the years, the effects of tax-deferred compounding can be awesome. Here's an example. If a 35-year-old earning $60,000 a year routinely contributes 6% of his salary to a taxable account earning 8% a year, he would have $185,744 by age 65 (assuming a 30% tax rate). But if he were to invest that money in a tax-deferred account, he would amass a hefty $407,820. And even if he then withdrew the entire amount and paid taxes at a 30% rate on the proceeds, he would still be ahead by 54%.

Many investors, however, do not take full advantage of their opportunities to shelter money. A recent survey of employers by accountant KPMG Peat Marwick found that only 61% of eligible workers participate in 401(k)s even though nearly 85% of employers match their contributions (typically 50¢

on the dollar up to a specified percentage of salary). Thus if your employer offers a 401(k), put in the maximum allowed. If you truly cannot afford to contribute the maximum, at least put in enough to get the full matching amount offered by your company.

What if you have no pension or company retirement plan? Self-employed people can use SEPs (simplified employee pensions) that allow you to defer taxes on 15% of your annual income, up to $30,000. A business owner can set up a Keogh plan. The three types are defined-benefit, profit-sharing and money-purchase, and you are allowed to contribute anywhere from 15% of gross income to $120,000. And don't overlook the humble IRA. Even though Congress has limited the deductibility of IRA deposits, you can still write off some or all of your contribution if you're not covered by a retirement plan at work or if you're married and have an adjusted gross income below $50,000 ($35,000 for single taxpayers). Even if you can't get an IRA deduction, you could still contribute $2,000 annually ($2,250 for married couples with one working spouse) and watch those earnings grow tax deferred.

Power your portfolio with stocks. The most effective way to build your retirement portfolio is to invest in stocks rather than bonds and cash. Over the past 68 years,

You're Fooling Yourself About Retirement

Although a majority of Americans profess to be preparing for a financially secure retirement, most lack the investment knowledge necessary to achieve their goal. That's the troubling conclusion of a national poll about retirement planning conducted for MONEY and Oppenheimer Management by the Wirthlin Group in McLean, Va. Wirthlin interviewed 1,238 adults ages 21 to 64 who had not yet retired. The outfit also surveyed 504 retirees age 65 and over. The margins of error on these surveys are plus or minus 2.8 and 4.4 percentage points respectively. Here are some key findings:

◆ **You often exaggerate about planning.** An overwhelming 95% of those polled say that retirement saving should start as early as possible, with more than 60% stating that people should begin putting away money before age 25. More than 70% say they regularly set aside money directly from their paychecks. Of those eligible to contribute to a 401(k) or other retirement savings plan, nine out of 10 say they participate. Respondents claimed to be stashing away an awesome 15% of their income. Of course, polls only report what people say they do. According to KPMG Peat Marwick, only 61% of eligible employees participate in their 401(k)s. That alleged 15% saving rate is also more hot air than cold cash. Government figures show that the national saving rate is hovering at only 4% of after-tax income. "People often forget their debts when they calculate savings rates," notes Oppenheimer chairman Jon Fossel. "It won't do you much good to save 10% if you're also running up a huge balance on your Visa card."

◆ **You seem to have a block against stock.** Asked to name the investment that delivered the highest returns over the past 30 years, only 36% correctly chose stocks. More than 40% picked low-returning, fixed-income investments, such as CDs and bonds. Many investors also believe stocks are far riskier than they really are. Nearly half think that most stock investors "get wiped out" at least once in their lifetime. In truth, stocks have never lost money when measured over every 20-year holding period since 1926.

◆ **You put too much faith in real estate.** When asked which asset would provide the highest returns over the next 20 years, only 29% of poll respondents picked stocks while 25% chose real estate. And an overwhelming three-quarters think that buying a house is one of the best ways to save for retirement. In fact, most investment experts figure real estate will struggle to stay ahead of inflation. Farther out, things could get even uglier. Warns Stanford economics professor Douglas Bernheim: "When the baby boomers reach retirement age and all try to sell their houses, the market may drop because there will be insufficient demand from the generations behind them."

stocks have returned an average of 10% annually, twice the 5% returns for long-term Treasury bonds. And cash investments like Treasury bills merely matched the inflation rate at 3%. Yet the MONEY/Oppenheimer poll found that less than 25% of the typical household's assets are currently invested in stocks, compared with roughly 50% in fixed-income assets, and the rest mainly in real estate.

True, stocks are likely to deliver a bumpy ride along with those higher average returns. Thus the percentage of your retirement portfolio that you devote to stocks should depend on your ability to tolerate the roller-coaster movements of the market. If you are at least 20 years from retirement, however, consider putting 60% or more of your assets in stocks because you will have many years to recover from any market swoons. Even if you have recently retired, you should keep about 40% in stocks. That's because you will need inflation-whipping growth to make your money last for the next 20 or more years.

To diversify right, purchase a variety of stocks including blue chips for relatively stable returns and small companies for zippy gains that have averaged 12% annually over the past 68 years. To add even more variety, spice up your mix with overseas stocks. Many investment experts predict that foreign stock markets are likely to outpace the U.S. over the remainder of this decade by two to four percentage points a year. As for the fixed-income portion of your portfolio, consider a no-load, low-cost fund that holds a mixture of government and corporate bonds. High-income investors might earn better after-tax returns in a muni fund.

Your smooth-running retirement plan requires regular tune-ups. You should plan to re-evaluate your investments once a year. Adjust your portfolio if needed, selling assets that have surged beyond your intended allocation and buying those that have slumped below. With a few adjustments and a bit of luck you can still look forward to sipping mai-tais alongside that manicured fairway.

Estimating How Much You'll Need

You know you must save regularly and invest wisely to have enough money for a worry-free retirement. But how much is enough? Instead of panicking about falling short or having to catch up, think about how your life will change when you leave work and then estimate the cost of that lifestyle.

The traditional rule of thumb that retirees need 80% of their pre-retirement income may not hold true for you. You may consider it a hardship to have to make do with less just when you have time to enjoy the fruits of years of work and savings. On the other hand, some frugal people may find they need

no more than 50% of their pre-retirement income. Health care aside, Americans over 65 spend 25% to 40% less than younger people do on food, clothing, housing, transportation and other everyday expenses. Whether to aim for 50% or 120% of your pre-retirement income depends on how you hope to live after you stop working. Do you envision a retirement of travel, two homes and a country club membership? Or quieter years making do with one car and fewer dinners out? Moreover, with retirement possibly lasting as long as 30 years, don't forget that your living costs will diminish as you age. Expenses tend to be highest for young retirees who travel extensively. Older retirees typically spend less on such discretionary items as well as necessities (except health care).

To find out the dollars and cents of all this, start with the worksheet "Your Costs After Calling It Quits" on page 100. Then let the worksheet "The Tab for Retiring in Style" on page 102 guide you to an annual savings goal based on your anticipated retirement lifestyle, your current savings and your expected pension and Social Security benefit. For example, housing (**line 1** in "Your Costs After Calling It Quits") will continue to be your biggest expense even if you don't have a mortgage. Figure that property taxes, homeowners insurance, utilities and upkeep will cost you no less than they do now unless you move to a smaller house or to a lower-cost area.

Your food costs (**line 3**) may decline 25% or so in retirement if you eat out less (obviously you won't continue to buy lunch at work every day). Transportation costs (**line 4**) will drop because you will no longer incur commuting expenses. And you may find that you don't need to replace a car so often or even keep two, especially later on. Unless your job never required pricey suits or dresses, you can expect to shave 20% to 35% off clothing costs (**line 2**). How much travel and entertainment costs (**line 12**) may change depends on your tastes. If retirement means that you'll be going on long trips, budget for them, since travel is often retirees' single biggest new expense.

Chances are (you hope) you will have finished paying for your children's education by the time you retire. But think about whether you want to take courses yourself (**line 7**). You may also want to help grown children buy a home or pay for their children's schooling. Members of the so-called sandwich generation may have to budget money for the care of their aging parents (**line 16**). As for

loan payments (**line 10**), financial planners suggest that you reduce credit-card and other debt while you are still working.

Life insurance costs (**line 8**) usually go down or, in the case of disability insurance, disappear in retirement, since you typically will no longer have earnings from work to protect. Your income from investments, including those in retirement plans, doesn't need to be safeguarded by life insurance. Nor does your pension plan because federal law requires that a surviving spouse be paid a reduced benefit—unless he or she has formally waived it. On the other hand, you may decide that you need life insurance to provide liquidity in your estate or supplement a small pension for a surviving spouse.

Your biggest savings on taxes (**line 15**), assuming that you don't work in retirement, will be the Social Security and Medicare tax on wages. In addition, some states exempt some income from Social Security benefits and pensions from taxes. But don't look for many other breaks. Under the new federal tax law, for example, as much as 85% of your Social Security benefits may be taxable, depending on your overall income.

Trying to predict medical expenses (**line 9**) is tough because you don't know what health problems you may face or the outcome of the health reform debate. Nonetheless, for purposes of the worksheet, assume that health care costs could be higher. In addition, early retirees may face higher medical costs until they qualify for Medicare at 65 if they have to buy their own insurance, which can cost a couple $6,000 a year. Also figure on your health costs staying high after 65 because of higher out-of-pocket medical expenses and insurance premiums. For example, a supplemental Medicare policy could run as much as $3,500 a year. And don't forget routine dental costs, which may mount with age and are unlikely to be covered by insurance.

Your Costs After Calling It Quits

While nearly everyone looks forward to retirement as a time of doing exactly as one pleases, there are as many ways to pursue your pleasures as there are people. That's an important retirement planning point, because the stuff of your post-working-life dreams—be it Caribbean cruises, relocating to the sunbelt or simply working on your golf score—helps determine how much money you should be putting toward those goals now. The rule of thumb among financial planners and benefit consultants is that you will need an annual retirement income amounting to roughly 70% to 80% of your family's current earnings.

Whatever the life style you envision, the best way to ensure that you can pay for it is to plan as far ahead as possible. The first step is to determine what your annual expenses are likely to be. The worksheet on the facing page is specifically designed to help you do that. Despite the diversity in retirement living, financial planners surveyed by MONEY note at least some similarities in spending patterns after age 65. For example, most retirees spend about the same amount on food, gifts, charitable contributions and personal care as they did while working. Medical and dental bills, on the other hand, are significantly higher, depending on how generous your company's retirement coverage is. Here are some general guidelines to help you fill out the worksheet on the right.

◆ **Line 1:** If you pay off your mortgage and take care of all necessary maintenance problems before you retire, housing costs should drop by as much as 25% to 30%. Count on even more shrinkage if you sell your house and buy a smaller one. Condominium owners and renters should factor in maintenance-fee and rent increases. And anyone who plans to spend more time at home should anticipate higher utilities charges.

◆ **Line 2:** Financial planners estimate that if you are moving from business suits to jeans, you can expect to reduce clothing expenses by 20% to 35%.

◆ **Line 4:** Scratch commuting costs. Other transportation expenses will increase if you intend to be very active. Planners recommend that two-car couples keep both autos during retirement, especially if both are fairly active.

◆ **Line 6:** Most people keep giving the same amounts to charitable, political and educational institutions, as well as to family members outside the immediate household. But the overall figure drops, usually by the amount you used to give at the office.

◆ **Line 7:** If your kids will be grown by the time you retire, you can eliminate education expenses, unless you plan to help pay your grandchildren's college bills. And if you intend to return to school yourself, check into reduced tuition costs for senior citizens.

◆ **Line 8:** There will be little change in your payout for property, liability and auto insurance, but retirees can generally reduce their life insurance coverage by at least 50% or, if their spouses are fully provided for under their pension plan, eliminate it altogether.

◆ **Line 9:** If you are currently covered by a company health plan, expect medical and dental costs to spurt by about 50% because of increased illnesses combined with reduced insurance coverage. Medicare pays part of doctors' fees and hospital bills. Check your company's coverage for retirees.

◆ **Line 10:** You should plan to be debt-free by the time you retire, thereby eliminating loan repayment expenses.

◆ **Line 12:** How much you spend for entertainment depends on how active you are. Expect such expenditures to rise an average of about 20% during your retirement.

◆ **Line 13:** Be prepared to budget for higher veterinary bills if you will have an aging dog, cat or other pet.

◆ **Line 14:** While your contributions to pension plans cease at retirement, many financial planners encourage clients to continue setting aside about 10% of their income as a hedge against inflation.

◆ **Line 15:** If you don't work, it's farewell to Social Security (FICA) taxes. Also check laws in your state because some don't tax income from retirement plans. The conventional wisdom that you will be in a lower tax bracket after retirement is no longer true for high earners. You will be taxed on up to 50% of your Social Security benefits if the total of your adjusted gross income, nontaxable interest, and half your Social Security benefits exceeds $25,000 ($32,000 if you are married). If that total is over $34,000 ($44,000 for couples), you'll owe tax on up to 85% of benefits.

◆ **Line 16:** With more adult kids expecting financial help from Mom and Dad and Americans' increasing longevity, you could be contributing to the down payment on a child's first house while paying for a parent's nursing home.

Total current expenditures should equal approximately 100% of your current before-tax income. By dividing your total expenditures at retirement by your current gross income, you will arrive at the percentage of your current income that you will need in retirement.

EXPENDITURES	AT RETIREMENT	CURRENT YEAR
1. Housing. Rent, mortgage, property taxes, utilities (gas, oil, electricity and water), telephone, home furnishings, household services, maintenance, improvements	_____	_____
2. Clothing. Purchases and cleaning	_____	_____
3. Food. (including tobacco and alcohol)	_____	_____
4. Transportation. Car repair and maintenance, installment payments, gas, commuting costs, other	_____	_____
5. Gifts.	_____	_____
6. Contributions.	_____	_____
7. Education.	_____	_____
8. Insurance. Life, medical, auto, property, liability	_____	_____
9. Medical and dental care. Premiums, deductible and out-of-pocket costs	_____	_____
10. Loan repayment costs.	_____	_____
11. Personal care. Grooming, health club, other	_____	_____
12. Entertainment. Vacations, dining out, movies, plays, concerts, sports events, cable TV, videocassettes, entertaining, sports, hobbies, other	_____	_____
13. Pet expenses.	_____	_____
14. Investments and retirement savings. Contribution to company plans, IRAs, Keoghs, SEPs and other investments	_____	_____
15. Taxes. Federal, FICA, state, local	_____	_____
16. Support of relatives.	_____	_____

TOTAL EXPENDITURES. (add lines 1 through 16) _____ _____

TOTAL CURRENT EXPENDITURES DIVIDED BY CURRENT GROSS INCOME. _____ _____

TOTAL EXPENDITURES AT RETIREMENT DIVIDED BY CURRENT GROSS INCOME. _____ _____

The Tab for Retiring in Style

The worksheet at right will tell you how much you need to start saving now to hold on to your standard of living in retirement. The multipliers used in lines 7, 9 and 11 allow for inflation by assuming your investments will grow at three percentage points over the inflation rate, before and after retirement. This keeps all figures in today's dollars.

◆ **Line 3:** You and your spouse can easily keep tabs on what you have coming to you. Just call Social Security (800-772-1213) and ask for a copy of its Personal Earnings and Benefits Estimate Statement (PEBES) request form. Two to three weeks after submitting it, you'll get a free statement that notes your annual earnings to date and estimates your monthly Social Security benefit if you retire at age 62, 65 or 70. If you're 60 or older, you can spare yourself a telephone call. Between now and Sept. 30, 1995, the folks at Social Security are sending a benefits statement to everyone age 60 and over who isn't already getting checks from the agency. Then, after September, anyone who turns 60 will get a statement during the year of his or her 60th birthday.

◆ **Line 4:** Your company benefits department may be able to estimate your pension. Make sure the estimate assumes that you continue working until your retirement age at your current salary. That will understate your likely eventual payout but will keep the figure in today's dollars.

◆ **Line 7:** The multipliers in column A incorporate the cautious assumption that men will live to 90 and women to 94—longer than 85% of them do now. Single men should use the multiplier under "men." Women and married couples should use the one under "women," since wives usually outlive their husbands.

◆ **Line 8:** Your personal retirement portfolio includes any investments you have specifically earmarked for retirement, aside from your IRA or Keogh. For your employer-sponsored savings plans, check the most recent statement from your 401(k), profit-sharing, thrift or stock ownership plan and total your vested balance in each.

◆ **Line 12:** Consult the annual statement from these plans to find the amount your company contributed on your behalf to each of the plans last year. Enter the total.

1. Current gross income _____

2. Annual income needed in retirement, in today's dollars (70% of line 1) _____

3. Annual Social Security retirement benefits _____

4. Annual pension benefits _____

5. Guaranteed annual retirement income (line 3 plus line 4) _____

6. Additional retirement income needed (line 2 minus line 5) _____

7. Capital required to provide additional retirement income (line 6 times multiplier from column A at right) _____

8. Amount you have saved already

_____ + _____ + _____ = _____
personal retirement portfolio   IRA/Keogh   employer-sponsored savings plans   total savings

9. What your current investments will have grown to by the time you retire (total from line 8 times multiplier from column B at right) _____

10. Additional retirement capital required (line 7 minus line 9) _____

11. Total annual savings still needed (line 10 times multiplier, column C at right) _____

12. Annual employer contributions to your company savings plans _____

13. Amount you need to set aside each year (line 11 minus line 12) _____

AGE AT WHICH YOU EXPECT TO RETIRE	MULTIPLIER A	
	men	women
55	22.1	23.5
56	21.8	23.2
57	21.4	22.8
58	21.0	22.5
59	20.6	22.1
60	20.2	21.8
61	19.8	21.4
62	19.3	21.0
63	18.9	20.6
64	18.4	20.2
65	17.9	19.8
66	17.4	19.3
67	16.9	18.9

TIME UNTIL YOU EXPECT TO RETIRE	MULTIPLIER B	MULTIPLIER C
1 year	1.03	1.000
3 years	1.09	.324
5 years	1.16	.188
7 years	1.23	.131
9 years	1.30	.098
11 years	1.38	.078
13 years	1.47	.064
15 years	1.56	.054
20 years	1.81	.037

Don't expect to stop saving because that's one of the only ways that you can counteract inflation. Experts recommend that you plan to save up to 10% of your income annually in the first few years after you stop working. Moreover, in your early retirement years, you might take a part-time job to supplement your income from pensions and taxable investments. That way your tax-deferred accounts can keep on growing to cover unexpected costs and provide income in late retirement when you stop working altogether.

Now fill out the worksheet "The Tab for Retiring in Style" (at left) to determine how much you must set aside every year until you stop working. As the line-by-line instructions specify, you'll need estimates of your future Social Security benefit and your company pension. If you're close to retirement, your company benefits department may be willing to project a pension benefit that's based on your planned retirement age, which will be more accurate than one based on your current years of service.

You'll most likely find that your pension and Social Security won't equal your expected retirement living costs. For example, if you retired last year and were earning $60,600, the maximum wage that's covered by Social Security, your government benefit would have replaced about 27% of that amount. If you had earned $85,000, that Social Security benefit would have made up only about 19%. Note that early retirees now collect 80% of the full benefit if they start receiving checks at age 62. That percentage will decline to 75% in 2005 and 70% in 2022 as the age for full benefits rises. Don't count on your pension to pick up what Social Security doesn't cover. What you collect will be based on years of service and your salary over the past three to five years on the job. Pensions typically replace about 30% of pre-retirement salary and rarely increase with inflation.

Don't Rely Solely on Your 401(k)

More and more Americans are counting on their 401(k) company savings plans to help them achieve a comfortable retirement. And to be sure, the 401(k) is one of the best ways to save for your future. But don't make the mistake of expecting the program alone to fund your retirement. A close examination of these plans shows that 401(k)s are likely to provide you with a lesser lifestyle than you would get from a traditional pension. By taking the right steps now, however, you can bridge the gulf and retire in comfort.

While traditional defined-benefit pensions remain available at many large companies, 401(k)s are becoming an increasingly important source of retirement income for millions of workers. The number of 401(k)s offered by U.S. employers as their primary retirement plan climbed 257% between 1985 and 1990, the most recent time frame for which figures are available, according to the Employee Benefit Research Institute, a public policy think tank. Meantime, the number of traditional pension plans has dropped 33%. By 1997, 401(k)s and other so-called defined-contribution plans will account for an estimated 43% of retirement assets, up from 30% a decade earlier. A defined-contribution plan can be a sweet deal because it lets you put away money for retirement on a pretax basis. And unlike a defined-benefit pension, your payout from a 401(k) doesn't depend on how much time you've slaved away for a single employer. In a typical 401(k) plan, you can set aside annually as much as 13% of your salary on a pretax basis, to a maximum of $9,240. (The amount rises annually with inflation.) Best of all, most companies match employee contributions (generally 50¢ on the dollar) on up to 6% of salary. "By the turn of the century, 401(k)s will be the backbone of the private retirement system," predicts Theodore Benna, a pension consultant who created the 401(k) savings plan in 1980.

But a 401(k) is no substitute for a pension. Many 401(k) plans carry high, hidden fees and will also leave you short if you retire early. More important, a 401(k) has no set benefit. Retirees can expect a pension to provide them with a fixed monthly check (say, 35% of final salary after 30 years on the job). But the size of your 401(k) cash-out at retirement depends on how much you invest in the plan and how wisely you manage your own account. And most people don't put nearly enough into their 401(k)s to provide for a cushy retirement, or they invest the money too conservatively. Worse, many participants reduce their retirement stash by cashing in their 401(k)s while still working. Here in greater detail are the ways 401(k) programs pale in comparison to traditional pensions. We also offer advice about what you should be doing to help secure your retirement.

They're not as well funded as pensions.

To be sure, a defined-benefit pension plan is far from perfect. To get the biggest pension benefits, you must spend 20 or 30 years with a single employer, since the benefits are typically based on your years of service and final salary before retirement. But with a defined-benefit pension, your employer does all the saving. Most of the money that goes into a 401(k) plan, by contrast, comes out of your own pocket, limiting the amount you can save outside the plan. And more money goes into pensions, which let companies develop formulas that provide more generous benefits. Employer contributions to defined-benefit pension plans run 10% to 12% of payroll. In generous 401(k)s, both employee contributions and employer matches typically average only about 7% of employees' annual pay. Even workers who want to save the maximum 13% of pay that many 401(k) plans allow may be stymied. That's because tax laws that originally were designed to keep 401(k)s from favoring highly paid workers limit contributions by anyone earning more than $66,000.

Their returns tend to lag pensions.

On average, 401(k)s deliver lower investment returns than pensions. The financial consulting firm Frank Russell estimates that companies need to put in just $18 for every $100 they'll pay out in pension benefits because they can expect investment gains to provide the other $82. "It could take two to three times as much to produce the same level of benefits in a 401(k)," says Eric Russell, the firm's director of defined-contribution services. The chief explanation for the difference is that 401(k) investors tend to be more conservative than pension managers. At last count, 27% of 401(k) assets were held in GICs (guaranteed investment contracts), which promise a fairly modest fixed return. Only 16% of 401(k) money was diversified among stocks, which have compounded 10% annually since 1926. Pension funds, by contrast, kept just 2% of their assets in GICs and had 54% of their money in stocks.

Employees who want to optimize returns and reduce risk by diversifying often have the odds stacked against them. While pension funds can spread their portfolios among lots of different investments, nearly a fifth of 401(k)s give investors only one or two choices. Many 401(k) plans entice employees into loading up on company stock, discouraging diversification. For example, defense contractor General Dynamics matches dollar for dollar the contributions that go into company

Money Helps

Q. My wife left her job at Inland Crop Dusters and wants to roll over her 401(k) into an IRA. But she couldn't shake the money loose from the company for eight months. What recourse do 401(k) participants have if their former employers delay paying?

ROB ARNESON, WASCO, CALIF.

A. The answer to your question highlights the often overlooked fact that employees still don't have many rights these days. The law requires only that the company pay out 401(k) funds to participants once they reach retirement age. That's right. Even if you are tossed out the door tomorrow, a company could technically hang on to your money until you are age 65. (Of course, you would continue to earn interest along the way.) Fortunately, most plans including your wife's at Inland voluntarily cough up your dough if you quit or get a pink slip—but usually at their own speed. Your spouse's 401(k), for instance, states only that such payments should be made "as soon as it is administratively feasible," according to Stan Nishikubo of Pension Services Corp., which keeps the books for the 401(k). But there's another catch. It turns out that Inland, not Pension Services, actually invests the money, a fairly common practice at small companies. Noel Wilson, Inland's president, says he didn't disburse your dough sooner because he needed time to determine which investments to sell in order to minimize any effect on the holdings of the other 10 employees in the plan. Your only recourse is to do what you did—pester the company with letters and phone calls until it hands over your cash.

stock but puts in only 50¢ for every dollar directed to the company's seven other investment options. Some 18% of employers report they fully or partially match worker contributions only in their company's shares.

Their fees are often exorbitant.

In fact, your 401(k) money gets eaten up by expenses that may be more than twice as high as those charged to pension plans. Employers, not their employees, pay their pension fund managers annual fees averaging just 0.4% of assets. In a 401(k), employees often pay these costs, and it's not uncommon for them to be docked an annual fee of 1% to 1.5%, sometimes as much as 3%. Some 401(k)s, particularly at small firms, also hit you with sales loads of up to 4% or surrender charges of as much as 8% when you withdraw the cash upon switching jobs or, worse, because your employer changes managers. And 401(k) charges are increasingly coming directly out of employees' pockets. More than 40% of companies now require their employees to pick up part of the tab for 401(k) plan expenses, up from just 28% in 1990. Some plans also charge participants $50 to $100 to take out loans against them.

They can clobber early retirees.

Call it quits at 62 with a traditional pension, and you're likely to get from your employer 80% to 100% of the benefit you would get if you waited till 65 to retire. With a 401(k), however, you bear the full cost of cashing out early. First, your pot of retirement savings is smaller than it would otherwise be because you will be eliminating three years of potential contributions. Second, you'll have to stretch your 401(k) money over three more years of retirement. Thus a person who retires at 62 with a 401(k) would wind up with 10% to 15% less than a person who retires at 62 with a pension, assuming they both would receive the same amount upon retirement at age 65.

The challenge for anyone who has a 401(k) is to get the biggest return you can out of the plan and to supplement it with other retirement savings. You should try to move on the following fronts:

Invest to the max in your 401(k).

If, like many eligible workers, you're not participating in your firm's 401(k), go to your benefits department and join up. If you are contributing, you probably ought to try to put in the maximum your company allows—or at least the maximum that your employer matches. Matching can make even mediocre returns look outstanding. But don't go overboard on company stock. Financial planners say that if you have 10 years or more before retirement, you should keep no more than 10% to 25% of your 401(k) in company stock.

Ask your firm for better choices.

A decent plan will offer at least four options. If yours has fewer, complain to your benefits manager. The latest wrinkle for some employers is to offer "lifestyle funds" that package several investment options into a single portfolio tailored to various ages or risk-tolerance levels. You should be aware of the fact that your employer has one incentive to add to its portfolio selection. New federal rules offer employers protection against lawsuits if their 401(k)s perform poorly as long as the firms offer at least three investment choices and meet certain other requirements.

Lobby hard for a traditional pension.

Employees often don't fully appreciate the value of the pension benefit and the cost to the company. Reason: in contrast to a pension, a 401(k) shows you just how much you're receiving on a quarterly basis. So if you want your company to keep its pension plan or start a new one, make sure your boss knows that. Silence could result in a less golden retirement.

Weighing an Early Retirement Offer

In 1991, Michael Yendrzeski and 5,800 other Eastman Kodak employees as young as 47 received buyout offers they felt they couldn't refuse. The package included full pensions, health insurance for life, two weeks' salary for each year of service and bridge payments of as much as $900 a month until they could collect Social Security at 62. Yendrzeski, then 50, walked away from his job as a senior product engineer with $400,000 counting a $900-a-month bridge benefit. With Michael pulling down $900 or so a week as a consultant and his wife Deborah earning $25,000 a year as a dental hygienist, the couple's annual income recently totaled nearly $73,000. And the lump sum from Kodak is quietly growing in a tax-deferred IRA. "We're living just as well as ever but our total assets have tripled," says Yendrzeski. "For me, the only question was, why would anyone not do this?"

That same question now must haunt the Kodak workers who didn't take the offer. Two

See the Difference a Few Years Make

Even a generous early-out package won't make up for the bigger pension you'd earn by staying on the job. In the table below, we analyze an offer to a 55-year-old who earns $50,000 and has worked 20 years for a company. The package adds five years to both his age and years of service, which gives him the pension he would normally get at 60, and pays him an additional $6,800 for seven years. That's two-thirds of his expected Social Security benefit at 62. The table shows that if he turns down the deal and works until 60 or 62, he will boost his annual retirement income by as much as $8,891—namely, $6,891 in additional pension, $1,600 from his fatter 401(k) and $400 from his higher Social Security benefit.

Age	Income with retirement at 55 without the package	Income with retirement at 55 with the package	Income with retirement at age 60	Income with retirement at age 62
55	$9,073	$21,177	$51,500	$51,500
56	9,073	21,177	53,000	53,000
57	9,073	21,177	54,600	54,600
58	9,073	21,177	56,300	56,300
59	9,073	21,177	58,000	58,000
60	9,073	21,177	17,354	59,700
61	9,073	21,177	17,354	61,500
62[1]	19,273	24,577	27,754	33,468
63	19,273	24,577	27,754	33,468
64	19,273	24,577	27,754	33,468
65	19,273	24,577	27,754	33,468

Note: The table assumes that the employee's pension is based on his five highest years of earnings, that he gets 3% annual pay hikes, and that he contributes 3% of salary to his 401(k), which he annuitizes at retirement. [1]Social Security kicks in. **Source**: Kwasha Lipton

How the Plans Stack Up

Plan	Available to	Best for	Maximum contribution	Tax break on contributions/earnings	Matching contributions	Charges/fees	Early withdrawal[6]	Number of investment options
401(k)	Employees of for-profit businesses	Everyone who qualifies	15% of salary, up to $9,240[1] in 1995	Yes/Yes	Anywhere from 0% to 100%,[3] but typically only up to 6% of salary	Depends on plan/annual expenses of 1% to 1.5% of assets[4]	Only in case of hardship	Three to 10, typically, depending on your employer's plan
403(b)	Employees of nonprofit organizations	Everyone who qualifies	20% of gross salary or $9,500, whichever is less	Yes/Yes	Generally not available	Depends on plan/annual expenses of 1% to 3% of assets	Only in case of hardship and employee contributions only	One to 10, typically, depending on your employer's plan
IRA	Anyone with earned income	Those who don't have company pension plans or who have put the maximum into their company plans	100% of wages up to $2,000; $2,250 if joint with spouse	Sometimes/Yes	None	Depends on investment/zero to $50 annual fee	Always permitted	Nearly everything except real estate, collectibles and other hard assets
SEP	The self-employed and employees of small businesses	Self-employed person who is a sole proprietor	13% of net self-employment income, or $22,500, whichever is less[2]	Yes/Yes	None	Depends on investment/$10 to $30 a year	Always permitted	Same as IRA
PROFIT-SHARING KEOGH	The self-employed and employees of unincorporated small businesses	Small-business owner who is funding a plan for himself and employees	Same as SEP[2]	Yes/Yes	None	Depends on investment/up to $2,000 in annual administrative expenses	Always permitted	Unlimited
MONEY-PURCHASE KEOGH	Same as profit-sharing Keogh	Small-business owner who wants to shelter more than allowed by profit-sharing Keogh	20% of net self-employment income, or $30,000, whichever is less[2]	Yes/Yes	None	Same as profit-sharing Keogh	Always permitted	Unlimited
DEFINED-BENEFIT KEOGH	Same as profit-sharing Keogh	Self-employed person nearing retirement who needs to set aside a high percentage of income	Maximum needed to fund $120,000[1] annual benefit, or three years' average income, whichever is less[2]	Yes/Yes	None	Depends on investment/$2,000 to $4,000 annual expenses	Always permitted	Unlimited
VARIABLE ANNUITY	Anyone	Someone who has put the maximum into other plans and won't need the money for 10 years	None	No/Yes	None	6% to 8% surrender charges[5]/annual expenses of 2% to 2.2% of assets	Always permitted	Anywhere from one to 22, but typically nine
FIXED ANNUITY	Anyone	Someone who has put the maximum into other plans and shuns risk	None	No/Yes	None	Surrender charges of 6% to 8%[5]	Always permitted	One

Notes: [1]Estimate [2]Small-business owners fund the SEPs and Keoghs of their employees. [3]Percentage of employee's contribution [4]Some plans charge $20 to $30 annual administrative fees. [5]Surrender charges last six to eight years and typically decline by 1% a year. [6]All plans are subject to 10% income tax penalty, except in case of death or disability.

years later, the company began involuntary layoffs that, by the end of this year, will reduce its work force by 10,000. Those getting the ax received a far less generous goodbye than the 1991 departees. The deal: up to a year of severance but no pension boosts and health insurance for just four months.

There's a costly lesson for employees of Kodak and other big corporations in the enduring era of buyouts. If you're offered a package that looks reasonable, take the money and run because a less generous deal may come your way in a year or two. And it may not be voluntary. How likely are you to face a buyout? If you're over 55 and a manager in a shrinking industry such as manufacturing or retailing, employment experts rate your chances at about one in four.

Companies generally use two types. First are early retirement offers made to workers of 55 and over. If you get one and you're lucky, it will include an enhanced pension such as Kodak's '91 deal. On the other hand, you might be presented with one that doesn't give you a bridge to Social Security or excludes health insurance. The number of downsizing companies that offer early retirement incentives fluctuates widely from year to year. One reason: these packages tend to be relatively expensive and must conform to elaborate federal nondiscrimination rules. As a cheaper alternative, employees of all ages are offered arrangements called voluntary separation packages. They typically add up to enough to tide a family over for a year at most.

Accepting either variety of buyout may make sense. First, however, you will need to explore these key issues to help determine whether the offer works in your favor.

What real choices do you have? Under federal law, you can't be forced to take a package. But the law doesn't prevent an employer from later firing you, eliminating your job, demoting you, cutting your pay or otherwise making you wish that you had taken the buyout. So before turning it down, make sure your company wants you to stay. For example, if your boss seems happy with your performance and the offer is company-wide, you can probably afford to ignore it. If your boss is unhappy, or the offer is targeted at a specific division or department, you ought to give it serious thought. Another tension heightener is that you usually won't have more than two or three months to think things over. If you feel you must take the package but worry that you aren't financially prepared to leave work, you might read the crash-course book *Retirement: Ready or Not* by New York financial planner Lee Rosenberg.

What to look for in early-out deals. In an offer extended only to employees older than 50 or 55, an employer will usually adjust your pension to make it bigger than you'd otherwise deserve. We're talking about a traditional defined-benefit pension. Vested money in a profit-sharing or 401(k) savings plan will be yours whenever you leave work. The most common pension adjustment technique is to add several years to your age, length of service or both so as to fatten your payout. Your company may also provide a financial bridge to Social Security that equals some or all of the payments you will be eligible to receive from the government starting at 62. If you're bridged from age 60, for example, the effect is like starting to get your Social Security checks two years early.

What to look for in separation deals.
Here you get only a cash incentive to leave, usually two or three weeks' salary for each year of your service, up to a maximum of a year's pay. A poor package might include only a week of pay for each year of service, or the offer might top out at 26 weeks and

Money Helps

Q. I am 71 years old and would like to retire. My expenses total about $1,200 a month. Each month I get $700 from Social Security, $50 from a Nuveen tax-exempt bond fund and $250 from my $38,000 IRA, which is now invested in growth and income stock funds. I have $60,000 in a savings account and my $62,000 condo is paid off. I need a safe investment for the next 30 years to accommodate my long-life genes. My mother died at age 98—in an accident. So you can understand my concern.

DOROTHY HARRIS, GAITHERSBURG, MD.

A. Sounds like you could be destined to be immortalized by TV weatherman Willard Scott, assuming he lasts as long as you do. Along the way, however, your finances could get pretty tight. Even now, with your biggest stash sitting in a bank account earning maybe 3.5% a year, you would have a monthly income shortfall of about $25. To bridge the gap and keep up with even minimal inflation of 3.5% a year, you'll have to get a bit more aggressive with your $60,000 in savings. Not too much though because you really can't afford to lose a penny. We recommend you split the $60,000 account in four equal parts. Buy a money-market fund (some pay as much as 4.9%); a no-load intermediate bond fund such as Benham Treasury Note Fund (recently yielding 7.1%); a conservative no-load stock fund such as Vanguard Windsor II (up 7.9% annually over the past three years and yielding about 3.5%); and a real estate mutual fund such as Cohen & Steers Realty Shares (up 15.6% annually over three years and yielding about 5.9%).

give you no health insurance. A good deal might offer as much as a month of pay per year plus health insurance for a year or more. In addition, if you're vested in your company's pension plan, you'll get it when you reach your employer's regular retirement age.

What if you don't have to accept.
Having to decide whether to volunteer for a package comes down to this question—can you afford to retire? Even if the buyout, plus your other assets, gives you enough to meet your short-term financial needs, you may not be able to finance all of your retirement years, particularly if your prospects for getting another job are dim. And bear in mind that even the most generous deal won't deliver the same income you would get by staying on until normal retirement. One reason is that your pension rises with your salary. After retirement, however, most pensions don't keep up with inflation. (Refer to the table "See the Difference a Few Years Make" on page 107 for an example of the advantages of hanging on to your job.)

What about health coverage.
While lots of early retirement offers include lifetime health insurance, voluntary severance packages typically don't. Of course, you always have the right to continue in your firm's medical plan for 18 months at your own expense. After that, you'll have to buy private coverage, which can cost as much as $5,000 a year if you're over 50, until Medicare kicks in at 65. If you're not healthy, you may not be able to obtain any coverage.

What about earnings in retirement.
If you have prospects of another job or plan to start your own business, you may have more latitude to accept an offer that isn't perfect, particularly if you have a working spouse. Consider the example of LaMarr Hamilton, 54, of Vista, Calif. He had worked as an IBM computer

technician for 26 years when he took a voluntary severance package. IBM offered him a year's salary of $45,000 plus full health, dental and life insurance. At 55, Hamilton could start collecting a $1,380-a-month pension. If he died before his wife Sally, 52, she would receive $700 a month for life. Bolstered by $350,000 in assets, Sally's $20,000 income as a medical secretary and the guarantee of another job, LaMarr decided to take the offer. Now earning $43,000 as a computer technician for a retailer, he has invested much of his buyout cash in stocks. He expects his investments to grow to $1.5 million by 2002, enabling him to retire early with an income of at least $3,000 a month. That's 80% of his old IBM salary.

Shield Your Stash From the Taxman

It's a frightening thought. You're ready to grab the retirement money you built up over your 25-year career, and you suddenly realize that this could be the largest single amount you'll ever see. When a lump-sum pension, 401(k) and other corporate savings plans are totted up, workers can walk away with $1 million or more. Thus your first task is to keep as much of it as possible from the IRS. But beware that your distribution has a short fuse. If you fritter away more than 60 days after receiving the money before deciding what to do with it, the amount may be subject to a 10% penalty as well as federal tax.

You have two ways to ease the blow. You can take the money and use a tax-cutting technique called special averaging. Or you can roll over your payout into an IRA and postpone paying the tax until you withdraw the money, presumably when you'll be in a lower tax bracket than you are now. Which method is better depends mostly on the size of your settlement and how long you have until you stop working altogether. Before making a choice, you need to understand the main points of both approaches.

Opt to average over five or 10 years. You may qualify for either five- or 10-year averaging, depending on your age. Both can yield after-tax results that are far more favorable than paying up in a single year. As the name suggests, this legerdemain computes your tax as if you received the distribution over a five- or 10-year period. There are entry rules, however. To use averaging, your lump-sum distribution must meet the following four requirements. It must be:

◆ From a qualified pension, profit-sharing or Keogh plan in which you participated for at least five years. Your plan administrator can tell you whether the plan qualifies.

◆ The entire balance due you from all of your employer's qualified plans.

◆ Paid to you within a single tax year. For example, if you retire this year and pay taxes on a calendar-year basis, you must receive your entire balance by Dec. 31, 1995.

◆ Paid after you turn 59.5. The age test doesn't apply, however, if you were born before Jan. 1, 1936.

If you meet all those tests, you can apply averaging to the taxable portion of your lump-sum distribution. This includes your employer's contributions to your account and its earnings over the years—but not your own nondeductible contributions. The taxable amount is listed on the Form 1099-R that you will receive from your employer.

If your distribution is less than $70,000, part of it is absolutely tax-free thanks to the minimum-distribution allowance. This break exempts 50% of the first $20,000 of a lump-sum distribution from tax. As the payout rises above $20,000, however, the tax-free portion phases out. At $30,000, $8,000 is tax-free. At $40,000, it's $6,000. At $50,000, it's $4,000. At $60,000, it's $2,000. And at $70,000 or more, it's zero.

The tax on the rest of the distribution is figured using grade school math. First, you divide the remaining distribution by five. Next, find the tax on the result using the rates for single taxpayers; the rates are listed in the IRS instruction booklet for filing your annual tax return. Finally, multiply that tax by five. Let's say you receive a lump-sum distribution of $180,000 that includes no nondeductible contributions by you. The payout is too big to benefit from the minimum-distrib-

ution allowance, so the entire amount will be taxable. Using five-year averaging, one-fifth of $180,000 is $36,000. Tax on that amount is about $7,214. Multiplying $7,214 by five gives you a tax bill of $36,070. Without using averaging, the tax could run as high as $71,280 (39.6% of $180,000).

If you were born before 1936, you may use 10-year averaging, which works the same way as its five-year cousin except that you divide and multiply by 10 instead of five. There's one catch, however: With 10-year averaging, you must use the higher and more steeply graduated 1986 tax rates for singles, which ranged from 11% to 50%.

If you qualify for five- and 10-year averaging, use Form 4972 to figure your tax both ways and choose the one that results in the lower bill. You might also compare it with what your tax would be if you didn't use averaging. If the difference is small and you don't plan to quit working altogether, you might want to pay the regular tax. Reason: you can use averaging only once. If you expect a bigger lump-sum distribution from another qual-

Check Your Social Security Benefits

Are you worried that you won't get all the Social Security benefits you're entitled to when you retire? If not, maybe you should be. The Social Security Administration recently discovered a computer glitch that shortchanged 426,000 retirees by some $478 million over a 10-year period. These retirees will have to wait up to six months to get reimbursed. But you can avoid a similar hassle by keeping tabs on what you have coming to you.

Just call Social Security (800-772-1213) and ask for a copy of its Personal Earnings and Benefits Estimate Statement (PEBES) request form. Two to three weeks after submitting it, you'll get a free statement that notes your annual earnings to date and estimates your monthly Social Security benefit if you retire at age 62, 65 or 70. If you're 60 or older, you can spare yourself making a telephone call. Between now and Sept. 30, 1995, the folks at Social

Security are sending a benefits statement to everyone age 60 and over who isn't already getting checks from the agency. Then, after September, anyone who turns 60 will get a statement during the year of his or her 60th birthday.

Check the figures carefully. Of the 1.2 million people who in the past year questioned their earnings reports, the agency confirmed errors in 13,000 cases. To avoid getting less than you deserve, request a PEBES every couple of years while you still have an accurate record of your recent earnings to compare it against. If you find a mistake, call 800-537-7005 to talk to a Social Security representative. Be prepared to send proof of your earnings to correct it. Incidentally, officials say they hope that in the year 2000 the agency will start mailing to everyone a free benefits statement every year. That's assuming, of course, that Social Security benefits will still be available in the year 2000.

ified plan in the future, you might postpone taking advantage of averaging until you retire for good. Your tax can be even lower if you were born before Jan. 1, 1936 and earned retirement benefits before 1974. In that case, you may treat part of the payout as a capital gain and pay a flat 20% tax on it. That can be a bargain compared with current income tax rates of up to 39.6% and the top capital-gains rate of 28%. Your employer will tell you how much qualifies.

The case for tax-free rollovers.

To postpone taxes on your lump sum, you can roll it over into an IRA and let the money grow tax deferred until you withdraw it. If you wish, you can stash the distribution in two or more IRAs, for example, putting part in a stock fund and the rest in a bond fund. If you have a Keogh retirement plan set up with self-employment earnings, you can fend off the IRS with a rollover and keep your five- or 10-year averaging. Invest your company-plan distribution in the Keogh. Then, if you later take a lump-sum distribution from it, you can use averaging to figure the tax.

The basic rollover rules are simple. It must be completed within 60 days of receiving the distribution. The money can then be placed in a new or existing IRA. If your lump sum is paid in installments over the calendar year, the 60-day rule applies to each of the payments. If you are unlucky enough to miss the deadline, you'll owe tax on all the money plus a 10% penalty if you're under age 59.5. Once made, the rollover can't be revoked. Ask your employer to transfer the money directly to the IRA of your choice. If you make the rollover yourself, 20% of the payout will be withheld under IRS rules, and you will have to claim a credit on your next tax return to get it back. Worse, if you're under 59.5, you'll have to pay the nonrefundable 10% early-withdrawal penalty on the 20%

unless you make it up out of your own pocket. Don't include your after-tax contributions to the plan or lump-sum severance pay in the rollover. If you do, the IRS will levy a 6% excise tax on the excess amount.

You should keep in mind that you don't have to roll over your entire distribution. You can take some of the money and pay regular tax on it plus a 10% penalty if you're under 59.5. (In this case, however, you can't use averaging.) The amount rolled over will still escape taxes until withdrawn from your IRA. You must report a rollover on line 16 of your 1040 but only for information purposes. If not, the IRS will assume you're omitting income and send you a bill for additional tax.

Which distribution method is better?

Don't rush into either one blindly. Remember too that a rollover merely postpones the tax man's inevitable payday. In fact, if you are in a higher tax bracket when you withdraw the money, a rollover could actually wind up costing you more than simply paying your tax when you take your distribution. Before electing a rollover, have your tax pro or financial planner compute the current tax on your lump-sum distribution using one or more of the methods described earlier. Compare this amount to his or her estimate of the tax you'll pay on future distributions from an IRA. Make sure your pro takes into account the money you'll earn in the IRA.

Chances are the rollover will win hands down. Consider a new retiree who at age 62 receives $250,000 from his company's 401(k) at the start of this year. He plans to let the money grow at 6.5% annually in an IRA until age 72 and then withdraw the money gradually over the next 15 years. He expects to be in the 34% federal and state bracket during those years. Thus his best bet is clearly a rollover. The $250,000, undiminished by taxes, will grow to $440,643 by the time he turns 72. By contrast, with 10-year averaging, his after-tax $205,882 (his $250,000 payout minus an immediate tax of $44,118) will increase to just $300,471 at age 72.

By choosing a rollover, you'll avoid the 15% tax penalty on what the government deems to be excess annual distributions from a retirement plan—$148,500 at last count.

(The amount rises each year with inflation.) Alternatively, you can take an amount that doesn't exceed the excise tax limit and shield the rest in an IRA. Of course, you may need all the money immediately. In that case, you should pay the tax using averaging and be assured that you've done all you can to shield your precious lump from tax meltdown.

Making Your Money Last a Lifetime

Your retirement dream is being in a position so comfortable that you can lavish gifts on your children and grandchildren. Your retirement nightmare is being in such dire straits that you must live off your offspring or, worse, the kindness of strangers. You're far from alone if the nightmare haunts you more than the dream inspires you. The No. 1 fear of many retirees is that they will outlive their assets. In reality, you don't have to be a millionaire or a miser to ensure that your money will last as long as you do. But you do have to take to heart the strategies that follow.

Consider working at least part time. In the event that you leave your current job in your fifties or early sixties, your retirement kitty probably won't be big enough for you to start drawing it down immediately and still have enough left over to last as long as you do. So by all means look for work preferably in a field where you can use your skills. By saving your earnings and allowing them to grow unmolested, you'll have a bigger fund to draw on when you stop working altogether.

Don't collect Social Security early. If you're 62 to 64, you couldn't have earned more than $8,040 last year and still received your full Social Security check. The penalty for earning more is a stiff 50¢ deducted from your benefit for each dollar in salary you made above $8,040. Retirees age 65 or older could have earned as much as $11,160 and collected full benefits. The penalty for earning more is 33¢ on each additional dollar. (The dollar limits increase annually with inflation.) After 70, there's no benefit loss no matter how much you make. Thus if you aim to earn more than the dollar limits but don't want to lose any of your benefit, put off collecting Social Security until you're at least 65. That way you will eventually receive fatter Social Security checks. For example, if you wait until age 65 instead of starting to collect your benefit at age 62, you will receive 100% of your full benefit rather than 80% of it.

Invest in stocks. A common delusion among people planning retirement is that they can make their assets last their lifetime simply by putting everything in bonds or CDs and living off the interest. That unfortunately won't work because fixed-income investments pay too little (only 5% a year on average for the past four decades) and leave you undefended against inflation's corrosive effects. Even at 4% a year, inflation can slash

the real value of your retirement money in half in just 18 years. As a result, you may have to invest about half of your assets in stocks to maintain the value of your portfolio over the long haul. Moreover, if you put the bulk of your assets into fixed-income securities, your stocks will have to perform spectacularly well for your portfolio to maintain a steady total return over many years. Let's say that you sink 80% of your stash into bonds and only 20% in stocks. If inflation averages 4% a year, your stocks must return a breathtaking 23% to ensure that your entire portfolio will grow 7%. Fat chance. Stocks historically have returned about 10% annually.

Dip into your principal.

This is an issue if you don't have enough income-producing assets to generate all the cash you need to supplement your pension and job earnings year after year. How do you do this without going broke? The best solution involves investing to maximize your total return (both capital gains and income) and then withdrawing a fixed percentage of your assets each year. For example, if you needed $40,000 to supplement your Social Security and pension benefits, and your nest egg totaled $500,000 including investment income, you would spend 8% of it. To determine how much of your assets you can spend each year without running out of money, hire a financial planner to crunch the numbers for you. Do the calculations several times with different assumptions about inflation and investment returns to figure out how far your money would stretch under various scenarios. To make sure it will last as long as you're expected to live, check the actuarial tables found in IRS Publication 590, *Individual Retirement Arrangements*, and Publication 939, *Pension General Rule* (for free copies call 800-829-3676). For example, if your portfolio were worth $500,000 when you began your retire-

Money Helps

Q. My widowed mother plans to remarry. Before Dad died, he put his estate into a revocable living trust. Mom is living off the interest of part of the trust, while another portion will go to her kids. Mom claims that if she remarries, the part of the estate held for the kids can never be touched by her new husband. She says she wants us to have the money Dad left for us. Shouldn't she sign a prenuptial agreement?

NAME WITHHELD, SAN JOSE

A. Sounds like Mother knows best. Revocable living trusts are meant to defer taxes and ensure that the kids eventually get something. Husband and wife put all their assets in the revocable trust, so called because it can be changed or dissolved by either spouse until one dies. Upon the death of the husband or wife, the estate is divided into two or more separate components. In this case, there's an "A" part (the mother's money) and the "B" portion, for the kids. The B part would typically hold $600,000, because that sum equals the federal estate-tax exemption. Estates larger than six hundred grand suffer a 37% to 55% tax bite.

In theory, the mother spends the A portion while the assets in B go to the kids upon her death. Let's say, however, the mother leaves her A wad to the kids. They would pay no estate tax on any amount up to $600,000 because her estate, like the B trust, would qualify for the $600,000 exclusion. Thus the family is able to pass $1.2 million to the kids without federal tax. The B trust remains separate legal property even if your mother remarries.

America's Top-Rated Spots for Retirees

The best places to retire are Prescott, Ariz.; Fairhope, Ala.; Mount Dora, Fla.; Las Vegas; and Chapel Hill, N.C. That's the consensus of a board of seven experts (see below) who helped MONEY choose the top retirement locations in the U.S. We first asked the experts what retirees want when they relocate. From the answers, we drew up a wish list of 10 attributes led by low crime rate, mild climate, affordable housing, attractive environment, proximity to cultural and educational activities, strong economic outlook and excellent health care. We then asked the experts to rank the 20 towns in America that best fulfilled the wishes. With their final responses, we awarded points on a sliding scale of 20 for a No. 1 choice down to one point for a No. 20.

You'll find our choices ranked in the table at right along with vital information about each, such as cost of living, average home price, tax rates and weather. What these places have in common is an abundance of available activities for today's retirees, who tend to be as energetic as when they had full-time jobs. Indeed, the idea of retirement is changing as more people leave the work force younger (the median retirement age is now around 63, down from 67 in the early 1950s) and stay healthy longer. "Retirement used to be viewed as an extended vacation," says Mark Fagan, a professor in social work at Alabama's Jacksonville State University who has studied retirees for a decade. "These days it's seen as an opportunity to pursue neglected hobbies, take a part-time job or become involved in community activities."

Each year about half a million Americans in their sixties make the move to new hometowns. For many this is the first time they have been able to choose a community they actually like, rather than one that is merely close to work, the right schools or a convenient commuter train. And the choice can be most invigorating. Of course, a place must suit your personal style, cautions Peter Dickinson, a member of our panel. He advises that before you put down cash for a new house, you should spend six months to a year visiting your prospective new community in as many seasons as possible. You can meet potential neighbors, shop in local markets, sample recreational facilities, get a sense of local politics and feel the fluctuations in the weather. Clear, mild days in Las Vegas, for instance, might seem lovely in February when there are 10 inches of ice and snow back home. But a summer of temperatures consistently over 100 degrees might make you long again for your northern environs.

MONEY's board of experts. These specialists helped us determine the top places to retire: Peter Dickinson, author of *Sunbelt Retirement* ; Norman Ford, author of *The 50 Healthiest Places to Live and Retire in the United States* ; Alan Fox, publisher of *Where to Retire* magazine (713-974-6903); John Howells, author of *Where to Retire* ; Saralee Rosenberg, co-author of *50 Fabulous Places to Retire in America* ; David Savageau, author of *Retirement Places Rated* ; and Robert Tillman, producer of the *Retirement in America* video series (for details, call 800-755-6555).

City and chamber of commerce phone number	Population	% of population over 65[1]	Nearest big city (miles away)	Cost of living vs. the national average[2]
1. Prescott, Ariz. 602-445-2000	28,211	22.5%	Phoenix (90)	+6%
2. Fairhope, Ala. 205-928-6387	9,000	23.3	Mobile (20)	0 to −5%
3. Mount Dora, Fla. 904-383-2165	7,500	27	Orlando (25)	0 to −6%
4. Las Vegas 702-735-1616	920,000	13	Phoenix (180)	+5%
5. Chapel Hill, N.C. 919-967-7075	41,524	13	Durham (8)	+4%
6. Naples, Fla. 813-262-6141	19,505	29	Fort Myers (30)	+1% to +11%
7. Sedona, Ariz. 602-282-7722	7,898	32	Flagstaff (27)	+6% to +11%
8. Palm Springs, Calif. 619-325-1577	41,674	26	Los Angeles (110)	+19%
9. Aiken, S.C. 803-641-1111	20,534	16	Augusta (20)	+1%
10. Fayetteville, Ark. 501-521-1710	42,962	10	Tulsa (115)	−9%
11. Kerrville, Texas 210-896-1155	18,068	30	San Antonio (60)	−6%
12. Brevard, N.C. 800-648-4523	5,476	19	Asheville (30)	+2% to +8%
13. Durango, Colo. 303-247-0312	13,091	11	Albuquerque (215)	+5% to +10%
14. Asheville, N.C. 704-258-3858	63,598	19	Greenville, S.C. (70)	+5%
15. Myrtle Beach, S.C. 803-626-7444; 800-356-3016	25,676	13 in county	Charleston (95)	−5%
16. St. George, Utah 801-628-1658	38,000	15 to 25	Las Vegas (120)	0
17. Hendersonville, N.C. 704-692-1413	7,403	23 in county	Asheville (22)	+5% to +10%
18. Sequim, Wash. 206-683-6197	4,075	52	Seattle (130)	+1% to +3%
19. Charleston, S.C. 803-577-2510	83,095	15	Savannah (120)	+3%
20. Clayton, Ga. 706-782-4812	1,613	29	Greenville, S.C. (86)	−7% to −10%

[1]Latest available figure from U.S. Census Bureau data or the area's local chamber of commerce. [2]Range is given to approximate the cost of living when the actual figure is unavailable. From ACCRA, the American Chamber Commerce Researchers Association. [3]Arizona allows a deduction of up to $8,400 for all residents 65 or older. [4]Alabama

Two-bedroom house or condominium					
Average monthly rent	Average cost	Average property tax	Highest state income tax rate	Sunny days per year	Special features
$800	$115,000	$1,000	7% over $300,000[3]	300	Four museums; three performing arts facilities; outdoor sports in 15-square-mile Granite Mountain wilderness area
$400- $600	$80,000	$300- $400	5% over $6,000[4]	219	Adult Recreation Center organizes dances, bridge games and social events.
$400- $600	$65,000- $70,000	$900- $1,000	No income tax	238	Boating, sailing and other water activities are available on six-mile-long Lake Dora.
$875- $1,150	$110,000- $115,000	$640- $670	No income tax	293	Opera, dance, symphony and major sports events; 197 gambling casinos draw top entertainment ranging from Frank Sinatra to the Bolshoi Ballet.
$800- $900	$100,000- $180,000	$1,000- $1,500	7.75% over $100,000[5]	217	University of North Carolina at Chapel Hill has a major sports center, an art museum and a planetarium.
$1,100	$80,000 (condo)	$650	No income tax	267	Forty golf courses; seven miles of beaches and shoreline with prime fishing, sailing and snorkeling; Philharmonic Center for the Arts attracts world-class talent.
$1,150- $1,350	$150,000- $200,000	$1,000- $1,500	7% over $300,000[3]	264	Picturesque Coconino National Forest; acclaimed art galleries
$850- $900	$92,000- $103,200 (condo)	$1,100- $1,300	11% over $424,760[6]	313	Door-to-door senior citizens bus service; 82 golf courses; McCallum Theater features top national tours.
$400- $850	$40,000- $85,000	$500	7% over $10,800[7]	218	Horse racing, polo, symphony, dance and theater
$500	$60,000	$375	7% over $25,000[8]	218	Theater, art exhibits, sports events and continuing education at the University of Arkansas
$750	$60,000- $80,000	$1,000	No income tax	224	Cowboy Artists of America museum and major touring entertainment
$350- $500	$68,000- $95,000	$513	7.75% over $100,000[5]	218	Pisgah National Forest has 200 miles of trout-fishing streams and 300 miles of hiking trails; Brevard Music Center attracts world-class musicians.
$850	$80,000- $110,000	$680- $750	Flat 5% on all taxable income[9]	300	Purgatory-Durango Ski Resort has nine lifts, 70 trails; historic Durango-Silverton narrow-gauge railroad operates during spring and summer.
$550- $750	$68,000- $95,000	$1,000 in city; $500 outside	7.75% over $100,000[5]	214	Scenic mountains, gorge, forest and parks nearby; cultural events at Asheville Civic Center
$450- $650	$70,000- $85,000	$650	7% over $10,800[7]	212	Top country-music concerts, 60 miles of beaches and 80 championship golf courses in the vicinity
$750	$85,000 (condo)	$550	7.2% over $7,500[10]	293	Hiking, climbing and picnicking in Snow Canyon State Park, Zion National Park and Joshua Tree Forest; concerts, ballet and opera
$400- $500	$68,000- $95,000	$513	7.75% over $100,000[5]	218	Lectures, classes and travel for retirees sponsored by Opportunity House, an organization for retirees; top summer-stock theater at Flat Rock Playhouse
$800	$120,000	$1,440	No income tax	303	Hiking and bird watching at seven-mile-long wildlife preserve, Dungeness Spit; cultural activities and art classes at Museum and Arts Center
$540	$85,000- $110,000	$600- $1,000	7% over $10,800[7]	212	Nine museums, historic houses and plantations; 32 annual festivals including Spoleto U.S.A., a 17-day showcase for performing arts
$350- $450	$80,000- $87,000	$700	6% over $10,000[11]	217	White-water rafting on Chattanooga River; classes and cultural events at Hambidge Center educational facility

exempts pensions. [5]North Carolina excludes up to $4,000 of pension income for retired residents and gives credit for the elderly, based on income. [6]California gives all residents 65 or older a $64 tax credit. [7]South Carolina exempts $10,000 of pension income for all residents 65 or older. [8]Arkansas excludes the first $6,000 of pension income for retired residents or gives nonpensioned residents 65 or older up to $60 tax credit. [9]Colorado exempts the first $20,000 of retirement income for all residents 55 or older. [10]Utah exempts up to $7,500 of pension income for all residents 65 or older. [11]Georgia exempts up to $10,000 of retirement income for all residents 62 or older. Real estate data provided by Century 21.

ment, your assets earned 5% annually and you spent $40,000 a year, your money would be gone in 21 years. Increase your return to 7%, and your money would last 31 years.

Tap taxable accounts first. This will allow tax-deferred accounts to grow undisturbed as long as possible. The law requires you to start making withdrawals from IRAs and 401(k)s once you reach 70.5. To calculate the minimum withdrawal necessary to satisfy Uncle Sam, divide the value of all your tax-deferred accounts by your life expectancy according to the IRS actuarial tables. Penalties are severe if you don't take out enough—50% on the amount you should have withdrawn but didn't.

Gains and Pains of Retiring Abroad

First the good news. Jane Parker, co-author with Allene Symons of the guide *Adventures Abroad*, figures that a couple can live in some foreign retirement Edens for a third to a half the cost of an equivalent lifestyle in the U.S. "You can manage comfortably for $1,800 to $2,000 a month in Portugal or $1,000 to $1,200 in Mexico," she estimates. On those budgets, you could afford a spacious home in a middle-class neighborhood, buy fresh food in open-air markets, dine out on local delicacies and attend plays and concerts for $8 or less. Weighing factors that American retirees consider important when moving abroad, Lifestyle Explorations, a Boston company, says these locations as particularly attractive—Canada's Maritime Provinces (New Brunswick, Nova Scotia and Prince Edward Island), Costa Rica, Honduras, Ireland, Portugal and Uruguay. Before you pack, however, the experts recommend you make the following moves.

Look before you relocate. In choosing where to retire abroad, consider most of the same criteria that apply Stateside, including an affordable cost of living, amenable climate and good health care. To be sure your needs will be met, visit an area several times before retiring there even part time. Extended visits will also help you learn the locals' attitude toward Americans and whether cultural habits are compatible with your personal tastes. For a free packet of information about living in any of the places recommended by Lifestyle Explorations, call 508-371-4814.

Make sure your taxes don't rise. Many countries have higher federal tax rates than the U.S. (the top rate is 57% in France, for example). Find out whether you must pay taxes to your new country, to the U.S. or to both. IRS Publication 901, *U.S. Tax Treaties*, spells out agreements with 40 countries. Also check out IRS Publication 593, *Tax Highlights for U.S. Citizens and Residents Going Abroad*. (Call 800-829-3676 for free copies of both.)

Be ready to revamp your investments. Municipal bond interest, for example, may be tax-free only for U.S. residents; your new host country may tax it. And you may want to reduce your portfolio's volatility. Technology makes it a cinch to trade anywhere in the world. But you may be slow to catch market movements. "I have a general rule," says financial planner Malcolm Makin of Westerly, R.I. "The more exotic the culture you're moving to, the more boring your investments."

5

Investing in Your Family's Future

As you and your child search for the right college, keep in mind the findings of a poll of nearly 1,000 undergraduates that was commissioned by MONEY last year.

◆ **Costs curtail choice**. Rising tuition, up 46% at public schools and 32% at private schools over the past five years, forced two-thirds of respondents to make price a major factor in deciding where to enroll. Even the well-to-do are not immune: Half of them from families earning more than $100,000 a year said money affected their choice.

◆ **Course closeouts are common**. Two out of five students said they have difficulty getting into the courses they need to complete their majors, and half of those fear they will not be able to graduate on time. The problem was twice as common at public colleges as at private schools.

◆ **Teachers get high marks**. Nine out of 10 students polled said their professors were doing a good job. More than eight out of 10 said the professors were as accessible as the students wanted them to be.

◆ **Overall satisfaction abounds**. Most of the students said college met their expectations. About one-third reported most aspects of college were even better than they had expected. While 48% feel college is preparing them for life after graduation, another 44% say they feel only "somewhat" prepared.

Drawing on results of our poll and on advice from students and education experts, we have created the following insider's guide to what you should look for in a college to get the most education for your dollar.

Students like smaller better.

Participants in our poll who attended schools with fewer than 5,000 students were more positive about their learning experiences than those at larger institutions. Similarly, undergraduates at private schools, which tend to be small, reported more satisfaction than those at public schools. These students were more upbeat about the accessibility of professors and the quality of classroom experiences, housing, safety and preparation for life after graduation. Large universities, of course, may provide facilities and possibilities that are important to your child and not available at smaller campuses. Among them are photon microscopes or multiple libraries or arcane majors such as geodetic science.

Tour the campus, stupid.

Visiting a school before you commit to going there may sound obvious. But one out of five students in our poll reported that they never saw the campus until the first day of freshman orientation. These students end up less satisfied with their teachers, classroom experience, accommodations and opportunity to learn from fellow students than those who visited the campus before applying for admission. When you visit, pay attention to whether the atmosphere reflects your child's personality and aspirations. Are most students hanging out on the quad or studying in the library? How friendly are they? Do fraternities dominate campus life? Are the college's facilities well maintained? When possible, ask the admissions department to arrange for your child to spend a weekend in a dorm. "That's how you will really see what a student's everyday experience is like," says John White, a Caltech senior. "Look at the level of stress students have about their work, how difficult they feel the tasks that they've been given are, and how satisfied with college they are overall."

More work often means less study.

To survive economically, two-thirds of the students in our survey must hold down paying jobs while in school. Most work more than 10 hours a week. And those who do are markedly less positive about college than others. For instance, they give lower marks overall to their social lives and their ability to meet one-on-one with faculty. Half of the students who worked more than 21 hours a week said they could be learning more if they did not have jobs, compared with only one in four of those who worked under 10 hours. Students who worked less than 10 hours a week were generally as satisfied with college as those who did not work at all. There are alternatives worth considering. Encourage your child to increase job hours during the summer when there are no school conflicts. And check out the availability of study jobs on campus. This is work that often has slow periods during which students can study. These positions are usually service jobs, such as checking books out of the library, assisting in a lab or serving as a police dispatcher.

Time in classes is well spent. We asked students to rank seven learning methods in order of personal importance. Classroom time was No. 1, with 72% of respondents rating it most useful or very useful. Textbooks, small lab or discussion groups, and contact with fellow students were each considered most useful or very useful by about 64%. Meetings with instructors (59%), library research (50%) and internships (28%) followed. During campus visits, have your child sit in on one or two classes. Classes ideally should be small (20 to 30 students) especially in elective courses for juniors and seniors. Large lecture classes should break down at least once a week into small discussion groups led by full-fledged faculty members, rather than teaching assistants. And professors should be easily accessible after hours. In conversations with students, ask whether professors make themselves available informally, perhaps by eating lunch in student

Money Helps

Q. I heard of something called a family limited partnership that's supposed to protect your assets from creditors and make it easier to pass them to your heirs. Would you explain exactly what this is and whether it's a good idea?

LARRY THOMPSON, BOONVILLE, CALIF.

A. The family limited partnership (let's call it a FLIP) that you describe may sound too good to be true. But legal experts endorse this arcane device for families that have more than $1 million in assets. Here's how it works. The parents create a partnership with themselves as general partners and their eventual heirs (usually the children) as limited partners. They then turn over to it some or all of their assets. As general partners, the parents run the partnership and may initially own most of its shares. But over the years, they gradually transfer the shares to each kid in annual gifts that can amount to as much as $10,000 per parent (the most they can give without incurring federal gift tax). Since the IRS considers partnership shares to be relatively illiquid, the parents may be able to value them at 10% to 30% less than the actual worth of the underlying assets. This lets them transfer more wealth while they are alive and reduces any tax owed by their estate after they die. And a FLIP helps protect assets because the parents' creditors can seize only the portion of partnership shares that's in their names. FLIPs are complex. But if you are game to try one, you should expect to pay between $3,000 and $6,000 to set up the partnership and another $500 to $700 a year to maintain it.

dining halls. Find out how often professors are in their offices. Are they there at hours when students can conveniently visit? And do they encourage drop-in conversations?

Beware of course gridlock. If you have qualms about supporting your child through five or more years of college, you should try to determine whether students are having difficulty registering for required courses. According to our poll, this problem was most extreme at public schools. Nearly half the students at public schools said they had trouble getting into courses required for graduation, and one in four feared that closeouts would jeopardize their chances of earning their degrees in four years. By contrast, only 25% of private school students had problems enrolling in courses they needed to graduate. So, far from saving money, having your child enroll in a public school may in fact cost you an extra year of tuition. And financial aid typically ends after four years. Thus you should ask the admissions office or registrar what percentage of students graduate in four years and in five. If more than 20% of all graduates need five years, it could be that course closings prevent students from getting out on time. Inquire about the departments your child figures to focus on. How crowded are the classes, and are any cutbacks planned? A few schools such as DePauw in Indiana guarantee students will be able to earn degrees in four years or can stay for a fifth free.

The appeal of dormitory life. According to our poll, students who lived on campus were generally more satisfied with important aspects of college than those who did not. "It's an instant community," says Caltech's John White. Students with housing on campus also reported feeling more prepared for life after college than those living away from the school. The reason may be because students living together tend to share information such as how to study for exams, how to find jobs and how to apply for graduate school. In addition, campus life provides an opportunity for students to develop social skills during those all-night bull sessions about the meaning of life. So be sure to explore the various housing opportunities on campus and in the surrounding community. Find out about the availability of dormitory rooms. Inquire about special-interest rooming (dorm suites for, say, French language or physics majors). And check out the options for off-campus housing because living close to campus in a house full of other students may prove just as beneficial to your kid's educaton as being in a dorm.

The Best Education for Your Money

You're in for a pleasant surprise if you assume you can get a deal on your child's education costs only by being needy enough to qualify for financial aid. There are many other means of slashing thousands of dollars from college expenses. And none requires sacrificing the quality of their education. Granted, some strategies can be used only by outstanding students, such as attending an honors college at a leading state university (see "The Bargains Available for Bright Kids" at right). But other options will work for just about anyone, such as enrolling in a topnotch commuter college and living at home (see the box "Commuter Schools Worth the Drive" on page 125).

Of course, any of these strategies can

backfire if, just to save money, you push your child to attend a college that he or she dislikes. So first work with your son or daughter to identify appropriate colleges and then look for ways to cut the costs. Says college counselor Steven Antonoff of Denver: "If your child finds a college that's a good fit and also happens to be a good value, congratulations! You've been good shoppers." To achieve that goal, check out our top money-saving moves for students of all abilities and aspirations.

Accelerate your scholar's studies. A

year's expenses can be saved by acquiring a bachelor's degree in three years instead of four or a master's degree in one year instead of two. Finishing earlier also adds a year's salary to your offspring's lifetime earnings. Whizzing through college isn't easy, however. So only well-disciplined students should attempt it. "The kids who successfully pull this off are career-oriented and motivated to get out into the work force faster," says David Mason, a college counselor in North Brunswick, N.J. While nearly all schools allow students to speed up studies, about 175 offer three-year programs leading to bachelor's degrees. For example, 5% of the 3,200 full-time undergraduates at Bentley College in Waltham, Mass. ($20,640 annual cost) are in the three-year program, which requires them to take summer classes or extra courses during the regular academic year. Another spin: Clark University in Worcester, Mass. offers tuition-free fifth years (worth nearly $18,000) to freshmen who maintain grade point averages of 3.25 or better as undergrads and go on to earn master's degrees in the school's one-year program.

High school students can earn credits toward college degrees by taking rigorous Advanced Placement (AP) courses. Such courses culminate in three-hour exams scored on a scale of 1 to 5. The exams, administered

The Bargains Available for Bright Kids

Searching for a small, selective school that costs less than $15,000 a year? Look at the first-rate honors programs sponsored by major state universities. Raves college counselor David Mason: "Honors programs are superb. Students are exposed to great professors, attend classes with the same kind of bright, inquisitive kids who go to selective private schools, and often have a chance to take interdisciplinary courses that aren't open to other students." Among the best programs are those at Arizona, Arizona State, Bloomsburg, Clemson, Colorado, Delaware, Florida, Florida State, Georgia, Indiana, James Madison, Maine, Miami (Ohio), Michigan, Michigan State, New York (at Buffalo), Ohio, Ohio State, Pennsylvania State, Pittsburgh, Rutgers, South Florida, Texas, Utah, Washington and Western Washington.

Honors programs typically offer special classes or tutorials, seminars and cultural events and sometimes separate dormitories. Moreover, honors students are often permitted to register for classes before other students. That's an important perk at large public universities where courses required for graduation fill up fast. Getting into an honors college isn't easy, though. In general, an applicant needs a high school grade point average of at least 3.5 and scores of 1,150 or higher on the combined SAT. But take heart if your son or daughter doesn't make the cut. Some programs admit upperclassmen who earn top grades as freshmen.

Once admitted, many honors students become eligible for special scholarships based on merit, not financial need. For example, most of the 200 students who attend Ohio University's Honors Tutorial College get awards of $1,000 to $1,500 a year and are also eligible to apply for school year or summer research apprenticeships that pay $3,000. These perks cover nearly two-thirds of the total annual expenses for in-state students ($7,650 tuition, fees, room and board) and more than one-third of the costs for out-of-staters ($11,700). In addition, honors students can skip the university's general education requirements and still get credit for them. As a result, many humanities or fine arts majors can graduate in three years instead of four, thereby lopping another quarter off the cost of their degrees.

by the Educational Testing Service, cost a stiff $71 each. But discounts are available (ask your child's guidance counselor whether you qualify). Most of the schools that award AP credits demand examination scores of three or higher. But selective private schools typically ask for fours or fives. Some schools, however, allow kids who perform well on AP tests to skip introductory courses but still insist that they take and pay for four years of classes.

Favor schools with fat scholarships.

With the exception of the Ivies and a few other exclusive institutions, colleges increasingly are awarding scholarships to top students regardless of their families' financial need. For a list of awards available at 1,200 schools, consult the book *The A's and B's of Academic Scholarships* (Octameron, $7). Another good source is *College Financial Aid* (Arco, $22). "Merit scholarships are sometimes used as loss leaders," explains Benny Walker of Furman University in Greenville, S.C., which gave 90 of them worth an average of $5,000 each to this year's 650 freshmen. "They attract students who will probably be successful, and thereby attract other good students."

Going to the college that offered the biggest merit scholarship proved a wise choice for Stephen Yoder, 21, of Accokeek, Md., who scored straight A's at private Queen Anne School and a combined 1,490 on the SAT. Boston University offered him a Trustee Scholarship covering tuition and fees (lately $18,700) that is annually renewable if he maintains a 3.5 GPA or better. Yoder was also accepted at Johns Hopkins, Rice and Yale, all more selective schools. But only Rice also offered a merit scholarship. He settled on BU after visiting Boston and Houston and deciding he liked Beantown and BU's choice of majors better. In addition to free tuition, Yoder and BU's 67 other Trustee Scholars enjoy their own brownstone dormitory, dis-

count tickets to cultural events and weekly receptions with prominent professors, university administrators and local politicians.

Start at a community college.
Students who use this strategy can save thousands of dollars because community colleges charge only $200 to $2,000 for tuition, vs. total costs of as much as $25,800 at four-year schools. While community colleges have traditionally appealed mostly to older students or those who didn't hit the books hard in high school, counselors report that more and more solid students counting dollars are taking this path to a B.A. They choose only courses that will earn them credits that can be easily transferred to a four-year school. (Most community colleges have so-called articulation agreements with at least one four-year school, ensuring that courses your child takes will be accepted there for full credit.) Advises Harriet Gershman, a college counselor in Evanston, Ill.: "Kids should identify the four-year school they eventually want to attend before they enter a community college. That way, they can find out in advance which courses they'll need to transfer into the four-year school as a junior."

Get paid to be schooled close to home.
Twenty-two states give promising native sons and daughters financial incentives to attend in-state schools. Take Georgia, for example. Its program called HOPE (Helping Outstanding Pupils Educationally), which is financed by the state lottery, will distribute $90 million to 55,000 students this year. Students who maintain at least B averages in high school and whose families earn less than $100,000 a year qualify for free tuition at any of the state's 34 public colleges plus $100 a quarter for books. If the kids choose instead to attend private colleges in the state, they receive $2,000 a year from HOPE and the Georgia Tuition Equalization Grant program.

Commuter Schools Worth the Drive

Here's a surefire way to slash your college costs as much as 60%. Simply have your child live at home and enroll at a local college. That will eliminate room and board expenses of as much as $7,000 a year. There are dozens of outstanding public and private institutions in major metropolitan areas that primarily serve students who live off-campus. The table at right lists 20 such schools where at least three-quarters of the undergraduates commute and at least 40% of entering freshmen graduate within six years. That's an accomplishment considering that many students who commute to college also hold full-time or temporary jobs and that the average six-year graduation rate for all schools is around 57%.

Most commuter schools are state supported, which keeps tuition low. Many are branches of flagship state universities, such as the University of Illinois at Chicago Circle (tuition: $3,800) and the University of Massachusetts at Boston ($4,300). Others are large, urban institutions, like Georgia State University in Atlanta, where nearly all 16,800 undergraduates commute, and the University of Houston, where 93% of the 22,000 undergraduates live off-campus. Some intellectually challenging commuter schools are the by-products of suburban growth, such as George Mason University in Fairfax, Va., which draws most of its 21,300 students from Washington, D.C.'s Virginia suburbs. Many technical colleges that primarily serve commuters majoring in engineering, computer science or other technological subjects

Top Commuter Colleges

Private schools

Alverno College (Wis.)
DePaul University (Ill.)
Holy Family College (Pa.)
Iona College (N.Y.)
Polytechnic University (N.Y.)
St. John's University (N.Y.)
St. Thomas Aquinas (N.Y.)
Suffolk University (Mass.)
U. of Detroit Mercy (Mich.)
Webster University (Mo.)

Private schools

Baruch College (City U. of N.Y.)
California State–Fresno
Florida International University
George Mason University (Va.)
N.J. Institute of Technology
University of Central Florida
University of Cincinnati (Ohio)
University of Minnesota
University of North Florida
Temple University (Pa.)

are also renowned for academic excellence. Among the best: Polytechnic University in Brooklyn, a private school with 1,600 undergraduates, and the New Jersey Institute of Technology in Newark, a public college with 7,500 students that boasts an impressive six-year graduation rate of 68%.

Topflight private schools with large commuter populations are often affiliated with the Roman Catholic church. Among them is DePaul University in Chicago with 9,800 undergraduates, nearly 80% of whom commute. While DePaul's $11,200 tuition is higher than the typical state university's, college counselors still call the school a bargain because it attracts a large following of strong students. Last year's freshmen averaged 1,082 on the SAT, and DePaul graduates 62% of its freshmen within six years.

Shopping for a commuter school is like searching for the ideal residential college. You and your child should visit campuses and ask plenty of questions about professors' qualifications, class size and other academic matters. In addition, talk to commuters about their experiences with parking and student lounges. Most schools that welcome commuters encourage them to develop friendships with faculty and other students. You can help too by gently reminding your offspring that he or she should spend more time on campus than on your rec room couch. Students who make the extra effort to join campus organizations and get to know professors will have a much more rewarding college experience than those who don't.

The awards can be renewed annually if the students maintain B averages and if their families continue to earn less than $100,000 a year. To find out whether your children are eligible for similar deals, call your state's department of higher education.

Find a well-paying job on campus. At Susquehanna University in Selinsgrove, Pa., four special student assistants earn $7,500 a year for performing tasks such as organizing

university archives 10 hours a week, thereby cutting the total cost (lately $20,800) of their education by about one-third. Many colleges also pay decent wages to residence hall assistants, student body presidents and school newspaper editors. At Ashland University in Ohio, for instance, residence hall assistants get free room and board, which knocks $4,700 off the school's $16,360 total cost. Ashland also pays student government officials $150 to $1,200 a year. For details on money-making opportunities on campus, see *College CheckMate: Innovative Tuition Plans That Make You a Winner* (Octameron, $7).

Search for offbeat discounts. These deals generally won't save you as much as the other cost-cutting strategies. But they're worth asking about when you look at a college. If your children are close enough in age and aren't repulsed by the idea of spending their college years on the same campus, consider one of the nearly 70 colleges that discounts tuition for the second member of a family who also enrolls. George Washington University in the District of Columbia cuts its tuition and fees (lately about $18,200) in half for siblings who attend at the same time. Sending Junior to your alma mater may also provide savings. Nearly 75 schools now offer such discounts, including private Franklin College in Indiana. Students whose parents or even grandparents graduated from Franklin (recent total cost: $14,500) receive grants of $2,000 a year that are renewable annually with a B average.

Creative Ways to Borrow for College

When savings and financial aid fall short of your child's college costs, you can usually borrow the difference. Before you do, however, consider strategies to lower your interest charges. Many parents act impulsively in borrowing for their children's college education. They take on a lot of debt and overextend themselves just when they should be gearing up their savings for retirement.

Start your search with the federal government's variable-rate student loan program. Any undergraduate can take out an unsubsidized Stafford Loan for $2,625 to $5,500 annually (the amount increases as the student progresses through school). The loan's 1994-95 interest rate is 7.25%. Payments can be deferred until six months after graduation. At that time, borrowers can choose from a number of repayment options, including one that requires him or her to pay a fixed percentage of annual income, say 5% or 10%, until the debt is retired. With subsidized Stafford Loans, which are part of colleges' financial aid packages, the government pays the interest while the student is in school.

Banks, credit unions and other lenders make most Stafford Loans, which are insured by state guarantee agencies and reinsured by the federal government. Applications are available from most banks and college financial aid offices. You might also ask aid officers for the names of Stafford lenders that sell their loans to the Student Loan Marketing Association (Sallie Mae). The company will knock two percentage points off a loan's interest rate after a borrower makes the first 48 monthly payments on time. Graduates who ask Sallie Mae to deduct their monthly payments directly from their bank accounts can get an additional quarter-point discount.

Your child can also cut borrowing costs by spending nine months to a year as a member of AmeriCorps, the federal government's new national-service organization. Last year some 20,000 volunteers were expected to participate in the program, which will be expanded to about 100,000 members in 1996. (Call 800-942-2677 for more information and an application.) In exchange for a living allowance of about $7,500, a participant works for a year in a community service program, such as an environmental task force, and then receives $4,725 for future college tuition or to help pay student loans.

Want to keep your child from taking on a load of debt? You might consider applying for a federal PLUS loan (1994-95 rate: 8.4%), usually through a bank or other private lender. A PLUS (Parent Loans to Undergraduate Students) can cover the full cost of your child's education minus any financial aid. And the interest rate is often one to three percentage points lower than private lenders charge. Moreover, up-front fees on PLUS as well as Stafford Loans now total only 4%, down from 8% in 1993-94. Some lenders will waive all or part of their 1% insurance fee on federally insured loans, cutting your up-front costs to as little as 3% of the amount borrowed, vs. 3% to 5% on a private loan. To qualify for a PLUS loan, you must have no loan delinquencies of more than 90 days, and your child must be attending college at least half time, which is generally defined as more than 12 classroom hours a week.

While private lenders make most federal loans, that will soon change. This year about 500 colleges will be enrolled in the Federal Direct Student Loan Program. Students at those schools and their parents will be eligible for Stafford or PLUS loans dispensed by the U.S. Department of Education, cutting out private lenders. The department plans to make these direct loans available to students at 60% of colleges by 1998. If Congress votes to continue the program, it will be expanded to all schools. Program sponsors claim that loans will be approved more quickly and at the same rate as those made through banks. On the other hand, borrowers will have to pay 1% insurance fees and won't get a rate discount from Sallie Mae.

Yet another low-cost option that's worth considering is a home-equity line of credit. Rates recently averaged a tax-deductible 9.5%. You can tap up to 80% of your home equity as you need the money. With a credit line, you can draw from the funds whenever tuition bills are due and typically pay as little as 1.5% of the amount you owe during the months when you are short of cash. There's a major caveat, of course. If you fail to make payments, you risk losing your house.

If you plan to combine a home-equity line of credit with other loans or with student financial aid, get the credit line first. Reason: many schools take the value of your home equity into account when calculating your family's financial need. Because an outstanding home-equity loan reduces your equity, it may boost your chances of qualifying for need-based scholarships and grants from a college's own funds. (The formula for federal financial aid doesn't take home equity into account.) And since it's easier to qualify for a line of credit when your monthly debt payments are less than 40% of your income, hold off your application, say, for a PLUS loan until you've arranged your home-equity line.

As a last resort, you may want to borrow against a cash-value life insurance policy, a 401(k) retirement account or a profit-sharing plan. For annual interest of 6% to 8%, an insurer will lend you the full cash value of a life insurance policy. You don't ever have to pay the money back. But if you die with a loan outstanding, your beneficiaries will get the policy's face value minus the unpaid balance. Your insurance agent can tell you how to arrange for a loan. For information on loans against your balance in a 401(k) or profit-sharing plan, see your company's benefits department. Most plans let you take out as much as half of your vested balance or $50,000, whichever is less, as long as you pay it back within five years with interest (typically the prime rate plus one percentage point). Otherwise, the loan will be considered a withdrawal, and you'll owe regular income taxes on it, as well as a 10% penalty.

Wheeling and Dealing for Financial Aid

Long gone are the days when parents had to accept whatever financial aid package a college offered. Today, growing numbers of people are bargaining hard and getting great deals. On reason is that the shrinking pool of high school graduates has made colleges compete more aggressively for attractive applicants. Pressure from the Justice Department has stopped an elite group of eastern schools from comparing notes in order to make similar financial aid offers to outstanding students. And tight budgets have led many colleges to hold in reserve money that decisive parents can frequently shake loose.

Consider Stephanie Neild, 18, who is a straight-A student from Chelmsford, Mass. She was initially offered only a one-year, $2,625 unsubsidized Stafford Loan and a $764 Perkins Loan by her first-choice school, Cornell University (total annual costs: $25,200). Then her father, a high school physical education teacher, learned at a financial aid seminar that he had a basis to appeal Cornell's award. In setting it, school officials had overlooked nearly $10,000 in family expenses, such as his and his wife's commuting costs and his graduate school tuition. Cornell also had overstated the value of the family's home by $17,000. After the father appealed to the financial aid office, Cornell boosted Stephanie's freshman-year award to a more acceptable $6,700 (the loans plus a $2,570 grant and a work/study job.

Why even top schools have to haggle.

Statistics show why colleges are more willing to bargain over aid today than they were in the 1980s. Of the $24 billion in aid awarded to undergraduates in 1987, the federal government anted up 78%, states gave 6% and colleges kicked in 16%. Yet federal funds recently accounted for only 74% of the $35 billion aid total, states put up 6% and colleges had to provide 20%—a $3 billion hike. Over the next decade, education experts expect that the colleges' share will continue to rise because the federal government is not likely to increase its grants budget. Forced to stretch their money, schools' initial offers often appear less generous. "In many cases, colleges want to see whether you will blink at the price," says financial aid specialist Kalman Chany of Campus Consultants in a New York City. "So they build room into their aid packages for negotiation."

For middle-income families, the colleges' willingness to negotiate means that financial aid may be easier to get than you might think. For example, a family with $50,000 in income and one child in college is likely to receive aid, especially if the parents have few assets beyond their home equity. And even parents with two children in college, total income above $100,000 a year and few assets outside of home equity have qualified for awards. You can get a rough idea whether your family is likely to obtain aid by filling out the worksheet "Calculate Your Share of the College Bills" on the right.

Your chances of persuading your child's first-choice school to boost its offer have never been better. Since 1992, for example, price-fixing has been forbidden. That year, the Justice Department pressured nine highly selective colleges, including Cornell, Harvard and MIT, to stop sharing financial aid information. The practice had enabled them to make similar offers to attractive applicants, thereby preventing the kids from bargaining for more money by playing one school off against another. Today, an applicant pursued by more

Calculate Your Share of the College Bills

This worksheet can help you estimate how much you will be expected to contribute to your child's college costs. The formulas are based on the so-called federal methodology—Uncle Sam's rules for determining your family's eligibility for federal financial aid. Regardless of whether the final amount bears any resemblance to your ability to pay, colleges must use it to calculate how much federal assistance to give to your son or daughter. This worksheet assumes there are two parents in your family and that the older one is 45. The figures are effective for the 1994-95 school year.

Complete sections 1 and 2 to determine your eligible income and assets. Those figures will be used in section 3 to calculate the parents' contribution. Then go to section 4 to figure out the student's share. Add the parents' and the student's shares to come up with what's officially called your "expected family contribution." If that figure is greater than a college's total annual cost (including tuition, fees, room, board and an allowance for books and transportation), you will probably not qualify for aid based on need. If it is less, your child will most likely be offered a financial aid package to help make up the difference.

1. PARENTS' INCOME

Enter your adjusted gross income from your '94 tax return. _____

Subtract any child support you paid out in '94. _____

Add the sum of all nontaxable income. _____

Add back '94 deductions for IRA and Keogh contributions. _____

Subtract '94 federal, state and Social Security (FICA) taxes. _____

If both parents work, subtract employment expenses: $2,500 or 35% of the lower salary, whichever is less. _____

Subtract your income protection allowance (from Table I). If the result is negative enter "0" on line A; if it is positive, enter the amount on line A.

A. $_____

2. PARENTS' ASSETS

If your adjusted gross income is $50,000 or less and you did not itemize deductions on your tax return, enter "0" on line B. Otherwise enter the total value of your investments, including stocks, bonds and real estate other than your principal home. _____

Add the sum of all cash, bank and money-market accounts. _____

Subtract $38,900. _____

If the result is negative, enter "0" on line B. If it is positive, multiply by 0.12 and enter the result on line B _____

B. $_____

3. PARENTS' CONTRIBUTION

Enter the total of lines A and B. _____

Use this number to find the parents' expected contribution from Table II. Divide that figure by the number of family members attending college and enter the result on line C. _____

C. $_____

4. STUDENT'S CONTRIBUTION

Enter the student's adjusted gross income as reported on his or her '94 tax return. _____

Subtract '94 federal, state and Social Security (FICA) taxes. _____

Subtract the $1,750 income protection allowance. _____

If the result is negative, enter "0." If it is positive, multiply by 0.5. _____

Add 35% of the student's investments and savings and enter the total on line D. _____

D. $_____

5. TOTAL FAMILY CONTRIBUTION

Add lines C and D and enter the sum on line E.   **E. $_____**

TABLE I: INCOME PROTECTION ALLOWANCE

Family size (including student)	Number of family members in college				
	1	2	3	4	5
2	$11,150	$9,240			
3	13,890	11,990	$10,080		
4	17,150	15,240	13,350	$11,440	
5	20,240	18,330	16,430	14,520	$12,620
6	23,670	21,760	19,860	17,960	16,060

TABLE II: PARENTS' CONTRIBUTION

If line A plus line B equals	Then the parents' contribution is
$3,408 or less	Minus $750
$3,409 to $10,000	22% of line A plus B
$10,001 to $12,500	$2,200 plus 25% of amount over $10,000
$12,501 to $15,100	$2,825 plus 29% of amount over $12,500
$15,101 to $17,600	$3,579 plus 34% of amount over $15,100
$17,601 to $20,100	$4,429 plus 40% of amount over $17,600
$20,101 or more	$5,429 plus 47% of amount over $20,100

Source: The College Board

Money Helps

Q. I would like to lend $10,000 to my mother-in-law for home improvements. This loan would be repaid from her estate after she dies. I want to charge her the lowest interest rate allowable without running afoul of the IRS. I hear it sets a minimum for what you charge, the applicable federal rate, which fluctuates. Must my loan be a variable rate that matchs the AFR?

TED STEVENS, EUGENE, ORE.

A. If your loan is less than $10,000 (and never exceeds $10,000 for the life of the loan), you don't have to charge your mom-in-law any interest at all. As far as the IRS is concerned, the money could be construed as a "gift" (even if she repays you), and any "gift" worth $10,000 or less is tax-free. If she needs a little more than that, you and your wife could each lend her as much as $10,000 and still ignore those tiresome AFR requirements. Just make sure that your in-law and you sign an agreement that the principal will be repaid from the sale of the house or other assets after her death. That way, your wife's siblings can't stop you from collecting what's owed you from the estate.

For the sake of argument, let's assume you and your wife want to lend her mom $100,000. In that case, yes, you could charge her a fixed rate of interest. But it would have to be the AFR at the time you make the loan. The IRS publishes its rates in its monthly bulletin (ask your accountant for a copy) and tells you which ones apply to short-term (less than three years), mid-term (three to nine years) and long-term loans (more than nine years).

than one of these schools often receives offers that differ by as much as $10,000, and negotiating is part of the game. Williams College reports that 77 of the 450 students who qualified for aid asked for more money. And the college hiked 80% of their packages an average of 20%. Moreover, in the past 20 years the pool of college applicants has shrunk 15%, setting off an intense bidding war, particularly among second-tier colleges. Pittsburgh's Carnegie Mellon University (total annual costs: $23,600) routinely asks its applicants who qualify for aid to give the university an opportunity to match any competing offers.

What's more, many small private colleges are now willing to discount their sticker prices 30%, on average, according to a recent study by the National Association of College and University Business Officers. (The association won't name the schools in the study.) Says Robin Jenkins, the group's director of research: "Price warfare is beginning to resemble the frequent-flier programs in the airline industry." Even without haggling, middle-class families can often win substantial aid by using the following rules to their advantage.

Tilt the odds in your child's favor. Urge your offspring to apply to schools where he or she stands the best chance of getting a large offer. In general, these schools will be either private colleges or your state's public schools. "State schools are sticking out-of-state students with higher costs, and most of their aid is earmarked for in-state students," says Chany. Also encourage your child to consider colleges that grant millions of dollars in aid out of their own funds. For example, your son or daughter might focus on schools with large ratios of endowment per student, especially if he or she seems likely to rank in the top quarter of the freshman class. You can find those ratios in the information packages that colleges will send you on request.

Send in aid forms promptly. In the fall of your child's senior year of high school, you must fill out the Free Application for Federal Student Aid (FAFSA). It's available at high school guidance offices or by calling 800-433-3243. You should apply even if you don't think you qualify for need-based aid. Reason: colleges use this information in processing applications for government loans that are available to all students and their parents, as well as some merit awards. The form will ask for detailed information about your income in the prior year and savings and investments in the current calendar year. Using the federal formula, processing firms will then calculate the amount the federal rules assume you can afford to pay toward college—your so-called expected family contribution. Be sure to mail in all the forms as soon as possible after Jan. 1 and before the deadlines of the colleges to which your child has applied. An early aid applicant won't get more money (in most cases, the total aid will be 65% to 100% of your assessed need). But tardy applicants may find that grants and work/study have run out and have to settle for loans.

Make the aid rules work for you. Unless you are certain that your child won't qualify for aid, don't save college money in his or her name. The reason is a quirk in the federal formula. It requires students to contribute 35% of their assets to college costs, vs. only 5.6% for parents. If you think your child will be eligible for aid, keep the savings in your name. And don't worry about stashing money in a 401(k) or other tax-sheltered retirement plan. The federal formula won't include them among your assets. To take advantage of another quirk in the formula, plan to sell investments earmarked for college costs by Dec. 31 of your child's junior year in high school—a year before you must fill out the federal aid questionnaire. That's because the formula assumes parents can afford to spend up to 47% of after-tax income on school bills but only 5.6% of assets. Since the federal formula treats capital gains as ordinary income, selling investments a year before applying for aid can help reduce your family's expected contribution to college costs.

Appeal a low-ball offer. It never hurts to ask for more money if you need it. At worst, the college will simply say no. It will not revoke the offer of admission or cancel its aid offer as punishment for asking. So you should delay accepting the college's offer of admission to the last possible moment before the deadline to maintain your bargaining leverage as long as you can. In negotiating for more money, focus on your child's first-choice college. After all, what you really want is the best possible price at the school that most suits your son or daughter. Your appeal's chances will be best if your child is an excellent student or has other sought-after qualities, such as leadership skills, musical talent or athletic ability. If the first-choice college offered less aid than other schools, ask it to match the best competing package. Make sure, however, that the schools are equally prestigious. Don't expect a Harvard or a Stanford to match a second-tier school's offer.

Provide proof that you need more aid. For example, list data that was not reflected in the aid questionnaires, such as support for other relatives or high living costs in your area. Correct any mistakes that you may have made in the aid questionnaires or that the college may have made in interpreting them. Chany estimates that errors occur at least 5% of the time. Then, with a dollar figure in mind, phone the financial aid officer in charge of your child's file. Explain that this college is your child's first choice. But you need more money or your child will not be able to attend. Schools will be most sympathetic if you have special reasons for requesting more money. A good example is that since you applied for aid, a close family member suffered a medical emergency or job loss. "What we can do in these situations will depend on how much money is still left," says Anne Sturtevant, director of financial aid at Emory University in Atlanta. "So the sooner we are notified, the more likely we can help." Don't hesitate to follow up your call to the aid officer with a letter restating the important argu-ments for your appeal and attach copies of any documentation. If you live within an easy drive of the school, you might consider visiting to make your case personally.

What if you simply don't have enough money for your child to enroll in his or her first-choice college? There's no need to panic as long as you have followed the cardinal rule that college counselors constantly stress. Make sure your child applies to at least one safety school—a place that is certain to admit him or her and that you can afford without aid.

Housing's Outlook Under Higher Rates

Higher mortgage rates are bound to make this year a more difficult one for the housing market. Economist Mark Zandi at Regional Financial Associates (RFA), a West Chester, Pa. consulting firm, sees fixed-rate mortgages rising to around 10% by year's end, up from 9.3% recently and a 28-year low of 6.8% in October 1993. Average adjustable-rate mortgages could rise from 6.5% to as high as 8%. Dampened by those ratcheting rates, sales of new and existing houses are expected to drop about 6% to 4.9 million in '95, according to estimates by the National Association of Realtors. Average prices will keep rising but at a subdued pace. An RFA forecast of housing prices shows that the median price in the 50 largest U.S. housing markets will rise a gentle 3.2% this year, vs. 3.5% in 1994.

To learn what's in store for housing where you live, see MONEY's 50-market ranking on the right. No. 1 Portland, Ore., where house prices rose an estimated 10.8% in 1994, towers above the crowd with a 9.7% hike forecast for this year. Among the reasons cited are expansion of the area's computer-based manufacturing industries and a steady stream of house-hungry refugees pouring in from megacities such as Los Angeles. Just behind Portland rank the Salt Lake City/Ogden metro area (7.8%), Orlando (5.4%), San Antonio (4.7%), Fort Lauderdale (4.5%) and Greensboro/Winston-Salem, N.C. (4.4%).

With Portland's economic strengths, it's hardly surprising that the metro area's home prices are now some $14,000 above the U.S. median of $102,575. Happily for buyers elsewhere, median prices in half of the 10 hottest housing markets fall below the U.S. figure. The five most affordable all have strong economies (Salt Lake City, Orlando, San Antonio, Greensboro/Winston-Salem, N.C., and Phoenix). And their states are attracting plenty of new residents. Still, predicts RFA's Zandi: "With prices up moderately and rates up sharply, affordability will be worse everywhere next year." So follow these strategies if you're about to edge into the housing market as a buyer or as a seller.

Advice for today's home buyers. Because higher mortgage rates tend to chill demand, fewer enthusiastic buyers will be competing

Today's Hot and Cold Housing Markets

This year's house prices are expected to spurt 9.7% in Portland, Ore. but rise less than 4% in most other big metro areas.

Rank	Metropolitan area	projected gain in '95	1994 median price	annual Income needed[1]
1	Portland, Ore.	9.7%	$116,190	$30,593
2	Salt Lake City	7.8	94,950	25,665
3	Orlando	5.4	91,300	22,503
4	San Antonio	4.7	78,470	20,380
5	Fort Lauderdale	4.5	102,890	25,168
6	Greensboro/Winston-Salem, N.C.	4.4	92,910	23,968
7	Phoenix	4.4	90,400	23,898
8	Denver	4.3	112,980	29,479
9	Charlotte, N.C.	4.3	104,120	27,147
10	Middlesex/Somerset counties, N.J.	4.2	176,930	44,629
11	Tampa/St. Petersburg	4.1	74,940	18,261
12	Nashville	4.0	94,370	25,301
13	Atlanta	3.8	91,900	23,441
14	Memphis	3.8	86,520	23,268
15	Houston	3.8	80,220	21,400
16	Chicago	3.8	141,750	37,205
17	Seattle	3.8	153,170	40,166
18	St. Louis	3.8	85,970	22,330
19	Columbus, Ohio	3.7	95,850	25,307
20	Minneapolis	3.6	99,360	26,690
21	Fort Worth	3.6	82,220	22,057
22	Dallas	3.5	94,960	25,203
23	Boston	3.4	178,720	44,493
24	Washington, D.C.	3.3	155,600	40,048
25	Milwaukee	3.3	108,260	28,758
26	Kansas City, Mo.	3.2	85,300	22,112
27	Newark	3.2	188,180	46,897
28	Cleveland/Lorain/Elyria	3.2	97,090	25,432
29	Sacramento	3.2	124,800	32,594
	U.S. median	**3.2**	**102,575**	**26,676**
30	Detroit	3.1	84,360	22,805
31	Indianapolis	3.0	90,730	23,712
32	Monmouth/Ocean counties, N.J.	3.0	134,090	33,860
33	Miami	3.0	102,210	25,575
34	Baltimore	2.8	118,060	30,749
35	Orange County, Calif.	2.7	212,270	56,477
36	Riverside/San Bernardino, Calif.	2.7	129,510	34,776
37	New Orleans	2.7	76,520	20,289
38	Cincinnati	2.6	94,170	24,641
39	Bergen/Passaic counties, N.J.	2.6	190,390	47,339
40	New York City	2.5	172,390	42,759
41	Rochester, N.Y.	2.5	86,490	22,254
42	San Francisco	2.4	250,270	65,078
43	New Haven/Bridgeport, Conn.	2.3	142,020	34,230
44	Nassau/Suffolk counties, N.Y.	2.3	157,670	39,525
45	Buffalo/Niagara Falls	2.1	81,160	20,466
46	Norfolk/Virginia Beach	2.1	102,260	26,662
47	Philadelphia	1.7	116,640	29,400
48	Hartford	1.5	132,330	30,844
49	San Diego	1.5	177,340	46,603
50	Los Angeles/Long Beach	1.0	184,900	44,891

Notes and sources: [1]Annual income needed to buy a house in each of the 50 largest metro areas assumes a 20% down payment, a 30-year loan term, and that no more than 30% of a household's income is used for the monthly mortgage payment. This analysis was prepared for MONEY by Regional Financial Associates, West Chester, Pa.

for desirable houses. To give yourself an edge, you might hire your own broker, which won't cost a penny. He or she will take 50% of the commission that the seller will pay his broker. While some real estate agents refuse to represent buyers, an estimated two-thirds will do it if asked. A knowledgeable broker can steer you to suitable neighborhoods, size up the positive and negative features of each house you view, and help you negotiate the lowest possible price on the one you want to buy. Even though this may reduce the broker's commission, it also makes it more likely that you'll buy a house through the broker.

"What a buyer's broker brings you is the ability to know all the pertinent facts," says Tim Stockwell, director of relocation and human-resource operations at Sprint. Each year, most of the company's 400 relocating employees who are seeking houses to buy use their own brokers. In a study several years ago, Sprint found that employees with buyer's brokers paid an average of 91% of the asking price, vs. 96% for those who bought homes without any help. On a $250,000 house, an employee who used a buyer's broker typically saved an impressive $22,500, compared with only $10,000 for one who didn't. Another wise move is paying for a competent home inspection (typically $200 to $400). For that outlay, you get cost savings and a negotiating chip if you still want the house. You can often negotiate several thousand dollars off the price just by knowing something like the life expectancy of the roof.

When you set out to get a mortgage, your first shock may be that adjustable-rate loans are no longer low-digit darlings. But if you're pretty sure you won't be living in your new house for more than a decade, you can consider an adjustable-rate loan known as a 10/1 ARM. You pay a fixed 8.8% rate for the first 10 years of the mortgage and then a rate that adjusts annually for the next 20 years.

Wise buyers should also keep an eye on local demographic changes when shopping for a home. "Think about how easy it will be eventually to sell the house," advises Stanley Duobinis, director of forecasting at the National Association of Home Builders in Washington, D.C. He is referring to the baby-bust generation now moving into the starter-house market. Adds Duobinis: "Prices for smaller homes will not continue to grow with the rest of the market." A particular scourge is condos, which buyers see as starter homes. "But condo prices are flat compared with five years ago, and many people aren't getting their initial investment back," warns Duobinis. He recommends against buying in real estate markets that were hot in the late '80s and are awash in condos today.

Advice for today's home sellers.

Timing will be even more critical this year as the pool of potential buyers shrinks. So it's essential to price your house to sell. Base the price on those for comparable homes that have sold in your neighborhood in the current market. Moreover, after you have found a broker you feel comfortable with, agree to let his or her agency list your house exclusively for no more than 90 days. If you have an attractive house that's priced right, at least four to eight people should be looking at it every two weeks or so. Otherwise the agent probably isn't doing the job and should be replaced. Another tip is to resist the temptation to invest in unnecessary improvements, such as an expensive new bathroom or kitchen, in hopes of getting a better price for your house. Instead, apply a fresh coat of paint, place vases of fresh-cut flowers in strategic spots and banish that old piano and maybe even the extra sofa to unclutter the living room. Otherwise you're stunting the imagination of the buyers, who like to fantasize about how their things will look there.

Great Places for Your Aging Loved Ones

Beverly Berger recalls fondly how, as a little girl, she would make the rounds of local nursing homes with her pharmacist father. Now it is her father's turn to live his last years with dignity. And like so many families, Berger and her siblings are struggling with the big dilemma of where to secure the best care for aging parents. Until recently her mother and father managed well on their own. But two strokes have impaired her father's abilities, and the strain of caring for him has begun to impair her mother's health. Says Berger, age 45: "Places are expensive, and some are overpriced. Several also have long waiting lists. We need help now."

You may well face similar circumstances. According to the American Association of Retired Persons, people over 65 account for 13% of the nation's population and will hit 20% by the year 2030. Back when Berger was a child, the elderly were cared for in their own home, usually by family, or in a nursing home. These days, however, the variety of options is vast and often overwhelming. To help you narrow your choices, we describe the major types of institutions providing care for seniors, analyzing which type generally works best for whom. Drawing on the recommendations of experts nationwide and personal visits by Money correspondents, we have also compiled a roster of outstanding facilities in every region of the nation. You'll find the establishments described in detail in the tables that begin on the following pages.

Because every family's needs are unique, you should also do some research on your own. Get in touch with your state unit on aging for free information on services for the elderly. The National Association of State Units on Aging (202-898-2578) will provide

data on the one that's closest to you. Another good free information source is the Eldercare Locator, funded by the U.S. Administration on Aging, which helps you find community assistance (800-677-1116). When you've narrowed your housing choices to a few facilities, try to visit at least six of them with these guidelines in mind. Is the institution willing to provide information and allow you to look over the premises? Be wary of those that are not. How much of a voice do residents have in the facility's management? Active resident councils are a reflection of a facility's respect for seniors. Must this type of institution be licensed in the state? If so, follow up your visit by checking its record with your state's long-term care ombudsman. You can locate that person through the state unit on aging.

Whatever kind of housing your family eventually chooses, it almost certainly won't come cheap. For example, you would pay $3,140 a month, plus a $149,600 entry fee, to live in a two-bedroom, double-occupancy apartment with all nursing services at lavish Kendal at Longwood in Kennett Square, Pa. Corporate retiree health benefits rarely pick up any of the cost, and Medicare will likely cover only so-called skilled care services such as those provided by doctors and nurses. Custodial care such as bathing and meals is not covered. To help handle most nursing home expenses, you might consider buying long-term care insurance. But be wary of policies that don't cover all levels of custodial and skilled nursing care, don't have inflation adjustment built in and aren't guaranteed renewable, which means the policies can't be canceled as long as you pay the premiums. Experts often recommend the policies of UNUM, CNA and John Hancock. If bought

Where Seniors Get Superior Care

Experts on aging helped Money create this regional guide to some of America's premier facilities for the elderly. Almost all have waiting lists ranging from a few weeks to a few years. Even if you need a place immediately, you can use these institutions as benchmarks for the quality you should look for during your search. Most of the places in this table welcome visits; call ahead to arrange one.

Facility	Entry fee	Rent or maintenance	Includes[1]	Assisted living
Continuing Care				
Kendal at Longwood/Crosslands Kennett Square, Pa. 215-388- 7001	$46,100 to $149,600	$1,440 to $3,140 a month	Housekeeping, meals, utilities	Included in monthly fee
Bentley Village Naples, Fla. 813-597-1121	$132,000 to $317,500	$1,161 to $2,639 a month	Cable TV, housekeeping, some meals, utilities	Included
John Knox Village Lee's Summit, Mo. 800-821-3098	$19,981 to $169,740	$400 to $1,709 a month	Landscaping, security, utilities	$1,715 a month
University Place Houston 713-541-2900	$54,400 to $102,000	$1,180 to $2,435 a month; lease without entry fee	Housekeeping, some meals, utilities	$750 a month
Freedom Village Lake Forest, Calif. 714-472-4700	$50,000 to $192,000	$1,050 to $1,580 a month	Local transport, security	$72 a day additional
Panorama City Lacey, Wash. 206-456-0111	$39,000 to $225,000	$575 to $1,050 a month	Lawn care, utilities	$1,803 a month
Congregate Housing				
The Esplanade New York City 212-874-5000	None	$2,200 to $4,300 a month	Housekeeping, laundry, meals, utilities	Not available
Friends Home West Greensboro, N.C. 910-292-9952	$75,000 to $115,000	$1,200 to $2,015 a month	Cable TV, some meals, utilities	$2,100 a month, plus a $45,000 entry fee
West Hills Village Rapid City, S.D. 605-342-0255	$47,972 to $126,000	$593 to $1,113 a month	Housekeeping, one meal daily, utilities	Not available
Burgundy Place Tulsa 918-299-0953	None	$985 to $1,455 a month	Cable TV, housekeeping, local transport, utilities	Can be arranged
The Fountains at La Cholla Tucson 602-797-2001	None	$945 to $1,925 a month	Housekeeping, one meal daily, utilities	$595 a month additional
Hidden Lakes Retirement Residence Salem, Ore. 503-588-2922	None	$925 to $2,050 a month	Cable TV, housekeeping, linens, meals, utilities	Not available
Active Communities				
Winslow Place Winslow, Maine 207-877-7064	None	$650 to $1,200 a month	Cable TV, housekeeping, meals, utilities	$149 a month additional
Carolina Meadows Chapel Hill, N.C. 919-942-4014	$78,500 to $280,000	$985 to $1,270 a month	Cable TV, some meals	$74 a day additional for limited assistance

Notes: [1]Additional services may be included in fees, and additional accommodations may be available. **Sources**: The facilities

Nursing care	Site	Number of residents	Special features	Wait for entry
Included in monthly fee	Longwood: 85 acres; Crosslands: 133 acres	370 in each facility	Putting greens, gardens, arts and crafts, bowling, swimming pools; residents plan own activities through 70 committees.	Three years
Included	86 acres	520	Golf course, five lakes, medical clinic; people on waiting list have access to golf course, dining room and nursing home.	Three to six months
$84 to $107 a day	420 acres	2,100	Fishing pond, swimming pools, golf course, hospital; large nursing-care division has 430 beds.	Three to 12 weeks
Not available	10 acres	205	Borders a hospital and a university where residents take classes and attend cultural events; refundable entry fee.	None
$108 a day additional	Three-story building in city	320	Library, lounges; registered nurse on duty daily; two guest apartments available for visitors	Six months
$105 to $150 a day	140 acres	1,200	Borders a lake; 18 miles of walking trails, two stock brokerages, two banks	Three to nine months
Can be arranged	Converted city hotel	150	Within walking distance of Lincoln Center	60 days
$115 a day additional	38 acres	166	Nonprofit; rural setting with walking trails, half a mile from international airport	None
$83 to $89 a day	15 acres	300	Formal dining room, bank, libraries	One to three years
Can be arranged	10-story high-rise on four acres	150	Beauty and gift shops, arts and crafts classes, located in a country setting	30 days
Not available	10 acres	310	Emergency call system in all units, 15 medical facilities are located nearby	Four to six months
Not available	20 acres	210	15-acre lake stocked with fish; billiard room, library, dance floor with jukebox	Two to three months
Not available	Less than one acre in town	27	Residents can use neighboring Muskie Center, a nationally known senior center.	None
$114 to $149 a month additional	160 acres in woods	435	Golf, tennis, swimming, croquet; close to four universities and teaching hospitals	One year

Where Seniors Get Superior Care

Facility	Entry fee	Rent or maintenance	Includes[1]	Assisted living
Edina Park Plaza Minneapolis 612-830-0909	None	$1,100 to $2,200 a month	Housekeeping, local transport, utilities	$90 to $140 a day additional
The Forum at Parklane Dallas 214-369-9902	None	$1,900 to $3,900 a month	Housekeeping, some meals, utilities	$1,900 to $2,500 a month
Del Webb's Sun City West Sun City West, Ariz. 800-341-6121	$90,000 to $230,000	$110 annual recreation fee	Landscaping for home-owners association members	Not available
Horizon House Seattle 206-624-3700	$17,100 to $218,300	$505 to $1,118 a month	Utilities	$55 to $91 a day
Assisted Living				
Woodside Place Oakmont, Pa. 412-826-6500	None	$95 to $99 a day	Housekeeping, meals, utilities	Included
Manor on the Square Roswell, Ga. 404-993-8040	None	$70 to $100 a day	Housekeeping, meals, utilities	Included
Karrington at Tucker Creek Worthington, Ohio 614-486-3213	None	$60 to $100 a day	Housekeeping, meals, utilities	Included
Sterling House Bethany, Okla. 405-787-9200	None	$1,199 to $1,899 a month	Housekeeping, laundry, meals, utilities	Included
Sunset Manor Brush, Colo. 303-842-2825	None	$875 to $1,850 a month	Housekeeping, meals, utilities	Included
Rackleff House Canby, Ore. 503-676-2242	None	$1,250 to $1,750 a month	Housekeeping, meals, utilities, laundry	Included
Nursing Homes				
Chase Memorial New Berlin, N.Y. 607-847-6117	None	$4,050 to $4,350 a month	Housekeeping, room and board, utilities	Not available
Joseph L. Morse Geriatric Center West Palm Beach, Fla. 407-471-5111	None	$118 to $162 a day	Laundry, meals, utilities	Not available
The Anchorage of Bensenville, Ill. 708-766-3570	None	$99 to $160 a day	Housekeeping, meals	Not available
Eden Home New Braunfels, Texas 210-625-6291	None	$65 to $81 a day	Meals, nonprescription medicine	$35 a day
Life Care Center of Las Vegas 702-648-4900	None	$100 to $146 a day	Housekeeping, laundry, meals	Not available
Benedictine Nursing Center Mount Angel, Ore. 503-845-6841	None	$130 to $211 a day	Housekeeping, laundry, meals	Not available

Notes: [1]Additional services may be included in fees, and additional accommodations may be available. **Sources**: The facilities

Nursing care	Site	Number of residents	Special features	Wait for entry
Can be arranged	18-story high-rise on four acres	230	Enclosed landscaped park kept at 72°F; heated parking, full-service restaurant	Varies
$89 to $120 a day	Eight acres	309	Spa, arts and crafts, billiards, greenhouse	Up to three months
Not available	7,100 acres	24,800	Eight 18-hole golf courses; four recreation centers; more than 90 clubs; hospital	None
$105 to $159 a day	Hise-rise next to city park	490	Exercise classes, educational forums	Varies
Can be arranged	2.5 acres	36	Innovative care of Alzheimer's sufferers emphasizes patients' freedom.	1.5 to two years
Not available	3.5 acres	35	Extra-wide halls for wheelchair mobility; adult day-care center on site	Three months
Limited	1.5 acres	64	Choice of nine different room designs; ice cream parlor	None
Not available	Four acres	26	Special service plan for each resident includes personalized diets.	Six months
$92 to $95 a day	Five acres	85	Residents are divided into groups of eight, each with nursing supervision of daily activities.	Based on need
Included	1.3 acres	25	Managed by Keren Brown Wilson, known for creating individual care in assisted living	Six to eight months
Included	Eight acres	80	Residence arranges visits from preschool children; residents encouraged to keep pets.	Three to five months
Included	20 acres	280	Community adult day-care center on premises; geriatric clinic scheduled to open soon	Varies
Included	27 acres	230	Garden club, pets; residence arranges visits from preschool children.	Less than 30 days
Included	11 acres	256	Special care unit for Alzheimer's patients	None
Included	3.5 acres	169	Special care unit for Alzheimer's patients	Varies
Included	11 acres	130	Residents interact with preschool kids from the child-development center on premises.	Varies

when you're 55, they cost between $767 and $799 a year, guaranteed for life. Premiums almost double if first bought when you're 65.

In the descriptions below, you will find additional advice that's specific to each of the categories of elder living. The categories appear in the order of the type of client they serve—active (and relatively affluent) elders; frail elderly who need help with daily activities such as getting dressed; or infirm seniors who often need medical care.

Continuing care communities.
These retirement facilities usually have at least three separate buildings or wings. The resident signs up for an apartment in what are called independent living quarters. Then, as his or her needs increase, the client is transferred to what is known as an assisted living apartment, where staff members help with daily functions such as meal preparation and bathing. Eventually, if necessary, he or she is moved to a nursing home on the premises for around-the-clock medical monitoring.

Many communities require substantial entry fees ranging from $15,000 to as much as $500,000, depending on their size and amenities. Monthly charges range from $150 to around $3,000, again depending upon the services you require. You make a long-term commitment when you buy in, so make sure that you're satisfied with the facilities at all three levels of care. The best places (166 in 24 states) are accredited by the Continuing Care Accreditation Commission, sponsored by the American Association of Homes and Services for the Aging (call 202-783-2242), which represents not-for-profit elderly living facilities and community organizations. Be sure to have your attorney or financial adviser check out a community's financial statements and admittance contract. Find out how much of the entry fee would be returned to your estate at death or refunded if you moved.

Congregate senior housing.
In these arrangements, residents have their own apartments but can eat their meals in a central dining room. Housekeeping is available, as well as social activities such as dances and field trips. Rent and fees can vary widely, from as much as $4,300 a month for a two-bedroom apartment in the posh Esplanade in New York City to as little as $380 a month (after a $25,000 entry fee) for a one-bedroom duplex in rustic Bristol Village in Waverly, Ohio. Assisted living apartments are often available in congregate senior housing facilities too.

Active adult communities.
These can range in size from Maine's Winslow Place, which houses 27 people, to complexes as big as Arizona's Sun City West, a town with a population of 24,800. Accommodations vary from studio apartments to three-bedroom houses, and some offer transportation, meals and in-home amenities like housekeeping. If nursing care and assistance with daily living are not available on site, however, a yearly lease can make better sense than a buy-in.

Shared housing.
Maggie Kuhn, founder of the advocacy group Gray Panthers, is also a pioneer of shared housing—communal living in a private home or a home sponsored by a local nonprofit group. Kuhn, 89, shares her house in Philadelphia with five other women ranging in age from their mid-twenties to 55. They share chores and pay an average of $250 a month for rent and utilities. The National Shared Housing Resource Center (410-235-4454) can provide information on more than 350 programs across the country.

Assisted living.
At such facilities, residents have small, private apartments or rooms. But a 24-hour staff is on hand to help them with daily tasks like getting out of bed, bathing and dressing. This kind of care is available in

specialized assisted living units. At $20 to $110 a day, it costs less than a nursing home. It is not an option for those who are in need of continual nursing treatment, though a growing number of assisted living facilities offer special care for Alzheimer's sufferers.

Residential care.
Some 32,000 homes are licensed to provide residential care, according to AARP. They are known by various names including "personal care" and "homes for the aged," and some states consider assisted living facilities part of this category. Residential care homes are not for people who need skilled nursing, but some do have nurses on staff. Monthly costs range from $350 to $4,000, depending on the services required.

Adult foster care.
For monthly fees that range from $500 to $3,000, families take older people generally in good health into their homes. "It can be a wonderful option," says Wayne Nelson, of Oregon's ombudsman office for long-term care. "But anyone who doesn't have a criminal record can go into business. It needs reform." For example, alleged crimes committed against adult foster-care residents have included abandonment and even murder.

Home care.
According to the National Association of Home Care, an estimated 7 million people will receive cost-effective help in their own homes, including homemaker services and various forms of physical therapy. For example, to keep a person who's hooked up to a life-sustaining ventilator would cost $21,570 a month in a hospital but only $7,050 at home. And, of course, there are psychological benefits to remaining in familiar quarters near family and friends.

Nursing homes.
Despite an image problem, nursing homes remain an important part of senior care at an average cost of $37,000 a year. A fancy building and decor don't ensure quality care. Ask residents how responsive the staff is, how flexible the daily schedule is, and how well the staff and residents interact—a sure sign of whether emotional needs are being met. Odors and a high usage of catheters suggest that calls for help often go unheeded. And no matter how well a place checks out, it is smart to choose one near the home of a relative or friend who can drop in easily. Even in the best homes, a resident who is visited regularly (and at unexpected times) will be attended to more carefully.

How to Help Manage Your Folks' Money

We usually learn the details of our parents' financial situation only after they become seriously ill or die. Then it's too late to be of much help. But if your parents are in their fifties or older, you might prevent trouble later on by having a conversation with your mother and father soon about their money.

Now, your folks might not want to have this talk. After all, it's seldom pleasant to contemplate one's own mortality. One way to break the ice is to pick up cues your parents drop indicating that they're concerned about money. For instance, they might talk about current financial troubles of their friends, particularly those who've been socked by steep medical bills. Use the opening to ask whether they are confident that their financial affairs are in order and what you can do to ensure that their wishes will be carried out if they die or cannot make decisions for themselves.

Money Helps

Q. I've heard that if a bank fails, the Federal Deposit Insurance Corporation can take as long as 25 years to repay your money. Is this statement true?

MARGARET SHEARBURN, GLENDALE, ARIZ.

A. No way. Only 13 of the nation's 13,000 banks and savings and loan institutions went under in the first 11 months of 1994, the latest period for which statistics were available. That's a puny failure rate of 0.1%. And the FDIC, which insures most U.S. bank accounts for up to $100,000 per person per bank, says that it has never taken more than three business days to issue refunds (except when the failed bank had a wrong address for a customer). So make sure that your bank knows your whereabouts. And endeavor to find a more reliable source of financial information.

If your parents don't bring up the topic of money, you will have to raise the subject yourself. And endeavor to cover these key issues.

◆ **Financial documents**. Urge your parents to let you know where you can find their bank, brokerage, mutual fund, IRA and loan statements in case of an emergency. Explain that you aren't interested in knowing how much money they have. You just want to make sure that if they have a sudden illness and can't handle their finances, their debts will get paid. And they'll get all their investment, pension and Social Security checks. Then make a copy for yourself of the key account numbers, contacts, addresses and phone numbers for future reference. To help your parents avoid overlooking any important document, buy them the workbook *One*

of These Days, We'll Have to Get Organized by Donald Upp ($22; JADLU Press, Box 554, Jenison, Mich. 49429). It will let them list everything from their checking account number to whom to call if their electricity goes out to how they want their funeral handled.

◆ **Wills and trusts**. Remember that these vehicles are the only ways to make sure your parents' assets will be disbursed according to their wishes. Experts recommend that anyone with a will or trust review it at least every three years to keep up with family changes, such as the arrival of grandchildren, and revisions in the tax law that can have a significant impact on how your estate is taxed. If your parents don't have an estate-planning attorney, you can help them find one and gently remind them to make an appointment. They can expect to pay about $100 for a simple will. Figure $200 to $2,000 for one with more sophisticated elements such as trusts.

◆ **Life insurance**. If your parents have a life insurance policy, discuss with them whether they really need it. They might be better off spending the premiums in other ways. That's because the primary reason to own life insurance is to replace income that is lost when a wage earner dies. Your parents may no longer need life insurance if they are living off their pensions, Social Security and investments.

◆ **Health care**. Ask your parents where they would like to stay if they become incapacitated. They may prefer home health care, moving in with family members or living in a nursing home or community care complex. If your parents favor a nursing home or continuous care center, start researching such places through your city or state's department for the aging. Knowing your parents' health care wishes now will make things easier for all of you if they need ongoing care someday.

6

How to Be a Smarter Fund Investor

Many Americans are conditioned to expect their standards of living to rise as their lives and careers progress. If you are in your forties or fifties, however, you could be stunned to discover when you add up your net worth that you already have amassed quite a bundle. Even if you're just starting a family, you could be surprised at your potential for accumulating serious money. According to government surveys, some 850,000 people had built up estates worth at least $500,000. Whether you aspire to or have attained such affluence, the challenge confronting you is to keep those assets growing without taking unacceptable risks.

The solution for more and more people is mutual funds, which in the 1990s have been as profitable in practice as they are sensible in theory. By pooling small investors' money to buy and sell securities on their behalf, a mutual fund provides many of the advantages once available only to the wealthy. These include professional management, diversified holdings and ready access to your cash, all at a reasonable price. For these services some funds impose a sales charge, or load, on top of annual management fees and operating expenses that average just 1.4% of stock funds' assets and 0.8% of bond funds' assets.

The rising popularity of funds comes fortuitously at a time when many investors face difficult financial issues ahead, including continued job insecurity, reduced health care benefits and an aging Social Security safety net. Let's face it. The days when employers, one's extended family and the government provided financial security to the grave are history. These days you have to rely primarily on yourself to make sure that your family's future is adequately provided for. The question no longer is if but when and how aggressively you need to get started as an investor.

The objective of this chapter is to answer such questions, as precisely as possible, so that you can be successful with mutual funds regardless of your experience or goals as an investor. Start by weighing our unvarnished "Answers on Safety, Ethics and Expenses" (see below) concerning these hot topics among fund investors. Also try to evaluate yourself as a fundholder using the quiz "What's Your Investment Rating?" on page 147. Later in the chapter we supply you with model fund portfolios that can be tailored to various stages of your financial life. Along the way we provide our insights about developing a strategy to achieve your goals, be they capital growth, income or a combination of the two. Then we'll teach you how to select funds that will help you reach those milestones without subjecting you to added risk. We also give tips on choosing a fund family to call your own.

Answers on Safety, Ethics and Expenses

Every day, 40 million Americans show a remarkable faith in the integrity of strangers, entrusting their savings to the largely anonymous professional money managers who run mutual funds. The industry has earned that trust during the past 50 years despite some embarrassing blemishes in the go-go funds era of the late 1960s. It has built a reputation as champion of the little guy in the often brutal global financial markets. Recently, however, the industry's bond with investors has been eroded by worrisome episodes involving the abuse of derivatives, the ethics of fund managers and other troubling issues.

Industry officials contend there's no reason for concern. "These minor blips show how well we do at maintaining our standards," says Matthew Fink, president of the Investment Company Institute (ICI) trade association. Yet one prominent fund watcher believes the torrent of dollars may have distracted some from their real mission. "The emphasis over the past few years seems to have moved from portfolio management to selling a product," says Kathryn McGrath, formerly the SEC's top fund regulator and now a securities lawyer in Washington, D.C. "Some people have forgotten that funds are a fiduciary business, which is disturbing." MONEY hasn't. Here are our answers to nagging questions investors now have about funds. We believe that the insights we've gathered will help you become a smarter fund investor—and ultimately a richer one.

Is my fund as safe as it claims?

In the race to stand out among today's nearly 5,000 funds, an increasing number of fund managers invested in highly volatile securities that can boost their portfolios' returns—and also subject them to sizable losses. For example, managers of some aggressive small-cap funds bought speculative issues of new and untested companies that do not trade on major stock exchanges. In bond and money-market funds, the new big risk comes from the arcane securities known as derivatives. These are complex instruments, such as inverse floaters and structured notes, whose value is based on some underlying asset, commodity or interest-rate index. Fund ranker Lipper Analytical Services estimates that more than half of the 3,800 or so fixed-income and money funds have used some form of derivatives to hedge their bets or boost yield. When rates began to shoot up early last year, derivatives soured far faster than the pros expected. As a result, many investors were stunned by sharp losses in supposedly conservative short-term bond funds. What's more, about 20 money-market funds had to be bailed out by their sponsors because of problems with derivatives. Analysts note that some funds are still carrying derivatives on their books at prices 5% to 20% above what they would fetch if they were actually sold.

Bruised shareholders have ample reason to feel betrayed. In most cases, even a careful inspection of a fund's prospectus might not have alerted them to the potential time bombs because the disclosure is worded so opaquely. Take a gander at this section from the prospectus of one battered short-term bond fund. "The fund may also invest in inverse or reverse floating CMOs. Inverse or reverse floating CMOs constitute a tranche of a CMO with a coupon rate that moves in the reverse direction to an applicable index such as LIBOR." Got that? Even reading a fund's portfolio might not have revealed the synthetics. Since funds are required to file their holdings only in their semiannual and annual reports, some managers engage in the sneaky technique called window dressing. That means dumping securities just before public filing dates so that they need not be reported, then buying them back later.

◆ **What you can do.** When investing in small-cap and aggressive growth funds, ask a fund representative how much of the portfolio is in stocks with market capitalizations of $10 million or less. If the fund keeps 5% or more in such issues, invest only if you are prepared to accept outsize risks. The only sure way to learn about your fund's use of derivatives is to question a representative directly. Remember that some derivatives can actually lower the riskiness of a fund, as when currency futures are used in a bond fund to dampen possible losses from foreign exchange fluctuations. What you want to know is whether your fund is using derivatives to pump up the fund's yield and, if so, how much the fund's value can drop if interest rates rise, say, one percentage point. Avoid funds that invest more than 5% of their assets in such derivatives. Or you can go with funds that have strict policies against or largely avoid using these toxic derivatives, such as Vanguard Fixed-Income Short-Term Corporate, Invesco Intermediate Government Bond, AIM Limited Maturity Treasury and Franklin Short/Intermediate U.S. Government Securities.

Is a manager looking after my interests?

An unethical one could hurt a fund several ways. He could buy some stocks for his own account and then drive up their price by having the fund make huge purchases of the same stocks (a practice that's known as front-running). In addition, a manager could accept profit-insuring deals on initial public stock offerings and feel obliged to have the fund buy other issues from the same firm regardless of whether they are good investments. Or a manager could use the fund's money to buy shares in which friends, associates or relatives have some financial stake. These issues surfaced last year when the Invesco Fund group fired star manager John Kaweske for failing to report stock trades in his personal account. Invesco insists that fund shareholders suffered no losses as a result of Kaweske's personal trading. In the wake of the incident, however, an Investment Company Institute panel issued a stringent set of new trading guidelines for fund personnel. Among the recommendations are a ban on managers' profiting from short-term transactions (buying and selling within 60 days) and investing in initial public offerings. Says Ronald Lynch, the Lord Abbett & Co. partner who led the ICI advisory panel: "These strict rules show we're serious about making sure not a single shareholder suffers economic harm."

◆ **What you can do.** Ask your fund whether it has adopted the tough new ICI code of ethics on personal trading. If not, you can urge it to do so or consider voting with your feet.

How much does my fund really cost?

This is basically a no-brainer if you own no-load funds. Simply look up the fund's expense ratio in the prospectus or a mutual fund rating guide such as Morningstar's or Value Line's. If the expense ratio is 1.25%, that means for every hundred dollars you have in the fund, you are paying $1.25 each year to cover the investment adviser's fee as well as marketing, advertising, custodial and administrative services. But for investors who buy funds sold only through brokers or financial planners, trying to answer this simple question can become a calculator-punching headache. Here's why. Seeking to make their commissions more palatable, many funds now offer two or three classes of shares (labeled A, B and C) with differing sales charges and annual expenses. Each share class gives you an interest in the same portfolio. But the fee structures differ, so no two classes have precisely the same net asset value or track record. A few enterprising firms, such as Paine Webber, have gone as far as D shares.

◆ **What you can do.** Stick with no-loads and avoid the incredible expanding share-class problem. If your fund's expenses are above average, find another one or write to your fund's independent directors to ask them to bring down costs in line with its peers.

Who's personally managing my fund?

Since 1993, the SEC has required all mutual funds to disclose the names of portfolio managers in their prospectuses and to inform shareholders whenever a manager departs. Score one for fund investors, right? Not exactly. In an irritating twist, it's getting more difficult to find out who's at the helm of many funds. That's

What's Your Investment Rating?

Anyone who keeps up with today's financial markets should have no trouble polishing off these queries. Score 10 points for each correct answer (explained below).

1. You can't lose money investing in a U.S. Treasury bond because it is backed by the United States Government. True or false?

2. Investing in a fund that holds a diversified portfolio of stocks protects your investment against market declines. True or false?

3. You meet a financial planner whose business card says that he or she is a Registered Investment Adviser. This means the planner
a) meets rigorous standards set by the SEC
b) is recommended by the SEC
c) has paid a $150 registration fee to the SEC

4. You're considering investing in a mutual fund that's announced its plans to distribute $1 a share in dividends. You should
a) buy now so you'll get the distribution
b) buy after the distribution is paid
c) buy either way, because it doesn't matter

5. You own a stock fund whose holdings loosely mirror the Standard & Poor's 500-stock index's recent price-earnings ratio of 19 and dividend yield of 2.8%. This means that the fund is
a) undervalued by historical standards
b) mildly overvalued
c) fairly valued

6. You put $1,000 in a stock fund two years ago. The fund's trading price declined 40% the first year and rose 40% the next. As a result, you've
a) lost money
b) made money
c) broken even

7. You hold bonds maturing in five years that are likely to be called, or redeemed, as early as next year. The best gauge of your return is their
a) current yield
b) yield to maturity
c) yield to call

8. You own shares in the closed-end Germany Fund. The value of your fund's investment expressed in U.S. dollars would be higher if
a) the dollar weakens vs. the Deutsche mark
b) the dollar strengthens against it
c) a change in the dollar doesn't matter

9. The statistical figure that best reflects a mutual fund's performance is
a) its current yield
b) the total of dividends and capital gains paid
c) its total return

10. If interest rates climb one percentage point, which of these would be hurt the least?
a) a 20-year zero-coupon bond
b) a 20-year bond selling at its face value
c) a 20-year bond selling above its face value

Answers: **1.** False. If interest rates rise, the market value of all bonds falls. **2.** False. A portfolio holding stocks alone cushions only against losses in specific stocks. **3.** c. Virtually anyone can register with the SEC as an investment adviser; no professional credentials are required. **4.** b. By waiting, you'll avoid taxes on the distribution. **5.** b. Stocks are generally considered overvalued when the market's price-earnings ratio is around 20 or higher and its dividend yield is lower than 3%. **6.** a. To make up your loss, you would need a 67% gain. **7.** c. The yield to call reflects both the shortened stream of interest payments and the faster principal repayment (sometimes more than the bond's face value) that occurs when a bond is redeemed early. **8.** a. The portfolio is valued in Deutsche marks. If it is converted to a dollar value, the stronger Deutsche mark will buy more dollars, thus increasing your return. **9.** c. Total return includes all income and capital gains distributions plus the change in the fund's share price. **10.** c. The lower a bond's coupon rate and the longer the maturity, the more its price fluctuates with interest rates. A zero has no coupon rate, and a premium bond has a higher coupon rate than one selling at face value. Thus the premium bond would be hurt least.

Scoring: 100: Congratulations! You could become the next fund phenom. 70 to 90: You've mastered the basics. 50 to 60: Bone up before making any big investments. 40 or lower: It's time to start learning about the fundamentals of investing in mutual funds.

because sponsors are still taking advantage of a regulation loophole that allows them to list multiple managers or to simply claim the fund is run by a team and give no names at all. According to Morningstar, nearly 35% of funds now say they are piloted by more than one person, up from 15% in 1989. Of course, some funds, such as those in the Twentieth Century group, really are run by an investment committee. But critics contend the team approach is often little more than an attempt to avoid revealing who is really calling the shots. Why? The fund doesn't want investors fleeing when a successful manager departs.

◆ **What you can do.** If your fund claims team management, ask for details such as which manager has the final say over decisions and how the team divvies up responsibilities. If the fund sponsor won't divulge this information, seek it from mutual fund rating companies. As long as the performance is sound, it doesn't make sense to pull out of the fund over this issue alone.

Is my fund accurately priced? You might have scoffed at this question until last year, when a manager at Fidelity Investments knowingly sent out day-old prices on 150 funds after a computer snafu delayed the tabulation of NAVs (net asset values). Fund ranker Lipper Analytical estimates that no more than 40 of the 3,800 quotes that appear in the newspaper each day are wrong, giving funds an accuracy rate of 99%. In most cases, the prices are off by a penny or two a share, usually because the fund has inadvertently mispriced one or more securities in the mad rush to meet the deadline for sending fund price data to the National Association of Securities Dealers, which distributes them to news services. This small margin of error overstates the problem, however. That's because most of the faulty NAVs printed in newspapers are

corrected before the fund actually processes shareholder transactions. In the Fidelity incident, for example, all trades were made using accurate prices, not the erroneous numbers printed in newspapers.

A more troubling pricing problem is whether a fund is assigning the proper market value to its securities. This is mainly a concern for bond funds that hold difficult-to-price securities such as municipal bonds, junk bonds or yield-boosting derivatives. For muni bond funds, the problem is that of the 1.5 million or so issues outstanding, maybe 180 or so trade on any given day and can be priced on the basis of actual sales. That means the majority of munis are priced by matrix. This is essentially a mathematical formula that takes into account factors like the bond's coupon rate, maturity, credit rating and call features. And those that don't quite fit into a pricing formula are priced by hand—that is, the fund or an independent pricing service calls several dealers to solicit so-called opinions, or estimates of the value of the bonds. Regardless of which method is used, none tells you what you would get if those bonds were sold. Similar difficulties complicate the pricing of junk bonds.

If a fund's NAV is slightly inflated compared with the value of the securities it holds, such a variance is most likely to surface during times of market turmoil. The culprit could be massive redemptions that force the fund to unload its most difficult-to-price holdings. While rare, sell-offs of fund shares large enough to expose shareholders to underlying pricing problems do occur. When assets in Paine Webber's Short-Term U.S. Government Income fund plummeted 57% in the first half of last year, the fund's derivative holdings zoomed to 24% of the portfolio, prompting Paine Webber to protect shareholders by buying derivatives from the fund at the price they were carried on its books.

◆ **What you can do.** Pricing uncertainties are just one more reason to avoid funds that use risky derivatives. But if you want the tax-free income of muni funds, or the double-digit payouts of junk bonds, you will just have to accept the fact that the issues' prices are more like appraisals than precise reflections of the most recent sale. To lower the chances of being stung by a fund with over-priced muni or junk holdings, stick to national muni funds such as SteinRoe Managed Municipals and Tax-Exempt Bond Fund of America that tend to have the most liquid portfolios. Ditto junk funds such as Vanguard Fixed-Income High-Yield Corporate.

Who's championing my interests?

Fund investors have two principal advocates—the independent directors on the fund's board and government regulators, the most prominent of which is the SEC. Independent directors, so named because they do not work for the fund company, usually meet quarterly with the fund management to weigh in on a number of issues, ranging from the size of the fund's expense ratio to the kinds of securities the fund buys. They also get together annually to review the fund's investment advisory contract. At least 40% of each board's directors must be independent (51% if the fund levies a so-called 12b-1 marketing fee). By law, the independents are there to champion the shareholders' rights, not to rubber-stamp the sponsor's requests. Despite the law, how-ever, independent directors too often go along with management on fee increases and other issues. The National Association of Securities Dealers, state securities regulators and even state attorneys general hold some sway over funds. But the SEC is the most visible watchdog for shareholders because it has the power to censure and fine funds.

Still, the SEC claims it needs more money to police the industry. One point of contention between the SEC and Congress is that funds pay much more in registration and other fees to the SEC than Congress budgets for the agency to spend on fund regulation. To correct this and make the SEC less dependent on annual congressional appropriations, some lawmakers are pushing for self-funding—that is, allowing the SEC to use the fees it collects to pay for its own operations. And reinforcements are on the way. The commission expects to hire another 100 or so fund examiners over the next two years, bringing the total number to 300. Even with these new recruits, the SEC will continue to inspect the 50 largest fund companies once every two years, as it does now. For the rest of the funds, inspections will increase to once every 3.5 years, vs. four to five years now.

◆ **What you can do.** Press Congress to make the SEC self-funding. Write to independent directors or buttonhole them at the fund's annual meeting to demand that they be more vigilant in looking after your interests.

Making Money in Riskier Markets

Last year fixed-income investors had to fight Federal Reserve rate hikes and fears of rising inflation, both of which depressed prices of long-term bonds. Stock investors also suffered losses. If history is any guide, however, those setbacks were merely pauses in the long march to profits for investors who stay the course. You can't afford to ignore stocks and stock funds if you're piling up money for a goal that's five or more years away—for example, the down payment on a house, your kids' college education or your secure retirement. "Anyone aiming to meet financial goals 10 to 20 years away has the best chance of being a winner with stocks," notes Peter Lynch, former manager of Fidelity Magellan Fund. The challenge for fund investors, of course, is to assemble and manage a portfolio of promising funds that performs well in different market conditions. The market downdraft was a timely reminder that you can't simply send checks to some mutual fund and count on totting up gains. To succeed in this era of skittish stock and bond markets, you must choose funds with excellent chances of achieving above-average returns year after year.

Today's investors no longer can expect the markets to rack up the exceptional gains over a recent 10-year period. For that decade, stocks returned 15% annually, five percentage points above their six-decade average, and long-term bonds earned almost 12%, more than double their 5% average over time. A return to the historic norms (or worse) was inevitable. "Falling interest rates and expansionary Federal Reserve policy translated to rising stock prices over the three years to 1994," explains James Stack of the investment newsletter *InvesTech Market Analyst*. Last year, however, those conditions were reversed, leading pessimistic forecasters like Stack to conclude the worst. "There is more than a 75% chance that we have entered a bear market," he says. More upbeat experts believe that sharp retreats in the Dow were merely corrections in a bull market. "This is a normal occurrence that should be of little concern to investors who own shares of strong, growing companies," says Bradlee Perry of adviser Babson Research in Boston.

There's a message for investors. The more insecure the markets, the more compelling the case for investing via mutual funds. First, the traditional benefits that you gain with funds (diversification and professional management at very little cost) become more valuable than ever. Second, you can take advantage of the industry's continual innovations to reduce your portfolio's overall risks and earn new profits by diversifying more broadly. Investors today can balance their predominately U.S. holdings with funds that invest as far afield as India and Korea. Moreover, discount brokers like Charles Schwab and Fidelity have made fund investing easier by setting up surrogate fund families that let you buy and sell hundreds of funds from various sponsors without paying a penny in commissions on your trades (discussed later in this chapter).

What bond fundholders are up against.

They are considered by many to be among the best minds in the bond business. But these days William Gross, head of Pimco, a Newport Beach money-management firm, and Dan Fuss of the Loomis Sayles fund group in Boston have very different ideas on how to make money in bonds.

Gross, who has been called the Peter Lynch of bonds, argues that 30-year Treasury bond yields will hover in the narrow 6% to 8% range for the next two to three years. Therefore, he advises income investors to forget about trying to snag capital gains that typically come from making correct bets on the direction of rates. Instead, they should go all-out for yields by choosing funds laden with long-term bonds, lower-quality corporate bonds and foreign issues. Gross is pursuing that strategy with his many Pimco bond funds sold through discount brokers. Some other prominent managers have also been moving to longer maturities.

Fuss shares Gross' view of rates but insists that capital gains are still crucial. To capture them, he searches for bonds and convertible securities whose prices are depressed because the companies that issued them are out of favor. As the economy grows, Fuss believes, these companies will recover and their securities will rise in price. Ken Gregory of newsletter *No-Load Fund Analyst* admires both men: "Fuss is a quintessential bond picker, while Gross looks more for secular trends in the economy." But he thinks investors will be slightly better off following Fuss for now. His opportunistic style, says Gregory, will produce superior returns in today's market. And if interest rates shoot higher, Fuss' portfolio of undervalued bonds will suffer less than Gross' flock of longer maturities.

Why stock funds perform well or not.

The answer depends largely on each fund's investment style (i.e., the kinds of stocks the fund manager prefers). Most fund captains, by training or inclination, favor stocks with certain characteristics year in and year out. Growth funds look for consistent increases in earnings. Thus these funds often shine in stagnant economies or recessions, when reliable profit rises are hard to come by. Value funds lean toward corporate turnarounds and cyclical companies (those whose fortunes are closely tied to the economy's cycles of expansion and recession). These funds tend to dominate the performance charts when the economy is pulling out of recession.

Managers typically also stick to stocks of a particular size. These include blue chips with market values of more than $5 billion or small-company stocks with market capitalizations of less than $500 million. Like both growth and value funds, large and small stock funds tend alternately to outperform and then underperform each other. These lead changes, rather than being tied to the economy, depend more on the evolving strategies of large institutions such as insurance companies. Every five to seven years or so, the giants shed their usual preference for big-name stocks and go looking for the higher returns among smaller stocks. That pushes up prices and begins a cycle of superior returns by Lilliputian firms—until the little guys get overvalued again and deflate, prompting institutions to retreat again to blue chips.

What's in Style This Year for Funds

Shunting your money between funds with different styles in an effort to catch each cycle on the upswing is likely to be as fruitless as any other kind of market timing. All-or-nothing bets are simply too dangerous. It's better to own funds of every investment style. That way, you're assured that at least one fund will be in the winner's circle even when your others are lagging. Nonetheless, it does make sense to use your knowledge of investment cycles to lean toward styles that seem especially promising over the coming year. Among the ones you should consider:

Small-cap funds have room to grow.

These funds as a group have handily outperformed the S&P 500 index from November 1990 until recently. Based on this record—and the tendency of small-company issues to outpace the big guys for five to seven years at a stretch—many experts think small-cap funds could continue to lead their large-company brethren in the year ahead. One reason is that annual earnings growth for small stocks figures to average about twice that expected for big ones, estimates research firm Frank Russell in Tacoma, Wash. On the other hand, "small stocks rarely come out of a serious bear market as shining stars," says analyst Claudia Mott of Prudential Securities. Thus you might keep just 15% to 20% of your stock portfolio allocated to small-company funds.

Growth excels as the economy slows.

The current economic expansion continues to favor value-oriented funds even though their average PE ratio has been as high as 1.75 times that of growth stocks. This suggests value hunters may have bid up the shares' prices beyond their historical norm, report both Prudential and the Leuthold Group, a Minneapolis investment research firm. "These relative valuation measures now look bullish for growth stocks," says Prudential analyst Melissa Brown, particularly if the economy slows down over the coming year. Many analysts recommend that investors have 30% of their stock portfolio in larger-company growth funds and 20% in value funds.

Keep bonds short- or medium-term.

Recurring inflation scares could continue to prop up interest rates. Therefore, it is safest to stick with short-term or intermediate bond funds, which are hurt the least by rising interest rates. Other good choices in these tricky times are the funds that invest in mortgage-backed securities such as GNMAs (commonly called Ginnie Maes) that yield over 8.5%, about one-half percentage point greater than U.S. Treasuries with comparable maturities. The rationale: GNMA funds could still deliver total returns of at least 4% even if long-term interest rates continue to rise.

Broaden your profit horizons abroad.

Overseas stock funds, like primarily U.S. ones, had a disappointing year in '94. Those specializing in Asian markets outside Japan were stung even worse. T. Rowe Price New Asia, for instance, was down 19% in '94 after a 79% run-up the year before. Despite those global swan dives, it still makes sense to keep at least 15% of your stock fund money in overseas funds. The single best reason is the promise of rapid economic growth abroad. Economists expect that some of the bustling economies of Asia and Latin America are capable of growing at rates of 7% or more, compared with 3% for the U.S. Such strong growth should eventually propel stocks higher.

Why We're So Bullish on Stock Funds

Try to look past 1994's market disappointments to the distant year 2000. Investors are on track for one of the great stock-buying opportunities of a lifetime. We have shifted from a nation of CD savers to mutual fund shareholders. Billions of dollars are pouring into the markets just as U.S. corporations have become more competitive. An all but irreversible shift toward long-term stock investing is transforming the market's fundamental outlook. This profound change in investors' behavior will lift stocks higher than they have gone in past bull markets and help them ride out declines such as those in '94. In fact, MONEY is convinced that the market is on the verge of another major advance that could last for the rest of the 1990s and carry the Dow, recently around 3,900, above the 5,000 mark well before the decade ends.

Fueling the boom is a deluge of dough.

Savers who used to squirrel away all they

could in bank savings accounts, money-market funds and CDs have decided they can earn much more investing in stocks, particularly through mutual funds (see the chart "While Banks Lose, Stocks Gain" on the next page). MONEY's Small Investor Index shows that the typical individual's investment portfolio has reached 43% stocks and 36% cash, compared with almost the opposite, 32% stocks and 44% cash, in '88. Despite the conventional wisdom on Wall Street, people are not investing for the short term and do not

panic when the market dips. Some 90% of all fund investors are shareholders for more than 18 months. "Individual investors have been the bull market's engine," says Lehman Bros. investment strategist Katherine Hensel. "And they will probably continue investing via stock funds for the rest of the decade."

Investors realize they can reach their goals only if they own stocks. To put it bluntly, the paltry payouts of bank CDs and savings accounts can't get you what you

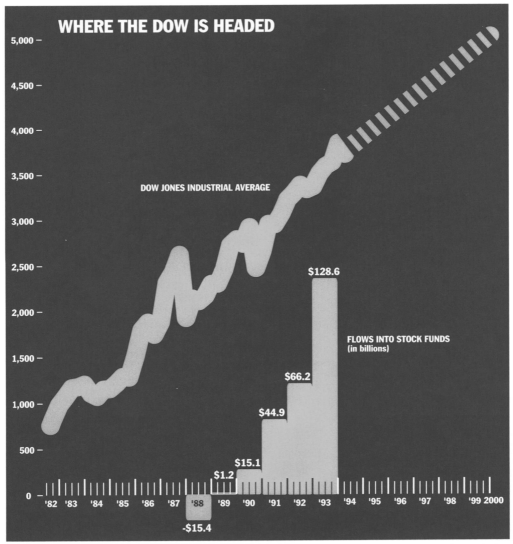

WHERE THE DOW IS HEADED

DOW JONES INDUSTRIAL AVERAGE

FLOWS INTO STOCK FUNDS
(in billions)

$128.6

$66.2

$44.9

$15.1

$1.2

-$15.4

'82 '83 '84 '85 '86 '87 '88 '89 '90 '91 '92 '93 '94 '95 '96 '97 '98 '99 2000

Charts by Paragraphics

Sources: Goldman Sachs, MONEY projections

want, be it college for your kids, a more luxurious home or a comfortable retirement. "Savers want to get a decent return on their money," says Craig Kelly of Banc One in Columbus, Ohio. Like many other bankers, Kelly thinks that the trend to making regular investments in stocks and stock funds is unstoppable. "Investors are more sophisticated and educated, and they're taking a much longer view," says Kelly. "We doubt there will ever be a big switch back to investing in CDs."

The cascade of cash into stock investments will only increase as workers step up their retirement saving to guard against eventually outliving their money. "There's a growing awareness that people will be on their own in funding their retirement," says SEC commissioner Carter Beese. "What's important for people is ongoing asset allocation. And with just income investments, you'll need to save more." That's particularly true now that the potential for double-digit returns from bond funds has been weakened by the Federal Reserve's policy of raising interest rates. As long as interest rates were falling, long-term bonds could provide total returns that rivaled what stocks could offer. In fact, in seven of the past 14 years, long-term government bond returns have actually topped those on stocks. Once the Fed began lifting interest rates, however, the bull market in bonds has looked very long in the hoof.

As a result, stocks clearly rank as the top investment choice. Since bonds can't offer the unparalleled returns they paid in the 1980s, stocks will once again be the top pick for

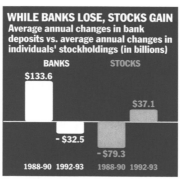

WHILE BANKS LOSE, STOCKS GAIN
Average annual changes in bank deposits vs. average annual changes in individuals' stockholdings (in billions)

BANKS: $133.6, -$32.5 (1988-90, 1992-93)
STOCKS: $37.1, -$79.3 (1988-90, 1992-93)

Sources: Federal Reserve, Goldman Sachs, Investment Company Institute

long-term wealth building. All the historical evidence suggests that stocks will comfortably outpace even 4% or 5% annual inflation. Consider that, over the past 20 years, blue-chip stocks have returned an average of 7% a year after inflation and taxes, compared with a 0.6% loss for long-term Treasury bonds and a 6% loss for money funds (see "Only Stocks Win" below).

People of most ages and incomes are investing in stocks via funds.

Investors' new interest in stocks began following the 1981-82 bear market, grew irregularly in the mid-1980s as the bull market gathered speed and then boomed after '88, when investors saw that even the '87 crash's huge plunge in share prices didn't end the market advance. Since 1988, small investors have been pouring money into stock funds at an accelerating rate. Over a recent 12-month period, inflows into such funds totaled $151 billion, vs. only $45 billion as recently as 1991.

And the fun has just begun. For example, banks have decided to join the mutual fund bandwagon. "As banks lose deposits, they will try to sell more funds," says Dan Smith of the American Bankers Association. He says 20% of the new money going into mutual funds comes from ones that were bought at banks. The big merger of the Mellon Bank and the Dreyfus fund organization only confirms the trend. Some three-quarters of the nation's 100 largest banking companies already sponsor proprietary funds. And some 3,500 banks and thrifts sell

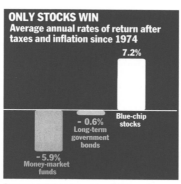

ONLY STOCKS WIN
Average annual rates of return after taxes and inflation since 1974

7.2% Blue-chip stocks
-0.6% Long-term government bonds
-5.9% Money-market funds

Sources: Ibbotson Associates, IBC/Donoghue, MONEY estimates

other mutual funds. Says Smith: "Banks will dominate the mutual fund industry within 10 years." A MONEY poll found that one out of five people said they would invest a $10,000 windfall in mutual funds, up from less than one in 10 in 1986. People also are becoming investors earlier. A Merrill Lynch poll found that today's 25- to 44-year-olds started saving or planning for retirement at the seemingly young age of 26, on average.

Workers are adding more stock funds to their IRAs, 401(k)s and other retirement plans. Even people whose sole investments are retirement accounts are relying more heavily on stocks. Since 1988, the nation's 18 million 401(k) savers have added $148 billion to funds that hold stocks or a balance of stocks and bonds, vs. $58 billion for short-term investments such as guaranteed investment contracts (GICs) and money funds (see the chart "401(k)s Opt for Stocks" at right). Retirees also are boosting their stockholdings. Those who are 65 now are likely to live at least another 17 years. Over that period, even 4% inflation would slash the purchasing power of their savings in half.

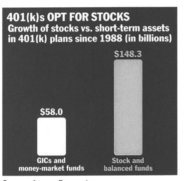

401(k)s OPT FOR STOCKS
Growth of stocks vs. short-term assets in 401(k) plans since 1988 (in billions)

$148.3

$58.0

GICs and money-market funds

Stock and balanced funds

Source: Access Research

The continuing torrent of cash will buoy stock prices in the 1990s.

The economic rebound that began in '91 is peculiar in one important respect. "This is a Silly Putty recovery—it keeps getting stretched out," says investment strategist Abby Joseph Cohen at Goldman Sachs in New York City. Although overall growth has been slower than in past recoveries, that will cause less inflationary pressure and the bull market will therefore be able to last longer. Professional investors may be forced to trade in and out of stocks to try to achieve market-beating results quarter after quarter. But today's seasoned small investors realize that they are best advised to hang on to investments, especially since good times are likely to keep rolling for years to come, argues Cohen. "The long-term view is terrific," she continues. "As the baby boom ages, they'll increasingly buy stocks. That means cash inflows will be favorable for the next five to 10 years."

The rush into stocks comes as American industry regains its global leadership. If all this money were gushing into stocks in the middle of a dead U.S. economy, we would have the ingredients of another market crash. But that's not happening. Corporate cutbacks over the past 10 years, accelerated by the 1990-91 recession, have turned American businesses into sinewy profit machines. Most economists say U.S. business looks leaner and feistier than at any time since the 1960s. In fact, this country is now poised to reassert its dominance in all three crucial economic areas—manufacturing, services and advanced technology. Foreign investors apparently recognize this potential; their holdings of U.S. stocks recently reached a record $20 billion. Consider:

◆ **Manufacturing.** The U.S. again ranks as the world's most efficient producer. After spending nearly $1 trillion on downsizing, restructuring and automation since 1980, U.S. companies are extremely competitive. Indeed, U.S. productivity per employee has sprinted ahead of the comparable figures for German and Japanese firms. Manufacturing costs in the U.S. have risen a mere 0.2% annually in recent years, while both Japanese and German manufacturing costs jumped 12% or more (see the chart "U.S. Stays Lean" on the right). Thus U.S. exports are expected to boom as foreign economies also recover over the coming years.

◆ **Services.** America also continues to dominate tomorrow's most promising service businesses, from finance to entertainment. And there is growing evidence that productivity enhancement is penetrating the all-important service sector. It accounts for nearly 80% of the U.S. economy. Among the most important reasons for the advances is the personal computer. The U.S. has 35 such PCs per 100 workers, compared with only 15 in Germany and nine in Japan (see the chart "We Lead in PCs" on the right).

◆ **Technology.** The U.S. leads in biotech, computers and other high-technology industries. "Advances in these fields come from recently formed companies, and there's a good environment for entrepreneurial firms in the U.S. now," says William Hambrecht of brokerage Hambrecht & Quist in San Francisco. Once again, the U.S. is in the forefront of technology. "The U.S. has dominance in microprocessors, networking, software and communications," he says. "And we're a leader in aerospace, environmental science and biotechnology." As a consequence, U.S. exports of advanced technology have soared (see the chart "U.S. High-Tech Sells" on the right).

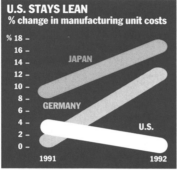

U.S. STAYS LEAN
% change in manufacturing unit costs

Source: Bureau of Labor Statistics

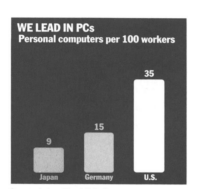

WE LEAD IN PCs
Personal computers per 100 workers

Source: International Data Corp.

U.S. HIGH-TECH SELLS
U.S. advanced technology exports (in billions)

Source: The Commerce Department

Investors in U.S. firms can bet on brisk 8% to 9% earnings growth.

After averaging only 3% annual earnings growth from '89 to '91, after-tax corporate profits exploded at double-digit rates in both '93 and '94. And there's more growth ahead. "The fundamentals for profits are all moving in favorable directions at the same time," says Prudential Securities economist Richard Rippe. Demand is expanding at a moderate rate of almost 3% a year, labor costs are rising less than 1% annually, and interest rates are still lower than they were three years ago. Rippe expects only 5% to 6% growth in 1995, mainly because slower growth owing to the current rise in interest rates could knock as much as 10 percentage points off corporate profit gains for the year. Starting in '96, however, the economy will have adjusted successfully to higher interest rates, allowing profits growth to accelerate to 8% to 9%. "A moderate increase in inflation would actually help corporate profits over the next few years," says strategist Joseph McAlinden at the investment firm Dillon Read in New York City. "As inflation fell over the past decade, companies weren't able to pass their cost increases through to customers. But a slight increase in inflation will let them raise prices, and those increases will go right to the bottom line." In addition, McAlinden notes that productivity is rising at an above-average rate. Over the next five years, he forecasts that 4% to 4.5% inflation, 1.5% yearly productivity gains and real economic growth averaging 2.5% to 3% a year will propel company profits 8% to 9% annually.

Confidence in the market and economy can push the Dow above 5,000 by 2000.

If current trends continue, the stock market weakness that began last year should be over soon, and prices will start to rise again. Here's why. The market has actually been following the typical pattern. A bull market begins late in a recession as interest rates fall. Then when the recession ends, corporate profits rebound powerfully from depressed levels. That combination provides jet fuel for stocks. Existing factories and service operations eventually are fully employed. At that point, companies have to borrow to expand or bottlenecks will start pushing up prices, causing inflation. Either way, interest rates begin rising, setting the stage for a market correction in which share prices plunge as investors reassess their expectations in light of higher rates. Once that adjustment is made, stocks typically stage a slower advance that can last for years. And if the economy has grown more efficient, the expansion can continue without boosting inflation and interest rates beyond moderate levels.

One financial menace that could derail this forecast would be an upsurge in inflation to more than 5% a year. Indeed, a few gloomsters, such as money manager Henry Kaufman, formerly chief economist at Salomon Bros., are saying that accelerating inflation and soaring interest rates could squash share prices in as little as two years. MONEY doesn't buy that bleak scenario. The kind of runaway inflation that would trigger a lengthy bear market seems nowhere in sight.

To appreciate the potential payoff that stocks offer, take the time to do some simple math. Let's assume that once this market correction runs its course, stocks' average PE ratio holds constant at around 15 times current-year earnings and that corporate profits increase an average of 8% annually. Over the next six years, that formula could translate into a stunning 59% gain in share prices. So even if the Dow falls before a sustainable market advance commences, the Dow would still top 5,000 before the year 2000.

Ride the upturn with growth funds.

In a market driven by earnings growth rather than rising PE ratios, it makes sense to invest in growth stock funds. You may want to put as much as 15% to 20% of your portfolio in small-cap funds. "Companies with revenues of $250 million to $750 million tend to be the best performers in periods of steady growth and moderate inflation," says McAlinden of Dillon Read. Get started by buying an index fund, such as the Vanguard Index 500, that holds the S&P 500 stocks and should keep pace with the market's future growth.

Profiting Through Life's Passages

Investors increasingly view diversification as their silver bullet, the one terminator to every threat. By dividing your money among a variety of complementary funds, you can reduce your risk and maintain (or even enhance) your return. Achieving the optimum combi-

Winning Portfolios for Life's Stages

Young Achiever

Single Woman, Age 25 - Investment: $10,000

With a long way to go before retirement, she can take the necessary risks to gun for high returns. Three stock funds diversified among large and small U.S. companies plus foreign shares do that work, while a single bond fund hedges against stock market declines. Four funds are a maximum. Any more would stretch her limited resources too much.

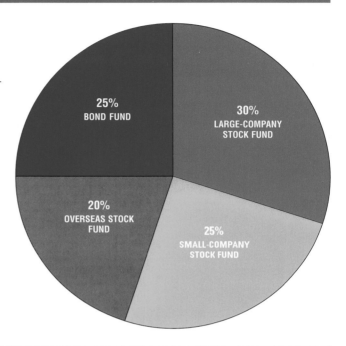

Nest Builders

Married Couple, Mid-Thirties, Two Preschoolers - Investment: $50,000

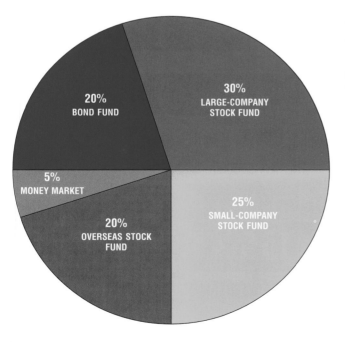

The children's eventual college bills add one more long-term expense to this family's financial picture, making high returns a must. Thus 75% of their assets should go into stock funds, including a 25% slice in small-company funds. Depending on their tax bracket, up to half of their bond investment should be in tax-free muni funds.

Peak Earners

Married Couple, Early Fifties, Three Teenagers - Investment: $250,000

We assume that about 60% of this couple's portfolio is already earmarked for their retirement. That portion should go entirely into U.S. and overseas stock funds that are invested for capital growth. Most of the remaining money should be stashed in relatively stable, income-generating bond funds to pay for their kids' college education.

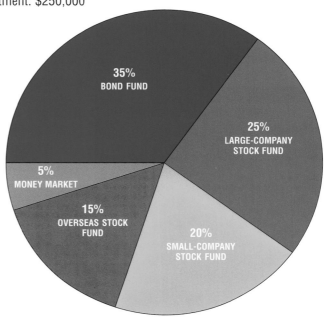

35%
BOND FUND

25%
LARGE-COMPANY
STOCK FUND

5%
MONEY MARKET

15%
OVERSEAS STOCK
FUND

20%
SMALL-COMPANY
STOCK FUND

The Enjoyers

Married Couple, Early Sixties, Two Grown Children - Investment: $350,000

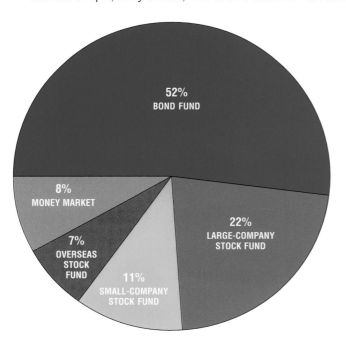

52%
BOND FUND

8%
MONEY MARKET

7%
OVERSEAS
STOCK
FUND

11%
SMALL-COMPANY
STOCK FUND

22%
LARGE-COMPANY
STOCK FUND

Their main goals are to conserve principal and generate income to live on. Accordingly, 60% of their assets goes into bond funds and money-market funds. To help keep pace with inflation during retirement, however, the couple still need stock funds. Indeed, we recommend an 18% stake in fairly volatile small-cap and overseas funds.

159

nation, however, is not as simple as dialing an 800 number. The passages in your life bring changes in the degree of diversification that you require as well as subtle shifts in your portfolio itself. No matter what your age is or how you apportion your assets, keep in mind that the best way to stay diversified is to formulate a strategy you will not feel trapped by later. The key is to find your comfort zone—and to know it may change as you progress through your life and career.

Starting out. A lifetime plan for building wealth and conquering risk begins when you first accumulate assets in your name, usually in your twenties. At that time you should diversify broadly in various categories of funds. Since you have plenty of time to ride out losses at this stage, you can afford to take somewhat greater risks than you would later in life. Therefore, your biggest bets should be in three types of stock funds focused, respectively, on large, established firms, smaller companies and those based overseas. As for bonds, funds that own corporate, U.S. government or municipal issues with intermediate terms (maturing in 10 years or fewer) provide the most generous combination of yield and possible appreciation.

Getting married. You may have a well-balanced portfolio for a single person. But what do you do if your newly betrothed loves racy sector funds invested solely in, say, technology stocks? The solution seems easy enough. You simply add up your combined assets and then reallocate them according to a mutually acceptable plan. In fact, the process often entails a fair amount of soul searching. You should think hard, for instance, before eliminating a category of volatile investments just because one party feels skittish about it. But keep in mind that both owners of a portfolio should be comfortable—and vigilant for any

potential land mines. Prominent among them is the increasingly common case of a two-career couple whose jobs are in the same field or even company. If they have been contributing regularly to their firms' stock-purchase plans, they both are doubly vulnerable to a cyclical downturn in the industry's profitability and payroll. Thus the couple should sell some shares, and reinvest the proceeds in a diversified fund, even if they're bet-the-farm bullish on their company's prospects.

Raising a family. Because your kids could become your biggest expense, each birth is likely to cause you to reconsider just how your wealth is divvied up. But the event shouldn't occasion a wholesale rejiggering. Instead, let your holdings ride while you try to meet short-term needs by extracting cash from money-market funds. Remember too that the amount you put aside for college is part of your total portfolio and not some segregated sector of it, even if the money is in your child's name. If you decide to load your kids' college account with growth-minded stock funds, for instance, you may need to lighten up on such funds in your portfolio as a whole. Be aware as well of when you will need to tap the savings. You should gradually reduce your holdings of stock funds as you approach those tuition bills. That way you won't get caught having to cash in during a sudden slump in the market.

Changing jobs. When you leave yours, you may have trouble keeping your portfolio properly poised. For example, you may receive a large lump sum from a company-sponsored savings plan and will need to decide how to allocate it. The best strategy depends mostly on the circumstances of your leave-taking. If you are moving directly to another job at comparable pay, you may simply want to roll the money over into a self-directed IRA and rebalance your other holdings as needed. If you expect to be out of work for a while, however, you should try to resist the immediate temptation to disrupt your portfolio mix by weeding out the riskier holdings and bulking up on cash and short-term bonds. A short-term disruption shouldn't upset a long-term plan. If you have an emergency fund equal to three months or more of expenses, you can probably ride out the episode without being forced to sell long-term holdings such as stock funds.

Splitting up. While divorce is often messy, disengaging your investments shouldn't be. That's because stockbrokers and mutual fund sponsors generally are willing to reissue jointly registered fund shares in separate names. The exception, of course, is real estate. Whatever you both own may have to be sold and divided, thus adding the task of integrating the proceeds into your own portfolio. Now is the perfect time to reassess whether you are comfortable owning singly what you invested in jointly only a while ago. Once you have determined that, you may still need to reallocate your portfolio (just as you may when a spouse dies). If you were depending on someone else's income as well as your own, you may want to shift a small percentage of growth-oriented assets, such as small-company stock funds or international funds, into income-generating bond funds.

Calling it quits. Once you reach your sixties, which will probably be the decade you retire, many of your financial problems will be behind you. Your children, if any, may be grown and even out of the house. Your home may be largely paid off. And you may be on the verge of making the classic mistake of unloading stock funds in a quest for greater income and capital preservation, thereby leaving yourself vulnerable to the risk of rising inflation. Assuming that inflation stays at around 3% annually, for example, it would cut the purchasing power of today's dollar in half in only 12 years. Thus you should still pursue a growth strategy via a hefty stake in stock funds. The rest of your portfolio should be stashed in sturdy, interest-paying bond funds and money-market funds.

Finding Funds That Fit Your Profile

The word portfolio conjures images of artists carrying samples of their best work that have been methodically chosen, updated and arranged for maximum effect. Savvy investors take the same kind of care assembling a fund portfolio, selecting funds not only for their particular promise but also for how well they complement the other funds in the portfolio. The result, when you do it right, is a kind of investing alchemy. Your portfolio becomes less risky than the sum of its components without a corresponding drop in return.

Diversify for risk reduction. If fund investing were a form of meditation, there would be no mistaking its mantra—diversify, diversify, diversify. The practice of offsetting one investment's vulnerabilities with another's strengths is the principal ingredient in a well-constructed portfolio. It's what curbs risk without canceling growth. Think of it as a way of hedging your bets. Individual funds, of course, are inherently diversified. But owning a bunch of stocks does you little good when the whole market plunges. So you want to own funds that embrace a wide variety of assets. The key is to mix and match funds invested in markets that are not correlated (that is, go up and down at different times).

Match your funds to your goals.

This process, the heart of managing a portfolio, starts with a simple question. What's the money for? Is it for retirement in 20 years or a new car next year? If you're sure you won't need the money for five to 10 years, you should tilt your portfolio toward stocks, the assets that provide the best long-term return, and ignore the inevitable market ups and downs in the meantime. If you expect to need the cash in five years or less, you'll have to play it safer by putting a larger share of your money in bonds and cash.

You'll also want to consider how much income you rely on from your investments. The more cash flow you require, the more you should tilt your portfolio toward bond funds or to income-producing stock funds. But you'll first need to square that advice with your own internal risk meter. Often there's a wide gap between what makes sense financially and what people feel comfortable with emotionally. Many investors can afford to be more aggressive but do not trust the stock market. If you are one of them, you owe it to yourself and your family to be candid about this concern.

If both indicators point to an aggressive portfolio, then consider putting as much as 75% of your money in stock funds, balancing small-cap funds against large, and U.S. stock funds against foreign to dampen some of the volatility. The remaining 25% should be split between investment-grade bonds and cash. If your temperament or circumstances don't permit such an aggressive stance, a better fit might be 60% stocks, 20% bonds and 20% cash. Over the past 10 years, that would have provided 95% of the return earned by the

aggressive portfolio with a loss in its worst year just 60% as large. And if your needs call for still more caution, try 50% stock funds, 20% bonds and 30% cash. This would have cut the worst-year loss to just 36% of the aggressive portfolio's and still have delivered 88% of the riskier brew's return.

Don't forget to stash enough cash.

Before you risk any of your money, set aside an emergency reserve equal to three to six months' living expenses in a safe, easily accessible investment like a money fund. This will keep you from having to sell long-term investments if you become ill or lose your job. If the cash portion of your portfolio is large enough, it can serve as the emergency stash. If not, you'll need a separate reserve fund. In addition, if you're counting on income from your investments to meet day-to-day expenses, make sure that you allocate enough to bond or total return stock funds to meet your income needs before apportioning the rest of your portfolio.

How many funds you can manage.

When diversifying, don't confuse quantity with quality. What matters is not how many funds you own but how distinct they are. A portfolio of 10 small-cap growth funds is less truly diversified than one holding just a stock fund and a money-market fund. In general, you should aim for the broadest portfolio you can afford using the following guidelines based on the amount of capital that you have on hand for investment.

With $5,000 or less, go for a single diversified fund. You might consider balanced funds, which divide your money between stocks and bonds. For still more diversification, try asset allocation funds. They create a portfolio in a single fund, holding stocks, bonds and cash, and occasionally real estate, and gold.

With $5,000 to $20,000, you can afford three or four funds. If you started with a balanced fund and can tolerate moderate risk, you probably should think about adding a couple of stock funds with different approaches (e.g., a large-company growth fund and a small-cap fund). If you hate paperwork, you should consider sticking to funds in a single no-load family that will report all your investment transactions on one statement.

With $20,000 to $50,000, five or six funds ought to be enough. Depending on how you're allocating your assets to match your circumstances, you could add an overseas fund and an intermediate-term bond fund (one with maturities between five and 10 years). For less volatility and more income, try two stock funds, two bond funds with intermediate maturities, and a money fund.

With $50,000 to $100,000, you can add another fund or two to further subdivide your stock and bond allocations. Among your stockholdings, you can balance growth against value funds; small-stock against large-company; domestic against foreign. Bond choices can be split among funds with varying maturities and levels of credit risk. Some investors also divide their stake in each subdi-vision between a couple of funds to balance one manager against the other.

With $100,000 or more, you have the wherewithal to hold 15 or 20 different funds. Note, however, that you would be adequately diversified with a well-chosen seven to 10. Owning more funds is fine if you have the time to track them. But if you break your holdings into many pieces smaller than $5,000, the diversification may not justify the record keeping. One way to streamline the office work is to buy no-load funds through the "no transaction fee" services of discount brokers like Charles Schwab and Fidelity Investments (discussed later in this chapter).

Move into the market methodically.

Once you decide how to allocate the money in your portfolio, try to resist the urge to invest it all at once. Instead, divide the money into equal dollar amounts and move it into your chosen funds once a month or once a quarter over a year or two. Such periodic investing, commonly called dollar cost averaging, forces you to buy more fund shares when the prices are low and fewer when they are high—one of investing's golden rules (see below). Another advantage of this technique is that it keeps you from yielding to panic in a market downturn.

Master Techniques That Reduce Risk

Are you sitting on the sidelines because the stock market looks too scary? Or waiting for prices to hit bottom before moving more money into stock funds? Either way, you are very likely to be disappointed. No one really knows when stock prices have no place to go but up. As a result, you may miss the chance to make some big profits. Thus investing experts often suggest that you use a risk-reducing technique for moving money into stock funds that will let you take full advantage of price dips, prevent you from getting badly hurt by sudden spikes and help assure that you reach your financial goals. The strategy, called periodic investing, has you invest regularly (e.g., every month or quarter) no matter what's happening in the market. Here are four variations of this disciplined approach to investing.

Dollar cost averaging.

With this most basic form of periodic investing, you put a set amount each month (say, $200) in a stock fund. When stock prices fall, your $200 buys more fund shares. When prices rise, your money buys fewer. That way, you keep your fund shares' average cost relatively low. As shown below in the table "Profit from the Installment Plan," if you had invested $200 a month beginning in 1984 in Vanguard Index 500 Fund, which mimics the S&P 500 index, your $24,000 would have more than doubled to approximately $49,400.

Dollar cost averaging is simple and very dependable. But you might prefer to boost your profits with a more advanced version, called progressive dollar cost averaging. This strategy takes into account inflation, the chief drawback of investing the same amount every month for years. With progressive averaging, you can increase your monthly contribution every year, or even every six months, by a set percentage. How much? Experts often recommend a manageable 10%. That will keep you far ahead of inflation as well as supercharge your savings. So an investor who starts out contributing $200 a month might step that up to $220 a year later. If you had used this technique beginning in '84, your $37,950 total investment in the Vanguard Index 500 Fund would have grown to $69,800.

Value averaging.

Think of this as dollar cost averaging with attitude. Rather than investing a set monthly amount, you put in whatever is necessary to hit your goal. Let's say you need $9,000 in three years for a down payment on a house. You first open a fund account with, perhaps, $200. Next, with the help of a financial calculator or compound interest tables found in your local library's reference section, you determine that your account's value must increase $200 a month to reach your target. The actual amount you invest each month will change as stock prices fluctuate. For example, if the

---

Profit From the Installment Plan

If you had used the value averaging method during the 1984 to 1993 bull market, you would have earned annual returns of 15%, far more than with any of the other risk-cutting strategies shown below and explained in this chapter. In today's skittish market, however, investing experts say the three other techniques may carry less risk. In our table, we assumed that a hypothetical investor had an account with the Vanguard Index 500 Fund, which closely mimics the S&P 500 index. In the case of two related strategies, constant ratio planning and variable installment, we linked the Index 500 Fund with the Vanguard Money Market Reserves Prime Fund.

STRATEGY	Monthly contribution	Total amt. invested	Portfolio value	Average annual return	Avg. cost per share
Value averaging	Varies	$23,540	$49,400	15.1%	$20.90
Dollar cost averaging	$200	24,000	49,400	13.8	21.30
Constant ratio planning	200	24,000	40,400	9.9	28.00
Variable installment	200	24,000	40,300	9.9	29.30

market is flat during the month you open your fund account, you simply invest an additional $200 in the second month, bringing your account's value to $400. On the other hand, if your fund's value falls by 12.5% during the second month, your account will dip to $350. Your third investment must then be $250, since your game plan calls for your account to be worth $600 in month three. If, however, stocks rise in the second month and boost your balance to $470, your third contribution must be only $130.

What happens if the value of your holdings rises so rapidly that your account's value exceeds your monthly target? In that case, value averaging calls for you to sell some shares. If your account increased to $700 in the third month, you would dump $100 of your holdings. Of course, your profit would be taxable if you were investing outside of a tax-deferred account, such as an IRA or 401(k) plan. Therefore, you might prefer a modified value averaging strategy called no-sell value averaging. With this technique, when your portfolio value exceeds the target, you simply do nothing that month.

Value averaging beats dollar cost averaging most of the time. To accumulate your $49,400 in the Vanguard Index 500 Fund using our example, you would have had to invest $24,000 beginning in '84 if you used dollar cost averaging but $23,540 with value averaging. That $460 saving may seem slim. Still, your money would have worked more efficiently, delivering both higher returns and a lower average cost per share.

Constant ratio planning.
This fairly conservative method calls for you to balance a stock fund investment against a less aggressive one, usually a money-market fund. You first decide how much risk you can take, then allocate your monthly investment between the two funds accordingly. Let's say you decide to split a $200 monthly investment evenly between a stock fund and a money fund. If stock prices rise, you eventually will have to shift money from your stock fund to your money fund to restore your fifty-fifty ratio. Investing experts recommend that you rebalance your portfolio whenever the ratio gets five percentage points out of whack (in our example, whenever the value of either fund rises to 55% of your portfolio). When stocks are rising, the more risk you're willing to take when you set the ratio, the more money you will make. In our example, a $200 monthly investment divided equally between the Vanguard Index 500 Fund and the Vanguard Money Market Reserves Prime funds would have grown to $40,400, about $9,000 less than with straight dollar averaging. But you would cut your risk roughly in half by stashing 50% of your cash in a money fund.

Variable installment strategy.
Like constant ratio, you start out by dividing your monthly investment equally between the funds. Then, when one fund lags the other, you direct your entire contribution to it. That way, you buy more shares when they are cheap and avoid putting money in investment categories that may be temporarily overvalued. Let's again assume you decide to invest $200 a month in a stock and a money fund. You start out by putting $100 into each. Whenever the stock fund's share price drops by an amount (let's say, 5%) that you have determined in advance, you put all of your next monthly investment into that fund. Conversely, if its share price rises 5%, you invest all your next monthly installment in the money fund. If you had invested a total of $24,000 since '84 using this 5% variable installment method, your portfolio would have grown to $40,300. Like constant ratio, variable installment would have earned you about $9,000 less than straight dollar cost averaging but would have carried less risk.

Rating the 25 Biggest Mutual Funds

Today's 15 biggest stock funds and the 10 brawniest national bond funds command $252 billion. That's an astounding 16% of total industry assets, and more money than was invested in the entire universe of stock and bond funds as recently as 1985. Only 10 years ago, four of these colossal 25 weren't even born; the other 21 had combined assets of roughly $18 billion. Does bigger mean better? The fattest funds would seem to get that way because their winning records boosted assets and drew flocks of fresh cash. But sometimes a fund's reputation can pull in shareholder dollars long after its glory days have ended. And growth can make it harder for funds to maintain their winning streaks. When managers start deploying billions instead of millions, they must often increase the number of stocks in their portfolios and buy larger issues. Such changes in strategy can sometimes lead to disappointing results.

To help the millions of shareholders who own a piece of these 25 fund Gibraltars, or anyone interested in joining their ranks, MONEY analyzed each portfolio, dissected performance rankings and consulted dozens of fund experts to rate each fund as a buy, sell or hold. Thirteen heavyweights, including Fidelity Magellan, Janus and Pimco Total Return, earned buy recommendations because we believe they are poised to outperform comparable funds over the next 12 months. In our book, a buy means new investors and current shareholders alike have ample reason to put fresh money in the fund. We put hold ratings on nine funds that seemed capable of merely average returns over the coming year. Because these funds have shone in the past, we think current investors would do well to sit tight in them. As veteran investors know,

success often comes from sticking with a few strong funds that produce superior gains over periods of five years or more, not from opening and closing accounts in a usually futile chase for the hot name of the week.

Finally, we recommend selling three of these funds—Dean Witter U.S. Government Securities, IDS High-Yield Tax Exempt and Dreyfus Municipal Bond. They all posted below-average results without showing much prospect for improvement soon, or they are simply too risky in our view. You can find detailed performance records as well as cost and portfolio data for all 25 funds in the rankings beginning on page 177. The risk figures cited are from Morningstar, the Chicago mutual fund rating service, and rely on its proprietary measures.

The 15 Biggest Stock Funds

Buy Fidelity Magellan. Since 1992, Jeff Vinik has managed the world's largest mutual fund (with assets of $37 billion) and followed in the stock-picking tradition of his predecessor, Peter Lynch. Vinik uses what pros call a bottom-up approach, checking out companies one by one, preferably in person, before adding them to the portfolio. But there have been a couple of notable changes in the fund since Lynch's departure. For one thing, assets have tripled. But the number of stocks in the portfolio has shrunk by more than half, from 1,300 under Lynch to 600. As a result, Vinik inevitably makes bigger bets on individual companies and sectors than did Lynch, though Lynch too swung for the fences from time to time. For example, 29% of Magellan's assets recently were invested in technology stocks (up from 18% a year ago), including chipmakers Motorola (among the fund's biggest holdings at 2.7%) and Intel (2.3%). Vinik believes such stocks will benefit from the irreversible trend of "computers and technology replacing people." His second biggest stake is the lagging financial services sector, at 11%, which he believes will flourish as aging baby boomers step up their investment activity. Eric Kobren of *Fidelity Insight*, an independent investment newsletter, believes Magellan is worth its 3% load, and we agree. Vinik's flexibility and stock-picking skills figure to help Magellan maintain its position as an above-average growth fund.

Buy Investment Company of America.

The largest of four American Funds stock portfolios on our list, this $20 billion growth and income entry exemplifies its family's style of steady performance that wins marathons rather than sprints. Its 10-year average annual return of 15% puts it in the top 12% of its group for the period, yet it never cracked the top decile in any one of those years. That consistency is rooted in American's unusual management system, where every fund has multiple managers (ICA has nine), each of whom exercises control over a portion of the portfolio. ICA's team recently had 77% of shareholders' money in large stocks such as AT&T and IBM. About 15% of the fund is in short- and intermediate-term government bonds that can cut the fund's share price volatility. Partly as a result, ICA registers between 30% to 40% less risk than the typical stock fund. While ICA charges a steep 5.75% sales commission, its 0.6% annual expense ratio is well below the 1.4% average for stock funds. Holders willing to stay in the fund for 10 years or so needn't fret about the initial load. Going forward, the fund's steady style could thrive no matter what fashions sweep the markets, making ICA a buy.

Hold Washington Mutual Investors.

This $13 billion fund seems to get better the longer you own it. Despite its failure to finish in the top 50% of growth and income funds in three of the past 10 years, this portfolio of large-capitalization stocks is nevertheless in the top 20% of its investment category for the past 10 and 15 years. "Even when it trails the leaders, it manages to remain competitive," says Morningstar analyst Laura Lallos. "Over the long term, it is impressive." Indeed, we would rate this 5.75% load fund a buy, rather than hold, if it weren't for the fact that its American sibling, Investment Company of America (see the previous item), earns first place honors among the family's growth and income funds. ICA's long-term gains not only top Washington Mutual's. But Morningstar also rates ICA as slightly less risky.

Hold Fidelity Asset Manager. Bob

Beckwitt, who has steered the $12 billion no-load fund since its 1988 launch, shifts assets among stocks, bonds and cash in response to changing market conditions. And when his calls are correct, his moves can reward shareholders handsomely. Bracing for what he believes will be a tough year, Beckwitt has dropped his stock stake to 38% of assets from 51% a year ago and increased cash to 29% of assets from 16% in '93. Beckwitt says he will wait for markets to improve before putting more cash to work. While he's waiting it out, we are rating this fund a hold.

Buy Vanguard Windsor. Manager John

Neff plans to retire at the end of this year with one of the best records in the business. Windsor has gained 4,766% since he started running it in June 1964, vs. 2,411% for stock funds as a group. Neff is a classic value hunter, feasting on stocks trading at discounts of 30% to 50% to the market's PE. And when he likes a stock, he scoops up a heaping helping. Neff's top 10 holdings account for 40% of the fund's nearly $12 billion in assets. Despite such large bets, no-load Windsor has been 14% less risky than the norm over the past 10 years. And we rate it a buy even though Neff is departing. Reason: his successor Charles Freeman has worked alongside Neff for the past 25 years. There is one major complication, however. The fund has been largely closed to new investors since 1985. So you can acquire shares only if you are one of the fund's current shareholders or participate in one of the many company savings plans with accounts in the fund.

Buy Fidelity Puritan.

Value has been the watchword over the seven years that Richard Fentin has managed this $11 billion fund. Any stock or bond he buys must be priced at less than half its worth as measured by book value, earnings, cash flow or assets. Like Windsor's John Neff, Fentin has shown that he can prosper under various market conditions. "Puritan is among the top-performing funds regardless of the time period you pick," says Sheldon Jacobs of the *No-Load Fund Investor* newsletter. "This shows the manager has a knack for being in the right part of the market at all times." We rate Puritan a buy. As a bonus, Fidelity is waiving Puritan's 2% load until December 1995.

Hold Income Fund of America.

This $11 billion American Funds portfolio aims to combine the high current income of a bond fund with the long-term gains of a stock fund. It fulfills that goal fairly well. Its six managers generate a strong yield (lately 5.8%) by investing in dividend-paying stocks such as Bristol-Myers Squibb as well as intermediate-term corporate and government bonds. The fund has produced a very respectable 13% average annual return over the past 10 years. Yet in our view, unless you

need every penny of the fund's income, you can improve your chances of piling up profits over the long haul with other conservative stock funds, such as Fidelity Puritan, by avoiding IFA's hefty 5.75% load. Therefore, we rate it a hold.

Hold Twentieth Century Ultra.

Call this $10 billion aggressive growth fund's recent performance ultra-disappointing. Its 3.6% loss last year landed it on the bottom rung of its group. Here's why. Ultra built its remarkable 10-year record (up 18% annually) by investing primarily in a handful of small-company stocks. But the fund has tripled in size in the past three years alone. All that cash has forced lead manager James Stowers to buy, buy, buy. The portfolio has swelled to 160 stocks from 80 at the beginning of 1992 and, says Stowers, figures to hit 250 by mid-1995. He insists that the expansion won't crimp Ultra's ability to score big gains. "Holding more names will dampen our upside, but we also expect it to dampen the downside too," he says. "So over time we expect to maintain returns in line with our historic rate." If that forecast proves true over the next year, Ultra would merit a buy.

Buy Janus Fund.

The name of this $9 billion fund suggests that manager James Craig has the ability to look in two directions at once. For the past two years, however, the market has favored cyclicals over the large growth companies that dominate his portfolio. Now that many market analysts expect this trend to reverse in '95, Craig is anticipating a sweet repeat of his stunning '89 rebound. "In '87 and '88, everyone flocked to cyclicals," says Craig. And Janus predictably lagged the S&P 500. "Then the economy slowed in '89 and attention shifted to growth stocks," he adds. Janus gained 46% that year, creaming the S&P 500 by 15 percentage points. We agree with many other analysts who believe Craig will return to form this year. Hence, we think that Janus is a buy.

Hold Fidelity Growth & Income.
Steve Kaye, who has managed this $9 billion fund since January 1993, looks for shares that are trading well below what corporate earnings or cash flow might otherwise suggest. His nose for value lately has led him to build big positions in health care (12% of the portfolio), including Columbia Healthcare, the nation's largest health maintenance organization, plus real estate (4%). We rate Growth & Income a hold largely because we favor a no-load alternative within the huge Fidelity family. The similar Fidelity Equity-Income II has both a better three-year record and is less risky than its larger sibling.

Hold Vanguard Wellington.
You won't go wrong hanging on to your shares of no-load Wellington. The $9 billion balanced fund, managed by Vincent Bajakian and Paul Kaplan, generally keeps the enormous portfolio anchored by a 60% to 70% stake in value stocks, most of them large-caps like drugmaker Pfizer (recently 2% of fund assets) and some 30% to 40% in intermediate-term government and high-grade corporate bonds. But we grade it no higher than a hold because we feel investors might fare better with the similar Fidelity Puritan, described earlier. Puritan has outperformed Wellington over the past one-, three-, five- and 10-year periods. Moreover, Puritan has been 19% less risky.

Buy Fidelity Contrafund.
Since Will Danoff took over Contrafund in 1990, assets have ballooned more than eightfold to around $8.5 billion. Danoff likes strong runners that have stumbled but are making the right moves to get back on track. Two examples are IBM, recently the fund's largest hold-

ing (at 2% of assets), and Philip Morris (2%). While the fund's size forces Danoff to buy larger companies, he still has $2 billion of his assets in stocks with market capitalizations of $1 billion or less. We believe Danoff's 22% stake in technology stocks and 10% holding of health care issues will help him produce superior results over the next 12 months, making Contrafund a buy.

Buy Vanguard Index 500.
By definition, investors who put their money in Vanguard Index 500 are happy to settle for average returns. And that's what they get. The $8.5 billion fund promises to trace the S&P 500-stock index to within a few tenths of a percentage point. For the past 10 years, the fund has gained 14.6% annually, practically matching the S&P's 14.9% advance. For keeping its promises to investors and achieving its goals, Index 500 earns a buy.

Buy Vanguard Windsor II.
Despite its copycat moniker, this $8 billion growth and income fund is no mere clone of its famous stablemate. Yes, like the original Windsor's Neff, lead manager James Barrow is a value seeker. His approach has produced a return of more than 217% since the fund's inception on June 30, 1985, vs. 183% for the typical growth and income fund during that time (and 222% for Windsor). But unlike Neff, Barrow doesn't make big bets even on companies he likes. For example, the top 10 holdings in his portfolio—mostly banks and energy firms—represent 25% of the fund's assets (vs. 40% for Windsor). Broad diversification has helped the fund remain about 21% less risky than the norm over the past five years. That low risk plus Barrow's shrewd instincts make Windsor II a buy.

Buy EuroPacific Growth.
Stamping a buy rating on this American Funds Group foreign

169

portfolio is très simple. After all, the $8 billion fund has produced above-average returns and below-average risk almost from the moment it was founded in 1984. EuroPacific outpaced 85% of all stock funds over the past five and 10 years while incurring 25% less risk than the norm, according to Morningstar. Fund assets lately were 40% invested in Europe, where many countries are in the early stages of economic recoveries, 25% in Japan and Pacific Rim countries, and 15% in Latin America, including a 1% stake in Teléfonos de México. We think the five-member management squad has positioned the fund to continue treating its shareholders to a luxury world tour.

The 10 Biggest Bond Funds

Hold Franklin U.S. Government. Unlike many bond funds that vigorously trade securities in search of capital gains, Franklin funds tend to follow a buy-and-hold approach. A case in point is the family's $12 billion U.S. Government Securities portfolio (one of two Franklin entries among the big 10 bond funds). It applies that slow-and-steady technique to intermediate-term Ginnie Maes, shorthand for mortgage-backed bonds issued by the Government National Mortgage Association. The fund's return over the past five years beats two-thirds of its peers, and its yield is above-average as well. As 10-year manager Jack Lemein proudly proclaims, "We're a plodding, high-quality fund." Lemein also can boast about avoiding risky derivatives, the complex financial instruments whose value is "derived" from the performance of some underlying asset or index. Many derivatives tied to the mortgage market melted down as rates heated up last year. Funds holding them generally had steep losses. Given the threat of additional interest-rate increases, many fixed-income specialists

believe the fund's duration of 5.8 years is optimal. (Duration indicates a fund's sensitivity to a one-point rise in interest rates. For instance, a fund with a three-year duration would fall about 3% in value while one with a 5.8-year duration would slide 5.8%.) But we think investors not already in the fund will get more bond profits for their bucks with no-load Vanguard Fixed Income GNMA Portfolio, a superior performer described below.

Sell Dean Witter U.S. Government. Rajesh Gupta, who has managed the $10 billion fund since 1992, invests in high-quality intermediate-term U.S. Treasury and mortgage securities. But the fund's 10-year performance places this lumbering laggard in the bottom 14% of all government bond funds for the period. Why the poor long-term showing? Look no further than the fund's stiff 1.2% annual expense ratio (vs. 1% for the typical U.S. bond entry). The fund also has a 5% maximum deferred sales charge. Worse, there are no signs that total returns will improve. Better alternatives abound including several below. We rate this fund a sell.

Hold Franklin Federal Tax-Free. Andrew Jennings is a typical Franklin bond fund manager. In his four years as the head of this $7 billion muni bond portfolio, Jennings has bought newly issued high-quality bonds at close to face value and held them to maturity. That staid strategy has helped the 4.25%-load fund grind out a five-year return that's better than 80% of its peers. But the fund's recent duration of 9.8 years (1.3 years longer than the norm) makes it 15% more vulnerable to rising interest rates than national muni funds as a group. Despite that flaw, we rate the fund a hold for its solid record.

Sell IDS High-Yield Tax-Exempt. You would think that the weight of this $6 billion fund's 5% load alone would cause it to sink hip-deep into the bog of high-yield (a.k.a. junk) tax-frees. Not so. Kurt Larson, the fund's manager for 15 years, stashes just 17% of his portfolio in below-investment-grade issues, vs. 34% for the average high-yield muni fund. This relative caution makes the fund less prone to price swings than the norm—but at a cost of slightly subpar total returns and yield. As a result, we rate IDS High-Yield a sell. We think municipal junk fans would be better off with T. Rowe Price Tax-Free High Yield. It's 24% less risky than muni bond funds overall yet boasts a yield and five-year return that are above average. Better yet, the T. Rowe Price fund is no load.

Buy Vanguard Fixed Income GNMA.

Long-term investors seeking safe income can't do much better than this $6 billion no-load, which we rate a buy. With its cut-rate expenses (0.3% of assets a year, lowest in its class) and strict ban on risky derivatives, the five-year return of this Vanguard fund has topped nearly all mortgage-backed bond funds. Manager Paul Kaplan took over the fund last year after serving as an assistant to his predecessor Paul Sullivan for 16 years. In today's dicey interest-rate environment, Kaplan acquires a mix of new bonds and older issues with slightly higher coupons. The portfolio's duration lately was 8.6 years. While he could pay extra to buy bonds with higher current yields, he believes they run the risk of being redeemed early if interest-rate declines set off another wave of mortgage refinancing. And in his view, rates will notch up a bit further and then begin drifting down again sometime this year. "We never make an investment decision merely to maximize income," he says. "Rather, we strive for the best total return."

Buy Pimco Total Return. Mutual fund analysts have dubbed William Gross the

Peter Lynch of bonds. And like the legendary stock picker who put Fidelity Magellan on the map, Gross has an eclectic style. He fills this no-load $6 billion intermediate-term portfolio with a mix of securities ranging from Ginnie Maes to European debt. The fund's recent five-year return beats 96% of its competitors in Morningstar's corporate bond category. But even Gross didn't survive last year's bond market bust unscathed largely because he held on too long to faltering European government bonds, which constituted up to 20% of the portfolio a year ago. Anticipating fairly steady interest rates over the next two to three years, Gross has shifted from seeking capital gains to emphasizing solid high yields. He's loading up on bargain-priced Ginnie Mae and Freddie Mac mortgage securities that yield about a percentage point more than U.S. Treasuries. (The portfolio's duration is rougly 4.5 years.) "For intermediate bonds, this is the best fund around," says Kurt Brouwer, president of Brouwer & Janachowski, an investment advisory firm in San Francisco. Pimco earns a buy.

Hold Kemper U.S. Government. Fund manager Patrick Beimford has been pursuing a less risky strategy at this 4.5%-load fund since his big bet on declining rates in 1992 backfired, saddling the $5 billion fund with a 2.3% loss in that year's first quarter. To reduce the fund's sensitivity to interest-rate swings, he has converted it to a pure Ginnie Mae portfolio (it had held more volatile long-term Treasury securities as well) and capped the fund's duration at 5.5 years (it had been as high as seven years). And he is now willing to retreat into cash when interest rates climb sharply. While these safety measures may limit potential gains when interest rates fall, Morningstar analyst Natalie Andrus says they represent an improvement for shareholders. For that reason, the fund warrants a hold.

Buy Bond Fund of America. Prior to 1994, this $5 billion high-quality corporate bond fund hadn't lost money in a calendar year since it was launched in 1974 (a record shared by only one of the eight other bond funds with 20-year histories). As interest rates soared last year, however, BFA's emphasis on total return over high current income saddled shareholders with a 5% annual loss. Lead manager Abner Goldstine and his team at Capital Research have shortened the fund's duration to five years from 9.8 years a year ago. Catherine Voss Sanders of newsletter *Morningstar's Mutual Funds* thinks this move will return BFA to its winning ways this year and beyond. We rate it a buy.

Buy Vanguard Municipal Intermediate.

Ian MacKinnon and Chris Ryon have deftly steered this $5 billion no-load, a specialist in intermediate-term munis, in bad times as well as good. During the bull market from '91 to '93, the twosome extended the portfolio's average duration to 6.5 years counting on rising bond prices to produce capital gains. The result was a fat 11% annualized return during that three-year span, vs. 10% for the fund's peers. But late in '93, they sensed an end to falling rates and gradually brought the portfolio's duration down to a risk-dampening 5.1 years, thereby limiting losses in '94. Believing the worst of the interest-rate rise is over, senior manager MacKinnon, in charge since 1981, has lately erased the fund's "bearish tilt" by extending duration to 5.8 years. "We look to the current weakness in the market as a buying opportunity," he says. Management's superb record, plus low expenses of 0.2%, earn the fund a buy. Like all Vanguard entries, this one eschews derivatives.

Sell Dreyfus Municipal Bond.

Last year's rising interest rates turned out to be a double-barreled menace for this $4 billion no-load. The fund's long duration of 9.5 years exposed it to sharp bond-market price declines. And a hefty stake in the risky derivatives known as inverse floaters deepened those losses when the market for those synthetics went splat. Richard Moynihan, who has managed the fund since its inception in 1976, has pared derivatives to 5% of assets. Why not unload all of them? He insists they will help boost yield during what he expects to be a year or more of relative interest-rate stability. Partly because of its long duration, the fund's yield was about a percentage point above the average for national muni bond funds. But we rate the fund a sell because investors are better off in less risky portfolios, including Vanguard Municipal Intermediate-Term (see above), that don't use derivatives.

Choosing the Best Family of Funds

What are the most telling traits that often distinguish great fund families—those one-stop emporia of stock, bond and money-market portfolios sponsored by a single investment company? It all depends on the family values that you prize most. Above-average returns? Superior customer service? Low fees?

MONEY has the answers. Most people know that the fund business has long been dominated by Fidelity, with assets of $250 billion, almost $100 billion more than the nearest competitor. Our study shows that Fidelity also ranks No. 1 overall in performance, the statistic that matters most to investors. In fact, the Boston powerhouse took three of the top six places in our exclusive ranking of the 25 biggest full-service fund houses and two discount brokerages that operate large no-load fund networks.

MONEY ranks the top fund clans.

In first was the $10 billion Fidelity Advisor series, which lately managed 16 funds sold through brokers and banks, followed by the $240 billion Fidelity retail group, which runs 156 funds sold directly to investors. Sixth was Fidelity FundsNetwork, part of a discount brokerage that markets 192 no-load funds (71 of them managed by its parent). That put the network well ahead of its only direct rival on our list, Charles Schwab's 249-fund OneSource, No. 20 in our ranking. In third, fourth and fifth place respectively were American Funds, Oppenheimer and Prudential. For a complete breakdown of the results, refer to the tables beginning on page 174.

There are sound reasons to choose funds in the strongest families. For one thing, it's easier than trying to judge every contender on its individual merits. "Investors want ways to narrow their search for a fund," says Don Phillips of Morningstar, the fund research service that helped us rank the families. "And a fund's family affiliation provides one." Moreover, investing in a family of funds offers great convenience. When you reallocate your portfolio, you can simply pick up the phone and switch from one fund to a stablemate, usually at no additional cost.

Which families deserve the most loyalty?

To find out, we pitted the 25 largest full-service fund families and the two leading discount brokerages' no-load programs against each other. We included the discounters because, like traditional families, these plans let you trade any fund on their roster over the phone with no transaction fee and track your holdings on a single monthly statement. We then asked Morningstar to compare the performance of each organization's funds with others of the same type according to their risk-adjusted return. This calculation rewards a fund for earning high returns with low volatility. A fund was rated on a scale of 1 to 100 (a so-called percentile ranking) over all three-year periods in which it existed. Morningstar then averaged each fund's various three-year percentiles to arrive at a single score for the fund. The scores of all the funds within an investment category were combined to produce an average for each of the five investment categories in a family. These scores, in turn, were averaged to come up with a single overall score for each family.

Whose research has the winning edge?

Critics of Fidelity sometimes accuse the firm of flooding the marketplace with funds to increase the chances that one will always top the performance charts. But in our ranking, the Fidelity Advisor and Fidelity funds stood out because of their consistency in all categories. The two families ranked 1 and 2, respectively, in the growth category, long a Fidelity specialty. In addition, both Fidelity families scored above the median in the four other asset categories, placing among the top five in three of them (growth, taxable bond and municipal bond). Fidelity also finished in the top five for total return funds, giving the company four top-five results, a feat matched only by the Phoenix group.

Fund specialists attribute Fidelity's strong performance mostly to the company's research department, whose analysts serve as a kind of farm team of future managers. Standout researchers get a chance to manage a single-industry sector fund. If they continue to do well, they may graduate to running one of the firm's diversified portfolios. Because most Fidelity managers have followed much the

Comparing Family Values

Spearheaded by its standout growth funds, Fidelity dominates our ranking of 27 full-service fund families and discount brokerages with no-load fund networks. Fidelity Advisor, the firm's family of broker-sold funds, ranks first with an overall percentile score of 68—meaning that the average Fidelity Advisor fund outscored 68% of its closest peers. The Fidelity funds sold directly to shareholders placed second with a score of 65. And Fidelity FundsNetwork, an arm of the group's discount brokerage that sells funds without transaction fees, scored 59 to come in sixth. To arrive at overall scores, we first averaged the rankings of a group's funds within their respective investment categories. For example, No. 4 Oppenheimer's overseas funds scored a remarkable 87, on average, while the firm's

	PERFORMANCE ANALYSIS						COMPANY PROFILE		
Fund Family (number of funds)	Overall score	Growth	Total Return	Overseas	Taxable Bond	Tax-exempt Bond	Average tenure of senior manager (years)	Best funds Stocks	Bonds
Fidelity Advisor (16)	68	81	64	58	66	73	4.5	Income & Growth	High-Income Muni
Fidelity (156)	65	75	76	51	61	61	3.8	Equity-Income II	Spartan High-Income
American (27)	60	58	74	89	56	21	9.2	Smallcap World	High-Income
Oppenheimer (38)	59	37	59	87	62	51	3.4	Main Street Income & Growth A	Strategic Income A
Prudential (69)	59	69	70	48	40	68	3.4	Equity-Income A	Structured Maturity A
Fidelity FundsNetwork (192)	59	62	59	72	54	47	4.4	Fidelity Equity-Income II	Fidelity Spartan High-Income
Putnam (77)	58	67	52	85	40	45	2.9	New Opportunities A	Municipal Income A
Dreyfus (136)	58	41	59	89	50	50	5.2	Peoples Index	Short-Intermediate Muni Bond
Franklin/Templeton(97)	57	64	58	81	31	53	6.5	Balance Sheet Investment	High-Yield Tax-Free Income
Phoenix (17)	57	64	76	18	63	65	4.6	Capital Appreciation	Multi-Sector Fixed Income A
Kemper (59)	55	56	74	70	29	47	4.6	Retirement II	Municipal Bond
Alliance Capital (50)	55	62	59	47	31	76	2.5	Growth A	Muni Income National A
Scudder (40)	53	40	47	75	53	49	5.4	Japan	Medium-Term Tax-Free
T. Rowe Price (56)	53	54	56	57	53	44	4.7	New Asia	Spectrum Income
Vanguard (75)	49	30	49	63	53	48	7.5	Asset Allocation	Municipal Limited-Term
MFS (50)	48	38	66	64	31	45	3.1	World Total Return A	Municipal High-Income A
USAA (26)	47	20	55	36	67	60	4.0	Mutual Income Stock	Tax-Exempt Short-Term
Merrill Lynch (203)	47	42	48	52	45	49	4.9	Global Allocation A	Muni Limited Maturity A
IDS (36)	46	43	70	42	43	29	5.3	Diversified Equity-Income	High-Yield Tax-Exempt
Schwab OneSource (249)	45	58	52	37	42	38	4.6	Evergreen Foundation	Strong Advantage
United (16)	44	36	39	73	20	51	8.1	Income	Municipal High-Income
Lord Abbett (22)	39	42	43	25	41	46	2.9	Equity 1990	Tax-Free Income National
Dean Witter (40)	39	35	37	75	31	16	5.3	Pacific Growth	Intermediate Income Secs.
Colonial (36)	37	27	61	12	41	45	2.9	Colonial A	U.S. Government A
Invesco (30)	37	40	60	33	33	18	4.0	Industrial Income	Tax-Free Long-Term Bond
Smith Barney Shearson (48)	36	43	59	20	24	35	4.2	Prin. Ret. 1998	Div. Strat. Inc. B
PaineWebber (25)	34	34	19	40	32	43	3.2	Growth A	Municipal High-Income A

Notes: (d): Max. deferred sales charge N.A.: Not applicable [1]Except Select Funds (unlimited exchanges for $7.50 each; 0.75% redemption fee if held for less than 30 days), Internationals (free, unlimited exchanges, except for Southeast Asia, Emerging Markets and Latin America, which charge 1.5% redemption fee if held less than 90 days) and Spartan ($5 per exchange); fees waived for exchanges using automated phone system [2]Free, unlimited exchanges with automated phone system [3]Unlimited, free exchanges for funds held six months or more [4]Sales load charged if shares held less than six months [5]Round-trip domestic growth funds earned only a 37. Combining those scores with the other three categories and averaging the total, we arrived at Oppenheimer's overall score of 59. Convenience and cost also matter a great deal to fund shareholders. No. 8 Dreyfus, for example, accepts orders 24 hours a day. But its stock and bond funds carry annual expenses averaging, respectively, 0.9% and 0.8% of assets. By contrast, rival Vanguard's phone reps are on duty only from 8 a.m. to 9 p.m. eastern time, Monday through Friday. But the firm's stock and bond funds carry annual expenses averaging just 0.4% and 0.2%. In addition, using fund ranker Morningstar's shareholder report grade, Vanguard's annual statements rate an A- for frankness and clarity, while Dreyfus' rate no better than C.

SERVICE				EXPENSES				
Number of free switches	Switching fee	Transaction hours (ET)	Morningstar shareholder report grade	% maximum sales load		Annual expenses (% of assets)		Phone (800)
				Stocks	Bonds	Stocks	Bonds	
Unlimited	None	8:30 to 6	B-	4.75	4.75	1.67	0.89	522-7297
4 per year[1]	None	24 hours	B	3.00[15]	0.40	1.49	0.66	544-8888
Unlimited	None	8 to 8	B	5.75	4.75	0.86	0.86	421-0180
None[2]	$5	8:30 to 8[9]	B	5.75	5.00(d)	1.41	1.38	525-7048
Unlimited	None	8 to 6	C+	5.25	5.00(d)	1.70	1.15	225-1852
4 per year[3]	None[8]	24 hours	N.A.	None	None	1.27	0.69	544-9697
Unlimited	None	8:30 to 8	B-	5.75	5.00(d)	1.48	1.14	225-1581
Unlimited	None	24 hours	C	4.50	4.50	0.93	0.75	782-6620
Unlimited[4]	None	8:30 to 8	C+	5.75[16]	4.50	1.01	0.69	342-5236[17]
Unlimited	None	8 to 4	C	5.00(d)	4.75	1.48	0.95	243-4361
Unlimited	None	8 to 7[10]	B	5.75	4.50	1.08	0.80	621-1048
Unlimited	None	9 to 4	B-	4.25	4.25	2.27	1.58	227-4618
4 per year[5]	None	8 to 6[11]	B+	None	None	1.42	0.84	225-2470
3 per year[5]	None	8 to 10[12]	A	None	None	1.08	0.74	638-5660
2 per year[5]	None	8 to 9	A-	None	None	0.39	0.22	851-4999
Unlimited	None	8 to 8	C+	5.75	5.00(d)	1.58	1.27	225-2606
6 per year	None	9 to 9	B-	None	None	1.13	0.45	531-8181
Unlimited	None	8:30 to 5:30	B+	6.50	4.00	1.66	1.03	637-3863
36 per year	None	8 to 6	C+	5.00	5.00	1.24	0.86	437-4332
4 per year[3]	None[8]	24 hours	N.A.	None	None	1.28	0.76	266-5623
Unlimited	None	8 to 4:30[13]	B-	5.75	5.75	0.98	0.69	366-5465
Unlimited	None	9:30 to 4	C+	5.75	4.75	1.34	0.54	874-3733
Unlimited[6]	None	Brokers only	C	5.00(d)	5.50	1.95	0.89	869-3863
Unlimited	None	8 to 8	C+	5.75	5.00(d)	1.75	1.19	525-8085
4 per year[7]	None	7 to midnight[14]	C	None	None	1.12	1.00	248-2828
Unlimited	None	Brokers only	B	5.00	4.50	1.90	1.22	221-8806
None	$5	9 to 4	C+	5.00(d)	5.00(d)	1.95	1.36	647-1568

exchanges [6]Sales load charged if shares held less than 30 days [7]Per fund [8]Transaction fee charged if short-term trades exceed four per year [9]Sat. 10 to 2 [10]Sat. 10 to 4 [11]Sat. 10 to 2 [12]Sat. and Sun. 9 to 5 [13]Exchanges by mail only [14]Hours for Mon. to Thurs.; Fri.: 7 a.m. to 10 p.m.; Sat.: 8 a.m. to 5 p.m.; Sun.: 6 p.m. to midnight [15]8.24% maximum sales load applies solely to company's contractual funds [16]9.00% maximum sales load applies solely to company's contractual funds [17]To contact Templeton Funds service reps, phone 800-237-0738 **Sources:** Morningstar Inc., Chicago, Illinois, 800-876-5005; the funds.

same career path and typically have worked together as analysts or junior portfolio managers, many funds have developed an informal team-management style. One result is that Fidelity funds often end up owning many of the same securities, which can magnify both successes and failures for the family.

Of the two discount brokerage fund networks, which charge no transaction fees, the Fidelity FundsNetwork owes its superior ranking mainly to the fact that it offers 71 Fidelity funds. Schwab's OneSource plan has none. Who pays the bill for Fidelity's and Schwab's no-fee networks, since you don't? The funds do. The brokers charge each fund sponsor about a quarter of one percent of the assets held through their accounts annually. The fund companies accept the tariff because they believe the brokers help attract new investors. Some experts predict, however, that the participating fund companies will try to recoup the added cost by passing it on in the form of higher expense ratios.

Which give investors the best service?

After returns, what you expect most from a fund are flawless record keeping and convenient switching privileges among funds in the group. Families give shareholders varying degrees of freedom to switch money from one fund to another. Some groups, including Fidelity and Vanguard, limit the number of exchanges you can make in a year. Others, including the two discount brokerages, discourage short-term trading by requiring that you own shares for six months before qualifying for unlimited free exchanges. Most fund groups permit transactions only during business hours, though at many groups the day is 12 hours or longer. Dreyfus, Fidelity, Fidelity FundsNetwork and Schwab's OneSource go even further with service representatives on hand 24 hours a day to take buy or sell orders. Fund groups differ in the quality of the infor-

mation that they provide. Our yardstick is Morningstar's shareholder report grade, an evaluation of every company's literature for clarity, frequency and openness. (Note that the two brokerage networks do not issue their own prospectuses and annual reports.)

How do expenses add up?

Fund costs come in two forms. Sales charges, extracted one way or another by every broker-sold fund and by some direct-sold funds as well, can be avoided by investing in no-loads. But all funds charge annual fees for management and administration. Most of the families in our study are sold by brokers who charge commissions of as much as 6.5% when you buy or sell shares. About half a dozen offer you the option instead of paying a so-called level load, which is lower than the normal front-end or back-end sales charge but is accompanied by higher annual expenses. One reason load funds dominate our rankings is that the brokers or financial advisers who sell them want to offer clients a full range of investment options. By contrast, no-load fund families, which sell directly to the public, often specialize in a single investment arena.

The Vanguard family has by far the lowest expenses. Shareholders benefit from the group's unique corporate structure, in which the funds own the management company. That allows Vanguard to provide management and administrative services to the funds at cost. (At virtually every other family, the sponsor aims to make a profit at managing and administering the fund.) The result: Vanguard stock funds nick shareholders for only 0.4% of assets a year, on average, compared with an industry average that's around 1.4%. Vanguard bond fund holders pay just 0.2%, compared with a norm of 0.8% for competitors. After Vanguard, the most cost-efficient fund families turned out to be American for stock funds and USAA for bonds.

MONEY's Rankings of 2,688 Funds

Let's face it, last year was a lousy one for most mutual funds. The Federal Reserve Board hiked interest rates an astonishing six times in 10 months, rocking stock and bond funds. Derivative issues unraveled like dime-store socks, steepening losses. Mexico, the blue-chip country of Latin America, unexpectedly devalued the peso, sending many international funds (and even some seemingly all-American entries) tumbling. "It was a year of constant headaches for fund investors," says John Rekenthaler of *Morningstar Mutual Funds* in Chicago. "There was one unpleasant surprise after another."

How severe was the battering? The table on page 179 shows all 14 fund categories tracked for MONEY by Morningstar lost money last year. Foreign regional funds were the biggest tankers of all, sinking 6.7%. U.S. stock portfolios proved no refuge, with the average domestic-stock fund dropping 2%, well below the 1.3% total return of the S&P 500-stock index. And taxable bonds fell 3.6%. Indeed, of the 2,688 funds we track, only 406 stock funds and 101 bond funds turned in winning results for 1994, as you can see for yourself using MONEY's comprehensive mutual fund tables that follow. To help you find these hardy survivors in our listings, we denote them with stars after their names.

Don't let the gloomy numbers get you down. At MONEY, we suspect that the worst is over and that the S&P 500 can return a solid 10% this year. Looking ahead, the Dow could soar to 5000 by the end of the decade. But the Fed is likely to continue lifting rates in 1995's first half, causing further setbacks for bonds. By summer, however, long-term rates are likely to peak at about 8.5% and make bonds more attractive as investments. Here's why no investing strategy seemed to work last year.

Interest rates rose and rose. The dispiriting tone of 1994 was set by the Federal Reserve Board's first interest-rate hike in February. By year's end, yields on 30-year Treasury bonds had climbed to around 8% (vs. 6.4% a year earlier), and prices on long-term bond funds were off 4.2%. Intermediate-term funds fell 3.7%, and even relatively safe short-term portfolios took a 0.7% hit. The Fed's moves also slammed the stock market, as investors were simultaneously tempted by rising fixed-income yields and worried that higher rates would slow the economy and slice corporate profits. The worst performing diversified stock fund was $57 million American Heritage. This aggressive growth fund fell a heart-stopping 35% mainly because of its heavy stakes in four skidding small stocks, including Spectrum Information Technologies.

Derivatives deepened the damage. Many fixed-income managers used these slippery instruments, whose value is tied to or derived from an underlying asset or index, to make hefty bets that rates would continue to fall. When rates swooshed up instead, many derivative securities swooned. Among the most notorious fund disasters was $565 million Piper Jaffray Institutional Government Income, which plummeted 29% as its huge derivatives stake cratered. Derivatives also played havoc in the normally sleepy money-market arena. One tiny institutional fund, $84 million Community Bankers U.S. Government, became the first money fund in more than a decade to break the buck—that is, see its net asset value fall below $1 per share. At least 16 fund sponsors were forced to bail out selected retail portfolios to avoid similar catastrophes. And in the muni market, already mangled by rising rates, tax-exempt bond prices were further mauled by December's news that an Orange County, Calif. investment fund had lost an estimated $2 billion from highly leveraged speculation in derivatives. California single-state muni funds, which naturally had the largest exposure to Orange County issues, ended the year with a painful 7% average loss.

The peso's fall hurt overseas funds.

Late December's 31% devaluation of the Mexican peso was the *coup de grâce* in a rocky 12 months for international stock portfolios, which had already toughed out a 30% drop in the Hong Kong market earlier in the year. All told, foreign stock funds gave up an average of 2.5%. Funds that focused exclusively on Latin America stocks, however, suffered even bigger losses. For example, $445 million TCW/DW Latin American Growth plunged 23.7% and $616 million Fidelity Latin America lost 23.2%. International bond funds were also hard hit, losing an average of 4.2%. And that number masked a few financial Titanics, such as the peso-propelled 30.8% drop in $1.6 billion Alliance North American Government Income B.

The peso claimed some unexpected victims as well. For example, $11.1 billion Fidelity Asset Manager lost 6.6% for the year, compared with a 2.7% drop for total-return stock funds overall, because of its 7% exposure to Mexico. And even some domestic bond funds turned out to have peso-denominated holdings. Take $1.5 billion Fidelity Short-term Bond, whose 6% Mexican stake contributed to its loss of 2.2% in the fourth quarter. Or $2.3 billion Scudder Short-term Bond, which lost 1.6% in the fourth quarter as a result of its 5% stake in Mexican debt.

Despite the many market crises, a few nimble funds did manage to make money last year. Indeed, stock portfolios that focused on the handful of sizzling sectors—technology, health care and Japan—posted double-digit gains. Leading the pack was $251 million Seligman Communications & Information A, up a lofty 35.3%. Among diversified stock funds, the top performer was $67 million Govett Smaller Companies, up 28.7% on the strength of its technology and Japanese stockholdings. In the fixed-income category, the prime mover was $8.6 million Fidelity Deutsche Mark Performance, which gained 16.4% on its holdings of German debt and currency. Among domestic portfolios, many that focused on the shortest maturities and avoided risky derivatives posted profits. The best was $71 million Hotchkis & Wiley Low Duration, up 5.2%.

Fundholders were further vexed in 1994 by several major confidence-rattling industry tremors. The year started with the firing by Denver's $10 billion Invesco group of former star manager John Kaweske for violating the company's code of ethics. Other controversies included an SEC settlement in which Milwaukee's Strong/Corneliuson Capital Management reimbursed $440,000 to three of its mutual funds to settle charges that it hadn't followed proper pricing procedures in moving securities from one fund to another (Strong neither admitted nor denied wrongdoing). And industry giant Fidelity Investments committed two embarrassing bloopers last year. In June, a computer snafu led an employee to report day-old prices on 166 of Fidelity Investments' 210 funds. In December, the company announced that the flagship $36.7 billion Magellan fund would not make a year-end distribution of capital gains and income, contrary to previous estimates of a $4.32 per share payout. The company later explained that the mistaken estimate occurred after an accountant accidentally dropped a minus sign in the course of making a computation.

The lesson of '94 is that, now more than ever, it pays to choose your portfolio carefully and to keep close tabs on its performance. That's where MONEY's comprehensive year-end guide to funds can help. Starting on page 181, we give you an X-ray analysis of the best-performing individual funds in six major categories for the past year, three years and five years. In the next section, we offer results of 2,688 funds broken into two groups—major funds and single-state muni funds. The major category includes 2,125 stock and bond funds (our most comprehensive listing ever) that are open to all retail investors in most states for an initial investment of $25,000 or less. This year we also include figures to help you gauge each fund's after-tax return and potential capital-gains liability. Tax-conscious investors will also want to check out our guide to 563 single-state muni bond portfolios. You will find funds specializing in the tax-free bonds of 42 states and Puerto Rico.

As always, the best way to achieve long-term gains is to diversify, spreading your money among several different types of funds. And you should strive to review all your fundholdings at least once a year to ensure that the manager and your fund company are living up to their promises. That's an essential strategy in any year.

Returns for '94 and Over Time

Better brace yourself before you look at the table below. As the abundance of negative numbers shows, not one broad or specific fund category made money in 1994. The best of the bunch was the growth and income fund group, which lost only 0.9%. The biggest losers, foreign regional funds, were hit by the Mexican peso's 31% free-fall in December.

| | % gain (or loss) to Jan. 1, 1995 | | |
Category	One year	Three years[1]	Five years[1]
GROWTH	(1.6)	7.1	10.0
Aggressive growth	(1.2)	8.7	11.7
Capital growth	(1.8)	6.3	9.1
TOTAL RETURN	(2.2)	6.2	7.9
Growth and income	(0.9)	6.3	8.0
Equity total return	(2.7)	5.8	7.4
Income total return	(4.2)	7.0	8.6
SPECIALTY	(4.0)	9.0	7.6
OVERSEAS	(3.7)	8.5	5.1
International/global	(2.5)	8.6	5.6
Foreign regional	(6.7)	8.2	2.8
TAXABLE BONDS	(3.6)	4.4	7.3
Government bond	(4.0)	3.5	6.4
Investment-grade corporate	(3.2)	4.5	7.1
High-yield corporate	(3.3)	10.7	10.4
Mortgage-backed security	(3.1)	2.7	6.4
World income	(4.2)	2.8	7.0
MUNICIPAL BONDS	(5.0)	4.7	6.3

Note: [1]Annualized **Source:** Morningstar Inc., 800-876-5005

Notes to MONEY's Rankings

N.A. Not available; [1]Closed to new investors; [2]As of fund's recent liquidation; [3]As of fund's recent merger; [4]Maximum deferred sales charge; [5]Area code 713; [6]Area code 212; [7]Area code 716; [8]Area code 312; [9]Area code 314; [10]Area code 612; [11]Area code 303; [12]Area code 414; [13]Area code 203; [14]Area code 617; [15]Area code 301; [16]Area code 502; [17]Area code 913; [18]Area code 415; [19]Area code 207; [20]Area code 808; [21]Area code 401;†Only available through a discount broker;††By contractual plan only; Yield cited is 30-day SEC yield.

How to Read Our Tables

Type We divide our funds into 14 types, depending on their investment objectives and the kinds of securities they buy. For example, capital-growth funds (abbreviated Gro; other abbreviations are explained below) focus on stocks that figure to appreciate, whether or not they pay dividends. Our tables group eight stock types and six bond types into categories and list funds alphabetically starting on page 184.

Risk Level Our risk measure is based on the number of months a fund has underperformed risk-free Treasury bills in any month over the past three years, and the extent of that underperformance. Using that yardstick, we compare all major stock and bond funds with three-year records and divide them into 12 equal groups. A fund's risk level indicates the group into which it falls, from 1 (least risky) through 12 (riskiest).

Tax Analysis Tax efficiency is the percentage of the fund's total return that an investor in the 28% federal tax bracket retained after paying taxes on the income and capital gains that the fund distributed over the past three years. For example, if the fund has a three-year annualized return of 12% and a tax-efficiency of 87%, the after-tax annual return would be 10.4% (87% of 12%). Potential tax liability indicates the estimated amount of unrealized investment gains (or losses) on holdings in the fund's portfolio, expressed as a percentage of assets. When the fund sells profitable investments, it must distribute the proceeds to shareholders, who then may owe taxes on them.

Fund name/★ 1994 winner	Type	Style	Risk level	% average annual return to Jan. 1, 1995			Tax analysis		Performance analysis (percentile ranking by type)				Expense analysis		Net assets (millions)	Telephone (800)
				One year	Three years	Five years	% tax efficiency	% tax liability	1994	1993	1992	1991	% max. sales charge	Five-year total per $1,000		
STOCK FUNDS																
AARP Capital Growth	Gro	**Md/Gro**	11	(10.0)	3.0	5.3	55	2	7	68	27	65	None	$62	$649.0	322-2282

Style For stock funds, this column tells you the market value (large, medium or small) of stocks the fund owns and whether it prefers growth stocks with rising earnings, relatively cheap value stocks or a blend of both. For fixed-income funds, style tells you the average weighted maturity of bonds in the portfolio (short, intermediate or long), and their overall credit quality (high, medium or low).

Performance Analysis Here we rank the fund's total return against all funds of the same type on a scale of 1 (lowest) to 100 (highest). High numbers are better, of course. A rank of 90, for example, means that the fund beat 90% of its peers that year. A fund that consistently scores above the median (50) is likely to have a higher cumulative return than one that pulls an 80 one year and a 10 the next.

Five-Year Total Cost Per $1,000 This figure, which is required by the Securities and Exchange Commission, is the best way to compare the expense of investing in funds with different cost structures. It shows the total amount you would pay in sales charges and other expenses on a hypothetical $1,000 investment, assuming the fund earns 5% annually and that you redeem your shares after five years.

STOCK/BOND TYPES: Agg—Aggressive growth; **ETR**—Equity total return; **G&I**—Growth and income; **Gov**—U.S. Government bond; **Gro**—Capital growth; **HYC**—High-yield corporate; **IGC**—Investment-grade corporate; **Intl**—International; **ITR**—Income total return; **MBS**—Mortgage-backed securities; **Muni**—Municipal bond; **Reg**—Foreign regional; **Spec**—Specialty; **WI**—World income. **STOCK FUND STYLES:** **Bl**—Buys stocks that blend growth and value characteristics; **Gro**—Buys companies with accelerating earnings; **Lg**—Buys stocks with total market values of more than $5 billion; **Md**—Buys stocks with total market values between $1 billion and $5 billion; **Sm**—Buys stocks with total market values under $1 billion; **Val**—Buys stocks that are inexpensive relative to their earnings or assets. **BOND FUND STYLES:** **Hi**—Buys bonds rated AA or better; **Med**—Buys bonds rated BBB or better; **Lo**—Buys bonds rated BB or lower; **Int**—Buys bonds with maturities between four and 10 years; **L**—Buys bonds with maturities over 10 years; **Sh**—Buys bonds with maturities under four years.

GROWTH

1994 WINNERS

Fund name	Type	Style	% return	Risk level
1 Govett Smaller Companies	Agg	Sm/Gro	28.7	—
2 PBHG Emerging Growth	Agg	Sm/Gro	23.8	—
3 Robertson Stephens Val. Plus	Agg	Sm/Bl	23.1	—
4 Montgomery Growth	Gro	Md/Gro	20.9	—
5 B.T. Investment Small Cap.	Agg	N.A.	19.3	—
6 Strong Growth	Gro	Md/Gro	17.3	—
7 AIM Aggressive Growth[1]	Agg	Sm/Bl	17.2	11
8 Franklin California Growth	Gro	Sm/Gro	16.4	10
9 Janus Mercury	Gro	Md/Gro	15.9	—
10 G.T. Global America Gro. A	Agg	Sm/Bl	15.7	10
11 Pioneer Capital Growth A	Gro	Sm/Bl	14.8	10
12 Berger Small Co. Growth	Agg	Sm/Gro	13.7	—
13 20th Century Giftrust Inv.	Agg	Sm/Gro	13.5	12
14 Waddell & Reed Growth	Gro	Sm/Gro	12.8	—
15 Parnassus	Gro	Sm/Val	12.0	9
16 Crabbe Huson Special	Gro	Sm/Bl	11.7	10
17 Vanguard Primecap	Gro	Md/Bl	11.4	10
18 United New Concepts	Agg	Sm/Gro	11.3	11
19 FPA Capital	Agg	Sm/Val	10.4	11
20 Fidelity Blue Chip Growth	Gro	Md/Gro	9.9	8
21 Franklin Small Cap. Growth	Agg	Sm/Gro	9.0	—
22 Kaufmann	Agg	Sm/Gro	9.0	11
23 Longleaf Partners	Gro	Md/Bl	9.0	4
24 Janus Enterprise	Gro	Md/Gro	8.9	—
25 Yacktman	Gro	Md/Gro	8.8	—
Average growth fund			**(1.6)**	

THREE-YEAR WINNERS

Fund name	Type	Style	% return	Risk level
1 Oakmark	Gro	Md/Bl	26.2	4
2 Crabbe Huson Special	Gro	Sm/Bl	26.1	10
3 PBHG Growth	Agg	Sm/Gro	25.4	12
4 AIM Aggressive Growth[1]	Agg	Sm/Bl	23.4	11
5 Parnassus	Gro	Sm/Val	21.6	9
6 20th Century Giftrust Inv.	Agg	Sm/Gro	20.7	12
7 Pioneer Capital Growth A	Gro	Sm/Bl	20.0	7
8 Skyline Special Equities[1]	Agg	Sm/Val	20.0	7
9 Putnam New Opp. A	Gro	Md/Gro	19.9	12
10 Heartland Value	Agg	Sm/Val	19.8	8
11 PIMCo Adv. Opportunity C1	Agg	Sm/Gro	18.6	12
12 Royce Micro-Cap.	Agg	Sm/Val	18.3	4
13 G.T. Global America Gro. A	Agg	Sm/Bl	18.2	10
14 Fidelity Low-Priced Stock	Agg	Sm/Val	17.6	6
15 Longleaf Partners	Gro	Md/Bl	17.1	4
16 Fidelity Value	Gro	Md/Bl	17.0	6
17 John Hancock Sp. Eq. A[1]	Agg	Sm/Gro	16.8	12
18 Fidelity Capital App.	Agg	Md/Gro	16.8	6
19 Gabelli Value	Gro	Md/Bl	16.3	9
20 Seligman Frontier A	Agg	Sm/Gro	16.2	12
21 FPA Capital	Agg	Sm/Val	16.1	11
22 Franklin Balance Sheet Inv.	Gro	Sm/Val	15.9	5
23 Berwyn	Agg	Sm/Val	15.5	9
24 Fidelity Destiny II2	Gro	Lg/Bl	15.2	7
25 Colonial Small Stock A	Agg	Sm/Gro	15.1	10
Average growth fund			**7.1**	

FIVE-YEAR WINNERS

Fund name	Type	Style	% return	Risk level
1 AIM Aggressive Growth1	Agg	Sm/Bl	23.5	11
2 20th Century Giftrust Invest.	Agg	Sm/Gro	22.0	12
3 PBHG Growth	Agg	Sm/Gro	22.0	12
4 John Hancock Sp. Eq. A1	Agg	Sm/Gro	21.8	12
5 MFS Emerging Growth B	Agg	Md/Gro	21.4	12
6 PIMCo Adv. Opportunity C1	Agg	Sm/Gro	21.0	12
7 United New Concepts	Agg	Sm/Gro	19.9	11
8 Crabbe Huson Special	Gro	Sm/Bl	19.5	10
9 20th Century Ultra Investors	Agg	Lg/Gro	19.4	12
10 Kaufmann	Agg	Sm/Gro	19.3	11
11 Strong Common Stock1	Gro	Md/Gro	19.0	8
12 Fidelity Low-Priced Stock	Agg	Sm/Val	18.9	6
13 CGM Capital Development1	Gro	Md/Gro	18.7	12
14 Fidelity Blue Chip Growth	Gro	Md/Gro	18.4	8
15 Seligman Frontier A	Agg	Sm/Val	18.4	12
16 Skyline Special Equities1	Agg	Sm/Val	18.3	7
17 Oberweis Emerging Growth	Agg	Sm/Gro	17.7	12
18 Keystone Custodian S-4	Agg	Md/Gro	17.5	12
19 Fidelity Contrafund	Gro	Md/Gro	17.5	8
20 AIM Constellation	Agg	Md/Gro	17.4	11
21 FPA Capital	Agg	Sm/Val	17.3	11
22 Cowen Opportunity A	Agg	Sm/Bl	17.3	11
23 Wasatch Aggressive Equity	Agg	Sm/Gro	17.2	11
24 Berger 100	Gro	Md/Gro	17.0	12
25 MainStay Capital App. B	Gro	Md/Gro	16.9	12
Average growth fund			**10.0**	

TOTAL RETURN

1994 WINNERS

Fund name	Type	Style	% return	Risk level
1 Safeco Equity	G&I	Md/Bl	9.9	9
2 Invesco Balanced	ETR	Sm/Bl	9.4	—
3 FPA Paramount	G&I	Md/Gro	9.4	8
4 Warburg Pincus Gro.& Inc.	G&I	Md/Bl	7.6	7
5 Goldman Sachs Gro.& Inc.	G&I	Md/Bl	5.9	—
6 Mutual Qualified	G&I	Md/Val	5.7	4
7 Mutual Beacon	G&I	Md/Val	5.6	3
8 Gateway Index Plus	G&I	Lg/Bl	5.6	2
9 General Securities	ETR	Lg/Bl	5.4	2
10 Dodge & Cox Stock	G&I	Lg/Val	5.2	8
11 Quest for Value Opp. A	ETR	Lg/Bl	4.9	7
12 Baird Blue Chip	G&I	Lg/Gro	4.7	9
13 Gabelli ABC1	ETR	Md/Val	4.5	—
14 Mutual Shares	G&I	Md/Val	4.5	5
15 T. Rowe Price Equity-Inc.	ETR	Lg/Bl	4.5	5
16 Pilgrim MagnaCap	G&I	Lg/Bl	4.1	8
17 Nicholas Equity Income	ETR	Md/Val	4.1	—
18 20th Century Value	G&I	Md/Val	4.0	—
19 Dreyfus Balanced	ETR	Lg/Bl	4.0	—
20 Affiliated	G&I	Lg/Val	3.9	7
21 First American Equity-Inc. A	ETR	N.A.	3.8	—
22 RIMCo Monument Stock	G&I	Lg/Bl	3.4	—
23 Princor Blue Chip	G&I	Lg/Bl	3.4	9
24 Oppenheimer Value Stock A	G&I	Lg/Val	3.3	7
25 Fidelity Equity-Income II	ETR	Lg/Val	3.2	6
Average total return fund			**(2.2)**	

THREE-YEAR WINNERS

Fund name	Type	Style	% return	Risk level
1 Oppen. Main St. I&G A	G&I	Md/Bl	20.5	10
2 Warburg Pincus Gro. & Inc.	G&I	Md/Bl	17.2	7
3 Mutual Beacon	G&I	Md/Val	16.9	3
4 Mutual Qualified	G&I	Md/Val	16.8	4
5 Safeco Equity	G&I	Md/Bl	16.3	9
6 Bond Fund for Growth	ITR	N.A.	15.7	4
7 Mutual Shares	G&I	Md/Val	15.4	5
8 Fidelity Equity-Income II	ETR	Lg/Val	13.5	6
9 Babson Value	G&I	Md/Val	13.3	7
10 FPA Paramount	G&I	Md/Gro	13.2	8
11 Fidelity Puritan	ETR	Md/Bl	12.6	5
12 Fidelity Convertible Sec.	ITR	N.A.	12.2	6
13 Berwyn Income	ITR	Int/Lo	12.1	2
14 SoGen International1	ETR	Sm/Bl	12.1	2
15 Fidelity Asset Manager–Gro.	ETR	Lg/Bl	12.0	8
16 Pacific Horizon Capital Inc.	ITR	N.A.	11.9	7
17 Fidelity Equity-Income	ETR	Lg/Val	11.7	7
18 Putnam Convert. I&G A	ITR	N.A.	11.6	3
19 MainStay Convertible B	ITR	N.A.	11.6	6
20 Vanguard Windsor1	G&I	Lg/Val	11.6	8
21 Neuberger & Ber. Guardian	G&I	Lg/Val	11.4	7
22 Dodge & Cox Stock	G&I	Lg/Val	11.3	8
23 IDS Diversified Equity-Inc.	ETR	Md/Val	11.3	5
24 Franklin Convertible Sec.	ITR	N.A.	11.3	5
25 UST Master Inc. & Gro.	G&I	Md/Bl	11.2	6
Average total return fund			**6.2**	

FIVE-YEAR WINNERS

Fund name	Type	Style	% return	Risk level
1 Oppen. Main St. I&G A	G&I	Md/Bl	22.2	10
2 Evergreen Foundation	ETR	Md/Val	15.0	7
3 Vista Growth & Income A	G&I	Lg/Val	14.9	8
4 MainStay Convertible B	ITR	N.A.	14.0	6
5 Fidelity Convertible Sec.	ITR	N.A.	13.7	6
6 Warburg Pincus Gro.& Inc.	G&I	Md/Bl	13.6	7
7 Pacific Horizon Capital Inc.	ITR	N.A.	13.1	7
8 Safeco Equity	G&I	Md/Bl	13.0	9
9 FPA Paramount	G&I	Md/Gro	12.9	8
10 Bond Fund for Growth	ITR	N.A.	12.9	4
11 Quest for Value Opp. A	ETR	Lg/Bl	12.7	7
12 Kemper Diversified Inc. A	ITR	N.A.	12.7	2
13 Fidelity Growth & Income	G&I	Lg/Bl	12.5	7
14 MainStay Value B	G&I	Md/Val	12.2	8
15 Invesco Industrial Income	ETR	Lg/Val	12.2	8
16 Neuberger & Ber. Guardian	G&I	Lg/Val	12.1	7
17 IDS Managed Retirement	G&I	Lg/Bl	11.9	10
18 Dreman High Return	G&I	Lg/Val	11.8	9
19 Berger 101	G&I	Md/Bl	11.8	10
20 Berwyn Income	ITR	Int/Lo	11.7	2
21 Franklin Convertible Sec.	ITR	N.A.	11.6	5
22 Mutual Qualified	G&I	Md/Val	11.6	4
23 Mutual Beacon	G&I	Md/Val	11.5	3
24 Lexington Convertible Sec.	ITR	N.A.	11.3	10
25 Smith Bar. Prem. Tot. Ret. B	ETR	Lg/Val	11.1	4
Average total return fund			**7.9**	

Notes: [1]Closed to new investors N.A.: Not available All data are to Jan.1, 1995. Telephone numbers and other performance data are available in the tables that follow. Fund types and styles are explained on page 180. **Source:** Morningstar Inc., 800-876-5005

The Top-Performing Funds

1994 WINNERS

Fund name	Type	Style	% return	Risk level
1 Fidelity Japan	Reg	Md/Bl	16.5	—
2 T. Rowe Price Japan	Reg	Md/Bl	15.1	12
3 Vanguard Intl. Equity Pacific	Reg	Lg/Gro	12.9	12
4 Wright EquiFund-Dutch Natl.	Reg	Sm/Val	11.7	9
5 Selig. Henders. Glob. Em. A	Intl	Sm/Gro	10.1	—
6 Japan	Reg	Md/Bl	10.0	12
7 One Fund International	Intl	Md/Val	9.7	—
8 Quantitative Intl. Equity	Intl	Lg/Val	9.0	11
9 New England Intl. Equity A	Intl	Lg/Val	8.1	—
10 SoGen Overseas	Intl	Md/Val	7.8	—
11 Dean Witter Global Div. Gro.	Intl	Lg/Val	7.1	—
12 Dean Witter European Gro.	Reg	Md/Bl	6.9	10
13 G.T. Global Japan Growth A	Reg	Md/Gro	6.6	12
14 Putnam Europe Growth A	Reg	Md/Val	6.4	10
15 Fidelity Europe	Reg	Md/Val	6.3	10
16 Pioneer Europe A	Reg	Md/Val	6.0	11
17 Alliance International A	Intl	Lg/Bl	5.7	11
18 Pierpont Intl. Equity	Intl	Lg/Val	5.7	12
19 Harbor International¹	Intl	Lg/Val	5.4	10
20 Nomura Pacific Basin	Reg	Lg/Bl	5.3	12
21 Vanguard/Trustees' Eq. Intl.	Intl	Md/Val	5.3	10
22 Wright EquiFund-Ital. Natl.	Reg	Sm/Val	5.0	12
23 B.T. Investment Intl. Equity	Intl	Md/Val	4.8	—
24 Invesco Pacific Basin	Reg	Lg/Val	4.7	12
25 Alliance New Europe A	Reg	Lg/Val	4.6	11
Average overseas fund			**(3.7)**	

THREE-YEAR WINNERS

Fund name	Type	Style	% return	Risk level
1 Newport Tiger	Reg	Lg/Gro	23.5	12
2 Putnam Asia Pacific Gro. A	Reg	Md/Bl	18.9	9
3 Dean Witter Pacific Gro.	Reg	Md/Gro	18.8	12
4 T. Rowe Price New Asia	Reg	Md/Gro	17.2	12
5 Fidelity Emerging Markets	Intl	Md/Gro	16.4	12
6 John Hancock Free. Pac. Bas. A	Reg	Lg/Bl	16.4	11
7 Keystone Amer. Glob. Opp. A	Intl	Sm/Gro	16.4	10
8 Ivy International A	Intl	Lg/Val	15.5	11
9 Harbor International¹	Intl	Lg/Val	15.2	10
10 Templeton Capital Accum.	Intl	Md/Val	15.2	8
11 Fidelity Worldwide	Intl	Md/Val	14.3	9
12 Franklin Pacific Growth	Reg	Md/Val	14.0	9
13 Sit International Growth	Intl	Lg/Bl	13.9	9
14 United International Growth	Intl	Md/Val	13.8	11
15 Fidelity Pacific Basin	Reg	Md/Gro	13.7	11
16 Managers Intl. Equity	Intl	Lg/Bl	13.7	8
17 Dean Witter European Gro.	Reg	Md/Bl	13.6	10
18 Lexington WW. Emer. Mkt.	Intl	N.A.	13.5	11
19 Prudential Global Genesis B	Intl	Sm/Gro	13.2	10
20 Janus Worldwide	Intl	Lg/Bl	13.2	9
21 Pacific European Growth	Intl	Md/Val	13.2	10
22 Warburg Pinc. Intl. Eq. Comm.	Intl	Md/Val	13.1	11
23 Templeton Developing Mkts.	Intl	Md/Gro	12.9	10
24 USAA Investment Intl.	Intl	Lg/Bl	12.8	9
25 Twentieth Century Intl. Eq.	Intl	Md/Bl	12.5	10
Average overseas fund			**8.5**	

FIVE-YEAR WINNERS

Fund name	Type	Style	% return	Risk level
1 Newport Tiger	Reg	Lg/Gro	15.0	12
2 Keystone Amer. Glob. Opp. A	Intl	Sm/Gro	14.0	10
3 Founders Worldwide Gro.	Intl	Lg/Gro	13.2	10
4 Smith Barney Intl. Equity A	Intl	Md/Bl	11.2	11
5 Harbor International¹	Intl	Lg/Val	10.9	10
6 Warburg Pinc. Intl. Eq. Comm.	Intl	Md/Val	10.8	11
7 Templeton Growth	Intl	Lg/Val	10.7	8
8 EuroPacific Growth	Intl	Lg/Bl	10.7	9
9 New Perspective	Intl	Lg/Bl	10.3	9
10 Templeton Foreign	Intl	Lg/Val	9.5	9
11 Managers Intl. Equity	Intl	Lg/Bl	9.4	8
12 Ivy International A	Intl	Lg/Val	9.4	11
13 Lexington WW Emerg. Mkt.	Intl	N.A.	9.3	11
14 Templeton Smaller Co. Gro.	Intl	Sm/Val	8.9	9
15 Templeton World	Intl	Lg/Val	8.7	9
16 United International Growth	Intl	Md/Val	8.6	11
17 Oppenheimer Global A	Intl	Md/Val	8.5	11
18 USAA Investment Intl.	Intl	Lg/Bl	8.1	9
19 Princor World	Intl	Md/Val	7.8	11
20 Scudder Global	Intl	Lg/Val	7.6	7
21 T. Rowe Price Intl. Stock	Intl	Lg/Bl	7.2	11
22 Merrill Lynch EuroFund B	Reg	Lg/Val	7.0	12
23 Putnam Global Growth A	Intl	Md/Bl	7.0	9
24 Prudential Global Genesis B	Intl	Sm/Gro	6.8	10
25 Babson-Stewart Ivory Intl.	Intl	Md/Gro	6.8	10
Average overseas fund			**5.1**	

1994 WINNERS

Fund name	Type	Style	% return	Risk level
1 Seligman Commun. & Info. A	Spec	Sm/Gro	35.3	12
2 Alliance Technology A	Spec	Md/Gro	28.5	12
3 Merrill Lynch Technology B	Spec	Md/Gro	25.5	—
4 Fidelity Select Health Care	Spec	Lg/Gro	21.4	12
5 Fidelity Select Computers	Spec	Md/Bl	20.5	12
6 Fidelity Select Med. Delivery	Spec	Md/Gro	19.8	12
7 Fidelity Select Electronics	Spec	Md/Bl	17.2	10
8 T. Rowe Price Sci. & Tech.	Spec	Md/Bl	15.8	12
9 Putnam Health Sciences A	Spec	Lg/Gro	15.2	12
10 Fidelity Select Dev. Commun.	Spec	Md/Gro	15.1	11
11 Fidelity Select Chemicals	Spec	Md/Bl	14.8	9
12 Franklin Global Health Care	Spec	Sm/Gro	14.2	—
13 Fidelity Sel. Paper & Forest Pr.	Spec	Md/Bl	14.1	11
14 Lexington Strategic Inv.	Spec	N.A.	11.3	12
15 Kemper Technology A	Spec	Md/Gro	11.2	12
16 Fidelity Select Technology	Spec	Lg/Gro	11.1	11
17 United Science & Tech.	Spec	Md/Gro	9.8	12
18 John Han. Free. Gl. Tech. A	Spec	Md/Gro	9.6	12
19 Vanguard Spec. Health Care	Spec	Md/Bl	9.5	11
20 John Han. Free. Global Rx A	Spec	Sm/Gro	8.8	12
21 Cohen & Steers Realty Shrs.	Spec	Sm/Bl	8.3	9
22 Fidelity Select Indust. Material	Spec	Md/Bl	8.2	9
23 Fidelity Select Food & Agri.	Spec	Md/Bl	6.1	8
24 Invesco Strat. Technology	Spec	Md/Gro	5.3	12
25 Franklin DynaTech	Spec	Lg/Gro	5.2	9
Average specialty fund			**(4.0)**	

THREE-YEAR WINNERS

Fund name	Type	Style	% return	Risk level
1 Seligman Commun. & Info. A	Spec	Sm/Gro	29.0	12
2 Fidelity Select Home Finance	Spec	Sm/Val	27.3	10
3 Fidelity Select Electronics	Spec	Md/Bl	25.4	10
4 Fidelity Select Computers	Spec	Md/Bl	23.7	12
5 Fidelity Sel. Software & Comp.	Spec	Md/Gro	21.8	12
6 Alliance Technology A	Spec	Md/Gro	21.8	12
7 Fidelity Sel. Develop. Commun.	Spec	Md/Gro	21.2	11
8 John Han. Free. Reg. Bank B	Spec	Sm/Val	21.0	8
9 Fidelity Select Multimedia	Spec	Md/Gro	20.4	8
10 T. Rowe Price Sci. & Tech.	Spec	Md/Gro	19.6	12
11 Fidelity Select Automotive	Spec	Md/Val	18.7	10
12 Fidelity Select Transport.	Spec	Sm/Val	18.5	7
13 Fidelity Select Regional Banks	Spec	Sm/Val	18.3	11
14 Fidelity Select Indust. Equip.	Spec	Md/Val	18.1	10
15 Fidelity Select Prec. Metals	Spec	Md/Val	17.8	12
16 Fidelity Select Fin. Svcs.	Spec	Md/Val	17.4	11
17 Lexington Strategic Inv.	Spec	N.A.	17.4	12
18 Invesco Strat. Leisure	Spec	Md/Gro	16.8	9
19 Fidelity Select Telecommun.	Spec	Lg/Gro	16.0	9
20 Fidelity Select Technology	Spec	Lg/Gro	15.8	11
21 Cohen & Steers Realty Shrs.	Spec	Sm/Bl	15.6	9
22 John Han. Free. Glob. Tech. A	Spec	Md/Gro	15.2	12
23 Fidelity Adv. Global Res. A	Spec	Md/Val	15.2	10
24 PaineWeb. Regnl. Fin. Gro. A	Spec	Sm/Val	14.9	9
25 Fidelity Sel. Paper & Forest Pr.	Spec	Md/Bl	14.9	11
Average specialty fund			**9.0**	

FIVE-YEAR WINNERS

Fund name	Type	Style	% return	Risk level
1 Seligman Commun.& Info. A	Spec	Sm/Gro	24.2	12
2 Fidelity Select Computers	Spec	Md/Bl	24.0	12
3 Fidelity Select Home Fin.	Spec	Sm/Val	23.6	10
4 Fidelity Select Electronics	Spec	Md/Bl	23.1	10
5 Invesco Strat. Technology	Spec	Md/Gro	22.5	12
6 Fidelity Select Technology	Spec	Lg/Gro	22.3	11
7 T. Rowe Price Sci. & Tech.	Spec	Md/Gro	22.0	12
8 Alliance Technology A	Spec	Md/Gro	22.0	12
9 Fidelity Sel. Software & Comp.	Spec	Md/Gro	21.6	12
10 Fidelity Select Health Care	Spec	Lg/Gro	18.6	12
11 John Hancock Free. Reg. B	Spec	Sm/Val	18.2	8
12 Invesco Strat. Fin. Svcs.	Spec	Md/Val	18.0	10
13 Fidelity Select Med. Delivery	Spec	Md/Gro	17.8	12
14 PaineWeb. Reg. Fin. Gro. A	Spec	Sm/Val	17.1	9
15 Fidelity Select Reg. Banks	Spec	Sm/Val	16.8	11
16 Invesco Strategic Leisure	Spec	Md/Gro	16.7	9
17 Fidelity Select Automotive	Spec	Md/Val	16.5	10
18 Fidelity Select Biotech.	Spec	Sm/Gro	16.3	12
19 Fidelity Select Retailing	Spec	Sm/Bl	15.9	11
20 Vanguard Sp. Health Care	Spec	Md/Bl	15.6	11
21 Fidelity Select Transport.	Spec	Sm/Val	15.0	7
22 Fidelity Select Brok. & Inv.	Spec	Md/Val	14.7	12
23 Fidelity Select Fin. Svcs.	Spec	Md/Val	14.6	11
24 Invesco Strat. Health Sci.	Spec	Sm/Gro	14.4	12
25 Fidelity Select Chemicals	Spec	Md/Bl	13.4	9
Average specialty fund			**7.6**	

Notes: ¹Closed to new investors N.A.: Not available All data are to Jan.1, 1995. Telephone numbers and other performance data are available in the tables that follow. Fund types and styles are explained on page 180. **Source:** Morningstar Inc., 800-876-5005

TAXABLE BONDS

1994 WINNERS

Fund name	Type	Style	% return	Risk level
1 Fidelity Deutsche Mark Perf.	WI	Sh/Hi	16.4	10
2 Franklin/Temp. Hard Curr.	WI	Sh/Hi	15.1	7
3 Fidelity Yen Performance	WI	Sh/Hi	12.6	8
4 Franklin/Templeton H/I Curr.	WI	Sh/Hi	10.2	9
5 Fidelity Sterling Performance	WI	Sh/Hi	9.9	11
6 Franklin/Templeton Ger. Gov.	WI	Int/Hi	9.6	—
7 Franklin/Templeton Glob. Curr.	WI	Sh/Hi	8.1	3
8 Hotchkis & Wiley Low Dur.	IGC	Sh/Hi	5.2	—
9 Keystone Australia Income A	WI	Int/Hi	4.5	11
10 Hotchkis & Wiley S/T Inv.	IGC	Sh/Hi	4.4	—
11 Smith Breeden Sh. Dur. Gov.	MBS	Sh/Hi	4.3	1
12 Smith Bree. Sh. Dur. Gov. Ser.	MBS	Sh/Hi	4.1	1
13 Seven Seas Yield Plus	IGC	Sh/Hi	4.1	—
14 Strong Advantage	IGC	Sh/Med	3.6	1
15 Eaton Vance Sh.-Term Treas.	Gov	Sh/Hi	3.5	1
16 Permanent Port. Treas. Bill	Gov	Sh/Hi	3.3	1
17 Goldman Sachs Adj./R Mort.	MBS	Sh/Hi	3.3	—
18 First American Mgd. Inc. A	IGC	Sh/Med	3.3	1
19 Pilgrim Sh.-Term Multi-Mkt.	WI	Sh/Hi	2.9	8
20 IAI Reserve	IGC	Sh/Hi	2.7	1
21 Harbor Short Duration	IGC	Int/Hi	2.7	1
22 Fidelity Spartan High-Income	HYC	N.A.	2.6	1
23 Permanent Port. Versatile	IGC	Sh/Hi	2.6	1
24 Pacifica Asset Preservation	IGC	Sh/Med	2.4	1
25 Smith Barney Adj./R Gov. A	MBS	Sh/Hi	2.3	—
Average taxable bond fund			**(3.6)**	

THREE-YEAR WINNERS

Fund name	Type	Style	% return	Risk level
1 Dean Witter H/Y Sec.[1]	HYC	Int/Lo	14.9	4
2 Fidelity Spartan High-Inc.	HYC	Int/Lo	14.7	1
3 Fidelity Capital & Income	HYC	Int/Lo	14.7	2
4 MainStay H/Y Corp. Bond B	HYC	Int/Lo	14.5	1
5 Northeast Investors	HYC	Int/Lo	14.1	1
6 Advantage High-Yield Bond	HYC	L/Lo	14.1	2
7 Venture Income Plus A	HYC	Int/Lo	13.8	1
8 Colonial High-Yield Sec. A	HYC	Int/Lo	13.1	1
9 Fidelity Adv. High-Yield A	HYC	Int/Lo	13.1	1
10 Seligman High-Yield Bond A	HYC	Int/Lo	13.0	1
11 MetLife-State Res. H/I A	HYC	Int/Lo	12.7	1
12 Keystone Amer. Strat. Inc. A	HYC	Int/Lo	12.4	6
13 Oppen. Champion H/Y A	HYC	Int/Lo	12.1	1
14 First Investors High-Yield	HYC	Int/Lo	11.5	1
15 Kemper High-Yield A	HYC	Int/Lo	11.4	2
16 AIM High-Yield A	HYC	Int/Lo	11.4	1
17 Eaton Vance Inc. of Boston	HYC	Int/Lo	11.3	1
18 First Investors Fund for Inc.	HYC	Int/Lo	11.2	1
19 Enterprise High-Yield Bond	HYC	Int/Lo	11.1	1
20 Putnam High Yield Adv. A	HYC	Int/Lo	10.8	2
21 MFS High-Income A	HYC	Int/Lo	10.8	1
22 Fortis Advantage H/Y A	HYC	Int/Lo	10.7	2
23 Liberty High-Income Bond A	HYC	Int/Lo	10.6	2
24 EV Marathon High-Income	HYC	Int/Lo	10.6	1
25 Smith Barney High-Inc. B	HYC	Int/Lo	10.6	2
Average taxable bond fund			**4.4**	

FIVE-YEAR WINNERS

Fund name	Type	Style	% return	Risk level
1 Fidelity Adv. High-Yield A	HYC	Int/Lo	15.9	1
2 Liberty High-Income Bond A	HYC	Int/Lo	13.6	2
3 Fidelity Capital & Income	HYC	Int/Lo	13.5	2
4 Oppen. Champion H/Y A	HYC	Int/Lo	13.5	1
5 Advantage High-Yield Bond	HYC	L/Lo	13.2	2
6 MainStay H/Y Corp. Bd. B	HYC	Int/Lo	12.9	1
7 Putnam High Yield Adv. A	HYC	Int/Lo	12.8	2
8 PaineWebber H/I A	HYC	Int/Lo	12.6	6
9 AIM High-Yield A	HYC	Int/Lo	12.3	1
10 Colonial High-Yield Sec. A	HYC	Int/Lo	12.1	1
11 Kemper High-Yield A	HYC	Int/Lo	12.1	2
12 Putnam High Yield A	HYC	Int/Lo	12.1	2
13 Seligman High-Yield Bond A	HYC	Int/Lo	11.8	1
14 Fortis Advantage H/Y A	HYC	Int/Lo	11.6	2
15 Franklin AGE High-Income	HYC	Int/Lo	11.4	1
16 Fortress Bond	IGC	Int/Med	11.3	3
17 Northeast Investors	HYC	Int/Lo	11.2	1
18 MFS High-Income A	HYC	Int/Lo	11.0	1
19 Scudder International Bond	WI	Int/Hi	11.0	7
20 American High-Income	HYC	Int/Lo	11.0	2
21 Fidelity Yen Performance	WI	Sh/Hi	11.0	8
22 Oppenheimer High-Yield A	HYC	Int/Lo	10.8	1
23 Eaton Vance Inc. of Boston	HYC	Int/Lo	10.6	1
24 SunAmerica H/I A	HYC	Int/Lo	10.6	4
25 Lord Abbett Bond-Debenture	HYC	Int/Lo	10.6	2
Average taxable bond fund			**7.3**	

TAX-EXEMPT BONDS

1994 WINNERS

Fund name	Type	Style	% return	Risk level
1 20th Cent. Tax-Ex. Sh.-Tm.	Muni	Sh/Hi	2.5	—
2 Calvert Tax-Fr. Res. Ltd./T A	Muni	Sh/Hi	2.4	1
3 Venture Muni Plus B	Muni	L/Med	2.3	1
4 Vanguard Muni Short-Term	Muni	Int/Hi	1.6	1
5 First American Ltd./T T/F A	Muni	Sh/Hi	1.6	—
6 Colonial Short-Term Tax-Ex.	Muni	Sh/Hi	1.2	—
7 USAA Tax-Exempt S/T	Muni	Sh/Hi	0.8	1
8 Managers Short Municipal	Muni	Sh/Hi	0.4	1
9 T. Rowe Price T/F Sh.-Int.	Muni	Sh/Hi	0.3	1
10 Amer. Cap. T/E H/Y Muni A[1]	Muni	L/Lo	0.2	1
11 Vanguard Muni Ltd.-Term	Muni	Int/Hi	0.1	1
12 United Svcs. Near-Term T/F	Muni	Int/Hi	0.0	1
13 Fidelity Spartan S/I Muni	Muni	Sh/Med	(0.1)	1
14 Smith Bar. Ltd. Mat. Munis A	Muni	Int/Hi	(0.2)	1
15 Dreyfus S/I Muni Bond	Muni	Sh/Med	(0.3)	1
16 UST Master T/E S/T Sec.	Muni	Sh/Hi	(0.3)	—
17 STI Classic Inv. Gr. T/E Inv.	Muni	L/Hi	(0.6)	—
18 Sit Tax-Free Income	Muni	L/Med	(0.6)	1
19 Forum Taxsaver Bond	Muni	L/Med	(0.9)	1
20 Strong H/Y Muni Bond	Muni	N.A.	(1.0)	—
21 Schwab Short/Int. T/F Bond	Muni	Sh/Hi	(1.1)	1
22 MFS Municipal Ltd. Mat. A	Muni	Sh/Med	(1.3)	1
23 Evergreen Short-Int. Muni	Muni	Sh/Med	(1.4)	1
24 AIM Tax-Free Intermediate	Muni	Int/Hi	(1.4)	1
25 Thornburg Ltd.-Term Natl. A	Muni	Int/Hi	(1.5)	1
Average tax-exempt bond fund			**(5.0)**	

THREE-YEAR WINNERS

Fund name	Type	Style	% return	Risk level
1 Smith Barney Mgd. Munis A	Muni	L/Med	6.6	4
2 United Municipal High-Inc.	Muni	L/Lo	6.5	1
3 Amer. Cap. T/E H/Y Muni A1	Muni	L/Lo	6.4	1
4 Franklin High-Yld. T/F Inc.	Muni	L/Med	6.4	1
5 Thornburg Intm. Muni A	Muni	Int/Med	6.3	2
6 Venture Muni Plus B	Muni	L/Med	6.3	1
7 Vista Tax-Free Income A	Muni	L/Hi	6.2	5
8 UST Master T/E Long-Tm.	Muni	L/Hi	6.2	7
9 Strong Municipal Bond	Muni	L/Med	6.2	3
10 Forum Taxsaver Bond	Muni	L/Med	6.1	1
11 Flagship All-American T/E A	Muni	L/Hi	6.0	5
12 Vanguard Muni I/T	Muni	Int/Hi	5.9	2
13 First Prairie Muni Bd. Ins. A	Muni	L/Hi	5.9	3
14 Great Hall National Tax-Ex.	Muni	L/Lo	5.9	1
15 Delaware Tax-Free USA A	Muni	L/Hi	5.9	1
16 T. Rowe Price Tax-Fr. H/Y	Muni	L/Med	5.8	2
17 Sit Tax-Free Income	Muni	L/Med	5.7	1
18 Strong Insured Muni Bond	Muni	L/Hi	5.7	6
19 Sierra National Muni A	Muni	L/Med	5.6	6
20 Franklin Insured T/F Inc.	Muni	L/Med	5.6	2
21 Premier Municipal Bond A	Muni	L/Med	5.6	4
22 Quest for Value National T/E	Muni	L/Hi	5.5	5
23 Vanguard Muni High-Yield	Muni	L/Med	5.5	6
24 Franklin Fed. Tax-Free Inc.	Muni	L/Med	5.5	2
25 Calvert Tax-Fr. Res. L/T A	Muni	L/Med	5.4	2
Average tax-exempt bond fund			**4.7**	

FIVE-YEAR WINNERS

Fund name	Type	Style	% return	Risk level
1 Vista Tax-Free Income A	Muni	L/Hi	8.0	5
2 Smith Barney Mgd. Munis A	Muni	L/Med	7.8	4
3 United Municipal H/I	Muni	L/Lo	7.7	2
4 UST Master T/E Long-Tm.	Muni	L/Hi	7.7	7
5 Flagship All-American T/E A	Muni	L/Hi	7.6	5
6 Fidelity Adv. High-Income A	Muni	L/Med	7.6	4
7 Premier Municipal Bond A	Muni	L/Med	7.6	4
8 First Prairie Muni Bd. Ins. A	Muni	L/Hi	7.5	3
9 Vanguard Muni I/T	Muni	Int/Hi	7.4	2
10 Vanguard Muni High-Yield	Muni	L/Med	7.4	6
11 General Municipal Bond	Muni	L/Med	7.3	6
12 Franklin High-Yld. T/F Inc.	Muni	L/Hi	7.3	1
13 Strong Municipal Bond	Muni	L/Med	7.3	3
14 Vanguard Muni Long-Term	Muni	L/Hi	7.2	6
15 T. Rowe Price T/F Hi-Yld.	Muni	L/Med	7.2	2
16 American Cap. T/E H/Y A[1]	Muni	L/Lo	7.1	1
17 Benham Natl. T/F L/T	Muni	L/Hi	7.1	6
18 Forum Taxsaver Bond	Muni	L/Med	7.1	1
19 Great Hall National Tax-Ex.	Muni	L/Lo	7.1	1
20 Smith Barney Muni Natl. A	Muni	L/Med	7.1	4
21 Fidelity Aggressive T/F	Muni	L/Hi	7.0	3
22 Vanguard Muni Insured L/T	Muni	L/Hi	7.0	6
23 Nuveen Insured Muni Bond[1]	Muni	L/Hi	7.0	6
24 Franklin Fed. Tax-Free Inc.	Muni	L/Med	7.0	2
25 Putnam Municipal Inc. A	Muni	L/Med	6.9	3
Average tax-exempt bond fund			**6.3**	

Notes: [1]Closed to new investors N.A.: Not available All data are to Jan.1, 1995. Telephone numbers and other performance data are available in the tables that follow. Fund types and styles are explained on page 180. **Source:** Morningstar Inc., 800-876-5005

The 2,125 Major Funds

Fund name/★ 1994 winner	Type	Style	Risk level	One year	Three years	Five years	% tax efficiency	% tax liability	1994	1993	1992	1991	% max. sales charge	Five-year total per $1,000	Net assets (millions)	Telephone (800)
				\% average annual return to Jan. 1, 1995			Tax analysis		Performance analysis (percentile ranking by type)				Expense analysis			

STOCK FUNDS

Fund name/★ 1994 winner	Type	Style	Risk level	One year	Three years	Five years	% tax efficiency	% tax liability	1994	1993	1992	1991	% max. sales charge	Five-year total per $1,000	Net assets (millions)	Telephone (800)
AARP Capital Growth	Gro	Md/Gro	11	(10.0)	3.0	5.3	55	2	7	68	27	65	None	$62	$649.0	322-2282
AARP Growth & Income ★	G&I	Md/Bl	7	3.1	9.2	10.0	85	10	91	79	61	38	None	50	2,284.7	322-2282
ABT Emerging Growth	Agg	Md/Gro	12	(9.3)	6.8	15.6	95	25	9	51	59	93	4.75	123	62.2	553-7838
ABT Growth & Income	G&I	Md/Bl	9	(4.1)	1.0	4.0	41	3	22	8	12	59	4.75	112	61.4	553-7838
ABT Utility Income	Spec	Md/Val	10	(12.2)	1.8	3.2	N.A.	(6)	16	16	67	44	4.75	109	99.9	553-7838
Accessor Growth ★	Gro	Lg/Bl	—	4.0	—	—	—	5	91	60	—	—	None	N.A.	23.2	759-3504
Accessor Small Cap	Agg	Sm/Val	—	(4.1)	—	—	—	2	30	35	—	—	None	N.A.	24.0	759-3504
Accessor Value & Income	ETR	Lg/Val	—	(2.0)	—	—	—	(1)	57	71	—	—	None	N.A.	19.9	759-3504
Acorn[1]	Agg	Sm/Gro	9	(7.4)	15.0	13.1	90	39	12	96	91	39	None	35	1,982.8	922-6769
Acorn International[1]	Intl	Sm/Gro	—	(3.8)	—	—	—	6	37	89	—	—	None	N.A.	1,364.8	922-6769
Addison Capital Shares	G&I	Md/Val	10	(6.7)	3.9	6.5	61	15	8	58	34	71	3.0	141	34.1	526-6397
Advantage Growth	Gro	Lg/Bl	10	(7.7)	3.3	7.6	61	10	14	41	49	61	4.0[4]	115	76.4	241-2039
Advantage Income	ITR	Md/Val	7	(5.3)	5.3	7.3	70	3	40	54	29	32	4.0[4]	99	73.8	241-2039
Advantage Special	Agg	Sm/Bl	11	(4.9)	9.4	13.4	95	10	25	64	62	64	4.0[4]	150	38.8	241-2039
Affiliated ★	G&I	Lg/Val	7	3.9	9.8	8.9	71	11	93	60	80	20	5.75	89	4,009.6	874-3733
AIM Aggressive Growth[1] ★	Agg	Sm/Bl	11	17.2	23.4	23.5	98	15	98	94	88	78	5.5	120	714.7	347-1919
AIM Balanced A	ETR	Lg/Val	10	(5.4)	6.2	10.5	87	(2)	19	75	69	96	4.75	156	37.6	347-1919
AIM Charter	G&I	Lg/Bl	9	(4.3)	2.1	9.6	45	5	19	40	7	90	5.5	116	1,475.1	347-1919
AIM Constellation ★	Agg	Md/Gro	11	1.3	11.0	17.4	97	19	73	49	63	85	5.5	118	3,703.5	347-1919
AIM Growth A	Gro	Md/Gro	12	(5.0)	(0.5)	5.1	N.A.	9	24	16	10	59	5.5	116	123.7	347-1919
AIM International Equity	Intl	Md/Bl	—	(3.3)	—	—	—	11	43	84	—	—	5.5	N.A.	653.4	347-1919
AIM Summit	Gro	Md/Bl	11	(2.8)	3.2	9.8	38	12	41	32	25	77	8.5	42	746.4	347-1919
AIM Utilities A	Spec	Md/Val	10	(11.6)	2.4	5.2	14	(14)	19	25	55	54	5.5	116	150.0	347-1919
AIM Value A ★	Gro	Md/Bl	9	3.3	12.5	15.8	87	6	87	79	86	76	5.5	115	1,358.3	347-1919
AIM Weingarten	Gro	Lg/Bl	11	(0.3)	(0.1)	9.1	N.A.	20	61	10	8	81	5.5	114	3,667.6	347-1919
Alger Balanced	ETR	Md/Gro	—	(6.6)	—	—	—	2	11	18	—	—	5.0[4]	202	2.9	992-3863
Alger Growth	Gro	Md/Bl	11	(1.6)	9.6	14.0	87	8	49	83	67	76	5.0[4]	144	71.4	992-3863
Alger Income & Growth	G&I	Md/Bl	11	(8.1)	1.9	3.8	56	(1)	4	22	42	24	5.0[4]	182	7.1	992-3863
Alger Leveraged AllCap	Agg	Md/Gro	—	(2.2)	—	—	—	4	42	—	—	—	5.0[4]	259	2.4	992-3863
Alger MidCap Growth ★	Gro	Md/Gro	—	0.6	—	—	—	4	71	—	—	—	5.0[4]	143	22.1	992-3863
Alger Small Capitalization	Agg	Sm/Gro	12	(4.6)	3.8	13.0	73	11	27	31	19	58	5.0[4]	136	294.3	992-3863
Alliance A	Gro	Lg/Bl	11	(2.5)	8.5	10.4	61	26	43	60	80	44	4.25	110	761.9	227-4618
Alliance Strategic Balanced A	ETR	Lg/Bl	7	(5.8)	3.4	5.4	69	0	16	29	41	23	4.25	127	145.9	227-4618
Alliance Conservative Inv. B	ETR	N.A.	—	(5.7)	—	—	—	(8)	17	21	—	—	4.0[4]	128	30.2	227-4618
Alliance Counterpoint A	Gro	Lg/Gro	11	(1.9)	3.2	7.0	N.A.	41	46	27	26	43	4.25	138	39.3	227-4618
Alliance Global Sm. Cap. A	Intl	Sm/Bl	11	(4.5)	2.9	0.5	22	14	33	4	35	88	4.25	173	59.8	227-4618
Alliance Growth & Income A ★	G&I	Lg/Bl	9	(4.2)	3.3	6.6	25	6	20	43	16	42	4.25	112	395.3	227-4618
Alliance Growth B	Gro	Md/Bl	9	(1.8)	11.6	15.8	81	(1)	47	98	63	95	4.0[4]	128	757.8	227-4618
Alliance Growth Investors B	ETR	Md/Bl	—	(4.3)	—	—	—	(2)	26	32	—	—	4.0[4]	128	39.5	227-4618
Alliance Income Builder C	ITR	Lg/Val	6	(5.8)	1.4	—	12	(12)	29	11	5	—	None	133	61.5	227-4618
Alliance International A ★	Intl	Lg/Bl	11	5.7	8.3	1.6	84	19	96	19	26	15	4.25	152	178.3	227-4618
Alliance New Europe A ★	Reg	Lg/Val	11	4.6	11.9	—	98	(5)	77	49	76	26	4.25	169	80.3	227-4618
Alliance Premier Growth B	Gro	Lg/Gro	—	(6.2)	—	—	—	4	20	38	—	—	4.0[4]	143	140.1	227-4618
Alliance Quasar A	Agg	Sm/Bl	12	(7.3)	3.5	2.6	30	31	13	42	19	14	4.25	138	134.3	227-4618
Alliance Balanced B	ETR	Md/Bl	10	(9.1)	(0.6)	6.9	N.A.	(3)	6	52	3	94	5.5[4]	128	40.6	227-4618
Alliance Technology A ★	Spec	Md/Gro	12	28.5	21.8	22.0	79	45	100	55	77	84	4.25	138	204.5	227-4618
Alliance Utility Income C	Spec	Md/Val	—	(11.4)	—	—	—	(5)	20	—	—	—	None	118	2.7	227-4618
Allmerica Growth & Inc.[2] ★	G&I	N.A.	—	2.8	—	—	—	0	—	—	—	—	4.5	N.A.	2.2	828-7084
Amana Income	ETR	Md/Bl	9	(6.5)	2.1	4.9	54	6	12	43	9	44	None	98	10.2	728-8762
AMCAP	Gro	Lg/Gro	9	(0.2)	5.9	9.3	57	23	62	45	43	56	5.75	97	2,877.2	421-4120
America's Utility	Spec	Md/Val	—	(13.1)	—	—	—	(14)	14	29	—	—	None	67	123.6	487-3863
American Balanced ★	ETR	Lg/Val	4	0.3	6.9	8.5	72	3	85	40	68	52	5.75	96	2,081.9	421-4120
American Cap. Comstock A	G&I	Lg/Bl	9	(3.7)	3.8	7.4	N.A.	20	23	30	35	76	5.75	110	871.8	421-5666
American Cap. Emerg. Gro. A	Agg	Md/Gro	12	(7.1)	8.1	15.6	83	14	14	83	42	71	5.75	117	677.6	421-5666
American Cap. Enterprise A	Gro	Md/Gro	10	(0.2)	6.3	10.2	46	11	63	45	53	64	5.75	109	749.3	421-5666

Source: Morningstar Inc. Chicago Ill.; 800-876-5005

Fund name/★ 1994 winner		Type	Style	Risk level	% average annual return to Jan. 1, 1995			Tax analysis		Performance analysis (percentile ranking by type)				Expense analysis		Net assets (millions)	Telephone (800)
					One year	Three years	Five years	% tax efficiency	% tax liability	1994	1993	1992	1991	% max. sales charge	Five-year total per $1,000		
American Cap. Equity-Inc. A		ETR	Lg/Bl	7	(2.0)	8.0	8.7	80	1	57	80	82	67	5.75	$110	$240.3	421-5666
American Cap. Exchange	★	Gro	Lg/Bl	9	4.8	5.7	9.3	93	N.A.	93	29	24	30	None	N.A.	37.7	421-5666
American Cap. Glob. Eq. A		Intl	Md/Bl	10	(1.7)	5.4	—	88	2	56	5	59	—	5.75	162	61.6	421-5666
American Cap. Growth & Inc.		G&I	Lg/Bl	8	(1.7)	7.8	9.1	59	10	36	80	64	65	5.75	117	205.4	421-5666
American Cap. Harbor A		ITR	N.A.	7	(6.4)	5.3	7.2	51	0	19	47	47	38	5.75	111	369.9	421-5666
American Cap. Pace A		Gro	Lg/Bl	9	(3.7)	3.7	6.7	N.A.	14	33	44	25	36	5.75	110	2,060.7	421-5666
American Cap. Util. Inc. B		Spec	Lg/Val	—	(8.1)	—	—	—	(7)	39	—	—	—	4.0⁴	N.A.	11.8	421-5666
American Gas Index		Spec	Md/Val	10	(9.7)	5.5	1.6	77	(7)	27	40	72	26	None	47	178.1	343-3355
American Growth		Gro	Lg/Val	9	(4.0)	10.3	9.2	63	19	30	93	73	15	5.75	158	70.8	525-2406
American Heritage		Agg	Sm/Gro	12	(35.3)	2.8	8.2	16	(56)	1	98	94	100	None	118	57.0	828-5060
American Leaders A		G&I	Lg/Val	8	0.0	7.7	10.0	77	17	58	51	76	72	5.5	107	239.8	245-5051
American Mutual	★	G&I	Lg/Val	7	0.3	7.3	8.2	66	20	61	68	50	19	5.75	89	5,278.6	421-4120
American National Growth	★	Gro	Lg/Bl	10	4.4	2.9	7.7	N.A.	15	92	31	5	58	5.75	113	113.3	231-4639
American National Income		ETR	Lg/Bl	8	(1.1)	4.1	8.0	29	11	67	32	18	75	5.75	119	114.2	231-4639
Amway Mutual		Gro	Md/Gro	11	(5.7)	1.8	8.6	N.A.	7	21	41	11	70	3.0	86	58.9	346-2670
Analytic Optioned Equity	★	G&I	Lg/Bl	4	2.5	5.1	6.0	54	4	86	17	32	3	None	56	48.2	374-2633
API Capital Income		ETR	Lg/Bl	8	(0.4)	3.7	5.5	82	N.A.	77	13	27	43	None	183	3.0	544-6060
API Growth		Gro	Md/Gro	10	(3.4)	5.2	8.4	69	N.A.	35	77	14	82	None	111	49.2	544-6060
API Special Markets		ETR	Lg/Bl	11	(6.9)	(1.0)	(2.2)	N.A.	N.A.	10	10	5	1	None	135	1.0	544-6060
API Total Return		ETR	Lg/Bl	10	(6.8)	2.6	2.4	75	N.A.	10	47	15	49	None	135	4.4	544-6060
Ariel Appreciation A		Gro	Sm/Val	9	(8.4)	3.9	8.0	77	15	10	30	75	42	None	125	128.5	292-7435
Ariel Growth¹		Agg	Sm/Bl	9	(4.2)	5.2	5.3	60	22	30	18	50	11	None	113	130.8	292-7435
Arrow Equity		Gro	Md/Val	—	(2.1)	—	—	—	(4)	46	7	—	—	3.5	N.A.	30.8	866-6040
ASM	★	G&I	Lg/Bl	8	1.1	6.6	—	80	9	74	61	26	—	None	43	7.3	445-2763
Atlanta Growth		Gro	Md/Gro	—	(4.8)	—	—	—	15	25	23	—	—	3.75	203	5.4	762-0227
Babson Enterprise¹	★	Agg	Sm/Val	7	2.4	14.1	12.3	77	24	77	43	92	31	None	64	190.5	422-2766
Babson Enterprise II		Agg	Sm/Val	10	(7.4)	9.2	—	97	7	12	62	75	—	None	99	36.8	422-2766
Babson Growth		Gro	Lg/Val	8	(0.6)	6.2	6.4	72	32	60	41	57	18	None	48	226.5	422-2766
Babson-Stewart Ivory Intl.	★	Intl	Md/Gro	10	1.3	10.0	6.8	90	16	77	43	56	51	None	86	55.2	422-2766
Babson Value	★	G&I	Md/Val	7	2.5	13.3	10.7	89	8	87	98	91	57	None	56	122.0	422-2766
Baird Blue Chip	★	G&I	Lg/Gro	9	4.7	4.0	8.6	77	28	96	10	10	66	5.75	129	58.4	792-2473
Baird Capital Development		Gro	Sm/Bl	8	(0.3)	8.2	11.4	81	14	62	48	78	80	5.75	138	52.6	792-2473
Baron Asset	★	Agg	Sm/Gro	9	7.4	14.8	10.5	95	27	93	81	60	12	None	92	84.3	992-2766
Bartlett Cap. Basic Value	★	G&I	Md/Val	8	0.4	7.3	7.1	80	11	63	51	70	36	None	66	93.2	800-4612
Bartlett Capital Val. Intl.		Intl	Lg/Val	11	(0.5)	8.6	5.9	91	6	61	34	54	81	None	108	56.4	800-4612
BayFunds Equity Investment		Gro	Md/Bl	—	(3.2)	—	—	—	2	37	—	—	—	None	N.A.	29.4	229-3863
Benham Equity Growth		Gro	Lg/Bl	8	(0.2)	5.0	—	72	4	63	47	21	—	None	42	97.6	331-8331
Benham Gold Equities Index		Spec	Md/Gro	12	(16.7)	11.3	(0.3)	99	1	6	92	21	6	None	42	570.6	331-8331
Benham Income & Growth		G&I	Lg/Bl	8	(0.5)	6.1	—	77	6	47	49	51	92	None	42	224.8	331-8331
Benham Utilities Income		Spec	Lg/Val	—	(10.0)	—	—	—	(16)	25	—	—	—	None	N.A.	152.3	331-8331
Berger 100		Gro	Md/Gro	12	(6.7)	7.1	17.0	100	11	18	87	54	100	None	107	2,113.0	333-1001
Berger 101		G&I	Md/Bl	10	(9.1)	5.6	11.8	96	0	2	99	17	100	None	145	368.3	333-1001
Berger Small Co. Growth	★	Agg	Sm/Gro	—	13.7	—	—	—	6	97	—	—	—	None	N.A.	291.2	333-1001
Bernstein Intl. Value	★	Intl	Md/Val	—	3.8	—	—	—	8	90	50	—	—	None	N.A.	1,392.8	756-4097⁶
Berwyn	★	Agg	Sm/Val	9	3.9	15.5	11.0	89	17	82	79	85	32	None	76	63.5	824-2249
Berwyn Income		ITR	Int/Lo	2	(1.1)	12.1	11.7	76	(4)	94	77	97	46	None	73	55.8	824-2249
Bhirud Mid Cap Growth		Gro	Sm/Bl	—	(10.6)	—	—	—	(4)	6	51	—	—	5.75	N.A.	9.8	845-8405
Biltmore Balanced		ETR	Lg/Val	—	(0.5)	—	—	—	(2)	74	—	—	—	4.5	N.A.	194.7	462-7538
Biltmore Equity	★	G&I	Lg/Bl	—	2.0	—	—	—	2	82	—	—	—	4.5	N.A.	86.9	462-7538
Biltmore Equity Index	★	G&I	Lg/Bl	—	0.9	—	—	—	1	70	—	—	—	4.5	N.A.	183.7	462-7538
Biltmore Special Values		Agg	Sm/Val	—	(3.3)	—	—	—	(3)	35	—	—	—	4.5	N.A.	17.4	462-7538
Blanchard American Equity		Gro	Lg/Gro	—	(4.1)	—	—	—	(3)	30	4	—	—	None	N.A.	11.1	922-7771
Blanchard Flexible Income		ITR	Int/Md	—	(5.5)	—	—	—	(14)	34	50	—	—	None	N.A.	300.4	922-7771
Blanchard Global Growth		ETR	Md/Bl	8	(7.5)	6.1	4.4	66	1	7	98	22	6	None	147	97.5	922-7771
Blanchard Precious Metals		Spec	Md/Gro	12	(15.0)	11.6	0.9	87	1	9	97	9	19	None	197	72.5	922-7771
BNY Hamilton Equity-Income		ETR	Lg/Bl	—	(2.6)	—	—	—	(2)	47	45	—	—	3.0	N.A.	135.1	426-9363
Bond Fund for Growth		ITR	N.A.	4	(2.5)	15.7	12.9	89	(3)	72	95	100	73	3.25	128	125.7	383-1300⁷
Brandywine		Gro	Md/Gro	11	0.0	12.4	16.3	84	6	65	90	84	86	None	61	2,299.3	656-3017
Bruce		ETR	N.A.	12	(16.1)	3.5	2.2	67	(20)	2	88	81	2	None	118	2.0	236-9160⁸
Brundage Story & Rose G&I		G&I	Lg/Bl	9	(0.5)	4.0	—	71	11	47	46	8	22	4.0	82	19.0	545-0103

Source: Morningstar Inc. Chicago Ill.; 800-876-5005

Fund name/★ 1994 winner	Type	Style	Risk level	% average annual return to Jan. 1, 1995			Tax analysis		Performance analysis (percentile ranking by type)				Expense analysis		Net assets (millions)	Telephone (800)
				One year	Three years	Five years	% tax efficiency	% tax liability	1994	1993	1992	1991	% max. sales charge	Five-year total per $1,000		
BT Investment Capital App. ★	Gro	Md/Gro	—	3.2	—	—	—	4	87	—	—	—	None	$69	$42.6	943-2222
BT Investment Equity App. ★	Gro	Md/Gro	—	3.5	—	—	—	0	89	—	—	—	None	55	31.0	943-2222
BT Investment Intl. Equity ★	Intl	Md/Val	—	4.8	—	—	—	12	94	61	—	—	None	82	56.1	949-9940
BT Inv. Latin Amer. Equity	Reg	N.A.	—	(10.8)	—	—	—	5	40	—	—	—	None	N.A.	18.7	949-9940
BT Inv. Lifecycle Long	ETR	Lg/Bl	—	(2.9)	—	—	—	(3)	41	—	—	—	None	55	12.0	943-2222
BT Inv. Lifecycle Mid.	ETR	N.A.	—	(3.4)	—	—	—	(7)	38	—	—	—	None	55	24.3	943-2222
BT Inv. Lifecycle Short	ETR	N.A.	—	(3.0)	—	—	—	(7)	40	—	—	—	None	55	21.4	943-2222
BT Inv. Pacific Basin Eq.	Reg	Md/Gro	—	(16.9)	—	—	—	0	25	—	—	—	None	N.A.	22.9	949-9940
BT Investment Small Cap. ★	Agg	N.A.	—	19.3	—	—	—	N.A.	99	—	—	—	None	N.A.	31.8	949-9940
BT Investment Utility	Spec	Sm/Val	—	(11.7)	—	—	—	(18)	17	20	—	—	None	69	16.9	949-9940
Bull & Bear Gold Investors	Spec	Md/Gro	12	(13.8)	10.2	0.6	90	23	12	94	10	20	None	156	33.9	847-4200
Bull & Bear Quality Growth	Gro	Lg/Bl	—	(7.9)	—	—	—	9	13	—	—	—	None	N.A.	4.2	847-4200
Bull & Bear Special Equity	Agg	Sm/Gro	12	(16.5)	7.6	2.2	72	(20)	2	44	94	25	None	161	45.0	847-4200
Bull & Bear US & Overseas	Intl	Md/Val	11	(13.1)	2.3	3.7	7	11	4	17	50	82	None	184	9.2	847-4200
Burnham A	G&I	Lg/Bl	7	(1.8)	5.0	6.0	53	4	35	34	49	8	3.0	106	102.3	874-3863
Calamos Convertible	ITR	N.A.	9	(7.0)	5.6	9.2	57	7	9	83	23	89	4.5	133	16.2	323-9943
Calvert Social Inv. Equity	Gro	Md/Bl	11	(12.2)	(0.9)	2.4	—	(3)	3	12	53	9	4.75	102	94.7	368-2748
Calvert Social Inv. Managed	ETR	Md/Bl	6	(4.7)	2.7	5.4	56	6	24	11	50	15	4.75	116	507.4	368-2748
Calvert World Val. Glob. Eq.	Intl	Md/Bl	—	(2.7)	—	—	—	2	50	14	—	—	4.75	150	182.4	368-2748
Cambridge Capital Growth B	Gro	Lg/Val	—	(3.4)	—	—	—	3	35	15	—	—	1.0[4]	119	39.1	382-0016
Cambridge Growth B	Gro	Md/Bl	—	(11.4)	—	—	—	(3)	4	18	—	—	1.0[4]	121	26.5	382-0016
Cambridge Income & Growth B	ETR	Md/Val	—	(1.9)	—	—	—	5	60	—	—	—	1.0[4]	N.A.	41.3	382-0016
Capital Growth Investment[2]	Gro	Md/Bl	N.A.	(12.9)	1.8	5.6	N.A.	N.A.	—	—	—	—	5.75	110	—	245-4770
Capital Income Builder	ETR	Lg/Val	7	(2.3)	7.4	10.1	79	2	52	74	73	59	5.75	100	3,596.5	421-4120
Capital World G & I ★	Intl	Lg/Val	—	1.2	—	—	—	6	75	—	—	—	5.75	N.A.	2,827.1	421-4120
Cappiello-Rushmore Emerg.Gro.	Agg	Sm/Bl	—	(6.9)	—	—	—	(1)	15	75	—	—	None	82	20.1	343-3355
Cappiello-Rushmore Gro. ★	Gro	Md/Bl	—	4.4	—	—	—	7	92	60	—	—	None	82	11.8	343-3355
Cappiello-Rushmore Util. Inc.	Spec	Md/Val	—	(14.1)	—	—	—	(21)	10	10	—	—	None	58	9.9	343-3355
Capstone Fund of the S.W.	Gro	Md/Bl	12	(28.7)	(5.7)	2.5	N.A.	N.A.	1	32	55	83	4.75	148	4.1	262-6631
Capstone Growth	Gro	Lg/Bl	10	(7.8)	(0.5)	5.2	N.A.	17	13	23	11	48	4.75	105	76.3	262-6631
Capstone New Zealand	Reg	N.A.	12	(8.3)	1.7	—	67	(2)	50	6	85	—	4.75	174	3.1	262-6631
Cardinal	G&I	Lg/Val	7	(3.2)	4.0	6.9	50	25	25	13	67	79	6.0	120	229.4	848-7734
Cardinal Aggressive Growth	Agg	Md/Gro	—	(2.2)	—	—	—	(1)	43	—	—	—	5.5	N.A.	9.4	848-7734
Cardinal Balanced	ETR	Lg/Val	—	(1.8)	—	—	—	(4)	60	—	—	—	5.5	N.A.	13.3	848-7734
Carillon Capital ★	ETR	Sm/Val	2	1.4	7.7	9.4	67	11	91	65	58	64	5.0	108	41.3	999-1840
Centurion Growth[3]	G&I	Sm/Val	—	(7.8)	(5.3)	(3.6)	N.A.	(5)	N.A.	—	—	—	4.75	227	3.4	448-6984
Century Shares	Spec	Md/Val	10	(3.9)	6.7	8.1	77	51	60	3	93	64	None	47	199.2	321-1928
CGM Capital Development[1]	Gro	Sm/Gro	12	(22.9)	5.2	18.7	34	(3)	1	98	89	100	None	49	401.7	345-4048
CGM Mutual	ETR	Lg/Val	10	(9.7)	5.3	10.7	60	(3)	4	94	32	93	None	51	1,063.4	345-4048
Chubb Growth & Income	G&I	Md/Val	9	(6.2)	4.9	8.3	71	0	9	77	38	81	5.0	117	19.3	258-3648
Chubb Total Return	ETR	Md/Val	7	(4.2)	5.1	8.3	63	0	28	58	45	76	5.0	117	17.0	258-3648
Clipper	Gro	Lg/Val	10	(2.5)	7.9	9.0	67	10	43	46	85	39	None	63	245.7	776-5033
Cohen & Steers Realty Shares ★	Spec	Sm/Bl	9	8.3	15.6	—	86	(8)	87	46	86	—	None	67	458.5	437-9912
Colonial A	G&I	Md/Val	7	(2.1)	8.2	8.1	76	15	31	71	83	35	5.75	116	537.0	248-2828
Colonial Global Equity B	Intl	Md/Val	—	(2.5)	—	—	—	16	52	49	—	—	5.04	N.A.	60.3	248-2828
Colonial Growth Shares A	Gro	Md/Val	10	(2.7)	5.9	7.3	50	13	42	39	66	45	5.75	119	151.4	248-2828
Colonial Intl. Fund/Gro. B	Intl	N.A.	—	(8.4)	—	—	—	N.A.	15	—	—	—	5.04	N.A.	99.2	248-2828
Colonial Natural Resources A	Spec	Md/Bl	—	(0.9)	—	—	—	14	70	73	—	—	5.75	N.A.	33.9	248-2828
Colonial Small Stock A ★	Agg	Sm/Val	10	6.3	15.1	6.7	100	19	91	58	85	3	5.75	168	26.9	248-2828
Colonial Strategic Income A	ITR	L/Med	2	(3.7)	6.7	7.7	61	(35)	60	61	49	67	4.75	113	643.4	248-2828
Colonial US Fund for Gro. B	Gro	Lg/Bl	—	(1.0)	—	—	—	9	55	55	—	—	5.04	N.A.	163.3	248-2828
Colonial Utilities A	Spec	Md/Val	8	(10.3)	5.6	7.1	73	(22)	24	17	87	57	4.75	114	373.3	248-2828
Columbia Balanced ★	ETR	Lg/Bl	5	0.1	7.4	—	81	0	84	61	65	—	None	45	249.7	547-1707
Columbia Common Stock ★	G&I	Lg/Bl	8	2.1	9.4	—	87	7	82	83	68	—	None	48	124.3	547-1707
Columbia Growth	Gro	Md/Bl	10	(0.6)	7.9	10.3	66	10	59	54	70	47	None	48	591.7	547-1707
Columbia International Stock	Intl	Lg/Bl	—	(2.5)	—	—	—	7	52	42	—	—	None	N.A.	118.5	547-1707
Columbia Special ★	Agg	Md/Gro	10	2.3	12.3	13.3	78	11	76	69	56	50	None	65	889.5	547-1707
Common Sense Growth	Gro	Lg/Bl	9	(2.3)	4.6	8.9	43	10	44	38	43	62	8.5	144	1,951.7	544-5445
Common Sense Gro. & Inc.	G&I	Lg/Bl	9	(3.2)	4.3	7.6	45	15	26	32	45	74	8.5	140	609.3	544-5445
Compass Cap. Equity-Inc. ★	ETR	Md/Val	9	0.6	8.1	10.1	68	(4)	86	83	46	61	3.75	89	279.0	451-8371

Source: Morningstar Inc. Chicago Ill.; 800-876-5005

Fund name/★ 1994 winner		Type	Style	Risk level	% average annual return to Jan. 1, 1995			Tax analysis		Performance analysis (percentile ranking by type)				Expense analysis		Net assets (millions)	Telephone (800)
					One year	Three years	Five years	% tax efficiency	% tax liability	1994	1993	1992	1991	% max. sales charge	Five-year total per $1,000		
Compass Capital Growth	★	Gro	Md/Bl	10	0.1	2.1	6.2	49	3	67	8	29	35	3.75	$91	$131.0	451-8371
Compass Cap. Intl. Equity	★	Intl	Lg/Bl	11	2.2	10.3	—	87	13	82	55	43	—	3.75	119	36.6	451-8371
Compass Cap. Small Cap. Value		Gro	Sm/Val	11	(4.4)	7.1	—	74	0	28	64	69	—	3.75	102	26.7	451-8371
Composite Bond & Stock		ETR	Lg/Val	6	(2.1)	5.5	7.4	74	2	53	25	71	34	4.5	105	183.4	543-8072
Composite Growth	★	G&I	Lg/Val	8	2.6	6.7	7.8	74	15	87	18	73	44	4.5	104	100.0	543-8072
Composite Northwest 50		Gro	Md/Bl	11	(1.4)	1.5	8.5	68	17	52	13	19	78	4.5	103	146.9	543-8072
Connecticut Mutual Growth		Gro	Md/Val	8	(0.3)	10.5	11.2	71	10	62	85	70	57	5.0	111	78.4	234-5606
Connecticut Mutual T/R		ETR	Md/Val	6	(2.1)	7.6	9.8	67	3	55	78	71	72	5.0	108	177.9	234-5606
Copley		G&I	Md/Val	8	(7.7)	6.2	6.7	100	8	7	45	94	4	None	76	73.5	424-8570
Cornerstone Growth	★	Gro	Sm/Val	9	8.1	3.3	4.3	98	(21)	97	21	6	45	None	108	5.5	728-0670
Cowen Income & Growth		ETR	Lg/Val	8	(6.3)	4.7	5.7	44	0	14	24	88	66	4.75	117	32.1	262-7116
Cowen Opportunity	★	Agg	Sm/Bl	11	3.9	12.8	17.3	60	10	83	93	22	37	4.75	146	34.5	262-7116
Crabbe Huson Asset Alloc.		ETR	Md/Val	4	(0.8)	9.6	9.6	81	6	70	86	87	30	None	86	108.0	541-9732
Crabbe Huson Equity	★	Gro	Md/Val	5	1.6	14.2	14.7	91	4	79	96	86	52	None	88	155.3	541-9732
Crabbe Huson Special	★	Gro	Sm/Bl	10	11.7	26.1	19.5	97	6	98	100	100	4	None	99	346.2	541-9732
CT&T Growth & Income	★	G&I	Lg/Bl	—	0.5	—	—	—	(1)	65	—	—	—	None	N.A.	12.5	992-8151
Dean Witter American Value		Gro	Lg/Gro	11	(6.7)	4.8	12.2	78	(2)	16	79	20	91	5.0[4]	106	1,490.1	869-3863
Dean Witter Capital Growth		Gro	Md/Bl	11	(3.0)	(4.2)	—	N.A.	(5)	39	1	9	85	5.0[4]	114	439.5	869-3863
Dean Witter Convertible		ITR	N.A.	8	(2.9)	6.8	6.1	85	N.A.	70	68	33	57	5.0[4]	124	175.0	869-3863
Dean Witter Developing Gro.		Agg	Sm/Gro	12	(4.6)	6.7	11.6	90	11	28	91	7	44	5.0[4]	121	338.1	869-3863
Dean Witter Diver. Income		ITR	N.A.	—	(1.3)	—	—	—	(8)	90	15	—	—	5.0[4]	116	412.7	869-3863
Dean Witter Dividend Growth		G&I	Lg/Bl	7	(3.2)	5.4	7.3	87	19	26	67	28	70	5.0[4]	98	6,696.0	869-3863
Dean Witter European Gro.	★	Reg	Md/Bl	10	6.9	13.6	—	92	15	90	54	74	39	5.0[4]	148	726.3	869-3863
Dean Witter Glob. Div. Gr.	★	Intl	N.A.	—	7.1	—	—	—	4	97	—	—	—	5.0[4]	N.A.	1,733.8	869-3863
Dean Witter Health Sciences		Spec	Sm/Gro	—	(6.5)	—	—	—	8	49	9	—	—	5.0[4]	N.A.	243.1	869-3863
Dean Witter Mgd. Assets	★	ETR	L/Hi	3	2.7	5.9	8.2	54	3	95	26	30	63	5.0[4]	117	408.7	869-3863
Dean Witter Natural Res.		Spec	Md/Bl	10	(0.9)	7.5	3.8	77	6	70	41	48	32	5.0[4]	126	136.5	869-3863
Dean Witter Pacific Growth		Reg	Md/Gro	12	(17.5)	18.8	—	96	9	19	100	93	95	5.0[4]	166	1,417.7	869-3863
Dean Witter P.M. & Mining		Spec	Md/Gro	12	(11.5)	7.5	—	97	(2)	20	84	19	13	5.0[4]	192	66.7	392-2550[6]
Dean Witter Strategist		ETR	Lg/Bl	8	(1.9)	4.4	9.1	66	6	59	19	48	85	5.0[4]	109	766.0	869-3863
Dean Witter Utilities		Spec	Lg/Val	8	(9.3)	3.4	5.6	58	2	33	25	59	45	5.0[4]	106	2,828.6	869-3863
Dean Witter Value Mkt. Eq.	★	G&I	Md/Bl	8	0.1	8.3	8.1	95	13	59	55	82	77	5.0[4]	115	495.2	869-3863
Dean Witter World Inv.		Intl	Md/Bl	10	(7.1)	5.9	4.9	87	11	22	75	15	72	5.0[4]	148	575.7	869-3863
Delaware		ETR	Md/Val	6	(1.4)	6.7	7.9	69	3	65	26	89	28	5.75	102	439.4	523-4640
Delaware Decatur Income		ETR	Lg/Bl	7	(0.8)	7.6	5.6	61	(1)	72	74	64	35	5.75	122	1,150.7	523-4640
Delaware Decatur Total Return		G&I	Lg/Bl	8	(0.5)	7.3	6.4	57	2	48	74	54	13	5.75	121	403.0	523-4640
Delaware DelCap		Gro	Md/Gro	12	(5.3)	2.6	8.2	61	17	22	49	12	74	5.75	129	761.8	523-4640
Delaware Intl. Equity	★	Intl	Lg/Val	10	1.9	8.8	—	85	6	79	21	57	—	5.75	122	53.8	523-4640
Delaware Trend		Agg	Sm/Gro	11	(10.0)	10.5	12.2	73	6	6	75	90	92	5.75	119	268.6	523-4640
Delaware Value		Gro	Sm/Val	7	(7.0)	8.3	10.7	90	5	15	79	81	88	5.75	142	180.3	523-4640
DG Equity	★	Gro	Lg/Bl	—	1.8	—	—	—	4	80	22	—	—	2.0	N.A.	233.3	748-8500
Dodge & Cox Balanced	★	ETR	Lg/Val	5	2.1	9.4	9.8	84	8	93	79	80	27	None	35	708.4	621-3979
Dodge & Cox Stock	★	G&I	Lg/Val	8	5.2	11.3	9.7	88	24	97	88	72	18	None	36	524.4	621-3979
Domini Social Equity		G&I	Lg/Bl	8	(0.4)	6.0	—	91	3	49	16	78	—	None	42	33.1	762-6814
Dreman Contrarian		Gro	Lg/Val	9	0.0	6.7	7.6	70	29	64	35	68	20	None	69	13.0	533-1608
Dreman High Return		G&I	Lg/Val	9	(1.2)	9.0	11.8	92	10	39	35	97	98	None	69	35.0	533-1608
Dreman Small Cap. Value	★	Agg	Sm/Val	—	1.7	—	—	—	1	73	3	—	—	None	69	6.9	533-1608
Dreyfus		G&I	Lg/Val	9	(4.3)	2.4	5.9	36	20	19	15	23	50	None	43	2,466.3	782-6620
Dreyfus Appreciation	★	Gro	Lg/Gro	10	3.6	2.9	8.1	83	11	90	7	23	61	None	63	228.5	782-6620
Dreyfus Asset Allocation	★	ETR	Lg/Bl	—	1.7	—	—	—	0	92	—	—	—	None	N.A.	49.6	782-6620
Dreyfus Balanced	★	ETR	Lg/Bl	—	4.0	—	—	—	2	97	37	—	—	None	N.A.	89.0	782-6620
Dreyfus Cap. Gro. (Premier)		Gro	Lg/Bl	8	(7.0)	4.3	8.2	35	6	16	63	37	40	3.0	87	555.8	782-6620
Dreyfus Cap. Val. A (Prem.)		ETR	Md/Gro	10	(3.9)	(1.0)	0.5	N.A.	(19)	32	53	2	4	4.5	132	377.4	782-6620
Dreyfus Core Value Inv.	★	Gro	Lg/Val	9	0.3	6.7	5.3	57	10	69	71	21	11	None	63	319.1	782-6620
Dreyfus Edison Electric		Spec	Md/Val	11	(12.7)	1.2	—	N.A.	(23)	15	19	52	—	None	72	71.7	782-6620
Dreyfus Focus Large Co. Gro.		Gro	N.A.	—	(0.7)	—	—	—	(1)	58	—	—	—	None	N.A.	5.0	782-6620
Dreyfus Focus Large Co. Val.		Gro	N.A.	—	(1.0)	—	—	—	(4)	55	—	—	—	None	N.A.	5.0	782-6620
Dreyfus Focus Small Co. Gro.		Agg	N.A.	—	(6.6)	—	—	—	(7)	17	—	—	—	None	N.A.	5.0	782-6620
Dreyfus Focus Small Co. Val.		Agg	N.A.	—	(1.2)	—	—	—	(4)	54	—	—	—	None	N.A.	5.0	782-6620
Dreyfus Global Growth		Intl	Lg/Bl	9	(7.3)	3.2	6.4	100	13	21	8	47	63	3.0	115	137.3	782-6620

Source: Morningstar Inc. Chicago Ill.; 800-876-5005

Fund name/★ 1994 winner	Type	Style	Risk level	% average annual return to Jan. 1, 1995			Tax analysis		Performance analysis (percentile ranking by type)				Expense analysis		Net assets (millions)	Telephone (800)
				One year	Three years	Five years	% tax efficiency	% tax liability	1994	1993	1992	1991	% max. sales charge	Five-year total per $1,000		
Dreyfus Glob. Inv. A (Prem.)	Intl	Md/Gro	—	(5.5)	—	—	—	4	26	10	—	—	4.5	$132	$75.3	782-6620
Dreyfus Growth & Income	G&I	Md/Bl	6	(5.2)	10.5	—	93	0	14	90	97	—	None	92	1,640.8	782-6620
Dreyfus Growth Opportunity	Gro	Lg/Bl	12	(6.3)	(3.0)	5.3	N.A.	(7)	19	11	5	88	None	55	366.7	782-6620
Dreyfus Intl. Equity	Intl	Md/Bl	—	(5.4)	—	—	—	1	28	—	—	—	None	109	167.8	782-6620
Dreyfus New Leaders	Agg	Sm/Bl	9	(0.1)	8.6	10.4	69	11	61	48	39	36	None	69	388.0	782-6620
Dreyfus Special Growth Inv.	Gro	Sm/Bl	12	(18.3)	7.4	8.8	73	(6)	1	82	99	29	None	97	68.3	782-6620
Dreyfus Strategic Growth ★	Agg	N.A.	9	2.7	2.7	6.0	100	24	78	86	1	10	3.0	124	103.4	782-6620
Dreyfus Strategic Income	ITR	L/Md	5	(6.3)	5.5	8.1	58	(13)	24	63	43	20	3.0	131	312.6	782-6620
Dreyfus Strat. Investing A	Gro	Md/Bl	12	(11.4)	(0.7)	6.9	N.A.	3	5	72	3	68	4.5	135	227.9	782-6620
Dreyfus Third Century	Gro	Md/Bl	11	(7.5)	(0.3)	7.2	N.A.	14	14	21	13	60	None	60	349.0	782-6620
Dreyfus-Wilshire Lrg. Co. Gro. ★	Gro	Lg/Gro	—	2.3	—	—	—	4	81	5	—	—	None	N.A.	10.3	782-6620
Dreyfus-Wilshire Lrg. Co. Val.	Gro	Lg/Val	—	(5.2)	—	—	—	(3)	23	55	—	—	None	N.A.	10.8	782-6620
Dreyfus-Wilshire Sm. Co. Gro.	Agg	Sm/Bl	—	(1.4)	—	—	—	9	52	40	—	—	None	N.A.	12.4	782-6620
Dreyfus-Wilshire Sm. Co. Val.	Agg	Sm/Val	—	(4.5)	—	—	—	(6)	28	27	—	—	None	N.A.	21.1	782-6620
Dreyfus/Laurel Contrar. Inv.	Gro	Sm/Val	10	(11.1)	6.0	9.1	69	13	5	87	64	69	None	108	2.6	782-6620
Dreyfus/Laurel Intl. Inv. ★	Intl	Lg/Val	12	3.5	4.9	0.1	97	(37)	89	12	11	7	None	98	4.8	782-6620
Eaton Vance Greater China	Reg	Md/Gro	—	(20.9)	—	—	—	21	10	93	—	—	4.75	N.A.	154.3	225-6265
Eaton Vance Investors	ETR	Lg/Bl	7	(1.8)	5.1	7.3	49	11	61	39	37	31	4.75	94	201.3	225-6265
EV Marathon Gold & Nat. Res.	Spec	Md/Gro	10	(2.1)	8.7	4.0	92	3	65	60	42	32	5.04	190	12.5	225-6265
EV Traditional Growth	Gro	Lg/Bl	11	(4.4)	(0.7)	5.3	N.A.	12	28	3	31	64	4.75	93	122.2	225-6265
EV Traditional Special Equities	Gro	Md/Bl	12	(9.6)	(2.1)	8.7	N.A.	23	8	8	15	93	4.75	97	64.4	225-6265
Eaton Vance Traditional Stock	G&I	Lg/Bl	9	(4.1)	2.2	5.5	N.A.	13	21	9	39	17	4.75	96	85.1	225-6265
Eaton Vance Total Return	G&I	Md/Val	10	(12.2)	0.9	4.9	N.A.	(1)	1	37	36	27	4.75	120	448.7	225-6265
Eagle Growth Shares	Gro	Sm/Bl	11	(15.6)	(2.4)	(0.4)	N.A.	19	2	8	56	43	8.5	207	2.3	749-9933
Eaton Vance Equity-Income	ETR	Sm/Val	9	(6.4)	0.5	1.6	N.A.	(3)	13	17	8	7	6.04	153	28.0	225-6265
EBI Equit ★	G&I	Lg/Bl	8	2.7	5.8	8.8	52	16	90	31	24	83	None	118	77.9	554-1156
EBI Flex ★	ETR	Lg/Val	6	0.6	6.2	8.8	75	11	87	33	54	76	None	118	243.8	554-1156
EBI MultiFlex	ETR	Sm/Bl	—	(1.0)	—	—	—	(4)	69	—	—	—	None	142	120.3	554-1156
Eclipse Fin. Asset Balanced	ETR	Md/Val	4	(0.1)	8.8	9.6	76	5	82	82	75	28	None	29	27.1	872-2710
Eclipse Fin. Asset Equity	Agg	Sm/Val	9	(4.7)	10.0	8.6	73	9	26	47	81	9	None	63	181.4	872-2710
Emerald Equity A	Gro	Lg/Bl	11	(6.9)	0.4	—	N.A.	2	16	18	22	—	4.5	85	19.4	637-6336
Enterprise Capital App.	Agg	Lg/Gro	11	(3.5)	2.6	12.3	82	18	35	8	25	69	4.75	138	101.2	432-4320
Enterprise Growth	Gro	Lg/Gro	11	(1.0)	5.2	10.1	62	20	55	43	38	71	4.75	130	88.4	432-4320
Enterprise Growth & Income	G&I	Lg/Bl	7	(0.5)	7.0	6.8	76	11	48	61	56	27	4.75	125	50.9	432-4320
Enterprise Intl. Growth	Intl	Lg/Bl	10	(2.8)	9.4	4.7	82	15	49	55	60	28	4.75	150	27.6	432-4320
Enterprise Small Co. ★	Agg	Sm/Val	—	0.3	—	—	—	(2)	66	—	—	—	4.75	N.A.	22.1	368-3527
EuroPacific Growth ★	Intl	Lg/Bl	9	1.1	11.9	10.7	93	14	73	53	76	68	5.75	122	8,269.5	421-4120
Evergreen ★	Agg	Sm/Val	10	0.7	5.2	7.6	53	45	70	9	35	24	None	63	489.6	235-0064
Evergreen American Ret.	ETR	Md/Val	5	(2.9)	7.4	7.9	74	(3)	43	64	86	21	None	99	37.4	235-0064
Evergreen Foundation	ETR	Md/Val	7	(1.1)	11.1	15.0	84	(3)	67	76	99	91	None	78	321.1	235-0064
Evergreen Limited Market	Agg	Sm/Val	12	(10.5)	2.6	7.9	N.A.	13	6	21	44	52	None	69	88.7	235-0064
Evergreen Real Estate	Spec	Sm/Bl	11	(14.0)	12.8	5.5	93	(4)	11	83	65	37	None	133	103.8	235-0064
Evergreen Small Cap. Eq. Inc.	Agg	Sm/Val	—	(2.1)	—	—	—	(4)	44	—	—	—	None	N.A.	3.5	235-0064
Evergreen Tax Strat. Found. ★	ETR	N.A.	—	1.4	—	—	—	(1)	91	—	—	—	None	N.A.	8.7	235-0064
Evergreen Total Return	ETR	Md/Val	7	(6.4)	5.2	6.0	51	(18)	13	55	74	40	None	66	953.0	235-0064
Evergreen U.S. Real Est. Eq.	Spec	Sm/Val	—	(10.9)	—	—	—	(18)	22	—	—	—	None	N.A.	7.8	235-0064
Evergreen Value Timing ★	G&I	Md/Bl	8	1.7	9.8	9.8	83	25	81	70	86	35	None	77	74.9	235-0064
Fairmont ★	Gro	Sm/Val	11	7.3	12.2	9.1	100	4	96	66	78	66	None	97	21.9	262-9936
FAM Value ★	Gro	Sm/Val	8	6.8	10.2	13.3	93	7	92	2	93	41	None	82	210.3	932-3271
Fasciano ★	Agg	Sm/Bl	8	3.7	6.5	10.0	78	20	81	14	31	14	None	92	17.5	848-6050
Fidelity ★	G&I	Lg/Bl	7	2.6	9.6	9.2	72	3	88	87	55	29	None	37	1,886.1	544-8888
Fidelity Advisor Glob. Res. A	Spec	Md/Bl	10	(2.3)	15.2	10.6	89	(3)	64	77	75	41	4.75	180	193.2	522-7297
Fidelity Advisor Gro. Opp. A ★	Gro	Lg/Bl	7	2.9	13.1	15.2	88	6	83	89	82	74	4.75	132	4,826.6	522-7297
Fidelity Advisor Inc. & Gro. A	ETR	N.A.	5	(5.1)	7.4	10.1	78	(3)	21	90	66	87	4.75	126	3,160.0	522-7297
Fidelity Advisor Overseas A ★	Intl	Lg/Val	11	2.0	11.2	—	98	3	80	78	36	9	4.75	169	659.2	522-7297
Fidelity Asset Manager	ETR	Lg/Bl	5	(6.6)	9.1	11.1	83	2	12	96	90	45	None	64	11,075.6	544-8888
Fidelity Ast. Manager: Gro.	ETR	Lg/Bl	8	(7.4)	12.0	—	92	(1)	7	99	100	—	None	66	2,852.9	544-8888
Fidelity Ast. Manager: Inc.	ITR	Int/Hi	—	(1.4)	—	—	—	(3)	87	67	—	—	None	N.A.	476.2	544-8888
Fidelity Balanced	ETR	L/Hi	5	(5.3)	6.8	9.0	71	(6)	19	87	59	67	None	53	4,999.1	544-8888
Fidelity Blue Chip Growth ★	Gro	Md/Gro	8	9.9	13.2	18.4	84	8	98	93	36	90	3.0	98	3,287.0	544-8888

Source: Morningstar Inc. Chicago Ill.; 800-876-5005

Fund name/★ 1994 winner	Type	Style	Risk level	% average annual return to Jan. 1, 1995			Tax analysis		Performance analysis (percentile ranking by type)				Expense analysis			
				One year	Three years	Five years	% tax efficiency	% tax liability	1994	1993	1992	1991	% max. sales charge	Five-year total per $1,000	Net assets (millions)	Telephone (800)
Fidelity Canada	Reg	Sm/Bl	11	(12.0)	2.4	3.6	98	(6)	37	30	63	88	3.0	$135	$332.9	544-8888
Fidelity Capital App. ★	Agg	Md/Gro	6	2.5	16.8	8.1	85	14	77	96	72	2	3.0	68	1,623.2	544-8888
Fidelity Contrafund	Gro	Md/Gro	8	(1.1)	11.6	17.5	86	2	53	87	85	91	3.0	88	8,682.4	544-8888
Fidelity Convertible Secs.	ITR	N.A.	6	(1.8)	12.2	13.7	81	(2)	80	86	99	93	None	53	891.3	544-8888
Fidelity Destiny I‡ ★	Gro	Lg/Bl	7	4.4	15.0	15.4	68	26	92	97	82	62	8.24	34	3,207.8	752-2347
Fidelity Destiny II‡ ★	Gro	Lg/Bl	7	4.5	15.2	16.1	76	17	93	97	83	68	8.24	49	1,468.2	752-2347
Fidelity Disciplined Equity ★	Gro	Md/Bl	8	3.0	9.9	12.4	82	6	85	58	75	55	None	64	1,160.1	544-8888
Fidelity Diver. Intl. ★	Intl	Lg/Val	12	1.1	6.0	—	91	9	72	59	3	—	3.0	N.A.	306.0	544-8888
Fidelity Emerging Growth	Agg	Md/Gro	11	(0.2)	9.0	—	77	8	60	63	32	82	3.0	88	635.2	544-8888
Fidelity Emer. Markets	Intl	Md/Gro	12	(17.9)	16.4	—	98	8	2	100	93	8	3.0	164	1,508.3	544-8888
Fidelity Equity-Income ★	ETR	Lg/Val	7	0.2	11.7	9.2	85	12	85	93	96	79	2.0	57	7,412.8	544-8888
Fidelity Equity-Income II ★	ETR	Lg/Val	6	3.2	13.5	—	86	6	96	87	98	99	None	56	7,697.5	544-8888
Fidelity Europe ★	Reg	Md/Val	10	6.3	9.6	5.5	96	16	85	32	65	29	3.0	97	478.9	544-8888
Fidelity Global Balanced	ITR	Md/Bl	—	(11.5)	—	—	—	(9)	2	—	—	—	None	N.A.	236.5	544-8888
Fidelity Growth & Income ★	G&I	Lg/Bl	7	2.3	10.9	12.5	75	7	85	93	75	95	3.0	76	9,344.9	544-8888
Fidelity Growth Company ★	Gro	Lg/Bl	10	(2.2)	7.0	13.5	73	6	44	69	49	85	3.0	88	2,993.4	544-8888
Fidelity Intl. Gro. & Inc.	Intl	Lg/Val	10	(2.9)	8.2	5.8	92	3	47	52	44	17	None	106	1,272.6	544-8888
Fidelity Japan ★	Reg	Md/Bl	—	16.5	—	—	—	2	100	15	—	—	3.0	74	389.0	544-8888
Fidelity Latin America	Reg	Lg/Gro	—	(23.2)	—	—	—	10	7	—	—	—	3.0	N.A.	616.1	544-8888
Fidelity Low-Priced Stock ★	Agg	Sm/Val	6	4.8	17.6	18.9	84	10	88	64	97	37	3.0	66	2,354.5	544-8888
Fidelity Magellan	Gro	Md/Bl	9	(1.8)	9.4	12.0	70	7	47	94	41	67	3.0	84	36,441.5	544-8888
Fidelity Market Index ★	G&I	Lg/Bl	8	1.0	5.9	—	87	16	72	38	45	67	None	75	306.7	544-8888
Fidelity New Millennium ★	Gro	Md/Gro	—	0.8	—	—	—	10	74	94	—	—	3.0	N.A.	319.7	544-8888
Fidelity OTC	Gro	Md/Gro	10	(2.7)	6.6	11.5	65	6	41	32	82	85	3.0	92	1,381.3	544-8888
Fidelity Overseas ★	Intl	Lg/Val	11	1.3	7.9	5.0	82	12	76	71	8	19	3.0	110	2,194.1	544-8888
Fidelity Pacific Basin	Reg	Md/Gro	11	(2.8)	13.7	3.8	89	24	62	75	46	67	3.0	127	475.5	544-8888
Fidelity Puritan ★	ETR	Md/Bl	5	1.8	12.6	10.7	75	3	93	93	96	50	2.0	44	11,769.4	544-8888
Fidelity Real Estate Inv. ★	Spec	Sm/Bl	10	2.0	11.1	11.8	89	(8)	79	26	84	76	None	68	555.7	544-8888
Fidelity Select Air Transport.	Spec	Sm/Val	12	(21.7)	3.0	4.1	59	(19)	3	67	47	72	3.0	166	7.5	544-8888
Fidelity Select Amer. Gold	Spec	Md/Gro	12	(15.5)	13.6	2.6	100	(6)	8	90	30	9	3.0	121	314.2	544-8888
Fidelity Select Automotive	Spec	Md/Val	10	(12.8)	18.7	16.5	89	12	14	76	97	73	3.0	120	64.0	544-8888
Fidelity Select Biotech.	Spec	Sm/Bl	12	(18.2)	(9.6)	16.3	N.A.	(12)	4	6	17	100	3.0	117	396.1	544-8888
Fidelity Select Broker./Inv.	Spec	Md/Gro	12	(17.3)	9.1	14.7	92	(5)	5	82	44	98	3.0	152	21.9	544-8888
Fidelity Select Chemicals ★	Spec	Md/Bl	9	14.8	12.1	13.4	79	3	94	28	61	75	3.0	137	167.8	544-8888
Fidelity Select Computers ★	Spec	Md/Bl	12	20.5	23.7	24.0	97	9	98	64	88	61	3.0	133	175.4	544-8888
Fidelity Select Con./Housing	Spec	Md/Bl	11	(16.0)	10.1	11.2	96	5	7	73	82	77	3.0	143	17.5	544-8888
Fidelity Select Cnsmr. Prod.	Spec	Sm/Bl	10	(7.1)	7.9	—	75	4	46	59	57	74	3.0	165	7.6	544-8888
Fidelity Select Def./Aerosp. ★	Spec	Md/Val	10	1.8	9.5	9.7	94	(13)	79	63	35	59	3.0	166	3.7	544-8888
Fidelity Select Devel. Com. ★	Spec	Md/Gro	11	15.1	21.2	—	92	11	95	68	79	90	3.0	136	276.1	544-8888
Fidelity Select Electronics ★	Spec	Md/Bl	10	17.2	25.4	23.1	93	(2)	97	70	94	69	3.0	127	156.6	544-8888
Fidelity Select Energy ★	Spec	Md/Bl	12	0.4	5.3	2.2	83	5	77	48	32	21	3.0	128	96.7	544-8888
Fidelity Select Energy Svc. ★	Spec	Sm/Bl	12	0.6	8.0	(0.4)	94	(3)	77	53	40	1	3.0	130	50.8	544-8888
Fidelity Select Environ.	Spec	Sm/Bl	12	(9.6)	(3.9)	(1.4)	N.A.	(20)	31	3	34	34	3.0	142	32.1	544-8888
Fidelity Select Fin. Svc.	Spec	Md/Val	11	(3.6)	17.4	14.6	81	5	61	42	98	90	3.0	119	94.2	544-8888
Fidelity Select Food/Agri. ★	Spec	Md/Bl	8	6.1	7.0	12.4	72	12	86	15	46	66	3.0	126	85.5	544-8888
Fidelity Select Health Care ★	Spec	Lg/Gro	12	21.4	0.9	18.6	N.A.	16	99	7	9	99	3.0	115	796.1	544-8888
Fidelity Select Home Fin. ★	Spec	Sm/Val	10	2.7	27.3	23.6	90	13	80	61	100	92	3.0	119	130.2	544-8888
Fidelity Select Indust. Equip. ★	Spec	Sm/Val	10	3.1	18.1	12.0	98	(5)	81	80	71	58	3.0	166	104.2	544-8888
Fidelity Select Indust. Matl. ★	Spec	Md/Bl	9	8.2	13.9	10.7	99	(9)	87	55	75	70	3.0	143	180.1	544-8888
Fidelity Select Insurance	Spec	Md/Val	10	(0.3)	9.7	10.2	82	(21)	72	13	90	71	3.0	166	10.1	544-8888
Fidelity Select Leisure	Spec	Md/Gro	9	(6.8)	14.8	9.3	88	2	48	79	78	64	3.0	137	61.3	544-8888
Fidelity Select Medic. Del. ★	Spec	Md/Gro	12	19.8	3.2	17.8	63	12	97	9	14	97	3.0	131	247.6	544-8888
Fidelity Select Brdcst./Med. ★	Spec	Md/Gro	8	4.0	20.4	12.2	90	3	83	78	88	74	3.0	166	26.6	544-8888
Fidelity Select Natural Gas	Spec	Md/Bl	—	(6.8)	—	—	—	(15)	49	—	—	—	3.0	160	79.0	544-8888
Fidelity Select Paper & For. ★	Spec	Md/Bl	11	14.1	14.9	11.6	95	4	93	45	73	68	3.0	152	76.3	544-8888
Fidelity Select P.M.	Spec	Md/Gro	12	(1.1)	17.8	5.6	97	1	68	98	5	23	3.0	129	453.3	544-8888
Fidelity Select Reg. Banks ★	Spec	Md/Val	11	0.2	18.3	16.8	81	1	74	21	100	94	3.0	116	108.4	544-8888
Fidelity Select Retailing	Spec	Sm/Bl	11	(5.0)	9.4	15.9	85	(10)	55	28	89	95	3.0	131	35.5	544-8888
Fidelity Select Soft./Comp. ★	Spec	Md/Gro	12	0.4	21.8	21.6	89	3	76	71	96	79	3.0	124	211.5	544-8888
Fidelity Select Technology ★	Spec	Lg/Gro	11	11.1	15.8	22.3	86	16	91	63	59	87	3.0	124	227.4	544-8888

Source: Morningstar Inc. Chicago Ill.; 800-876-5005

Fund name/★ 1994 winner	Type	Style	Risk level	% average annual return to Jan. 1, 1995			Tax analysis		Performance analysis (percentile ranking by type)				Expense analysis		Net assets (millions)	Telephone (800)
				One year	Three years	Five years	% tax efficiency	% tax liability	1994	1993	1992	1991	% max. sales charge	Five-year total per $1,000		
Fidelity Select Tele. ★	Spec	Lg/Gro	9	4.3	16.0	11.3	89	3	83	66	76	62	3.0	$129	$363.8	544-8888
Fidelity Select Transport. ★	Spec	Sm/Val	7	3.9	18.5	15.0	87	13	82	65	92	83	3.0	166	11.1	544-8888
Fidelity Select Utilities Growth	Spec	Lg/Val	9	(7.4)	4.8	7.0	46	(5)	43	27	68	48	3.0	113	202.4	544-8888
Fidelity Southeast Asia	Reg	Md/Gro	—	(21.8)	—	—	—	2	9	—	—	—	3.0	N.A.	660.9	544-8888
Fidelity Stock Selector ★	Gro	Lg/Bl	9	0.8	9.9	—	86	5	73	58	83	79	None	64	786.7	544-8888
Fidelity Strat. Opp. Initial[1]	Gro	Md/Val	8	(6.4)	8.7	8.2	74	(1)	19	86	76	14	4.75	93	17.6	544-8888
Fidelity Trend	Gro	Md/Gro	10	(6.7)	9.1	9.1	75	19	17	80	88	56	None	31	1,193.8	544-8888
Fidelity Utilities	Spec	Md/Val	8	(5.3)	6.7	8.4	68	5	54	38	70	48	None	53	1,079.6	544-8888
Fidelity Value ★	Gro	Md/Bl	6	7.6	17.0	12.0	91	8	96	91	95	19	None	55	3,720.4	544-8888
Fidelity Worldwide	Intl	Md/Val	9	3.0	14.3	—	93	7	86	58	94	16	3.0	110	703.9	544-8888
Fiduciary Capital Growth ★	Gro	Sm/Val	8	0.4	9.5	9.6	72	11	70	61	80	56	None	73	39.3	338-1579
First Amer. Diver. Gro. A	Gro	Lg/Gro	—	(1.0)	—	—	—	N.A.	55	4	—	—	4.5	85	1.8	637-2548
First American Eq.-Inc. A ★	ETR	N.A.	—	3.8	—	—	—	(37)	97	6	—	—	4.5	N.A.	1.8	637-2548
First Eagle Fund of America	Gro	Md/Val	10	(2.6)	14.5	8.4	77	6	42	92	98	8	None	119	105.1	451-3623
First Investors Blue Chip	G&I	Lg/Bl	9	(3.0)	3.7	6.5	52	12	27	22	36	45	6.25	144	121.0	423-4026
First Investors Global	Intl	Lg/Bl	10	(3.8)	4.1	2.9	90	4	39	9	37	60	6.25	161	213.6	423-4026
First Investors G&I	G&I	N.A.	—	(0.8)	—	—	—	(2)	43	—	—	—	6.25	N.A.	35.2	423-4026
First Invest. Made in USA ★	Gro	Md/Bl	—	0.5	—	—	—	(1)	71	5	—	—	6.25	N.A.	7.4	423-4026
First Investors Spec. Sit.	Agg	Sm/Gro	11	(3.7)	10.8	—	86	9	33	66	75	50	6.25	153	88.6	423-4026
First Investors Total Return	ETR	Md/Bl	9	(3.5)	0.8	—	N.A.	1	36	15	6	32	6.25	146	51.0	423-4026
First Investors Util. Inc.	Spec	Lg/Val	—	(8.5)	—	—	—	(14)	37	—	—	—	6.25	N.A.	61.5	423-4026
First Prairie Diver. Asset	ITR	Lg/Val	4	(1.6)	5.8	8.8	66	(2)	84	22	41	50	4.5	142	45.9	346-3621
First Union Value B Invest. ★	Gro	Lg/Val	7	1.9	6.3	7.6	68	5	80	37	49	17	4.75	94	188.4	326-3241
Flag Inv. Emerging Growth ★	Agg	Sm/Gro	12	5.0	(1.8)	2.3	N.A.	18	88	1	2	46	4.5	126	23.5	767-3524
Flag Inv. International	Intl	Md/Val	11	(7.4)	7.7	0.8	92	(22)	20	91	12	3	4.5	126	13.8	767-3524
Flag Inv. Quality Growth	Gro	Lg/Bl	11	(3.1)	(1.2)	5.1	N.A.	29	38	2	32	27	4.5	113	33.7	767-3524
Flag Inv. Telephone Inc. A	Spec	Lg/Bl	10	(6.3)	7.6	7.2	83	19	51	43	74	53	4.5	95	436.2	767-3524
Flag Inv. Val. Builder A	ETR	Lg/Bl	—	(0.4)	—	—	—	2	78	44	—	—	4.5	N.A.	136.2	767-3524
Flagship Utility Income A	Spec	Md/Val	6	(7.2)	3.8	4.1	52	N.A.	45	19	58	37	4.2	105	24.3	227-4648
Flex-funds Growth	ETR	N.A.	7	(0.7)	4.2	7.5	91	(15)	73	16	36	33	None	82	22.0	325-3539
Flex-funds Muirfield ★	ETR	N.A.	3	2.7	6.1	9.7	47	1	95	21	53	82	None	77	81.8	325-3539
Fortis Adv. Asset Allocation A	ETR	Md/Gro	8	(0.8)	5.5	8.5	74	11	70	41	35	78	4.5	127	116.3	800-2638
Fortis Adv. Capital App. A	Agg	Sm/Gro	12	(7.2)	4.4	10.2	85	24	13	41	25	80	4.5	132	68.9	800-2638
Fortis Capital A ★	Gro	Md/Gro	10	2.5	4.0	8.7	54	32	82	13	39	86	4.75	112	237.7	800-2638
Fortis Fiduciary A ★	Gro	Md/Gro	11	3.4	4.4	9.1	60	34	89	14	41	89	4.75	125	48.6	800-2638
Fortis Global Growth A	Intl	Md/Gro	11	(4.3)	6.7	—	100	7	35	3	95	—	4.75	162	53.6	800-2638
Fortis Growth A	Gro	Md/Gro	12	(8.2)	0.8	9.9	—	33	11	42	11	96	4.75	107	545.3	800-2638
Fortress Utility	Spec	Md/Val	8	(7.9)	4.9	8.0	69	(4)	41	36	60	58	1.0	70	781.1	245-5051
Founders Balanced	ETR	Lg/Val	6	(1.9)	8.2	8.1	77	0	58	95	31	40	None	95	96.0	525-2440
Founders Blue Chip ★	G&	Md/Bl	9	0.5	4.7	8.2	31	10	66	72	3	52	None	61	312.2	525-2440
Founders Discovery	Agg	Sm/Bl	12	(7.7)	5.6	16.7	94	8	10	24	64	73	None	97	187.5	525-2440
Founders Frontier	Agg	Sm/Gro	11	(2.8)	7.3	11.3	84	14	39	45	35	45	None	92	249.2	525-2440
Founders Growth	Gro	Md/Gro	12	(3.3)	8.2	10.8	76	10	36	95	24	82	None	80	310.1	525-2440
Founders Passport	Intl	Sm/Gro	—	(10.4)	—	—	—	(10)	9	—	—	—	None	114	16.5	525-2440
Founders Special	Agg	Md/Bl	12	(4.9)	6.1	11.9	61	9	24	41	32	76	None	64	300.9	525-2440
Founders Worldwide Growth	Intl	Lg/Gro	10	(2.2)	8.9	13.2	94	15	54	28	73	97	None	104	104.9	525-2440
Fountain Square Balanced	ETR	Lg/Bl	—	(1.0)	—	—	—	(7)	69	4	—	—	4.5	N.A.	49.8	334-0483
Fountain Square Mid Cap. ★	Gro	Md/Bl	—	1.5	—	—	—	0	79	9	—	—	4.5	N.A.	29.6	334-0483
Fountain Square Quality Gro. ★	Gro	Lg/Bl	—	0.1	—	—	—	(6)	66	5	—	—	4.5	N.A.	58.3	334-0483
FPA Capital ★	Agg	Sm/Val	11	10.4	16.1	17.3	86	34	95	46	89	78	6.5	121	180.8	982-4372
FPA Paramount ★	G&I	Md/Gro	8	9.4	13.2	12.9	76	9	100	95	67	30	6.5	113	463.8	982-4372
FPA Perennial	G&I	Md/Bl	7	0.0	5.8	7.8	70	24	57	11	84	18	6.5	122	51.5	982-4372
Franklin Balance Sheet Inv. ★	Gro	Sm/Val	5	1.5	15.9	—	91	2	78	95	97	51	1.5	151	137.4	342-5236
Franklin California Growth ★	Gro	Sm/Gro	10	16.4	12.8	—	87	14	100	75	27	—	4.5	161	7.7	342-5236
Franklin Convertible Secs.	ITR	N.A.	5	(1.6)	11.3	11.6	79	3	82	92	81	85	4.5	83	66.2	342-5236
Franklin Corp. Qual. Div. ★	ITR	Md/Val	1	0.4	7.7	9.2	82	(38)	97	4	83	40	1.5	73	28.0	342-5236
Franklin DynaTech ★	Spec	Lg/Gro	9	5.2	5.6	10.5	80	39	85	11	42	69	4.5	101	69.5	342-5236
Franklin Equity	Gro	Md/Bl	9	(1.3)	3.5	5.1	18	11	52	33	19	22	4.5	77	281.2	342-5236
Franklin Equity-Income	ETR	Lg/Bl	6	(0.3)	10.0	9.2	80	2	78	84	92	73	4.5	83	92.7	342-5236
Franklin Global Health Care ★	Spec	Sm/Gro	—	14.2	—	—	—	15	93	11	—	—	4.5	N.A.	10.5	342-5236

Source: Morningstar Inc. Chicago Ill.; 800-876-5005

Fund name/★ 1994 winner	Type	Style	Risk level	% average annual return to Jan. 1, 1995			Tax analysis		Performance analysis (percentile ranking by type)				Expense analysis		Net assets (millions)	Telephone (800)
				One year	Three years	Five years	% tax efficiency	% tax liability	1994	1993	1992	1991	% max. sales charge	Five-year total per $1,000		
Franklin Global Utilities	Spec	Lg/Val	—	(8.9)	—	—	—	(6)	33	68	—	—	4.5	N.A.	$121.8	342-5236
Franklin Gold	Spec	Md/Gro	12	(4.7)	9.7	2.4	95	16	58	89	6	31	4.5	$81	379.1	342-5236
Franklin Growth ★	Gro	Lg/Bl	9	2.9	4.3	8.0	88	24	84	27	17	21	4.5	92	523.4	342-5236
Franklin Income	ITR	Int/Lo	4	(6.4)	9.5	11.1	71	(2)	22	97	77	95	4.25	79	4,882.5	342-5236
Franklin Intl. Equity	Intl	Md/Val	10	(0.2)	10.2	—	89	5	63	42	72	—	4.5	172	55.0	342-5236
Franklin Pacific Growth	Reg	Md/Val	11	(10.7)	14.2	—	94	2	42	71	90	—	4.5	172	54.0	342-5236
Franklin Premier Return ★	G&I	Lg/Bl	5	1.1	11.0	8.8	92	(15)	73	89	88	22	4.5	89	25.3	342-5236
Franklin Rising Dividends	G&I	Md/Val	9	(5.2)	0.3	6.6	N.A.	(3)	14	2	71	88	4.5	114	241.4	342-5236
Franklin Small Cap. Gro. ★	Agg	Sm/Gro	—	9.0	—	—	—	8	95	69	—	—	4.5	N.A.	37.0	342-5236
Franklin Utilities	Spec	Md/Val	10	(11.7)	2.4	6.0	33	(5)	18	22	63	55	4.25	80	2,569.8	342-5236
Fremont Global	ETR	Lg/Gro	5	(4.2)	6.4	7.0	85	4	29	89	29	19	None	62	436.8	548-4539
Fremont Growth ★	Gro	Lg/Bl	—	0.4	—	—	—	(2)	70	25	—	—	None	62	23.4	548-4539
FT International Equity A ★	Intl	Lg/Bl	11	0.5	7.5	3.4	91	16	68	34	25	13	5.5	126	261.1	245-5051
FundTrust Aggressive Growth	Agg	N.A.	11	(5.7)	2.8	7.8	45	9	20	66	4	34	1.5	88	38.0	344-9033
FundTrust Growth	Gro	N.A.	10	(0.5)	5.3	8.2	51	9	60	97	2	53	1.5	87	33.7	344-9033
FundTrust Growth & Income	G&I	N.A.	8	(0.1)	6.3	6.9	71	9	55	80	13	40	1.5	82	50.0	344-9033
FundTrust Managed T/R	ETR	N.A.	3	(1.2)	4.7	6.4	56	6	66	44	21	20	1.5	130	16.3	522-7297
Fundamental Investors ★	G&I	Lg/Bl	8	1.3	9.7	10.0	73	11	79	86	69	68	5.75	92	2,611.1	421-4120
Gabelli ABC[1] ★	ETR	Md/Val	—	4.5	—	—	—	5	98	—	—	—	2.0	N.A.	26.1	422-3554
Gabelli Asset	Gro	Md/Gro	7	(0.2)	11.8	9.2	89	21	64	88	81	4	None	72	979.3	422-3554
Gabelli Convertible Secs.[1]	ITR	N.A.	1	(0.2)	8.4	8.8	69	4	95	40	69	6	None	118	113.1	422-3554
Gabelli Equity-Income ★	ETR	Lg/Bl	5	1.1	9.0	—	78	11	89	85	63	—	4.5	104	48.5	422-3554
Gabelli Global Tele.	Spec	Lg/Gro	—	(3.7)	—	—	—	(2)	60	—	—	—	4.5	N.A.	138.9	422-3554
Gabelli Growth	Gro	Md/Gro	10	(3.4)	3.9	8.1	54	23	36	46	25	46	None	77	493.2	422-3554
Gabelli Small Cap. Growth	Agg	Sm/Bl	8	(2.9)	12.7	—	92	18	38	77	84	—	4.5	146	196.5	422-3554
Gabelli Value	Gro	Md/Bl	9	0.0	16.3	11.3	78	23	65	100	73	3	5.5	133	441.4	422-3554
Galaxy Asset Alloc. Retail	ETR	Lg/Bl	6	(2.5)	4.0	—	83	(1)	49	20	37	—	None	63	67.7	628-0414
Galaxy Eq. Growth Retail ★	Gro	Lg/Bl	9	0.6	4.0	—	86	50	71	21	35	32	None	53	68.1	628-0414
Galaxy Equity-Inc. Retail ★	ETR	Lg/Bl	7	1.2	5.5	—	80	2	90	20	49	38	None	57	61.0	628-0414
Galaxy Eq. Value Retail ★	Gro	Lg/Val	7	3.5	8.7	9.0	77	34	90	64	51	12	None	52	73.6	628-0414
Galaxy Intl. Equity Retail	Intl	Lg/Val	10	(2.5)	7.8	—	97	16	51	39	45	—	None	90	32.3	628-0414
Galaxy Sm. Co. Eq. Retail	Agg	Sm/Gro	12	(0.1)	7.5	—	97	24	62	76	14	—	None	63	27.1	628-0414
Galaxy II Lg. Co. Index Retail ★	G&I	Lg/Bl	8	1.0	5.8	—	84	13	N.A.	—	—	—	None	73	137.8	628-0414
Galaxy II Sm. Co. Index Retail	Agg	Md/Bl	10	(3.7)	6.4	—	83	11	N.A.	—	—	—	None	73	230.7	628-0414
Galaxy II Utility Index Retail	Spec	Lg/Val	—	(8.6)	—	—	—	(14)	35	—	—	—	None	73	53.3	628-0414
Gateway Index Plus ★	G&I	Lg/Bl	2	5.6	6.0	9.2	74	10	97	21	21	7	None	61	161.1	354-6339
Gateway Mid-Cap. Index	Gro	Md/Bl	—	(5.1)	—	—	—	(5)	23	20	—	—	None	82	8.1	354-6339
Gateway Small-Cap. Index	Agg	Sm/Bl	—	(6.0)	—	—	—	(8)	19	—	—	—	None	94	10.6	354-6339
General Securities ★	ETR	Lg/Bl	2	5.4	5.9	10.0	65	9	100	11	32	89	None	121	26.5	331-4923
Geo. Putnam Fund of Boston A	ETR	Lg/Val	6	(0.4)	6.1	7.7	62	(2)	76	38	60	39	5.75	113	895.9	225-1581
Gintel	Gro	Sm/Bl	11	(16.5)	3.2	3.5	51	0	2	22	98	3	None	93	88.3	243-5808
GIT Equity Income	ETR	Md/Val	9	(5.8)	2.1	4.2	25	11	17	27	16	12	None	116	3.2	336-3063
GIT Special Growth	Agg	Sm/Bl	9	(1.2)	6.6	5.1	64	22	53	38	27	5	None	76	30.2	336-3063
Global Utility A	Spec	Lg/Val	9	(7.9)	7.3	10.6	74	4	41	56	64	51	5.0	127	118.8	225-1852
Goldman Sachs Capital Gro.	Gro	Md/Bl	8	(1.1)	11.7	—	77	11	54	59	97	37	5.5	134	862.7	762-5035
Goldman Sachs G&I ★	G&I	Md/Bl	—	5.9	—	—	—	(1)	99	—	—	—	5.5	N.A.	169.5	526-7384
Goldman Sachs Intl. Equity	Intl	Sm/Gro	—	(6.9)	—	—	—	4	22	5	—	—	5.5	N.A.	312.8	526-7384
Goldman Sachs Select Equity ★	G&I	Lg/Bl	10	1.3	4.5	—	58	9	78	56	4	—	5.5	N.A.	91.3	762-5035
Goldman Sachs Sm. Cap. Eq.	Agg	Sm/Bl	—	(14.8)	—	—	—	(4)	2	92	—	—	5.5	N.A.	352.4	526-7384
Govett Emerging Markets	Intl	N.A.	—	(12.7)	—	—	—	12	6	100	—	—	4.95	176	91.0	634-6838
Govett International Equity	Intl	Md/Bl	—	(8.4)	—	—	—	15	14	95	—	—	4.95	176	34.7	634-6838
Govett Smaller Cos. ★	Agg	Sm/Gro	—	28.7	—	—	—	24	100	100	—	—	4.95	N.A.	66.6	634-6838
Gradison-McDonald Est. Val. ★	Gro	Md/Val	7	0.2	10.1	8.4	87	17	68	84	62	10	None	72	260.2	869-5999
Gradison-McDonald Opp. Val.	Agg	Sm/Val	8	(2.2)	7.5	8.0	84	15	42	26	61	15	None	81	82.9	869-5999
Green Century Balanced	ETR	Lg/Gro	—	(4.3)	—	—	—	(4)	27	2	—	—	None	133	3.0	934-7336
Greenspring ★	Gro	Sm/Val	1	2.9	11.2	8.9	75	4	84	63	87	6	None	81	49.1	366-3863
Growth Fund of America	Gro	Lg/Gro	9	0.0	7.1	9.9	87	28	66	61	44	53	5.75	99	5,274.2	421-4120
Growth Fund of Washington	Gro	Md/Val	10	(9.3)	6.3	4.4	84	N.A.	9	52	90	20	4.75	128	33.7	972-9274
G.T. Glob. America Growth A ★	Agg	Sm/Bl	10	15.7	18.2	12.8	85	19	98	15	99	4	4.75	129	199.9	824-1580
G.T. Global Emerg. Mkt. A	Intl	Md/Gro	—	(3.8)	—	—	—	18	39	98	—	—	4.75	169	333.8	824-1580

Source: Morningstar Inc. Chicago Ill.; 800-876-5005

| Fund name/★ 1994 winner | Type | Style | Risk level | % average annual return to Jan. 1, 1995 | | | Tax analysis | | Performance analysis (percentile ranking by type) | | | | Expense analysis | | Net assets (millions) | Telephone (800) |
				One year	Three years	Five years	% tax efficiency	% tax liability	1994	1993	1992	1991	% max. sales charge	Five-year total per $1,000		
G.T. Global Europe Growth A	Reg	Lg/Val	12	(5.8)	2.4	(0.9)	90	(19)	55	36	26	33	4.75	$149	$647.3	824-1580
G.T. Global Gro. & Inc. A	Intl	Lg/Val	8	(3.6)	8.0	—	83	4	42	18	78	73	4.75	142	299.7	824-1580
G.T. Global Health Care A ★	Spec	Md/Gro	12	0.3	(3.8)	9.7	N.A.	23	75	8	13	86	4.75	150	387.5	824-1580
G.T. Global Intl. Growth A	Intl	Md/Gro	11	(7.8)	5.2	2.5	81	17	16	48	28	43	4.75	139	431.0	824-1580
G.T. Global Japan Growth A ★	Reg	Md/Gro	12	6.6	3.7	(5.0)	94	9	89	47	10	12	4.75	154	100.3	824-1580
G.T. Pacific Growth A	Reg	Md/Bl	12	(19.7)	5.9	3.6	84	10	12	69	40	74	4.75	144	405.9	824-1580
G.T. Global Tele. A	Spec	Lg/Gro	—	(4.4)	—	—	—	13	59	81	—	—	4.75	162	1,481.0	824-1580
G.T. Glob. Worldwide Growth A	Intl	Lg/Bl	10	(6.7)	7.1	5.3	85	14	23	20	84	75	4.75	144	182.2	824-1580
G.T. Latin America Growth A	Reg	Md/Gro	12	(6.6)	11.7	—	86	19	54	62	68	—	4.75	168	283.1	824-1580
Guardian Asset Allocation	ETR	Lg/Val	—	(2.1)	—	—	—	(4)	54	—	—	—	4.5	113	54.9	221-3253
Guardian Baillie Giff Intl.	Intl	Lg/Bl	—	(0.6)	—	—	—	8	60	—	—	—	4.5	N.A.	37.5	221-3253
Guardian Park Avenue	Gro	Md/Bl	8	(1.4)	12.6	11.1	87	13	52	83	94	52	4.5	89	640.7	221-3253
Hancock Capital Growth	Agg	Md/Bl	12	(11.3)	(0.2)	5.2	N.A.	5	5	10	23	17	5.75	130	68.6	225-5291
Hancock Discovery B	Agg	Sm/Gro	12	(1.5)	6.1	—	69	13	50	11	58	—	5.0[4]	N.A.	25.6	225-5291
Hancock Emerging Growth B	Agg	Sm/Gro	12	(1.5)	7.3	14.2	100	19	50	28	51	68	5.0[4]	149	268.4	225-5291
Hancock Freedom Environ. A[3]	Spec	Md/Gro	N.A.	(15.3)	(5.4)	(4.6)	N.A.	(46)	—	—	—	—	5.0	155	10.9	225-5291
Hancock Freedom Global B	Intl	Lg/Gro	11	(5.4)	8.1	4.6	76	23	27	47	62	85	5.0[4]	163	30.0	225-5291
Hancock Freedom Global Rx ★	Spec	Sm/Gro	12	8.8	9.2	—	100	23	88	6	81	—	5.0	N.A.	19.1	225-5291
Hancock Free. Glob. Tech. ★	Spec	Md/Gro	12	9.6	15.2	10.7	81	21	89	69	45	65	5.0	157	50.7	225-5291
Hancock Freedom Gold/Gov. B	ETR	Md/Gro	10	(15.5)	0.3	2.6	N.A.	(23)	2	78	13	7	5.0[4]	138	34.3	225-5291
Hancock Freedom Natl. Avi.	Spec	Md/Bl	11	(14.2)	2.3	2.5	N.A.	53	10	52	39	63	5.0	129	61.3	225-5291
Hancock Freedom Pac. Basin A	Reg	Lg/Bl	11	(9.3)	16.4	6.4	96	0	49	84	82	70	5.0	187	43.5	225-5291
Hancock Freedom Reg. Bank B	Spec	Sm/Val	8	(0.2)	21.0	18.2	90	4	73	50	99	91	5.0[4]	126	484.8	225-5291
Hancock Global Resources B	Spec	Sm/Bl	10	(9.6)	6.5	3.2	100	4	29	57	55	39	5.0[4]	202	34.6	225-5291
Hancock Growth & Income A	G&I	Lg/Bl	9	(8.5)	2.1	7.0	9	0	4	40	30	78	5.75	127	114.5	225-5291
Hancock Growth A	Gro	Md/Gro	11	(7.6)	3.5	10.4	49	22	14	55	35	70	5.0	113	145.8	225-5291
Hancock Sovereign Achiever B	Gro	Md/Bl	10	(6.0)	3.0	5.4	31	(1)	20	34	40	33	5.0[4]	142	88.5	225-5291
Hancock Sovereign Bal. B	ETR	Lg/Bl	—	(4.2)	—	—	—	(6)	28	36	—	—	5.0[4]	202	78.7	225-5291
Hancock Sovereign Invest. A	G&I	Lg/Bl	7	(1.9)	3.6	8.7	71	(1)	33	12	44	69	5.0	109	1,081.0	225-5291
Hancock Special Equities A[1] ★	Agg	Sm/Gro	12	2.0	16.8	21.8	100	16	75	61	98	95	5.0	162	303.8	225-5291
Hancock Special Opp. B	Gro	Md/Gro	—	(9.4)	—	—	—	(9)	8	—	—	—	5.0[4]	N.A.	128.3	225-5291
Hancock Strategic Income A	ITR	Int/Med	2	(3.1)	5.8	7.4	55	(15)	67	49	19	83	4.5	133	321.9	225-5291
Hanover Blue Chip Growth Inv.	Gro	Lg/Bl	—	(3.9)	—	—	—	(1)	31	—	—	—	None	N.A.	46.7	821-2371
Hanover Small Cap. Gro. Inv.	Agg	Sm/Val	—	(9.4)	—	—	—	(6)	8	—	—	—	3.0	N.A.	17.5	821-2371
Harbor Capital Appreciation ★	Gro	Lg/Gro	11	3.4	8.4	14.1	77	17	88	50	61	90	None	51	226.9	422-1050
Harbor Growth	Gro	Md/Bl	12	(11.4)	(0.6)	6.7	N.A.	10	4	78	3	87	None	50	132.6	422-1050
Harbor International Growth	Intl	Lg/Gro	—	(7.7)	—	—	—	1	18	—	—	—	None	N.A.	71.8	422-1050
Harbor International[1] ★	Intl	Lg/Val	10	5.4	15.2	10.9	94	24	95	82	63	80	None	71	2,982.2	422-1050
Harbor Value ★	G&I	Lg/Val	9	0.7	5.5	6.1	55	5	68	26	48	15	None	52	56.6	422-1050
Harris Insight Convertible	ITR	N.A.	4	(5.1)	6.9	5.0	78	N.A.	45	25	79	61	4.5	87	1.4	982-8782
Harris Insight Equity	Gro	Md/Val	9	(2.0)	7.9	8.1	64	14	46	77	54	24	4.5	96	39.2	982-8782
Heartland Value ★	Agg	Sm/Val	8	1.7	19.8	16.4	89	7	74	58	100	46	None	80	325.0	432-7856
Heartland Value & Income	ETR	Sm/Val	—	(4.9)	—	—	—	(9)	22	—	—	—	None	N.A.	9.7	432-7856
Hercules European Value ★	Reg	N.A.	—	2.3	—	—	—	0	72	—	—	—	None	N.A.	18.4	584-1317
Hercules Latin American Val.	Reg	N.A.	—	(18.1)	—	—	—	(20)	17	—	—	—	None	N.A.	28.3	584-1317
Hercules N. American G&I	Intl	N.A.	—	(13.0)	—	—	—	(13)	5	—	—	—	None	N.A.	15.9	584-1317
Hercules Pacific Basin Value	Reg	N.A.	—	(1.8)	—	—	—	(3)	64	—	—	—	None	N.A.	39.5	584-1317
Heritage Capital App.	Gro	Md/Bl	9	(2.4)	9.0	8.8	69	23	44	78	71	51	4.0	130	69.5	421-4184
Heritage Income-Growth	G&I	Lg/Bl	7	(0.9)	7.2	8.2	73	5	41	48	76	83	4.0	135	31.2	421-4184
Heritage Small Cap Stock ★	Agg	Sm/Bl	—	0.5	—	—	—	8	67	—	—	—	4.75	N.A.	41.7	421-4184
Hodges ★	Gro	Md/Bl	—	1.0	—	—	—	(2)	75	24	—	—	2.5	N.A.	8.7	388-8512
Homestead Value ★	G&I	Md/Val	7	2.5	10.8	—	93	9	86	90	75	5	None	67	90.1	258-3030
Hotchkis & Wiley Bal. Inc. ★	ETR	Lg/Val	3	0.8	7.5	8.3	66	1	88	50	67	24	None	57	34.1	346-7301
Hotchkis & Wiley Eq.-Inc.	ETR	Lg/Val	8	(3.5)	8.4	7.0	81	10	37	77	93	88	None	57	106.7	346-7301
Hotchkis & Wiley Intl.	Intl	Md/Val	11	(2.9)	11.3	—	91	5	46	83	48	76	None	57	27.7	346-7301
Hotchkis & Wiley Sm. Cap. ★	Agg	Sm/Val	9	1.1	9.0	11.7	80	17	72	30	57	42	None	57	14.8	346-7301
Household Personal Eq.-Inc.	ETR	Md/Val	—	(5.0)	—	—	—	(1)	22	—	—	—	None	N.A.	5.3	231-0180
Household Personal Gro. Eq.	Gro	Md/Bl	—	(3.4)	—	—	—	4	35	—	—	—	None	N.A.	5.4	231-0180
Hudson Capital Appreciation	Gro	Md/Bl	11	(11.2)	4.3	—	64	10	5	76	55	—	4.5	181	15.9	221-5588
IAI Balanced	ETR	Lg/Bl	—	(1.4)	—	—	—	(1)	65	8	—	—	None	N.A.	41.2	945-3863

Source: Morningstar Inc. Chicago III.; 800-876-5005

Fund name/★ 1994 winner		Type	Style	Risk level	% average annual return to Jan. 1, 1995			Tax analysis		Performance analysis (percentile ranking by type)				Expense analysis		Net assets (millions)	Telephone (800)
					One year	Three years	Five years	% tax efficiency	% tax liability	1994	1993	1992	1991	% max. sales charge	Five-year total per $1,000		
IAI Emerging Growth	★	Agg	Md/Gro	12	0.2	12.1	—	90	7	64	37	91	—	None	$69	$292.9	945-3863
IAI Growth	★	Gro	Md/Bl	—	0.4	—	—	—	0	70	—	—	—	None	N.A.	22.6	945-3863
IAI Growth & Income		G&I	Md/Gro	9	(4.8)	2.9	5.2	28	1	16	44	14	42	None	69	106.1	945-3863
IAI International		Intl	Lg/Val	10	(0.1)	9.8	5.9	86	9	64	74	31	57	None	109	157.3	945-3863
IAI Midcap Growth	★	Gro	Md/Gro	—	5.7	—	—	—	10	94	91	—	—	None	N.A.	75.4	945-3863
IAI Regional	★	Gro	Md/Bl	9	0.7	4.3	8.9	58	3	72	35	18	53	None	69	513.2	945-3863
IAI Value		Gro	Md/Bl	9	(9.1)	7.5	5.7	73	(6)	9	88	69	6	None	69	35.8	945-3863
IDS Blue Chip Advantage	★	G&I	Lg/Bl	9	1.2	6.7	—	67	8	77	54	39	59	5.0	104	146.9	328-8300
IDS Discovery		Agg	Md/Gro	12	(7.8)	3.2	10.9	82	14	11	20	34	56	5.0	101	647.0	328-8300
IDS Diversified Equity-Inc.		ETR	Md/Val	5	(3.7)	11.3	—	83	1	34	98	95	60	5.0	107	945.9	328-8300
IDS Equity Plus		G&I	Md/Bl	9	(8.0)	5.2	8.4	62	20	5	73	71	79	5.0	139	580.4	328-8300
IDS Global Growth		Intl	Md/Bl	11	(7.3)	8.0	—	94	5	20	68	52	45	5.0	139	640.4	328-8300
IDS Growth	★	Gro	Md/Gro	12	2.9	6.5	12.9	51	32	84	33	50	81	5.0	96	1,007.0	328-8300
IDS International		Intl	Lg/Val	11	(2.2)	6.8	5.0	83	12	54	38	29	33	5.0	125	769.8	328-8300
IDS Managed Retirement		G&I	Lg/Bl	10	(4.6)	6.2	11.9	60	14	17	74	62	97	5.0	100	2,248.7	328-8300
IDS Mutual		ETR	Md/Val	6	(3.0)	7.0	8.0	58	1	41	66	78	46	5.0	91	2,924.8	328-8300
IDS New Dimensions		Gro	Lg/Gro	11	(3.0)	5.2	13.1	72	15	39	59	31	87	5.0	100	4,458.4	328-8300
IDS Precious Metals		Spec	Md/Gro	12	(9.6)	14.3	1.8	99	(28)	31	92	21	16	5.0	142	69.8	328-8300
IDS Progressive	★	Gro	Sm/Val	6	1.4	10.9	7.1	83	4	77	50	93	18	5.0	106	278.0	328-8300
IDS Stock		G&I	Lg/Bl	8	(2.8)	6.6	9.5	49	10	29	83	38	47	5.0	88	2,259.2	328-8300
IDS Strat. Aggressive Equity		Agg	Md/Gro	12	(6.9)	(0.2)	8.4	N.A.	14	16	13	11	53	5.0[4]	119	726.0	328-8300
IDS Strategic Equity		G&I	Lg/Val	7	(3.3)	8.2	8.9	71	4	24	82	81	53	5.0[4]	112	1,192.3	328-8300
IDS Strat. Worldwide Growth		Intl	Lg/Bl	11	(2.8)	5.9	2.4	97	4	49	32	21	22	5.0[4]	176	316.6	328-8300
IDS Utilities Income		Spec	Lg/Val	8	(8.5)	6.3	7.5	63	(2)	38	47	66	50	5.0	99	585.9	328-8300
Income Fund of America		ITR	Lg/Val	3	(2.5)	7.6	8.4	71	0	74	52	59	44	5.75	92	10,502.7	421-4120
Indep. Cap. Opportunities		Gro	Md/Val	11	(6.5)	2.4	—	43	2	18	20	58	5	4.5	141	25.1	833-4264
Indep. Cap. T/R Growth		Gro	Md/Gro	12	(8.3)	(0.6)	—	N.A.	15	11	51	4	49	4.5	122	24.2	833-4264
Invesco Balanced	★	ETR	Sm/Bl	—	9.4	—	—	—	3	100	—	—	—	None	N.A.	10.2	525-8085
Invesco Dynamics		Agg	Md/Gro	11	(1.9)	9.8	15.6	72	4	45	60	55	81	None	65	313.0	525-8085
Invesco Emerging Growth		Agg	Sm/Bl	11	(3.7)	14.3	—	84	12	32	81	94	—	None	N.A.	171.1	525-8085
Invesco European		Reg	Md/Val	12	(3.0)	3.7	4.0	89	(1)	60	25	43	50	None	71	272.4	525-8085
Invesco Growth		Gro	Lg/Bl	11	(8.8)	3.5	9.2	19	17	9	76	17	73	None	58	457.9	525-8085
Invesco Industrial Income		ETR	Lg/Val	8	(3.9)	4.2	12.2	49	4	31	81	8	98	None	54	3,768.1	525-8085
Invesco Intl. Growth	★	Intl	Lg/Bl	12	0.6	4.0	0.6	83	5	69	21	5	10	None	75	119.2	525-8085
Invesco Multi-Asset Alloc.		ETR	Md/Val	—	(2.0)	—	—	—	(3)	58	—	—	—	None	N.A.	6.0	525-8085
Invesco Pacific Basin	★	Reg	Lg/Bl	12	4.7	8.9	2.6	83	13	79	58	18	77	None	97	272.1	525-8085
Invesco Small Company		Agg	Sm/Bl	—	(1.4)	—	—	—	(4)	52	—	—	—	None	N.A.	13.0	525-8085
Invesco Strategic Energy		Spec	Md/Gro	12	(7.3)	(2.1)	(5.4)	N.A.	(10)	45	41	13	16	None	95	57.1	525-8085
Invesco Strat. Environ. Svcs.		Spec	Sm/Bl	12	(11.4)	(11.8)	—	N.A.	(38)	21	2	8	43	None	101	24.2	525-8085
Invesco Strat. Fin. Svc.		Spec	Md/Val	10	(5.9)	12.2	18.0	74	(7)	52	44	92	95	None	59	239.7	525-8085
Invesco Strategic Gold		Spec	Sm/Gro	12	(27.9)	4.6	(4.0)	100	(20)	2	88	22	6	None	78	208.7	525-8085
Invesco Strat. Health Sci.	★	Spec	Sm/Gro	12	0.9	(7.3)	14.4	N.A.	6	78	1	11	100	None	55	473.7	525-8085
Invesco Strat. Leisure		Spec	Md/Gro	9	(5.0)	16.8	16.7	89	8	56	76	91	82	None	83	271.8	525-8085
Invesco Strat. Technology	★	Spec	Md/Gro	12	5.3	12.9	22.5	87	12	85	33	84	96	None	62	312.2	525-8085
Invesco Strat. Utilities		Spec	Md/Val	8	(9.9)	6.5	6.8	54	(10)	26	54	69	60	None	63	126.4	525-8085
Investment Co. of America	★	G&I	Lg/Bl	8	0.2	6.2	8.8	74	20	60	50	41	39	5.75	88	19,279.6	421-4120
Investors Research		Gro	Lg/Bl	10	(4.0)	(2.7)	5.2	N.A.	12	30	26	1	73	5.75	113	33.5	732-1733
Investors Trust Growth		Gro	Md/Gro	—	(2.8)	—	—	—	0	41	—	—	—	5.0[4]	N.A.	7.2	656-6626
Investors Trust Value B		ETR	Lg/Bl	—	(2.7)	—	—	—	(1)	46	—	—	—	5.0[4]	N.A.	9.4	656-6626
Ivy Canada A		Reg	N.A.	11	(14.2)	8.3	(1.6)	87	(13)	32	67	49	8	5.75	192	23.9	456-5111
Ivy China Region A		Reg	Md/Gro	—	(25.2)	—	—	—	(13)	4	—	—	—	5.75	169	13.9	456-5111
Ivy Emerging Growth A	★	Agg	Sm/Gro	—	2.9	—	—	—	4	78	—	—	—	5.75	N.A.	19.6	456-5111
Ivy Global A		Intl	Lg/Val	10	(5.1)	8.1	—	78	7	30	26	80	—	5.75	160	19.9	456-5111
Ivy Growth A		Gro	Md/Bl	10	(3.1)	4.6	7.5	34	4	38	50	30	34	5.75	144	229.9	456-5111
Ivy Growth with Income A		G&I	Md/Bl	10	(2.4)	5.2	9.5	60	5	30	81	9	87	5.75	172	25.7	456-5111
Ivy International A	★	Intl	Lg/Val	11	3.9	15.5	9.4	95	24	92	88	67	61	5.75	145	228.5	456-5111
Jackson National Growth	★	Gro	Lg/Bl	—	1.0	—	—	—	7	76	38	—	—	4.75	N.A.	33.2	888-3863
Jackson National T/R		ETR	Lg/Val	—	(0.4)	—	—	—	2	75	45	—	—	4.75	N.A.	34.1	888-3863
Janus		Gro	Lg/Gro	8	(1.1)	5.4	10.7	74	8	54	44	41	75	None	54	9,400.6	525-8983
Janus Balanced		ETR	Lg/Bl	—	(0.8)	—	—	—	4	71	35	—	—	None	N.A.	93.4	525-8983

Source: Morningstar Inc. Chicago Ill.; 800-876-5005

Fund name/★ 1994 winner		Type	Style	Risk level	% average annual return to Jan. 1, 1995			Tax analysis		Performance analysis (percentile ranking by type)				Expense analysis		Net assets (millions)	Telephone (800)
					One year	Three years	Five years	% tax efficiency	% tax liability	1994	1993	1992	1991	% max. sales charge	Five-year total per $1,000		
Janus Enterprise	★	Gro	Sm/Gro	—	8.9	—	—	—	14	97	68	—	—	None	N.A.	$354.1	525-8983
Janus Flexible Income		ITR	Int/Lo	2	(2.9)	7.9	8.6	67	(8)	69	70	57	59	None	$55	353.9	525-8983
Janus Growth & Income		G&I	Lg/Bl	11	(4.9)	2.3	—	78	5	16	16	22	—	None	83	456.5	525-8983
Janus Mercury	★	Gro	Md/Gro	—	15.9	—	—	—	9	100	—	—	—	None	N.A.	690.1	525-8983
Janus Twenty[1]		Gro	Lg/Gro	12	(6.7)	(0.5)	10.9	N.A.	10	17	16	13	99	None	62	2,504.3	525-8983
Janus Venture[1]	★	Agg	Sm/Gro	8	5.5	7.3	12.7	75	18	89	20	29	43	None	59	1,496.1	525-8983
Janus Worldwide	★	Intl	Lg/Bl	9	3.6	13.2	—	92	13	90	22	99	—	None	94	1,542.6	525-8983
Japan	★	Reg	Md/Bl	12	10.0	4.2	(0.5)	69	8	94	23	15	22	None	78	600.8	535-2726
Jefferson Pilot Cap. App.		Gro	Lg/Bl	9	(4.7)	2.7	7.2	N.A.	22	27	29	32	38	4.5	91	32.4	458-4498
Kaufmann	★	Agg	Sm/Gro	11	9.0	12.8	19.3	99	19	94	52	47	94	None	157	1,590.6	237-0132
Kemper Blue Chip A		G&I	Lg/Bl	11	(5.2)	(1.0)	7.5	—	2	15	7	2	96	5.75	133	143.7	621-1048
Kemper Diversified Income A		ITR	Int/Med	2	(3.7)	11.1	12.7	74	(30)	59	93	87	100	4.5	107	462.8	621-1048
Kemper Growth A		Gro	Md/Gro	12	(5.9)	(2.0)	10.3	N.A.	5	21	10	8	96	5.75	111	1,505.3	621-1048
Kemper International A		Intl	Lg/Bl	11	(4.0)	7.4	4.6	85	12	37	54	38	20	5.75	128	361.7	621-1048
Kemper Retirement I[1]		ETR	Md/Gro	9	(6.3)	2.1	—	N.A.	12	14	41	10	97	5.0	N.A.	99.9	621-1048
Kemper Retirement II[1]		ETR	Md/Gro	9	(6.8)	2.6	—	18	9	11	50	15	94	5.0	N.A.	164.5	621-1048
Kemper Retirement III[1]		ETR	Md/Bl	—	(7.3)	—	—	—	5	8	60	—	—	5.0	N.A.	117.9	621-1048
Kemper Retirement IV		ETR	Md/Gro	—	(8.2)	—	—	—	(11)	6	—	—	—	5.0	N.A.	141.4	621-1048
Kemper Small Cap Equity A		Agg	Md/Gro	12	(3.3)	4.2	12.6	54	27	37	47	12	84	5.75	124	459.4	621-1048
Kemper Technology A	★	Spec	Md/Gro	12	11.2	7.1	12.2	56	36	91	23	34	79	5.75	100	681.6	621-1048
Kemper Total Return A		ETR	Md/Bl	10	(9.2)	1.3	8.7	N.A.	0	5	42	11	92	5.75	113	1,648.9	621-1048
Keystone Amer. Fund for T/R A		ETR	Lg/Bl	9	(4.0)	4.3	6.8	60	11	30	54	25	55	5.75	155	23.2	343-2898
Keystone Amer. Glob. Opp. A	★	Intl	Sm/Gro	10	2.7	16.4	14.0	99	5	86	63	100	93	5.75	196	69.8	343-2898
Keystone Amer. Hart. Em. Gro.A		Agg	Sm/Gro	12	(1.0)	1.4	13.1	38	17	55	5	13	89	5.75	132	121.4	343-2898
Keystone Amer. Hart. Gro.A		Gro	Lg/Gro	12	(9.0)	0.7	7.0	N.A.	40	9	39	15	95	5.75	156	19.0	343-2898
Keystone Amer. Omega A		Agg	Md/Gro	11	(5.7)	5.4	12.1	54	4	21	60	20	57	5.75	140	98.9	343-2898
Keystone Custodian K-1		ETR	Lg/Bl	7	(4.7)	2.9	5.8	37	5	24	31	20	48	4.0[4]	107	1,294.8	343-2898
Keystone Custodian K-2		Gro	Md/Gro	11	(3.0)	6.0	9.4	59	12	40	54	52	69	4.0[4]	86	414.5	343-2898
Keystone Custodian S-1		G&I	Lg/Bl	9	(5.9)	1.1	4.9	N.A.	6	9	41	4	56	4.0[4]	112	188.9	343-2898
Keystone Custodian S-3		Gro	Md/Gro	10	(4.7)	2.9	7.2	25	11	26	34	30	72	4.0[4]	92	231.1	343-2898
Keystone Custodian S-4	★	Agg	Md/Gro	12	0.2	11.3	17.5	71	26	64	88	43	90	4.0[4]	80	1,171.0	343-2898
Keystone Fund of Amer. B		Intl	Md/Gro	—	(9.3)	—	—	—	(6)	9	—	—	—	3.0[4]	N.A.	141.9	343-2898
Keystone International		Intl	Lg/Bl	9	(6.2)	7.8	1.7	85	3	25	30	77	46	4.0[4]	188	142.9	343-2898
Keystone Precious Metals		Spec	Sm/Gro	12	(13.3)	14.8	3.8	99	3	13	98	12	35	4.0[4]	143	199.5	343-2898
Kidder Peabody Eq.-Inc. A		ETR	Lg/Bl	10	(4.6)	(2.0)	7.0	N.A.	20	25	3	5	97	5.75	124	65.5	854-2505
Kidder Peabody Glob. Eq. A		Intl	Lg/Bl	10	(2.3)	9.7	—	88	22	53	31	83	—	5.75	144	169.6	854-2505
Laidlaw Covenant	★	G&I	Md/Val	—	3.0	—	—	—	8	91	8	—	—	4.5	172	4.2	275-2683
Landmark Balanced		ETR	Lg/Bl	7	(2.1)	4.3	—	82	(3)	56	23	42	80	4.75	123	227.4	559-7117[6]
Landmark Equity		Gro	Lg/Bl	9	(0.4)	6.3	—	92	4	61	51	45	35	4.75	123	184.0	559-7117[6]
Landmark Intl. Equity		Intl	Md/Bl	11	(11.5)	4.0	—	99	5	7	27	53	—	4.75	140	29.0	559-7117[6]
Leeb Personal Finance		Gro	Lg/Bl	4	(3.1)	1.9	—	55	(4)	38	15	36	—	None	N.A.	38.5	545-0103
Legg Mason Amer. Lead. Co.		G&I	Lg/Bl	—	(4.2)	—	—	—	(5)	21	—	—	—	None	N.A.	56.1	882-5544
Legg Mason Special Inv.		Agg	Sm/Bl	11	(13.1)	7.6	11.8	89	8	3	84	65	22	None	115	605.7	822-5544
Legg Mason Total Return		G&I	Lg/Val	9	(7.1)	6.6	7.2	78	2	7	66	88	93	None	125	193.3	822-5544
Legg Mason Value	★	Gro	Lg/Val	10	1.4	8.0	7.1	96	30	77	48	68	48	None	103	967.3	822-5544
Lepercq-Istel		G&I	Md/Val	8	(5.0)	4.4	4.5	59	13	15	62	23	5	None	89	19.2	338-1579
Lexington Convertible Secs.	★	ITR	N.A.	10	1.3	6.9	11.3	67	29	100	6	65	97	None	137	7.6	526-0057
Lexington Corp. Leaders		G&I	Lg/Val	9	(0.8)	8.6	7.9	63	36	43	85	66	12	None	N.A.	154.6	526-0057
Lexington Global	★	Intl	Md/Bl	10	1.8	9.0	4.5	69	21	78	37	40	54	None	83	72.8	526-0057
Lexington Goldfund		Spec	Md/Gro	12	(7.3)	11.3	0.5	99	(3)	44	93	5	10	None	96	151.2	526-0057
Lexington Growth & Income		G&I	Md/Bl	8	(3.1)	7.2	6.7	55	7	27	60	79	31	None	75	125.0	526-0057
Lexington Strat. Invest.	★	Spec	N.A.	12	11.3	17.4	(5.5)	98	(83)	92	100	1	2	5.75	207	96.0	526-0057
Lexington Strategic Silver		Spec	Sm/Gro	12	(8.4)	12.7	(3.7)	100	(24)	39	90	16	5	5.75	207	50.4	526-0057
Lexington Worldwide Emer.		Intl	N.A.	11	(13.8)	13.5	9.3	89	7	3	97	86	86	None	102	332.2	526-0057
Liberty Equity-Income A		ETR	Lg/Val	7	(3.8)	8.2	9.5	84	(6)	32	91	69	95	5.5	97	100.0	245-5051
Liberty Financial Gro. & Inc.		G&I	Lg/Val	—	(1.1)	—	—	—	(2)	40	23	—	—	4.5	N.A.	36.3	872-5426
Liberty Financial Utilities		Spec	Md/Val	7	(6.9)	5.7	—	70	(6)	47	33	67	—	4.5	111	248.3	872-5426
Liberty Utility A		Spec	Md/Val	8	(8.0)	5.0	8.2	58	(4)	40	35	63	56	5.5	102	737.8	245-5051
Lincoln Enterprise A		Gro	Md/Gro	—	(10.5)	—	—	—	(12)	6	—	—	—	5.5	N.A.	10.5	923-8476
Lincoln Growth & Income A		G&I	Md/Val	—	(7.0)	—	—	—	(7)	8	—	—	—	5.5	N.A.	10.2	923-8476

Fund name/★ 1994 winner	Type	Style	Risk level	% average annual return to Jan. 1, 1995			Tax analysis		Performance analysis (percentile ranking by type)				Expense analysis		Net assets (millions)	Telephone (800)
				One year	Three years	Five years	% tax efficiency	% tax liability	1994	1993	1992	1991	% max. sales charge	Five-year total per $1,000		
Lincoln New Pacific A	Reg	Lg/Bl	—	(11.0)	—	—	—	(3)	39	—	—	—	5.5	N.A.	$10.6	923-8476
Lincoln U.S. Growth A	Gro	Lg/Gro	—	(3.4)	—	—	—	(3)	36	—	—	—	5.5	N.A.	10.2	923-8476
Lincoln World Growth A ★	Intl	Md/Bl	—	4.2	—	—	—	2	92	—	—	—	5.5	N.A.	11.2	923-8476
Lindner	Gro	Sm/Bl	7	(0.7)	10.3	8.0	83	11	58	81	74	13	None	$44	1,503.0	727-5305[9]
Lindner Dividend	ITR	Md/Val	2	(3.3)	10.4	9.9	75	(6)	65	59	93	65	None	42	1,605.2	727-5305[9]
Lindner Utility	Spec	Md/Bl	—	(1.0)	—	—	—	1	69	—	—	—	None	61	43.4	727-5305[9]
LMH ★	G&I	Md/Val	8	2.6	6.1	2.9	91	(51)	88	19	58	8	None	142	5.9	847-6002
Longleaf Partners ★	Gro	Md/Bl	4	9.0	17.1	13.3	86	15	98	89	94	63	None	82	753.5	445-9469
Longleaf Partners Sm.-Cap. ★	Agg	Sm/Val	9	3.7	9.9	3.3	94	12	82	62	28	6	None	82	99.6	445-9469
Loomis Sayles Growth	Gro	Lg/Gro	11	(3.6)	3.0	—	85	8	33	36	20	—	None	82	36.9	633-3330
Loomis Sayles Growth & Inc.	G&I	Md/Val	9	(0.9)	8.2	—	85	6	42	53	87	—	None	82	25.7	633-3330
Loomis Sayles Intl. Equity	Intl	Md/Val	10	(1.8)	8.9	—	85	9	56	67	34	—	None	82	71.6	633-3330
Loomis Sayles Small Cap	Agg	Sm/Bl	11	(8.3)	9.0	—	76	(3)	10	86	54	—	None	82	74.1	633-3330
Lord Abbett Developing Gro. ★	Agg	Sm/Gro	11	6.2	5.1	11.2	58	56	91	30	6	64	5.75	125	130.3	874-3733
Lord Abbett Fund. Value	Gro	Lg/Val	7	(0.9)	8.1	8.4	62	9	56	56	72	5	5.75	140	30.1	874-3733
Lord Abbett Global Eq.	Intl	Lg/Val	10	(0.1)	7.4	4.5	81	9	64	15	55	49	5.75	151	84.2	874-3733
Lord Abbett Value App.	Gro	Md/Val	8	(3.2)	7.8	8.8	69	20	38	59	76	23	5.75	121	186.4	874-3733
L. Roy Papp Stock	Gro	Md/Bl	8	(1.4)	4.4	9.3	90	10	51	10	77	43	None	71	36.6	421-4004
Mackenzie American	Gro	Md/Bl	9	(4.7)	8.1	3.3	58	4	26	91	47	1	5.75	160	25.6	456-5111
Mackenzie North Amer. A	ETR	Md/Bl	7	(4.9)	5.0	4.4	66	N.A.	23	62	43	13	5.75	158	29.7	456-5111
MainStay Capital App.	Gro	Md/Gro	12	(1.5)	7.6	16.9	94	12	50	58	66	98	5.0[4]	128	481.4	522-4202
MainStay Convertible B	ITR	N.A.	6	(1.3)	11.6	14.0	74	(7)	89	100	71	99	5.0[4]	143	167.0	522-4202
MainStay Equity Index ★	G&I	Lg/Bl	8	0.4	5.2	—	89	13	63	21	52	51	5.5	103	60.7	522-4202
MainStay Global	Intl	Md/Val	11	(6.3)	2.4	1.2	86	2	24	13	20	39	5.0[4]	170	39.5	522-4202
MainStay Nat. Res./Gold	Spec	Md/Bl	12	(8.9)	6.3	(1.0)	97	5	34	79	25	27	5.0[4]	170	16.7	522-4202
MainStay Total Return	ETR	Md/Gro	9	(2.4)	3.8	9.9	78	5	50	35	20	90	5.0[4]	129	638.3	522-4202
MainStay Value	G&I	Md/Val	7	(0.2)	10.6	12.4	83	(1)	52	63	95	94	5.0[4]	124	436.8	522-4202
Mairs & Power Growth ★	Gro	Md/Bl	8	5.6	8.7	13.6	86	66	93	53	48	72	None	54	41.9	222-8478[10]
Mairs & Power Income	ITR	Lg/Val	5	(2.1)	4.7	7.9	68	22	75	24	11	63	None	59	13.0	222-8478[10]
Managers Balanced	ETR	Md/Bl	7	(3.1)	2.8	6.2	N.A.	12	40	14	27	84	None	92	1.6	835-3879
Managers Capital App.	Gro	Md/Bl	9	(1.5)	10.0	11.7	71	6	50	72	86	41	None	60	87.6	835-3879
Managers Income Equity ★	ETR	Lg/Bl	7	1.0	7.7	7.1	54	10	89	49	72	82	None	68	50.5	835-3879
Managers Intl. Equity ★	Intl	Lg/Bl	8	2.0	13.7	9.4	97	15	81	67	89	66	None	82	88.4	835-3879
Managers Special Equity	Agg	Sm/Bl	10	(2.0)	10.2	11.0	79	11	44	49	72	47	None	73	112.0	835-3879
Marshall Balanced	ETR	Md/Bl	—	(5.6)	—	—	—	(15)	18	—	—	—	None	N.A.	10.5	236-8560
Marshall Equity-Income	ETR	N.A.	—	(1.6)	—	—	—	(5)	62	—	—	—	None	N.A.	54.0	236-8560
Marshall Mid-Cap Stock	Gro	N.A.	—	(5.6)	—	—	—	(5)	22	—	—	—	None	N.A.	61.7	236-8560
Marshall Stock	G&I	Lg/Bl	—	(5.8)	—	—	—	(3)	11	6	—	—	None	N.A.	220.6	236-8560
Marshall Value Equity ★	G&I	N.A.	—	2.1	—	—	—	(2)	83	—	—	—	None	N.A.	211.1	236-8560
Massachusetts Investors A	G&I	Lg/Bl	9	(1.0)	5.4	8.3	18	21	41	45	46	47	5.75	95	1,535.2	637-2929
Mass. Investors Gro. Stock A	Gro	Lg/Gro	12	(6.7)	4.4	9.5	31	32	17	61	38	83	5.75	100	965.9	637-2929
Mathers	Gro	N.A.	7	(5.9)	(0.3)	3.7	N.A.	(7)	21	11	17	2	None	49	293.3	962-3863
Matrix Growth	Gro	Md/Bl	10	(4.8)	3.0	7.0	59	22	25	37	28	46	None	91	15.4	354-6339
Medical Research Investment	Spec	Md/Gro	11	(6.4)	6.8	12.8	61	8	50	62	38	78	4.75	173	13.5	262-6631
Mentor Growth	Gro	Sm/Bl	10	(4.5)	8.5	11.2	72	25	27	67	84	87	5.0[4]	127	189.5	825-5353
Mentor Strategy	ETR	Md/Bl	—	(3.4)	—	—	—	(3)	38	—	—	—	5.0[4]	N.A.	176.4	825-5353
Merger ★	Gro	Sm/Val	1	7.1	9.9	9.4	81	4	95	75	31	3	None	147	170.3	343-8959
Meridian ★	Agg	Sm/Gro	10	0.6	9.5	16.6	92	3	69	33	67	66	None	95	256.6	446-6662
Merrill Lynch Bal. Inv.& Ret.B	ETR	Md/Bl	9	(7.4)	2.7	5.6	N.A.	10	8	71	10	54	4.0[4]	100	324.2	637-3863
Merrill Lynch Dragon B	Reg	Md/Gro	—	(17.0)	—	—	—	21	24	97	—	—	4.0[4]	N.A.	950.7	637-3863
Merrill Lynch EuroFund B ★	Reg	Lg/Val	12	3.2	8.1	7.0	86	15	74	41	51	84	4.0[4]	114	991.0	637-3863
Merrill Lynch Tomorrow B	Gro	Lg/Bl	11	(8.5)	2.0	5.0	N.A.	11	10	40	29	34	4.0[4]	107	139.4	637-3863
Merrill Lynch Fund. Gro. C	Gro	Lg/Gro	—	(6.3)	—	—	—	(1)	19	20	—	—	1.0[4]	N.A.	38.4	637-3863
Merrill Lynch Glob. Alloc. B	ETR	Lg/Val	3	(2.9)	9.0	10.7	82	0	42	90	83	70	4.0[4]	112	6,266.1	637-3863
Merrill Lynch Glob. Conv. B	ITR	N.A.	4	(1.5)	7.1	5.4	89	(2)	85	43	51	14	4.0[4]	181	76.0	637-3863
Merrill Lynch Glob. Res. B ★	Spec	Md/Bl	11	0.2	3.5	2.7	95	(11)	74	46	25	29	4.0[4]	108	223.5	637-3863
Merrill Lynch Glob. Util. B	Spec	Lg/Val	9	(10.6)	6.1	—	85	(1)	23	57	56	38	4.0[4]	96	459.2	637-3863
Merrill Lynch Inv. B ★	Gro	Sm/Gro	10	0.7	12.8	12.0	87	19	73	99	56	15	4.0[4]	101	1,321.9	637-3863
Merrill Lynch Latin Amer. B	Reg	N.A.	12	(15.9)	11.6	—	94	12	29	73	79	—	4.0[4]	141	937.6	637-3863
Merrill Lynch Strat. Div. B	ETR	Lg/Val	8	(0.2)	5.0	4.2	49	14	81	18	57	11	4.0[4]	103	138.3	637-3863

Source: Morningstar Inc. Chicago Ill.; 800-876-5005

| Fund name/★ 1994 winner | Type | Style | Risk level | % average annual return to Jan. 1, 1995 | | | Tax analysis | | Performance analysis (percentile ranking by type) | | | | Expense analysis | | Net assets (millions) | Telephone (800) |
				One year	Three years	Five years	% tax efficiency	% tax liability	1994	1993	1992	1991	% max. sales charge	Five-year total per $1,000		
Merrill Lynch Tech. B ★	Spec	Md/Gro	—	25.5	—	—	—	7	99	52	—	—	4.0[4]	$135	$572.0	637-3863
Merriman Asset Allocation	ETR	Md/Gro	4	(2.9)	5.8	6.1	61	6	42	86	13	8	None	83	25.8	423-4893
Merriman Cap. App.	Gro	N.A.	6	(0.6)	2.4	6.2	8	7	59	17	23	8	None	80	23.8	423-4893
Merriman Growth & Income	G&I	N.A.	5	(0.2)	0.4	4.6	N.A.	8	53	5	2	10	None	87	9.9	423-4893
Merriman Leveraged Gro.	Gro	N.A.	—	(0.1)	—	—	—	3	64	17	—	—	None	165	5.8	423-4893
MetL.-St. Res. Cap. App. A	Agg	Md/Gro	12	(2.5)	9.3	14.5	75	9	40	78	37	91	4.5	123	254.1	882-3302
MetLife-State Res. Eq. Inv. A	Gro	Lg/Bl	10	(4.9)	5.5	7.5	54	5	24	53	59	50	4.5	123	26.9	882-3302
MetLife-State Res. Eq.-Inc. A	ETR	Md/Bl	6	(4.9)	9.5	6.8	84	0	23	96	91	16	4.5	123	39.2	882-3302
MetLife-State Res. Managed A	ETR	Md/Bl	7	(5.9)	7.4	7.2	73	(5)	16	95	61	29	4.5	111	179.7	882-3302
MFS Capital Growth B	Gro	Lg/Val	9	(0.9)	3.8	7.4	57	13	56	19	51	32	4.0[4]	140	394.9	637-2929
MFS Emerging Gro. Class B ★	Agg	Md/Gro	12	4.0	13.0	21.4	96	30	84	83	49	98	4.0[4]	145	801.4	637-2929
MFS Gold & Natural Res. B	Spec	Md/Gro	12	(17.7)	7.2	(1.7)	99	(8)	4	82	36	18	4.0[4]	153	29.6	637-2929
MFS Growth Opportunities A	Gro	Md/Gro	11	(4.2)	6.3	7.0	64	14	29	70	47	11	5.75	107	588.8	637-2929
MFS Intermediate Income B	ITR	Int/Med	6	(6.4)	1.5	4.6	N.A.	(16)	20	13	7	4	4.0[4]	138	285.7	637-2929
MFS Managed Sectors B	Gro	Md/Gro	12	(3.5)	1.3	7.4	N.A.	11	34	17	21	94	4.0[4]	147	197.5	637-2929
MFS OTC B ★	Gro	Sm/Gro	—	3.0	—	—	—	2	85	—	—	—	4.0[4]	N.A.	56.9	637-2929
MFS Research A	Gro	Md/Gro	9	0.0	10.6	11.0	73	12	65	88	67	39	5.75	107	321.4	637-2929
MFS Strategic Income A	ITR	N.A.	3	(5.9)	3.9	7.2	43	(13)	25	42	9	53	4.75	151	41.2	637-2929
MFS Total Return A	ETR	Lg/Val	5	(2.7)	7.2	7.9	76	7	45	73	74	34	4.75	92	1,825.1	637-2929
MFS Utilities A	Spec	Md/Val	—	(5.0)	—	—	—	(7)	56	49	—	—	4.75	N.A.	40.6	637-2929
MFS Value A	Gro	Md/Bl	9	(2.5)	13.0	9.5	72	11	43	95	92	16	5.75	129	142.8	637-2929
MFS Worldwide Equity B	Intl	Md/Bl	8	(3.7)	8.1	5.2	81	19	41	24	74	11	4.0[4]	173	163.7	637-2929
MFS World Growth B ★	Intl	Md/Gro	—	2.0	—	—	—	4	81	—	—	—	4.0[4]	N.A.	229.7	637-2929
MFS World Total Return A	Intl	Lg/Bl	7	(3.1)	7.4	—	74	1	44	7	92	79	4.75	158	95.4	637-2929
Midwest Strategic Equity C	Gro	Md/Val	—	(2.4)	—	—	—	(24)	44	—	—	—	1.0	N.A.	2.6	543-8721
Midwest Leshner Fin. Util. A	Spec	Md/Val	7	(2.0)	4.5	7.5	54	(2)	66	12	53	52	4.0	132	40.4	543-8721
MIM AFA Equity Income	ETR	Md/Bl	7	(6.0)	3.1	—	57	(6)	15	7	84	—	None	176	2.3	233-1240
MIM Bond Income	ITR	Lg/Bl	7	(3.6)	2.0	4.2	68	(26)	62	2	15	12	None	148	1.9	233-1240
MIM Stock Appreciation	Gro	Sm/Gro	12	(10.4)	1.5	14.3	49	0	6	42	33	100	None	141	41.0	233-1240
MIM Stock Growth	Gro	Md/Bl	11	(11.7)	(4.0)	1.1	N.A.	3	3	12	7	22	None	150	6.6	233-1240
MIM Stock Income	G&I	Lg/Bl	9	(1.8)	0.8	3.4	N.A.	(1)	34	4	20	11	None	138	5.4	233-1240
MIMLIC Asset Allocation	ETR	Lg/Gro	8	(2.1)	3.1	7.8	56	3	53	9	34	71	5.0	120	53.9	443-3677
MIMLIC Investors I ★	G&I	Lg/Gro	10	0.7	3.3	8.8	75	23	68	9	18	91	5.0	123	31.6	443-3677
Monetta[1]	Agg	Sm/Gro	11	(6.2)	(0.2)	11.5	N.A.	(4)	19	3	24	62	None	82	364.9	666-3882
Monetta Tr. Mid-Cap. Eq. ★	Gro	Md/Bl	—	3.8	—	—	—	3	90	—	—	—	None	N.A.	11.7	241-9772
Monitrend Gold	Spec	N.A.	12	(50.2)	(24.8)	(19.4)	N.A.	N.A.	1	51	3	7	4.5	171	1.3	251-1970
Monitrend Summation	G&I	Lg/Bl	9	(2.0)	(5.2)	(1.8)	N.A.	N.A.	32	1	1	2	4.5	171	1.6	251-1970
Montgomery Emerging Mkt.	Intl	Md/Gro	—	(7.7)	—	—	—	11	17	96	—	—	None	104	878.0	572-3863
Montgomery Global Comm.	Spec	Lg/Gro	—	(13.4)	—	—	—	(2)	12	—	—	—	None	N.A.	216.4	572-3863
Montgomery Global Opp.	Intl	Md/Bl	—	(8.6)	—	—	—	(4)	13	—	—	—	None	N.A.	13.2	572-3863
Montgomery Growth ★	Gro	Md/Gro	—	20.9	—	—	—	5	100	—	—	—	None	N.A.	592.7	572-3863
Montgomery Intl. Small Cap.	Intl	Sm/Val	—	(13.3)	—	—	—	(18)	3	—	—	—	None	N.A.	29.3	572-3863
Montgomery Small Cap.[1]	Agg	Sm/Gro	12	(10.0)	7.1	—	80	11	7	85	41	100	None	82	202.5	572-3863
Morgan Stan. Asian Gro. A	Reg	Lg/Gro	—	(14.2)	—	—	—	8	34	—	—	—	4.75	N.A.	158.5	282-4404
Muhlenkamp	G&I	Md/Val	10	(9.2)	7.5	9.0	98	(1)	2	86	92	96	None	N.A.	16.3	860-3863
Munder Multi-Seas. Gro. B	Gro	Md/Bl	—	(3.3)	—	—	—	1	37	—	—	—	5.0[4]	N.A.	46.0	239-3334
Mutual Beacon ★	G&I	Md/Val	3	5.6	16.9	11.5	89	11	98	98	100	6	None	46	2,017.9	553-3014
Mutual Benefit ★	Gro	Md/Bl	4	2.8	7.3	8.4	51	24	83	34	64	25	4.75	101	47.9	559-5535
Mutual Discovery[1] ★	Agg	Md/Val	—	3.6	—	—	—	9	81	97	—	—	None	N.A.	736.8	553-3014
Mutual Qualified ★	G&I	Md/Val	4	5.7	16.8	11.6	86	21	98	97	99	15	None	47	1,766.2	553-3014
Mutual Shares ★	G&I	Md/Val	5	4.5	15.4	10.9	85	23	96	95	99	14	None	45	3,713.0	553-3014
National Industries	Gro	Lg/Gro	11	(0.8)	(1.6)	5.4	N.A.	N.A.	57	9	3	37	None	82	30.8	220-8500[11]
Nations Equity-Index Tr. A ★	Gro	N.A.	—	1.0	—	—	—	(2)	76	—	—	—	None	N.A.	123.1	321-7854
Nationwide ★	G&I	Md/Gro	9	0.6	3.4	7.6	39	30	66	18	11	64	4.5	78	636.8	848-0920
Nationwide Growth ★	Gro	Lg/Bl	9	1.5	6.3	8.6	82	21	78	47	37	55	4.5	80	439.8	848-0920
Neuberger/Berman Focus ★	Gro	Lg/Val	9	0.9	12.4	10.8	79	27	75	70	95	16	None	50	596.3	877-9700
Neuberger/Berman Genesis	Agg	Sm/Val	9	(1.8)	8.9	8.9	86	12	46	35	68	28	None	90	108.5	877-9700
Neuberger/Berman Guard. ★	G&I	Lg/Val	7	1.4	11.4	12.1	89	16	80	72	95	85	None	46	2,375.7	877-9700
Neuberger/Ber. Manhattan	Gro	Md/Bl	10	(3.6)	7.7	8.5	54	14	34	40	90	35	None	59	458.9	877-9700
Neuberger/Berman Partners	Gro	Md/Bl	9	(1.9)	10.3	9.3	72	11	47	71	90	10	None	48	1,249.3	877-9700

Source: Morningstar Inc. Chicago Ill.; 800-876-5005

Fund name/★ 1994 winner	Type	Style	Risk level	% average annual return to Jan. 1, 1995			Tax analysis		Performance analysis (percentile ranking by type)				Expense analysis		Net assets (millions)	Telephone (800)
				One year	Three years	Five years	% tax efficiency	% tax liability	1994	1993	1992	1991	% max. sales charge	Five-year total per $1,000		
New Economy	Gro	Md/Gro	9	(8.1)	12.0	10.3	84	19	11	99	88	29	5.75	$104	$2,594.4	421-4120
New England Balanced A	ETR	Lg/Bl	7	(2.6)	8.2	7.9	84	4	46	66	93	77	5.75	134	197.5	225-7670
New England Capital Growth A	Gro	Md/Gro	—	(1.6)	—	—	—	4	49	30	—	—	5.75	N.A.	95.7	225-7670
New England Growth A[1]	Gro	Lg/Val	11	(7.1)	(1.2)	9.7	N.A.	7	15	47	2	92	6.5	124	989.0	225-7670
New England Growth Opp. A ★	G&I	Lg/Bl	8	1.0	6.0	8.3	80	27	70	24	63	69	5.75	119	103.5	225-7670
New England Intl. Equity A ★	Intl	Lg/Val	—	8.1	—	—	—	7	98	25	—	—	5.75	N.A.	140.6	225-7670
New England Value A	G&I	Lg/Val	9	(1.4)	9.8	7.8	80	14	37	76	93	43	5.75	126	195.4	225-7670
New Perspective ★	Intl	Lg/Bl	9	3.0	10.8	10.3	88	24	87	17	87	84	5.75	102	6,540.2	421-4120
Newport Tiger	Reg	Lg/Gro	12	(12.0)	23.5	15.0	99	23	35	88	100	98	5.0	145	444.7	776-5455
New USA Mutual	Gro	Sm/Gro	—	(3.6)	—	—	—	2	33	37	—	—	5.0	N.A.	184.0	222-2872
New York Venture A ★	Gro	Lg/Val	11	3.2	10.3	12.9	78	16	87	69	71	65	4.75	95	1,090.5	279-0279
Nicholas	Gro	Md/Bl	8	(2.8)	5.0	9.4	68	26	40	22	72	72	None	43	2,820.2	272-6133[12]
Nicholas Equity Income ★	ETR	Md/Val	—	4.1	—	—	—	(1)	98	—	—	—	None	N.A.	10.9	272-6133[12]
Nicholas II ★	Agg	Sm/Bl	8	1.0	5.6	9.1	69	38	70	11	38	23	None	37	603.9	272-6133[12]
Nicholas Limited Edition[1]	Agg	Sm/Bl	8	(3.0)	7.3	11.7	74	36	38	19	74	32	None	52	142.6	272-6133[12]
Nicholas-Applegate Bal. B	ETR	Md/Bl	—	(6.9)	—	—	—	(6)	9	—	—	—	1.0[4]	N.A.	16.7	551-8043
Nicholas-Applegate Core B	Gro	Md/Gro	—	(11.5)	—	—	—	(11)	4	—	—	—	1.0[4]	N.A.	134.8	551-8043
Nicholas-Applegate Gro. Eq A	Agg	Md/Gro	11	(9.5)	5.8	11.6	76	1	7	65	36	60	5.0	139	90.5	225-1852
Nicholas-Applegate Inc. B	G&I	Int/Lo	—	(8.7)	—	—	—	(8)	3	—	—	—	1.0[4]	N.A.	65.1	551-8043
Nicholas-Applegate World B ★	Intl	Md/Bl	—	1.9	—	—	—	4	79	—	—	—	1.0[4]	N.A.	77.6	551-8043
Nomura Pacific Basin ★	Reg	Lg/Bl	12	5.3	8.3	3.7	84	9	82	56	24	60	None	82	55.3	833-0018
North American Asset Alloc.	ETR	Md/Val	7	(2.8)	4.6	3.6	73	6	44	30	44	16	None	143	82.2	872-8037
North Amer. Global Growth C ★	Intl	Lg/Bl	10	1.2	8.4	—	95	8	75	25	46	31	None	163	95.5	872-8037
North American Gro.& Inc. C ★	G&I	Lg/Bl	8	2.1	6.5	—	89	5	83	32	54	—	None	143	45.5	872-8037
North American Growth C	Gro	Md/Val	8	(2.2)	8.9	6.3	93	9	45	44	92	16	None	143	69.3	872-8037
North American Strat. Inc. A	ITR	Int/Lo	—	(6.6)	—	—	—	(14)	15	—	—	—	4.75	125	10.5	733-3098
Northeast Investors Growth	Gro	Lg/Bl	11	0.0	0.5	7.1	N.A.	21	65	12	9	58	None	77	35.3	225-6704
Norwest Val. Gro. St. Inv. A	Gro	Md/Bl	10	(4.2)	3.9	8.7	84	9	29	26	60	57	4.5	108	11.7	338-1348
NWNL Northstar I&G A	ETR	Lg/Val	—	(3.6)	—	—	—	(6)	35	—	—	—	4.75	N.A.	69.4	863-6215[13]
NWNL Northstar Multi-Sect. A	ITR	L/Lo	—	(9.7)	—	—	—	(18)	5	—	—	—	4.75	N.A.	24.3	595-7827
Oak Hall Equity	Agg	Sm/Gro	—	(11.6)	—	—	—	(8)	3	99	—	—	None	N.A.	20.3	625-4255
Oakmark ★	Gro	Md/Bl	4	3.3	26.2	—	94	14	87	98	100	—	None	92	1,622.0	625-6275
Oakmark International	Intl	Md/Val	—	(9.1)	—	—	—	5	10	94	—	—	None	N.A.	1,192.1	625-6275
Oberweis Emerging Growth	Agg	Sm/Gro	12	(3.5)	6.4	17.7	95	13	34	22	57	97	None	106	90.1	323-6166
Old Westbury International	Intl	Md/Val	—	(11.1)	—	—	—	0	8	—	—	—	4.5	N.A.	89.6	545-1074
ONE Fund Growth ★	Gro	Md/Val	—	0.6	—	—	—	14	71	73	—	—	5.0	118	6.0	578-8078
ONE Fund Income & Growth ★	ETR	Md/Bl	—	0.5	—	—	—	10	86	83	—	—	5.0	106	6.8	578-8078
ONE Fund International ★	Intl	Md/Val	—	9.7	—	—	—	12	100	—	—	—	5.0	161	10.4	578-8078
Oppenheimer A ★	Gro	Md/Bl	8	0.3	7.8	9.1	73	26	68	65	52	28	5.75	114	246.1	525-7048
Oppenheimer Asset Alloc. A	ETR	Md/Bl	6	(1.6)	7.2	7.3	76	13	63	81	52	9	5.75	118	240.2	525-7048
Oppenheimer Discovery A	Agg	Sm/Gro	12	(11.2)	6.9	12.3	90	12	5	50	73	88	5.75	136	592.0	525-7048
Oppenheimer Equity-Income A	ETR	Lg/Val	7	(2.8)	6.0	6.6	69	6	45	68	42	14	5.75	100	1,715.8	525-7048
Oppenheimer Global G&I A	Intl	Md/Bl	9	(4.7)	7.6	—	80	9	32	69	24	50	5.75	146	124.1	525-7048
Oppenheimer Global A	Intl	Md/Bl	11	(3.1)	5.8	8.5	66	24	43	80	2	90	5.75	128	1,879.5	525-7048
Oppenheimer Glob. Emer. Gro.	Intl	Sm/Gro	12	(27.5)	(17.8)	6.7	N.A.	(19)	1	1	1	100	5.75	129	169.3	525-7048
Oppenheimer Gold/Spec. Min.	Spec	Md/Gro	12	(6.0)	11.0	0.1	98	6	52	86	18	22	5.75	129	175.5	525-7048
Oppenheimer Growth A ★	Gro	Lg/Bl	10	2.4	6.0	10.9	68	36	37	100	100	100	5.75	133	1,187.9	525-7048
Oppenheimer Main St. I&G A	G&I	Md/Bl	10	(1.5)	20.5	22.2	87	(1)	35	8	—	—	4.75	N.A.	41.2	525-7048
Oppenheimer Str. I&G A	ITR	Lg/Bl	—	(5.5)	—	—	—	(4)	35	8	—	—	4.75	N.A.		525-7048
Oppenheimer Strat. Inc. A	ITR	Sh/Md	3	(4.7)	7.1	9.9	57	(9)	47	88	25	28	4.75	108	3,096.9	525-7048
Oppenheimer Target A ★	Agg	Md/Bl	10	0.5	4.8	9.7	63	29	67	5	44	28	5.75	113	303.6	525-7048
Oppenheimer Time	Gro	Md/Gro	12	(12.8)	2.0	6.5	1	22	3	81	12	63	5.75	108	313.9	525-7048
Oppenheimer Total Return A	G&I	Md/Bl	10	(7.9)	8.1	10.6	77	3	5	96	82	88	5.75	107	1,230.8	525-7048
Oppenheimer Val. Stock A ★	G&I	Lg/Val	7	3.3	7.3	8.8	78	16	92	29	65	32	5.75	119	89.9	525-7048
O.R.I. Growth ★	Gro	Sm/Bl	—	3.2	—	—	—	0	86	—	—	—	None	N.A.	2.6	407-7298
Overland Exp. Ast. Alloc. A	ETR	Lg/Bl	7	(0.7)	6.3	9.2	55	4	73	51	49	25	4.5	111	40.3	552-9612
Overland Express G&I A	G&I	Md/Val	9	(0.5)	7.5	—	80	5	49	28	89	75	4.5	70	16.5	552-9612
Pacific Advisors Balanced	ETR	N.A.	—	(2.4)	—	—	—	2	49	—	—	—	5.75	138	1.3	282-6693
Pacific Advisors Income ★	ITR	N.A.	—	1.0	—	—	—	(1)	99	—	—	—	4.75	134	0.6	282-6693
Pacific Advisors Small Cap	Agg	N.A.	—	(4.0)	—	—	—	(2)	31	—	—	—	5.75	167	3.3	282-6693

Source: Morningstar Inc. Chicago Ill.; 800-876-5005

Fund name/★ 1994 winner	Type	Style	Risk level	% average annual return to Jan. 1, 1995 One year	Three years	Five years	Tax analysis % tax efficiency	% tax liability	Performance analysis (percentile ranking by type) 1994	1993	1992	1991	Expense analysis % max. sales charge	Five-year total per $1,000	Net assets (millions)	Telephone (800)
Pacific European Growth	Intl	Lg/Bl	10	(3.6)	13.2	—	94	19	41	92	61	29	4.0	$156	$165.7	866-7778
Pacific Horizon Agg. Growth	Agg	Md/Gro	12	(11.5)	(2.4)	10.8	N.A.	21	4	13	10	86	4.5	120	125.5	332-3863
Pacific Horizon Cap. Inc.	ITR	N.A.	7	(5.9)	11.9	13.1	83	(7)	27	99	95	91	4.5	45	200.6	332-3863
Pacifica Balanced	ETR	Md/Val	6	(3.8)	8.1	—	69	3	33	89	70	19	4.5	100	102.1	662-8417
Pacifica Equity Value	Gro	Md/Val	7	(1.7)	11.0	—	77	9	48	96	64	7	4.5	99	167.1	662-8417
PaineWebber Asset Alloc. B	ETR	Lg/Bl	9	(10.5)	2.3	5.3	12	9	4	70	23	18	5.0⁴	129	48.9	647-1568
PaineWebber Atlas Glob. Gro. A	Intl	Md/Bl	12	(12.8)	4.2	2.7	84	3	5	79	18	21	4.5	134	189.8	647-1568
PaineWebber Blue Chip Gro. B	Gro	Md/Bl	10	(5.2)	4.2	5.8	27	27	23	52	33	40	5.0⁴	137	34.2	647-1568
PaineWebber Cap. App. D	Gro	Md/Gro	—	(2.1)	—	—	—	1	45	65	—	—	None	124	25.0	647-1568
PaineWebber Dividend Gro. A	G&I	Lg/Bl	10	(5.8)	(1.6)	5.0	N.A.	3	10	3	13	86	4.5	109	190.0	647-1568
PaineWebber Europe Gro. A	Reg	Md/Val	12	(8.2)	3.2	—	89	(14)	52	45	32	15	4.5	150	73.4	647-1568
PaineWebber Global Energy B	Spec	Md/Bl	11	(9.9)	(0.3)	0.6	N.A.	(12)	27	32	29	36	5.0⁴	180	15.2	647-1568
PaineWebber Glob. G&I A	ETR	Md/Bl	10	(10.5)	5.3	5.5	84	4	3	100	4	5	4.5	134	55.1	647-1568
PaineWebber Growth A	Gro	Md/Gro	11	(10.9)	3.4	8.5	77	15	6	80	22	82	4.5	120	127.5	647-1568
PaineWebber Regional Fin. Gro.A	Spec	Sm/Val	9	(0.8)	14.9	17.1	87	30	72	17	96	93	4.5	134	46.9	647-1568
PaineWebber S/C Value B	Agg	Sm/Val	—	(2.0)	—	—	—	(2)	45	—	—	—	5.0⁴	N.A.	47.6	647-1568
Parnassus ★	Gro	Sm/Val	9	12.0	21.6	16.6	88	18	99	74	100	89	3.5	112	151.8	999-3505
Parnassus Income Balanced	ITR	Sm/Val	—	(5.4)	—	—	—	(9)	39	74	—	—	None	69	16.9	999-3505
Pasadena Balanced Return A	ETR	Lg/Gro	9	(4.4)	0.8	7.2	48	5	26	5	25	91	5.5	161	54.6	882-2855
Pasadena Growth A	Gro	Lg/Gro	12	(3.8)	(2.5)	8.2	N.A.	10	33	2	15	98	5.5	137	402.2	882-2855
Pasadena Nifty Fifty A ★	Gro	Lg/Gro	10	1.1	1.4	—	100	13	76	6	19	97	5.5	149	101.3	882-2855
Pax World ★	ETR	Md/Bl	7	2.6	0.7	6.4	N.A.	(7)	94	1	7	25	None	58	388.3	767-1729
PBHG Emerging Growth	Agg	Sm/Gro	—	23.8	—	—	N.A.	14	100	—	—	—	None	N.A.	142.7	433-0051
PBHG Growth ★	Agg	Sm/Gro	12	4.8	25.4	22.0	91	4	87	100	96	54	None	169	657.9	433-0051
Penn Square Mutual ★	G&I	Lg/Bl	8	0.2	7.2	8.2	67	16	60	57	58	44	4.75	98	243.5	523-8440
Pennsylvania Mutual	Agg	Sm/Val	6	(0.7)	8.8	8.5	74	31	57	28	71	10	None	50	785.8	221-4268
Peoples Index ★	G&I	Lg/Bl	8	0.7	5.9	8.0	68	14	67	37	49	61	None	36	233.8	645-6561
Peoples S&P MidCap Index	Gro	Md/Bl	10	(4.0)	6.9	—	80	7	30	56	70	—	None	64	73.4	645-6561
Permanent Portfolio	ETR	Md/Bl	5	(2.9)	4.8	3.6	91	0	43	75	12	4	None	102	72.0	531-5142
Permanent Port. Agg. Gro. ★	Agg	Md/Bl	10	1.0	13.9	—	97	20	71	71	82	7	None	102	6.2	531-5142
Perritt Capital Growth	Agg	Sm/Val	11	(5.1)	2.1	4.2	45	16	23	7	26	20	None	121	6.2	338-1579
Philadelphia	G&I	Md/Bl	—	(8.6)	8.8	3.8	84	15	3	85	96	1	None	97	80.5	749-9933
Phoenix Balanced A	ETR	Lg/Bl	6	(4.6)	2.7	7.9	52	(2)	25	12	40	61	4.75	99	2,502.5	243-4361
Phoenix Capital App. A	Gro	Lg/Bl	10	(3.8)	4.6	15.3	72	6	31	40	50	84	4.75	121	419.8	243-4361
Phoenix Convertible A	ITR	N.A.	2	(3.8)	6.1	7.0	63	(2)	55	18	67	8	4.75	111	218.4	243-4361
Phoenix Equity Opp. A	Gro	Lg/Bl	9	(5.1)	7.9	7.7	50	5	24	62	84	12	4.75	128	173.9	243-4361
Phoenix Growth A	Gro	Lg/Bl	7	(1.6)	2.3	7.8	49	6	49	19	23	26	4.75	109	2,036.6	243-4361
Phoenix Income & Gro. A	ETR	Lg/Bl	6	(6.3)	6.3	7.9	61	1	15	67	86	43	4.75	129	499.9	243-4361
Phoenix International	Intl	Md/Bl	11	(0.2)	6.4	4.9	89	10	62	63	7	27	4.75	150	168.0	243-4361
Phoenix Multi-Sector F/I A	ITR	Int/Md	4	(6.8)	6.4	10.2	53	(12)	10	65	61	69	4.75	124	167.7	243-4361
Phoenix Total Return A	ETR	Lg/Bl	4	(2.3)	6.0	9.9	68	(1)	52	33	76	73	4.75	118	337.0	243-4361
Phoenix US Stock A	Gro	Lg/Bl	7	(3.9)	4.9	7.1	53	8	31	48	47	30	4.75	113	132.5	243-4361
Phoenix Worldwide Opp. A	Intl	Md/Bl	9	0.0	12.5	6.5	86	18	65	64	81	87	4.75	168	137.9	243-4361
Pierpont Capital App.	Agg	Sm/Bl	12	(5.9)	6.7	8.0	64	0	20	17	80	69	None	50	177.3	521-5411
Pierpont Diversified	ETR	Lg/Bl	—	(0.4)	—	—	—	(1)	75	—	—	—	None	54	13.3	521-5411
Pierpont Emerging Mkts. Eq.	Intl	Md/Gro	—	(8.5)	—	—	—	2	13	—	—	—	None	100	51.7	521-5411
Pierpont Equity	G&I	Lg/Bl	9	(0.6)	6.3	10.3	55	2	45	47	59	84	None	50	235.1	521-5411
Pierpont Intl. Equity ★	Intl	Lg/Val	12	5.7	6.0	—	85	7	96	16	9	26	None	76	200.2	521-5411
Pilgrim MagnaCap ★	G&I	Lg/Bl	8	4.1	7.1	8.4	74	28	95	33	52	32	5.0	130	198.1	334-3444
Pilot Kleinwort Intl. Eq. B	Intl	Md/Bl	11	(0.3)	7.4	3.4	95	18	62	23	42	35	4.5	N.A.	34.9	237-4218
PIMCo Adv. Equity-Inc. C†	ETR	Lg/Bl	8	(5.1)	7.5	6.9	89	1	21	92	54	86	1.0⁴	113	168.7	426-0107
PIMCo Adv. Growth C†	Gro	Lg/Gro	10	(0.7)	3.8	9.7	54	15	57	42	14	71	1.0⁴	103	1,062.7	426-0107
PIMCo Adv. International C†	Intl	Lg/Bl	11	(8.2)	4.9	3.2	78	3	15	44	27	74	1.0⁴	138	274.6	426-0107
PIMCo Adv Opportunity C1,†	Agg	Sm/Gro	12	(4.7)	18.6	21.0	93	27	25	98	95	83	1.0⁴	108	539.7	426-0107
PIMCo Adv. Precious Metals C†	Spec	Md/Gro	12	(9.7)	14.5	1.3	100	0	29	95	15	11	1.0⁴	138	52.4	426-0107
PIMCo Adv. Target C† ★	Gro	Md/Gro	—	3.1	—	—	N.A.	9	85	94	—	—	1.0⁴	N.A.	557.2	426-0107
Pioneer	G&I	Md/Bl	6	(0.6)	8.9	7.3	77	32	46	67	86	23	5.75	109	1,985.2	225-6292
Pioneer Capital Growth A ★	Gro	Sm/Bl	7	14.8	20.0	—	89	13	99	72	99	58	5.75	134	411.8	225-6292
Pioneer Equity-Income A	ETR	Md/Val	6	(1.3)	10.5	—	86	1	66	56	100	64	5.75	146	171.1	225-6292
Pioneer Europe A ★	Reg	Md/Val	11	6.0	8.7	—	85	16	84	28	60	—	5.75	159	63.4	225-6292

Source: Morningstar Inc. Chicago Ill.; 800-876-5005

Fund name/★ 1994 winner	Type	Style	Risk level	% average annual return to Jan. 1, 1995			Tax analysis		Performance analysis (percentile ranking by type)				Expense analysis		Net assets (millions)	Telephone (800)
				One year	Three years	Five years	% tax efficiency	% tax liability	1994	1993	1992	1991	% max. sales charge	Five-year total per $1,000		
Pioneer Gold Shares	Spec	Sm/Gro	12	(11.7)	11.5	—	100	1	16	87	23	11	5.75	$147	$23.3	225-6292
Pioneer Growth	Agg	Sm/Gro	12	(2.6)	2.3	9.7	—	29	39	16	15	72	5.75	108	129.4	225-6292
Pioneer II	G&I	Md/Val	8	(1.7)	8.5	7.2	63	17	35	91	63	34	5.75	107	4,337.9	225-6292
Pioneer Income	ITR	Lg/Bl	5	(4.3)	4.3	6.9	48	(3)	52	20	21	16	4.5	100	260.6	225-6292
Pioneer International Gro. A	Intl	Lg/Bl	—	(5.4)	—	—	—	2	28	—	—	—	5.75	N.A.	281.3	225-6292
Pioneer Three	Agg	Sm/Val	9	(5.7)	9.7	9.4	79	24	22	45	82	16	5.75	102	955.4	225-6292
Pioneer Winth Real Est. Inv. ★	Spec	Sm/Bl	—	0.2	—	—	—	(18)	75	—	—	—	5.75	N.A.	25.5	225-6292
Piper Jaffray Balanced	ETR	Lg/Bl	6	(0.2)	5.8	8.0	77	4	80	14	81	70	4.0	109	42.4	866-7778
Piper Jaffray Emerging Gro.	Agg	Sm/Gro	12	(4.9)	6.5	—	100	21	24	55	29	79	4.0	109	209.2	866-7778
Piper Jaffray Sector Perf.	Agg	Md/Bl	9	(2.5)	6.5	11.1	98	2	41	26	47	26	4.0	109	70.1	866-7778
Piper Jaffray Growth & Inc. ★	G&I	Lg/Bl	—	1.1	—	—	—	3	75	14	—	—	4.0	109	65.2	866-7778
Piper Jaffray Value	Gro	Lg/Bl	11	(3.5)	1.4	9.3	85	23	34	20	16	84	4.0	108	176.1	866-7778
PNC Value Equity Inv. ★	Gro	Lg/Val	—	0.7	—	—	—	N.A.	73	76	—	—	4.5	100	12.1	422-6538
Portico Balanced	ETR	Md/Bl	—	(4.3)	—	—	—	2	27	23	—	—	None	N.A.	93.2	228-1024
Portico Equity Index ★	G&I	Lg/Bl	8	1.0	5.6	7.8	88	16	72	31	40	63	None	30	103.6	228-1024
Portico Growth & Income ★	G&I	Md/Bl	8	0.1	4.1	6.5	69	6	59	15	25	21	None	50	158.0	228-1024
Portico MidCore Growth	Gro	Md/Bl	—	(5.3)	—	—	—	1	22	39	—	—	None	N.A.	107.0	228-1024
Portico Special Growth	Gro	Sm/Bl	11	(2.0)	4.3	12.6	92	14	46	30	43	93	None	50	377.4	228-1024
PRA Real Estate Securities ★	Spec	Sm/Bl	11	3.0	13.3	7.0	76	(5)	81	49	80	53	None	74	103.4	435-1405
Preferred Asset Allocation	ETR	Lg/Bl	—	(2.6)	—	—	—	0	48	36	—	—	None	N.A.	61.0	662-4769
Preferred Growth	Gro	Lg/Gro	—	(1.1)	—	—	—	14	53	69	—	—	None	N.A.	241.1	662-4769
Preferred International ★	Intl	Md/Val	—	3.3	—	—	—	14	88	77	—	—	None	N.A.	107.6	662-4769
Preferred Value ★	G&I	Lg/Bl	—	0.5	—	—	—	10	64	28	—	—	None	N.A.	148.6	662-4769
Premier Growth B ★	Intl	Lg/Gro	—	1.2	—	—	—	3	74	—	—	—	4.0⁴	N.A.	11.4	544-4611
Primary Trend	G&I	Md/Bl	8	(0.1)	3.7	5.5	53	0	55	50	5	13	None	66	20.1	443-6544
Principal Pres. Balanced	ETR	Md/Val	—	(1.7)	—	—	—	(4)	62	3	—	—	4.5	114	10.2	826-4600
Principal Pres. Div. Achiev. ★	G&I	Lg/Bl	10	1.2	(0.3)	6.8	N.A.	10	76	2	12	91	4.5	108	20.0	826-4600
Principal Pres. S&P 100 Plus ★	G&I	Lg/Bl	8	1.1	5.2	7.6	81	19	74	39	19	48	4.5	112	39.9	826-4600
Princor Balanced	ETR	Md/Val	7	(3.4)	4.0	7.1	65	4	37	8	79	85	5.0	117	52.1	451-5447
Princor Blue Chip ★	G&I	Lg/Bl	9	3.4	4.0	—	88	11	92	5	30	—	5.0	N.A.	27.5	451-5447
Princor Capital Accumulation ★	Gro	Md/Val	8	0.2	5.6	7.6	61	7	68	29	57	59	5.0	99	282.9	451-5447
Princor Emerging Growth ★	Agg	Sm/Bl	9	3.0	9.9	13.7	98	17	79	29	63	55	5.0	140	94.8	451-5447
Princor Growth ★	Gro	Md/Bl	9	3.2	6.9	13.6	81	25	86	28	62	92	5.0	112	117.2	451-5447
Princor Utilities	Spec	Md/Val	—	(11.1)	—	—	—	(18)	22	14	—	—	5.0	N.A.	56.1	451-5447
Princor World	Intl	Md/Val	11	(5.3)	11.8	7.8	93	15	30	84	71	52	5.0	137	115.1	451-5447
Prudent Speculator	Agg	Sm/Val	12	(8.9)	(1.8)	(0.6)	N.A.	(6)	9	4	13	77	None	197	2.5	444-4778
Prudential Alloc. Cons. Mgd. B	ETR	Md/Bl	6	(3.6)	5.4	7.9	67	1	35	63	39	31	5.0⁴	122	427.6	225-1852
Prudential Alloc. Strategy B	ETR	Lg/Bl	7	(5.2)	3.2	6.8	41	4	20	46	19	57	5.0⁴	121	326.0	225-1852
Prudential Equity B ★	Gro	Lg/Val	8	1.6	11.5	10.4	85	9	79	86	74	14	5.0⁴	104	1,891.0	225-1852
Prudential Equity-Income B	ETR	Md/Val	7	(0.8)	9.0	8.9	79	2	71	92	62	58	5.0⁴	119	919.0	225-1852
Prudential Global B	Intl	Md/Gro	10	(5.5)	9.8	4.4	98	17	26	87	33	38	5.0⁴	138	388.2	225-1852
Prudential Glob. Genesis B	Intl	Sm/Gro	10	(8.9)	13.2	6.8	98	6	11	96	65	55	5.0⁴	182	183.4	225-1852
Prudential Glob. Nat. Res. B	Spec	Md/Gro	11	(5.6)	8.0	1.8	100	5	53	65	38	24	5.0⁴	186	76.3	225-1852
Prudential Growth Opp. B	Agg	Sm/Val	10	(3.9)	11.1	10.7	77	0	31	57	83	19	5.0⁴	124	379.1	225-1852
Prudential IncomeVertible B	ITR	N.A.	8	(4.2)	4.8	5.3	69	6	54	27	17	26	5.0⁴	125	245.4	225-1852
Prudential Multi-Sector B ★	Gro	Md/Bl	8	2.7	8.2	—	64	3	82	90	10	21	5.0⁴	122	164.5	225-1852
Prudential Pacific Growth B	Reg	Md/Gro	—	(9.5)	—	—	—	5	45	80	—	—	5.0⁴	N.A.	418.7	225-1852
Prudential Strategist B	ETR	Md/Bl	10	(7.0)	1.4	3.0	N.A.	4	9	24	18	47	5.0⁴	124	164.3	225-1852
Prudential Utility B	Spec	Md/Val	9	(8.5)	4.8	5.1	62	9	37	38	62	46	5.0⁴	98	3,660.4	225-1852
Putnam Asia Pacific Growth A	Reg	Md/Bl	9	(0.5)	18.9	—	98	5	67	78	88	—	5.75	167	149.7	225-1581
Putnam Convert Inc. Gro. A	ITR	N.A.	3	(1.9)	11.6	10.1	78	6	79	79	91	79	5.75	115	670.2	225-1581
Putnam Corporate Asset	ITR	Lg/Val	2	(3.8)	5.7	7.5	62	N.A.	57	29	45	36	2.5	73	118.6	225-1581
Putnam Diversified Income A	ITR	Int/Md	2	(5.6)	7.1	9.8	61	(9)	32	72	63	42	4.75	115	1,456.0	225-1581
Putnam Dividend Growth A ★	G&I	Md/Val	8	0.8	4.4	—	53	(2)	69	19	21	73	5.75	154	45.3	225-1581
Putnam Equity-Income A ★	ETR	Lg/Val	7	1.3	7.7	7.6	83	(45)	90	84	26	52	5.75	120	303.7	225-1581
Putnam Europe Growth A ★	Reg	Md/Val	10	6.4	11.2	—	95	8	87	43	71	81	5.75	187	82.1	225-1581
Putnam Fund for G/I A	G&I	Lg/Bl	7	(0.3)	8.5	9.3	75	3	50	70	77	10	5.75	112	5,768.2	225-1581
Putnam Global Growth A	Intl	Md/Bl	9	(0.9)	9.4	7.0	93	12	59	35	69	64	5.75	138	1,442.3	225-1581
Putnam Health Sciences A ★	Spec	Lg/Gro	12	15.2	0.9	12.1	N.A.	26	95	4	17	81	5.75	120	793.0	225-1581
Putnam Investors A	Gro	Lg/Bl	9	(3.2)	7.0	8.9	47	16	37	74	48	27	5.75	110	766.3	225-1581

Source: Morningstar Inc. Chicago Ill.; 800-876-5005

Fund name/★ 1994 winner		Type	Style	Risk level	% average annual return to Jan. 1, 1995			Tax analysis		Performance analysis (percentile ranking by type)				Expense analysis		Net assets (millions)	Telephone (800)
					One year	Three years	Five years	% tax efficiency	% tax liability	1994	1993	1992	1991	% max. sales charge	Five-year total per $1,000		
Putnam Managed Income A		ITR	Lg/Val	4	(1.2)	7.3	8.3	70	(8)	92	33	55	48	5.75	$117	$437.8	225-1581
Putnam Natural Resources A		Spec	Md/Bl	11	(2.8)	5.6	3.7	52	(6)	62	30	50	33	5.75	139	119.6	225-1581
Putnam New Opportunities A	★	Gro	Md/Gro	12	3.4	19.9	—	98	15	88	99	98	97	5.75	142	855.7	225-1581
Putnam OTC Emerging Gro. A	★	Agg	Sm/Gro	12	2.2	15.0	14.1	80	29	75	95	53	27	5.75	129	495.5	225-1581
Putnam Util. G&I A		Spec	Md/Val	9	(7.0)	4.4	—	59	(9)	47	30	50	40	5.75	126	522.4	225-1581
Putnam Vista A		Gro	Md/Gro	9	(3.8)	10.0	11.2	73	5	32	75	91	60	5.75	115	656.8	225-1581
Putnam Voyager A	★	Agg	Md/Gro	11	0.4	9.3	13.8	86	20	66	54	41	48	5.75	120	3,362.9	225-1581
Quantitative Gro. & Inc. Ord.		G&I	Lg/Bl	8	(0.7)	5.7	8.4	34	15	44	53	33	49	1.0^4	111	34.0	331-1244
Quantitative Intl. Eq. Ord.	★	Intl	Lg/Val	11	9.0	7.6	(0.3)	95	(1)	99	40	4	25	1.0^4	125	29.2	331-1244
Quantitative Numeric Ord.	★	Agg	Sm/Val	—	4.3	—	—	—	6	85	90	—	—	1.0^4	119	46.3	331-1244
Quest for Value A	★	Gro	Md/Bl	8	0.9	8.2	9.4	80	16	74	26	91	40	5.5	145	223.0	232-3863
Quest for Value Global Eq. A	★	Intl	Lg/Bl	8	3.2	9.4	—	78	20	88	13	75	56	5.5	145	148.0	232-3863
Quest for Value G&I A	★	G&I	Lg/Bl	6	1.1	7.1	—	57	4	75	52	57	—	4.75	161	29.7	232-3863
Quest for Value Opp. A	★	ETR	Lg/Bl	7	4.9	10.2	12.7	91	9	99	22	97	100	5.5	170	163.6	232-3863
Quest for Value Sm. Cap. A		Agg	Sm/Bl	8	(0.3)	12.6	12.9	86	5	60	53	88	41	5.5	162	116.3	232-3863
Rea-Graham Balanced		ETR	Sm/Val	7	(5.3)	(0.3)	1.4	—	(19)	20	2	22	10	4.75	153	15.3	433-1998
Reich & Tang Equity	★	Gro	Md/Bl	5	1.7	10.6	9.4	71	26	80	57	88	11	None	63	92.8	676-6779
Retirement Plan. Conv. Sec. A		ITR	L/Lo	—	(6.7)	—	—	—	(4)	14	81	—	—	4.75	118	47.8	279-0279
Retirement Plan. Fin. Val. A		Spec	Md/Val	10	(4.8)	13.3	—	87	6	57	36	95	—	4.75	134	57.6	279-0279
Retirement Planning Growth B		Gro	Md/Val	12	(8.3)	(0.3)	5.9	N.A.	28	11	46	7	67	4.0^4	136	42.4	279-0279
Reynolds Blue Chip Growth		Gro	Lg/Gro	11	(0.6)	(1.9)	5.1	N.A.	14	59	2	9	54	None	92	23.7	338-1579
Rightime	★	G&I	N.A.	6	0.8	4.3	8.4	43	15	69	24	15	61	None	131	143.0	242-1421
Rightime Blue Chip	★	G&I	N.A.	3	2.2	4.5	7.3	55	22	85	20	15	25	4.75	167	221.1	242-1421
Rightime MidCap	★	G&I	N.A.	5	1.9	6.3	—	79	3	81	12	74	—	4.75	164	67.8	242-1421
Rightime Social Awareness	★	G&I	N.A.	5	1.5	3.8	—	60	(1)	80	3	80	25	4.75	172	7.2	242-1421
RIMCO Monument Stock	★	G&I	Lg/Bl	—	3.4	—	—	—	9	93	89	—	—	3.5	88	57.4	934-3883
Robertson Stephens Contrar.		ETR	Sm/Gro	—	(5.5)	—	—	—	(11)	18	—	—	—	None	N.A.	485.7	766-3863
Robertson Steph. Emer. Gro.	★	Agg	Sm/Gro	12	8.0	4.1	14.4	70	5	94	12	7	67	None	87	176.1	766-3863
Robertson Stephens Val./Gro.	★	Agg	Sm/Bl	—	23.1	—	—	—	13	99	56	—	—	None	N.A.	132.5	766-3863
Rodney Square Intl. Equity		Intl	Lg/Bl	11	(2.9)	4.7	1.9	80	10	47	51	6	37	4.0	131	22.6	336-9970
Rodney Square M/M Growth		Gro	Md/Bl	10	(0.2)	6.6	9.7	67	27	63	62	34	69	4.0	117	65.3	336-9970
Rodney Square M/M Gro.& Inc.		G&I	Md/Val	8	(5.8)	4.6	7.3	2	7	10	69	32	33	4.0	119	6.5	336-9970
Royce Equity-Income		ETR	Sm/Val	3	(3.3)	9.3	7.6	76	(2)	39	56	98	83	None	58	81.7	221-4268
Royce Micro-Cap.	★	Agg	Sm/Val	4	3.6	18.3	—	86	4	80	82	97	—	None	107	26.4	221-4268
Royce Premier	★	Agg	Sm/Val	1	3.3	12.5	—	92	2	80	59	69	—	None	84	196.1	221-4268
Royce Value		Agg	Sm/Val	6	(1.6)	8.1	7.4	76	23	48	23	69	8	None	113	166.7	221-4268
Rydex Nova		Agg	N.A.	—	(6.7)	—	—	—	(7)	16	—	—	—	None	N.A.	58.4	820-0888
Rydex Precious Metals		Spec	Md/Gro	—	(25.4)	—	—	—	(14)	2	—	—	—	None	N.A.	30.9	820-0888
Safeco Equity	★	G&I	Md/Bl	9	9.9	16.3	13.0	88	11	100	99	62	49	None	53	438.2	426-6730
Safeco Growth		Agg	Sm/Bl	12	(1.6)	5.2	10.0	66	20	49	73	5	73	None	50	153.8	426-6730
Safeco Income		ETR	Lg/Val	6	(1.1)	7.5	6.4	80	7	68	51	85	41	None	50	181.2	426-6730
Safeco Northwest		Gro	Sm/Bl	10	(1.6)	4.3	—	86	13	50	7	79	—	None	61	34.5	426-6730
Salomon Bros. Capital		Gro	Md/Val	12	(14.2)	1.7	5.0	N.A.	6	2	73	28	42	None	73	91.1	725-6666
Salomon Bros. Investors		G&I	Lg/Bl	9	(0.8)	7.1	8.2	43	17	42	77	47	58	None	38	353.3	725-6666
Salomon Bros. Opportunity	★	Gro	Md/Val	8	0.8	9.0	7.3	81	45	74	53	78	33	None	69	109.0	725-6666
SBC World Growth		Intl	Lg/Bl	—	(3.7)	—	—	—	4	40	50	—	—	4.8	143	27.9	524-9984
SBSF		G&I	Md/Bl	7	(5.6)	6.6	7.0	57	12	11	94	37	9	None	66	108.0	422-7273
SBSF Capital Growth		Gro	Md/Bl	—	(3.0)	—	—	—	(4)	39	—	—	—	None	79	4.5	422-7273
SBSF Convertible Securities		ITR	N.A.	4	(6.5)	7.7	8.8	69	4	17	90	53	71	None	74	57.9	422-7273
Schafer Value		Gro	Md/Val	8	(4.3)	12.1	12.3	83	1	28	92	92	66	None	113	71.7	343-0481
Schwab 1000		G&I	Lg/Bl	8	(0.1)	5.9	—	90	11	56	38	56	—	None	25	542.6	526-8600
Schwab International Index	★	Intl	Lg/Bl	—	3.8	—	—	—	3	91	—	—	—	None	N.A.	137.7	526-8600
Schwab Small Cap. Index		Agg	Sm/Bl	—	(3.1)	—	—	—	(4)	37	—	—	—	None	N.A.	67.5	526-8600
Scottish Widows Intl.		Intl	Md/Bl	11	(1.4)	7.1	—	71	19	58	45	22	14	5.5	160	35.5	523-5903
Scudder Balanced		ETR	Lg/Bl	—	(2.4)	—	—	—	(4)	50	5	—	—	None	N.A.	64.0	225-2470
Scudder Capital Growth		Gro	Md/Gro	11	(9.9)	5.0	6.6	59	10	7	82	42	75	None	54	1,294.5	225-2470
Scudder Development		Agg	Sm/Gro	12	(5.3)	0.4	12.0	N.A.	29	23	18	10	87	None	71	589.5	225-2470
Scudder Global		Intl	Lg/Val	7	(4.2)	9.5	7.6	93	10	35	33	90	62	None	87	1,131.3	225-2470
Scudder Global Small Co.		Intl	Sm/Gro	9	(7.7)	8.4	—	95	6	18	66	66	—	None	82	239.3	225-2470
Scudder Gold		Spec	Sm/Gro	12	(7.4)	10.3	0.8	92	(1)	43	85	20	8	None	135	125.7	225-2470

Source: Morningstar Inc. Chicago Ill.; 800-876-5005

Fund name/★ 1994 winner	Type	Style	Risk level	% average annual return to Jan. 1, 1995			Tax analysis		Performance analysis (percentile ranking by type)				Expense analysis		Net assets (millions)	Telephone (800)
				One year	Three years	Five years	% tax efficiency	% tax liability	1994	1993	1992	1991	% max. sales charge	Five-year total per $1,000		
Scudder Growth & Income ★	G&I	Md/Bl	7	2.6	9.1	10.2	75	13	89	78	65	52	None	$51	$1,988.7	225-2470
Scudder International	Intl	Lg/Bl	10	(3.0)	8.8	5.6	86	10	45	56	49	34	None	71	2,299.8	225-2470
Scudder Latin America	Reg	Lg/Gro	—	(9.4)	—	—	—	(7)	47	86	—	—	None	N.A.	799.3	225-2470
Scudder Pacific Opp.	Reg	Md/Gro	—	(17.1)	—	—	—	6	20	65	—	—	None	N.A.	447.7	225-2470
Scudder Quality Growth	Gro	Lg/Bl	11	(1.3)	1.7	—	44	8	52	6	39	—	None	69	108.5	225-2470
Scudder Value ★	Gro	Md/Val	—	1.6	—	—	—	1	79	49	—	—	None	N.A.	34.8	225-2470
Security Equity	Gro	Lg/Bl	9	(2.6)	7.3	9.7	54	15	42	62	65	49	5.75	113	349.9	888-2461
Security Growth & Income A	G&I	Lg/Bl	9	(7.8)	1.5	4.3	N.A.	1	6	25	17	20	5.75	123	60.3	888-2461
Security Ultra	Agg	Sm/Bl	12	(6.6)	3.4	5.0	47	13	17	22	30	70	5.75	126	58.1	888-2461
Selected American	G&I	Lg/Val	11	(3.3)	2.6	8.7	N.A.	9	25	11	28	98	None	64	503.0	243-1575
Selected Special	Agg	Sm/Val	10	(2.5)	5.4	6.4	52	15	41	25	33	5	None	77	45.2	243-1575
Seligman Capital A	Agg	Md/Gro	12	(7.1)	2.8	11.3	N.A.	31	14	6	48	59	4.75	111	172.3	221-2783
Seligman Common Stock A	G&I	Lg/Bl	9	(1.9)	6.0	8.3	67	22	33	75	26	62	4.75	100	541.1	221-2783
Seligman Commun./Info. A ★	Spec	Sm/Gro	12	35.3	29.0	24.2	85	27	100	74	80	85	4.75	138	250.9	221-2783
Seligman Frontier A ★	Agg	Sm/Gro	12	7.0	16.2	18.4	71	10	92	88	70	75	4.75	119	61.6	221-2783
Seligman Growth A	Gro	Md/Bl	11	(3.8)	4.4	8.3	18	23	32	24	68	61	4.75	103	557.5	221-2783
Selig. Henders. Glob. Emer. A ★	Intl	Sm/Gro	—	10.1	—	—	—	13	100	72	—	—	4.75	N.A.	46.2	221-2450
Seligman Henderson Intl. A ★	Intl	Lg/Bl	—	2.6	—	—	—	11	83	62	—	—	4.75	138	62.9	221-2450
Seligman Income A	ITR	Int/Md	4	(5.4)	8.9	9.0	77	(2)	37	75	85	81	4.75	107	309.3	221-2783
Sentinel Balanced	ETR	Lg/Bl	6	(3.6)	3.9	7.1	63	5	36	29	33	42	5.0	111	228.0	282-3863
Sentinel Common Stock	G&I	Lg/Bl	9	(1.2)	4.5	7.8	61	41	38	34	27	71	5.0	102	842.0	282-3863
Sentinel Emerging Growth ★	Agg	Sm/Bl	—	0.1	—	—	—	26	63	—	—	—	5.0	126	90.0	282-3863
Sentinel Growth	Gro	Md/Bl	10	(7.5)	0.4	5.1	N.A.	33	14	16	35	19	5.0	123	50.2	282-3863
Sentinel World	Intl	Lg/Val	—	1.1	—	—	—	4	73	—	—	—	5.0	152	42.5	282-3863
Sentry	Gro	Md/Bl	8	(1.1)	4.0	8.8	57	30	54	23	45	27	None	50	75.7	533-7827
Sequoia[1] ★	Gro	Md/Val	8	3.7	8.5	11.5	77	32	90	52	59	64	None	56	1,548.3	245-4500[6]
Seven Seas Growth & Income	G&I	Lg/Bl	—	(0.3)	—	—	—	(11)	51	—	—	—	None	N.A.	26.5	647-7327
Seven Seas Matrix Equity	Gro	Lg/Bl	—	(0.4)	—	—	—	1	61	66	—	—	None	31	131.0	647-7327
Seven Seas S&P 500 Index ★	G&I	Lg/Bl	—	1.3	—	—	—	0	79	25	—	—	None	N.A.	396.8	647-7327
Seven Seas Small Cap.	Agg	Md/Bl	—	(0.9)	—	—	—	(18)	56	32	—	—	None	N.A.	4.1	647-7327
Shadow Stock	Agg	Sm/Val	8	(4.3)	9.0	7.9	67	9	29	39	76	23	None	69	33.5	422-2766
Sierra Emerging Growth A	Agg	Sm/Gro	10	(0.3)	12.0	—	89	8	59	74	66	21	4.5	128	146.3	222-5852
Sierra Growth & Income A ★	G&I	Lg/Bl	9	0.1	4.6	7.1	53	3	58	48	10	46	4.5	121	152.2	222-5852
Sierra Growth A ★	Gro	Md/Bl	—	0.7	—	—	—	4	72	—	—	—	5.75	N.A.	122.1	222-5852
Sierra International Growth A	Intl	Lg/Val	11	(1.3)	5.3	—	85	7	58	38	10	47	4.5	138	122.3	222-5852
Sit Balanced	ETR	Lg/Gro	—	(0.3)	—	—	—	(3)	79	—	—	—	None	N.A.	1.5	332-5580
Sit Growth	Gro	Md/Gro	12	(0.5)	1.9	11.4	43	25	60	33	7	95	None	46	300.2	332-5580
Sit Growth & Income ★	G&I	Lg/Gro	10	2.8	3.6	7.7	58	18	90	6	19	81	None	82	36.1	332-5580
Sit International Growth	Intl	Lg/Bl	9	(3.0)	13.9	—	97	23	45	88	79	—	None	101	66.0	332-5580
Skyline Europe[3]	Reg	Lg/Val	—	(13.9)	—	—	—	(19)	—	—	—	—	None	N.A.	13.0	458-5222
Skyline Special Equities II	Agg	Sm/Val	—	(1.5)	—	—	—	2	49	—	—	—	None	N.A.	89.5	458-5222
Skyline Special Equities[1]	Agg	Sm/Val	7	(1.2)	20.0	18.3	83	12	55	77	100	40	None	120	202.0	458-5222
Smallcap World	Intl	Sm/Gro	9	(2.9)	10.5	—	85	16	48	29	97	94	5.75	125	3,482.7	421-4120
Smith Bar. Agg. Gro. A	Agg	Md/Gro	12	(1.6)	6.7	10.2	95	47	48	68	17	30	5.0	118	176.4	451-2010
Smith Barney App. A	Gro	Lg/Bl	8	(0.8)	4.5	7.6	70	14	57	31	37	22	5.0	105	1,697.6	451-2010
Smith Barney Cap. App. C	Gro	Lg/Bl	—	(8.5)	—	—	—	5	10	36	—	—	1.0[4]	N.A.	71.3	544-7835
Smith Barney Convertible B	ITR	N.A.	6	(6.8)	6.0	6.3	78	(21)	12	34	73	55	5.0[4]	112	45.1	451-2010
Smith B. Div. St. Inc. B	ITR	N.A.	3	(3.4)	4.9	8.4	49	(8)	64	36	13	18	4.5[4]	98	2,280.1	451-2010
Smith Barney Euro. B	Reg	Lg/Val	11	(3.1)	2.9	2.1	100	5	59	21	35	19	5.0[4]	151	28.5	451-2010
Smith Barney Val. A ★	Gro	Lg/Bl	7	1.1	11.6	10.9	77	9	—	—	—	—	5.0	128	257.6	451-2010
Smith Barney Glob. Opp. A	Intl	Lg/Bl	11	(3.8)	2.1	1.2	63	5	38	2	23	41	5.0	145	51.8	451-2010
Smith Barney G&I A	G&I	Md/Bl	—	(4.3)	—	—	—	(1)	18	27	—	—	5.0	N.A.	95.0	451-2010
Smith Barney Inc. & Growth A	G&I	Lg/Bl	8	(4.2)	6.1	6.4	68	8	20	82	43	37	5.0	94	559.6	544-7835
Smith Barney Intl. Eq. A	Intl	Md/Bl	11	(8.9)	11.8	11.2	98	9	11	93	70	98	5.0	128	519.2	544-7835
Smith Bar. P.M.& Min. A	Spec	Md/Gro	12	(9.6)	12.6	2.0	100	(16)	30	87	28	15	5.0	153	38.3	451-2010
Smith Bar. Prem. Tot. Ret. B ★	ETR	Lg/Val	4	2.9	8.8	11.1	74	6	96	39	88	74	5.0[4]	102	1,386.6	451-2010
Smith Bar. Sp. Eq. B	Agg	Sm/Gro	12	(6.3)	10.5	8.0	98	14	18	94	38	33	5.0[4]	133	93.2	451-2010
Smith Barney Strat. Inv. B	ETR	Lg/Val	7	(2.1)	6.2	8.2	57	1	54	69	38	65	5.0[4]	121	219.5	451-2010
Smith Barney Tele. Gr A	Spec	Md/Gro	11	(6.4)	14.9	9.7	93	4	50	75	85	47	5.0	125	86.0	573-9410[14]
Smith Bar. Tele. Inc.[1]	Spec	Lg/Bl	11	(1.9)	8.0	5.0	54	67	66	39	71	27	5.0	51	67.8	573-9410[14]

Source: Morningstar Inc. Chicago Ill.; 800-876-5005

| Fund name/★ 1994 winner | Type | Style | Risk level | % average annual return to Jan. 1, 1995 | | | Tax analysis | | Performance analysis (percentile ranking by type) | | | | Expense analysis | | Net assets (millions) | Telephone (800) |
				One year	Three years	Five years	% tax efficiency	% tax liability	1994	1993	1992	1991	% max. sales charge	Five-year total per $1,000		
Smith Barney Utility B	Spec	Lg/Val	8	(10.1)	2.5	6.2	21	(10)	25	22	51	49	5.0⁴	$96	$1,501.6	451-2010
Smith Barney Utility A	Spec	Md/Val	8	(8.6)	2.8	—	23	(5)	35	18	54	43	5.0	101	69.3	544-7835
SoGen Gold	Spec	Md/Bl	—	(0.8)	—	—	—	(3)	71	—	—	—	3.75	N.A.	47.8	628-0252
SoGen International¹ ★	ETR	Sm/Bl	2	2.5	12.1	10.5	90	12	94	99	64	22	3.75	110	1,822.5	628-0252
SoGen Overseas ★	Intl	Md/Val	—	7.8	—	—	—	1	98	—	—	—	3.75	N.A.	437.9	628-0252
Sound Shore ★	Gro	Md/Bl	6	0.3	10.8	10.0	74	4	69	49	96	38	None	75	56.7	551-1980
SouthTrust Vulcan Stock	Gro	Lg/Gro	—	(1.7)	—	—	—	0	48	14	—	—	4.5	69	118.9	239-7470
Stagecoach Diversified Inc. ★	ETR	Lg/Val	—	0.1	—	—	—	(1)	83	48	—	—	4.5	98	44.8	222-8222
Star Relative Value	G&I	Lg/Val	8	(2.6)	7.2	—	91	5	29	64	73	—	4.5	111	74.0	677-3863
State St. Exchange¹ ★	Gro	Lg/Bl	9	3.5	5.0	7.1	77	N.A.	89	19	40	31	None	N.A.	200.6	562-0032
State St. Res. Global Ener. A	Spec	Sm/Gro	12	(4.4)	10.5	—	100	(16)	58	71	49	3	4.5	136	26.9	882-3302
SteinRoe Capital Opp.	Agg	Sm/Gro	11	0.0	9.3	8.6	100	17	62	89	18	74	None	58	159.7	338-2550
SteinRoe Prime Equities	G&I	Md/Bl	8	(0.1)	7.4	10.0	76	19	54	56	69	80	None	54	119.6	338-2550
SteinRoe Special	Gro	Md/Gro	8	(3.3)	9.9	10.9	80	19	36	84	79	45	None	55	1,213.6	338-2550
SteinRoe Stock	Gro	Lg/Gro	10	(3.8)	2.3	9.6	N.A.	35	32	14	52	79	None	51	307.9	338-2550
SteinRoe Total Return	ETR	Lg/Bl	7	(4.1)	5.1	8.2	55	8	29	48	57	79	None	47	216.1	338-2550
Stellar Investment	ETR	Md/Val	7	(2.1)	5.0	—	81	(1)	55	57	24	—	4.5	125	50.6	677-3863
STI Classic Cap. Gro. Inv.	Gro	Lg/Bl	—	(8.0)	—	—	—	(1)	12	36	—	—	3.75	N.A.	154.0	428-6970
Stock & Bond A	ETR	Lg/Val	5	(1.9)	5.2	6.7	72	4	59	34	47	17	None	57	121.0	245-5040
Stratton Growth ★	Gro	Md/Val	7	7.2	6.8	6.8	68	14	95	25	39	9	None	75	26.6	634-5726
Stratton Monthly Dividend	ETR	Md/Val	10	(12.1)	1.1	6.1	—	(24)	3	12	76	88	None	60	121.9	634-5726
Strong American Utilities	Spec	Lg/Val	—	(2.6)	—	—	—	(10)	64	—	—	—	None	N.A.	37.6	368-1030
Strong Asia Pacific	Reg	Md/Bl	—	(5.3)	—	—	—	(8)	57	—	—	—	None	N.A.	59.0	368-1030
Strong Common Stock¹	Agg	Md/Gro	8	(0.5)	14.6	19.0	90	11	59	87	86	65	None	78	791.0	368-1030
Strong Discovery	Agg	Md/Gro	11	(5.7)	5.5	13.9	55	(1)	21	73	16	82	None	82	381.2	368-1030
Strong Growth ★	Gro	Md/Gro	—	17.3	—	—	—	3	100	—	—	—	None	N.A.	91.7	368-1030
Strong International Stock	Intl	Md/Val	—	(1.6)	—	—	—	3	57	86	—	—	None	N.A.	267.7	368-1030
Strong Investment	ETR	Md/Bl	5	(1.5)	5.2	7.4	55	(1)	64	68	17	22	None	66	250.1	368-1030
Strong Opportunity ★	Gro	Md/Bl	8	3.2	13.6	11.4	91	11	86	86	89	37	None	82	794.5	368-1030
Strong Total Return	G&I	Md/Gro	9	(1.4)	6.7	8.6	94	(2)	38	96	6	82	None	70	589.1	368-1030
SunAmerica Bal. Assets B	ETR	Lg/Bl	8	(2.6)	5.5	7.8	41	0	48	65	30	68	4.0⁴	114	175.7	858-8850
SunAmerica Blue Chip Gro. B	Gro	Lg/Bl	10	(4.8)	7.2	3.7	84	6	25	81	54	32	4.0⁴	144	71.0	858-8850
SunAmerica MidCap Gro. A	Gro	Md/Gro	11	(4.8)	5.9	7.6	66	1	25	43	72	74	5.75	147	31.2	858-8850
SunAmerica Sm. Co. Gro. A ★	Agg	Sm/Gro	11	4.7	11.3	9.2	90	13	87	34	66	60	5.75	154	41.1	858-8850
Target International Equity ★	Intl	Lg/Val	—	0.3	—	—	—	(1)	—	—	—	—	None	153	192.8	225-1852
Target Large Cap. Growth	Gro	Lg/Gro	—	(0.7)	—	—	—	1	—	—	—	—	None	136	142.5	225-1852
Target Large Cap. Value ★	G&I	Lg/Bl	—	2.2	—	—	—	1	—	—	—	—	None	136	141.5	225-1852
Target Small Cap. Growth	Agg	Sm/Bl	—	(2.2)	—	—	—	0	—	—	—	—	None	136	94.6	225-1852
Target Small Cap. Value	Agg	Sm/Bl	—	(11.1)	—	—	—	(9)	—	—	—	—	None	136	84.5	225-1852
TCW/DW Balanced	ETR	Lg/Val	—	(9.7)	—	—	—	(9)	5	—	—	—	None	N.A.	138.4	392-2550⁶
TCW/DW Core Equity	Gro	Md/Val	—	(7.8)	—	—	—	9	13	80	—	—	5.0⁴	N.A.	694.3	392-2550⁶
TCW/DW Income & Growth	ETR	Int/Lo	—	(3.3)	—	—	—	(15)	39	—	—	—	None	N.A.	58.1	392-2550⁶
TCW/DW Latin American Gro.	Reg	N.A.	—	(23.7)	—	—	—	3	5	60	—	—	5.0⁴	N.A.	444.9	526-3143
TCW/DW Small Cap. Growth	Agg	Sm/Gro	—	(4.6)	—	—	—	(10)	27	—	—	—	5.0⁴	N.A.	61.1	392-2550⁶
Templeton American ★	ETR	Md/Val	8	1.6	8.4	—	84	16	92	77	61	—	5.0⁴	176	37.9	292-9293
Templeton Capital Accum. ★	Intl	Md/Val	8	2.7	15.2	—	93	11	84	70	96	—	9.0	54	43.1	292-9293
Templeton Developing Mkt.	Intl	Md/Gro	10	(8.6)	12.9	—	94	9	12	99	13	—	5.75	160	2,000.9	292-9293
Templeton Foreign ★	Intl	Lg/Val	9	0.4	11.2	9.5	84	8	67	59	68	67	5.75	122	5,305.8	292-9293
Templeton Global Opp.	Intl	Md/Val	10	(4.0)	12.3	—	78	13	36	65	98	96	5.75	124	476.6	292-9293
Templeton Growth ★	Intl	Lg/Val	8	0.8	11.7	10.7	76	14	71	41	88	92	5.75	117	5,475.7	292-9293
Templeton Real Estate Sec.	Spec	Sm/Val	8	(7.7)	8.5	8.4	92	(5)	42	72	41	67	5.75	155	128.5	292-9293
Templeton Smaller Co. Gro.	Intl	Sm/Val	9	(4.6)	9.3	8.9	72	18	32	36	85	99	5.75	131	1,275.9	292-9293
Templeton World ★	Intl	Lg/Val	9	0.9	11.6	8.7	72	16	71	46	82	91	5.75	115	5,020.2	292-9293
Third Avenue Value	Gro	Sm/Val	6	(1.5)	13.9	—	94	8	51	92	96	47	4.5	176	183.4	443-1021
Tocqueville	Gro	Md/Val	7	(0.8)	13.8	10.9	78	20	57	90	96	2	None	98	27.9	697-3863
Torray ★	Gro	Md/Val	8	2.5	9.7	—	90	10	81	24	94	7	None	69	23.4	493-4600¹⁵
Tower Capital Appreciation	G&I	Lg/Bl	9	(2.6)	3.7	7.5	36	3	30	69	6	74	3.0	89	128.3	999-0124
Trademark Equity ★	Gro	Lg/Bl	—	0.2	—	—	—	1	68	—	—	—	None	N.A.	135.3	566-3653¹⁶
Triflex ★	ETR	Lg/Bl	8	0.8	3.2	6.8	36	2	88	9	14	51	5.75	117	19.0	231-4639
T. Rowe Price Balanced	ETR	Lg/Bl	6	(2.1)	6.0	9.3	69	5	56	59	47	37	None	55	386.7	638-5660

Source: Morningstar Inc. Chicago Ill.; 800-876-5005

Fund name/★ 1994 winner	Type	Style	Risk level	One year	Three years	Five years	% tax efficiency	% tax liability	1994	1993	1992	1991	% max. sales charge	Five-year total per $1,000	Net assets (millions)	Telephone (800)
T. Rowe Price Blue Chip Gro. ★	Gro	Lg/Bl	—	0.8	—	—	—	3	73	—	—	—	None	$69	$37.6	638-5660
T. Rowe Price Capital App. ★	Gro	Md/Bl	2	3.8	9.5	9.5	81	12	91	67	58	8	None	60	648.1	638-5660
T. Rowe Price Dividend Gro. ★	G&I	Lg/Bl	—	2.2	—	—	—	3	84	93	—	—	None	N.A.	51.0	638-5660
T. Rowe Price Equity Index ★	G&I	Lg/Bl	8	1.0	5.8	—	85	5	71	35	43	57	None	50	266.4	638-5660
T. Rowe Price Equity-Inc. ★	ETR	Lg/Bl	5	4.5	11.1	9.9	80	10	99	72	94	55	None	54	3,143.9	638-5660
T. Rowe Price Euro. Stock ★	Reg	Lg/Bl	11	4.1	7.7	—	95	9	75	34	54	46	None	81	355.5	638-5660
T. Rowe Price Gro. & Inc.	G&I	Lg/Bl	7	(0.1)	9.2	8.7	83	12	53	57	91	76	None	47	1,219.8	638-5660
T. Rowe Price Growth Stock ★	Gro	Lg/Gro	9	0.9	7.3	9.6	72	31	75	67	34	44	None	46	2,054.8	638-5660
T. Rowe Price Intl. Dis.	Intl	Sm/Bl	11	(7.6)	8.0	4.1	91	8	19	90	16	32	None	82	467.1	638-5660
T. Rowe Price Intl. Stock	Intl	Lg/Bl	11	(0.8)	10.3	7.2	88	13	60	73	41	58	None	58	5,982.0	638-5660
T. Rowe Price Japan ★	Reg	Md/Bl	12	15.1	6.3	—	76	5	99	17	21	—	None	82	177.8	638-5660
T. Rowe Price Latin America	Reg	N.A.	—	(15.9)	—	—	—	(3)	27	—	—	—	None	107	195.4	638-5660
T. Rowe Price Mid-Cap. Gro.	Gro	Sm/Gro	—	0.3	—	—	—	9	69	96	—	—	None	N.A.	96.4	638-5660
T. Rowe Price New Am. Gro.	Gro	Md/Gro	11	(7.4)	6.1	11.2	89	19	15	74	60	94	None	69	636.8	638-5660
T. Rowe Price New Asia	Reg	Md/Gro	12	(19.2)	17.2	—	90	8	14	91	96	91	None	79	2,061.7	638-5660
T. Rowe Price New Era ★	Spec	Lg/Gro	7	5.2	7.4	5.3	74	23	84	37	37	42	None	45	987.7	638-5660
T. Rowe Price New Horizons	Agg	Sm/Gro	12	0.3	10.6	13.3	68	33	65	72	45	55	None	51	1,617.3	638-5660
T. Rowe Price OTC Sec. ★	Agg	Sm/Bl	9	0.1	10.5	8.3	56	30	63	54	60	19	None	69	190.2	638-5660
T. Rowe Price Science/Tech. ★	Spec	Md/Gro	12	15.8	19.6	22.0	89	20	96	58	83	89	None	69	844.7	638-5660
T. Rowe Price Sm.-Cap. Val.[1]	Agg	Sm/Val	6	(1.4)	13.7	11.8	90	21	53	79	87	13	None	69	415.8	638-5660
T. Rowe Price Spectrum Gro. ★	Gro	Lg/Gro	7	1.4	9.6	—	78	7	78	85	44	31	None	49	862.4	638-5660
T. Rowe Price Spectrum Inc.	ITR	Int/Md	2	(1.9)	5.9	—	62	(5)	77	31	27	24	None	49	622.6	638-5660
Tweedy Browne Amer. Val.	Gro	Md/Val	—	(0.6)	—	—	—	(1)	60	—	—	—	None	N.A.	30.9	432-4789
Tweedy Browne Global Val. ★	Intl	Md/Val	—	4.4	—	—	—	1	93	—	—	—	None	N.A.	556.3	432-4789
20th Century Balanced Inv.	ETR	Lg/Gro	10	(0.1)	0.2	8.5	N.A.	6	82	17	3	100	None	55	683.2	345-2021
20th Century Giftrust Inv. ★	Agg	Sm/Gro	12	13.5	20.7	22.0	87	31	96	92	77	96	None	55	274.2	345-2021
20th Century Growth Inv.	Gro	Lg/Bl	12	(1.5)	(0.7)	9.7	N.A.	23	51	18	5	98	None	55	4,158.0	345-2021
20th Century Heritage Inv.	Gro	Md/Gro	11	(6.3)	7.5	9.0	75	8	19	84	62	54	None	55	851.6	345-2021
20th Century Intl. Equity	Intl	Md/Bl	10	(4.8)	12.5	—	89	8	31	80	91	—	None	55	1,272.4	345-2021
20th Century Select Inv.	Gro	Lg/Bl	11	(8.0)	0.3	5.7	N.A.	14	12	63	4	36	None	55	3,995.2	345-2021
20th Century Ultra Inv.	Agg	Lg/Gro	12	(3.6)	5.9	19.4	95	19	34	70	16	96	None	55	9,850.8	345-2021
20th Century Value ★	G&I	Md/Val	—	4.0	—	—	—	(5)	94	—	—	—	None	N.A.	153.1	345-2021
20th Century Vista Inv. ★	Agg	Sm/Gro	12	4.7	2.6	9.6	27	26	86	7	9	91	None	55	820.2	345-2021
UMB Heartland ★	Agg	Sm/Val	3	0.7	5.8	3.4	89	2	69	9	46	1	None	58	28.0	422-2766
UMB Stock ★	Gro	Md/Bl	7	2.8	6.8	8.2	69	10	83	43	42	17	None	48	120.9	422-2766
United Accumulative ★	Gro	Lg/Bl	8	0.1	7.6	6.7	62	1	67	35	80	14	5.75	103	967.6	366-5465
United Continental Income	ETR	Lg/Bl	6	(0.4)	7.6	8.0	81	6	77	57	79	62	5.75	126	417.8	366-5465
United Gold & Gov.	ETR	Sm/Gro	12	(17.4)	8.1	0.1	97	(74)	1	100	1	3	5.75	180	37.5	366-5465
United Income	ETR	Lg/Bl	8	(1.8)	8.1	9.1	88	30	61	80	83	81	5.75	105	3,144.3	366-5465
United International Growth ★	Intl	Md/Val	11	1.8	13.8	8.6	86	25	77	85	58	69	5.75	144	638.5	366-5465
United New Concepts ★	Agg	Sm/Gro	11	11.3	8.8	19.9	90	32	96	24	21	99	5.75	143	273.2	366-5465
United Retirement Shares	ETR	Lg/Bl	5	(0.4)	8.2	9.5	79	12	76	54	91	37	5.75	127	473.6	366-5465
United Science & Tech. ★	Spec	Md/Gro	12	9.8	4.6	11.9	70	38	90	14	30	88	5.75	130	496.4	366-5465
United Svcs. All American	G&I	Md/Bl	9	(5.3)	3.2	4.3	47	13	13	44	25	41	None	98	9.2	873-8637
United Svcs. Euro. Income	Reg	N.A.	11	(0.6)	(0.5)	(5.1)	N.A.	(25)	65	8	29	36	None	165	2.0	873-8637
United Svcs. Glob. Resource	Spec	Md/Gro	11	(9.7)	1.3	(1.7)	41	5	28	44	31	30	None	136	20.4	873-8637
United Svcs. Gold Shares	Spec	N.A.	12	(2.7)	2.3	(9.9)	68	(62)	63	100	2	4	None	101	291.6	873-8637
United Svc. Growth	Gro	Sm/Gro	12	(5.2)	(1.7)	0.9	N.A.	28	22	54	1	23	None	138	3.3	873-8637
United Svcs. Income	ITR	Md/Val	10	(10.3)	4.5	3.6	66	8	4	84	31	10	None	114	10.0	873-8637
United Svcs. Real Estate	Spec	Sm/Val	12	(11.6)	(2.5)	2.9	N.A.	(27)	18	5	43	85	None	98	11.0	873-8637
United Services World Gold	Spec	Sm/Gro	12	(16.9)	14.5	0.9	100	(14)	6	95	27	17	None	129	182.5	873-8637
United Vanguard ★	Gro	Lg/Gro	10	6.2	7.8	9.0	85	29	94	60	18	24	5.75	134	1,017.7	366-5465
USAA Investment Balanced	ETR	Lg/Val	5	(2.6)	5.1	6.2	69	0	47	62	28	10	None	51	124.7	382-8722
USAA Inv. Cornerstone	ETR	Md/Bl	7	(1.0)	9.2	6.6	83	3	68	97	35	13	None	65	841.3	382-8722
USAA Investment Gold	Spec	Md/Gro	12	(9.4)	9.7	(1.5)	99	(54)	32	84	24	12	None	78	158.5	382-8722
USAA Investment Intl. ★	Intl	Lg/Bl	9	2.7	12.8	8.1	92	6	85	71	64	44	None	92	337.8	382-8722
USAA Inv. World Gro. ★	Intl	Lg/Bl	—	0.6	—	—	—	5	69	11	—	—	None	N.A.	185.3	382-8722
USAA Mutual Agg. Gro.	Agg	Sm/Gro	12	(0.8)	(0.6)	8.2	N.A.	8	56	15	3	87	None	48	283.8	382-8722
USAA Mutual Growth ★	Gro	Md/Bl	9	3.3	6.9	9.3	57	1	88	28	61	25	None	59	677.2	382-8722
USAA Mutual G&I ★	G&I	Lg/Val	—	1.3	—	—	—	(1)	77	—	—	—	None	N.A.	150.5	382-8722

Source: Morningstar Inc. Chicago Ill.; 800-876-5005

Fund name/★ 1994 winner	Type	Style	Risk level	% average annual return to Jan. 1, 1995			Tax analysis		Performance analysis (percentile ranking by type)				Expense analysis		Net assets (millions)	Telephone (800)
				One year	Three years	Five years	% tax efficiency	% tax liability	1994	1993	1992	1991	% max. sales charge	Five-year total per $1,000		
USAA Mutual Income	ITR	L/Hi	5	(5.2)	4.1	7.7	46	(9)	44	17	35	22	None	$23	$1,611.8	382-8722
USAA Mutual Income Stock	ETR	Lg/Val	8	(0.7)	6.1	8.4	69	(3)	72	42	55	69	None	39	1,171.7	382-8722
USAffinity Green	Gro	N.A.	—	(8.0)	—	—	—	(76)	12	85	—	—	4.5	172	2.0	800-3030
USAffinity Growth	Gro	N.A.	—	(6.7)	—	—	—	(2)	17	65	—	—	4.5	148	5.9	800-3030
USAffinity Growth & Income	G&I	N.A.	—	(3.0)	—	—	—	0	28	43	—	—	4.5	148	3.2	800-3030
UST Master Aging of America	Gro	Md/Bl	—	(2.9)	—	—	—	(2)	40	25	—	—	4.5	N.A.	17.0	233-1136
UST Master Business & Ind. ★	Gro	Md/Val	—	2.6	—	—	—	5	82	100	—	—	4.5	N.A.	26.2	233-1136
UST Master Comm. & Enter. ★	Gro	Md/Gro	—	1.2	—	—	—	10	77	100	—	—	4.5	N.A.	28.4	233-1136
UST Master Early Life Cycle ★	Agg	Sm/Bl	—	5.3	—	—	—	6	89	90	—	—	4.5	N.A.	42.3	233-1136
UST Master Emerging Amer.	Intl	Md/Bl	—	(11.6)	—	—	—	9	7	76	—	—	4.5	N.A.	48.5	233-1136
UST Master Envir.-Rel. Prods.	Gro	Sm/Bl	—	(6.4)	—	—	—	(15)	18	1	—	—	4.5	N.A.	4.4	233-1136
UST Master Equity ★	Gro	Md/Gro	9	0.2	10.7	9.9	91	24	67	70	87	48	4.5	107	120.9	233-1136
UST Master Glob. Competitors	Gro	Lg/Bl	—	(1.6)	—	—	—	1	49	71	—	—	4.5	N.A.	17.4	233-1136
UST Master Income & Growth	G&I	Md/Bl	6	(4.3)	11.2	7.3	89	3	18	92	98	37	4.5	111	103.9	233-1136
UST Master International	Intl	Lg/Bl	11	(2.0)	6.6	3.1	92	6	55	57	14	5	4.5	127	64.9	233-1136
UST Master L/T Supp. Energy	Spec	Md/Bl	—	(2.7)	—	—	—	(4)	62	31	—	—	4.5	N.A.	13.6	233-1136
UST Master Pacific/Asia	Reg	Md/Val	—	(14.7)	—	—	—	(2)	30	82	—	—	4.5	N.A.	53.1	233-1136
UST Master Pan-European	Reg	Lg/Val	—	0.0	—	—	—	4	69	10	—	—	4.5	N.A.	41.6	233-1136
UST Master Prod. Enhanc. ★	Gro	Md/Bl	—	0.7	—	—	—	1	72	40	—	—	4.5	N.A.	17.1	233-1136
Valley Forge ★	Gro	Md/Val	1	5.9	10.7	6.7	81	(1)	94	73	58	1	None	77	10.8	548-1942
Value Line	Gro	Md/Bl	11	(4.5)	2.2	10.2	N.A.	20	27	27	26	90	None	47	273.1	223-0818
Value Line Convertible	ITR	N.A.	7	(5.3)	7.4	8.9	59	(6)	42	58	75	77	None	63	46.1	223-0818
Value Line Income	ITR	Md/Bl	8	(4.4)	1.8	6.7	N.A.	(1)	50	9	3	75	None	49	133.9	223-0818
Value Line Lev. Gro. Inv.	Agg	Md/Gro	12	(3.7)	3.0	9.5	42	23	32	43	8	38	None	51	261.7	223-0818
Value Line Sp. Situations ★	Agg	Sm/Gro	12	1.0	3.3	7.8	68	33	71	32	4	18	None	60	88.7	223-0818
Van Eck Asia Dynasty A	Reg	Md/Gro	—	(18.7)	—	—	—	6	15	—	—	—	4.75	144	88.4	544-4653
Van Eck Global Balanced A	ETR	N.A.	—	(3.9)	—	—	—	N.A.	30	—	—	—	4.75	N.A.	14.8	544-4653
Van Eck Gold/Resources	Spec	Md/Gro	12	(15.6)	12.8	0.3	100	(34)	8	91	26	14	5.75	138	175.2	544-4653
Van Eck Intl. Growth[2]	Over	Md/Val	—	(7.4)	—	—	—	12	N.A.	—	—	—	4.75	151	0.3	544-4653
Van Eck Intl. Investors Gold	Spec	Md/Gro	12	(1.0)	14.4	2.3	92	39	68	99	4	25	5.75	119	610.8	544-4653
Van Eck World Trends ★	Intl	Lg/Bl	10	2.3	4.6	3.5	37	58	83	9	19	40	4.75	138	25.6	544-4653
Vanguard Asset Allocation	ETR	Lg/Bl	7	(2.3)	6.0	8.6	74	0	51	59	51	58	None	29	1,117.0	851-4999
Vanguard Balanced Index	ETR	Lg/Bl	—	(1.6)	—	—	—	(2)	64	30	—	—	None	62	392.0	851-4999
Vanguard Convertible Sec.	ITR	N.A.	8	(5.7)	8.4	9.5	74	(4)	30	45	89	87	None	47	175.5	851-4999
Vanguard Equity-Income	ETR	Lg/Val	7	(1.6)	7.2	6.4	76	5	63	69	66	56	None	25	868.8	851-4999
Vanguard Explorer ★	Agg	Sm/Gro	10	0.5	9.5	12.8	81	14	68	39	54	61	None	38	1,092.6	851-4999
Vanguard Index 500 ★	G&I	Lg/Bl	8	1.2	6.1	8.5	86	11	76	42	47	64	None	60	9,204.0	851-4999
Vanguard Ind. Extended Mkt.	Agg	Sm/Bl	9	(1.8)	8.2	9.1	91	13	47	36	52	29	None	71	956.9	851-4999
Vanguard Index Growth ★	Gro	Lg/Gro	—	2.9	—	—	—	2	84	9	—	—	None	61	79.3	851-4999
Vanguard Sm. Cap. Stock	Agg	Sm/Bl	10	(0.5)	11.8	10.7	89	8	58	56	78	35	None	70	585.1	851-4999
Vanguard Ind. Tot. Stk. Mkt.	G&I	Lg/Bl	—	(0.2)	—	—	—	4	52	47	—	—	None	64	761.1	851-4999
Vanguard Index Value	G&I	Lg/Val	—	(0.6)	—	—	—	(2)	44	87	—	—	None	61	298.4	851-4999
Vanguard Intl. Equity Euro. ★	Reg	Lg/Val	11	1.9	8.4	—	92	11	70	38	57	64	None	77	711.8	851-4999
Vanguard Intl. Eq. Pacific ★	Reg	Lg/Gro	12	12.9	7.8	—	94	14	97	51	13	57	None	77	688.6	851-4999
Vanguard Intl. Growth ★	Intl	Lg/Bl	10	0.8	11.2	4.8	96	14	70	81	30	4	None	32	2,947.2	851-4999
Vanguard Preferred Stock	ITR	L/Med	5	(7.9)	4.1	7.7	44	(16)	7	38	37	30	None	33	286.2	851-4999
Vanguard/Primecap ★	Gro	Md/Bl	10	11.4	12.8	13.2	92	24	98	77	56	41	None	38	1,472.4	851-4999
Vanguard Quantitative	G&I	Lg/Val	9	(0.6)	6.6	9.0	65	5	46	64	41	66	None	22	584.8	851-4999
Vanguard Sp. Energy	Spec	Md/Bl	12	(1.6)	9.7	5.5	82	0	67	60	46	22	None	30	458.6	851-4999
Vanguard Sp. Gold & P.M.	Spec	Md/Gro	12	(5.4)	13.8	4.3	95	12	54	96	7	28	None	32	637.2	851-4999
Vanguard Sp. Health Care ★	Spec	Md/Bl	11	9.5	6.4	15.6	69	22	89	24	33	80	None	30	692.7	851-4999
Vanguard Sp. Utilities Inc.	Spec	Md/Val	—	(8.6)	—	—	—	(14)	36	34	—	—	None	22	566.8	851-4999
Vanguard STAR	ETR	Lg/Val	5	(0.3)	6.9	7.9	75	5	79	38	77	49	None	21	3,756.8	851-4999
Vanguard/Trustees' Eq. Intl. ★	Intl	Md/Val	10	5.3	7.8	3.9	87	17	94	30	17	23	None	24	1,110.2	851-4999
Vanguard/Trustees' Eq. U.S.	G&I	Md/Bl	10	(3.9)	6.2	6.8	77	4	22	84	34	40	None	36	114.8	851-4999
Vanguard US Growth ★	Gro	Lg/Gro	9	3.9	1.7	10.1	76	13	91	4	16	80	None	27	2,038.8	851-4999
Vanguard/Wellesley Income	ITR	Lg/Val	6	(4.4)	6.0	8.5	63	(4)	49	56	39	34	None	20	5,710.8	851-4999
Vanguard/Wellington	ETR	Lg/Val	7	(0.5)	6.8	7.9	76	8	74	60	59	46	None	19	8,638.3	851-4999
Vanguard/Windsor[1]	G&I	Lg/Val	8	(0.1)	11.6	8.6	78	0	54	92	93	54	None	15	10,858.1	851-4999
Vanguard/Windsor II	G&I	Lg/Val	8	(1.2)	7.9	7.8	79	4	40	63	78	54	None	23	7,896.0	851-4999

Source: Morningstar Inc. Chicago Ill.; 800-876-5005

| Fund name/★ 1994 winner | Type | Style | Risk level | % average annual return to Jan. 1, 1995 | | | Tax analysis | | Performance analysis (percentile ranking by type) | | | | Expense analysis | | Net assets (millions) | Telephone (800) |
				One year	Three years	Five years	% tax efficiency	% tax liability	1994	1993	1992	1991	% max. sales charge	Five-year total per $1,000		
Van Kampen Gro. & Inc. A	G&I	Md/Bl	9	(5.2)	5.6	7.0	58	4	13	73	53	60	4.65	$137	$49.1	225-2222
Van Kampen Utility B	Spec	Md/Val	—	(10.4)	—	—	—	(15)	24	—	—	—	4.0⁴	N.A.	80.2	225-2222
Vision Growth & Income	G&I	N.A.	—	(1.6)	—	—	—	N.A.	36	—	—	—	4.5	N.A.	30.7	836-2211
Vista Balanced A ★	ETR	Md/Val	—	0.2	—	—	—	(1)	84	53	—	—	4.5	72	21.1	648-4782
Vista Capital Growth	Gro	Sm/Val	10	(1.3)	10.2	16.6	94	2	53	83	74	99	4.75	117	543.2	648-4782
Vista Equity-Income	ETR	Lg/Val	—	(3.8)	—	—	—	5	33	—	—	—	4.5	123	10.0	648-4782
Vista Growth & Income	G&I	Lg/Val	8	(3.4)	7.9	14.9	91	0	24	58	89	99	4.75	121	1,340.8	648-4782
Vista International Equity A	Intl	Md/Val	—	(4.3)	—	—	—	(1)	34	6	—	—	4.75	150	32.3	648-4782
Volumetric	Gro	Md/Val	10	(2.1)	3.5	7.2	44	5	45	11	66	50	None	108	11.1	541-3863
Vontobel EuroPacific	Intl	Md/Bl	10	(5.3)	9.2	6.3	98	19	29	75	51	70	None	107	142.6	527-9500
Vontobel US Value	G&I	Md/Val	8	0.0	6.9	—	58	3	57	14	90	89	None	105	27.8	527-9500
Voyageur Growth Stock	Gro	Lg/Bl	10	(0.2)	0.2	8.2	N.A.	2	63	3	33	93	4.75	154	22.1	553-2143
Waddell & Reed Growth ★	Gro	Sm/Gro	—	12.8	—	—	—	13	99	93	—	—	3.0⁴	N.A.	80.7	236-2000¹⁷
Waddell & Reed Total Return	G&I	Lg/Bl	—	(2.1)	—	—	—	1	32	66	—	—	3.0⁴	N.A.	93.2	236-2000¹⁷
Warburg Pincus Balanced	ETR	Lg/Bl	6	(0.2)	7.1	9.6	34	14	81	63	56	53	4.75	0	0.8	257-5614
Warburg Pincus Cap. App. Com.	Gro	Md/Gro	10	(2.7)	6.6	7.7	68	22	41	68	45	19	None	59	145.3	257-5614
Warburg Pincus Emer. Gro. Com.	Agg	Sm/Gro	11	(1.4)	9.3	12.9	92	13	51	52	50	63	None	68	222.8	257-5614
Warburg Pincus Gro. & Inc. ★	G&I	Md/Bl	7	7.6	17.2	13.6	82	(1)	99	100	60	3	None	113	628.0	257-5614
Warburg Pincus Intl. Eq. Com. ★	Intl	Md/Val	11	0.1	13.1	10.8	96	9	66	92	39	78	None	81	1,551.7	257-5614
Wasatch Aggressive Equity ★	Agg	Sm/Gro	11	5.5	10.9	17.2	83	14	90	80	22	49	None	82	50.3	345-7460
Wasatch Growth ★	Gro	Sm/Gro	11	2.7	6.1	13.2	38	24	82	45	27	66	None	82	11.6	345-7460
Wasatch Mid-Cap. ★	Gro	Sm/Gro	—	8.1	—	—	—	(10)	96	3	—	—	None	N.A.	1.2	345-7460
Washington Mutual Inv. ★	G&I	Lg/Val	8	0.5	7.4	8.0	79	18	65	59	60	26	5.75	96	12,668.3	421-4120
Wayne Hummer Growth	Gro	Md/Bl	7	(0.9)	4.1	8.9	87	17	66	15	63	28	None	68	86.7	621-4477
Weitz Value	Gro	Md/Bl	8	(9.8)	7.1	8.3	81	5	7	82	77	24	None	87	107.7	232-4161
Westcore Modern Val. Eq. ★	G&I	Lg/Val	9	0.4	4.8	9.1	57	11	62	54	8	86	4.5	86	40.8	392-2673
William Blair Growth ★	Gro	Md/Gro	9	6.5	9.8	13.4	74	25	95	66	46	77	None	46	182.2	742-7272
William Blair Intl. Growth ★	Intl	Md/Bl	—	0.1	—	—	—	7	66	46	—	—	None	N.A.	71.1	742-7272
Winthrop Focus Agg. Growth	Agg	Sm/Val	7	(0.7)	12.7	13.4	75	(9)	57	71	79	51	4.04	82	147.4	225-8011
Winthrop Focus Growth	Gro	Lg/Bl	10	(4.2)	3.6	5.7	28	11	29	57	13	26	4.04	69	49.7	225-8011
Winthrop Focus Gro. & Inc.	G&I	Lg/Bl	9	(2.4)	6.1	7.5	68	12	31	79	29	28	4.04	71	66.1	225-8011
Women's Equity Growth	Gro	Sm/Bl	—	(1.5)	—	—	—	0	51	—	—	—	None	N.A.	1.2	296-9135¹⁸
Working Assets Citizens Bal.	ETR	Md/Gro	—	(2.3)	—	—	—	(4)	51	6	—	—	4.0	N.A.	41.9	223-7010
Working Assets Cit. Growth	Gro	Md/Bl	—	(0.7)	—	—	—	1	58	6	—	—	4.0	N.A.	50.8	223-7010
WPG Dividend Income	EqTR	Sm/Val	N.A.	(16.0)	1.0	4.0	N.A.	(16)	N.A.	—	—	—	None	104	19.2	223-3332
WPG Growth & Income	G&I	Md/Bl	9	(5.5)	5.6	8.3	42	4	12	36	85	93	None	75	58.3	223-3332
WPG International	Intl	Lg/Bl	11	(6.3)	6.7	0.9	99	8	24	60	32	2	None	124	16.9	223-3332
WPG Quantitative Equity ★	G&I	Lg/Bl	—	0.3	—	—	—	2	61	65	—	—	None	N.A.	65.2	223-3332
WPG Tudor	Gro	Sm/Gro	12	(9.8)	2.5	8.3	—	19	8	56	29	79	None	68	159.2	223-3332
Wright EquiFund-Dutch Natl. ★	Reg	Sm/Val	9	11.7	7.0	—	58	35	95	12	38	53	None	108	3.3	888-9471
Wright EquiFund-Hong Kong	Reg	Md/Bl	12	(37.0)	10.5	—	94	(20)	2	95	99	100	None	108	19.5	888-9471
Wright Equifund Ital. Natl. ★	Reg	Sm/Val	12	5.0	(8.1)	—	N.A.	(30)	80	4	4	5	None	108	1.5	888-9471
Wright EquiFund-Span. Natl.	Reg	Md/Val	12	(9.5)	(9.6)	—	N.A.	(21)	44	19	7	43	None	108	6.7	888-9471
Yacktman ★	Gro	Md/Gro	—	8.8	—	—	—	3	97	1	—	—	None	N.A.	295.1	525-8258
Zweig Appreciation A	Agg	Sm/Val	7	(1.8)	7.2	—	88	11	46	37	40	—	5.5	142	218.2	444-2706
Zweig Managed Assets C	ETR	Int/Hi	—	(3.7)	—	—	—	(3)	34	—	—	—	1.25⁴	N.A.	582.4	444-2706
Zweig Priority Selection A	Gro	Md/Bl	9	(4.4)	1.6	6.7	1	(9)	28	57	6	50	5.5	151	46.5	444-2706
Zweig Strategy A ★	Gro	Md/Val	7	1.1	7.8	8.6	67	1	76	64	46	13	5.5	136	427.0	444-2706

BOND FUNDS

Fund name/★ 1994 winner	Type	Style	Risk level	One year	Three years	Five years	% tax efficiency	% tax liability	1994	1993	1992	1991	% max. sales charge	Five-year total per $1,000	Net assets (millions)	Telephone (800)
AARP GNMA & US Treasury	Gov	Int/Hi	2	(1.7)	3.6	6.9	45	(9)	78	20	66	50	None	40	5,336.4	322-2282
AARP High-Quality Bond	IGC	L/Hi	5	(4.5)	4.0	6.9	51	(8)	30	62	26	43	None	62	535.4	322-2282
AARP Ins. T/F General Bond	Muni	L/Hi	6	(6.2)	4.7	6.5	91	(6)	37	69	50	73	None	41	1,738.5	322-2282
Accessor Intm. F/I	IGC	Int/Hi	—	(5.2)	—	—	—	(10)	21	47	—	—	None	N.A.	31.3	759-3504
Accessor Mortgage Sec.	MBS	Int/Hi	—	(1.7)	—	—	—	(7)	55	81	—	—	None	N.A.	33.0	759-3504
Accessor Short-Intm. F/I	IGC	Sh/Hi	—	(1.4)	—	—	—	(4)	75	11	—	—	None	N.A.	32.3	759-3504
Advantage Gov. Sec.	Gov	L/Hi	8	(9.8)	5.5	7.9	67	(26)	5	99	98	55	4.0⁴	76	152.6	241-2039
Advantage High-Yield Bond	HYC	L/Lo	2	(2.2)	14.1	13.2	75	(9)	64	53	99	87	4.0⁴	82	136.3	241-2039
Advantage Muni Bond Natl.	Muni	L/Med	—	(10.4)	—	—	—	(18)	1	—	—	—	4.0⁴	N.A.	27.5	241-2039

Source: Morningstar Inc. Chicago Ill.; 800-876-5005

| Fund name/★ 1994 winner | Type | Style | Risk level | % average annual return to Jan. 1, 1995 | | | Tax analysis | | Performance analysis (percentile ranking by type) | | | | Expense analysis | | Net assets (millions) | Telephone (800) |
				One year	Three years	Five years	% tax efficiency	% tax liability	1994	1993	1992	1991	% max. sales charge	Five-year total per $1,000		
AIM Gov. Securities A	Gov	Int/Hi	3	(3.4)	3.2	6.3	31	(8)	54	34	55	28	4.75	$100	$157.6	347-1919
AIM High-Yield A	HYC	Int/Lo	1	(1.7)	11.4	12.3	72	(16)	72	48	67	74	4.75	108	575.6	347-1919
AIM Income A	IGC	Int/Med	7	(7.6)	4.6	7.0	48	(13)	7	93	59	75	4.75	100	200.6	347-1919
AIM Ltd. Mat. Treas. Ret. ★	Gov	Sh/Hi	1	0.8	3.6	6.0	61	(4)	97	10	37	9	1.0	37	266.0	347-1919
AIM Municipal Bond A	Muni	L/Hi	3	(3.8)	5.4	6.9	96	(1)	69	48	69	88	4.75	100	257.6	347-1919
AIM Tax-Free Intermediate	Muni	Int/Hi	1	(1.4)	5.1	6.3	100	(2)	90	14	31	15	1.0	49	87.8	347-1919
Alliance Bond Corp. Bond A	IGC	L/Med	9	(12.7)	9.0	10.0	69	(11)	2	100	99	78	4.25	109	218.0	227-4618
Alliance Bond US Gov. A	Gov	Int/Hi	4	(4.4)	3.6	6.8	37	(12)	38	72	48	75	4.25	87	438.5	227-4618
Alliance Mort. Sec. Inc. A	MBS	Sh/Hi	4	(6.1)	3.7	7.4	40	(16)	15	97	94	76	4.25	92	582.4	227-4618
Alliance Mortgage Strat. B	MBS	N.A.	—	(0.4)	—	—	—	(5)	73	46	—	—	3.0⁴	127	136.6	227-4618
Alliance Multi-Mkt. Strat. B	WI	Sh/Hi	8	(13.3)	(2.6)	—	—	(17)	13	45	13	—	3.0⁴	169	222.0	227-4618
Alliance Muni Inc. Natl. A	Muni	L/Hi	6	(9.6)	4.2	6.3	95	(15)	3	80	94	58	4.25	89	318.9	227-4618
Alliance Muni Ins. Natl. A	Muni	L/Hi	7	(9.2)	3.9	6.1	89	(14)	6	74	71	71	4.25	88	148.7	227-4618
Alliance N. Amer. Gov. Inc. B	WI	N.A.	—	(30.8)	—	—	—	(24)	2	83	—	—	3.0⁴	154	1,634.8	227-4618
Alliance S/T Multi-Mkt. A	WI	Sh/Hi	5	(8.7)	(0.5)	3.9	—	(13)	20	35	36	34	4.25	89	573.8	227-4618
Alliance S/T US Gov. A	Gov	Sh/Hi	—	(1.7)	—	—	—	(5)	77	24	N.A.	N.A.	4.25	104	2.5	227-4618
Alliance World Income	WI	Sh/Hi	2	(4.3)	0.4	—	—	(51)	51	12	52	8	None	87	94.7	227-4618
Allmerica Inv. Grade Inc.	N.A.	L/Hi	—	(4.9)	—	—	—	0	N.A.	—	—	—	4.5	N.A.	9.0	828-7084
American Cap. Corp. Bond A	IGC	L/Med	3	(4.3)	5.1	7.7	58	(15)	35	72	81	60	4.75	100	161.0	421-5666
American Cap. Fed. Mort. A ★	MBS	Sh/Hi	1	0.2	2.1	5.1	34	(24)	81	14	8	8	2.25	72	41.1	421-5666
American Cap. Glob. Gov. B	WI	N.A.	6	(6.9)	2.2	—	—	(16)	30	69	34	N.A.	4.0⁴	143	127.8	421-5666
American Cap. Gov. Sec. A	Gov	Int/Hi	3	(4.3)	3.3	6.9	37	(43)	40	54	66	80	4.75	99	2,580.4	421-5666
Amer. Cap. Gov. Target '97¹	Gov	Int/Hi	5	(3.0)	3.2	—	—	(8)	62	20	76	100	3.0	N.A.	17.4	421-5666
American Cap. H/Y Inv. A	HYC	Int/Lo	2	(3.6)	10.5	9.9	70	(67)	39	59	57	70	4.75	105	361.7	421-5666
American Cap. Muni Bond A	Muni	L/Med	2	(3.5)	5.3	6.6	100	(2)	72	38	57	60	4.75	96	295.8	421-5666
Amer. Cap. T/E H/Y Muni A¹ ★	Muni	L/Lo	1	0.2	6.4	7.1	100	(9)	97	22	68	25	4.75	103	418.1	421-5666
Amer. Cap. T/E Insured A	Muni	L/Hi	1	(3.4)	4.3	5.7	100	(9)	73	14	31	11	4.75	110	66.8	421-5666
American Cap. US Gov. B	Gov	Int/Hi	—	(4.9)	—	—	—	(18)	33	16	—	—	4.0⁴	N.A.	208.4	421-5666
American High-Income	HYC	Int/Lo	2	(5.1)	8.3	11.0	65	(8)	22	27	17	36	4.75	93	798.2	421-4120
American Natl. Gov. Inc.	Gov	N.A.	—	(5.6)	—	—	—	(7)	23	70	—	—	4.5	101	18.3	231-4639
American Natl. Tax-Free	Muni	L/Hi	—	(5.9)	—	—	—	(12)	43	—	—	—	4.5	98	7.3	231-4639
API T-1 Treasury	WI	N.A.	6	(4.1)	(0.4)	3.3	—	N.A.	52	21	22	46	None	113	3.2	544-6060
Arch Gov. & Corp. Bond Inv.	IGC	Int/Hi	3	(2.9)	3.9	6.5	53	(6)	58	40	19	41	4.5	94	5.2	551-3731
Arrow Fixed-Income	IGC	L/Hi	—	(6.6)	—	—	—	(9)	11	60	—	—	3.5	N.A.	32.8	866-6040
Arrow Municipal Income	Muni	L/Hi	—	(4.5)	—	—	—	(7)	63	—	—	—	3.5	N.A.	20.5	866-6040
Asset Mgmt. Adj. Rate ★	MBS	Int/Hi	1	2.0	3.7	—	64	(4)	96	39	27	N.A.	None	44	862.9	527-3713
Ast. Management Intm. Mort.	MBS	L/Hi	1	(1.8)	4.3	7.0	59	(11)	52	71	99	89	None	34	210.5	527-3713
Ast. Mgmt. Sh. US Gov. Sec. ★	Gov	Sh/Hi	1	0.2	4.2	6.7	60	(12)	94	17	76	16	None	28	165.1	527-3713
Ast. Mgmt US Gov. Mort. Sec.	MBS	L/Hi	2	(2.7)	3.5	7.0	38	(8)	36	69	68	60	None	30	59.3	527-3713
Babson Bond L	IGC	Int/Hi	3	(3.3)	5.1	7.5	53	(14)	50	65	72	36	None	54	139.0	422-2766
Babson Bond S	IGC	Int/Hi	2	(2.1)	4.3	7.0	49	(10)	70	34	50	31	None	38	29.0	422-2766
Babson Tax-Free Income L	Muni	L/Hi	6	(7.4)	4.1	6.1	80	(7)	21	59	44	73	None	55	26.6	422-2766
Babson Tax-Free Income S	Muni	Int/Hi	1	(1.7)	3.7	5.4	96	(2)	88	6	7	9	None	55	28.4	422-2766
Baird Adjustable Rate Inc.	MBS	N.A.	—	(6.6)	—	—	—	(16)	13	31	—	—	3.25	N.A.	140.9	792-2473
Baird Quality Bond	IGC	L/Hi	—	(5.2)	—	—	—	(12)	21	57	—	—	4.0	N.A.	8.5	792-2473
Bartlett Fixed-Income	IGC	Int/Hi	2	(2.9)	3.6	6.1	53	(7)	60	20	48	29	None	55	90.7	800-4612
BayFunds Bond Investment	IGC	Int/Hi	—	(2.4)	—	—	—	(7)	67	—	—	—	None	67	5.4	229-3863
BayFunds S/T Yield Inv.	IGC	Sh/Hi	—	(3.4)	—	—	—	(12)	47	—	—	—	None	N.A.	38.5	229-3863
Bear Stearns Emer. Mkt. Debt	WI	N.A.	—	(17.8)	—	—	—	N.A.	6	—	—	—	4.5	N.A.	35.7	766-4111
Benham Adjustable Rate Gov.	MBS	Sh/Hi	1	(1.2)	2.5	—	38	(15)	64	19	36	—	None	33	443.3	331-8331
Benham Euro. Gov. Bond ★	WI	Int/Hi	—	1.5	—	—	—	(5)	86	73	—	—	None	50	193.7	331-8331
Benham GNMA Income	MBS	Int/Hi	2	(1.5)	4.2	7.6	53	(8)	60	67	95	78	None	32	952.3	331-8331
Benham L/T Treas. & Agency	Gov	L/Hi	—	(9.3)	—	—	—	(13)	7	97	—	—	None	42	28.6	331-8331
Benham Natl. T/F Intm.	Muni	Int/Hi	3	(3.5)	4.4	6.3	95	(3)	72	23	15	50	None	40	62.1	331-8331
Benham Natl. T/F Long-Term	Muni	L/Hi	6	(6.1)	5.4	7.1	91	(4)	38	92	74	86	None	40	45.2	331-8331
Benham Target Mat. 1995 ★	Gov	Sh/Hi	2	0.6	4.2	5.3	48	(1)	96	21	49	2	None	35	80.5	331-8331
Benham Target Mat. 2000	Gov	Int/Hi	8	(7.2)	4.6	7.8	53	(8)	14	91	88	97	None	37	255.0	331-8331
Benham Target Mat. 2005	Gov	L/Hi	10	(9.4)	4.7	7.2	35	3	6	94	96	99	None	35	101.6	331-8331
Benham Target Mat. 2010	Gov	L/Hi	11	(12.0)	5.8	7.1	51	(4)	3	100	95	98	None	39	55.6	331-8331
Benham Target Mat. 2015	Gov	L/Hi	12	(14.2)	3.3	4.9	5	3	2	99	83	100	None	35	124.0	331-8331

Source: Morningstar Inc. Chicago Ill.; 800-876-5005

| Fund name/★ 1994 winner | Type | Style | Risk level | % average annual return to Jan. 1, 1995 | | | Tax analysis | | Performance analysis (percentile ranking by type) | | | | Expense analysis | | Net assets (millions) | Telephone (800) |
				One year	Three years	Five years	% tax efficiency	% tax liability	1994	1993	1992	1991	% max. sales charge	Five-year total per $1,000		
Benham Target Mat. 2020	Gov	L/Hi	12	(17.7)	4.0	8.0	48	(5)	2	100	7	91	None	$37	$125.5	331-8331
Benham Treasury Note	Gov	Sh/Hi	2	(2.3)	3.9	6.9	46	(7)	69	47	67	37	None	30	296.2	331-8331
Bernstein Diversified Muni	Muni	L/Hi	2	(2.5)	4.0	5.8	97	(4)	82	11	9	20	None	39	538.0	756-4097[6]
Bernstein Gov. Short Dur. ★	Gov	Sh/Hi	1	0.3	3.4	6.0	52	(3)	96	10	27	13	None	39	152.1	756-4097[6]
Bernstein Intm. Duration	IGC	Int/Hi	3	(3.2)	4.6	7.4	53	(5)	52	55	49	66	None	38	837.7	756-4097[6]
Bernstein Sh. Duration Plus ★	IGC	Sh/Hi	1	0.5	4.0	6.4	56	(3)	90	10	26	12	None	37	516.3	756-4097[6]
Biltmore Fixed-Income	IGC	L/Hi	—	(3.8)	—	—	—	(10)	43	—	—	—	4.5	N.A.	149.0	462-7538
Biltmore Short-Term F/I ★	IGC	Sh/Hi	—	1.2	—	—	—	(6)	91	—	—	—	4.5	N.A.	148.3	462-7538
BJB Global Income A	WI	Int/Hi	—	(6.6)	—	—	—	(21)	32	54	—	—	4.0	133	24.8	435-4659
Blackrock Gov. Income A ★	MBS	Int/Hi	1	1.5	2.1	—	23	(14)	94	8	6	—	3.0	93	56.8	225-1852
Blanchard Flex. T/F Bond	Muni	L/Hi	—	(5.6)	—	—	—	(17)	49	—	—	—	None	96	18.5	922-7771
Blanchard Short-Term Bond ★	IGC	Sh/Hi	—	1.0	—	—	—	(5)	91	—	—	—	None	N.A.	27.7	992-7771
Blanchard S/T Global Inc.	WI	Sh/Hi	2	(4.6)	2.4	—	21	(9)	49	40	77	—	None	96	351.3	922-7771
BNY Hamilton Intm. Gov.	Gov	Int/Hi	—	(5.2)	—	—	—	(12)	27	52	—	—	3.0	N.A.	59.3	426-9363
Bond Fund of America	IGC	Int/Med	3	(5.0)	6.5	8.6	60	(7)	24	90	97	98	4.75	86	4,941.2	421-4120
Brundage Story Rose S/I F/I	IGC	Sh/Hi	2	(2.3)	4.1	—	57	(7)	68	31	32	17	None	28	33.5	545-0103
BT Inv. Glob. H/Y Sec.	HYC	L/Hi	—	(3.1)	—	—	—	N.A.	46	—	—	—	None	N.A.	15.4	949-9940
BT Investment Intm. T/F	Muni	Int/Med	—	(3.8)	—	—	—	(6)	68	16	N.A.	N.A.	None	47	25.2	949-9940
BT Inv. Ltd.-Term US	Gov	N.A.	—	(0.5)	—	—	—	(2)	88	25	N.A.	N.A.	None	33	31.0	943-2222
Bull & Bear Global Income	WI	L/Med	7	(13.5)	6.9	6.9	67	(164)	12	95	100	97	None	N.A.	42.8	847-4200
Bull & Bear Municipal Inc.	Muni	L/Med	7	(9.7)	1.9	4.6	79	(10)	2	28	6	93	None	87	16.1	847-4200
Bull & Bear US Government	Gov	Int/Hi	4	(4.7)	3.4	6.6	58	(19)	35	78	21	69	None	101	16.4	847-4200
Calvert Income A	IGC	L/Hi	6	(6.2)	4.2	6.9	48	(8)	13	77	60	80	3.75	104	43.8	368-2748
Calvert Natl. Muni Intm. A	Muni	Int/Hi	—	(1.6)	—	—	—	(6)	89	18	—	—	2.75	N.A.	40.7	368-2748
Calvert Social Inv. Bond A	IGC	L/Hi	5	(5.3)	4.1	7.2	48	(7)	20	71	38	47	3.75	88	59.4	368-2748
Calvert T/F Res. Ltd.-Term A ★	Muni	Sh/Hi	1	2.4	3.8	4.9	100	0	100	3	3	2	2.0	59	600.0	368-2748
Calvert T/F Res. Long-Term A	Muni	L/Med	2	(2.3)	5.4	6.5	100	(4)	83	37	34	55	3.75	89	46.6	368-2748
Calvert US Government A	Gov	Int/Hi	4	(5.1)	2.8	5.7	25	(12)	31	59	25	24	3.75	113	9.4	368-2748
Cambridge Government Inc. B	Gov	Int/Hi	—	(5.4)	—	—	—	(21)	26	7	—	—	1.0[4]	89	71.9	382-0016
Cambridge Municipal Inc. B	Muni	L/Med	—	(8.4)	—	—	—	(9)	10	97	—	—	1.0[4]	92	41.4	382-0016
Capital World Bond	WI	L/Hi	5	(1.4)	5.1	8.4	63	(6)	73	79	42	81	4.75	119	563.2	421-4120
Capstone Gov. Income ★	Gov	Sh/Hi	1	1.1	2.7	2.7	76	(8)	99	5	5	4	None	51	75.6	262-6631
Cardinal Gov. Obligations	MBS	L/Hi	1	(0.9)	3.3	6.5	28	(21)	69	32	65	21	4.5	84	158.1	848-7734
CGM American Tax-Free	Muni	L/Med	—	(8.2)	—	—	—	(11)	12	—	—	—	None	N.A.	10.1	345-4048
CGM Fixed-Income	IGC	L/Lo	—	(8.0)	—	—	—	(13)	5	99	—	—	None	47	28.7	345-4048
Chubb Government Securities	Gov	Int/Hi	5	(3.3)	4.1	7.3	41	(11)	56	58	86	78	3.0	104	12.5	258-3648
Chubb Tax-Exempt	Muni	L/Hi	4	(6.4)	4.7	6.0	99	(5)	33	60	71	28	3.0	104	13.9	258-3648
Colonial Adj. Rate US Gov. A ★	MBS	Sh/Hi	—	0.8	—	—	—	(5)	90	21	—	—	3.25	N.A.	15.0	248-2828
Colonial Federal Sec. A	Gov	L/Hi	5	(5.8)	3.9	6.6	43	(22)	21	87	54	70	4.75	109	1,245.1	248-2828
Colonial High-Yield Muni B	Muni	L/Med	—	(3.4)	—	—	—	(10)	74	12	—	—	5.04	128	113.6	248-2828
Colonial High-Yield Secs. A	HYC	Int/Lo	1	(0.3)	13.1	12.1	77	(15)	85	65	84	82	4.75	114	383.6	248-2828
Colonial Income A	IGC	L/Med	4	(4.1)	5.3	7.3	57	(18)	38	76	82	92	4.75	108	130.0	248-2828
Colonial Intermediate T/E A	Muni	Int/Hi	—	(3.3)	—	—	—	(7)	75	—	—	—	3.25	N.A.	16.5	248-2828
Colonial Short-Term T/E ★	Muni	Sh/Hi	—	1.2	—	—	—	(2)	98	—	—	—	1.0	N.A.	13.7	248-2828
Colonial Tax-Exempt A	Muni	L/Med	4	(6.3)	4.0	6.0	100	(8)	36	29	41	54	4.75	103	2,855.3	248-2828
Colonial Tax-Exempt Ins. A	Muni	L/Hi	4	(6.1)	3.8	5.9	100	(6)	38	35	23	52	4.75	106	198.8	248-2828
Colonial US Government A	Gov	Int/Hi	1	(1.8)	2.9	5.8	30	(7)	75	15	17	12	4.75	108	679.1	248-2828
Columbia Fixed-Income Sec.	IGC	Int/Hi	4	(3.4)	4.9	7.9	50	(8)	49	58	74	63	None	37	252.1	547-1707
Columbia High-Yield	HYC	Int/Lo	—	(0.9)	—	—	—	(7)	81	—	—	—	None	N.A.	12.8	547-1707
Columbia US Gov. Sec.	Gov	Sh/Hi	1	0.0	3.9	6.5	58	(4)	92	19	42	23	None	42	33.5	547-1707
Common Sense Government	Gov	Int/Hi	4	(5.1)	3.1	6.5	21	(15)	29	55	74	73	6.75	117	326.2	544-5445
Common Sense Muni Bond	Muni	L/Hi	2	(4.7)	4.8	6.3	100	(3)	60	40	49	40	4.75	107	108.4	544-5445
Compass Cap. Fixed-Income	IGC	L/Hi	4	(3.8)	4.8	7.3	53	(6)	43	63	63	49	3.75	85	243.9	451-8371
Compass Cap. Intl. Fixed-Inc.	WI	Int/Hi	3	(3.7)	4.6	—	64	(5)	55	74	70	N.A.	3.75	108	45.3	451-8371
Compass Cap. Muni Bond	Muni	L/Hi	4	(5.5)	4.1	5.9	92	(10)	52	43	16	16	3.75	78	30.1	451-8371
Compass Cap. Short/Intm.	IGC	Sh/Hi	1	(0.5)	4.3	6.6	58	(4)	83	20	35	13	3.75	83	207.7	451-8371
Composite Income A	IGC	L/Med	4	(4.8)	4.3	7.5	54	(25)	26	61	57	69	4.0	101	88.1	543-8072
Composite Tax-Exempt Bond A	Muni	L/Hi	5	(6.5)	4.7	6.4	96	(6)	29	66	66	43	4.0	87	215.4	543-8072
Composite US Gov. Sec. A	Gov	Int/Hi	4	(4.9)	2.9	6.5	37	(12)	32	54	50	54	4.0	97	188.1	543-8072
Connecticut Mutual Gov. Sec.	Gov	Int/Hi	4	(4.2)	3.7	7.0	33	(10)	41	71	49	62	4.0	94	60.2	234-5606

Source: Morningstar Inc. Chicago Ill.; 800-876-5005

Fund name/★ 1994 winner	Type	Style	Risk level	% average annual return to Jan. 1, 1995			Tax analysis		Performance analysis (percentile ranking by type)				Expense analysis		Net assets (millions)	Telephone (800)
				One year	Three years	Five years	% tax efficiency	% tax liability	1994	1993	1992	1991	% max. sales charge	Five-year total per $1,000		
Connecticut Mutual Income	IGC	Sh/Med	1	(1.0)	4.4	6.7	55	(8)	81	27	33	26	2.0	$73	$46.5	234-5606
Crabbe Huson Income	IGC	L/Hi	3	(3.6)	2.9	6.0	26	(8)	46	15	27	53	None	51	5.2	541-9732
Crabbe Huson US Gov. Inc.	Gov	Sh/Hi	2	(2.3)	3.0	5.9	50	(5)	70	21	31	30	None	45	9.0	541-9732
CT&T Intm. Fixed-Inc.	IGC	N.A.	—	(2.8)	—	—	—	(8)	61	—	—	—	None	N.A.	12.9	992-8151
CT&T Intermediate Muni	Muni	N.A.	—	(2.2)	—	—	—	(6)	84	—	—	—	None	N.A.	10.4	992-8151
Dean Witter Federal Sec.	Gov	Int/Hi	5	(5.1)	3.3	6.2	42	(14)	30	63	63	47	5.0[4]	101	809.6	869-3863
Dean Witter Global S/T Inc. ★	WI	N.A.	1	0.1	2.8	—	32	(8)	84	22	58	22	3.0[4]	84	148.3	869-3863
Dean Witter High-Yield Sec.[1]	HYC	Int/Lo	4	(7.1)	14.9	8.7	73	N.A.	16	99	97	100	5.5	95	432.2	869-3863
Dean Witter Intm. Income	IGC	Int/Med	3	(3.1)	3.8	5.9	53	(8)	54	35	29	56	5.0[4]	108	224.6	869-3863
Dean Witter Ltd. Term Muni	Muni	L/Hi	—	(8.0)	—	—	—	(21)	14	N.A.	N.A.	N.A.	None	N.A.	85.3	869-3863
Dean Witter Premier Income ★	IGC	L/Hi	1	1.5	2.2	—	1	(23)	92	1	5	N.A.	3.0	114	38.6	869-3863
Dean Witter Sel. Muni Reinv.	Muni	L/Med	5	(6.2)	4.6	6.2	97	(3)	37	54	59	65	None	63	84.7	869-3863
Dean Witter S/T US Treas.	Gov	Sh/Hi	1	(1.3)	3.0	—	52	(7)	82	12	27	N.A.	None	N.A.	329.3	392-2550[6]
Dean Witter Tax-Exempt Sec.[1]	Muni	L/Hi	3	(5.6)	4.6	6.5	99	(3)	49	40	70	82	4.0	66	1,292.3	869-3863
Dean Witter US Government	Gov	Int/Hi	2	(3.6)	3.0	5.7	33	(28)	51	36	39	14	5.0[4]	85	8,199.9	869-3863
Dean Witter World Income	WI	Int/Hi	6	(4.4)	2.7	5.0	36	(17)	50	44	67	4	5.0[4]	121	164.5	869-3863
Delaware Delchester A	HYC	Int/Lo	2	(4.6)	9.2	10.4	64	(23)	30	14	55	80	4.75	104	930.8	523-4640
Delaware Tax-Free Insured A	Muni	L/Hi	1	(2.9)	4.5	6.2	98	0	79	17	25	40	4.75	100	83.7	523-4640
Delaware Tax-Free USA A	Muni	L/Med	1	(3.0)	5.9	6.8	98	3	78	47	86	76	4.75	94	693.5	523-4640
Delaware Treas. Res. Intm. A	Gov	Sh/Hi	1	(1.9)	3.0	6.2	32	(14)	74	13	35	29	3.0	78	810.2	523-4640
Delaware US Government A	Gov	Int/Hi	4	(5.8)	2.6	6.2	9	(19)	21	46	60	66	4.75	109	207.9	523-4640
DG Government Income	IGC	Int/Hi	—	(3.4)	—	—	—	(6)	47	48	N.A.	N.A.	2.0	N.A.	176.9	748-8500
DG Limited-Term Gov. Inc. ★	IGC	Sh/Hi	—	0.3	—	—	—	(5)	89	13	N.A.	N.A.	2.0	N.A.	104.5	748-8500
DG Municipal Income	Muni	L/Hi	—	(6.8)	—	—	—	(10)	29	71	N.A.	N.A.	2.0	N.A.	37.1	748-8500
Dodge &Cox Income	IGC	L/Hi	4	(2.9)	5.2	8.1	58	(3)	59	68	67	77	None	35	194.1	621-3979
Dreman Fixed-Income	IGC	Int/Hi	1	(1.2)	3.3	6.3	41	(4)	78	13	12	10	None	42	4.5	533-1608
Dreyfus 100% US Intm.	Gov	Int/Hi	4	(4.0)	4.6	7.4	54	(5)	44	83	82	70	None	53	180.3	782-6620
Dreyfus 100% US Long-Term	Gov	L/Hi	7	(9.2)	4.4	7.6	54	6	7	94	86	95	None	54	126.0	782-6620
Dreyfus 100% US Short-Term	Gov	Sh/Hi	1	(0.3)	4.6	6.5	50	(9)	90	36	79	27	None	62	176.7	782-6620
Dreyfus A Bonds Plus	IGC	L/Hi	6	(6.2)	5.3	7.8	53	(8)	14	92	77	86	None	49	486.6	782-6620
Dreyfus GNMA	MBS	Int/Hi	2	(2.8)	3.5	6.8	44	(16)	34	79	61	54	None	53	1,445.0	782-6620
Dreyfus Insured Muni Bond	Muni	L/Hi	7	(8.6)	3.5	5.7	87	(9)	9	65	28	43	None	53	212.7	782-6620
Dreyfus Intermediate Muni	Muni	Int/Hi	3	(4.6)	5.0	6.6	93	(2)	61	46	53	35	None	39	1,487.8	782-6620
Dreyfus Investors GNMA	MBS	Int/Hi	2	(1.1)	4.8	7.2	56	(6)	66	93	83	26	None	70	45.2	782-6620
Dreyfus Municipal Bond	Muni	L/Hi	5	(6.9)	4.4	6.3	89	(6)	26	69	45	62	None	38	3,495.6	782-6620
Dreyfus Short-Intm. Gov.	Gov	Sh/Hi	1	(0.8)	4.5	7.3	50	(9)	86	39	79	32	None	43	495.2	782-6620
Dreyfus Short-Intm. Muni Bond	Muni	Sh/Med	1	(0.3)	4.3	5.5	100	(3)	94	5	11	4	None	42	458.2	782-6620
Dreyfus Short-Term Income ★	IGC	Sh/Med	—	0.1	—	—	—	(8)	87	43	—	—	None	N.A.	230.6	782-6620
Dreyfus/Laurel S/T Bd. Inv. ★	IGC	Sh/Hi	N.A.	0.2	3.0	6.1	—	(4)	—	—	—	—	None	54	4.2	782-6620
EV Marathon High-Income	HYC	Int/Lo	1	(1.8)	10.6	8.8	70	(22)	67	21	61	63	5.0[4]	137	405.3	225-6265
EV Mar. Natl. Ltd. Mat. T/F	Muni	Int/Hi	—	(3.2)	—	—	76	(4)	76	13	—	—	3.0[4]	79	144.6	225-6265
EV Marathon S/T Strat. Inc.	WI	Int/Hi	6	(5.3)	1.4	—	—	(19)	42	50	31	32	3.0[4]	105	223.2	225-6265
EV Traditional Gov. Oblg.	Gov	Int/Hi	2	(2.0)	4.1	7.1	43	(13)	73	67	22	52	4.75	121	397.7	225-6265
Eaton Vance Income Boston	HYC	Int/Lo	1	(1.3)	11.3	10.6	71	(21)	79	42	65	76	4.75	104	98.9	225-6265
Eaton Vance Muni Bond	Muni	L/Med	6	(7.3)	4.7	6.8	100	6	23	86	61	91	4.75	87	89.3	225-6265
Eaton Vance S/T Treasury ★	Gov	Sh/Hi	1	3.5	3.0	—	100	5	100	2	4	—	None	33	6.1	225-6265
EBI Income	Gov	Int/Hi	2	(1.8)	3.4	6.0	57	(12)	75	41	12	21	None	122	25.5	554-1156
EBI Relative Return Bond	IGC	N.A.	—	(2.0)	—	—	—	(6)	71	—	—	—	None	85	3.2	554-1156
Emerald US Gov. Secs. A	Gov	L/Hi	3	(3.3)	4.1	—	50	(9)	58	64	74	N.A.	4.5	60	29.7	637-6336
Enterprise Government Sec.	Gov	Int/Hi	4	(7.8)	3.5	6.4	30	(18)	11	67	100	22	4.75	115	84.7	432-4320
Enterprise High-Yield Bond	HYC	Int/Lo	1	(0.1)	11.1	10.0	76	(12)	92	34	42	38	4.75	115	45.0	432-4320
Enterprise Tax-Exempt Inc.	Muni	L/Hi	3	(5.9)	4.0	5.7	100	(5)	42	30	32	34	4.75	113	34.3	432-4320
Evergreen National Tax-Free	Muni	L/Hi	—	(7.9)	—	—	—	(13)	15	100	—	—	None	N.A.	36.2	235-0064
Evergreen S/I Muni	Muni	Sh/Med	1	(1.4)	4.8	—	99	(2)	91	7	63	—	None	48	47.7	235-0064
Evergreen US Gov. Secs.	Gov	Sh/Hi	—	(7.8)	—	—	—	(15)	11	—	—	—	None	N.A.	8.7	235-0064
Executive Inv. High-Yield	HYC	Int/Lo	1	(2.6)	9.7	9.6	70	(40)	53	23	31	57	4.75	133	15.2	423-4026
Federated US Gov. Bond	Gov	L/Hi	6	(6.3)	4.8	7.3	61	(9)	17	89	93	35	None	49	131.7	245-5040
Fidelity Advisor Gov. Inv. A	MBS	L/Med	4	(3.8)	3.9	6.7	48	(8)	24	96	64	36	4.75	79	123.6	522-7297
Fidelity Advisor High-Income A	Muni	L/Med	4	(8.0)	5.2	7.6	98	(12)	14	90	98	69	4.75	99	506.4	522-7297
Fidelity Advisor High-Yield A	HYC	Int/Lo	1	(2.1)	13.1	15.9	78	(4)	65	68	91	50	4.75	112	682.8	522-7297

Source: Morningstar Inc. Chicago Ill.; 800-876-5005

Fund name/★ 1994 winner	Type	Style	Risk level	% average annual return to Jan. 1, 1995			Tax analysis		Performance analysis (percentile ranking by type)				Expense analysis		Net assets (millions)	Telephone (800)
				One year	Three years	Five years	% tax efficiency	% tax liability	1994	1993	1992	1991	% max. sales charge	Five-year total per $1,000		
Fidelity Advisor Short F/I A	IGC	Sh/Med	1	(3.4)	4.4	6.5	55	(9)	48	46	63	20	1.5	$74	$690.7	522-7297
Fidelity Aggressive Tax-Free	Muni	L/Med	3	(5.9)	5.4	7.0	92	(9)	44	89	72	56	None	38	793.8	544-8888
Fidelity Capital &Income	HYC	Int/Lo	2	(5.1)	14.7	13.5	83	(12)	23	95	100	25	None	44	2,039.8	544-8888
Fidelity Deutsche Mark Perf. ★	WI	Sh/Hi	10	16.4	5.1	8.3	100	31	100	3	47	11	0.4	74	8.6	544-8888
Fidelity Ginnie Mae	MBS	Int/Hi	2	(2.0)	3.6	6.9	45	(2)	46	58	81	39	None	44	704.5	544-8888
Fidelity Global Bond	WI	Int/Lo	8	(16.7)	1.7	5.9	—	(22)	7	93	83	57	None	75	382.9	544-8888
Fidelity Gov. Secs.	Gov	L/Hi	5	(5.2)	4.7	7.9	49	(10)	28	88	90	77	None	39	611.2	544-8888
Fidelity High-Yield T/F	Muni	L/Med	4	(7.4)	4.4	6.3	88	(10)	19	79	46	20	None	31	1,671.3	544-8888
Fidelity Insured Tax-Free	Muni	L/Hi	6	(7.7)	4.3	6.3	91	(11)	17	91	34	47	None	36	318.3	544-8888
Fidelity Intermediate Bond	IGC	Int/Hi	2	(2.0)	5.2	7.5	58	(4)	71	75	23	33	None	36	2,127.4	544-8888
Fidelity Invest. Grade Bond	IGC	L/Hi	3	(5.4)	6.0	8.5	62	(4)	19	96	78	91	None	39	995.1	544-8888
Fidelity Ltd.-Term Muni	Muni	Int/Hi	3	(4.8)	5.0	6.6	93	(6)	60	58	39	39	None	38	881.3	544-8888
Fidelity Mortgage Securities ★	MBS	Int/Hi	1	1.9	4.5	7.4	59	(4)	95	68	31	41	None	44	349.4	544-8888
Fidelity Municipal Bond	Muni	L/Hi	6	(9.1)	4.0	6.1	79	(10)	7	80	67	61	None	28	1,005.6	544-8888
Fidelity Short-Intm. Gov.	Gov	Sh/Hi	1	(1.4)	2.9	—	37	(12)	80	13	15	N.A.	None	71	151.2	544-8888
Fidelity Short-Term Bond	IGC	Sh/Hi	1	(4.1)	4.0	6.3	49	(9)	39	41	58	25	None	48	1,514.8	544-8888
Fidelity S/T World Inc.	WI	Sh/Med	3	(5.9)	3.5	—	42	(14)	38	58	86	—	None	66	265.8	544-8888
Fidelity Spartan Ginnie Mae	MBS	Int/Hi	2	(1.5)	3.5	—	41	(11)	62	62	41	47	None	41	347.8	544-8888
Fidelity Spartan Gov. Inc.	Gov	L/Hi	3	(3.6)	3.5	6.8	30	(11)	51	39	78	65	None	41	231.9	544-8888
Fidelity Spartan High-Income ★	HYC	Int/Lo	1	2.6	14.7	—	74	(3)	100	76	85	46	None	44	617.5	544-8888
Fidelity Spartan Inv. Gr. Bd.	IGC	L/Med	—	(4.6)	—	—	—	(9)	29	96	—	—	None	N.A.	118.0	544-8888
Fidelity Spartan Ltd. Mat.	Gov	Int/Hi	1	(1.0)	3.7	6.4	48	(8)	84	27	40	16	None	41	830.6	544-8888
Fidelity Spartan Long-Term	Gov	L/Hi	9	(12.3)	3.4	—	31	(10)	3	95	92	90	None	41	71.7	544-8888
Fidelity Spartan Muni Inc.	Muni	L/Med	5	(8.1)	4.5	—	86	(13)	12	95	47	81	None	29	535.6	544-8888
Fidelity Spartan S/I Gov.	Gov	Sh/Hi	—	(0.5)	—	—	—	(11)	87	15	—	—	None	N.A.	48.0	544-8888
Fidelity Spartan S/I Muni	Muni	Sh/Med	1	(0.1)	4.5	5.7	100	(3)	95	8	7	7	None	36	913.1	544-8888
Fidelity Spartan S/T Inc.	IGC	Sh/Med	—	(4.6)	—	—	—	(11)	28	38	—	—	None	N.A.	610.3	544-8888
Fidelity Sterling Perf. ★	WI	Sh/Hi	11	9.9	(0.4)	7.5	—	23	95	9	4	13	0.4	86	3.4	544-8888
Fidelity Yen Performance ★	WI	Sh/Hi	8	12.6	9.3	11.0	100	39	98	64	63	74	0.4	86	3.5	544-8888
First American Ltd./T T/F A ★	Muni	Sh/Hi	—	1.6	—	—	—	(14)	99	1	—	—	2.0	N.A.	0.6	637-2548
First American Mgd. Inc. A ★	IGC	Sh/Med	—	3.3	—	—	—	(63)	98	5	—	—	2.0	4.9	637-2548
First Investors Fund Income	HYC	Int/Lo	1	(0.2)	11.2	10.3	75	N.A.	86	44	44	78	6.25	144	397.9	423-4026
First Investors Government	MBS	Int/Hi	4	(3.8)	1.9	5.9	10	(9)	26	23	40	73	6.25	137	219.5	423-4026
First Investors High-Yield	HYC	Int/Lo	1	(0.4)	11.5	9.2	76	N.A.	83	25	70	44	6.25	156	170.0	423-4026
First Investors Insured T/E	Muni	L/Hi	3	(6.1)	3.7	5.5	95	(3)	40	21	38	22	6.25	128	1,284.6	423-4026
First Investors Inv. Grade	IGC	Int/Med	5	(5.2)	4.6	—	56	(6)	22	73	68	N.A.	6.25	135	46.0	423-4026
First Prairie Muni Bd. Ins. A	Muni	L/Hi	3	(2.0)	5.9	7.5	84	(7)	86	30	79	58	4.5	128	7.6	346-3621
First Prairie Muni Bd. Int. A	Muni	Int/Hi	1	(2.4)	4.8	6.8	88	(6)	83	21	19	60	3.0	45	25.9	346-3621
First Priority Ltd. Mat. Gov. ★	Gov	Sh/Hi	—	0.3	—	—	—	(4)	95	—	—	—	2.0	N.A.	48.5	433-2829
First Union F/I B Inv.	IGC	L/Hi	2	(2.6)	3.9	6.6	47	(8)	64	30	31	23	4.75	88	19.7	326-3241
First Union H/G T/F B Inv.	Muni	L/Hi	—	(7.7)	—	—	—	(8)	17	82	—	—	4.75	88	58.8	326-3241
First Union US Gov. C Inv.	Gov	Int/Hi	—	(3.7)	—	—	—	(13)	48	—	—	—	5.04	N.A.	199.7	326-3241
Flag Investors Intm.-Term	IGC	Int/Hi	3	(3.3)	3.7	—	48	(9)	50	38	18	—	1.5	54	78.2	767-3524
Flagship All-Amer. T/E A	Muni	L/Hi	5	(5.9)	6.0	7.6	96	(4)	44	93	96	98	4.2	90	168.0	227-4648
Flagship Intermediate T/E A	Muni	Int/Hi	—	(4.8)	—	—	—	(7)	59	87	—	—	3.0	N.A.	38.1	227-4648
Flagship Ltd.-Term T/E A	Muni	Int/Med	1	(1.9)	5.2	6.4	100	(3)	86	15	58	17	2.5	63	574.7	227-4648
Flex-funds Bond	IGC	Sh/Hi	2	(1.0)	3.4	6.7	64	(15)	80	29	3	42	None	55	12.9	325-3539
Flex-funds S/T Global Inc. ★	WI	Sh/Hi	—	2.2	—	—	—	(5)	89	5	—	—	None	N.A.	3.9	325-3539
Fortis Adv. Gov. Total Ret. A	Gov	Int/Hi	6	(7.7)	1.7	4.8	—	(41)	12	60	14	4	4.5	111	66.3	800-2638
Fortis Advantage High-Yield A	HYC	Int/Lo	2	(3.5)	10.7	11.6	70	(12)	43	87	23	97	4.5	115	95.6	800-2638
Fortis Tax-Free National E	Muni	L/Med	4	(5.2)	5.1	6.7	99	(3)	56	60	60	87	4.5	95	69.5	800-2638
Fortis US Gov. Sec. E	Gov	Int/Hi	4	(5.6)	2.6	6.3	12	(15)	22	56	33	41	4.5	86	489.4	800-2638
Fortress Adj. Rate US Gov.	MBS	Sh/Hi	1	(0.3)	2.6	—	46	(10)	75	18	25	N.A.	None	57	468.0	245-5051
Fortress Bond	IGC	Int/Med	3	(3.4)	9.2	11.3	73	(9)	49	97	100	100	1.0	67	145.3	245-5051
Fortress Muni Income	Muni	L/Med	4	(5.7)	4.2	6.0	100	(9)	47	36	35	33	1.0	69	414.8	245-5051
Forum Investors Bond	IGC	Int/Lo	2	(2.2)	5.7	8.4	57	(3)	68	84	41	51	3.75	75	23.1	879-8900[19]
Forum Taxsaver Bond	Muni	L/Med	1	(0.9)	6.1	7.1	94	(3)	93	27	60	23	3.75	67	16.3	879-8900[19]
Founders Government Sec.	Gov	Sh/Hi	7	(7.5)	2.1	5.0	—	(16)	12	69	22	60	None	65	21.5	525-2440
Founders Opportunity Bond	IGC	Int/Med	—	(10.0)	—	—	—	(15)	3	—	—	—	None	96	3.8	525-2440
Fountain Sq. Quality Bond	IGC	N.A.	—	(3.9)	—	—	—	(10)	42	25	—	—	4.5	N.A.	45.5	334-0483

Source: Morningstar Inc. Chicago Ill.; 800-876-5005

Fund name/★ 1994 winner	Type	Style	Risk level	% average annual return to Jan. 1, 1995			Tax analysis		Performance analysis (percentile ranking by type)				Expense analysis		Net assets (millions)	Telephone (800)
				One year	Three years	Five years	% tax efficiency	% tax liability	1994	1993	1992	1991	% max. sales charge	Five-year total per $1,000		
Fountain Sq. US Gov.	Gov	Int/Hi	—	(2.2)	—	—	—	(9)	72	25	—	—	4.5	N.A.	$23.4	334-0483
FPA New Income ★	IGC	Int/Hi	1	1.5	7.5	9.9	69	(1)	92	52	96	89	4.5	$86	127.9	982-4372
Franklin AGE High-Income	HYC	Int/Lo	1	(1.5)	10.5	11.4	73	(39)	76	36	38	93	4.25	71	1,696.5	342-5236
Franklin Adj. Rate Sec. ★	MBS	Int/Hi	1	0.2	3.5	—	63	(4)	83	33	45	—	2.25	N.A.	36.7	342-5236
Franklin Adj. US Gov.	MBS	Sh/Hi	1	(1.9)	1.1	4.2	—	(16)	48	5	16	6	2.25	66	714.5	342-5236
Franklin Fed. I/T T/F Inc.	Muni	Int/Med	—	(3.1)	—	—	—	(6)	77	72	N.A.	N.A.	2.25	N.A.	71.7	342-5236
Franklin Federal T/F Income	Muni	L/Med	2	(3.7)	5.5	7.0	100	(3)	70	41	82	87	4.25	67	6,463.7	342-5236
Franklin Glob. Gov. Income	WI	Int/Lo	8	(7.8)	2.9	6.0	10	(14)	25	87	33	64	4.25	83	181.9	342-5236
Franklin H/Y T/F Income	Muni	L/Med	1	(2.6)	6.4	7.3	100	(3)	81	79	69	76	4.25	68	3,137.3	342-5236
Franklin Insured T/F Income	Muni	L/Hi	2	(3.6)	5.6	6.9	100	(1)	71	52	73	42	4.25	68	1,588.0	342-5236
Franklin Inv. Grade Inc.	IGC	Sh/Hi	2	(1.2)	4.6	7.4	64	(8)	79	39	25	57	4.25	98	28.0	342-5236
Franklin Short-Intm. Gov.	Gov	Sh/Hi	3	(2.6)	3.8	6.6	55	(5)	67	44	69	17	2.25	58	220.8	342-5236
Franklin Strategic Mortgage	MBS	N.A.	—	(2.5)	—	—	—	(8)	39	—	—	—	4.25	N.A.	5.2	342-5236
Franklin Tax-Adv. US Gov.	MBS	L/Hi	4	(5.3)	3.2	6.8	43	(11)	16	92	87	56	4.25	76	467.1	342-5236
Franklin/Templtn. Ger. Gov. ★	WI	Int/Hi	—	9.6	—	—	—	7	94	19	N.A.	N.A.	3.0	N.A.	12.5	342-5236
Franklin/Templtn. Glob. Curr. ★	WI	Sh/Hi	3	8.1	5.9	7.9	58	13	93	24	79	25	3.0	119	55.3	342-5236
Franklin/Templtn. Hard Curr. ★	WI	Sh/Hi	7	15.1	7.2	9.9	55	8	99	16	59	29	3.0	121	59.6	342-5236
Franklin/Templtn H/I Curr. ★	WI	Sh/Hi	9	10.2	1.4	6.7	—	42	97	2	17	55	3.0	119	14.4	342-5236
Franklin US Government	MBS	Int/Hi	2	(2.7)	3.8	7.1	42	(13)	37	70	90	43	4.25	78	11,092.7	342-5236
Fremont Bond	IGC	Int/Hi	—	(4.0)	—	—	—	(3)	41	—	—	—	None	N.A.	59.8	548-4539
Fund for US Gov. Sec. A	MBS	Int/Hi	1	(1.9)	2.7	6.1	19	(18)	49	43	37	34	4.5	92	1,377.7	245-5051
FundTrust Income	IGC	N.A.	4	(4.3)	4.1	6.1	59	(8)	34	51	55	37	1.5	70	74.1	344-9033
Fundamental US Gov. Strat.	Gov	L/Hi	—	(25.6)	—	—	—	(81)	1	52	—	—	None	89	19.1	322-6864
Galaxy H/Q Bond Ret.	IGC	L/Hi	6	(6.5)	4.0	—	46	(20)	12	81	44	39	None	42	25.1	628-0414
Galaxy II Muni Bond Ret.	Muni	Int/Hi	—	(5.4)	—	—	—	(9)	54	—	—	—	None	34	24.7	628-0414
Galaxy II US Treas. Ind. Ret.	Gov	Int/Hi	4	(3.7)	4.3	—	48	(7)	N.A.	—	—	—	None	73	104.8	628-0414
Galaxy Intm. Bond Retail	IGC	Int/Med	5	(3.8)	2.9	5.9	34	(13)	44	10	51	48	None	41	84.3	628-0414
Galaxy S/T Bond Retail	IGC	Sh/Hi	1	(0.4)	3.9	—	64	(6)	84	16	19	—	None	N.A.	30.9	628-0414
Galaxy T/E Bond Retail	Muni	L/Hi	5	(5.4)	5.0	—	98	(12)	54	53	73	—	None	N.A.	31.3	628-0414
General Municipal Bond	Muni	L/Med	6	(7.3)	4.9	7.3	93	(6)	22	81	88	99	None	42	821.4	645-6561
GIT Government	Gov	L/Hi	4	(3.6)	3.7	6.4	35	(10)	50	73	25	40	None	83	7.5	336-3063
GIT Maximum Income	HYC	Int/Lo	2	(2.7)	7.9	7.8	68	(50)	51	6	4	12	None	84	6.7	336-3063
GIT Tax-Free National	Muni	L/Hi	6	(8.8)	3.3	5.1	72	(14)	8	52	39	22	None	62	31.7	336-3063
Goldman Sachs Adj./R Mort. ★	MBS	Sh/Hi	—	3.3	—	—	—	(1)	98	N.A.	N.A.	N.A.	3.0	N.A.	16.9	526-7384
Goldman Sachs Global Inc.	WI	Int/Hi	3	(5.3)	4.7	—	55	(10)	41	63	95	N.A.	4.5	117	383.6	762-5035
Goldman Sachs Gov. Income	Gov	N.A.	—	(2.6)	—	—	—	(7)	66	—	—	—	4.5	N.A.	16.6	526-7384
Goldman Sachs Muni Income	Muni	L/Hi	—	(6.1)	—	—	—	—	39	—	—	—	4.5	N.A.	45.8	526-7384
Government Income Sec.	MBS	Int/Hi	1	(1.9)	2.9	6.2	25	(37)	50	37	53	25	1.0[4]	62	1,377.7	245-5051
Govett Global Gov. Income	WI	Int/Med	—	(9.2)	—	—	—	(23)	19	80	—	—	4.95	140	56.0	634-6838
Gradison-McDonald Gov. Inc.	Gov	Int/Hi	3	(3.7)	3.3	6.4	37	(12)	49	42	57	44	2.0	71	184.0	869-5999
Great Hall National T/E	Muni	L/Lo	1	(3.1)	5.9	7.1	99	(4)	77	45	89	41	4.5	92	67.1	934-6674
G.T. Global Gov. Income A	WI	L/Hi	8	(14.4)	3.1	6.2	3	(21)	11	96	54	62	4.75	127	458.8	824-1580
G.T. Global High-Income B	WI	Int/Lo	—	(19.6)	—	—	—	(4)	4	100	N.A.	N.A.	5.0[4]	N.A.	209.5	824-1580
G.T. Global Strategic Inc. A	WI	L/Med	11	(20.9)	4.9	7.7	42	(17)	3	99	49	85	4.75	140	229.9	824-1580
Guardian Inv. Quality Bond	IGC	N.A.	—	(4.7)	—	—	—	(6)	27	—	—	—	4.5	N.A.	43.3	221-3253
Guardian Tax-Exempt		N.A.	—	(9.3)	—	—	—	(16)	4	—	—	—	4.5	N.A.	15.9	221-3253
Hancock Adj. US Gov. A ★	MBS	Int/Hi	1	1.1	3.9	—	63	(6)	91	22	72	—	3.5	75	15.6	225-5291
Hancock Freedom Glob. Inc. B	WI	L/Hi	7	(1.1)	1.9	5.7	N.A.	(13)	78	43	20	53	5.0[4]	123	113.2	225-5291
Hancock Gov. Income B	Gov	Int/Hi	6	(5.3)	2.4	5.7	13	(14)	26	43	24	45	5.0[4]	125	237.2	225-5291
Hancock Gov. Secs. B	Gov	Int/Hi	5	(4.0)	3.3	7.0	31	(79)	42	55	52	86	4.75	110	510.2	225-5291
Hancock H/Y Bond B	HYC	Int/Lo	3	(6.1)	8.9	10.1	66	(11)	18	80	10	42	5.0[4]	129	155.7	225-5291
Hancock H/Y T/F B	Muni	L/Med	2	(5.7)	4.5	5.8	94	(10)	47	43	46	71	5.0[4]	128	146.2	225-5291
Hancock Intm. Gov. A	Gov	Int/Hi	3	(3.8)	3.1	6.2	43	(13)	47	31	69	24	4.75	71	8.3	225-5291
Hancock Invest. Quality A	IGC	Int/Hi	5	(5.7)	2.9	6.8	23	(27)	16	42	22	76	4.75	114	82.3	225-5291
Hancock Ltd.-Term Gov. A	Gov	Sh/Hi	1	(1.3)	3.3	6.0	50	(4)	81	37	8	20	3.0	120	223.9	225-5291
Hancock Managed T/E B	Muni	L/Hi	6	(6.0)	4.9	6.4	94	(3)	42	53	84	50	5.0[4]	94	207.0	225-5291
Hancock S/T Strat. Inc. B ★	WI	Sh/Med	1	1.6	2.7	—	16	(30)	88	14	65	18	3.0[4]	111	97.2	225-5291
Hancock Sovereign Bond A	IGC	L/Med	3	(2.8)	5.4	7.8	55	(9)	61	67	75	58	4.5	120	1,328.8	225-5291
Hancock Sovereign US Gov. B	Gov	L/Hi	5	(4.6)	3.1	6.2	32	(14)	36	65	20	53	5.0[4]	103	193.0	225-5291
Hancock Tax-Exempt Inc. A	Muni	L/Med	5	(5.9)	4.5	6.3	86	(5)	43	55	42	66	4.5	112	459.4	225-5291

Source: Morningstar Inc. Chicago Ill.; 800-876-5005

Fund name/★ 1994 winner	Type	Style	Risk level	% average annual return to Jan. 1, 1995			Tax analysis		Performance analysis (percentile ranking by type)				Expense analysis		Net assets (millions)	Telephone (800)
				One year	Three years	Five years	% tax efficiency	% tax liability	1994	1993	1992	1991	% max. sales charge	Five-year total per $1,000		
Hancock Tax-Free Bond A	Muni	L/Med	7	(9.3)	5.0	—	89	(15)	5	98	98	100	4.75	$83	$117.2	225-5291
Hancock US Gov. A	Gov	Int/Hi	5	(3.9)	3.2	6.5	30	N.A.	45	51	38	51	4.75	69	19.7	225-5291
Hanover S/T US Gov. Inv. ★	Gov	Sh/Hi	—	0.2	—	—	—	(7)	93	—	—	—	None	N.A.	17.6	821-2371
Hanover US Gov. Secs. Inv.	Gov	Int/Hi	—	(4.0)	—	—	—	(7)	42	—	—	—	None	N.A.	83.6	821-2371
Harbor Bond	IGC	Int/Hi	3	(3.8)	5.7	8.8	59	(9)	44	79	88	94	None	46	159.5	422-1050
Harbor Short Duration ★	IGC	Int/Hi	1	2.7	3.9	—	38	(12)	97	7	8	N.A.	None	85	87.7	422-1050
Harris Insight Mgd. F/I	IGC	Int/Hi	2	(1.3)	4.5	—	53	(10)	77	50	14	N.A.	4.5	77	42.3	982-8752
Heartland US Gov. Secs.	Gov	Int/Hi	7	(9.6)	5.5	8.6	52	(17)	5	98	100	88	None	59	65.2	432-7856
Hercules Global Short-Term	WI	N.A.	—	(0.5)	—	—	—	(3)	81	—	—	—	None	N.A.	1.2	584-1317
Hercules World Bond	WI	N.A.	—	(6.2)	—	—	—	(8)	36	—	—	—	None	N.A.	26.4	584-1317
Heritage Income Diversified	IGC	Int/Med	1	(4.0)	5.3	—	52	(10)	42	46	97	100	4.0	105	32.8	421-4184
Heritage Inc. Ltd. Maturity	Gov	Sh/Hi	1	(0.1)	1.7	—	12	(13)	92	1	5	8	2.0	69	31.6	421-4184
Homestead Short-Term Bond	IGC	Sh/Hi	1	(0.4)	4.2	—	67	(3)	84	18	30	—	None	41	52.1	258-3030
Hotchkis & Wiley Low Dur. ★	IGC	Sh/Hi	—	5.2	—	—	—	(1)	100	—	—	—	None	N.A.	70.8	346-7301
Hotchkis & Wiley S/T Inv. ★	IGC	Sh/Hi	—	4.4	—	—	—	(1)	100	—	—	—	None	N.A.	13.6	346-7301
Household Personal F/I	IGC	N.A.	—	(5.7)	—	—	—	(11)	17	—	—	—	None	N.A.	4.9	231-0180
Household Personal S/T	IGC	N.A.	—	(2.0)	—	—	—	(6)	72	—	—	—	None	N.A.	5.1	231-0180
Household Personal T/E	Muni	N.A.	—	(3.2)	—	—	—	(5)	76	—	—	—	None	N.A.	5.2	231-0180
Hyperion Short Duration I ★	MBS	Sh/Hi	1	0.8	1.4	—	N.A.	(68)	89	3	11	N.A.	3.0	83	23.3	497-3746
Hyperion Short Duration II ★	MBS	Sh/Hi	1	0.4	0.7	—	N.A.	(30)	85	2	2	N.A.	4.04	105	41.1	497-3746
IAI Bond	IGC	L/Hi	6	(4.9)	4.5	7.5	26	(11)	25	78	45	70	None	61	80.6	945-3863
IAI Government	Gov	Int/Hi	2	(2.3)	3.9	—	48	(7)	70	57	35	N.A.	None	61	38.4	945-3863
IAI Reserve ★	IGC	Sh/Hi	1	2.7	3.1	5.1	60	(3)	98	3	2	2	None	47	78.9	945-3863
IAI Tax-Free	Muni	L/Hi	—	(8.7)	—	—	—	(12)	8	67	—	—	None	N.A.	6.9	945-3863
IDS Bond	IGC	L/Med	3	(4.3)	6.9	9.1	62	(4)	34	94	95	96	5.0	88	2,135.5	328-8300
IDS Extra Income	HYC	Int/Lo	4	(7.6)	9.8	10.4	70	(26)	15	67	76	67	5.0	94	1,526.0	328-8300
IDS Federal Income	MBS	Int/Hi	1	(0.3)	4.0	6.5	49	(7)	76	49	66	10	5.0	91	1,010.5	328-8300
IDS Global Bond	WI	L/Hi	7	(6.3)	6.1	9.3	65	(5)	34	85	99	83	5.0	122	449.8	328-8300
IDS High-Yield T/E	Muni	L/Med	3	(5.0)	4.2	5.9	98	(3)	57	19	53	63	5.0	83	5,604.9	328-8300
IDS Insured Tax-Exempt	Muni	L/Hi	5	(6.1)	5.1	6.6	100	(3)	40	85	66	49	5.0	84	488.6	328-8300
IDS Selective	IGC	L/Hi	4	(4.4)	5.6	8.0	58	(2)	33	83	86	67	5.0	89	1,392.9	328-8300
IDS Strat. Income	IGC	L/Med	6	(7.8)	5.3	7.6	59	(6)	6	95	90	62	5.0[4]	113	643.2	328-8300
IDS Strat. Short-Term Inc.	IGC	Sh/Hi	2	(2.2)	2.3	4.5	47	(4)	69	9	6	3	5.0[4]	119	215.3	328-8300
IDS Tax-Exempt Bond	Muni	L/Hi	6	(7.4)	3.8	5.6	93	(7)	21	75	12	19	5.0	84	1,087.8	328-8300
Independence Cap Muni Bond	Muni	L/Hi	6	(6.9)	4.7	—	92	(1)	28	77	64	97	4.5	98	4.3	833-4264
Independence Cap S/I Gov. ★	Gov	Sh/Hi	—	0.3	—	—	—	(7)	95	8	—	—	1.5	78	18.6	833-4264
Indep. Cap. T/R Bond	IGC	L/Med	4	(6.2)	5.0	—	44	(11)	12	89	71	87	4.5	109	30.7	833-4264
Intermediate Bond Fund Amer.	IGC	Int/Hi	3	(3.0)	4.0	6.8	49	(9)	58	41	30	28	4.75	95	1,449.3	421-4120
International Income A	WI	Int/Hi	8	(4.6)	6.1	—	58	(11)	47	98	27	—	4.5	123	209.2	245-5051
Invesco High-Yield	HYC	Int/Lo	2	(5.0)	8.0	8.3	67	(10)	27	8	19	6	None	55	207.1	525-8085
Invesco Select Income	IGC	L/Med	1	(1.2)	6.7	8.6	61	(8)	79	69	94	85	None	64	133.0	525-8085
Invesco Short-Term Bond	IGC	Int/Med	—	(0.6)	—	—	—	(6)	83	—	—	—	None	N.A.	8.9	525-8085
Invesco Tax-Free Intm. Bond	Muni	L/Med	—	(4.4)	—	—	—	(9)	64	—	—	—	None	N.A.	4.2	525-8085
Invesco Tax-Free L/T Bond	Muni	L/Med	4	(5.5)	4.8	6.8	87	(1)	51	55	57	79	None	57	260.9	525-8085
Invesco US Gov. Sec.	Gov	L/Hi	7	(7.2)	2.7	6.1	32	(10)	13	79	43	74	None	70	27.0	525-8085
Investors Trust Adj/R A	MBS	Sh/Hi	—	(2.1)	—	—	—	(6)	43	—	—	—	4.5	95	5.1	656-6626
Investors Trust Gov. B	Gov	Int/Hi	6	(9.3)	1.1	5.3	N.A.	(20)	6	47	40	39	5.0[4]	106	1,203.0	656-6626
Investors Trust Tax-Free A	Muni	L/Hi	—	(3.7)	—	—	—	(9)	70	—	—	—	4.5	105	14.2	656-6626
ISI Managed Municipal	Muni	L/Hi	6	(6.3)	3.7	—	96	(3)	36	42	13	30	4.45	93	80.5	955-7175
ISI North Amer. Gov. Bond	WI	Int/Hi	—	(12.7)	—	—	—	(12)	15	—	—	—	3.0	N.A.	73.4	955-7175
ISI Total Return US Treas.	Gov	Int/Hi	5	(4.0)	4.5	7.1	37	(11)	43	91	10	84	4.45	86	195.0	955-7175
Ivy Bond A	IGC	Int/Med	5	(4.5)	5.9	7.0	50	(13)	31	93	64	29	4.75	125	112.1	456-5111
Ivy Short-Term US Gov. A ★	MBS	Sh/Hi	1	0.3	2.6	—	50	(6)	84	17	18	—	1.0	76	8.6	456-5111
Jackson National Income	IGC	N.A.	—	(5.2)	—	—	—	(7)	22	73	—	—	4.75	N.A.	29.3	888-3863
Jackson National Tax-Ex.	Muni	L/Hi	—	(4.6)	—	—	—	(4)	61	64	—	—	4.75	N.A.	29.3	888-3863
Janus Federal Tax-Exempt	Muni	L/Hi	—	(7.8)	—	—	—	(14)	16	—	—	—	None	N.A.	24.2	525-8983
Janus Intm. Gov. Sec.	Gov	Sh/Hi	2	(2.4)	1.6	—	1	(14)	68	3	15	—	None	36	35.0	525-8983
Janus Short-Term Bond ★	IGC	Sh/Med	—	0.3	—	—	—	(7)	89	14	—	—	None	36	45.5	525-8983
Jefferson Pilot Inv. Grade	IGC	L/Hi	5	(6.0)	3.4	6.0	44	(5)	14	54	34	24	4.5	94	21.0	458-4498
Kemper Adj./R US Gov. A	MBS	Int/Hi	1	(0.4)	3.5	6.1	57	(7)	74	42	48	38	3.5	83	167.7	621-1048

Source: Morningstar Inc. Chicago Ill.; 800-876-5005

Fund name/★ 1994 winner	Type	Style	Risk level	% average annual return to Jan. 1, 1995			Tax analysis		Performance analysis (percentile ranking by type)				Expense analysis		Net assets (millions)	Telephone (800)
				One year	Three years	Five years	% tax efficiency	% tax liability	1994	1993	1992	1991	% max. sales charge	Five-year total per $1,000		
Kemper Global Income A	WI	Int/Hi	4	(1.5)	2.1	7.8	N.A.	(3)	72	47	24	48	4.5	$125	$122.9	621-1048
Kemper High-Yield A	HYC	Int/Lo	2	(1.7)	11.4	12.1	75	(12)	69	70	51	89	4.5	88	2,025.0	621-1048
Kemper Inc. & Cap. Pres. A	IGC	Int/Hi	3	(3.4)	5.2	7.9	58	(10)	48	72	67	73	4.5	88	492.1	621-1048
Kemper Municipal Bond A	Muni	L/Hi	6	(6.4)	4.8	6.7	91	(5)	32	78	54	83	4.5	71	3,402.8	621-1048
Kemper S/I Gov. B	Gov	Sh/Hi	2	(1.9)	2.6	5.2	36	(9)	74	11	23	12	4.0[4]	110	232.9	621-1048
Kemper US Gov. Secs. A	MBS	Int/Hi	3	(3.1)	2.5	6.8	13	(17)	32	59	28	99	4.5	79	4,811.7	621-1048
Kemper US Mortgage B	MBS	Int/Hi	4	(4.1)	1.6	5.6	N.A.	(38)	21	40	23	95	4.0[4]	107	1,808.8	621-1048
Keystone Amer. Cap. Pres. A ★	MBS	N.A.	1	1.1	3.2	—	57	(11)	92	44	12	—	3.0	75	25.3	343-2898
Keystone Amer. Cap. Pres.II B ★	MBS	Sh/Hi	1	0.1	2.2	—	47	(7)	80	25	3	—	3.0[4]	82	91.3	343-2898
Keystone Amer. Gov. A	Gov	L/Hi	3	(3.5)	4.2	7.1	35	(12)	52	59	91	56	4.75	121	32.3	343-2898
Keystone Amer. I/T A	IGC	Int/Hi	3	(3.2)	4.6	7.2	57	(13)	52	44	75	61	4.75	100	15.1	343-2898
Keystone Amer. Strat. Inc. A	HYC	Int/Lo	6	(9.6)	12.4	8.9	76	(23)	6	100	74	84	4.75	140	95.4	343-2898
Keystone Amer. T/F Income A	Muni	L/Med	4	(7.7)	3.4	5.3	86	(9)	18	28	38	44	4.75	110	95.7	343-2898
Keystone Amer. World Bond A	WI	N.A.	8	(9.2)	1.7	6.4	N.A.	(12)	17	82	29	92	4.75	160	5.9	343-2898
Keystone Australia Inc. A ★	WI	Int/Hi	11	4.5	5.2	9.3	60	3	91	72	15	90	4.75	174	6.5	343-2898
Keystone Custodian B-1	IGC	Int/Hi	5	(5.1)	2.4	5.6	17	(15)	24	36	4	36	4.0[4]	108	320.2	343-2898
Keystone Custodian B-2	IGC	L/Med	3	(6.9)	5.2	6.2	56	(24)	10	88	92	86	4.0[4]	107	744.3	343-2898
Keystone Custodian B-4	HYC	Int/Lo	7	(12.2)	9.4	7.7	69	(80)	2	97	63	72	4.0[4]	116	661.3	343-2898
Keystone Tax-Exempt	Muni	L/Hi	5	(7.1)	3.3	5.2	87	(7)	25	25	21	32	4.0[4]	101	677.0	343-2898
Keystone Tax-Free[1]	Muni	L/Hi	5	(7.3)	3.5	5.5	85	(7)	22	39	24	29	4.0[4]	76	1,217.4	343-2898
Kidder Peabody Gov. Inc. A	MBS	L/Hi	3	(4.3)	2.6	5.3	35	(21)	19	56	62	30	2.25	86	49.4	854-2505
Kidder Peabody Intm. F/I A	IGC	L/Hi	—	(3.8)	—	—	—	(11)	46	26	—	—	2.25	95	28.6	854-2505
Landmark US Gov. Inc.	Gov	Sh/Hi	1	(1.7)	3.3	6.2	57	(11)	77	23	32	38	1.5	73	53.0	559-7117[6]
Legg Mason Global Gov.	WI	Int/Med	—	(1.6)	—	—	—	(3)	71	—	—	—	None	N.A.	145.1	822-5544
Legg Mason Inv. Grade Inc.	IGC	Int/Med	4	(5.1)	4.1	6.8	38	(11)	23	66	45	50	None	47	66.0	822-5544
Legg Mason Gov. Intm.	Gov	Int/Hi	1	(2.2)	3.5	6.8	44	(9)	72	28	56	49	None	48	235.0	822-5544
Legg Mason T/F I/T Income	Muni	Int/Hi	—	(2.2)	—	—	—	(4)	84	22	—	—	2.0	37	47.5	822-5544
Lexington GNMA Income	MBS	Sh/Hi	3	(2.1)	3.6	7.1	45	(10)	44	85	35	82	None	56	130.1	526-0057
Lexington S/I Gov. Secs.	Gov	L/Hi	—	(1.3)	—	—	—	(5)	83	—	—	—	None	55	5.8	526-0057
Lexington Tax-Exempt Bond	Muni	L/Hi	5	(6.5)	3.4	5.3	100	(7)	30	33	9	18	None	82	11.6	526-0057
Liberty Fin. Ins. Muni	Muni	L/Hi	5	(5.8)	4.2	—	98	(10)	46	64	14	—	4.5	N.A.	45.3	872-5426
Liberty Fin. T/F Bond	Muni	L/Hi	3	(4.6)	4.9	6.5	99	(5)	61	35	62	41	4.5	74	230.6	872-5426
Liberty Fin. US Gov.	MBS	Int/Hi	1	(1.6)	3.3	6.8	38	(12)	59	48	47	49	4.5	92	704.9	872-5426
Liberty High-Inc. Bond A	HYC	Int/Lo	2	(1.7)	10.6	13.6	72	(18)	74	31	53	99	4.5	107	431.8	245-5051
Liberty Muni Securities A	Muni	L/Med	2	(3.8)	4.8	6.5	95	0	69	23	43	80	4.5	89	643.1	245-5051
Limited Term A	IGC	Sh/Hi	1	(1.3)	4.0	—	58	(2)	78	23	24	—	1.0	65	179.1	245-5040
Limited Term Municipal A	Muni	Sh/Med	—	(1.8)	—	—	—	(8)	87	—	—	—	1.0	N.A.	32.6	235-4669
Limited Term T/E Bond Amer.	Muni	L/Med	—	(2.9)	—	—	—	(8)	80	—	—	—	4.75	N.A.	182.4	421-4120
Lincoln Corporate Income A	IGC	Int/Med	—	(5.9)	—	—	—	(14)	15	—	—	—	4.5	N.A.	9.7	923-8476
Lincoln Government Income A	Gov	N.A.	—	(4.3)	—	—	—	(10)	39	—	—	—	4.5	N.A.	9.7	923-8476
Lincoln Tax-Free Inc. A	Muni	Int/Hi	—	(7.4)	—	—	—	(14)	20	—	—	—	4.5	N.A.	9.5	923-8476
Loomis Sayles Bond	IGC	L/Med	3	(4.1)	10.3	—	70	(10)	39	100	100	—	None	55	82.5	633-3330
Loomis Sayles Global Bond	WI	L/Hi	9	(8.7)	1.8	—	N.A.	(14)	21	70	40	—	None	82	25.7	633-3330
Loomis Sayles Muni Bond	Muni	L/Hi	6	(5.4)	4.9	—	97	(8)	53	47	78	—	None	55	7.3	633-3330
Loomis Sayles S/T Bond ★	IGC	Sh/Med	—	1.8	—	—	—	(5)	93	21	—	—	None	55	19.2	633-3330
Loomis Sayles US Gov. Sec.	Gov	Int/Hi	8	(6.3)	5.7	—	46	(17)	18	92	94	—	None	55	17.3	633-3330
Lord Abbett Bond-Debenture	HYC	Int/Lo	2	(3.9)	9.0	10.6	68	(18)	36	10	33	65	4.75	92	989.9	874-3733
Lord Abbett Bond-Deben. Tr.	HYC	Int/Med	—	(2.3)	—	—	—	(6)	57	—	—	—	1.0[4]	N.A.	60.7	874-3733
Lord Abbett Global Inc.	WI	Int/Hi	6	(3.4)	4.4	7.8	37	(14)	60	53	92	67	4.75	111	255.2	874-3733
Lord Abbett Global Inc. Tr.	WI	Int/Hi	—	(2.9)	—	—	—	(7)	64	—	—	—	1.0[4]	N.A.	6.7	874-3733
Lord Abbett Ltd. Dur. US Gov.	Gov	Sh/Hi	—	(3.5)	—	—	—	(9)	97	—	—	—	3.0	N.A.	10.4	874-3733
Lord Abbett Ltd./D US Gov. Tr.	Gov	Int/Hi	—	(3.2)	—	—	—	(15)	60	—	—	—	1.0[4]	N.A.	13.9	874-3733
Lord Abbett Natl. T/F Inc. Tr.	Muni	L/Hi	—	(9.1)	—	—	—	(18)	6	—	—	—	1.0[4]	N.A.	37.6	874-3733
Lord Abbett T/F Inc. Natl.	Muni	L/Hi	6	(7.9)	4.3	6.5	87	(11)	15	81	56	79	4.75	91	604.3	874-3733
Lord Abbett US Gov.	Gov	Int/Hi	5	(4.3)	3.9	7.6	33	(2)	41	66	81	93	4.75	93	3,232.0	874-3733
Lord Abb. US Gov. Sec. Tr.	Gov	Int/Hi	—	(5.5)	—	—	—	(17)	24	—	—	—	None	N.A.	330.0	426-1130
Mackenzie L/T Municipal A	Muni	Int/Hi	1	(2.2)	3.6	—	100	(9)	85	8	4	—	3.0	82	139.1	456-5111
Mackenzie National Muni A	Muni	L/Hi	4	(5.1)	4.0	5.7	95	(9)	56	45	6	24	4.75	105	31.6	456-5111
MainStay Gov. B	Gov	Int/Hi	2	(2.8)	2.2	5.3	4	(18)	63	18	6	31	5.0[4]	116	1,032.5	522-4202
MainStay High-Yield Corp. B ★	HYC	Int/Lo	1	1.5	14.5	12.9	79	(4)	95	84	87	34	5.0[4]	121	1,118.0	522-4202

Source: Morningstar Inc. Chicago Ill.; 800-876-5005

Fund name/★ 1994 winner	Type	Style	Risk level	% average annual return to Jan. 1, 1995			Tax analysis		Performance analysis (percentile ranking by type)				Expense analysis		Net assets (millions)	Telephone (800)
				One year	Three years	Five years	% tax efficiency	% tax liability	1994	1993	1992	1991	% max. sales charge	Five-year total per $1,000		
MainStay Tax-Free Bond B	Muni	L/Hi	4	(6.0)	4.0	5.5	92	(10)	41	24	45	31	5.0[4]	$91	$507.8	522-4202
Managers Bond	IGC	L/Med	6	(7.3)	3.7	7.5	27	(15)	8	70	69	93	None	65	32.4	835-3879
Managers Intm. Mortgage	MBS	Int/Hi	10	(25.0)	(2.6)	3.8	—	(99)	2	99	100	100	None	45	85.4	835-3879
Managers Municipal Bond	Muni	L/Hi	4	(5.6)	4.0	5.7	90	0	50	31	21	26	None	57	12.2	835-3879
Managers Short & Intm. Bond	IGC	L/Hi	3	(8.4)	3.5	6.1	40	(28)	4	35	98	14	None	49	60.1	835-3879
Managers Short Government	Gov	L/Hi	3	(6.1)	0.5	3.8	N.A.	(55)	19	5	8	10	None	43	25.1	835-3879
Managers Short Municipal ★	Muni	Sh/Hi	1	0.4	2.8	3.9	100	(78)	97	2	2	1	None	33	2.7	835-3879
Marshall Government Income	Gov	Int/Hi	—	(2.7)	—	—	—	(10)	65	22	—	—	None	N.A.	76.8	236-8560
Marshall Intm. Bond	IGC	Sh/Hi	—	(3.1)	—	—	—	(11)	57	16	—	—	None	N.A.	321.4	236-8560
Marshall Short-Term Inc. ★	IGC	Sh/Hi	—	1.8	—	—	—	(4)	95	4	—	—	None	N.A.	97.2	236-8560
Medalist US Gov. Sec. Inv.	MBS	Sh/Hi	3	(3.2)	3.3	—	40	(11)	29	80	54	63	None	79	105.9	444-7123
Merrill Lynch Adj./R Sec. B	MBS	Sh/Hi	1	(0.1)	1.8	—	36	(13)	78	10	7	—	4.0[4]	80	256.4	637-3863
Merrill Lynch Corp. I/T A	IGC	Int/Med	4	(4.7)	4.4	7.3	51	(10)	27	78	23	45	1.0	54	160.2	637-3863
Merrill Lynch Federal Sec. D	Gov	Int/Hi	3	(3.5)	3.0	6.5	44	(15)	53	38	36	35	4.0	83	1,050.3	637-3863
Merrill Lynch Global Bond B	WI	N.A.	4	(6.2)	3.7	8.1	34	(12)	37	57	93	78	4.0[4]	96	725.2	637-3863
Merrill Lynch Muni I/T B	Muni	L/Hi	3	(4.1)	4.5	5.9	100	(6)	66	29	24	33	1.0[4]	64	129.8	637-3863
Merrill Lynch S/T Glob. B	WI	Sh/Hi	5	(3.5)	(0.4)	—	N.A.	(15)	59	25	11	15	4.0[4]	82	704.0	637-3863
Merriman Flex. Bond	IGC	L/Hi	3	(1.7)	5.6	7.2	55	(3)	73	90	7	19	None	82	9.4	423-4893
MetLife-St. Res. Gov. Sec. A	Gov	Int/Hi	3	(3.5)	4.0	7.1	50	(9)	52	70	61	76	4.5	111	82.5	882-3302
MetLife-State Res. H/I A	HYC	Int/Lo	1	(2.8)	12.7	10.3	73	(10)	50	89	82	53	4.5	106	603.9	882-3302
MetLife-State Res. T/E A	Muni	L/Med	5	(6.9)	4.5	6.0	98	(6)	28	56	75	56	4.5	111	237.8	882-3302
MFS Bond A	IGC	L/Med	4	(4.5)	5.0	7.9	44	(12)	31	88	28	79	4.75	95	434.6	637-2929
MFS Gov. Ltd. Maturity A	Gov	Sh/Hi	1	(0.8)	4.2	5.2	55	(8)	86	32	64	5	2.5	78	256.2	637-2929
MFS Gov. Mortgage A	MBS	Int/Hi	2	(2.2)	3.4	5.3	35	(15)	41	65	56	28	4.75	121	374.0	637-2929
MFS Gov. Securities A	Gov	Int/Hi	3	(3.3)	4.4	7.0	52	(14)	59	71	83	47	4.75	113	313.9	637-2929
MFS High-Income A	HYC	Int/Lo	1	(2.6)	10.8	11.0	74	(42)	55	63	50	95	4.75	104	501.7	637-2929
MFS Limited Maturity A ★	IGC	Sh/Med	—	0.1	—	—	—	(6)	87	14	—	—	2.5	N.A.	87.2	637-2929
MFS Muni Bond A	Muni	L/Hi	6	(6.9)	5.0	6.8	94	(2)	25	88	77	86	4.75	80	1,886.6	637-2929
MFS Muni High-Inc. A[1]	Muni	L/Lo	1	(2.9)	4.8	5.6	100	(13)	80	20	36	23	4.75	102	896.3	637-2929
MFS Muni Income B	Muni	L/Med	4	(5.3)	4.3	5.5	97	(2)	54	32	33	45	4.0[4]	129	419.8	637-2929
MFS Muni Ltd. Maturity A	Muni	Sh/Med	—	(1.3)	—	—	—	(3)	91	9	—	—	2.5	N.A.	70.4	637-2929
MFS World Gov. A	WI	N.A.	7	(6.6)	3.9	8.4	38	(7)	33	86	50	60	4.75	127	358.8	637-2929
Midwest Adj. Rate US Gov. ★	MBS	Int/Hi	—	0.5	—	—	—	(6)	86	—	—	—	1.0	N.A.	21.4	543-8721
Midwest Intermediate-Term A	Muni	L/Hi	1	(2.9)	5.1	6.1	100	(5)	79	34	28	9	1.0	68	59.0	543-8721
Midwest Intm.-Term Gov. A	Gov	Int/Hi	5	(6.3)	3.2	6.3	48	(9)	17	76	64	64	1.0	65	59.0	543-0407
Midwest Strat. Treas. T/R A	Gov	L/Hi	7	(7.1)	3.4	5.8	30	(9)	14	90	13	74	4.0	106	25.6	543-8721
Midwest US Gov. Long Mat.	Gov	L/Hi	8	(8.9)	4.2	—	6	(16)	8	96	46	27	1.0	83	6.9	543-8721
Midwest US Gov. Sec.	MBS	L/Hi	6	(7.9)	2.0	5.3	N.A.	(17)	12	90	57	23	1.0	103	31.1	543-8721
MIMLIC Fixed-Inc. Sec. A	IGC	L/Med	5	(5.8)	4.0	7.0	40	(11)	15	67	56	54	5.0	102	13.6	443-3677
MIMLIC Mort. Sec. Inc. A	MBS	Int/Hi	5	(3.6)	3.5	7.0	31	(11)	27	91	44	88	5.0	115	26.4	443-3677
Monetta Intermediate Bond	IGC	Int/Hi	—	(1.7)	—	—	—	(6)	74	—	—	—	None	N.A.	3.0	241-9772
Monitrend Gov. Income	Gov	L/Hi	5	(3.4)	1.7	3.7	17	(41)	55	85	1	7	4.5	93	0.9	251-1970
Montgomery Short Gov. Bond ★	Gov	Sh/Hi	—	1.1	—	—	—	(5)	98	53	—	—	None	N.A.	19.0	572-3863
Nations Divers. Inc. Tr. A	IGC	L/Med	—	(2.5)	—	—	—	(9)	65	94	—	—	None	42	22.3	321-7854
Nationwide Bond	IGC	L/Med	7	(7.9)	3.2	6.8	32	(16)	6	59	73	65	4.5	80	121.6	848-0920
Nationwide Tax-Free Inc.	Muni	L/Hi	6	(9.1)	3.9	5.7	95	(9)	7	70	80	30	5.0[4]	64	237.3	848-0920
Nationwide US Gov. Inc.	Gov	Int/Hi	—	(3.6)	—	—	—	(9)	49	60	—	—	5.0[4]	65	36.9	848-0920
Neuberger & Berman Gov. Inc.	Gov	Int/Hi	—	(3.3)	—	—	—	(11)	57	—	—	—	None	N.A.	10.4	877-9700
Neuberger/Berman Ltd. Mat.	IGC	Sh/Med	1	(0.3)	3.8	6.4	55	(5)	85	19	13	9	None	36	301.5	877-9700
Neuberger/Berman Muni	Muni	Int/Hi	3	(4.0)	4.0	5.6	95	(8)	68	18	14	8	None	28	48.7	877-9700
Neuberger/Berman Ultra Sh. ★	IGC	Sh/Hi	1	2.2	3.0	5.0	59	(5)	95	2	4	1	None	36	98.6	877-9700
New England A/R US Gov. A ★	MBS	Sh/Hi	1	0.8	3.2	—	60	(4)	88	24	33	—	3.0	62	584.9	225-7670
New England Bond Income A	IGC	Int/Med	4	(4.2)	4.8	7.9	52	(9)	36	75	60	79	4.5	102	199.6	225-7670
New England Global Gov. A	WI	Int/Hi	5	(5.1)	3.3	6.1	32	(10)	45	60	74	41	4.5	157	18.5	225-7670
New England Gov. Sec. A	Gov	Int/Hi	5	(5.5)	3.2	6.0	33	(13)	24	61	75	61	4.5	110	152.2	225-7670
New England High-Income A	HYC	Int/Lo	2	(3.3)	9.3	9.1	70	(20)	44	16	29	55	4.5	148	33.7	225-7670
New England Ltd./T US Gov. A	Gov	Sh/Hi	2	(2.2)	3.2	6.7	39	(10)	71	28	37	39	3.0	92	425.0	225-7670
New England T/E Inc. A	Muni	L/Hi	6	(8.1)	4.1	5.7	90	(9)	13	67	63	48	4.5	95	182.2	225-7670
Nicholas Income	HYC	Int/Lo	1	(0.2)	7.6	8.7	67	(14)	88	4	2	4	None	38	140.9	272-6133[12]
Nicholas-Applegate Gov. B	Gov	Int/Hi	—	(3.1)	—	—	—	(8)	61	—	—	—	1.0[4]	N.A.	4.7	551-8043

Source: Morningstar Inc. Chicago Ill.; 800-876-5005

213

Fund name/★ 1994 winner	Type	Style	Risk level	% average annual return to Jan. 1, 1995			Tax analysis		Performance analysis (percentile ranking by type)				Expense analysis		Net assets (millions)	Telephone (800)
				One year	Three years	Five years	% tax efficiency	% tax liability	1994	1993	1992	1991	% max. sales charge	Five-year total per $1,000		
North Amer. Inv. Qual. A	IGC	Int/Hi	5	(5.4)	3.8	—	50	(12)	18	44	78	—	4.75	$106	$10.2	872-8037
North American Natl. Muni A	Muni	L/Med	—	(9.2)	—	—	—	(20)	5	—	—	—	4.75	100	7.4	872-8037
North Amer. US Gov. A	MBS	Int/Hi	2	(1.7)	4.3	6.8	56	(9)	56	86	74	32	4.75	106	91.1	872-8037
Northeast Investors ★	HYC	Int/Lo	1	2.2	14.1	11.2	77	(22)	99	93	59	14	None	44	554.6	225-6704
Norwest Adj. US Gov. Inv. A	MBS	Sh/Hi	—	(2.1)	—	—	—	(10)	42	45	—	—	1.5	46	52.3	338-1348
Norwest Gov. Income Inv. A	Gov	Int/Hi	5	(8.0)	2.0	6.5	N.A.	(16)	9	49	77	87	3.75	77	17.0	338-1348
Norwest Inc. Investor A	IGC	Int/Hi	4	(7.0)	3.0	7.3	17	(15)	9	37	71	90	3.75	77	5.7	338-1348
Norwest Tax-Free Inc. Inv. A	Muni	L/Hi	3	(4.9)	3.8	5.3	98	(11)	58	17	20	10	3.75	77	30.0	338-1348
Nuveen Ins. Muni Bond R[1]	Muni	L/Hi	6	(6.3)	5.2	7.0	98	(7)	35	86	85	84	None	86	675.6	351-4100
Nuveen Municipal Bond	Muni	L/Hi	1	(1.8)	5.0	6.2	95	(2)	87	11	48	28	4.75	80	2,552.1	351-4100
NWNL Northstar H/Y Bond A	HYC	Int/Lo	—	(9.4)	—	—	—	(16)	8	—	—	—	4.75	N.A.	52.3	595-7827
111 Corcoran Bond	IGC	Int/Hi	—	(4.2)	—	—	—	(12)	37	70	—	—	4.5	82	86.1	422-2080
One Fund Income	IGC	N.A.	—	(5.4)	—	—	—	(9)	19	66	—	—	3.0	90	4.7	578-8078
Oppenheimer Champion H/Y A	HYC	Int/Lo	1	(0.1)	12.1	13.5	75	(4)	90	78	36	29	4.75	118	169.2	525-7048
Oppenheimer High-Yield A	HYC	Int/Lo	1	(2.3)	10.3	10.8	69	(21)	58	72	12	17	4.75	96	961.0	525-7048
Oppenheimer Ins. T/E Bond A	Muni	L/Hi	6	(7.7)	4.5	6.2	97	(9)	18	68	82	45	4.75	118	63.0	525-7048
Oppenheimer Intm. T/E Bond A	Muni	Int/Hi	2	(3.9)	4.8	6.4	93	(7)	68	19	76	59	3.5	101	77.5	525-7048
Oppenheimer Inv. Gr. Bond A	IGC	Int/Hi	4	(4.4)	4.0	6.9	54	(11)	32	54	42	81	4.75	105	96.6	525-7048
Oppenheimer Ltd./T Gov. A ★	MBS	Sh/Hi	1	0.5	4.2	7.6	53	(7)	87	82	22	80	3.5	99	239.5	525-7048
Oppenheimer Mort. Inc. A	MBS	Int/Med	2	(0.7)	3.8	7.1	47	(9)	70	83	24	50	4.75	120	75.8	525-7048
Oppenheimer Strat. Inv. Gr. A	IGC	Int/Med	—	(4.0)	—	—	—	(10)	41	60	—	—	4.75	N.A.	24.0	525-7048
Oppenheimer Strat. S/T Inc. A	IGC	Sh/Med	—	(1.1)	—	—	—	(8)	80	32	—	—	3.5	N.A.	22.3	525-7048
Oppenheimer T/F Bond A	Muni	L/Hi	6	(9.3)	4.1	6.0	92	(10)	4	85	80	68	4.75	97	528.1	525-7048
Oppenheimer US Gov. A	Gov	Int/Hi	2	(1.3)	3.9	6.8	49	(6)	83	50	18	72	4.75	108	291.6	525-7048
Overland Exp. Muni Inc A	Muni	L/Hi	5	(6.8)	5.0	—	100	(12)	29	76	89	—	3.0	43	73.8	552-9612
Overland Express S/T Gov.	Gov	Int/Hi	—	(4.8)	—	—	—	(29)	34	4	—	—	3.0	68	14.4	552-9612
Overland Express US Gov. A	Gov	L/Hi	5	(4.8)	3.6	7.7	39	(12)	33	81	34	94	4.5	70	35.8	552-9612
Overland Exp. Var. Rate A	MBS	Sh/Hi	1	(3.8)	1.7	—	17	(11)	25	41	20	4	3.0	70	1,215.5	552-9612
Pacific Advisors Gov. Secs.	Gov	L/Hi	—	(0.2)	—	—	—	(1)	90	—	—	—	4.75	118	3.0	282-6693
Pacific Horizon US Gov.	MBS	L/Hi	2	(3.9)	3.4	7.0	35	(13)	23	72	93	69	4.5	65	89.7	332-3863
Pacifica Asset Preservation ★	IGC	Sh/Med	1	2.4	3.9	—	65	(2)	96	8	9	4	None	41	95.3	662-8417
Pacifica Government Income	Gov	Int/Hi	4	(6.9)	2.4	—	13	(14)	16	68	26	67	4.5	87	110.5	662-8417
PaineWebber Glob. Inc. B	WI	L/Hi	5	(4.7)	2.7	7.2	33	(12)	46	66	38	43	5.0[4]	127	693.0	647-1568
PaineWebber High-Inc. A	HYC	Int/Lo	6	(11.7)	10.4	12.6	68	(44)	4	91	95	91	4.0	92	268.4	647-1568
PaineWebber Inv. Grade A	IGC	L/Med	5	(5.6)	5.2	8.0	59	(20)	17	85	84	83	4.0	94	271.6	647-1568
PaineWebber Muni H/I A	Muni	L/Med	6	(7.1)	4.6	6.5	93	(8)	24	57	87	89	4.0	106	62.9	647-1568
PaineWebber Natl. T/F Inc. A	Muni	L/Hi	6	(7.1)	4.1	5.9	95	(6)	23	61	37	36	4.0	88	341.3	647-1568
PaineWebber S/T US Gov. Inc. D[1]	Gov	Sh/Hi	—	(4.9)	—	—	—	(29)	32	—	—	—	None	N.A.	296.1	647-1568
PaineWebber US Gov. Inc. A	MBS	Int/Hi	6	(10.5)	0.4	5.0	N.A.	(45)	10	64	58	65	4.0	89	428.7	647-1568
Parnassus Inc. Fixed-Inc.	IGC	L/Hi	—	(6.8)	—	—	—	(13)	11	63	—	—	None	55	4.5	999-3505
Permanent Port. Treas. Bill ★	Gov	Sh/Hi	1	3.3	2.8	4.2	79	1	100	2	3	3	None	75	122.4	531-5142
Permanent Port. Vers. Bd. ★	IGC	Sh/Hi	1	2.6	4.0	—	91	0	97	4	16	—	None	82	26.4	531-5142
Phoenix Asset Reserve A	IGC	Sh/Med	—	(1.9)	—	—	—	(5)	72	37	—	—	2.25	77	9.9	243-4361
Phoenix High-Yield A	HYC	Int/Lo	4	(8.0)	9.4	10.0	71	(81)	13	82	46	10	4.75	104	512.0	243-4361
Phoenix Tax-Exempt Bond A	Muni	L/Hi	6	(7.4)	5.2	6.6	94	(6)	20	87	96	46	4.75	87	141.6	243-4361
Phoenix US Gov. Securities A	Gov	Int/Hi	3	(3.5)	4.0	6.8	45	(86)	54	49	91	43	4.75	88	256.1	243-4361
Pierpont Bond	IGC	Int/Hi	6	(4.0)	2.7	6.3	37	(8)	40	11	43	21	None	45	113.0	521-5411
Pierpont Short-Term Bond	IGC	Sh/Hi	—	(0.9)	—	—	—	(5)	81	—	—	—	None	37	7.5	521-5411
Pierpont Tax-Exempt Bond	Muni	Int/Hi	3	(3.6)	3.9	5.9	93	(2)	71	16	12	32	None	43	352.6	521-5411
Pilgrim Adj. Rate Secs. I[1]	MBS	Sh/Hi	7	(20.0)	(3.1)	—	N.A.	(10)	4	54	86	—	4.0[4]	N.A.	60.6	334-3444
Pilgrim Adj. Rate Secs. I-A	MBS	Sh/Hi	—	(20.5)	—	—	—	(17)	3	60	—	—	4.0[4]	N.A.	154.7	334-3444
Pilgrim Adj. Rate Secs. II	MBS	Sh/Hi	7	(19.9)	(2.6)	—	N.A.	(44)	5	74	97	—	3.0	96	20.8	334-3444
Pilgrim Adj. Rate Secs. III	MBS	Sh/Hi	7	(19.0)	(2.2)	—	N.A.	(49)	6	73	98	—	5.0	N.A.	12.3	334-3444
Pilgrim Adj. US Gov. I[1]	MBS	Sh/Hi	5	(12.6)	(1.5)	—	N.A.	(85)	8	15	43	—	4.0[4]	N.A.	309.5	334-3444
Pilgrim Adj. US Gov. I-A	MBS	Sh/Hi	—	(12.9)	—	—	—	(25)	7	11	—	—	4.0[4]	N.A.	187.8	334-3444
Pilgrim Adj. US Gov. II	MBS	Sh/Hi	—	(12.5)	—	—	—	(25)	9	27	—	—	3.0	96	12.4	334-3444
Pilgrim GNMA	MBS	Int/Hi	3	(4.1)	2.6	5.4	21	(75)	22	35	91	13	3.0	89	51.6	334-3444
Pilgrim High-Yield	HYC	Int/Lo	2	(2.2)	10.4	9.6	75	(82)	62	51	34	23	3.0	136	16.1	334-3444
Pilgrim S/T Multi-Market ★	WI	Sh/Hi	8	2.9	(3.9)	(5.2)	N.A.	N.A.	90	6	2	6	3.0	100	16.8	334-3444
Pilgrim S/T Multi-Mkt. II ★	WI	Sh/Hi	6	0.2	(2.8)	—	N.A.	(32)	85	8	6	—	4.0[4]	140	4.8	334-3444

Source: Morningstar Inc. Chicago Ill.; 800-876-5005

Fund name/★ 1994 winner	Type	Style	Risk level	% average annual return to Jan. 1, 1995			Tax analysis		Performance analysis (percentile ranking by type)				Expense analysis		Net assets (millions)	Telephone (800)
				One year	Three years	Five years	% tax efficiency	% tax liability	1994	1993	1992	1991	% max. sales charge	Five-year total per $1,000		
PIMCo Advisors H/I C	IGC	Int/Med	7	(7.1)	2.2	4.1	N.A.	(77)	8	23	56	11	1.0[4]	$103	$154.6	426-0107
PIMCo Advisors S/I C †	Gov	Sh/Hi	1	(0.9)	1.3	—	—	(12)	85	4	2	—	1.0[4]	82	77.1	426-0107
PIMCo Advisors T/E C †	Muni	L/Hi	7	(9.5)	3.0	4.8	90	(7)	3	62	23	15	1.0[4]	97	60.3	426-0107
PIMCo Advisors US Gov. C †	Gov	Int/Hi	5	(5.3)	1.3	5.1	N.A.	(38)	27	34	3	77	1.0[4]	97	326.4	426-0107
Pioneer America Income A	Gov	Int/Hi	3	(4.0)	3.8	6.4	48	(6)	43	62	70	19	4.5	98	162.9	225-6292
Pioneer Bond A	IGC	L/Hi	3	(4.2)	4.8	7.4	56	(6)	37	69	70	46	4.5	102	100.2	225-6292
Pioneer Intermediate T/F A	Muni	L/Hi	4	(6.0)	4.3	6.1	97	(5)	41	37	52	37	4.5	90	76.3	225-6292
Pioneer Short-Term Inc. A ★	IGC	Sh/Hi	—	0.2	—	—	—	(6)	88	12	—	—	2.5	N.A.	59.0	225-6292
Pioneer Tax-Free Income	Muni	L/Hi	5	(6.4)	4.8	6.8	92	(3)	34	73	55	78	4.5	93	445.6	225-6292
Piper Jaffray Gov. Income	Gov	Int/Hi	8	(9.1)	1.5	6.2	N.A.	(22)	8	75	9	96	4.0	100	112.5	866-7778
Piper Jaffray Natl. T/E	Muni	L/Hi	7	(8.5)	4.5	6.5	91	(9)	10	96	51	64	4.0	90	61.3	866-7778
Portico Bond IMMDEX	IGC	Int/Hi	3	(3.1)	5.0	7.9	59	(5)	57	61	62	58	None	30	252.9	228-1024
Portico S/T Bond Mkt. ★	IGC	Sh/Hi	1	1.0	4.7	7.0	60	(4)	90	17	47	22	None	30	119.1	228-1024
Preferred Fixed-Income	IGC	L/Hi	—	(2.4)	—	—	—	(6)	66	55	—	—	None	N.A.	46.8	662-4769
Preferred S/T Gov. Sec.	Gov	Sh/Hi	—	(0.7)	—	—	—	(4)	87	14	—	—	None	N.A.	29.4	662-4769
Premier GNMA A	MBS	L/Hi	2	(2.9)	3.8	7.4	42	(10)	33	89	70	75	4.5	101	147.4	554-4611
Premier Ltd./T Gov. A	Gov	Int/Hi	4	(4.3)	3.3	6.1	51	(5)	40	63	30	33	None	69	18.0	554-4611
Premier Ltd./T Muni A	Muni	L/Hi	3	(4.2)	4.9	6.4	87	(3)	65	41	40	48	None	42	21.9	554-4611
Premier Managed Inc. A	IGC	Int/Med	4	(5.1)	5.7	7.5	52	(12)	23	91	83	65	None	60	83.3	554-4611
Premier Muni Bond A	Muni	L/Med	4	(6.4)	5.6	7.6	97	(5)	31	95	90	95	4.5	95	483.2	554-4611
Principal Pres. Government	Gov	Int/Hi	5	(5.4)	3.6	6.9	48	(9)	25	77	72	66	4.5	100	47.2	826-4600
Principal Pres. Insured T/E	Muni	L/Hi	6	(6.9)	4.4	5.8	85	(8)	27	77	37	12	4.5	104	17.7	826-4600
Principal Pres. Tax-Exempt	Muni	L/Hi	5	(6.4)	5.1	6.3	100	(23)	33	93	52	17	4.5	93	55.3	826-4600
Princor Bond	IGC	L/Med	4	(4.4)	5.4	7.6	60	(6)	33	82	82	72	5.0	96	89.8	451-5447
Princor Gov. Sec. Income	MBS	L/Hi	6	(4.9)	3.3	7.1	36	(11)	18	95	52	93	5.0	100	248.0	451-5447
Princor High-Yield	HYC	Int/Lo	2	(1.3)	7.2	7.0	68	(19)	78	2	8	19	5.0	123	19.7	451-5447
Princor Tax-Exempt Bond	Muni	L/Med	6	(9.4)	3.7	5.7	94	(12)	4	63	84	66	5.0	102	161.6	451-5447
Prudential Adj. Rate Sec. A ★	MBS	N.A.	—	1.1	—	—	—	(13)	93	7	—	—	1.0	79	69.5	225-1852
Prudential GNMA B	MBS	Int/Hi	2	(2.7)	2.4	5.4	23	(15)	35	28	39	15	5.0[4]	97	250.2	225-1852
Prudential Gov. Income B	Gov	Int/Hi	5	(4.8)	2.7	5.8	28	(14)	34	31	59	50	5.0[4]	102	1,578.3	225-1852
Prudential Gov. Intm. A	Gov	Sh/Hi	2	(2.6)	3.5	6.3	43	(36)	66	38	51	31	None	44	242.6	225-1852
Prudential High-Yield B	HYC	Int/Lo	1	(3.0)	9.4	9.7	69	(25)	48	17	27	40	5.0[4]	89	3,337.0	225-1852
Prudential Int. Glob. Inc. A	WI	Int/Hi	6	(7.0)	3.7	5.0	34	(43)	28	76	81	20	3.0	104	218.7	225-1852
Prudential Muni H/Y B	Muni	L/Med	2	(3.4)	5.1	6.2	100	(5)	74	33	42	63	5.0[4]	72	978.6	225-1852
Prudential Muni Ins. B	Muni	L/Hi	5	(5.7)	4.3	6.1	89	(5)	48	42	35	51	5.0[4]	72	622.7	225-1852
Prudential Muni Modified B	Muni	L/Hi	3	(5.6)	3.9	5.7	91	(5)	50	27	22	27	5.0[4]	100	58.4	225-1852
Prudential National Muni B	Muni	L/Hi	5	(6.4)	4.4	6.3	83	(6)	33	56	49	77	5.0[4]	72	668.4	225-1852
Prudential S/T Glob. Ast. A	WI	Sh/Hi	2	(1.3)	1.3	—	N.A.	(33)	75	15	45	—	1.0	82	46.4	225-1852
Prudential S/T Glob. Inc. B	WI	Sh/Hi	7	(5.2)	0.1	—	N.A.	(29)	43	34	25	39	3.0[4]	104	178.8	225-1852
Prudential Struc. Mat. A	IGC	Sh/Med	1	(1.4)	4.0	6.9	48	(7)	74	22	38	16	3.25	77	95.8	225-1852
Prudential US Government B	Gov	L/Hi	7	(6.1)	3.1	5.5	48	(14)	18	82	30	59	5.0[4]	107	121.4	225-1852
Putnam Adj. Rate US Gov. A	MBS	Sh/Hi	1	(0.2)	1.4	3.9	N.A.	(23)	77	4	15	2	3.25	94	105.9	225-1581
Putnam Amer. Gov. Inc. A	Gov	L/Hi	3	(2.9)	3.0	5.1	20	(59)	63	23	47	6	4.75	98	2,284.9	225-1581
Putnam Balanced Gov. A	MBS	Int/Hi	—	(1.0)	—	—	—	(7)	67	—	—	—	3.25	N.A.	53.9	225-1581
Putnam Federal Income A	Gov	Int/Hi	4	(3.1)	2.5	6.1	16	(60)	61	12	45	71	4.75	106	438.3	225-1581
Putnam Global Gov. Inc. A	WI	L/Hi	7	(10.0)	2.2	7.4	N.A.	(16)	16	67	84	76	4.75	123	446.8	225-1581
Putnam High Yield A	HYC	Int/Lo	2	(4.7)	10.4	12.1	68	(25)	29	50	72	68	4.75	105	2,725.7	225-1581
Putnam H/Y Advantage A	HYC	Int/Lo	2	(5.1)	10.8	12.8	69	(19)	20	74	68	85	4.75	107	654.5	225-1581
Putnam Income A	IGC	Int/Med	2	(3.3)	5.9	8.0	61	(8)	51	74	93	82	4.75	99	769.3	225-1581
Putnam Muni Income A	Muni	L/Med	3	(6.4)	5.3	6.9	98	(11)	34	54	99	74	4.75	110	789.4	225-1581
Putnam Tax Exempt Inc. A	Muni	L/Hi	6	(7.9)	4.9	6.4	94	(8)	16	83	95	81	4.75	93	2,075.0	225-1581
Putnam Tax-Free H/Y B	Muni	L/Med	3	(5.9)	5.4	6.3	98	(8)	43	66	95	51	5.0[4]	99	1,396.7	225-1581
Putnam Tax-Free Ins. B	Muni	L/Hi	5	(6.4)	3.7	5.4	95	(5)	32	39	16	35	5.0[4]	117	388.6	225-1581
Putnam US Gov. Income A	MBS	Int/Hi	2	(2.5)	3.2	6.2	30	(7)	38	47	73	12	4.75	101	3,036.7	225-1581
Quest for Value Global Inc. A	WI	Int/Lo	8	(6.9)	(0.4)	—	N.A.	(20)	29	61	8	—	3.0	129	16.8	232-3863
Quest for Value Inv. Qual. A	IGC	L/Med	6	(6.8)	5.1	—	59	(9)	10	87	89	15	4.75	118	45.1	232-3863
Quest for Value Natl. T/E	Muni	L/Hi	5	(5.8)	5.5	—	96	(8)	45	74	94	85	4.75	79.4	82.4	232-3863
Quest for Value US Gov. A	Gov	L/Hi	3	(3.8)	3.0	6.3	39	(13)	48	30	61	25	4.75	108	119.0	232-3863
RBB Government Securities	Gov	Int/Hi	3	(3.5)	3.9	—	45	(12)	53	65	62	—	4.75	81	52.5	888-9723
RBB Tax-Free	Muni	L/Hi	6	(8.1)	5.0	6.5	80	(4)	13	92	93	57	4.75	56	4.6	888-9723

Source: Morningstar Inc. Chicago Ill.; 800-876-5005

Fund name/★ 1994 winner		Type	Style	Risk level	% average annual return to Jan. 1, 1995			Tax analysis		Performance analysis (percentile ranking by type)				Expense analysis		Net assets (millions)	Telephone (800)
					One year	Three years	Five years	% tax efficiency	% tax liability	1994	1993	1992	1991	% max. sales charge	Five-year total per $1,000		
Retirement Planning Bond B		MBS	Sh/Hi	1	(1.1)	2.2	4.9	N.A.	(14)	65	20	19	17	4.0[4]	$134	$19.2	279-0279
Rightime Government Sec.		Gov	L/Hi	2	(0.4)	5.3	3.3	73	(12)	89	42	97	1	4.75	152	25.3	242-1421
RIMCo Monument Bond		IGC	Int/Hi	—	(4.4)	—	—	—	(11)	32	64	—	—	3.5	70	44.5	934-3883
Rodney Sq. Diver. Income		IGC	Int/Hi	2	(2.5)	4.0	—	56	(4)	65	26	46	—	3.5	75	31.6	336-9970
Rushmore US Gov. Intm.		Gov	Int/Hi	7	(7.3)	3.5	6.6	15	(16)	13	86	80	82	None	45	10.0	343-3355
Rushmore US Gov. L/T		Gov	L/Hi	9	(9.9)	3.3	6.1	13	(11)	4	92	52	85	None	45	30.8	343-3355
Safeco GNMA		MBS	Int/Med	3	(4.3)	3.0	6.4	37	(12)	20	75	75	58	None	52	43.6	426-6730
Safeco High-Yield Bond		HYC	Int/Lo	1	(2.3)	9.2	9.3	69	(10)	60	19	14	8	None	58	24.1	426-6730
Safeco Intm.-Term US		Gov	Int/Hi	4	(3.6)	4.4	6.7	53	(6)	50	81	65	34	None	54	12.4	426-6730
Safeco Muni Bond		Muni	L/Hi	7	(8.2)	4.0	6.4	91	(2)	11	72	56	94	None	30	445.4	426-6730
SBC Short-Term World Inc.		WI	Sh/Hi	—	(3.6)	—	—	—	(14)	56	27	—	—	3.5	—	36.9	524-9984
Schwab L/T Gov. Bond		Gov	L/Hi	—	(5.9)	—	—	—	(10)	20	—	—	—	None	—	8.0	526-8600
Schwab L/T T/F Bond		Muni	L/Hi	—	(6.9)	—	—	—	(11)	26	83	—	—	None	—	37.9	526-8600
Schwab S/I Government		Gov	Sh/Hi	2	(2.8)	3.6	—	52	(8)	65	45	47	—	None	33	166.4	526-8600
Schwab Short/Intm. T/F Bond		Muni	Sh/Hi	—	(1.1)	—	—	—	(5)	92	—	—	—	None	N.A.	56.1	526-8600
Scudder GNMA		MBS	Int/Hi	3	(3.1)	3.2	6.8	32	(13)	31	52	82	62	None	55	423.3	225-2470
Scudder H/Y Tax-Free		Muni	L/Med	6	(8.4)	5.0	6.8	91	(8)	11	90	97	90	None	54	253.7	225-2470
Scudder Income		IGC	L/Hi	5	(4.5)	4.7	7.9	48	(7)	29	81	41	71	None	51	460.1	225-2470
Scudder Intl. Bond		WI	Int/Hi	7	(8.6)	4.4	11.0	35	(14)	23	77	97	100	None	75	1,162.6	225-2470
Scudder Mgd. Muni Bonds		Muni	L/Hi	6	(6.0)	5.1	6.8	87	(5)	40	82	64	72	None	35	712.8	225-2470
Scudder Medium-Term T/F		Muni	Int/Hi	2	(3.5)	5.3	6.8	98	(5)	73	34	62	67	None	0	738.9	225-2470
Scudder Short-Term Bond		IGC	Sh/Hi	1	(2.9)	3.4	6.8	40	(8)	60	25	15	27	None	42	2,302.9	225-2470
Scudder S/T Global Income		WI	Sh/Hi	1	(1.1)	3.6	—	35	(11)	80	29	90	—	None	55	537.7	225-2470
Scudder Zero Coupon 2000		Gov	Int/Hi	8	(7.9)	4.9	7.7	30	(10)	10	93	93	97	None	55	24.5	225-2470
Security Inc. Corp. Bond A		IGC	L/Hi	6	(8.3)	4.4	7.1	42	(17)	5	87	86	52	4.75	101	90.6	888-2461
Security Inc. US Gov. A		MBS	Int/Hi	5	(6.5)	3.1	6.5	20	(18)	14	100	32	45	4.75	106	8.3	888-2461
Security Tax-Exempt A		Muni	L/Hi	6	(8.3)	3.4	5.6	93	(14)	11	62	20	53	4.75	92	23.9	888-2461
Select. US Gov. Income		Gov	L/Hi	3	(2.4)	3.5	6.5	35	(4)	69	48	20	36	None	79	10.3	243-1575
Seligman H/Y Bond A	★	HYC	Int/Lo	1	0.8	13.0	11.8	77	(23)	93	61	80	27	4.75	115	57.6	221-2783
Seligman Tax-Ex. National A		Muni	L/Hi	7	(9.9)	3.5	5.5	80	(16)	2	91	32	46	4.75	93	101.6	221-2783
Seligman US Gov. Sec. A		Gov	Int/Hi	3	(3.9)	3.0	5.8	34	(52)	46	41	41	43	4.75	103	57.7	221-2783
Sentinel Bond		IGC	Int/Hi	5	(4.9)	4.8	7.8	48	(10)	25	79	66	74	5.0	99	80.7	282-3863
Sentinel Gov. Sec.		Gov	Int/Hi	4	(4.3)	3.9	7.1	49	(12)	38	68	84	68	5.0	101	103.2	282-3863
Sentinel Tax-Free Income		Muni	L/Med	4	(5.3)	5.2	—	97	(2)	55	70	65	68	5.0	99	99.2	282-3863
Seven Seas Intermed. Bond		Gov	Int/Hi	—	(4.6)	—	—	—	(1)	36	—	—.	—	None	N.A.	19.5	647-7327
Seven Seas S/T Term Gov.	★	Gov	Sh/Hi	—	0.2	—	—	—	(5)	94	9	—	—	None	N.A.	21.9	647-7327
Seven Seas Yield Plus	★	IGC	Sh/Hi	—	4.1	—	—	—	0	99	2	—	—	None	N.A.	1,353.3	647-7327
Sierra Corporate Income A		IGC	L/Med	7	(10.3)	4.6	—	49	(16)	2	97	91	95	4.5	110	361.2	222-5852
Sierra National Muni A		Muni	L/Med	6	(7.0)	5.6	—	96	(4)	25	98	91	100	4.5	91	274.4	222-5852
Sierra S/T Glob. Government A		WI	N.A.	—	(1.2)	—	—	—	(4)	76	31	—	—	3.5	74	152.6	222-5852
Sierra S/T High-Qual. A		IGC	N.A.	—	(2.2)	—	—	—	(2)	70	—	—	—	3.5	N.A.	70.3	222-5852
Sierra US Government A		Gov	Int/Hi	4	(5.9)	2.3	6.1	8	(18)	20	30	59	58	4.5	83	461.4	222-5852
Sit Bond		IGC	Int/Hi	—	(1.3)	—	—	—	(8)	77	—	—	—	None	N.A.	3.4	332-5580
Sit Tax-Free Income		Muni	L/Med	1	(0.6)	5.7	6.8	98	(4)	93	25	30	10	None	44	252.9	332-5580
Sit US Gov. Secs.	★	Gov	Sh/Hi	1	1.8	4.8	7.6	58	(3)	99	40	28	26	None	55	36.1	332-5580
Smith Barney A/R Gov. A	★	MBS	Sh/Hi	—	2.3	—	—	N.A.	(4)	97	12	—	—	None	82	199.5	451-2010
Smith Barney Global Bond B		WI	Int/Hi	5	(2.9)	4.0	7.3	53	(2)	65	56	75	88	4.5[4]	119	54.5	451-2010
Smith Barney Global Gov. A		WI	N.A.	7	(4.0)	4.9	—	52	(3)	54	89	43	—	4.5	114	75.0	544-7835
Smith Barney Gov. Secs. B		Gov	Int/Hi	5	(3.3)	4.1	7.0	56	N.A.	57	80	29	81	4.5[4]	90	172.7	451-2010
Smith Barney High-Income B		HYC	Int/Lo	2	(5.0)	10.6	9.6	73	(46)	25	55	78	48	4.5[4]	100	402.2	451-2010
Smith Barney Inc. Return A	★	IGC	Sh/Hi	1	1.8	3.9	6.3	64	(9)	94	6	20	7	4.5	43	19.7	544-7835
Smith Barney Inv./G Bond B		IGC	L/Med	8	(9.3)	5.1	7.9	53	(16)	3	99	79	99	4.5[4]	94	217.6	451-2010
Smith Bar. Lim. Mat. Munis A		Muni	Int/Hi	1	(0.2)	4.8	—	100	(3)	95	7	27	—	2.0	58	76.3	451-2010
Smith Bar. Lim Mat. Treas. A		Gov	Int/Hi	5	(5.1)	4.2	—	47	(7)	30	57	99	—	2.0	58	74.7	451-2010
Smith Barney Mgd. Gov. A		MBS	Int/Hi	4	(2.0)	4.3	7.9	56	(18)	47	94	50	97	4.5	101	556.1	451-2010
Smith Barney Mgd. Munis A		Muni	L/Med	4	(4.5)	6.6	7.8	85	(6)	62	100	78	97	4.0	84	1,639.4	451-2010
Smith Bar. Monthly Paymt. A		MBS	L/Hi	2	(1.5)	3.9	7.2	47	(9)	63	66	78	71	4.5	69	42.2	544-7835
Smith Barney Muni Ltd./T B		Muni	Int/Hi	—	(1.8)	—	—	—	(3)	88	—	—	—	1.0[4]	49	26.6	544-7835
Smith Barney Muni Natl. A		Muni	L/Hi	4	(5.8)	5.3	7.1	99	(5)	45	84	75	84	4.5	69	384.8	544-7835
Smith Barney S/T US Treas.		Gov	N.A.	2	(1.6)	3.3	—	59	(8)	78	17	44	—	None	50	103.5	698-5349[6]

Source: Morningstar Inc. Chicago Ill.; 800-876-5005

Fund name/★ 1994 winner	Type	Style	Risk level	% average annual return to Jan. 1, 1995			Tax analysis		Performance analysis (percentile ranking by type)				Expense analysis		Net assets (millions)	Telephone (800)
				One year	Three years	Five years	% tax efficiency	% tax liability	1994	1993	1992	1991	% max. sales charge	Five-year total per $1,000		
Smith Barney T/E Inc. B	Muni	L/Hi	4	(6.5)	4.3	5.8	97	(6)	30	50	55	38	4.5[4]	$90	$736.5	451-2010
Smith Bar. US Gov. Secs. A	MBS	Int/Hi	2	(1.5)	3.8	7.3	42	(11)	61	61	77	86	4.5	68	367.4	544-7835
Smith Breeden Intm. Dur. Gov.	MBS	L/Hi	—	(1.7)	—	—	—	(4)	54	98	—	—	None	N.A.	33.3	221-3138
Smith Breeden Sh. Dur. Gov. ★	MBS	Sh/Hi	—	4.3	—	—	—	(2)	100	36	—	—	None	N.A.	225.0	221-3138
Smith Br. Sh. Dur. Gov. Svc. ★	MBS	Sh/Hi	—	4.1	—	—	—	(2)	99	29	—	—	None	N.A.	195.3	221-3138
SouthTrust Vulcan Bond	IGC	L/Hi	—	(4.7)	—	—	—	(4)	28	57	—	—	4.0	66	76.3	239-7470
Star US Government Inc.	Gov	L/Hi	—	(3.3)	—	—	—	(6)	59	—	—	—	3.5	N.A.	88.1	677-3863
Starburst Gov. Income	Gov	Int/Hi	—	(1.5)	—	—	—	(11)	79	33	—	—	2.5	96	53.7	239-1930
Starburst Muni Income	Muni	Int/Hi	2	(3.3)	4.6	—	98	(6)	75	24	19	—	2.5	93	25.0	239-1930
State St. Research Gov. Inc. A	Gov	L/Hi	3	(2.9)	4.4	7.6	57	(29)	62	74	71	79	4.5	100	622.6	882-3302
SteinRoe Gov. Income	Gov	L/Hi	4	(3.3)	3.2	6.5	34	(9)	60	35	53	62	None	55	40.3	338-2550
SteinRoe High-Yield Muni	Muni	L/Med	3	(4.2)	3.7	5.7	91	(9)	65	26	3	14	None	38	276.1	338-2550
SteinRoe Income	IGC	Int/Med	3	(4.1)	5.9	8.1	64	(9)	40	86	87	68	None	50	153.4	338-2550
SteinRoe Intm. Bond	IGC	Int/Hi	2	(2.8)	4.6	7.1	52	(10)	62	43	65	38	None	39	297.3	338-2550
SteinRoe Intm. Muni	Muni	Int/Hi	3	(3.5)	4.8	6.5	95	(3)	72	32	27	27	None	44	209.7	338-2550
SteinRoe Limited Mat. Inc.	IGC	Sh/Hi	—	(0.1)	—	—	—	(6)	86	—	—	—	None	25	27.2	338-2550
SteinRoe Managed Munis	Muni	L/Hi	4	(5.5)	4.3	6.7	92	(3)	51	36	41	94	None	36	632.2	338-2550
Stepstone Ltd. Mat. Gov. Inst.	Gov	N.A.	—	(0.9)	—	—	—	(6)	85	—	—	—	None	31	34.2	342-5734
STI Classic Inv./Gr. T/E Inv.	Muni	L/Hi	—	(0.6)	—	—	—	(1)	93	94	—	—	3.75	98	61.7	428-6970
Strong Advantage ★	IGC	Sh/Med	1	3.6	6.7	7.4	73	(1)	99	28	80	6	None	55	878.3	368-1030
Strong Gov. Securities	Gov	Int/Hi	3	(3.4)	6.0	8.6	55	(10)	56	88	98	85	None	64	259.0	368-1030
Strong H/Y Muni Bond	Muni	N.A.	—	(1.0)	—	—	—	(7)	92	—	—	—	None	N.A.	99.7	368-3863
Strong Income	IGC	L/Med	2	(1.3)	8.0	6.3	72	(49)	76	98	89	35	None	72	121.4	368-1030
Strong Insured Muni Bond	Muni	L/Hi	6	(6.5)	5.7	—	97	(13)	31	49	100	—	None	63	40.2	368-1030
Strong Muni Bond	Muni	L/Med	3	(4.6)	6.2	7.3	91	(11)	62	50	99	89	None	49	286.3	368-1030
Strong S/T Bond	IGC	Sh/Med	1	(1.8)	4.6	6.7	57	(8)	73	45	39	34	None	52	1,129.9	368-1030
Strong S/T Muni Bond	Muni	Sh/Hi	1	(1.5)	4.1	—	98	(6)	90	6	17	—	None	46	177.1	368-1030
SunAmerica Diver. Inc. B	IGC	Int/Lo	5	(8.9)	1.0	—	N.A.	(17)	4	85	1	—	4.0[4]	92	155.7	858-8850
SunAmerica Fed. Sec. B	MBS	L/Hi	3	(1.6)	1.5	5.6	N.A.	(10)	57	6	29	52	4.0[4]	125	66.4	858-8850
SunAmerica High-Income A	HYC	Int/Lo	4	(9.0)	8.8	10.6	60	(34)	9	12	89	59	4.75	130	26.0	858-8850
SunAmerica T/Ex. Ins. A	Muni	L/Hi	2	(4.0)	3.4	4.9	100	(11)	67	9	13	5	4.75	113	140.5	858-8850
SunAmerica US Gov. Secs B	Gov	L/Hi	1	(1.4)	2.7	5.3	34	(10)	81	6	32	8	4.0[4]	114	633.1	858-8850
Sunburst S/I Gov. Bond	Gov	Sh/Hi	—	(2.4)	—	—	—	(7)	67	—	—	—	1.0	N.A.	11.9	467-2506
Target Intm.-Term Bond	IGC	N.A.	—	(2.4)	—	—	—	(6)	N.A.	—	—	—	None	100	66.0	225-1852
Target Mort. Backed Secs.	MBS	N.A.	—	(0.3)	—	—	—	(8)	N.A.	—	—	—	None	100	62.5	225-1852
Target Total Return Bond	IGC	N.A.	—	(3.3)	—	—	—	(8)	N.A.	—	—	—	None	100	31.0	225-1852
Tax-Ex. Bond Fund Amer.	Muni	L/Med	3	(4.8)	5.1	6.5	97	(3)	59	49	67	38	4.75	85	1,253.1	421-4120
TCW/DW N. Amer. Gov. Inc.	WI	N.A.	—	(15.6)	—	—	—	(26)	10	38	—	—	None	N.A.	1,231.0	392-2550[6]
Templeton Income	WI	Int/Hi	7	(3.6)	3.1	6.7	21	(13)	58	48	68	71	4.25	107	198.6	292-9293
Thornburg Intm. Muni A	Muni	Int/Med	2	(2.5)	6.3	—	100	(3)	82	59	87	—	3.5	N.A.	209.3	847-0200
Thornburg Ltd.-Term Inc. A	IGC	Int/Hi	—	(3.1)	—	—	—	(7)	54	47	—	—	2.5	79	20.9	847-0200
Thornburg Ltd./T Muni Natl. A	Muni	Int/Hi	1	(1.5)	4.9	6.0	100	(2)	90	12	29	7	2.5	83	1,028.3	847-0200
Thornburg Ltd./T US Gov. A	MBS	Int/Hi	1	(2.1)	3.8	6.5	55	(4)	45	57	89	19	2.5	76	178.4	847-0200
Torchmark Gov. Securities	Gov	N.A.	—	(6.7)	—	—	—	(14)	16	—	—	—	None	55	1.3	733-3863
Torchmark Ins. Tax-Free	Muni	L/Hi	—	(8.6)	—	—	—	(13)	9	—	—	—	None	55	2.1	733-3863
Tower Total Return Bond	IGC	L/Hi	—	(2.6)	—	—	—	(6)	63	29	—	—	3.0	N.A.	72.5	999-0124
Tower US Government Inc.	Gov	L/Hi	3	(3.3)	3.0	6.4	33	(10)	58	44	16	54	3.0	82	50.5	999-0124
Trademark Government Inc.	Gov	Int/Hi	—	(5.2)	—	—	—	(11)	29	—	—	—	None	N.A.	99.9	566-3653[16]
Trademark Sh.-Intm. Gov.	Gov	Sh/Hi	—	(2.4)	—	—	N.A.	(10)	68	—	—	—	None	N.A.	44.6	566-3653[16]
T. Rowe Price Adj. Rate US	MBS	Sh/Hi	1	(0.6)	2.0	—	24	(19)	72	9	14	—	None	14	131.2	638-5660
T. Rowe Price GNMA	MBS	Int/Hi	2	(1.6)	3.6	7.1	42	(10)	58	55	69	67	None	48	757.8	638-5660
T. Rowe Price Global Gov.	WI	Int/Hi	4	(3.1)	3.6	—	43	(7)	63	51	72	50	None	66	40.0	638-5660
T. Rowe Price High-Yield	HYC	Int/Lo	4	(8.0)	8.7	8.4	69	(25)	11	85	21	31	None	49	1,090.8	638-5660
T. Rowe Price Intl. Bond	WI	Int/Hi	8	1.8	6.5	10.5	57	(5)	69	90	61	95	None	60	760.6	638-5660
T. Rowe Price New Income	IGC	L/Hi	3	(2.2)	3.8	7.1	50	(4)	69	40	11	44	None	48	1,370.0	638-5660
T. Rowe Price S/T Bond	IGC	Sh/Hi	1	(2.9)	2.8	5.6	37	(9)	59	17	12	8	None	42	490.2	638-5660
T. Rowe Price S/T Glob. Inc.	WI	Sh/Hi	—	(2.9)	—	—	—	(15)	67	37	—	—	None	55	59.9	638-5660
T. Rowe Price Summ. GNMA	MBS	L/Hi	—	(2.3)	—	—	—	(8)	40	—	—	—	None	N.A.	17.6	638-5660
T. Rowe P. Summ. Muni Intm.	Muni	Int/Hi	—	(1.7)	—	—	—	(6)	89	—	—	—	None	N.A.	12.7	638-5660
T. Rowe Price T/F High-Yield	Muni	L/Med	2	(4.4)	5.8	7.2	95	(4)	63	73	83	55	None	45	810.8	638-5660

Source: Morningstar Inc. Chicago Ill.; 800-876-5005

Fund name/★ 1994 winner	Type	Style	Risk level	% average annual return to Jan. 1, 1995			Tax analysis		Performance analysis (percentile ranking by type)				Expense analysis		Net assets (millions)	Telephone (800)
				One year	Three years	Five years	% tax efficiency	% tax liability	1994	1993	1992	1991	% max. sales charge	Five-year total per $1,000		
T. Rowe Price T/F Income	Muni	L/Hi	5	(5.5)	5.3	6.7	96	(5)	53	71	77	70	None	$34	$1,233.3	638-5660
T. Rowe Price T/F S/I ★	Muni	Sh/Hi	1	0.3	4.2	5.3	100	(1)	97	5	5	4	None	35	465.5	638-5660
T. Rowe P. US Treas. Intm.	Gov	Sh/Hi	3	(2.2)	3.9	7.0	50	(4)	71	50	57	58	None	44	165.0	638-5660
T. Rowe P. US Treas L/T	Gov	L/Hi	7	(5.7)	4.0	6.9	40	(6)	22	89	42	81	None	44	56.1	638-5660
20th Century L/T Bond	IGC	Int/Med	5	(4.5)	3.6	6.7	40	(6)	30	53	17	72	None	55	119.9	345-2021
20th Century T/E Intm.	Muni	Int/Hi	1	(1.9)	4.7	6.0	94	(2)	86	15	17	19	None	34	77.3	345-2021
20th Century T/E Long-Term	Muni	L/Hi	5	(5.5)	4.5	6.3	89	(5)	52	57	25	64	None	34	49.1	345-2021
20th Century T/E Short-Term ★	Muni	Sh/Hi	—	2.5	—	—	—	(1)	100	—	—	—	None	N.A.	60.3	345-2021
20th Century US Gov. S/T	Gov	Sh/Hi	1	(0.4)	2.7	5.4	56	(7)	89	9	10	15	None	55	390.7	345-2021
UMB Bond	IGC	Int/Hi	2	(3.1)	3.8	6.5	55	(5)	56	32	36	18	None	48	75.2	422-2766
United Bond	IGC	Int/Med	6	(5.8)	4.7	7.3	48	(11)	16	84	61	88	5.75	104	518.0	366-5465
United Gov. Securities	Gov	Int/Hi	5	(3.9)	4.3	7.3	60	(14)	45	76	81	89	4.25	82	152.4	366-5465
United High-Income	HYC	Int/Lo	1	(3.7)	9.8	9.1	73	(55)	37	38	40	61	5.75	123	908.0	366-5465
United High-Income II	HYC	Int/Lo	1	(4.1)	9.2	10.1	72	(20)	34	33	25	33	5.75	128	343.9	366-5465
United Municipal Bond	Muni	L/Hi	7	(7.1)	5.2	6.9	87	(6)	24	84	91	91	4.25	73	897.8	366-5465
United Muni High-Income	Muni	L/Lo	2	(3.1)	6.5	7.7	96	(4)	78	78	92	61	4.25	81	339.5	366-5465
United Services Intm. Treas.	Gov	Int/Hi	—	(4.9)	—	—	—	(8)	31	86	—	—	None	N.A.	4.2	873-8637
United Svcs. Near-Term T/F	Muni	Int/Hi	1	0.0	5.4	—	99	(3)	96	20	10	13	None	157	9.2	873-8637
United Svcs. Spec. Term Gov.	Gov	Int/Hi	—	(1.4)	—	—	—	(11)	79	—	—	—	None	N.A.	7.4	873-8637
United Svcs. Tax-Free	Muni	L/Hi	5	(5.2)	4.3	5.8	97	(9)	55	51	18	14	None	78	16.1	873-8637
USAA Investment GNMA	MBS	Int/Hi	2	0.0	4.4	—	51	(8)	79	78	49	—	None	21	244.9	382-8722
USAA Mutual S/T Bond	IGC	Sh/Med	—	0.0	—	—	—	(5)	86	—	—	—	None	N.A.	50.6	382-8722
USAA Tax-Exempt I/T	Muni	Int/Med	2	(4.0)	5.1	6.6	98	(4)	67	44	48	37	None	25	1,416.1	382-8722
USAA T/E Long-Term	Muni	L/Hi	5	(7.9)	4.5	6.5	86	(8)	15	65	92	75	None	22	1,661.2	382-8722
USAA T/E Short-Term ★	Muni	Sh/Hi	1	0.8	4.1	5.1	100	(2)	98	3	5	3	None	27	810.8	382-8722
USAffinity Gov. Income	Gov	N.A.	—	0.0	—	—	—	(10)	93	26	—	—	4.5	136	2.3	800-3030
USAffinity Tax-Free Muni	Muni	N.A.	—	(7.3)	—	—	—	(12)	22	96	—	—	4.5	136	1.9	800-3030
US Government Securities	Gov	Int/Hi	4	(4.6)	4.3	7.2	48	(10)	35	80	87	46	4.75	93	1,290.1	421-4120
UST Master I/T Mgd.	IGC	Int/Hi	—	(3.8)	—	—	—	(10)	45	34	—	—	4.5	84	42.8	233-1136
UST Master T/E I/T	Muni	Int/Hi	2	(4.2)	4.8	6.2	83	(9)	65	31	50	21	4.5	80	236.6	233-1136
UST Master Mgd. Inc.	IGC	L/Hi	6	(5.6)	4.0	7.4	32	(12)	18	80	21	59	4.5	102	99.2	233-1136
UST Master S/T Gov. ★	Gov	Sh/Hi	—	1.0	—	—	—	(3)	98	7	—	—	4.5	78	26.8	233-1136
UST Mst. L/T Tax-Exempt	Muni	L/Hi	7	(5.8)	6.2	7.7	79	(11)	46	99	91	82	4.5	91	74.5	233-1136
UST Mst. S/T T/E Sec.	Muni	Sh/Hi	—	(0.3)	—	—	—	(3)	94	4	—	—	4.5	78	54.9	233-1136
Value Line Adj./R US Gov.	MBS	L/Hi	—	(9.9)	—	—	—	(27)	11	53	—	—	None	58	23.4	223-0818
Value Line Aggressive Income	HYC	Int/Lo	2	(4.1)	8.6	9.3	69	(59)	32	57	6	16	None	65	29.9	223-0818
Value Line T/E High-Yield	Muni	L/Hi	6	(6.9)	3.8	6.0	95	(9)	27	44	30	74	None	32	225.9	223-0818
Value Line US Government	Gov	Int/Hi	6	(10.7)	1.4	6.0	N.A.	(21)	4	73	58	83	None	36	299.0	223-0818
Van Eck Global Income A	WI	Int/Hi	10	(2.8)	(0.5)	6.6	N.A.	(18)	68	18	9	99	4.75	116	142.8	544-4653
Van Kampen Adj./R US Gov. B	MBS	Int/Hi	—	(0.7)	—	—	—	(5)	71	34	—	—	3.0[4]	89	24.5	225-2222
Van Kampen High-Yield A	HYC	Int/Lo	2	(3.6)	9.9	9.7	66	(44)	41	40	48	51	4.65	121	245.1	225-2222
Van Kampen Ins. T/F Inc. A	Muni	L/Hi	6	(6.3)	4.8	6.4	97	(3)	36	61	81	25	4.65	90	1,081.6	225-2222
Van Kamp. Ltd./T Muni Inc. B	Muni	L/Hi	—	(4.0)	—	—	—	(8)	66	—	—	—	3.0[4]	51	17.6	225-2222
Van Kampen Muni Inc. A	Muni	L/Med	5	(6.4)	4.8	—	98	(8)	35	58	85	96	4.65	92	491.8	225-2222
Van Kampen S/T Glob. Inc. A	WI	Sh/Hi	4	(7.4)	1.5	—	N.A.	(11)	26	32	88	36	3.0	100	106.9	225-2222
Van Kampen Strat. Inc. B	IGC	L/Med	—	(16.8)	—	—	—	(22)	1	—	—	—	4.0[4]	N.A.	48.9	225-2222
Van Kampen T/F High-Inc. A	Muni	L/Med	3	(4.9)	3.3	4.3	100	(15)	58	99	1	6	4.65	103	598.4	225-2222
Van Kampen US Gov. A	MBS	Int/Hi	4	(5.1)	2.9	6.7	18	(21)	17	84	60	84	4.65	90	2,936.9	225-2222
Vanguard Bond Ind. Tot. Bond	IGC	Int/Hi	3	(2.7)	4.6	7.5	54	(6)	64	49	52	40	None	61	1,728.3	851-4999
Vanguard F/I GNMA	MBS	Int/Hi	2	(1.0)	3.9	7.6	49	(5)	68	50	79	91	None	16	5,804.0	851-4999
Vanguard F/I H/Y Corp.	HYC	Int/Lo	2	(1.7)	9.9	10.0	72	(11)	71	46	16	21	None	19	2,130.8	851-4999
Vanguard F/I I/T Corp. Bond	IGC	Int/Hi	—	(4.2)	—	—	—	(8)	36	—	—	—	None	15	133.0	851-4999
Vanguard F/I Intm.-Term	Gov	Int/Hi	5	(4.3)	4.7	—	55	(11)	39	84	88	—	None	15	815.2	851-4999
Vanguard F/I L/T Corp. Bond	IGC	L/Hi	6	(5.3)	6.0	8.9	57	(6)	20	91	93	97	None	18	2,538.8	851-4999
Vanguard F/I Long-Term US	Gov	L/Hi	7	(7.0)	5.3	7.7	45	(5)	15	96	85	92	None	15	634.3	851-4999
Vanguard F/I S/T Corp.	IGC	Sh/Med	1	(0.1)	4.7	7.2	59	(5)	85	22	54	15	None	15	3,050.4	851-4999
Vanguard F/I S/T Fed.	Gov	Sh/Hi	1	(0.9)	4.0	6.7	55	(5)	84	33	54	20	None	15	1,532.5	851-4999
Vanguard F/I Short-Term US	Gov	Sh/Hi	1	(0.5)	4.1	—	62	(5)	88	26	73	—	None	15	691.2	851-4999
Vanguard Muni High-Yield	Muni	L/Med	6	(5.1)	5.5	7.4	89	(6)	57	68	88	99	None	13	1,584.8	851-4999
Vanguard Muni Insured Long	Muni	L/Hi	6	(5.6)	5.2	7.0	92	(3)	50	75	70	78	None	13	1,742.7	851-4999

Source: Morningstar Inc. Chicago Ill.; 800-876-5005

Fund name/★ 1994 winner	Type	Style	Risk level	% average annual return to Jan. 1, 1995			Tax analysis		Performance analysis (percentile ranking by type)				Expense analysis		Net assets (millions)	Telephone (800)
				One year	Three years	Five years	% tax efficiency	% tax liability	1994	1993	1992	1991	% max. sales charge	Five-year total per $1,000		
Vanguard Muni Intermediate	Muni	Int/Hi	2	(2.1)	5.9	7.4	95	(1)	85	46	59	69	None	$13	$4,656.2	851-4999
Vanguard Muni Limited-Term ★	Muni	Int/Hi	1	0.1	4.2	5.8	99	(2)	96	4	8	12	None	13	1,711.7	851-4999
Vanguard Muni Long-Term	Muni	L/Hi	6	(5.8)	5.3	7.2	89	(4)	47	84	74	92	None	13	909.9	851-4999
Vanguard Muni Short-Term ★	Muni	Int/Hi	1	1.6	3.4	4.8	99	(1)	99	2	2	2	None	13	1,543.5	851-4999
Venture Income Plus ★	HYC	Int/Lo	1	1.6	13.8	6.0	75	(49)	97	29	93	2	4.75	147	57.0	279-0279
Venture Muni Plus B ★	Muni	L/Med	1	2.3	6.3	6.6	95	(1)	100	10	44	53	4.0⁴	129	143.2	279-0279
Victory S/T Gov. Inc.	Gov	N.A.	—	(0.1)	—	—	—	(5)	91	—	—	—	2.0	63	34.5	539-3863
Vision US Gov. Secs.	Gov	L/Hi	—	(5.5)	—	—	—	(8)	25	—	—	—	4.5	N.A.	28.0	836-2211
Vista Global F/I A	WI	N.A.	—	(1.2)	—	—	—	(4)	77	41	—	—	4.5	141	1.4	648-4782
Vista Tax-Free Income A	Muni	L/Hi	5	(7.6)	6.2	8.0	95	(13)	18	97	100	96	4.5	45	82.1	648-4782
Vista US Gov. Income A	Gov	Int/Hi	5	(4.5)	3.7	6.8	43	(12)	37	78	44	57	4.5	85	94.7	648-4782
Voyageur National Ins T/F A	Muni	L/Hi	—	(7.5)	—	—	—	(14)	19	48	—	—	4.75	48	32.3	553-2143
Voyageur US Gov. Sec. A	Gov	Int/Hi	6	(5.6)	3.9	7.9	42	(14)	23	83	68	93	4.75	105	75.0	553-2143
Waddell & Reed Glob. Inc. ★	WI	N.A.	—	0.1	—	—	—	(5)	82	11	—	—	3.0⁴	N.A.	10.9	236-2000¹⁷
Waddell & Reed Ltd./T Bond	IGC	Int/Hi	—	(3.1)	—	—	—	(6)	56	24	—	—	3.0⁴	N.A.	11.1	236-2000¹⁷
Waddell & Reed Muni Bond	Muni	L/Med	—	(8.8)	—	—	—	(14)	8	89	—	—	3.0⁴	107	24.0	236-2000¹⁷
Warburg Pincus Fixed-Inc.	IGC	Int/Hi	2	(0.8)	5.5	7.1	65	(6)	82	64	40	64	None	42	105.2	257-5614
Warburg Pincus Global F/I	WI	Int/Hi	6	(5.5)	5.0	—	60	(5)	39	92	56	69	None	25	85.0	257-5614
Warburg Pincus Intm. Mat.	Gov	Sh/Hi	3	(1.8)	4.2	7.2	37	(4)	76	46	71	63	None	33	44.1	257-5614
Wasatch Income ★	IGC	Int/Hi	1	1.6	3.4	6.8	42	(6)	93	5	10	22	None	55	3.2	345-7460
Wayne Hummer Income	IGC	L/Med	—	(2.4)	—	—	—	(9)	55	58	—	—	None	N.A.	25.8	621-4477
Weitz Fixed-Income	IGC	Int/Hi	2	(2.3)	3.6	6.2	55	(6)	67	28	15	8	None	58	18.5	232-4161
Westcore Bonds Plus	IGC	Int/Hi	3	(2.8)	4.0	7.2	37	(9)	62	31	37	50	4.5	74	53.7	392-2673
Westcore Long-Term Bond	IGC	L/Hi	8	(7.1)	4.3	7.3	26	(9)	9	76	85	93	4.5	75	25.7	392-2673
Westcore Quality T/E Income	Muni	Int/Hi	—	(4.3)	—	—	—	(8)	64	—	—	—	3.5	N.A.	12.7	392-2673
William Blair Income	IGC	Int/Hi	2	(0.7)	4.9	—	54	(8)	82	33	52	55	None	49	143.9	742-7272
Wm. Penn US Gov. Income	Gov	L/Hi	3	(3.8)	5.3	7.4	56	(9)	47	84	96	18	4.75	103	43.8	523-8440
Winthrop Focus Fixed-Inc.	IGC	Int/Hi	3	(3.7)	4.3	7.3	55	(5)	45	52	53	32	4.0⁴	50	39.2	225-8011
Winthrop Focus Muni Tr.	Muni	N.A.	—	(3.4)	—	—	—	(7)	75	—	—	—	4.0⁴	N.A.	33.7	225-8011
Working Assets Citizens Inc.	IGC	Int/Med	—	(3.1)	—	—	—	(7)	55	50	—	—	2.0	N.A.	25.2	223-7010
WPG Government Securities	Gov	Int/Hi	6	(8.8)	2.3	5.9	—	(22)	9	62	89	42	None	44	226.0	223-3332
WPG Intm. Muni Bond	Muni	L/Hi	—	(2.2)	—	—	—	(7)	83	—	—	—	None	N.A.	13.9	223-3332
Zweig Government Sec. A	Gov	Int/Hi	4	(2.8)	3.8	6.3	58	(79)	64	75	11	48	4.75	121	47.5	444-2706

The 563 State Funds

Fund name/★ 1994 winner	Yield	One year	Three years	Telephone (800)
ALABAMA				
Alabama Tax-Free Bond	4.8%	(3.6)	N.A.	443-4249
EV Marathon AL Tax-Free	5.2	(8.1)	N.A.	225-6265
Franklin AL Tax-Free Income	5.3	(4.4)	5.2	342-5236
MFS AL Municipal Bond A	5.5	(4.7)	5.3	637-2929
ARIZONA				
Dean Witter M/S Muni AZ	5.5	(6.6)	4.7	869-3863
EV Marathon AZ Tax-Free	5.4	(9.7)	3.9	225-6265
First Invest. M/S Ins. T/F AZ	5.6	(6.1)	6.1	423-4026
Flagship AZ Double Tax-Ex. A	5.3	(5.6)	5.5	227-4648
Franklin AZ Insured T/F Inc.	5.8	(8.3)	N.A.	342-5236
Franklin AZ Tax-Free Income	4.9	(4.0)	5.4	342-5236
GIT AZ Tax-Free	4.9	(8.6)	3.6	336-3063
Merrill Lynch AZ Ltd. Mat. B ★	3.6	1.2	N.A.	637-3863
Merrill Lynch AZ Muni B	5.0	(6.5)	4.6	637-3863
Norwest AZ Tax-Free Inv. A	5.6%	(3.8)	N.A.	338-1348
Nuveen AZ Tax-Free Value R¹	6.2	(6.3)	N.A.	351-4100
Premier State Muni AZ A	6.5	(7.8)	N.A.	554-4611
Prudential Municipal AZ B	4.9	(5.0)	4.7	225-1852
Putnam AZ Tax Exempt Inc. A	6.0	(6.7)	4.4	225-1581
Smith Barney AZ Munis A	5.1	(6.4)	5.1	451-2010
Tax-Free Trust of AZ	6.1	(5.3)	4.8	437-1020
Voyageur AZ Insured T/F A	5.4	(7.4)	4.6	553-2143
Westcore AZ Intm. T/F	5.2	(3.3)	N.A.	392-2673
ARKANSAS				
EV Marathon AR Tax-Free	5.2	(8.4)	N.A.	225-6265
MFS AR Municipal Bond A	5.8	(6.1)	N.A.	637-2929
CALIFORNIA				
Alliance Muni Income CA A	6.4	(10.1)	3.6	227-4618
Alliance Muni Insured CA A	5.8%	(11.0)	3.3	227-4618
Atlas CA Insured Intm. A	4.7	(4.1)	N.A.	933-2852
Atlas CA Municipal Bond A	5.6	(5.8)	4.9	933-2852
Benham CA Muni High-Yield	6.6	(5.4)	5.4	331-8331
Benham CA T/F Insured	6.0	(6.6)	5.0	331-8331
Benham CA T/F Intm.-Term	5.3	(3.7)	4.5	331-8331
Benham CA T/F Long-Term	6.3	(6.5)	4.8	331-8331
Benham CA T/F Short-Term	4.6	(0.6)	N.A.	331-8331
Bernstein CA Municipal	5.2	(3.2)	3.8	756-4097⁶
California Inv. CA Insured	5.0	(5.0)	N.A.	225-8778
California Inv. T/F Income	6.0	(8.6)	4.5	225-8778
California Muni	7.4	(20.0)	0.1	322-6864
California Muni Income Fort	6.8	(10.5)	N.A.	245-5040
Calvert CA Municipal Intm.A	4.7	(2.6)	N.A.	368-2748
Colonial CA Tax-Exempt A	5.4	(7.3)	3.4	248-2828
Dean Witter CA T/F Income	4.9	(6.0)	4.0	869-3863

Source: Morningstar Inc. Chicago Ill.; 800-876-5005

Fund name/★ 1994 winner	Yield	% return to Jan 1,1995 One year	% return to Jan 1,1995 Three years	Telephone (800)
Dean Witter M/S Muni CA	5.8%	(8.5)	4.4	869-3863
Dreyfus CA Intm. Muni	5.4	(5.5)	N.A.	645-6561
Dreyfus CA T/E Bond	5.8	(7.1)	3.5	645-6561
EV Marathon CA Ltd. Mat.T/F	4.4	(4.9)	N.A.	225-6265
EV Marathon CA Municipals	5.4	(9.1)	2.5	225-6265
Evergreen Sh.-Intm. Muni CA	4.5	(1.8)	N.A.	235-0064
Fidelity CA T/F High-Yield	6.4	(8.9)	4.0	544-8888
Fidelity CA Tax-Free Insured	6.2	(10.2)	3.7	544-8888
Fidelity Spartan CA I/M	5.9	(4.7)	N.A.	544-8888
Fidelity Spartan CA Muni H/Y	8.6	(9.0)	4.2	544-8888
First Invest M/S Ins. T/F CA	5.3	(6.5)	4.7	423-4026
Franklin CA High-Yield Muni	6.8	(6.2)	N.A.	342-5236
Franklin CA Insured T/F Inc.	5.0	(5.3)	5.1	342-5236
Franklin CA Intm.-Term T/F	5.4	(4.3)	N.A.	342-5236
Franklin CA Tax-Free Income	5.4	(2.8)	5.2	342-5236
Fremont CA Intm. Tax-Free	5.2	(4.9)	3.9	548-4539
General CA Municipal Bond	5.9	(7.0)	4.7	242-8671
Griffin CA Tax-Free A	5.7	(8.9)	N.A.	676-4450
Hancock Tax-Exempt CA	5.5	(6.1)	4.6	225-5291
IDS CA Tax-Exempt	5.6	(5.2)	4.8	328-8300
Kemper State T/F Inc. CA A	5.1	(5.4)	4.9	621-1048
Lord Abbett CA T/F Inc. Tr.	5.6	(11.3)	N.A.	874-3733
Lord Abbett CA T/F Income	5.6	(10.5)	3.7	874-3733
Mackenzie CA Municipal A	4.3	(5.0)	4.1	456-5111
MainStay CA Tax-Free	5.2	(4.8)	5.0	522-4202
Merrill Lynch CA Ins. Muni B	5.1	(8.0)	N.A.	637-3863
Merrill Lynch CA Ltd. Mat. B	3.8	(0.9)	N.A.	637-3863
Merrill Lynch CA Muni Bond B	5.3	(7.5)	3.9	637-3863
MFS CA Municipal A	6.0	(8.1)	4.2	637-2929
Montgomery CA T/F Free	4.5	0.0	N.A.	572-3863
N. American CA Muni A	5.3	(12.6)	N.A.	873-8037
New England I/T T/F CA A	5.0	(5.0)	N.A.	225-7670
Nuveen CA Ins. T/F Val. R[1]	6.2	(6.9)	4.6	351-4100
Nuveen CA T/F Value R[1]	6.3	(6.5)	4.4	351-4100
Oppenheimer CA T/E A	5.6	(8.5)	4.0	525-7048
Oppen. Main St. CA T/E A	5.8	(7.7)	4.1	525-7048
Overland Exp. CA T/F Bond A	5.6	(4.3)	5.6	552-9612
Pacific Horizon CA T/E Bond	5.5	(5.7)	4.8	332-3863
Pacifica CA Tax-Free	5.1	(6.3)	4.3	662-8417
Pacifica Short-Term CA T/F★	4.2	1.1	N.A.	662-8417
PaineWebber CA T/F Inc. A	5.6	(8.1)	3.4	647-1568
Parnassus Inc. CA Tax-Ex.	5.9	(6.4)	N.A.	999-3505
Phoenix CA T/E Bonds A	5.0	(5.2)	3.5	243-4361
Pioneer CA Double Tax-Free	6.2	(10.6)	N.A.	225-6292
Premier CA Ins. Muni Bond B	5.1	(10.5)	N.A.	554-4611
Premier CA Muni Bond A	5.6	(6.0)	4.9	554-4611
Premier Ltd./T CA Muni A	4.3	(3.7)	5.0	554-4611
Prudential CA Muni CA B	5.4	(6.2)	4.3	225-1852
Prudential CA Muni CA Inc.A	6.6	(3.7)	6.6	225-1852
Putnam CA T/E Income A	5.9	(6.7)	4.6	225-1581
Quest for Value CA Tax-Ex.	5.4	(6.5)	4.7	232-3863
Safeco CA Tax-Free Income	6.1	(9.2)	3.6	426-6730
Schwab CA L/T T/F Bond	6.5	(8.9)	N.A.	526-8600
Schwab CA Sh./Intm. T/F	4.7	(2.1)	N.A.	526-8600
Scudder CA Tax-Free	5.3	(7.3)	4.9	225-2470
Seligman T/E CA Qual. A	6.0	(8.3)	3.9	221-2783
Seligman T/E CA H/Y A	6.1	(2.8)	5.4	221-2783
Sierra CA Municipal A	6.1	(8.6)	4.3	222-5852
Smith Barney CA Munis A	5.1	(6.7)	4.3	451-2010
Smith Barney I/Mat. CA A	5.0	(4.9)	4.5	451-2010
Smith Barney Muni CA A	N.A.	(5.7)	4.6	544-7835
Smith Barney Muni CA L/T A	N.A.	(3.1)	N.A.	544-7835
Stagecoach CA T/Free Bond	5.7%	(7.3)	4.7	222-8222
Stagecoach CA Tax-Free Inc.	4.3	(1.1)	N.A.	222-8222
Tax-Exempt Fund of CA	5.5	(5.1)	5.1	421-4120
Thornburg L/T Muni CA A	4.6	(2.1)	4.4	847-0200
Transamerica CA T/F Inc. A	6.0	(9.3)	4.0	225-5291
T. Rowe Price CA T/F Bond	6.1	(5.7)	4.9	638-5660
USAA Tax-Exempt CA Bond	6.6	(9.3)	3.5	382-8722
Van Kampen CA Ins. T/F A	5.2	(8.6)	4.8	225-2222
Vanguard CA T/F Ins. L/T	6.5	(5.7)	5.2	662-7447
Vista CA Intermediate T/F	5.0	(3.2)	N.A.	648-4782
Voyageur CA Ins. T/F A	6.2	(9.4)	N.A.	553-2143
Working Assets Cit. Muir CA	4.9	(7.1)	4.1	223-7010

COLORADO

Fund name/★ 1994 winner	Yield	One year	Three years	Telephone (800)
EV Marathon CO Tax-Free	5.7	(9.5)	N.A.	225-6265
First Invest. M/S Ins. T/F CO	5.8	(6.7)	N.A.	423-4026
Flagship CO Double T/E A	5.7	(5.8)	5.1	227-4648
Franklin CO T/F Income	5.2	(5.4)	5.4	342-5236
Hanifen Imhoff CO Bd. Shrs. ★	6.2	6.3	7.8	525-9989
Merrill Lynch CO Muni B	5.0	(8.7)	N.A.	637-3863
Norwest CO Tax-Free Inv. A	5.6	(5.9)	N.A.	338-1348
Seligman Tax-Exempt CO A	6.8	(5.1)	4.3	221-2783
Tax-Free Fund of CO	6.0	(3.8)	5.2	872-2652
Voyageur CO Tax-Free A	5.9	(9.1)	4.5	553-2143
Westcore CO Tax-Exempt	5.3	(3.2)	4.8	392-2673

CONNECTICUT

Fund name/★ 1994 winner	Yield	One year	Three years	Telephone (800)
AIM Tax-Exempt Bond of CT	5.3	(3.3)	5.4	347-1919
Colonial CT Tax-Exempt A	6.0	(7.2)	4.5	248-2828
Dreyfus CT Intm. Muni	5.4	(4.7)	N.A.	645-6561
EV Classic CT Ltd. Mat. T/F	4.7	(4.3)	N.A.	225-6265
EV Marathon CT Tax-Free	5.6	(10.4)	N.A.	225-6265
Fidelity Spartan CT Muni H/Y	6.4	(7.0)	4.4	544-8888
First Invest. M/S Ins. T/F CT	5.2	(7.2)	5.1	423-4026
Flagship CT Double T/E A	5.7	(6.2)	4.7	227-4648
Franklin CT T/Free Income	5.3	(5.4)	4.8	342-5236
Lord Abbett T/F Income CT	5.7	(7.4)	4.5	874-3733
Premier State Muni Bd. CT A	5.8	(5.7)	4.9	554-4611

FLORIDA

Fund name/★ 1994 winner	Yield	One year	Three years	Telephone (800)
ABT FL H/I Muni Bond	6.8	(4.6)	N.A.	553-7838
ABT FL Tax-Free	5.7	(4.6)	5.5	553-7838
Alliance Muni Income II FL C	5.9	(12.5)	N.A.	221-5672
Colonial FL Tax-Exempt B	5.6	(8.0)	N.A.	248-2828
Dean Witter M/S Muni FL	5.6	(6.3)	5.2	869-3863
Dreyfus FL Intm. Muni	5.1	(4.9)	N.A.	645-6561
EV Marathon FL Ltd. Mat. T/F	4.4	(4.1)	N.A.	225-6265
EV Marathon FL Tax-Free	5.6	(9.0)	3.5	225-6265
Emerald FL Tax-Exempt	5.5	(6.9)	5.5	637-6336
Fidelity Spartan FL Muni Inc.	6.2	(6.7)	N.A.	544-8888
First Invest. M/S Ins. T/F FL	5.2	(5.8)	5.9	423-4026
First Union FL Muni C Inv.	5.1	(9.7)	N.A.	326-3241
Flagship FL Double T/E A	5.7	(5.6)	5.2	227-4648
Florida Municipal Income	4.6	(15.3)	N.A.	245-5040
Franklin FL Ins. T/F Income	5.6	(9.9)	N.A.	342-5236
Franklin FL Tax-Free Income	5.4%	(3.4)	5.6	342-5236
Hough FL Tax-Free S/T ★	5.1	0.2	N.A.	557-7555
Kemper State T/F Inc. FL A	5.1	(3.9)	6.0	621-1048
Keystone Amer. FL T/F A	6.1	(7.9)	4.0	343-2898
Lord Abbett FL T/F Inc. Tr.	5.4	(10.0)	N.A.	874-3733
Lord Abbett T/F Income FL	5.7	(8.2)	4.9	874-3733
Merrill Lynch FL Ltd. Mat.B	4.1	(0.5)	N.A.	637-3863
Merrill Lynch FL Muni Bd.B	5.1	(8.4)	3.4	637-3863
MFS FL Municipal Bond A	5.8	(8.8)	N.A.	637-2929
Nations FL Int. Muni Inv. A	4.7	(4.3)	N.A.	321-7854
Nations FL Muni Inv. N	5.7	(8.8)	N.A.	321-7854
Nuveen FL Tax-Free Value R[1]	6.0	(6.1)	N.A.	351-4100
Oppenheimer FL Tax-Ex. A	5.6	(7.0)	N.A.	525-7048
Premier State Muni FL A	5.6	(4.5)	5.2	554-4611
Prudential Municipal FL A	6.4	(7.2)	4.9	225-1852
Putnam FL T/E Income A	5.8	(6.2)	4.6	225-1581
Seligman Tax-Exempt FL A	7.0	(5.5)	5.4	221-2783
Sierra FL Insured Muni A	5.9	(8.5)	N.A.	222-5852
Smith Barney FL Munis B	5.0	(8.5)	N.A.	451-2010
Smith Barney Muni FL A	N.A.	(5.1)	5.3	554-7835
Smith Barney Muni FL L/T A	N.A.	(3.2)	N.A.	544-7835
State St. Research FL T/F A	5.0	(4.0)	N.A.	882-3302
T. Rowe Price FL Ins. Int. T/F	5.3	(2.9)	N.A.	638-5660
USAA State T/F FL T/F Inc.	6.3	(10.0)	N.A.	382-8722
Vanguard FL Ins. Tax-Free	6.3	(4.7)	N.A.	662-7447
Voyageur FL Insured T/F A	6.1	(8.7)	N.A.	553-2143

GEORGIA

Fund name/★ 1994 winner	Yield	One year	Three years	Telephone (800)
EV Marathon GA Tax-Free	5.3	(9.6)	2.9	225-6265
First Inv. M/S Ins. T/F GA	5.8	(5.1)	N.A.	423-4026
First Union GA Muni C Inv.	5.1	(10.5)	N.A.	326-3241
Flagship GA Dbl. Tax-Ex. A	5.6	(6.1)	4.2	227-4648
Franklin GA Tax-Free Inc.	5.0	(3.7)	5.4	342-5236
MFS GA Municipal Bond A	5.3	(6.9)	4.3	637-2929
Nations GA Muni Bd. Inv. N	5.7	(9.2)	N.A.	321-7854
Premier State Muni Bd. GA A	6.3	(7.7)	N.A.	554-4611
Prudential Municipal GA B	5.0	(7.0)	4.4	225-1852
Seligman Tax-Exempt GA A	7.0	(7.6)	4.2	221-2783
T. Rowe Price GA Tax-Free	6.2	(6.0)	N.A.	638-5660

HAWAII

Fund name/★ 1994 winner	Yield	One year	Three years	Telephone (800)
First Hawaii Muni Bond	5.0	(6.2)	4.1	599-2400[20]
Franklin HI Municipal Bond	6.0	(8.2)	N.A.	342-5236
Hawaiian Tax-Free	6.0	(4.6)	4.3	228-4227
Leahi Tax-Free Inc.	5.6	(7.1)	4.4	522-7777[20]
Lord Abbett T/F Income HI	5.5	(8.4)	4.3	874-3733

IDAHO

Fund name/★ 1994 winner	Yield	One year	Three years	Telephone (800)
Northwest Investors ID T/E	6.0	(3.4)	3.7	728-8762

INDIANA

Fund name/★ 1994 winner	Yield	One year	Three years	Telephone (800)
Franklin IN Tax-Free Income	5.1	(5.0)	5.6	342-5236

IOWA

Fund name/★ 1994 winner	Yield	One year	Three years	Telephone (800)
Voyageur IA Tax-Free	5.9	(10.3)	N.A.	553-2143

Source: Morningstar Inc. Chicago Ill.; 800-876-5005

Fund name/★ 1994 winner	Yield	One year	Three years	Telephone (800)
KANSAS				
Flagship KS Triple T/E A	5.8%	(8.3)	N.A.	227-4648
Kansas Ins. Muni Ltd. Mat.	5.0	(5.3)	N.A.	345-2363
Kansas Municipal	5.7	(6.3)	5.1	345-2363
Voyageur KS Tax-Free	5.8	(7.2)	N.A.	553-2143
KENTUCKY				
Churchill Tax-Free of KY	6.0	(3.4)	5.0	872-5859
Dupree KY T/F Short-Med. ★	3.5	1.0	4.5	866-0614
Dupree KY Tax-Free Income	5.6	(2.1)	6.2	866-0614
EV Marathon KY Tax-Free	5.6	(9.3)	3.1	225-6265
Flagship KY Triple Tax-Ex. A	5.7	(5.4)	5.1	227-4648
Franklin KY Tax-Free Inc.	5.7	(8.5)	4.8	342-5236
Trademark KY Muni Bond	5.2	(5.7)	N.A.	566-3653[16]
LOUISIANA				
EV Marathon LA Tax-Free	5.6	(10.3)	N.A.	225-6265
Flagship LA Double T/E A	5.9	(6.2)	5.0	227-4648
Franklin LA Tax-Free Inc.	5.3	(4.8)	4.8	342-5236
Marquis LA Tax-Free Inc. A	4.9	(5.5)	N.A.	462-9511
MFS LA Municipal Bond A	6.4	(7.7)	N.A.	637-2929
Paragon LA Tax-Free	5.4	(3.2)	4.9	777-5143
Seligman Tax-Exempt LA A	7.4	(5.9)	4.2	221-2783
Tower LA Muni Income	6.2	(4.6)	5.2	999-0124
MAINE				
Forum ME Muni Bond	5.6	(4.2)	4.8	879-8900[19]
MARYLAND				
Calvert Muni Intm. MD A	5.2	(2.9)	N.A.	368-2748
EV Marathon MD Tax-Free	5.3	(9.9)	N.A.	225-6265
Fidelity Spart. MD Muni Inc.	6.7	(7.5)	N.A.	544-8888
First Invest M/S Ins. T/F MD	5.5	(6.0)	5.8	423-4026
Flag Inv MD Intm. T/F Inc.	5.9	(5.4)	N.A.	767-3524
Franklin MD Tax-Free Inc.	5.3	(5.1)	5.0	342-5236
GIT MD Tax-Free	5.2	(8.9)	N.A.	336-3063
Legg Mason MD T/F Inc.	5.5	(3.3)	5.3	822-5544
Maryland Muni Inc.	5.5	(17.0)	N.A.	245-5040
Medalist MD Muni Bd. Inv.	4.9	(7.0)	3.8	444-7123
Merrill Lynch MD Muni B	5.2	(10.5)	N.A.	637-3863
MFS MD Municipal Bond A	5.5	(6.1)	3.6	637-2929
Nations MD Muni Inv. N	5.4	(9.8)	N.A.	321-7854
Nuveen MD T/F Value R[1]	6.0	(6.1)	N.A.	351-4100
Premier St. Muni MD A	5.6	(4.7)	4.8	554-4611
Prudential Municipal MD B	5.5	(7.7)	3.6	225-1852
Rushmore MD Tax-Free	5.7	(5.2)	4.6	343-3355
Seligman Tax-Exempt MD A	7.2	(5.5)	4.6	221-2783
Tax-Exempt Fund of MD	5.2	(4.8)	4.4	421-4120
T. Rowe Price MD S/T T/F ★	4.2	0.6	N.A.	638-5660
T. Rowe Price MD Tax-Free	6.1	(5.0)	5.1	638-5660
MASSACHUSETTS				
1784 MA Tax-Exempt Inc.	5.6	(5.4)	N.A.	252-1784
Colonial MA Tax-Exempt A	5.7	(5.7)	4.9	248-2828
Dean Witter M/S Muni MA	5.8	(6.8)	5.4	869-3863
Dreyfus MA Intm. Muni	5.1%	(6.4)	N.A.	645-6561
Dreyfus MA Tax-Ex. Bond	5.6	(6.0)	4.3	645-6561
EV Marath. MA Ltd. Mat. T/F	4.3	(3.5)	N.A.	225-6265
EV Marathon MA Tax-Free	5.6	(9.0)	3.3	225-6265
Fidelity MA T/F High-Yield	6.6	(6.6)	4.9	544-8888
First Invest M/S Ins. T/F MA	5.5	(5.7)	5.1	423-4026
Franklin MA Insured T/F Inc.	4.9	(3.6)	5.4	342-5236
Hancock Tax-Exempt MA	5.7	(5.5)	5.3	225-5291
IDS MA Tax-Exempt	5.8	(5.2)	5.1	328-8300
Mer. Lynch MA Ltd. Mat. B ★	4.7	0.3	N.A.	637-3863
Merrill Lynch MA Muni B	5.2	(7.9)	N.A.	637-3863
MFS MA Municipal Bond A	5.8	(5.6)	4.4	637-2929
New England MA T/F Inc. A	5.6	(7.4)	4.3	225-7670
Nuveen MA Ins. T/F Val. R[1]	5.9	(4.8)	5.2	351-4100
Nuveen MA T/F Value R[1]	6.2	(5.0)	5.4	351-4100
Pioneer MA Double T/F	6.0	(8.7)	N.A.	225-6292
Premier L/T MA Muni A	4.3	(2.9)	5.3	554-4611
Premier St. Muni MA A	5.9	(4.6)	5.4	554-4611
Prudential Municipal MA B	5.2	(5.5)	4.7	225-1852
Putnam MA T/E Inc. IIA	6.1	(6.1)	5.3	225-1581
Scudder MA Tax-Free	5.9	(6.2)	5.9	225-2470
Seligman Tax-Exempt MA A	7.3	(4.4)	5.2	221-2783
Smith Barney MA Munis A	5.3	(8.3)	4.1	451-2010
MICHIGAN				
Calvert Municipal Intm. MI A	5.0	(2.8)	N.A.	368-2748
Colonial MI Tax-Exempt A	5.8	(6.0)	4.4	248-2828
Dean Witter M/S Muni MI	5.8	(7.0)	5.0	869-3863
EV Marathon MI Ltd. Mat. T/F	4.4	(4.4)	N.A.	225-6265
EV Marathon MI Tax-Free	5.4	(8.5)	3.3	225-6265
Fidelity MI T/F High-Yield	6.5	(7.5)	4.9	544-8888
First Invest. M/S Ins. T/F MI	5.3	(6.8)	5.8	423-4026
Flagship MI Triple T/E A	5.4	(5.0)	5.2	227-4648
Franklin MI Insured T/F Inc.	4.8	(3.9)	5.6	342-5236
IDS MI Tax-Exempt	5.3	(4.9)	5.3	328-8300
Lord Abbett T/F Income MI	6.0	(7.9)	N.A.	874-3733
Merrill Lynch MI Muni B	5.1	(8.0)	N.A.	637-3863
Michigan Intermediate Muni	5.4	(4.7)	4.8	245-5040
Nuveen MI T/Free Value R[1]	6.2	(5.7)	N.A.	351-4100
Premier State Muni MI A	5.8	(4.6)	5.8	554-4611
Prudential Municipal MI B	5.3	(5.5)	4.8	225-1852
Putnam MI T/E Inc. IIA	6.0	(5.4)	4.7	225-1581
Seligman Tax-Exempt MI A	7.9	(4.8)	5.1	221-2783
Woodward MI Muni Ret.	5.6	(5.4)	N.A.	688-3350
MINNESOTA				
Alliance Muni Inc. II MN C	6.0	(9.5)	N.A.	247-4154
Colonial MN Tax-Exempt A	5.6	(4.8)	4.2	248-2828
Dean Witter M/S Muni MN	6.0	(7.2)	4.6	869-3863
EV Marathon MN Tax-Free	5.5	(9.0)	3.0	225-6265
Fidelity MN Tax-Free	6.4	(6.4)	4.2	544-8888
First Inv. M/S Ins. T/F MN	5.6	(6.4)	4.4	423-4026
Fortis Tax-Free MN A	6.0	(4.3)	5.1	800-2638
Franklin MN Ins. T/F Inc.	4.8	(3.5)	5.1	342-5236
Great Hall MN Insured T/E	5.3	(8.0)	3.7	934-6674
IDS MN Tax-Exempt	5.9	(4.4)	4.9	328-8300
Merrill Lynch MN Muni B	5.0	(6.8)	N.A.	637-3863
Norwest MN T/F Inv. A	5.4	(6.0)	4.1	338-1348
Piper Jaffray MN T/E	5.8%	(5.6)	4.6	866-7778
Premier State Muni MN A	5.9	(4.4)	5.2	554-4611
Prudential Municipal MN B	4.9	(6.0)	3.5	225-1852
Putnam MN T/E Inc. IIA	5.8	(5.4)	4.4	225-1581
Seligman Tax-Exempt MN A	7.4	(2.5)	5.5	221-2783
Sit MN Tax-Free Inc. ★	6.5	0.6	N.A.	332-5580
State Bond MN Tax-Free Inc.	4.9	(4.5)	4.2	328-4735
Voyageur MN Insured A	5.9	(7.9)	4.4	553-2143
Voyageur MN L/T T/F A	4.3	(1.9)	4.1	553-2143
Voyageur MN Tax-Free A	5.3	(6.7)	4.3	553-2143
MISSISSIPPI				
EV Marathon MS Tax-Free	5.6	(9.9)	N.A.	225-6265
MFS MS Municipal Bond A	6.3	(7.1)	N.A.	637-2929
MISSOURI				
Arch MO Tax-Exempt Inv.	5.5	(5.8)	4.6	551-3731
EV Marathon MO Tax-Free	5.3	(9.3)	N.A.	225-6265
First Invest M/S Ins. T/F MO	5.8	(7.1)	N.A.	423-4026
Flagship MO Double T/E A	5.7	(6.1)	5.1	227-4648
Franklin MO Tax-Free Inc.	5.1	(5.1)	5.4	342-5236
GIT MO Tax-Free	4.9	(8.5)	3.2	336-3063
Lord Abbett T/F Income MO	5.6	(8.7)	4.4	874-3733
Seligman Tax-Exempt MO A	7.0	(6.3)	3.8	221-2783
Voyageur MO Insured T/F A	5.9	(9.0)	N.A.	553-2143
NEBRASKA				
Heartland NE Tax-Free	5.8	(9.3)	N.A.	432-7856
Nebraska Municipal	6.1	(6.3)	N.A.	822-8460
NEW HAMPSHIRE				
Forum NH Bond	5.4	(4.6)	N.A.	879-8900[19]
NEW JERSEY				
Alliance Muni Inc. II NJ B	5.9	(10.8)	N.A.	227-4618
Compass Cap NJ Muni Bond	5.1	(4.7)	5.0	451-8371
Dean Witter M/S Muni NJ	5.7	(7.2)	4.7	869-3863
Dreyfus NJ Intm. Muni Bond	5.3	(5.2)	N.A.	645-6561
Dreyfus NJ Muni Bond	6.0	(6.0)	4.9	645-6561
EV Marathon NJ Ltd. Mat. T/F	4.4	(3.6)	N.A.	225-6265
EV Marathon NJ Tax-Free	5.6	(8.2)	3.7	225-6265
FFB NJ Tax-Free Income	5.0	(6.1)	4.8	437-8790
Fidelity Spartan NJ Muni H/Y	6.3	(5.7)	5.1	544-8888
First Invest. M/S Ins. T/F NJ	5.4	(6.4)	5.1	423-4026
Flagship NJ Double T/Ex. A	6.1	(5.7)	N.A.	227-4648
Flagship NJ Intm. Tax-Ex. A	5.1	(3.8)	N.A.	227-4648
Franklin NJ T/F Income	5.1	(5.2)	4.7	342-5236
Lord Abbett T/F Income NJ	5.6	(6.4)	5.4	874-3733
Merr. Lynch NJ Ltd. Mat. B ★	3.7	0.8	N.A.	637-3863
Merrill Lynch NJ Muni B	5.0	(6.5)	3.9	637-3863
New Jersey Muni Income	5.5	(17.1)	N.A.	245-5040
Nuveen NJ T/F Value R[1]	5.8	(4.0)	N.A.	351-4100
Prudential Municipal NJ B	5.4	(6.4)	4.6	225-1852
Putnam NJ T/E Inc. A	6.0	(6.3)	4.6	225-1581
Seligman NJ Tax-Exempt A	6.9	(6.1)	4.8	221-2783

Source: Morningstar Inc. Chicago Ill.; 800-876-5005

Fund name/★ 1994 winner	Yield	% return to Jan 1, 1995		Telephone (800)
		One year	Three years	
Smith Barney Muni NJ A	5.1%	(6.2)	5.0	544-7835
Smith Barney NJ Munis A	5.2	(7.1)	4.7	451-2010
T. Rowe Price NJ Tax-Free	6.1	(6.1)	5.5	638-5660
Vanguard NJ T/F Ins. L/T	6.3	(5.2)	5.5	662-7447

NEW MEXICO

Fund name/★ 1994 winner	Yield	One year	Three years	Telephone (800)
Flagship NM Double T/E A	5.8	(7.0)	N.A.	227-4648
Thornburg NM Intm. Muni A	4.9	(1.9)	5.5	847-0200
Voyageur NM Tax-Free A	6.2	(6.9)	N.A.	553-2143

NEW YORK

Fund name/★ 1994 winner	Yield	One year	Three years	Telephone (800)
Advantage Muni Bond NY	5.7	(11.0)	N.A.	241-2039
Alliance Muni Income NY A	6.5	(10.1)	3.9	227-4618
Bernstein NY Muni	5.2	(2.6)	4.2	756-4097[6]
BNY Hamilton Intm. NY T/E	4.3	(3.9)	N.A.	426-9363
Calvert Municipal Intm. NY A	5.2	(2.3)	N.A.	368-2748
Colonial NY Tax-Exempt A	6.1	(7.9)	3.9	248-2828
Dean Witter M/S Muni NY	5.5	(8.2)	4.5	869-3863
Dean Witter NY T/F Inc.	4.8	(7.7)	3.9	869-3863
Dreyfus NY Insured T/E	5.4	(6.6)	4.0	645-6561
Dreyfus NY Tax-Ex. Bond	5.7	(7.0)	4.5	645-6561
Dreyfus NY Tax-Ex. Intm.	5.0	(5.1)	5.0	645-6561
EV Marathon NY Ltd. Mat.T/F	4.4	(4.3)	N.A.	225-6265
EV Marathon NY Tax-Free	5.7	(9.4)	4.0	225-6265
Empire Builder Tax-Free	4.9	(5.2)	4.7	845-8406
Fidelity NY T/F High-Yield	6.2	(8.0)	4.2	544-8888
Fidelity NY Tax-Free Insured	6.0	(8.0)	4.1	544-8888
Fidelity Spartan NY Intm.Muni	6.0	(4.3)	N.A.	544-8888
Fidelity Spartan NY Muni H/Y	6.6	(8.5)	4.4	544-8888
First Invest. NY Insured T/F	5.4	(5.5)	4.1	423-4026
Flagship NY Tax-Exempt A	6.2	(7.1)	6.1	227-4648
Fortis Tax-Free NY	5.7	(3.0)	5.7	800-2638
Franklin NY Insured T/F Inc.	5.3	(8.6)	4.6	342-5236
Franklin NY Intm. T/F Inc.	5.7	(5.3)	N.A.	342-5236
Franklin NY Tax-Free Inc.	4.9	(3.6)	6.2	342-5236
Galaxy NY Muni Bond Ret.	5.5	(7.3)	4.1	628-0414
General NY Municipal Bond	6.0	(7.2)	5.3	645-6561
Hancock Tax-Exempt NY	5.5	(6.5)	5.4	225-5291
IDS NY Tax-Exempt	5.6	(5.1)	5.1	328-8300
Independence Cap NY Muni	5.5	(6.8)	5.1	833-4264
Kemper State T/F Inc. NY A	5.0	(4.9)	5.6	621-1048
Landmark NY Tax-Free Inc.	5.7	(7.5)	3.8	559-7117[6]
Lebenthal NY Municipal	6.2	(8.7)	4.5	221-5822
Limited-Term NY Municipal	5.2	(0.5)	6.6	383-1300[7]
Lord Abbett NY T/F Inc. Tr.	5.6	(9.4)	N.A.	874-3733
Lord Abbett T/F Income NY	5.6	(8.9)	3.9	874-3733
Mackenzie NY Municipal A	4.3	(4.0)	4.7	456-5111
MainStay NY Tax-Free	5.8	(4.7)	5.2	522-4202
Mariner NY Tax-Free Bond	5.2	(8.1)	5.1	634-2536
Merr.Lynch NY Ltd.Mat.B ★	3.9	0.1	N.A.	637-3863
Merrill Lynch NY Muni B	4.9	(9.1)	3.6	637-3863
MFS NY Municipal Bond A	5.5	(6.1)	5.3	637-2929
New England I/T T/F NY A	5.3	(4.2)	N.A.	225-7670
New York Muni	4.9	(20.4)	0.1	322-6864
New York Muni Inc. Fort	6.7	(9.9)	N.A.	245-5040
Nuveen NY Ins. T/F Val R[1]	6.1	(6.1)	5.2	351-4100
Nuveen NY T/F Value R[1]	6.4	(6.0)	5.5	351-4100
Oppenheimer NY T/E A	5.5	(8.8)	4.2	525-7048
PaineWebber NY T/F Inc. A	5.4%	(7.9)	4.5	647-1568
Pioneer NY Triple Tax-Free	5.9	(8.5)	N.A.	225-6292
Premier L/T NY Muni A	6.1	(3.4)	4.6	554-4611
Premier NY Muni Bond A	5.6	(6.8)	5.4	554-4611
Prudential Muni NY B	5.5	(6.8)	4.9	225-1852
Putnam NY T/E Opp. A	5.6	(2.8)	4.8	225-1581
Putnam NY Tax Ex. Inc. A	5.9	(7.4)	5.0	225-1581
Quest for Value NY T/E	5.4	(6.5)	5.6	232-3863
Rochester Fund Municipals	6.3	(8.3)	5.3	383-1300[7]
Scudder NY Tax-Free	5.1	(7.2)	4.9	225-2470
Seligman T/E NY A	7.0	(7.9)	4.5	221-2783
Smith Barney Intm. Mat. NY A	5.0	(3.9)	5.3	451-2010
Smith Barney Muni NY A	5.2	(5.9)	5.2	544-7835
Smith Barney NY Muni A	5.3	(6.7)	4.2	451-2010
T. Rowe Price NY Tax-Free	6.1	(5.9)	5.6	638-5660
USAA Tax-Exempt NY Bond	6.4	(9.0)	4.0	382-8722
UST Master T/E NY I/T	3.9	(4.3)	3.7	233-1136
Value Line NY Tax-Exempt	5.4	(7.7)	4.8	223-0818
Vanguard NY Insured T/F	6.3	(5.6)	5.4	662-7447
Victory NY Tax-Free A	4.7	(4.6)	5.1	539-3863
Vision NY Tax-Free	5.5	(5.4)	N.A.	836-2211
Vista NY Tax-Free Inc. A	5.4	(6.1)	5.6	648-4782
Warburg Pincus NY Muni	5.0	(0.6)	5.5	257-5614

NORTH CAROLINA

Fund name/★ 1994 winner	Yield	One year	Three years	Telephone (800)
Colonial NC T/E B	5.7	(9.1)	N.A.	248-2828
EV Marathon NC Tax-Free	5.4	(9.3)	3.0	225-6265
First Invest. M/S Ins. T/F NC	5.8	(7.3)	N.A.	423-4026
First Union NC Muni C Inv.	5.1	(9.6)	N.A.	326-3241
Flagship NC Triple T/E A	5.4	(5.6)	4.6	227-4648
Franklin NC T/F Income	5.1	(5.7)	4.7	342-5236
Merrill Lynch NC Muni B	5.0	(7.3)	N.A.	637-3863
MFS NC Municipal Bond A	5.5	(6.3)	3.6	637-2929
Nations NC Muni Inv. N	3.7	(9.7)	N.A.	321-7854
North Carolina Tax-Free	4.4	(4.1)	N.A.	525-3863
111 Corcoran NC Muni Sec.	5.3	(6.0)	N.A.	422-2080
Premier State Muni NC A	6.0	(8.5)	4.7	554-4611
Prudential Municipal NC B	5.3	(6.9)	4.1	225-1852
Seligman Tax-Exempt NC A	6.9	(7.3)	4.2	221-2783

NORTH DAKOTA

Fund name/★ 1994 winner	Yield	One year	Three years	Telephone (800)
Voyageur ND Tax-Free A	6.0	(5.5)	4.9	553-2143

OHIO

Fund name/★ 1994 winner	Yield	One year	Three years	Telephone (800)
Alliance Muni Inc. II OH C	6.0	(10.9)	N.A.	247-4154
Carnegie T/E OH Gen Muni	4.3	(3.3)	4.8	321-2322
Colonial OH Tax-Exempt A	5.6	(6.3)	4.2	248-2828
Dean Witter M/S Muni OH	5.8	(7.4)	5.1	869-3863
EV Marathon OH Ltd. Mat.T/F	4.4	(4.0)	N.A.	225-6265
EV Marathon OH Tax-Free	5.4	(8.9)	3.7	225-6265
Fidelity OH Tax-Free H/Y	6.4	(5.5)	4.9	544-8888
First Invest. M/S Ins. T/F OH	5.4	(6.3)	5.2	423-4026
Flagship OH Double Tax-Ex A	5.2	(4.7)	4.9	227-4648
Fountain Sq. OH T/F Bond	5.7	(4.0)	N.A.	334-0483
Franklin OH Insured T/F Inc.	4.9	(4.5)	5.3	342-5236
Gradison-McDonald OH T/F Inc.	5.1	(6.5)	N.A.	869-5999
IDS OH Tax-Exempt	5.6	(4.8)	5.0	328-8300
Kemper State T/F Inc. OH A	5.7%	(3.7)	N.A.	621-1048
Merrill Lynch OH Muni Bd. B	4.9	(7.5)	N.A.	637-3863
Midwest OH Ins. Tax-Free A	5.7	(5.4)	5.0	543-8721
NCC OH Tax-Exempt Ret	5.4	(4.5)	3.7	624-6450
Nuveen OH Tax-Free Val. R[1]	6.2	(5.2)	5.4	351-4100
Ohio Intermediate Muni	5.6	(6.4)	N.A.	245-5040
Ohio Municipal Income Fort	6.1	(6.4)	4.7	245-5040
PNC OH Tax-Free Inc. Inv. A	6.2	(6.5)	N.A.	422-6538
Premier State Muni Bd. OH A	5.9	(4.1)	5.6	554-4611
Prudential Municipal OH B	5.2	(5.2)	4.8	225-1852
Putnam OH T/E Inc. IIA	5.5	(4.8)	5.0	225-1581
Scudder OH Tax-Free	6.0	(5.5)	4.9	225-2470
Seligman Tax-Exempt OH A	7.5	(4.9)	4.8	221-2783
Vanguard OH T/F Ins. L/T	6.3	(5.1)	5.4	662-7447
Victory OH Municipal Bond	4.3	(4.5)	5.1	539-3863

OREGON

Fund name/★ 1994 winner	Yield	One year	Three years	Telephone (800)
Columbia Municipal Bond	5.4	(4.7)	4.0	547-1707
Crabbe Huson OR Muni Bond	4.8	(2.7)	4.4	541-9732
EV Marathon OR Tax-Free	5.3	(9.5)	4.0	225-6265
First Invest. M/S Ins. T/F OR	5.5	(7.1)	N.A.	423-4026
Franklin OR T/F Income	5.2	(4.9)	4.6	342-5236
Merrill Lynch OR Muni Bd. B	5.0	(10.5)	N.A.	637-3863
Seligman Tax-Exempt OR A	7.1	(4.6)	4.5	221-2783
Tax-Free Trust of OR	5.8	(3.8)	4.5	872-6734
Voyageur OR Insured T/F A	5.7	(7.6)	N.A.	553-2143
Westcore OR Tax-Exempt	5.3	(6.5)	4.3	392-2673

PENNSYLVANIA

Fund name/★ 1994 winner	Yield	One year	Three years	Telephone (800)
Advantage Muni Bond PA	6.3	(10.0)	N.A.	241-2039
Alliance Muni Inc. II PA B	5.9	(10.5)	N.A.	247-4154
Compass Cap PA Muni Bd.	5.5	(4.4)	N.A.	451-8371
Conestoga PA Tax-Free	5.6	(4.1)	N.A.	344-2716
Dean Witter M/S Muni PA	5.7	(6.9)	5.2	869-3863
Delaware Tax-Free PA A	5.0	(3.9)	5.2	523-4640
Dreyfus PA Intm. Muni Bd.	5.8	(1.5)	N.A.	645-6561
EV Marathon PA Ltd. Mat. T/F	4.3	(3.8)	N.A.	225-6265
EV Marathon PA Tax-Free	5.6	(9.6)	3.1	225-6265
Fidelity Spartan PA Muni H/Y	6.9	(5.0)	5.5	544-8888
First Invest. M/S Ins. T/F PA	5.3	(6.7)	5.4	423-4026
Flagship PA Triple T/E A	5.4	(4.2)	5.4	227-4648
Franklin PA Tax-Free Inc.	5.4	(3.3)	5.8	342-5236
Keystone Amer. PA T/F A	6.2	(8.3)	4.6	343-2898
Legg Mason PA Tax-Free Inc.	5.5	(4.0)	5.7	822-5544
Lord Abbett T/F Income PA	5.7	(8.8)	N.A.	874-3733
Merrill Lynch PA Ltd. Mat. B ★	3.7	0.6	N.A.	637-3863
Merrill Lynch PA Muni Bd. B	5.1	(6.0)	4.9	637-3863
MFS PA Municipal Bond A	6.4	(7.1)	N.A.	637-2929
Nuveen PA Tax-Free Val. R[1]	6.1	(6.8)	N.A.	351-4100
Oppenheimer PA Tax-Ex. A	5.5	(7.7)	4.1	525-7048
Pennsylvania Intm. Muni	5.6	(6.2)	N.A.	245-5040
Pennsylvania Muni Inc. A	6.2	(6.5)	4.7	245-5040
PNC PA T/F Income Inv. A	5.3	(7.1)	N.A.	422-6538
Premier State Muni Bd. PA A	5.9	(5.3)	5.4	554-4611
Prudential Municipal PA B	5.6	(6.4)	4.8	225-1852
Putnam PA Tax Ex. Inc. A	5.7	(4.8)	5.5	225-1581
Scudder PA Tax-Free	6.0	(5.9)	5.1	225-2470
Seligman PA T/E A	7.0	(7.0)	4.7	221-2783

Source: Morningstar Inc. Chicago Ill.; 800-876-5005

Fund name/★ 1994 winner	Yield	% return to Jan 1, 1995 One year	Three years	Telephone (800)
Sentinel PA Tax-Free	4.5%	(4.9)	4.5	282-3863
State St. Research PA T/F A	5.5	(3.6)	N.A.	882-3302
Van Kampen PA T/F Inc. A	5.4	(5.7)	5.5	225-2222
Vanguard PA T/F Ins. L/T	6.4	(4.5)	5.8	662-7447
William Penn PA T/F Inc.	5.1	(4.2)	4.6	523-8440

PUERTO RICO

Fund name/★ 1994 winner	Yield	One year	Three years	Telephone (800)
Franklin PR Tax-Free Income	5.0	(4.3)	5.0	342-5236

RHODE ISLAND

Fund name/★ 1994 winner	Yield	One year	Three years	Telephone (800)
EV Marathon RI Tax-Free	5.7	(10.2)	N.A.	225-6265
Narragansett Ins. T/F Inc.	7.3	(6.5)	N.A.	453-6864
Ocean State Tax-Exempt	5.3	(2.9)	5.1	421-1411[21]

SOUTH CAROLINA

Fund name/★ 1994 winner	Yield	One year	Three years	Telephone (800)
Biltmore SC Muni Bond	5.7	(3.8)	5.4	763-7277
EV Marathon SC Tax-Free	5.2	(9.6)	N.A.	225-6265
Flagship SC Double T/E A	5.8	(6.4)	N.A.	227-4648
MFS SC Muni Bond A	5.4	(5.7)	4.3	637-2929
Nations SC Muni Bd. Inv. N	5.7	(6.8)	N.A.	321-7854
Seligman Tax-Exempt SC A	7.2	(6.7)	4.2	221-2783

TENNESSEE

Fund name/★ 1994 winner	Yield	One year	Three years	Telephone (800)
Dupree TN Tax-Free Income	5.6	(1.2)	N.A.	866-0614
EV Marathon TN Tax-Free	5.5	(9.6)	N.A.	225-6265
Flagship TN Double T/E A	5.5	(5.5)	4.8	227-4648
MFS TN Municipal Bond A	5.6	(4.1)	4.7	637-2929
Nations TN Muni Bd. Inv. N	5.6	(7.2)	N.A.	321-7854
Riverside Cap. TN Muni Oblg.	5.8%	(6.1)	N.A.	874-8376
Tennessee Tax-Free Bond	5.4	(4.4)	N.A.	245-4270

TEXAS

Fund name/★ 1994 winner	Yield	One year	Three years	Telephone (800)
American Cap TX Muni Secs.A	4.9	(3.6)	N.A.	421-5666
EV Marathon TX Tax-Free	6.4	(8.1)	N.A.	225-6265
Franklin TX T/F Income	5.1	(2.8)	5.6	342-5236
Kemper State T/F Inc. TX A	5.5	(2.6)	6.9	621-1048
Keystone Amer. TX Tax-Free A	6.2	(7.5)	N.A.	343-2898
Lord Abbett T/F Income TX	5.7	(6.6)	4.8	874-3733
Merrill Lynch TX Muni Bd. B	5.4	(5.9)	5.3	637-3863
MFS TX Municipal Bond A	6.3	(7.2)	N.A.	637-2929
Nations TX Muni Bd. Inv. N	5.7	(9.0)	N.A.	321-7854
Premier State Muni Bd. TX A	6.2	(4.9)	5.9	554-4611
Texas Municipal Income	4.8	(15.5)	N.A.	245-5040

UTAH

Fund name/★ 1994 winner	Yield	One year	Three years	Telephone (800)
Tax-Free Fund for UT	7.2	(6.4)	N.A.	882-4937
Voyageur UT Tax-Free	6.3	(6.4)	N.A.	553-2143

VERMONT

Fund name/★ 1994 winner	Yield	One year	Three years	Telephone (800)
Calvert T/F Res. VT Muni A	5.4	(2.9)	5.0	368-2748
Tax-Free Fund of VT	5.6	(0.9)	3.2	675-3333

VIRGINIA

Fund name/★ 1994 winner	Yield	One year	Three years	Telephone (800)
Calvert Muni Intm. VA A	4.8	(2.0)	N.A.	368-2748
EV Marathon VA Tax-Free	5.4	(8.9)	2.9	226-6265
First Invest. M/S Ins. T/F VA	5.0	(6.4)	5.3	423-4026
First Union VA Muni C Inv.	5.0	(9.5)	N.A.	326-3241
Flagship VA Dbl. Tax-Ex A	5.8%	(5.5)	5.2	227-4648
Franklin VA Tax-Free Inc.	5.1	(4.6)	5.3	342-5236
GIT VA Tax-Free	5.2	(8.3)	3.5	336-3063
MarketWatch VA Muni Bd.	4.6	(6.0)	N.A.	232-9091
Medalist VA Muni Bond Inv.	4.9	(6.9)	4.0	444-7123
MFS VA Municipal Bond A	5.6	(6.7)	3.6	637-2929
Nations VA Muni Bd. Inv. N	5.8	(10.0)	N.A.	321-7854
Nuveen VA Tax-Free Val. R[1]	6.2	(5.7)	N.A.	351-4100
Premier State Muni Bd. VA A	6.1	(7.6)	5.3	554-4611
Rushmore VA Tax-Free	5.8	(5.0)	4.7	343-3355
Tax-Exempt Fund of VA	5.1	(4.8)	4.5	421-4120
T. Rowe Price VA Tax-Free	6.1	(5.1)	5.3	638-5660
USAA Tax-Exempt VA Bond	6.5	(6.3)	4.6	382-8722
Virginia Municipal Income	4.3	(15.9)	N.A.	245-5040

WASHINGTON

Fund name/★ 1994 winner	Yield	One year	Three years	Telephone (800)
Franklin WA Muni Bond	6.1	(9.7)	N.A.	342-5236
Lord Abbett T/F Income WA	5.9	(8.2)	N.A.	874-3733
MFS WA Municipal Bond A	6.6	(6.2)	N.A.	637-2929
Northwest Investors WA T/E	6.0	(6.4)	N.A.	728-8762
Voyageur WA Ins. Tax-Free	6.3	(7.6)	N.A.	553-2143

WEST VIRGINIA

Fund name/★ 1994 winner	Yield	One year	Three years	Telephone (800)
EV Marathon WV Tax-Free	5.8	(9.3)	N.A.	225-6265
MFS WV Municipal Bond A	5.5	(5.3)	4.6	637-2929

WISCONSIN

Fund name/★ 1994 winner	Yield	One year	Three years	Telephone (800)
Heartland WI Tax-Free	6.1	(6.5)	N.A.	432-7856
Voyageur WI Tax-Free	5.9	(8.4)	N.A.	553-2143

Source: Morningstar Inc. Chicago Ill.; 800-876-5005

Index